Regulation	Page
BUILDING REGULATIONS 2010 (SI 2010 NO. 2214)	
CARRIAGE OF DANGEROUS GOODS AND USE OF TRANSPORTABLE PRESSURE EQUIPMENT REGULATIONS 2009 (SI 2009 NO. 1348) (AS AMENDED)	7
CHEMICALS (HAZARD INFORMATION AND PACKAGING FOR SUPPLY) REGULATIONS 2009 (SI 2009 NO. 716)	11
CLASSIFICATION, LABELLING AND PACKAGING OF CHEMICALS (AMENDMENTS TO SECONDARY LEGISLATION) REGULATIONS 2015 (SI 2015 NO. 21)	15
CLASSIFICATION, LABELLING AND PACKAGING OF SUBSTANCES AND MIXTURES REGULATION (THE CLP REGULATION) (EU REGULATION (EC) NO. 1272/2008) AS APPLIES TO GREAT BRITAIN	17
COMPENSATION ACT 2006	20
CONFINED SPACES REGULATIONS 1997 (SI 1997 NO. 1713)	22
CONSTRUCTION (DESIGN AND MANAGEMENT) REGULATIONS 2015 (SI 2015 NO. 51)	24
CONSUMER PROTECTION ACT 1987	40
CONTROL OF ARTIFICIAL OPTICAL RADIATION AT WORK REGULATIONS 2010 (SI 2010 NO. 1140)	45
CONTROL OF ASBESTOS REGULATIONS 2012 (SI 2012 NO. 632)	50
CONTROL OF ELECTROMAGNETIC FIELDS AT WORK REGULATIONS 2016 (SI 2016 NO. 588)	65
CONTROL OF LEAD AT WORK REGULATIONS 2002 (SI 2002 NO. 2676)	70
CONTROL OF MAJOR ACCIDENT HAZARDS REGULATIONS 2015 (COMAH) (SI 2015 NO. 483)	77
CONTROL OF NOISE AT WORK REGULATIONS 2005 (SI 2005 NO. 1643)	82
CONTROL OF PESTICIDES REGULATIONS 1986 (SI 1986 NO. 1510)	86
CONTROL OF SUBSTANCES HAZARDOUS TO HEALTH REGULATIONS 2002 (SI 2002 NO. 2677)	88
CONTROL OF VIBRATION AT WORK REGULATIONS 2005 (SI 2005 NO. 1093)	96
CORPORATE MANSLAUGHTER AND CORPORATE HOMICIDE ACT 2007	100
CRIMINAL LAW ACT 1967	103
DANGEROUS SUBSTANCES AND EXPLOSIVE ATMOSPHERES REGULATIONS 2002 (SI 2002 NO. 2776)	104
DANGEROUS SUBSTANCES (NOTIFICATION AND MARKING OF SITES) REGULATIONS 1990 (SI 1990 NO. 304)	111
DATA PROTECTION ACT 2018	114
DEREGULATION ACT 2015	118
ELECTRICITY AT WORK REGULATIONS 1989 (SI 1989 NO. 635)	120
ELECTRICITY SAFETY, QUALITY AND CONTINUITY REGULATIONS 2002 (SI 2002 NO. 2665)	122
EMPLOYERS' HEALTH AND SAFETY POLICY STATEMENTS (EXCEPTION) REGULATIONS 1975 (SI 1975 NO. 1584)	127
EMPLOYERS' LIABILITY (COMPULSORY INSURANCE) ACT 1969	128
EMPLOYER'S LIABILITY (DEFECTIVE EQUIPMENT) ACT 1969	130
EMPLOYMENT RIGHTS ACT 1996	131
ENTERPRISE AND REGULATORY REFORM ACT 2013	140
ENVIRONMENTAL DAMAGE (PREVENTION AND REMEDIATION) (ENGLAND) REGULATIONS 2015 (SI 2015 NO. 810)	141
ENVIRONMENTAL DAMAGE (PREVENTION AND REMEDIATION) (WALES) REGULATIONS 2009 (SI 2009 NO. 995)	147
ENVIRONMENTAL LIABILITY (SCOTLAND) REGULATIONS 2009 (SI 2009 NO. 266)	153
ENVIRONMENTAL PERMITTING (ENGLAND AND WALES) REGULATIONS 2016 (SI 2016 NO. 1154)	159
ENVIRONMENTAL PROTECTION ACT 1990	167
EQUALITY ACT 2010	176
EUROPEAN UNION (WITHDRAWAL AGREEMENT) ACT 2020	180
FATAL ACCIDENTS ACT 1976	183
FIRE SAFETY (SCOTLAND) REGULATIONS 2006 (SI 2006 NO. 456)	185
FIRE (SCOTLAND) ACT 2005	193
FOOD SAFETY ACT 1990	200
GAS SAFETY (MANAGEMENT) REGULATIONS 1996 (SI 1996 NO. 551)	201
HAZARDOUS WASTE (ENGLAND AND WALES) REGULATIONS 2005 (SI 2005 NO. 894)	202
HAZARDOUS WASTE (MISCELLANEOUS AMENDMENTS) REGULATIONS 2015 (SI 2015 NO. 1360)	205
HEALTH ACT 2006	206
HEALTH AND SAFETY AND NUCLEAR (FEES) REGULATIONS 2021 (SI 2021 NO. 33)	208
HEALTH AND SAFETY AT WORK, ETC. ACT 1974	209
HEALTH AND SAFETY AT WORK, ETC. ACT 1974 (CIVIL LIABILITY) (EXCEPTIONS) REGULATIONS 2013 (SI 2013 NO. 1667)	223
HEALTH AND SAFETY AT WORK, ETC. ACT 1974 (GENERAL DUTIES OF SELF-EMPLOYED PERSONS) (PRESCRIBED UNDERTAKINGS) REGULATIONS 2015 (SI 2015 NO. 1583)	224
HEALTH AND SAFETY (CONSULTATION WITH EMPLOYEES) REGULATIONS 1996 (SI 1996 NO. 1513)	226
HEALTH AND SAFETY (DISPLAY SCREEN EQUIPMENT) REGULATIONS 1992 (SI 1992 NO. 2792)	229
HEALTH AND SAFETY (ENFORCING AUTHORITY) REGULATIONS 1998 (SI 1998 NO. 494)	231
HEALTH AND SAFETY (FIRST-AID) REGULATIONS 1981 (SI 1981 NO. 917)	232
HEALTH AND SAFETY INFORMATION FOR EMPLOYEES REGULATIONS 1989 (SI 1989 NO. 682)	239
HEALTH AND SAFETY (MISCELLANEOUS AMENDMENTS) REGULATIONS 2002 (SI 2002 NO. 2174)	241
HEALTH AND SAFETY (OFFENCES) ACT 2008	244
HEALTH AND SAFETY (SAFETY SIGNS AND SIGNALS) REGULATIONS 1996 (SI 1996 NO. 341)	246
HEALTH AND SAFETY (SHARP INSTRUMENTS IN HEALTHCARE) REGULATIONS 2013 (SI 2013 NO. 645)	248

Contents

IONISING RADIATION (MEDICAL EXPOSURE) REGULATIONS 2017 (SI 2017 NO. 1322) (AS AMENDED)	250
IONISING RADIATIONS REGULATIONS 2017 (SI 2017 NO. 1075)	252
LIFTING OPERATIONS AND LIFTING EQUIPMENT REGULATIONS 1998 (SI 1998 NO. 2307)	258
LIMITATION ACT 1980	262
MANAGEMENT OF HEALTH AND SAFETY AT WORK REGULATIONS 1999 (SI 1999 NO. 3242)	266
MANUAL HANDLING OPERATIONS REGULATIONS 1992 (SI 1992 NO. 2793)	272
NEW ROADS AND STREET WORKS ACT 1991	275
NITRATE POLLUTION PREVENTION REGULATIONS 2015 (SI 2015 NO. 668)	276
NITRATE POLLUTION PREVENTION (WALES) REGULATIONS 2013 (SI 2013 NO. 2506)	277
OCCUPIERS' LIABILITY ACT 1957	278
OCCUPIERS' LIABILITY ACT 1984	280
OCCUPIERS' LIABILITY (SCOTLAND) ACT 1960	282
PERSONAL PROTECTIVE EQUIPMENT (PPE) AT WORK REGULATIONS 1992 (SI 1992 NO. 2966)	283
PRESSURE EQUIPMENT (SAFETY) REGULATIONS 2016 (SI 2016 NO. 1105)	286
PRESSURE SYSTEMS SAFETY REGULATIONS 2000 (SI 2000 NO. 128)	288
PROHIBITION OF SMOKING IN CERTAIN PREMISES (SCOTLAND) REGULATIONS 2006 (SI 2006 NO. 90)	293
PROVISION AND USE OF WORK EQUIPMENT REGULATIONS 1998 (SI 1998 NO. 2306)	295
PUBLIC INTEREST DISCLOSURE ACT 1998	305
PUBLIC ORDER ACT 1986	308
REGULATORY REFORM (FIRE SAFETY) ORDER 2005 (RRFSO) (SI 2005 NO. 1541)	309
REPORTING OF INJURIES, DISEASES AND DANGEROUS OCCURRENCES REGULATIONS 2013 (RIDDOR) (SI 2013 NO. 1471)	312
RESTRICTION OF THE USE OF CERTAIN HAZARDOUS SUBSTANCES IN ELECTRICAL AND ELECTRONIC EQUIPMENT REGULATIONS 2012 (SI 2012 NO. 3032)	316
SAFETY REPRESENTATIVES AND SAFETY COMMITTEES REGULATIONS 1977 (SI 1977 NO. 500)	318
SIMPLE PRESSURE VESSELS (SAFETY) REGULATIONS 2016 (SI 2016 NO. 1092)	321
SMOKE-FREE (PREMISES AND ENFORCEMENT) REGULATIONS 2006 (SI 2006 NO. 3368)	323
SMOKE-FREE PREMISES, ETC. (WALES) REGULATIONS 2007 (SI 2007 NO. 787)	324
SMOKING, HEALTH AND SOCIAL CARE (SCOTLAND) ACT 2005	327
SOCIAL ACTION, RESPONSIBILITY AND HEROISM ACT 2015	329
SOCIAL SECURITY ADMINISTRATION ACT 1992	330
SOCIAL SECURITY (CLAIMS AND PAYMENTS) REGULATIONS 1979 (SI 1979 NO. 628)	331
SUPPLY OF MACHINERY (SAFETY) REGULATIONS 2008 (SI 2008 NO. 1597)	333
TRADE UNION AND LABOUR RELATIONS (CONSOLIDATION) ACT 1992 AS AMENDED	337
TREATY ON THE FUNCTIONING OF THE EUROPEAN UNION	342
UK REACH	346
UNFAIR CONTRACT TERMS ACT 1977	347
WASTE ELECTRICAL AND ELECTRONIC EQUIPMENT REGULATIONS 2013 (SI 2013 NO. 3113)	354
WORK AT HEIGHT REGULATIONS 2005 (SI 2005 NO. 735)	357
WORKING TIME REGULATIONS 1998 (SI 1998 NO. 1833)	363
WORKPLACE (HEALTH, SAFETY AND WELFARE) REGULATIONS 1992 (SI 1992 NO. 3004)	373
CASE LAW	377

BUILDING REGULATIONS 2010 (SI 2010 NO. 2214)

Introduction

These Regulations impose duties on people carrying out "building work", which is defined in regulation 3 as the erection or extension of a building; the provision or extension of a controlled service or fitting; the material alteration of a building or controlled service or fitting; work required in relation to a material change of use; insertion of insulating material into a cavity wall; work involving underpinning of a building; work required to replace or renovate thermal elements; work relating to a change in a building's energy status; and work relating to improvement of the energy status of certain large existing buildings.

The Regulations require that building work must be carried out so that it complies with the applicable requirements set out in Parts A to P of Schedule 1 and they provide for the oversight of building works by the local authority.

The Regulations are lengthy and split into 10 Parts with six Schedules. They also link to 18 Approved Documents that have special legal status and provide practical guidance on compliance with the requirements.

PART 1: General

Regulations 1 and 2: Citation and commencement and Interpretation

Gives the meaning of various words and phrases used in the Regulations (see also reg. 3).

PART 2: Control of Building Work

Regulation 3: Meaning of building work

Gives the full interpretation of the phrase 'building work' such as:

(a) the erection or extension of a building;

(b) the provision or extension of a controlled service or fitting in or in connection with a building;

(c) the material alteration of a building, or a controlled service or fitting, ... etc.

Regulation 4: Requirements relating to building work

(1) Subject to paragraph (2) building work shall be carried out so that:

  (a) it complies with the applicable requirements contained in Schedule 1; and

  (b) in complying with any such requirement there is no failure to comply with any other such requirement.

(2) Where:

  (a) building work is of a kind described in regulation 3(1)(g), (h) or (i); and

  (b) the carrying out of that work does not constitute a material alteration;

  that work need only comply with the applicable requirements of Part L of Schedule 1.

(3) Building work shall be carried out so that, after it has been completed:

  (a) any building which is extended or to which a material alteration is made; or

  (b) any building in, or in connection with, which a controlled service or fitting is provided, extended or materially altered; or

  (c) any controlled service or fitting,

  complies with the applicable requirements of Schedule 1 or, where it did not comply with any such requirement, is no more unsatisfactory in relation to that requirement than before the work was carried out.

Regulation 5: Meaning of material change of use

Defines the phrase.

Regulation 6: Requirements relating to material change of use

(1) Where there is a material change of use of the whole of a building, such work, if any, shall be carried out as is necessary to ensure that the building complies with the applicable requirements of Schedule 1.

Regulation 7: Materials and workmanship

Building work shall be carried out:

(a) with adequate and proper materials which:

    (i) are appropriate for the circumstances in which they are used,

    (ii) are adequately mixed or prepared,

    (iii) are applied, used or fixed so as adequately to perform the functions for which they are designed; and

(b) in a workmanlike manner.

Regulations 8 to 11

Deal with limitations, exemptions and local authorities' powers to relax the requirements.

PART 3: Notices, Plans and Certificates

Regulation 12: Giving of a building notice or deposit of plans

(1) This regulation applies to a person who intends to:

    (a) carry out building work;

    (b) replace or renovate a thermal element in a building to which the energy efficiency requirements apply;

    (c) make a change to a building's energy status; or

    (d) make a material change of use.

(2) Subject to following provisions of this regulation, a person to whom this regulation applies shall:

    (a) give to the local authority a building notice in accordance with regulation 13; or

    (b) deposit full plans with the local authority in accordance with regulation 14.

Regulation 13: Particulars and plans where a building notice is given

(1) A building notice shall state the name and address of the person intending to carry out the work and shall be signed by that person or on that person's behalf, and shall contain or be accompanied by:

    (a) a statement that it is given for the purpose of regulation 12(2)(a);

    (b) a description of the proposed building work, renovation or replacement of a thermal element, change to the building's energy status or material change of use; and

    (c) particulars of the location of the building to which the proposal relates and the use or intended use of that building.

(2) In the case of the erection or extension of a building, a building notice shall be accompanied by:

    (a) a plan to a scale of not less than 1:1250 showing:

        (i) the size and position of the building, or the building as extended, and its relationship to adjoining boundaries;

        (ii) the boundaries of the curtilage of the building, or the building as extended, and the size, position and use of every other building or proposed building within that curtilage;

        (iii) the width and position of any street on or within the boundaries of the curtilage of the building or the building as extended;

    (b) a statement specifying the number of storeys (each basement level being counted as one storey), in the building to which the proposal relates; and

    (c) particulars of:

        (i) the provision to be made for the drainage of the building or extension; and

        (ii) the steps to be taken to comply with any local enactment which applies.

Regulations 14 and 15

Deal with full plans and consultation with sewerage undertaker.

Regulation 16: Notice of commencement and completion of certain stages of work

(1) Subject to paragraphs (8) and (9) [application], a person who proposes to carry out building work shall not commence that work unless:

(a) that person has given the local authority notice of intention to commence work; and

(b) at least two days have elapsed since the end of the day on which the notice was given.

(2) Subject to paragraph (8) [application], a person carrying out building work shall not:

(a) cover up any excavation for a foundation, any foundation, any damp-proof course or any concrete or other material laid over a site; or

(b) cover up in any way any drain or sewer to which these Regulations apply, unless that person has given the local authority notice of intention to commence that work, and at least one day has elapsed since the end of the day on which the notice was given.

Regulation 17: Completion certificates

(1) A local authority shall within the specified period give a completion certificate in all cases (including a case where a certificate has already been given under regulation 17A [Certificate for building occupied before work is completed]) where they are satisfied, after taking all reasonable steps, that, following completion of building work carried out on it, a building complies with the relevant provisions.

(2) The specified period referred to in paragraph (1) is eight weeks starting from the date on which the person carrying out the building work notifies the local authority that the work has been completed.

Regulation 18: Unauthorised building work

(1) This regulation applies where it appears to a local authority that unauthorised building work has been carried out on or after 11 November 1985.

PART 4: Supervision of Building Work Otherwise than by Local Authorities

Regulation 19: Supervision of building work otherwise than by local authorities

PART 5: Self-certification Schemes

Regulation 20: Provisions applicable to self-certification schemes

PART 6: Energy Efficiency Requirements

Regulations 21 to 35

Deal with energy performance, CO_2 emission rates and energy assessors.

PART 7: Water Efficiency

Regulations 36 and 37

Deal with water efficiency and water consumption calculation.

PART 8: Information to be Provided by the Person Carrying Out Work

Regulation 38: Fire safety information

(1) This regulation applies where building work:

(a) consists of or includes the erection or extension of a relevant building; or

(b) is carried out in connection with a relevant change of use of a building,

and Part B of Schedule 1 imposes a requirement in relation to the work.

(2) The person carrying out the work shall give fire safety information to the responsible person not later than the date of completion of the work, or the date of occupation of the building or extension, whichever is the earlier.

(3) In this regulation:

 (a) "fire safety information" means information relating to the design and construction of the building or extension, and the services, fittings and equipment provided in or in connection with the building or extension which will assist the responsible person to operate and maintain the building or extension with reasonable safety;

 (b) a "relevant building" is a building to which the Regulatory Reform (Fire Safety) Order 2005 applies, or will apply after the completion of building work;

 (c) a "relevant change of use" is a material change of use where, after the change of use takes place, the Regulatory Reform (Fire Safety) Order 2005 will apply, or continue to apply, to the building; and

 (d) "responsible person" has the meaning given by article 3 of the Regulatory Reform (Fire Safety) Order 2005.

Regulations 39 and 40

Deal with information about ventilation and use of fuel and power.

PART 9: Testing and Commissioning

Regulations 41 to 44

Deal with sound insulation testing, ventilation air flow rate testing, pressure testing and commissioning.

PART 10: Miscellaneous

Regulation 45: Testing of building work

The local authority may make such tests of any building work as may be necessary to establish whether it complies with regulation 7 or any of the applicable requirements contained in Schedule 1.

Regulation 46: Sampling of material

The local authority may take such samples of the material to be used in the carrying out of building work as may be necessary to enable them to ascertain whether such materials comply with the provisions of these Regulations.

Regulations 47 to 54

Deal with contraventions, transitional provisions and revocations and amendments.

SCHEDULES

SCHEDULE 1: Requirements

SCHEDULE 2: Exempt buildings and work

SCHEDULE 3: Self-certification schemes and exemptions from requirement to give building notice or deposit full plans

SCHEDULE 4: Descriptions of work where no building notice or deposit of full plans required

SCHEDULE 5: Revocation of regulations

SCHEDULE 6: Consequential amendments

APPROVED DOCUMENTS

The **Building Act 1984** gives the Secretary of State power to approve and issue documents containing practical guidance with respect to the requirements contained in these Regulations. The following publications, originally approved for the purposes of the 2000 Regulations, are approved for the purposes of these Regulations:

Part A- Structure

Part B- Fire safety

Part C- Site preparation and resistance to contaminates and moisture

Part D- Toxic substances

Part E- Resistance to the passage of sound

Part F- Ventilation

Part G- Sanitation, hot water safety and water efficiency

Part H- Drainage and waste disposal

Part J- Combustion appliances and fuel storage systems

Part K- Protection from falling, collision and impact

Part L- Conservation of fuel and power

Part M- Access to and use of buildings

Part N- Glazing safety (withdrawn)

Part P- Electrical safety

Part Q- Security

Part R- Physical infrastructure for high speed electronic communications networks

Regulation 7- Materials and workmanship

Two of the Approved Documents, *B: Fire Safety Volume 2: Buildings other than dwellings* and *P: Electrical safety - Dwellings* are briefly summarised below.

APPROVED DOCUMENT B: FIRE SAFETY

2019 edition – for use in England

Volume 2: Buildings other than dwellings

Requirement B1: Means of warning and escape

Requirement B2: Internal fire spread (linings)

Requirement B3: Internal fire spread (structure)

Requirement B4: External fire spread

Requirement B5: Access and facilities for the fire service

Regulations: 6(3), 7(2) and 38

Summary

This approved document gives guidance on how to comply with Part B of the **Building Regulations**. It contains the following sections:

- Volume 1 deals solely with dwellings, including blocks of flats.
- Volume 2 deals with all other types of building covered by the **Building Regulations**.

Requirement B1: When there is a fire, ensure both:

(a) satisfactory means of sounding an alarm;

(b) satisfactory means of escape for people.

Requirement B2: Inhibit the spread of fire over internal linings of buildings.

Requirement B3: The building must be built such that all of the following are achieved in the event of a fire:

(a) The premature collapse of the building is avoided.

(b) Sufficient fire separation is provided within buildings and between adjoining buildings.

(c) Automatic fire suppression is provided where necessary.

(d) The unseen spread of fire and smoke in cavities is restricted.

Requirement B4: Restrict both:

(a) the potential for fire to spread over external walls and roofs (including compliance with regulations 6(4) and 7(2));

(b) the spread of fire from one building to another.

Requirement B5: Ensure both:

(a) satisfactory access for the fire service and its appliances;

(b) facilities in buildings to help firefighters save the lives of people in and around buildings.

Regulation 38: Provide fire safety information to building owners.

Appendices: Information common to more than one requirement of Part B

Appendix A: Key terms

Appendix B: Performance of materials, products and structures

Appendix C: Fire door sets

Appendix D: Methods of measurement

Appendix E: Sprinklers

Appendix F: Standards referred to

Appendix G: Documents referred to

APPROVED DOCUMENT P: ELECTRICAL SAFETY – DWELLINGS

2013 edition – for use in England

P1: Design and installation of electrical installations

This approved document gives guidance on how to comply with Part P of the **Building Regulations**. It contains the following sections:

- Section 1: Technical requirements for electrical work in dwellings.
- Section 2: The types of building and electrical installation within the scope of Part P and the types of electrical work that are notifiable.
- Section 3: The different procedures that may be followed to show that electrical work complies with Part P.
- Appendix A: Key terms.
- Appendix B: Standards referred to.

CARRIAGE OF DANGEROUS GOODS AND USE OF TRANSPORTABLE PRESSURE EQUIPMENT REGULATIONS 2009 (SI 2009 NO. 1348) (AS AMENDED)

Introduction

These Regulations, although lengthy, are simplifications of earlier Regulations of the same name. They are split into seven parts and have three schedules:

- Part 1: Introductory Provisions.
- Part 2: Prohibitions and Requirements.
- Part 3: Exemptions.
- Part 4: Transportable Pressure Equipment.
- Part 5: Radiological Emergencies.
- Part 6: GB Competent Authority Functions.
- Part 7: Miscellaneous.

This is a very technical piece of legislation and is the preserve of specialist dangerous goods safety advisers. Some of the technical content is not obvious because, rather than being self-contained, it makes extensive reference to existing legally binding international agreements. This is an eminently sensible approach because the experts already refer to the international agreements. These agreements are: ADR (The European Agreement concerning the International Carriage of Dangerous Goods by Road) and RID (The Regulations concerning the International Carriage of Dangerous Goods by Rail). These international agreements deal with, in turn, the operational requirements for the carriage of dangerous goods by road and rail across Europe. There is also a brief mention of carriage of dangerous goods by inland waterways. The Regulations therefore need to be read in conjunction with these agreements to fully understand the requirements.

Only a summary will be given here. Where details of a particular regulation would not be helpful, only the regulation number and title has been included.

Part 1: Introductory Provisions

Regulation 1: Citation and Commencement

Regulation 2: Interpretation - General

Any reference to a part, chapter, section, or subsection relates to that part of ADR (in relation to carriage of goods by road), RID (in relation to carriage of goods by rail) and ADN (in relation to carriage of goods by inland waterway) unless the context requires otherwise.

Regulation 3: Interpretation of ADR, RID, and ADN for the Purposes of These Regulations

Notably, the Regulations extend the scope of these agreements to also include national carriage (technically they only cover international carriage, so this is harmonising national and international carriage requirements).

Regulation 4: Application

These Regulations apply to the carriage of dangerous goods by road and by rail (excluding the Channel Tunnel). They also apply to inland waterways but only in respect of the training and examination system for safety advisers.

Part 2: Prohibitions and Requirements

Regulation 5: Carriage to be in Accordance with ADR and RID

With a simple sentence, these Regulations reference completely the existing international agreements. These are weighty external tomes containing an extreme amount of technical detail. In practice, experts in this field already use these documents extensively, so it is reflecting reality. Copies of ADR can be downloaded free from www.unece.org/trans/danger/publi/adr/adr_e.html

Regulation 6: Alternative Placarding Requirements to Apply to Certain National Carriage

In certain cases, it is permissible to use alternative placards, marks and plate markings on UK-registered vehicles for **UK domestic** carriage. The detail of this derogation is given in Schedule 1 and covers such things as the UK's "HazChem" style plates, incorporating the familiar UK Emergency Action Codes (EACs), instead of the European Hazard Identification Numbers (HINs). Both systems are designed to assist the emergency services when dealing with an incident.

Regulation 7: Additional Security Requirements for Carriage by Road

This concerns extra security when carrying Class 1 goods (i.e. explosives) by road. This is in addition to those already required by ADR.

Regulation 8: Additional Security Requirements Relating to Access

A person involved in the carriage of dangerous goods must take all reasonable steps to ensure that unauthorised access to those goods is prevented.

Regulation 9: Application of ADR to Carriage by Private Individuals

Private individuals carrying Class 1 goods by road must follow the provisions of ADR (ADR itself exempts such individuals in most cases). There is an exemption in the case of carrying small quantities (e.g. less than 50Kg of fireworks or 30Kg of other explosives or a combination of explosives and fireworks).

Regulation 10: Application of ADR to Carriage by Certain Enterprises

Part 3: Exemptions

Regulation 11: Derogations and Transitional Provisions

The Secretary of State for Transport may issue exemptions from any of the provisions in certain cases. These are published collectively from time to time in the approved document entitled *Carriage of dangerous goods: approved derogations and transitional provisions*.

Regulation 12: Authorisations

The Secretary of State for Transport, the Secretary of State for Defence (in relation to the armed forces), the Secretary of State for Energy and Climate Change and also the HSE can authorise national carriage contrary to the forgoing provisions. These are clearly for exceptional circumstances.

Regulation 13: Reference Temperatures and Standards

Regulation 14: Old Pressure Receptacles

Regulation 15: Carriage within the Perimeter of an Enclosed Area

Regulation 16: Carriage by Road Other Than in Vehicles

Regulation 17: Instruments of War and Related Material

Regulation 18: Nuclear Material

Part 4: Transportable Pressure Equipment

Regulation 19: Scope of Obligations

A **manufacturer, importer, distributor, owner** or **operator:**

- May only place on the market or use equipment if they ensure that the equipment meets the requirements of the **Dangerous Goods Directive**.
- Must identify on request to the HSE any manufacturer, importer, distributor or owner who has supplied them with, or to whom they have supplied, equipment over at least the previous 10 years.

A **manufacturer** (and any **importer** or **distributor** placing equipment on the market under their own name, or significantly modifying equipment) must:

- Ensure a conformity assessment is carried out, mark equipment accordingly and make sure that technical documents are retained for the appropriate period of time.
- Take appropriate action if equipment they have placed on the market is not in compliance with relevant standards.
- Record instances of non-compliance and corrective measures taken.

- On receipt of a request from a competent authority, provide all information and documents necessary to show that the equipment meets specified requirements.

Importers and **distributors** also have certain responsibilities relating to manufacturers' compliance with conformity assessment, marking of equipment, its storage and transport, technical documentation, non-compliance with Directives, informing the manufacturer and the HSE of any risk and provision of information to/co-operation with a competent authority.

An **owner** (excluding certain private individuals) must:

- Ensure that equipment for which they are responsible is stored and transported in conditions that do not jeopardise the compliance of that equipment with relevant standards.
- Inform the manufacturer, importer or distributor and the HSE if the equipment is considered to present a risk.
- Record instances of non-compliance and corrective measures taken.

An **operator** must inform the owner and the HSE if they consider that equipment presents a risk.

Regulation 20: Authorised Representatives

A **manufacturer** may appoint in writing a person ('an authorised representative') to carry out some of the duties imposed by Regulation 19.

Regulation 21: Reassessment of Conformity

Regulation 22: Periodic Inspection and Repeated Use

Regulation 23: Misleading and Other Marks

It sounds obvious but they have to say it. Misleading information is prohibited as is anything else which might reduce the visibility and legibility of the conformity mark.

An amendment to the original Regulations added requirements for tanks for the storage of volatile organic compounds (VOCs).

Part 5: Radiation Emergencies and Notifiable Events

Regulation 24: Radiation Emergencies and Notifiable Events

This covers Class 7 goods (i.e. radioactives) and refers you to Schedule 2 for the detail of what to do in an emergency (armed forces are exempted).

Part 6: GB Competent Authority Functions

Regulation 25: Competent Authority

The Secretary of State for Transport is the competent authority for most functions. However, the HSE is the competent authority for specific aspects of Class 1 goods (i.e. explosives). Military use of explosives and radioactives is the preserve of the Secretary of State for Defence and the Secretary of State for Energy and Climate Change is the competent authority for carriage of radioactive goods where the Secretary of State for Defence is not.

Regulation 26: Functions of the GB Competent Authority arising under ADR, RID and ADN

Regulation 27: Fees in Relation to the Functions of the GB Competent Authority

Regulation 28: GB Competent Authority Functions relating to Reference Temperatures and Standards

Regulation 29: Appointments by the GB Competent Authority

Regulation 30: Certain Functions Deemed to Have Been Performed by the GB Competent Authority

Part 7: Miscellaneous

Regulation 31: Keeping and Provision of Information

Any accident reports produced in accordance with ADR/RID/ADN must be made available to the GB competent authority upon request. The information contained in the transport document (again as required by ADR/RID/ADN) must be kept for at least three months after completion of carriage of those goods.

Regulation 32: Enforcement

Enforcement is shared between the HSE, the Secretary of State for Transport, the Office of Rail Regulation, the Secretary of State for Energy and Climate Change, the Secretary of State for Defence and the Police.

Regulation 33: Revocation

This Regulation formally revokes the 2007 Regulations.

Regulation 34: Duty to Review

This is a new requirement, inserted by the 2011 amendment. The Secretary of State must publish a five-yearly review of the operation and effect of these Regulations.

Schedules

Schedule 1: PLACARDS, MARKS AND PLATE MARKINGS FOR NATIONAL CARRIAGE

Part 1: Carriage of Goods by Road

Details are given of the design and use of hazard warning panels.

Part 2: Carriage of Goods by Rail

Schedule 2: RADIOLOGICAL EMERGENCIES

Schedule 3: APPOINTMENTS

CHEMICALS (HAZARD INFORMATION AND PACKAGING FOR SUPPLY) REGULATIONS 2009 (SI 2009 NO. 716)

Summary

These Regulations, commonly referred to as **CHIP 4**, have been largely revoked by the **Biocidal Products and Chemicals (Appointment of Authorities and Enforcement) Regulations 2013 (SI 2013 No. 1506)**. This change has been made necessary by the coming into force on 1 June 2015 of the EU's **Classification, Labelling and Packaging Regulation (CLP) (EC 1272/2008)**, which implements the Globally Harmonised System of Classification (GHS) within Europe.

Regulation 1: Citation, Commencement and Extent

The Regulations came into force on 6 April 2009. They do not extend to Northern Ireland.

Regulation 2: Interpretation

This defines the terms and expressions used in the Regulations. Many of these are common with other legislation. Of particular relevance are:

- Approved Classification and Labelling Guide (ACLG) which contains information on how to self-classify and label chemicals.

- 'Category of danger' means, in relation to a substance or preparation dangerous for supply, one of the categories of danger specified in column 1 of Schedule 1.

- 'The CLP Regulation' means **Regulation (EC) No. 1272/2008** of the European Parliament and of the Council of 16 December 2008 on classification, labelling and packaging of substances and mixtures, amending and repealing **Directives 67/548/EEC and 1999/45/EC**, and amending **Regulation (EC) No. 1907/2006**, of which articles 6(5), 11(3), 12, 14, 18(3)(b), 23, 25 to 29, 35(2) second and third sub-paragraph and Annexes I to VII are as amended from time to time.

- 'Community workplace exposure limit' means, in respect of a substance, an exposure limit for that substance established in an EU instrument. These values are included in EH40 as Workplace Exposure Limits in the UK or are incorporated into specific legislation such as **COSHH** or the **Control of Asbestos Regulations**.

- 'Dangerous substance' means a substance which is either included in Table 3.2 of Part 3 of Annex VI of the **CLP Regulation (EC 1272/2008)** or, if not so listed, which is in one or more of the categories of danger specified in column 1 of Schedule 1.

- 'Indication of danger' means, in relation to a dangerous substance or dangerous preparation, one or more of the indications of danger referred to in column 1 of Schedule 2 and:

    - In the case of a dangerous substance listed in Table 3.2 of Part 3 of Annex VI of the **CLP Regulation**, it is one or more indications of danger specified for that substance by a symbol-letter in that list.

    - In the case of any other dangerous substance or a dangerous preparation, it is one or more indications of danger determined in accordance with the classification of that substance or preparation in accordance with Regulation 4 and the Approved Classification and Labelling Guide.

- 'Package' means the package in which the substance or preparation is supplied and includes the receptacle containing the substance or preparation, or a pallet or other device which enables more than one receptacle to be handled as a unit. It does not include a container used for transport unless that is retained by the recipient for the purpose of storing the product.

- 'Preparation' means a mixture or solution of two or more substances.

- 'Receptacle' means a container together with any material, wrapping and component, including any closure or fastener, associated with the container which enables the container to perform its containment function.

- 'Risk phrase' means a risk phrase listed in Annex III of **Council Directive 67/548/EEC**.

- 'Safety phrase' means a safety phrase listed in Annex IV of **Council Directive 67/548/EEC**.

- 'Substance' means a chemical element and its compounds in the natural state or obtained by any production process, including any additive necessary to preserve the stability of the product and any impurity deriving from the process used, but excluding any solvent which may be separated without affecting the stability of the substance or changing its composition.

- 'Supply' in relation to a substance or preparation means making that substance or preparation available to another person and includes importation of the substance or preparation into Great Britain, and 'supplier' shall be construed accordingly.

- Where reference is made to a quantity in litres, that reference shall mean:

    - in the case of a liquid, the volume in litres of that liquid;

- in the case of a compressed gas, the volume in litres of the receptacle containing that gas; and
- in the case of a compressed gas dissolved in a solvent, liquefied gas or solid, the same number of kilograms of that gas or solid; and for the purposes of aggregation, one kilogram of a solid shall be deemed to be equivalent to one litre of liquid or gas.

NB: This regulation will not apply on or after 1 June 2018 (see Part 4, regulation 36 of the **Biocidal Products and Chemicals (Appointment of Authorities and Enforcement) Regulations 2013**).

Regulation 3: Application

These Regulations do not apply to chemicals such as foods, medicines, controlled drugs and cosmetics for which specific regulatory regimes are in place. Nor do they apply to the carriage of substances or preparations by rail, road, inland waterway, sea or air. A full list of the exemptions appears in Regulation 3.

NB: This regulation will not apply on or after 1 June 2018 (see Part 4, regulation 36 of the **Biocidal Products and Chemicals (Appointment of Authorities and Enforcement) Regulations 2013**).

Regulation 4: *This regulation was revoked as of 1 June 2015 (see Part 4, regulation 36 of the **Biocidal Products and Chemicals (Appointment of Authorities and Enforcement) Regulations 2013**).*

Regulation 5: This regulation was revoked as of 31 May 2015 (see Part 4, regulation 36 of the **Biocidal Products and Chemicals (Appointment of Authorities and Enforcement) Regulations 2013**).

Regulation 5A: Advertisements for Dangerous Preparations: *This regulation will not apply on or after 1 June 2017 (see Part 4, regulation 36 of the **Biocidal Products and Chemicals (Appointment of Authorities and Enforcement) Regulations 2013**).*

Regulations 6 to 11: *These regulations were revoked as of 1 June 2015 (see Part 4, regulation 36 of the **Biocidal Products and Chemicals (Appointment of Authorities and Enforcement) Regulations 2013**).*

Regulation 12: Retention of Data for Dangerous Preparations

Those who first supply dangerous preparations must maintain records of information used for the purpose of classifying and labelling or relating to any child-resistant fastening or any tactile warning which forms part of the packaging. The records must be kept for at least three years after the date on which the dangerous preparation was supplied by the supplier for the last time. The record (or a copy of it) shall be made available to the appropriate enforcing authority within 28 days of the request. When requested by the enforcing authority, the supplier shall provide a copy of any certificate issued by a qualified test house.

NB: This regulation will not apply on or after 1 June 2018 (see Part 4, regulation 36 of the **Biocidal Products and Chemicals (Appointment of Authorities and Enforcement) Regulations 2013**).

Note: The **REACH Regulation (EC 1907/2006)** similarly contains data retention requirements, but the time limit being 10 years (Article 36) for information used for the compilation of safety data sheets.

Regulations 13 to 16: Revoked

NB: Except to the extent that they continue to apply for the purposes of enforcing regulation 12 of the 2009 Regulations, regulations 14 to 16 and 18 were revoked with effect from 1 June 2015.

Schedules

Following the Regulations are 7 Schedules, all of which remain in force:

Schedule 1	Classification of Dangerous Substances and Dangerous Preparations	See below
Schedule 2	Indications of Danger and Symbols for Dangerous Substances and Dangerous Preparations	Not included here
Schedule 3	Provisions for Classifying Dangerous Preparations	Not included here
Schedule 4	Labelling Particulars for Dangerous Substances and Dangerous Preparations and for Certain Other Preparations	Not included here
Schedule 5	British and International Standards Relating to Child-Resistant Fastenings and Tactile Warning Devices	Not included here
Schedule 6	Amendments	Not included here
Schedule 7	Revocations	Not included here

SCHEDULE 1

CLASSIFICATION OF SUBSTANCES AND PREPARATIONS DANGEROUS FOR SUPPLY

Part 1		
Categories of Danger		
Column 1	Column 2	Column 3
Category of danger	**Property**	**Symbol-letter**
PHYSICO-CHEMICAL PROPERTIES		
Explosive	Solid, liquid, pasty or gelatinous substances and preparations which may react exothermically without atmospheric oxygen thereby quickly evolving gases, and which under defined test conditions detonate, quickly deflagrate or upon heating explode when partially confined.	E
Oxidising	Substances and preparations which give rise to a highly exothermic reaction in contact with other substances, particularly flammable substances.	O
Extremely flammable	Liquid substances and preparations having an extremely low flash point and a low boiling point and gaseous substances and preparations which are flammable in contact with air at ambient temperature and pressure.	F +
Highly flammable	The following substances and preparations, namely: (c) substances and preparations which may become hot and finally catch fire in contact with air at ambient temperature without any application of energy; (d) solid substances and preparations which may readily catch fire after brief contact with a source of ignition and which continue to burn or to be consumed after removal of the source of ignition; (e) liquid substances and preparations having a very low flash point; or (f) substances and preparations which, in contact with water or damp air, evolve highly flammable gases in dangerous quantities.	F
Flammable	Liquid substances and preparations having a low flash point.	none
HEALTH EFFECTS		
Very toxic	Substances and preparations which in very low quantities cause death or acute or chronic damage to health when inhaled, swallowed or absorbed via the skin.	T +
Toxic	Substances and preparations which in low quantities cause death or acute or chronic damage to health when inhaled, swallowed or absorbed via the skin.	T
Harmful	Substances and preparations which may cause death or acute or chronic damage to health when inhaled, swallowed or absorbed via the skin.	Xn
Harmful	Substances and preparations which may, on contact with living tissues, destroy them.	C

Corrosive	Non-corrosive substances and preparations which, through immediate, prolonged or repeated contact with the skin or mucous membrane, may cause inflammation.	Xi
Sensitising	Substances and preparations which, if they are inhaled or if they penetrate the skin, are capable of eliciting a reaction by hyper-sensitisation such that on further exposure to the substance or preparation, characteristic adverse effects are produced.	
Sensitising by inhalation		Xn
Sensitising by skin contact		Xi
Carcinogenic	Substances and preparations which, if they are inhaled or ingested or if they penetrate the skin, may induce cancer or increase its incidence.	
Category 1		T
Category 2		T
Category 3		Xn
Mutagenic	Substances and preparations which, if they are inhaled or ingested or if they penetrate the skin, may induce heritable genetic defects or increase their incidence.	
Category 1		T
Category 2		T
Category 3		Xn
Toxic for reproduction	Substances and preparations which, if they are inhaled or ingested or if they penetrate the skin, may produce or increase the incidence of non-heritable adverse effects in the progeny and/or an impairment of male or female reproductive functions or capacity.	
Category 1		T
Category 2		T
Category 3		Xn
ENVIRONMENTAL EFFECTS		
Dangerous for the environment	Substances which, were they to enter into the environment, would present or might present an immediate or delayed danger for one or more components of the environment.	N

CLASSIFICATION, LABELLING AND PACKAGING OF CHEMICALS (AMENDMENTS TO SECONDARY LEGISLATION) REGULATIONS 2015 (SI 2015 NO. 21)

Introduction

EU Regulation (EC) No. 1272/2008 on classification, labelling and packaging of substances and mixtures (the **CLP Regulation**) introduces the new EU classification system for hazardous chemicals. **Directive 2014/27/EU** amends five health and safety Directives to align them with the **CLP Regulation**. The **Classification, Labelling and Packaging of Chemicals (Amendments to Secondary Legislation) Regulations 2015** transpose **Directive 2014/27/EU** by amending the relevant domestic legislation.

The five Directives amended by **Directive 2014/27/EU** are:

- The **Safety Signs at Work Directive (92/58/EEC)**.
- The **Chemical Agents Directive (98/24/EC)**.
- The **Carcinogens and Mutagens Directive (2004/37/EC)**.
- The **Pregnant Workers Directive (92/85/EEC)**.
- The **Young Persons at Work Directive (94/33/EC)**.

The policy objective is to align domestic regulations with the new EU classification system contained in the **CLP Regulation**. Clear alignment of relevant domestic regulations with **CLP** ensures that the regulations remain workable and avoids confusion.

The amendments as set out in these Regulations ensure that the original policy intention of the regulations in relation to the protection of workers from hazardous substances can continue to be met when **CHIP** is revoked.

The Regulations also make amendments to domestic health and safety and related regulations to replace references to the current classification system, contained in the **Chemicals (Hazard Information and Packaging for Supply) Regulations 2009 (CHIP)** to be revoked, with references to the **CLP Regulation**.

These Regulations amend the following legislation:

- The **Health and Safety (Safety Signs and Signals) Regulations 1996 (SI 1996/341)**.
- The **Pipelines Safety Regulations 1996 (SI 1996/825)**.
- The **Merchant Shipping and Fishing Vessels (Health and Safety at Work) Regulations 1997 (SI 1997/2962)**.
- The **Health and Safety (Enforcing Authority) Regulations 1998 (SI 1998/494)**.
- The **Merchant Shipping and Fishing Vessels (Health and Safety at Work) (Employment of Young Persons) Regulations 1998 (SI 1998/2411)**.
- The **Management of Health and Safety at Work Regulations 1999 (SI 1999/3242)**.
- The **Merchant Shipping and Fishing Vessels (Safety Signs and Signals) Regulations 2001 (SI 2001/3444)**.
- The **Health and Safety at Work, etc. Act 1974 (Application to Environmentally Hazardous Substances) Regulations 2002 (SI 2002/282)**.
- The **Control of Lead at Work Regulations 2002 (SI 2002/2676)**.
- The **Control of Substances Hazardous to Health Regulations 2002 (SI 2002/2677)**.
- The **Dangerous Substances and Explosive Atmospheres Regulations 2002 (SI 2002/2776)**.
- The **Regulatory Reform (Fire Safety) Order 2005 (SI 2005/1541)**.
- The **Fire Safety (Scotland) Regulations 2006 (SI 2006/456)**.
- The **Merchant Shipping and Fishing Vessels (Health and Safety at Work) (Carcinogens and Mutagens) Regulations 2007 (SI 2007/3100)**.
- The **Legislative and Regulatory Reform (Regulatory Functions) Order 2007 (SI 2007/3544)**.
- The **REACH Enforcement Regulations 2008 (SI 2008/2852)**.
- The **Co-Ordination of Regulatory Enforcement (Regulatory Functions in Scotland and Northern Ireland) Order 2009 (SI 2009/669)**.

- The **Merchant Shipping and Fishing Vessels (Health and Safety at Work) (Chemical Agents) Regulations 2010 (SI 2010/330)**.
- The **Control of Asbestos Regulations 2012 (SI 2012/632)**.
- The **Biocidal Products and Chemicals (Appointment of Authorities and Enforcement) Regulations 2013 (SI 2013/1506)**.

CLASSIFICATION, LABELLING AND PACKAGING OF SUBSTANCES AND MIXTURES REGULATION (THE CLP REGULATION) (EU REGULATION (EC) NO. 1272/2008) AS APPLIES TO GREAT BRITAIN

Introduction

GB CLP is based around the **European Regulation on the classification, labelling and packaging of substances and mixtures** that has been amended (mainly by the **Chemicals (Health and Safety) and Genetically Modified Organisms (Contained Use) (Amendment etc.) (EU Exit) Regulations 2019**) so that it works effectively following UK withdrawal from the EU.

GB CLP adopts the United Nations' Globally Harmonised System on the classification and labelling of chemicals and applies to substances and mixtures placed on the market in England, Wales and Scotland. Substances and mixtures placed on the market in Northern Ireland are subject to the **EU CLP Regulation**.

GB CLP is enforced by the HSE and local authorities. In cases that involve environmental hazards, the Environment Agency and the Scottish Environment Protection Agency provide technical and scientific support.

A summary of the key features is given below; you should refer to the Regulation and amendments themselves for full details.

The Articles

Article 1 outlines the purpose and scope of the Regulation

Article 2: Definitions

Some of the definitions included in this Article are as follows:

- 'Hazard class' means the nature of the physical, health or environmental hazard.
- 'Hazard category' means the division of criteria within each hazard class, specifying hazard severity.
- 'Hazard pictogram' means a graphical composition that includes a symbol plus other graphic elements, such as a border, background pattern or colour that is intended to convey specific information on the hazard concerned.
- 'Signal word' means a word that indicates the relative level of severity of hazards to alert the reader to a potential hazard; the following two levels are distinguished:
  - 'Danger' means a signal word indicating the more severe hazard categories.
  - 'Warning' means a signal word indicating the less severe hazard categories.
- 'Hazard statement' means a phrase assigned to a hazard class and category that describes the nature of the hazards of a hazardous substance or mixture, including, where appropriate, the degree of hazard.
- 'Precautionary statement' means a phrase that describes recommended measure(s) to minimise or prevent adverse effects resulting from exposure to a hazardous substance or mixture due to its use or disposal.
- 'The Agency' means the Health and Safety Executive. 'Competent authority' means the authority or authorities or bodies established by Great Britain to carry out the obligations arising from this Regulation.
- 'Use' means any processing, formulation, consumption, storage, keeping, treatment, filling into containers, transfer from one container to another, mixing, production of an article or any other utilisation.

Article 3: Hazardous Substances and Mixtures and Specification of Hazard Classes

Makes reference to Annex I, which identifies hazardous substances or mixtures.

Article 4: General Obligations to Classify, Label and Package

Places obligations on manufacturers, importers and downstream users to classify substances or mixtures before placing them on the market.

Articles 5 to 8: Identification and Examination of Information

These articles place obligations on manufacturers, importers and downstream users of a substance to identify and examine available information on substances and mixtures. Testing on animals shall only be undertaken when no other alternatives which provide adequate reliability and quality of data are possible. Tests on non-human primates are prohibited, as are tests on humans for the purposes of **GB CLP**. New tests can be performed by manufacturers, importers or downstream users in cases where other means of generating information have been exhausted but it is still necessary to determine whether a substance or mixture entails a health or environmental hazard.

Articles 9 to 16: Evaluation of Hazard Information and Decision on Classification

Manufacturers, importers and downstream users of a substance or mixture shall evaluate information so as to ascertain hazards associated with the substance or mixture. Provision is made for the setting of specific concentration limits and generic concentration limits, which must be set by the manufacturer, importer or downstream user where adequate and reliable scientific information shows that the hazard of a substance is evident. Impurities, additives, etc. need to be taken into account for the purposes of classification if their concentration is at or above a certain value.

Specific cases requiring further evaluation are set out in Article 12. Article 13 deals with the decision to classify substances and mixtures.

Article 14 covers specific rules for the classification of mixtures, whereas Article 15 covers arrangements for the review of classification for substances and mixtures.

Article 16 sets out arrangements for classification of substances included in the classification and labelling inventory.

Articles 17 to 34: Hazard Communication in the Form of Labelling

This group of articles sets out general rules for the content of labels and provides that labels shall include details that permit the identification of the substance or mixture (so-called 'product identifiers'). Arrangements for inclusion of hazard pictograms, signal words, hazard statements and precautionary statements are included in Articles 19 to 22. Some substances may need to have supplemental information included on the label; this is provided for at Article 25. Hazard pictograms, hazard statements, and precautionary statements are to be shown in order of precedence.

Exemptions from labelling and packaging requirements are provided for within Article 29.

Article 30 covers arrangements for updating information on labels. Article 31 provides the general rules for the application of labels and Article 32 covers the location of information on labels. Specific rules for labelling of outer packaging, inner packaging and single packaging are set out at Article 33.

Article 35: Packaging

This article sets out rules for design and construction of packaging and mandates the use of child-resistant fastenings and tactile warnings in some circumstances.

Articles 36 to 42: Harmonisation of Classification and Labelling of Substances and the Classification and Labelling Inventory

Article 36 sets out the harmonisation of classification and labelling of substances covering respiratory sensitisation, germ cell mutagenicity, carcinogenicity and reproductive toxicity. The procedure for harmonisation of classification and labelling of substances is set out at Article 37. Articles 39 to 42 deal with the classification and labelling inventory.

Articles 43 to 47: Competent Authorities and Enforcement

These articles set out arrangements for the appointment of competent authorities and enforcement authorities and for co-operation between them. They also cover arrangements for the establishment of national help desks to provide advice to manufacturers, importers, distributors, downstream users and any other interested parties on their respective responsibilities and on obligations under **GB CLP**. This group of articles also features arrangements for the appointment of bodies responsible for receiving information relating to emergency health response, arrangements for enforcement and reporting and for the introduction of effective, proportionate and dissuasive penalties for non-compliance with **GB CLP**.

Articles 48 to 62: Common and Final Provisions

Article 48 requires that any advertisement for a substance classified as hazardous shall mention the hazard classes or hazard categories concerned. Suppliers are obliged to assemble and keep all information used for the purposes of classification and labelling for a period of at least 10 years after the substance or mixture was last supplied (Article 49).

Article 52 allows the Secretary of State or a Devolved Authority to take "appropriate provisional measures" in cases where it has justifiable grounds for believing that a substance or mixture constitutes a serious risk to human health or the environment.

Article 53 enables the Secretary of State to amend articles of **GB CLP** due to technical and scientific progress and/or development of the GHS.

The remaining articles deal with administrative provisions.

The Annexes

Extensive annexes are provided with **GB CLP**. They are as follows:

- ANNEX I: Classification and labelling requirements for hazardous substances and mixtures
- ANNEX II: Special rules for labelling and packaging of certain substances and mixtures
- ANNEX III: List of hazard statements, supplemental hazard information and supplemental label elements
- ANNEX IV: List of precautionary statements
- ANNEX V: Hazard pictograms
- ANNEX VI: Harmonised classification and labelling for certain hazardous substances
- ANNEX VII: Translation table from classification under **Directive 67/548/EEC** to classification under this Regulation

COMPENSATION ACT 2006

The text below focuses on those sections of direct interest in relation to health and safety.

Section 1: Deterrent Effect of Potential Liability

A court considering a claim in negligence or breach of statutory duty may, in determining whether the defendant should have taken particular steps to meet a standard of care (whether by taking precautions against a risk or otherwise), have regard to whether a requirement to take those steps might:

(a) prevent a desirable activity from being undertaken at all, to a particular extent or in a particular way, or

(b) discourage persons from undertaking functions in connection with a desirable activity.

Section 2: Apologies, Offers of Treatment or Other Redress

An apology, an offer of treatment or other redress, shall not of itself amount to an admission of negligence or breach of statutory duty.

Section 3: Mesothelioma - Damages

(1) This section applies where:

   (a) a person ("the responsible person") has negligently or in breach of statutory duty caused or permitted another person ("the victim") to be exposed to asbestos,

   (b) the victim has contracted mesothelioma as a result of exposure to asbestos,

   (c) because of the nature of mesothelioma and the state of medical science, it is not possible to determine with certainty whether it was the exposure mentioned in paragraph (a) or another exposure which caused the victim to become ill, and

   (d) the responsible person is liable in tort, by virtue of the exposure mentioned in paragraph (a), in connection with damage caused to the victim by the disease (whether by reason of having materially increased a risk or for any other reason).

(2) The responsible person shall be liable:

   (a) in respect of the whole of the damage caused to the victim by the disease (irrespective of whether the victim was also exposed to asbestos:

      (i) other than by the responsible person, whether or not in circumstances in which another person has liability in tort, or

      (ii) by the responsible person in circumstances in which he has no liability in tort), and

   (b) jointly and severally with any other responsible person.

(3) Subsection (2) does not prevent:

   (a) one responsible person from claiming a contribution from another, or

   (b) a finding of contributory negligence.

(4) In determining the extent of contributions of different responsible persons in accordance with subsection (3)(a), a court shall have regard to the relative lengths of the periods of exposure for which each was responsible; but this subsection shall not apply:

   (a) if or to the extent that responsible persons agree to apportion responsibility amongst themselves on some other basis, or

   (b) if or to the extent that the court thinks that another basis for determining contributions is more appropriate in the circumstances of a particular case.

(5) In subsection (1) the reference to causing or permitting a person to be exposed to asbestos includes a reference to failing to protect a person from exposure to asbestos.

(6) In the application of this section to Scotland:

    (a) a reference to tort shall be taken as a reference to delict, and

    (b) a reference to a court shall be taken to include a reference to a jury.

(7) The Treasury may make Regulations about the provision of compensation to a responsible person where:

    (a) he claims, or would claim, a contribution from another responsible person in accordance with subsection (3)(a), but

    (b) he is unable or likely to be unable to obtain the contribution, because an insurer of the other responsible person is unable or likely to be unable to satisfy the claim for a contribution.

(8) The Regulations may, in particular:

    (a) [Repealed by the **Financial Services Act 2012**];

    (b) replicate or apply (with or without modification) a transitional compensation provision;

    (c) provide for a specified person to assess and pay compensation;

    (d) provide for expenses incurred (including the payment of compensation) to be met out of levies collected in accordance with section 213(3)(b) of the **Financial Services and Markets Act 2000** (c. 8) (the Financial Services Compensation Scheme);

    (e) modify the effect of a transitional compensation provision;

    (f) enable the Financial Conduct Authority or the Prudential Regulation Authority to amend the Financial Services Compensation Scheme;

    (g) modify the **Financial Services and Markets Act 2000** in its application to an amendment pursuant to paragraph (f);

    (h) make, or require the making of, provision for the making of a claim by a responsible person for compensation whether or not he has already satisfied claims in tort against him;

    (i) make, or require the making of, provision which has effect in relation to claims for contributions made on or after the date on which this Act is passed.

(9) [Repealed by the **Financial Services Act 2012**]

(10) In subsections (7) and (8):

    (a) a reference to a responsible person includes a reference to an insurer of a responsible person, and

    (b) "transitional compensation provision" means a provision of an enactment which is made under the **Financial Services and Markets Act 2000** and:

        (i) preserves the effect of the **Policyholders Protection Act 1975** (c. 75), or

        (ii) applies the Financial Services Compensation Scheme in relation to matters arising before its establishment.

(11) Regulations under subsection (7):

    (a) may include consequential or incidental provision,

    (b) may make provision which has effect generally or only in relation to specified cases or circumstances,

    (c) may make different provision for different cases or circumstances,

    (d) shall be made by statutory instrument, and

    (e) may not be made unless a draft has been laid before and approved by resolution of each House of Parliament.

CONFINED SPACES REGULATIONS 1997 (SI 1997 NO. 1713)

Summary

These Regulations came into force in January 1998. The employer's duty to provide a safe place and safe system of work must extend to cover those situations in which employees, by the very nature of the work, have to enter and work in confined and cramped conditions. The following are the main regulations.

Regulation 1: Interpretation

'Confined Space'

Any place, including any chamber, tank, vat, silo, pit, trench, pipe, sewer, flue, well or other similar space in which, by virtue of its enclosed nature, there arises a reasonably foreseeable specified risk.

'Free Flowing Solid'

Any substance consisting of solid particles and which is of, or is capable of being in, a flowing or running consistency, and includes flour, grain, sugar, sand or other similar materials.

'Specified Risk'

- A serious risk of injury to any person at work arising from a fire or explosion.
- The loss of consciousness of any person at work arising from an increase in body temperature.
- The loss of consciousness or asphyxiation of any person at work arising from gas, fume, vapour or the lack of oxygen.
- The drowning of any person at work arising from an increase in the level of a liquid.
- The asphyxiation of any person at work arising from a free flowing solid or the inability to reach a respirable environment due to entrapment by a free flowing solid.

'System of Work'

- Includes the provision of suitable equipment which is in good working order.

Regulation 2: Disapplication

The Regulations do not apply to:

- The master or crew of a sea-going ship in respect of normal ship-board activities carried out solely by a ship's crew under the direction of the master.
- Any place below ground in a mine.
- Any diving project to which the **Diving at Work Regulations 1997** apply.

Regulation 3: Duties

Every employer shall:

- Ensure compliance with the provisions of these Regulations in respect of any work carried out by his employees.
- Ensure compliance, so far as is reasonably practicable, with the provisions of these Regulations in respect of any work carried out by persons other than his employees insofar as the provisions relate to matters which are within his control.

Every self-employed person shall:

- Comply with the provisions of these Regulations in respect of his own work.
- Ensure compliance, so far as is reasonably practicable, with the provisions of these Regulations in respect of any work carried out by other persons insofar as the provisions relate to matters which are within his control.

Regulation 4: Work in Confined Spaces

No person at work shall enter a confined space to carry out work for any purpose unless it is not reasonably practicable to achieve that purpose without such entry.

So far as is reasonably practicable, no person at work shall enter or carry out any work in, or (other than as a result of an emergency) leave, a confined space otherwise than in accordance with a system of work which, in relation to any relevant specified risks, renders that work safe and without risks to health.

Regulation 5: Emergency Arrangements

No person at work shall enter or carry out work in a confined space unless suitable and sufficient arrangements for the rescue of persons in the event of an emergency have been prepared in respect of it whether or not arising out of a specified risk. Those arrangements will not be suitable and sufficient unless they reduce, so far as is reasonably practicable, the risks to the health and safety of any person required to put the arrangements for rescue into operation. Furthermore, the arrangements require, where resuscitation of any persons is needed, as a result of a relevant specified risk, the provision and maintenance of resuscitation equipment and procedures. Where rescue arrangements are necessary they must immediately be put into operation.

Regulation 6: Exemption Certificates

The Health and Safety Executive may issue a certificate in writing, exempting any person or class of persons, or any type or class of confined space, from the Regulations, subject to certain conditions and to a time limit. The exemption may be revoked at any time by the Executive by a further certificate in writing.

Exemption will not be granted unless, having regard to the circumstances of the case, the conditions which it proposes and any other requirements imposed by or under any enactments which apply to the case, the HSE is satisfied that the health and safety of persons who are likely to be affected by the exemption will not be prejudiced as a result of it.

Regulation 7: Defence in Proceedings

In any proceedings for an offence concerning the failure to implement rescue arrangements immediately, it shall be a defence for the person to prove that the contravention was due to the act or default of another person not being one of his employees and that he took all reasonable precautions and exercised all due diligence to avoid the contravention. The defence cannot be relied on, however, unless, within a period ending seven clear days before the hearing to determine mode of trial, he has served on the prosecutor a notice in writing giving such information identifying or assisting in the identification of the other person as was then in his possession.

Where a contravention is due to the act or default of some other person, that other person shall be guilty of the offence.

CONSTRUCTION (DESIGN AND MANAGEMENT) REGULATIONS 2015 (SI 2015 NO. 51)

Regulation 1: Citation and Commencement

These Regulations may be cited as the **Construction (Design and Management) Regulations 2015** and came into force on 6 April 2015.

Regulation 2: Interpretation

(1) In these Regulations, unless the context otherwise requires:

"business" means a trade, business or other undertaking (whether for profit or not); "client" means any person for whom a project is carried out;

"construction phase" means the period of time beginning when construction work in a project starts and ending when construction work in that project is completed;

"construction phase plan" means a plan drawn up under regulations 12 or 15;

"construction site" includes any place where construction work is being carried out or to which the workers have access, but does not include a workplace within the site which is set aside for purposes other than construction work;

"construction work" means the carrying out of any building, civil engineering or engineering construction work and includes:

(a) the construction, alteration, conversion, fitting out, commissioning, renovation, repair, upkeep, redecoration or other maintenance (including cleaning which involves the use of water or an abrasive at high pressure or the use of corrosive or toxic substances), de-commissioning, demolition or dismantling of a structure;

(b) the preparation for an intended structure, including site clearance, exploration, investigation (but not site survey) and excavation, and the clearance or preparation of the site or structure for use or occupation at its conclusion;

(c) the assembly on site of prefabricated elements to form a structure or the disassembly on site of prefabricated elements which, immediately before such disassembly, formed a structure;

(d) the removal of a structure or of any product or waste resulting from demolition or dismantling of a structure or from disassembly of prefabricated elements which immediately before such disassembly formed such a structure; and

(e) the installation, commissioning, maintenance, repair or removal of mechanical, electrical, gas, compressed air, hydraulic, telecommunications, computer or similar services which are normally fixed within or to a structure;

but does not include the exploration for, or extraction of, mineral resources or activities preparatory thereto carried out at a place where such exploration or extraction is carried out;

"contractor" means any person (including a non-domestic client) who, in the course or furtherance of a business, carries out, manages or controls construction work;

"design" includes drawings, design details, specification and bill of quantities (including specification of articles or substances) relating to a structure, and calculations prepared for the purpose of a design;

"designer" means any person (including a client, contractor or other person referred to in these Regulations) who in the course or furtherance of a business:

(a) prepares or modifies a design; or

(b) arranges for or instructs any person under his control to do so,

relating to a structure or to a product or mechanical or electrical system intended for a particular structure, and a person is deemed to prepare a design where a design is prepared by a person under his control;

"domestic client" means a client for whom a project is being carried out which is not in the course or furtherance of a business of that client;

"excavation" includes any earthwork, trench, well, shaft, tunnel or underground working;

"the general principles of prevention" means the general principles of prevention specified in Schedule 1 to the **Management of Health and Safety at Work Regulations 1999**;

"health and safety file" means a file prepared under regulation 12(5);

"Inspector for the Executive" means an inspector within the meaning given in section 53 (1) of the 1974 Act; "loading bay" means any facility for loading or unloading;

"place of work" means any place which is used by any person at work for the purposes of construction work or for the purposes of any activity arising out of or in connection with construction work;

"pre-construction information" means the information in the client's possession or which is reasonably obtainable by or on behalf of the client, which is relevant to the construction work and is of an appropriate level of detail and proportionate to the risks involved, including:

(a) information about:

   (i) the project;

   (ii) planning and management of the project;

   (iii) health and safety hazards, including design and construction hazards and how they will be addressed; and

(b) information in any existing health and safety file;

"pre-construction phase" means any period of time during which design or preparatory work is carried out for a project and may continue during the construction phase;

"principal contractor" means the contractor appointed under regulation 5(1)(b) to perform the specified duties in regulations 12 to 14;

"principal designer" means the designer appointed under regulation 5(1)(a) to perform the specified duties in regulations 11 and 12;

"project" means a project which includes or is intended to include construction work and includes all planning, design, management or other work involved in a project until the end of the construction phase;

"site rules" means the rules which are drawn up for a particular construction site and are necessary for health or safety purposes; "structure" means:

(a) any building, timber, masonry, metal or reinforced concrete structure, railway line or siding, tramway line, dock, harbour, inland navigation, tunnel, shaft, bridge, viaduct, waterworks, reservoir, pipe or pipe-line, cable, aqueduct, sewer, sewage works, gasholder, road, airfield, sea defence works, river works, drainage works, earthworks, lagoon, dam, wall, caisson, mast, tower, pylon, underground tank, earth retaining structure or structure designed to preserve or alter any natural feature and fixed plant;

(b) any structure similar to anything specified in paragraph (a);

(c) any formwork, falsework, scaffold or other structure designed or used to provide support or means of access during construction work;

and any reference to a structure includes a part of a structure;

"traffic route" means a route for pedestrian traffic or for vehicles and includes any doorway, gateway, loading bay or ramp; "vehicle" includes any mobile work equipment;

"work equipment" means any machinery, appliance, apparatus, tool or installation for use at work (whether exclusively or not); "working day" means any day on which construction work takes place;

"workplace" means a workplace within the meaning of regulation 2(1) of the **Workplace (Health, Safety and Welfare) Regulations 1992** other than a construction site.

(2) Any reference in these Regulations to a plan, rule, document, report or copy includes a copy or electronic version which is:

    (a) capable of being retrieved or reproduced when required; and

    (b) secure from loss or unauthorised interference.

Regulation 3: Application In and Outside Great Britain

These Regulations shall apply:

(a) in Great Britain; and

(b) to premises and activities outside Great Britain to which sections 1 to 59 and 80 to 82 of the 1974 Act applied by virtue of articles 9 and 11(1)(a) of the **Health and Safety at Work, etc. Act 1974 (Application outside Great Britain) Order 2013**.

Regulation 4: Client Duties in Relation to Managing Projects

(1) A client must make suitable arrangements for managing a project, including the allocation of sufficient time and other resources.

(2) Arrangements are suitable if they ensure that:

    (a) the construction work can be carried out, so far as is reasonably practicable, without risks to the health or safety of any person affected by the project; and

    (b) the facilities required by Schedule 2 are provided in respect of any person carrying out construction work.

(3) A client must ensure that these arrangements are maintained and reviewed throughout the project.

(4) A client must provide pre-construction information as soon as is practicable to every designer and contractor appointed, or being considered for appointment, to the project.

(5) A client must ensure that:

    (a) before the construction phase begins, a construction phase plan is drawn up by the contractor if there is only one contractor, or by the principal contractor; and

    (b) the principal designer prepares a health and safety file for the project, which:

        (i) complies with the requirements of regulation 12(5);

        (ii) is revised from time to time as appropriate to incorporate any relevant new information; and

        (iii) is kept available for inspection by any person who may need it to comply with any relevant legal requirements.

(6) A client must take reasonable steps to ensure that:

    (a) the principal designer complies with any other principal designer duties in regulations 11 and 12; and

    (b) the principal contractor complies with any other principal contractor duties in regulations 12 to 14.

(7) If a client disposes of the client's interest in the structure, the client complies with the duty in paragraph (5)(b)(iii) by providing the health and safety file to the person who acquires the client's interest in the structure and ensuring that that person is aware of the nature and purpose of the file.

(8) Where there is more than one client in relation to a project:

    (a) one or more of the clients may agree in writing to be treated for the purposes of these Regulations as the only client or clients; and

(b) except for the duties specified in sub-paragraph (c) only the client or clients agreed in paragraph (a) are subject to the duties owed by a client under these Regulations;

(c) the duties in the following provisions are owed by all clients:

(i) regulation 8(4); and

(ii) paragraph (4) and regulation 8(6) to the extent that those duties relate to information in the possession of the client.

Regulation 5: Appointment of the Principal Designer and the Principal Contractor

(1) Where there is more than one contractor, or if it is reasonably foreseeable that more than one contractor will be working on a project at any time, the client must appoint in writing:

(a) a designer with control over the pre-construction phase as principal designer; and

(b) a contractor as principal contractor.

(2) The appointments must be made as soon as is practicable, and, in any event, before the construction phase begins.

(3) If the client fails to appoint a principal designer, the client must fulfil the duties of the principal designer in regulations 11 and 12.

(4) If the client fails to appoint a principal contractor, the client must fulfil the duties of the principal contractor in regulations 12 to 14.

Regulation 6: Notification

(1) A project is notifiable if the construction work on a construction site is scheduled to:

(a) last longer than 30 working days and have more than 20 workers working simultaneously at any point in the project; or

(b) exceed 500 person days.

(2) Where a project is notifiable, the client must give notice in writing to the Executive as soon as is practicable before the construction phase begins.

(3) The notice must:

(a) contain the particulars specified in Schedule 1;

(b) be clearly displayed in the construction site office in a comprehensible form where it can be read by any worker engaged in the construction work; and

(c) if necessary, be periodically updated.

(4) Where a project includes construction work of a description for which the Office of Rail Regulation is the enforcing authority by virtue of regulation 3 of the **Health and Safety (Enforcing Authority for Railways and Other Guided Transport Systems) Regulations 2006**, the client must give notice to the Office of Rail Regulation instead of the Executive.

(5) Where a project includes construction work on premises which are or are on:

(a) a GB nuclear site (within the meaning given in section 68 of the **Energy Act 2013**);

(b) an authorised defence site (within the meaning given in regulation 2(1) of the **Health and Safety (Enforcing Authority) Regulations 1998**); or

(c) a new nuclear build site (within the meaning given in regulation 2A of those Regulations), the client must give notice to the Office for Nuclear Regulation instead of the Executive.

Regulation 7: Application to Domestic Clients

(1) Where the client is a domestic client the duties in regulations 4(1) to (7) and 6 must be carried out by:

    (a) the contractor for a project where there is only one contractor;

    (b) the principal contractor for a project where there is more than one contractor; or

    (c) the principal designer where there is a written agreement that the principal designer will fulfil those duties.

(2) Where a domestic client fails to make the appointments required by regulation 5:

    (a) the designer in control of the pre-construction phase of the project is the principal designer;

    (b) the contractor in control of the construction phase of the project is the principal contractor.

Regulation 8: General Duties

(1) A designer (including a principal designer) or contractor (including a principal contractor) appointed to work on a project must have the skills, knowledge and experience, and, if they are an organisation, the organisational capability, necessary to fulfil the role that they are appointed to undertake, in a manner that secures the health and safety of any person affected by the project.

(2) A designer or contractor must not accept an appointment to a project unless they fulfil the conditions in paragraph (1).

(3) A person who is responsible for appointing a designer or contractor to carry out work on a project must take reasonable steps to satisfy themselves that the designer or contractor fulfils the conditions in paragraph (1).

(4) A person with a duty or function under these Regulations must co-operate with any other person working on or in relation to a project, at the same or an adjoining construction site, to the extent necessary to enable any person with a duty or function to fulfil that duty or function.

(5) A person working on a project under the control of another must report to that person anything they are aware of in relation to the project which is likely to endanger their own health or safety or that of others.

(6) Any person who is required by these Regulations to provide information or instruction must ensure the information or instruction is comprehensible and provided as soon as is practicable.

(7) To the extent that they are applicable to a domestic client, the duties in paragraphs (3), (4) and (6) must be carried out by the person specified in regulation 7(1).

Regulation 9: Duties of Designers

(1) A designer must not commence work in relation to a project unless satisfied that the client is aware of the duties owed by the client under these Regulations.

(2) When preparing or modifying a design the designer must take into account the general principles of prevention and any pre-construction information to eliminate, so far as is reasonably practicable, foreseeable risks to the health or safety of any person:

    (a) carrying out or liable to be affected by construction work;

    (b) maintaining or cleaning a structure; or

    (c) using a structure designed as a workplace.

(3) If it is not possible to eliminate these risks, the designer must, so far as is reasonably practicable:

    (a) take steps to reduce or, if that is not possible, control the risks through the subsequent design process;

    (b) provide information about those risks to the principal designer; and

(c) ensure appropriate information is included in the health and safety file.

(4) A designer must take all reasonable steps to provide, with the design, sufficient information about the design, construction or maintenance of the structure, to adequately assist the client, other designers and contractors to comply with their duties under these Regulations.

Regulation 10: Designs Prepared or Modified Outside Great Britain

(1) Where a design is prepared or modified outside Great Britain for use in construction work to which these Regulations apply:

(a) the person who commissions it, if established within Great Britain; or

(b) if that person is not so established, the client for the project,

must ensure that regulation 9 is complied with.

(2) This regulation does not apply to a domestic client.

Regulation 11: Duties of a Principal Designer in Relation to Health and Safety at the Pre-Construction Phase

(1) The principal designer must plan, manage and monitor the pre-construction phase and co-ordinate matters relating to health and safety during the pre-construction phase to ensure that, so far as is reasonably practicable, the project is carried out without risks to health or safety.

(2) In fulfilling the duties in paragraph (1), and in particular when:

(a) design, technical and organisational aspects are being decided in order to plan the various items or stages of work which are to take place simultaneously or in succession; and

(b) estimating the period of time required to complete such work or work stages,

the principal designer must take into account the general principles of prevention and, where relevant, the content of any construction phase plan and any health and safety file.

(3) In fulfilling the duties in paragraph (1), the principal designer must identify and eliminate or control, so far as is reasonably practicable, foreseeable risks to the health or safety of any person:

(a) carrying out or liable to be affected by construction work;

(b) maintaining or cleaning a structure; or

(c) using a structure designed as a workplace.

(4) In fulfilling the duties in paragraph (1), the principal designer must ensure all designers comply with their duties in regulation 9.

(5) In fulfilling the duty to co-ordinate health and safety matters in paragraph (1), the principal designer must ensure that all persons working in relation to the pre-construction phase co-operate with the client, the principal designer and each other.

(6) The principal designer must:

(a) assist the client in the provision of the pre-construction information required by regulation 4(4); and

(b) so far as it is within the principal designer's control, provide pre-construction information, promptly and in a convenient form, to every designer and contractor appointed, or being considered for appointment, to the project.

(7) The principal designer must liaise with the principal contractor for the duration of the principal designer's appointment and share with the principal contractor information relevant to the planning, management and monitoring of the construction phase and the co-ordination of health and safety matters during the construction phase.

Regulation 12: Construction Phase Plan and Health and Safety File

(1) During the pre-construction phase, and before setting up a construction site, the principal contractor must draw up a construction phase plan, or make arrangements for a construction phase plan to be drawn up.

(2) The construction phase plan must set out the health and safety arrangements and site rules taking account, where necessary, of the industrial activities taking place on the construction site and, where applicable, must include specific measures concerning work which falls within one or more of the categories set out in Schedule 3.

(3) The principal designer must assist the principal contractor in preparing the construction phase plan by providing to the principal contractor all information the principal designer holds that is relevant to the construction phase plan including:

(a) pre-construction information obtained from the client;

(b) any information obtained from designers under regulation 9(3)(b).

(4) Throughout the project the principal contractor must ensure that the construction phase plan is appropriately reviewed, updated and revised from time to time so that it continues to be sufficient to ensure that construction work is carried out, so far as is reasonably practicable, without risks to health or safety.

(5) During the pre-construction phase, the principal designer must prepare a health and safety file appropriate to the characteristics of the project which must contain information relating to the project which is likely to be needed during any subsequent project to ensure the health and safety of any person.

(6) The principal designer must ensure that the health and safety file is appropriately reviewed, updated and revised from time to time to take account of the work and any changes that have occurred.

(7) During the project, the principal contractor must provide the principal designer with any information in the principal contractor's possession relevant to the health and safety file, for inclusion in the health and safety file.

(8) If the principal designer's appointment concludes before the end of the project, the principal designer must pass the health and safety file to the principal contractor.

(9) Where the health and safety file is passed to the principal contractor under paragraph (8), the principal contractor must ensure that the health and safety file is appropriately reviewed, updated and revised from time to time to take account of the work and any changes that have occurred.

(10) At the end of the project, the principal designer, or where there is no principal designer the principal contractor, must pass the health and safety file to the client.

Regulation 13: Duties of a Principal Contractor in Relation to Health and Safety at the Construction Phase

(1) The principal contractor must plan, manage and monitor the construction phase and co-ordinate matters relating to health and safety during the construction phase to ensure that, so far as is reasonably practicable, construction work is carried out without risks to health or safety.

(2) In fulfilling the duties in paragraph (1), and in particular when:

(a) design, technical and organisational aspects are being decided in order to plan the various items or stages of work which are to take place simultaneously or in succession; and

(b) estimating the period of time required to complete the work or work stages, the principal contractor must take into account the general principles of prevention.

(3) The principal contractor must:

(a) organise co-operation between contractors (including successive contractors on the same construction site);

(b) co-ordinate implementation by the contractors of applicable legal requirements for health and safety; and

(c) ensure that employers and, if necessary for the protection of workers, self-employed persons:

(i) apply the general principles of prevention in a consistent manner, and in particular when complying with the provisions of Part 4; and

(ii) where required, follow the construction phase plan.

(4) The principal contractor must ensure that:

(a) a suitable site induction is provided;

(b) the necessary steps are taken to prevent access by unauthorised persons to the construction site; and

(c) facilities that comply with the requirements of Schedule 2 are provided throughout the construction phase.

(5) The principal contractor must liaise with the principal designer for the duration of the principal designer's appointment and share with the principal designer information relevant to the planning, management and monitoring of the pre-construction phase and the co-ordination of health and safety matters during the pre-construction phase.

Regulation 14: Principal Contractor's Duties to Consult and Engage with Workers

The principal contractor must:

(a) make and maintain arrangements which will enable the principal contractor and workers engaged in (b) construction work to co-operate effectively in developing, promoting and checking the effectiveness of measures to ensure the health, safety and welfare of the workers;

(b) consult those workers or their representatives in good time on matters connected with the project which may affect their health, safety or welfare, in so far as they or their representatives have not been similarly consulted by their employer;

(c) ensure that those workers or their representatives can inspect and take copies of any information which the principal contractor has, or which these Regulations require to be provided to the principal contractor, which relate to the health, safety or welfare of workers at the site, except any information:

(i) the disclosure of which would be against the interests of national security;

(ii) which the principal contractor could not disclose without contravening a prohibition imposed by or under an enactment;

(iii) relating specifically to an individual, unless that individual has consented to its being disclosed;

(iv) the disclosure of which would, for reasons other than its effect on health, safety or welfare at work, cause substantial injury to the principal contractor's undertaking or, where the information was supplied to the principal contractor by another person, to the undertaking of that other person;

(v) obtained by the principal contractor for the purpose of bringing, prosecuting or defending any legal proceedings.

Regulation 15: Duties of Contractors

(1) A contractor must not carry out construction work in relation to a project unless satisfied that the client is aware of the duties owed by the client under these Regulations.

(2) A contractor must plan, manage and monitor construction work carried out either by the contractor or by workers under the contractor's control, to ensure that, so far as is reasonably practicable, it is carried out without risks to health and safety.

(3) Where there is more than one contractor working on a project, a contractor must comply with:

(a) any directions given by the principal designer or the principal contractor; and

(b) the parts of the construction phase plan that are relevant to that contractor's work on the project.

(4) If there is only one contractor working on the project, the contractor must take account of the general principles of prevention when:

(a) design, technical and organisational aspects are being decided in order to plan the various items or stages of work which are to take place simultaneously or in succession; and

(b) estimating the period of time required to complete the work or work stages.

(5) If there is only one contractor working on the project, the contractor must draw up a construction phase plan, or make arrangements for a construction phase plan to be drawn up, as soon as is practicable prior to setting up a construction site.

(6) The construction phase plan must fulfil the requirements of regulation 12(2).

(7) A contractor must not employ or appoint a person to work on a construction site unless that person has, or is in the process of obtaining, the necessary skills, knowledge, training and experience to carry out the tasks allocated to that person in a manner that secures the health and safety of any person working on the construction site.

(8) A contractor must provide each worker under their control with appropriate supervision, instructions and information so that construction work can be carried out, so far as is reasonably practicable, without risks to health and safety.

(9) The information provided must include:

   (a) a suitable site induction, where not already provided by the principal contractor;

   (b) the procedures to be followed in the event of serious and imminent danger to health and safety;

   (c) information on risks to health and safety:

      (i) identified by the risk assessment under regulation 3 of **MHSWR**; or

      (ii) arising out of the conduct of another contractor's undertaking and of which the contractor in control of the worker ought reasonably to be aware; and

   (d) any other information necessary to enable the worker to comply with the relevant statutory provisions.

(10) A contractor must not begin work on a construction site unless reasonable steps have been taken to prevent access by unauthorised persons to that site.

(11) A contractor must ensure, so far as is reasonably practicable, that the requirements of Schedule 2 are complied with so far as they affect the contractor or any worker under that contractor's control.

Regulation 16: Application of Part 4

(1) This Part applies only to a construction site.

(2) A contractor carrying out construction work must comply with the requirements of this Part so far as they affect the contractor or any worker under the control of the contractor or relate to matters within the contractor's control.

(3) A domestic client who controls the way in which any construction work is carried out by a person at work must comply with the requirements of this Part so far as they relate to matters within the client's control.

Regulation 17: Safe Places of Construction Work

(1) There must, so far as is reasonably practicable, be suitable and sufficient safe access to and egress from:

   (a) every construction site to every other place provided for the use of any person whilst at work; and

   (b) every place construction work is being carried out to every other place to which workers have access within a construction site.

(2) A construction site must be, so far as is reasonably practicable, made and kept safe for, and without risks to, the health of a person at work there.

(3) Action must be taken to ensure, so far as is reasonably practicable, that no person uses access to or egress from or gains access to any construction site which does not comply with the requirements of paragraph (1) or (2).

(4) A construction site must, so far as is reasonably practicable, have sufficient working space and be arranged so that it is suitable for any person who is working or who is likely to work there, taking account of any necessary work equipment likely to be used there.

Regulation 18: Good Order and Site Security

(1) Each part of a construction site must, so far as is reasonably practicable, be kept in good order and those parts in which construction work is being carried out must be kept in a reasonable state of cleanliness.

(2) Where necessary in the interests of health and safety, a construction site must, so far as is reasonably practicable, and in accordance with the level of risk posed, comply with either or both of the following:

    (a) have its perimeter identified by suitable signs and be arranged so that its extent is readily identifiable; or

    (b) be fenced off.

(3) No timber or other material with projecting nails (or similar sharp object) must:

    (a) be used in any construction work; or

    (b) be allowed to remain in any place,

if the nails (or similar sharp object) may be a source of danger to any person.

Regulation 19: Stability of Structures

(1) All practicable steps must be taken, where necessary to prevent danger to any person, to ensure that any new or existing structure does not collapse if, due to the carrying out of construction work, it:

    (a) may become unstable; or

    (b) is in a temporary state of weakness or instability.

(2) Any buttress, temporary support or temporary structure must:

    (a) be of such design and installed and maintained so as to withstand any foreseeable loads which may be imposed on it; and

    (b) only be used for the purposes for which it was designed and installed and is maintained.

(3) A structure must not be so loaded as to render it unsafe to any person.

Regulation 20: Demolition or Dismantling

(1) The demolition or dismantling of a structure must be planned and carried out in such a manner as to prevent danger or, where it is not practicable to prevent it, to reduce danger to as low a level as is reasonably practicable.

(2) The arrangements for carrying out such demolition or dismantling must be recorded in writing before the demolition or dismantling work begins.

Regulation 21: Explosives

(1) So far as is reasonably practicable, explosives must be stored, transported and used safely and securely.

(2) An explosive charge may be used or fired only if suitable and sufficient steps have been taken to ensure that no person is exposed to the risk of injury from the explosion or from projected or flying material caused by the explosion.

Regulation 22: Excavations

(1) All practicable steps must be taken to prevent danger to any person, including, where necessary, the provision of supports or battering, to ensure that:

    (a) no excavation or part of an excavation collapses;

    (b) no material from the walls or roof of, or adjacent to, any excavation is dislodged or falls; and

(c) no person is buried or trapped in an excavation by material which is dislodged or falls.

(2) Suitable and sufficient steps must be taken to prevent any person, work equipment, or any accumulation of material from falling into any excavation.

(3) Suitable and sufficient steps must be taken, where necessary, to prevent any part of an excavation or ground adjacent to it from being overloaded by work equipment or material.

(4) Construction work must not be carried out in an excavation where any supports or battering have been provided in accordance with paragraph (1) unless:

   (a) the excavation and any work equipment and materials which may affect its safety have been inspected by a competent person:

       (i) at the start of the shift in which the work is to be carried out;

       (ii) after any event likely to have affected the strength or stability of the excavation; and

       (iii) after any material unintentionally falls or is dislodged; and

   (b) the person who carried out the inspection is satisfied that construction work can be safely carried out there.

(5) Where the person carrying out an inspection informs the person on whose behalf the inspection is carried out of any matter about which they are not satisfied (under regulation 24 (1)), construction work must not be carried out in the excavation until the matter has been satisfactorily remedied.

Regulation 23: Cofferdams and Caissons

(1) A cofferdam or caisson must be:

   (a) of suitable design and construction;

   (b) appropriately equipped so that workers can gain shelter or escape if water or materials enter it; and

   (c) properly maintained.

(2) A cofferdam or caisson must not be used to carry out construction work unless:

   (a) the cofferdam or caisson and any work equipment and materials which may affect its safety have been inspected by a competent person:

       (i) at the start of the shift in which the work is to be carried out; and

       (ii) after any event likely to have affected the strength or stability of the cofferdam or caisson; and

   (b) the person who carried out the inspection is satisfied that construction work can be safely carried out there.

(3) Where the person carrying out an inspection informs the person on whose behalf the inspection is carried out of any matter about which they are not satisfied (under regulation 24(1)), construction work must not be carried out in the cofferdam or caisson until the matter has been satisfactorily remedied.

Regulation 24: Reports of Inspections

(1) Where a person who carries out an inspection under regulation 22 or 23 is not satisfied that construction work can be carried out safely at the place inspected, that person must:

   (a) inform the person on whose behalf the inspection was carried out, before the end of the shift within which the inspection is completed, of the matters that could give rise to a risk to the safety of any person;

   (b) prepare a report, which must include:

       (i) the name and address of the person on whose behalf the inspection was carried out;

       (ii) the location of the place of construction work inspected;

  (iii) a description of the place of construction work or part of that place inspected (including any work equipment and materials);

  (iv) the date and time of the inspection;

  (v) details of any matter identified that could give rise to a risk to the safety of any person;

  (vi) details of any action taken as a result of any matter identified in sub-paragraph (v);

  (vii) details of any further action considered necessary; and

  (viii) the name and position of the person making the report; and

 (c) provide the report, or a copy of it, to the person on whose behalf the inspection was carried out, within 24 hours of completing the inspection to which the report relates.

(2) Where the person who carries out an inspection works under the control of another (whether as an employee or otherwise) the person in control must ensure the person who carries out the inspection complies with the requirements of paragraph (1).

(3) The person on whose behalf the inspection was carried out must:

 (a) keep the report or a copy of it available for inspection by an inspector for the Executive:

  (i) at the site where the inspection was carried out until the construction work is completed; and

  (ii) after that for 3 months; and

 (b) send to the inspector such extracts from or copies of the report as the inspector may from time to time require.

(4) This regulation does not require the preparation of more than one report where more than one inspection is carried out under regulation 22(4)(a)(i) or 23(2)(a)(i) within a seven-day period.

Regulation 25: Energy Distribution Installations

(1) Where necessary to prevent danger, energy distribution installations must be suitably located, periodically checked and clearly indicated.

(2) Where there is a risk to construction work from overhead electric power cables:

 (a) they must be directed away from the area of risk; or

 (b) the power must be isolated and, where necessary, earthed.

(3) If it is not reasonably practicable to comply with paragraph (2)(a) or (2)(b), suitable warning notices must be provided together with one or more of the following:

 (i) barriers suitable for excluding work equipment which is not needed;

 (ii) suspended protections where vehicles need to pass beneath the cable; or

 (iii) measures providing an equivalent level of safety.

(4) Construction work which is liable to create a risk to health or safety from an underground service, or from damage to or disturbance of it, must not be carried out unless suitable and sufficient steps (including any steps required by this regulation) have been taken to prevent such risk, so far as is reasonably practicable.

Regulation 26: Prevention of Drowning

(1) Where, in the course of construction work, a person is at risk of falling into water or other liquid with a risk of drowning, suitable and sufficient steps must be taken to:

 (a) prevent, so far as is reasonably practicable, the person falling;

 (b) minimise the risk of drowning in the event of a fall; and

(c) ensure that suitable rescue equipment is provided, maintained and, when necessary, used so that a person may be promptly rescued in the event of a fall.

(2) Suitable and sufficient steps must be taken to ensure the safe transport of any person conveyed by water to or from a place of work.

(3) Any vessel used to convey any person by water to or from a place of work must not be overcrowded or overloaded.

Regulation 27: Traffic Routes

(1) A construction site must be organised in such a way that, so far as is reasonably practicable, pedestrians and vehicles can move without risks to health or safety.

(2) Traffic routes must be suitable for the persons or vehicles using them, sufficient in number, in suitable positions and of sufficient size.

(3) A traffic route does not satisfy paragraph (2) unless suitable and sufficient steps are taken to ensure that:

(a) pedestrians or vehicles may use it without causing danger to the health or safety of persons near it;

(b) any door or gate for pedestrians which leads onto a traffic route is sufficiently separated from that traffic route to enable pedestrians to see any approaching vehicle or plant from a place of safety;

(c) there is sufficient separation between vehicles and pedestrians to ensure safety or, where this is not reasonably practicable:

(i) other means for the protection of pedestrians are provided; and

(ii) effective arrangements are used for warning any person liable to be crushed or trapped by any vehicle of its approach;

(d) any loading bay has at least one exit for the exclusive use of pedestrians; and

(e) where it is unsafe for pedestrians to use a gate intended primarily for vehicles, at least one door for pedestrians is provided in the immediate vicinity of the gate, is clearly marked and is kept free from obstruction.

(4) Each traffic route must be:

(a) indicated by suitable signs where necessary for reasons of health or safety;

(b) regularly checked; and

(c) properly maintained.

(5) No vehicle is to be driven on a traffic route unless, so far as is reasonably practicable, that traffic route is free from obstruction and permits sufficient clearance.

Regulation 28: Vehicles

(1) Suitable and sufficient steps must be taken to prevent or control the unintended movement of any vehicle.

(2) Where a person may be endangered by the movement of a vehicle, suitable and sufficient steps to give warning to any person who is liable to be at risk from the movement of the vehicle must be taken by either or both:

(a) the driver or operator of the vehicle; or

(b) where another person is directing the driver or operator because, due to the nature of the vehicle or task, the driver or operator does not have full visibility, the person providing directions.

(3) A vehicle being used for the purposes of construction work must, when being driven, operated or towed, be:

(a) driven, operated or towed in such a manner as is safe in the circumstances; and

(b) loaded in such a way that it can be driven, operated or towed safely.

(4) A person must not ride, or be required or permitted to ride, on any vehicle being used for the purposes of construction work otherwise than in a safe place in that vehicle provided for that purpose.

(5) A person must not remain, or be required or permitted to remain, on any vehicle during the loading or unloading of any loose material unless a safe place of work is provided and maintained for that person.

(6) Suitable and sufficient measures must be taken to prevent a vehicle from falling into any excavation or pit, or into water, or overrunning the edge of any embankment or earthwork.

Regulation 29: Prevention of Risk from Fire, Flooding or Asphyxiation

Suitable and sufficient steps must be taken to prevent, so far as is reasonably practicable, the risk of injury to a person during the carrying out of construction work arising from:

(a) fire or explosion;

(b) flooding; or

(c) any substance liable to cause asphyxiation.

Regulation 30: Emergency Procedures

(1) Where necessary in the interests of the health or safety of a person on a construction site, suitable and sufficient arrangements for dealing with any foreseeable emergency must be made and, where necessary, implemented, and those arrangements must include procedures for any necessary evacuation of the site or any part of it.

(2) In making arrangements under paragraph (1), account must be taken of:

    (a) the type of work for which the construction site is being used;

    (b) the characteristics and size of the construction site and the number and location of places of work on that site;

    (c) the work equipment being used;

    (d) the number of persons likely to be present on the site at any one time; and

    (e) the physical and chemical properties of any substances or materials on, or likely to be on, the site.

(3) Where arrangements are made under paragraph (1), suitable and sufficient steps must be taken to ensure that:

    (a) each person to whom the arrangements extend is familiar with those arrangements; and

    (b) the arrangements are tested by being put into effect at suitable intervals.

Regulation 31: Emergency Routes and Exits

(1) Where necessary in the interests of the health or safety of a person on a construction site, a sufficient number of suitable emergency routes and exits must be provided to enable any person to reach a place of safety quickly in the event of danger.

(2) The matters in regulation 30(2) must be taken into account when making provision under paragraph (1).

(3) An emergency route or exit must lead as directly as possible to an identified safe area.

(4) An emergency route or exit and any traffic route giving access to it must be kept clear and free from obstruction and, where necessary, provided with emergency lighting so that it may be used at any time.

(5) Each emergency route or exit must be indicated by suitable signs.

Regulation 32: Fire Detection and Fire-Fighting

(1) Where necessary in the interests of the health or safety of a person on a construction site, suitable and sufficient fire-fighting equipment and fire detection and alarm systems must be provided and located in suitable places.

(2) The matters in regulation 30(2) must be taken into account when making provision under paragraph (1).

(3) Fire-fighting equipment or fire detection and alarm systems must be examined and tested at suitable intervals and properly maintained.

(4) Fire-fighting equipment which is not designed to come into use automatically must be easily accessible.

(5) Each person at work on a construction site must, so far as is reasonably practicable, be instructed in the correct use of fire-fighting equipment which it may be necessary for the person to use.

(6) Where a work activity may give rise to a particular risk of fire, a person must not carry out work unless suitably instructed.

(7) Fire-fighting equipment must be indicated by suitable signs.

Regulation 33: Fresh Air

(1) Suitable and sufficient steps must be taken to ensure, so far as is reasonably practicable, that each construction site, or approach to a construction site, has sufficient fresh or purified air to ensure that the site or approach is safe and without risks to health or safety.

(2) Any plant used for the purpose of complying with paragraph (1) must, where necessary for reasons of health or safety, include an effective device to give visible or audible warning of any failure of the plant.

Regulation 34: Temperature and Weather Protection

(1) Suitable and sufficient steps must be taken to ensure, so far as is reasonably practicable, that during working hours the temperature at a construction site that is indoors is reasonable having regard to the purpose for which that place is used.

(2) Where necessary to ensure the health or safety of persons at work on a construction site that is indoors, the construction site must, so far as is reasonably practicable, be arranged to provide protection from adverse weather, having regard to:

   (a) the purpose for which the site is used; and

   (b) any protective clothing or work equipment provided for the use of any person at work there.

Regulation 35: Lighting

Each construction site and approach and traffic route to that site must be provided with suitable and sufficient lighting, which must be, so far as is reasonably practicable, by natural light.

The colour of any artificial lighting provided must not adversely affect or change the perception of any sign or signal provided for the purposes of health or safety.

Suitable and sufficient secondary lighting must be provided in any place where there would be a risk to the health or safety of a person in the event of the failure of primary artificial lighting.

Regulation 36: Enforcement in Respect of Fire

The enforcing authority for regulations 30 and 31 (so far as those regulations relate to fire) and regulation 32, in respect of a construction site which is contained within or forms part of premises occupied by persons other than those carrying out construction work, or any activity related to this work, is:

(a) in England and Wales, the enforcing authority within the meaning of article 25 of the **Regulatory Reform (Fire Safety) Order 2005** in respect of premises to which that Order applies; or

(b) in Scotland, the enforcing authority within the meaning of section 61 of the **Fire (Scotland) Act 2005** in respect of premises to which Part 3 of that Act applies.

Schedules

Schedule 1: Particulars to be notified under regulation 6.

Schedule 2: Minimum welfare requirements for construction sites.

Schedule 3: Work involving particular risks.

CONSUMER PROTECTION ACT 1987

(Relevant sections only)

Part I - Product Liability

Section 2: Liability for Defective Products

Where any damage is caused wholly or partly by a defect in a product, the following persons shall be liable for the damage:

- the producer of the product;
- any person who, by putting his name on the product or using a trademark or other distinguishing mark in relation to the product, has held himself out to be the producer of the product;
- any person who has imported the product into a member State from a place outside the member States in order, in the course of any business of his, to supply it to another.

Where any damage is caused wholly or partly by a defect in a product, any person who supplied the product shall be liable for the damage if:

- the person who suffered the damage requests the supplier to identify one or more of the persons (whether still in existence or not) to whom the above subsection applies in relation to the product;
- that request is made within a reasonable period after the damage occurs and at a time when it is not reasonably practicable for the person making the request to identify all those persons; and
- the supplier fails, within a reasonable period after receiving the request, either to comply with the request or to identify the person who supplied the product to him.

Where two or more persons are liable for the same damage, their liability shall be joint and several.

This section shall be without prejudice to any liability arising otherwise than by virtue of this Part.

Section 3: Meaning of "Defect"

Subject to the following provisions of this section, **there is a defect in a product for the purposes of this Part if the safety of the product is not such as persons generally are entitled to expect**; and for those purposes "safety", in relation to a product, shall include safety with respect to products comprised in that product and safety in the context of risks of damage to property, as well as in the context of risks of death or personal injury.

In determining (for the purposes of the above) what persons generally are entitled to expect in relation to a product all the circumstances shall be taken into account, including:

- the manner in which, and purposes for which, the product has been marketed, its get-up, the use of any mark in relation to the product and any instructions for, or warnings with respect to, doing or refraining from doing anything with or in relation to the product;
- what might reasonably be expected to be done with or in relation to the product; and
- the time when the product was supplied by its producer to another;

and nothing in this section shall require a defect to be inferred from the fact alone that the safety of a product which is supplied after that time is greater than the safety of the product in question.

Section 4: Defences

In any civil proceedings against any person ("the person proceeded against") in respect of a defect in a product it shall be a defence for him to show:

- that the defect is attributable to compliance with any requirement imposed by or under any enactment or with any EU obligation; or
- that the person proceeded against did not at any time supply the product to another; or
- that the following conditions are satisfied, that is to say:
  - that the only supply of the product to another by the person proceeded against was otherwise than in the course of a business of that person's; and
  - that section 2 above does not apply to that person or applies to him by virtue only of things done otherwise than with a view to profit; or

- that the defect did not exist in the product at the relevant time; or
- that the state of scientific and technical knowledge at the relevant time was not such that a producer of products of the same description as the product in question might be expected to have discovered the defect if it had existed in his products while they were under his control; or
- that the defect:
  - constituted a defect in a product ("the subsequent product") in which the product in question had been comprised; and
  - was wholly attributable to the design of the subsequent product or to compliance by the producer of the product in question with instructions given by the producer of the subsequent product.

In this section "the relevant time", in relation to electricity, means the time at which it was generated, being a time before it was transmitted or distributed, and in relation to any other product, means:

- if the person proceeded against is a person to whom section 2 above applies in relation to the product, the time when he supplied the product to another;
- if that section does not apply to that person in relation to the product, the time when the product was last supplied by a person to whom that section does apply in relation to the product.

Section 5: Damage Giving Rise to Liability

Subject to the following provisions of this section, in this Part "damage" means death or personal injury or any loss of or damage to any property (including land).

A person shall not be liable under section 2 ('Liability for defective products') above in respect of any defect in a product for the loss of or any damage to the product itself or for the loss of or any damage to the whole or any part of any product which has been supplied with the product in question comprised in it.

A person shall not be liable under section 2 above for any loss of or damage to any property which, at the time it is lost or damaged, is not:

- of a description of property ordinarily intended for private use, occupation or consumption; and
- intended by the person suffering the loss or damage mainly for his own private use, occupation or consumption.

No damages shall be awarded to any person by virtue of this Part in respect of any loss of or damage to any property if the amount which would fall to be so awarded to that person, apart from this section and any liability for interest, does not exceed £275.

In determining who has suffered any loss of or damage to property and when any such loss or damage occurred, the loss or damage shall be regarded as having occurred at the earliest time at which a person with an interest in the property had knowledge of the material facts about the loss or damage.

For this purpose the material facts about any loss or damage are such as would lead a reasonable person with an interest in the property to consider the loss or damage sufficiently serious to justify instituting proceedings for damages against a defendant who did not dispute liability and was able to satisfy a judgment.

For the above purpose a person's knowledge includes knowledge which he might reasonably have been expected to acquire:

- from facts observable or ascertainable by him; or
- from facts ascertainable by him with the help of appropriate expert advice which it is reasonable for him to seek;

but a person shall not be taken to have knowledge of a fact ascertainable by him only with the help of expert advice unless he has failed to take all reasonable steps to obtain (and, where appropriate, to act on) that advice.

Section 6: Application of Certain Enactments

Any damage for which a person is liable under section 2 above shall be deemed to have been caused for the purposes of the **Fatal Accidents Act 1976** (and relevant Scottish legislation) by that person's wrongful act, neglect or default.

Where a person's death is caused wholly or partly by a defect in a product, and a request is made to a supplier of the product by that person's personal representatives or by any dependant or relative of that person and the specified conditions are satisfied in relation to that request, this Part shall have effect for the purposes of the **Law Reform (Miscellaneous Provisions) Act 1934**, the **Fatal Accidents Act 1976** and the **Damages (Scotland) Act 1976** as if liability of the supplier to that person under that section did not depend on that person having requested the supplier to identify certain persons or on the said conditions having been satisfied in relation to a request made by that person.

The **Congenital Disabilities (Civil Liability) Act 1976** shall have effect if a person were answerable to a child in respect of any effect of an occurrence on a parent of the child, or would be so liable if the occurrence caused a parent of the child to suffer damage.

Where any damage is caused partly by a defect in a product and partly by the fault of the person suffering the damage, the **Law Reform (Contributory Negligence) Act 1945** and section 5 of the **Fatal Accidents Act 1976** (contributory negligence) shall have effect as if the defect were the fault of every person liable by virtue of this Part for the damage caused by the defect.

Part II - Consumer Safety

Section 10: The General Safety Requirement

This requirement was repealed by the **General Product Safety Regulations 2005 (SI 2005/1803)**, reg. 46(2).

Section 11: Safety Regulations

Safety Regulations may contain provision:

- with respect to the composition or contents, design, construction, finish or packing of goods to which this section applies, with respect to standards for such goods and with respect to other matters relating to such goods;
- with respect to the giving, refusal, alteration or cancellation of approvals of such goods, of descriptions of such goods or of standards for such goods;
- with respect to the conditions that may be attached to any approval given under the Regulations;
- for requiring such fees as may be determined by or under the Regulations to be paid on the giving or alteration of any approval under the Regulations and on the making of an application for such an approval or alteration;
- with respect to appeals against refusals, alterations and cancellations of approvals given under the Regulations and against the conditions contained in such approvals;
- for requiring goods to which this section applies to be approved under the Regulations or to conform to the requirements of the Regulations or to descriptions or standards specified in or approved by or under the Regulations;
- with respect to the testing or inspection of goods to which this section applies (including provision for determining the standards to be applied in carrying out any test or inspection);
- with respect to the ways of dealing with goods of which some or all do not satisfy a test required by or under the Regulations or a standard connected with a procedure so required;
- for requiring a mark, warning or instruction or any other information relating to goods to be put on or to accompany the goods or to be used or provided in some other manner in relation to the goods, and for securing that inappropriate information is not given in relation to goods either by means of misleading marks or otherwise;
- for prohibiting persons from supplying, or from offering to supply, agreeing to supply, exposing for supply or possessing for supply, goods to which this section applies and component parts and raw materials for such goods;
- for requiring information to be given to any such person as may be determined by or under the Regulations for the purpose of enabling that person to exercise any function conferred on him by the Regulations.

Safety Regulations may contain provision:

- for requiring persons on whom functions are conferred by these Regulations to have regard, in exercising those functions, to matters specified in a direction issued by the Secretary of State with respect to that provision;
- for securing that a person shall not be guilty of an offence against the safety Regulations unless it is shown that the goods in question do not conform to a particular standard;
- for securing that proceedings for such an offence are not brought in England and Wales or Northern Ireland except by or with the consent of the relevant Secretaries of State or the Directors of Public Prosecutions;
- for enabling a magistrates' court in England and Wales or Northern Ireland to try an information or a complaint in respect of such an offence if the information was laid or the complaint made within 12 months from the time when the offence was committed and in Scotland for enabling summary proceedings to commence at any time within 12 months from the date of the commission of the offence.

Where the Secretary of State proposes to make safety Regulations he must consult such organisations and persons who are likely to be affected by such proposals and in the case of proposed Regulations relating to goods suitable for use at work he must consult the Health and Safety Executive.

The power to make safety Regulations shall be exercisable by statutory instrument subject to annulment in pursuance of a resolution of either House of Parliament.

Section 12: Offences Against the Safety Regulations

(1) Where safety regulations prohibit a person from supplying or offering or agreeing to supply any goods or from exposing or possessing any goods for supply, that person shall be guilty of an offence if he contravenes the prohibition.

(2) Where safety regulations require a person who makes or processes any goods in the course of carrying on a business:

  (a) to carry out a particular test or use a particular procedure in connection with the making or processing of the goods with a view to ascertaining whether the goods satisfy any requirements of such regulations; or

  (b) to deal or not to deal in a particular way with a quantity of the goods of which the whole or part does not satisfy such a test or does not satisfy standards connected with such a procedure, that person shall be guilty of an offence if he does not comply with the requirement.

(3) If a person contravenes a provision of safety regulations which prohibits or requires the provision, by means of a mark or otherwise, of information of a particular kind in relation to goods, he shall be guilty of an offence.

(4) Where safety regulations require any person to give information to another for the purpose of enabling that other to exercise any function, that person shall be guilty of an offence if he fails without reasonable cause to comply with the requirement, or in giving the information he knowingly or recklessly makes a false statement.

(5) A person guilty of an offence under this section shall be liable on summary conviction to imprisonment for a term not exceeding six months and/or to a fine not exceeding level 5 on the standard scale.

Section 13: Prohibition Notices and Notices to Warn

The Secretary of State may serve on any person a notice ('a prohibition notice') prohibiting that person from supplying, offering to supply, agreeing to supply, exposing for supply or possessing for supply, any relevant goods which the Secretary of State considers are unsafe and which are described in the notice.

The Secretary of State may also serve on any person a notice ('a notice to warn') requiring that person at his own expense to publish a warning about any relevant goods which the Secretary of State considers are unsafe, which that person supplies or has supplied and which are described in the notice.

Schedule 2 to this Act shall have effect with respect to prohibition notices and notices to warn; and the Secretary of State may by Regulations make provision specifying the manner in which information is to be given to any person under that Schedule.

A consent given by the Secretary of State for the purposes of a prohibition notice may impose such conditions on the doing of anything for which the consent is required as he considers appropriate.

A person who contravenes a prohibition notice or a notice to warn shall be guilty of an offence and liable on summary conviction to imprisonment for a term not exceeding three months or to a fine not exceeding level 5 on the standard scale or to both.

Section 14: Suspension Notices

Where an enforcement authority has reasonable grounds for suspecting that any safety provision has been contravened in relation to any goods, the authority may serve a notice ('a suspension notice') prohibiting the person on whom it is served, for such period ending not more than six months after the date of the notice, without the consent of the authority, from supplying the goods, offering to supply them, agreeing to supply them or exposing them for supply.

Such suspension notice shall describe the goods sufficient to identify them; set out the grounds on which the authority suspects that a safety provision has been contravened and state that, and the manner in which, the person on whom the notice is served may appeal against the notice.

The suspension notice may also require that person to keep the authority informed of the whereabouts throughout that period of any of those goods in which he has an interest.

Where a suspension notice has been served, no further such notice shall be served on that person in respect of the same goods unless proceedings against that person for an offence in respect of a contravention in relation to the goods, or proceedings for the forfeiture of the goods, are pending at the end of the period specified in the first-mentioned notice.

A consent given by an enforcement authority for the purposes of the above may impose such conditions on the doing of anything for which the consent is required as the authority considers appropriate.

Any person who contravenes a suspension notice shall be guilty of an offence and liable on summary conviction to imprisonment for a term not exceeding three months or to a fine not exceeding level 5 on the standard scale or to both.

Where an enforcement authority serves a suspension notice in respect of any goods, the authority shall be liable to pay compensation to any person having an interest in the goods in respect of any loss or damage caused by reason of the service of the notice if there has been no contravention in relation to the goods of any safety provision and the exercise of the power is not attributable to any neglect or default by that person.

Any disputed question as to the right to, or the amount of, any compensation payable under this section shall be determined by arbitration or, in Scotland, by a single arbiter appointed, failing agreement between the parties, by the sheriff.

Section 15: Appeals Against Suspension Notices

Applications to set aside suspension notices may be made to the Magistrates' Court in England, Wales or Northern Ireland, or to the Sheriff Court in Scotland.

The decision of the Magistrates' Court in England or Wales may be appealed to a Crown Court. The decision of the Magistrates' Court in Northern Ireland may be appealed to a County Court.

Section 18: Power to Obtain Information

If the Secretary of State considers that he requires information, which another person is likely to be able to furnish, for the purpose of deciding whether to make, vary or revoke any safety Regulations or to serve, vary or revoke a prohibition notice or to serve or revoke a notice to warn, he may serve on the other person a notice under this section.

Such notice may require that person to furnish such information within a specified period or to produce such records as are specified at a time and place so specified and to permit a person appointed by the Secretary of State to take copies of the records at that time and place.

A person shall be guilty of an offence if he fails, without reasonable cause, to comply with a notice served on him under this section. He shall also be guilty of an offence if, in purporting to comply with a requirement, he furnishes information which he knows is false in a material particular or recklessly furnishes information which is false in a material particular.

A person guilty of an offence under this section shall in the case of failing to comply be liable on summary conviction to a fine not exceeding level 5 on the standard scale; and in the case of an offence of furnishing false information shall be liable:

- on conviction on indictment, to a fine;
- on summary conviction, to a fine not exceeding the statutory maximum.

CONTROL OF ARTIFICIAL OPTICAL RADIATION AT WORK REGULATIONS 2010 (SI 2010 NO. 1140)

Amending Legislation

None as yet.

Summary

These Regulations implement in Great Britain **European Directive 2006/25/EC** on the minimum health and safety requirements regarding the exposure of workers to risks arising from physical agents (artificial optical radiation). They impose duties on employers to protect both employees who may be exposed to risk from exposure to artificial optical radiation (AOR) at work and other persons at work who might be affected by that work. A specific form of risk assessment is required where there is a reasonably foreseeable risk of adverse health effects to the eyes or skin and where those risks have not already been eliminated or controlled. In these circumstances there is also a duty to eliminate, or where this is not reasonably practicable, to reduce the risk to as low a level as is reasonably practicable. Specific control measures are required.

AOR includes light emitted from all artificial sources in all its forms such as ultraviolet, infrared and laser beams, but excludes sunlight. It is likely that workers will be exposed to some form of artificial light at work, whether from general lighting, equipment or from a work process. The majority of light sources are safe, but some forms of artificial light can be harmful to workers unless protective measures are in place.

Note: HSE *Guidance for employers on the control of artificial optical radiation at work regulations (AOR) 2010* (available on the HSE website) will help decide whether workers are already adequately protected, or whether more should be done.

Citation and Commencement (Reg. 1(1))

The Regulations cited as the **Control of Artificial Optical Radiation at Work Regulations 2010** came into force on 27 April 2010.

Interpretation (Reg. 1(2))[Part]

AOR means any electromagnetic radiation in the wavelength range between 100nm and 1mm which is emitted by non-natural sources.

The **exposure limit values** mean:

- for non-coherent radiation, those exposure limit values set out in Annex I to the Directive; and
- for laser radiation those exposure limit values set out in Annex II to the Directive.

Health surveillance means assessment of the state of health of an employee, as related to exposure to artificial optical radiation and its effects on the skin.

Irradiance means the radiant power incident per unit area upon a surface expressed in watts per sq. metre (Wm^{-2}).

Laser (i.e. light amplification by stimulated emission of radiation) means any device which can be made to produce or amplify electromagnetic radiation in the optical radiation wavelength range primarily by the process of controlled stimulated emission.

Laser radiation means artificial optical radiation from a laser.

Non-coherent radiation means any artificial optical radiation other than laser radiation.

Radiance means the radiant flux or power output per unit solid angle per unit area expressed in watts per square metre per steradian ($Wm^{-2}\ sr^{-1}$).

Radiant exposure means the time integral of the irradiance, expressed in joules per square metre (Jm^{-2}).

Application (Reg. 2)

(1) Where a duty is placed on an employer in respect of its employees, the employer must, so far as is reasonably practicable, be under a like duty in respect of any other person at work who may be affected by the work carried out by the employer, except that the duties of the employer:

   (a) under Regulation 5 (information and training) do not extend to persons who are not its employees, unless those persons are present in the workplace where the work is being carried out; and

   (b) under Regulation 6 (health surveillance) do not extend to persons who are not its employees.

(2) These Regulations do not apply to the master or a crew of a ship, or to the employer of such persons, in respect of the normal shipboard activities of a ship's crew which are carried out solely by the crew under the direction of the master, and for the purposes of this paragraph "ship" includes every description of vessel used in navigation, other than a ship forming part of Her Majesty's Navy.

Risk Assessment (Reg. 3)

(1) Where:

   (a) the employer carries out work which could expose any of its employees to levels of AOR that could create a reasonably foreseeable risk of adverse health effects to the eyes or skin of the employee; and

   (b) that employer has not implemented any measures to either eliminate or, where this is not reasonably practicable, reduce to as low a level as is reasonably practicable, that risk based on the general principles of prevention set out in Schedule 1 to **MHSWR 1999**;

   the employer must make a suitable and sufficient assessment of that risk for the purpose of identifying the measures it needs to take to meet the requirements of these Regulations.

(2) The employer must as part of that risk assessment assess, and if necessary, measure or calculate, the levels of artificial optical radiation to which employees are likely to be exposed.

(3) In carrying out the assessment, measurement or calculation, the employer must follow the following standards or recommendations:

   (a) for laser radiation, the standards of the IEC; or

   (b) for non-coherent radiation, the standards of the IEC and the recommendations of the CIE and the CEN.

(4) In exposure situations which are not covered by those standards or recommendations, the assessment, measurement or calculation must follow national or international science-based guidelines.

(5) The assessment must also include consideration of:

   (a) the level, wavelength and duration of exposure;

   (b) the exposure limit values;

   (c) the effects of exposure on employees or groups of employees whose health is at particular risk from exposure;

   (d) any possible effects on the health and safety of employees resulting from interactions between artificial optical radiation and photosensitising chemical substances;

   (e) any indirect effects of exposure on the health and safety of employees such as temporary blinding, explosion or fire;

   (f) the availability of alternative equipment designed to reduce levels of exposure;

   (g) appropriate information obtained from health surveillance, including where possible published information;

   (h) multiple sources of exposure;

   (i) any class 3B or 4 laser that is classified in accordance with the relevant IEC standard that is in use by the employer and any artificial optical radiation source that is capable of presenting the same level of hazard; and

   (j) information provided by the manufacturers of artificial optical radiation sources and associated work equipment in accordance with the relevant European Union Directives.

(6) The risk assessment must be reviewed regularly if:

    (a) there is reason to suspect that it is no longer valid; or

    (b) there has been a significant change in the work to which the assessment relates.

(7) The employer must record:

    (a) the significant findings of the risk assessment as soon as is practicable after it is made or changed; and

    (b) the measures which have been taken and which the employer intends to take to meet the requirements of Regulations 4 and 5.

(8) In paragraphs (3) and (4):

    (a) a reference to standards or recommendations is a reference to standards or recommendations as revised or reissued from time to time;

    (b) "CEN" means the European Committee for Standardisation;

    (c) "CIE" means the International Commission for Illumination; and

    (d) "IEC" means the International Electrotechnical Commission.

(9) In paragraph (5)(a) "level" means the combination of irradiance, radiant exposure and radiance to which an employee is exposed.

Obligations to Eliminate or Reduce Risks (Reg. 4)

(1) An employer must ensure that any risk of adverse health effects to the eyes or skin of employees as a result of exposure to artificial optical radiation which is identified in the risk assessment is eliminated or, where this is not reasonably practicable, reduced to as low a level as is reasonably practicable.

(2) For the purposes of paragraph (1) measures to eliminate or reduce the risk must be based on the general principles of prevention set out in Schedule 1 to **MHSWR 1999**.

(3) If the risk assessment indicates that employees are exposed to levels of artificial optical radiation which exceed the exposure limit values, the employer must devise and implement an action plan comprising technical and organisational measures designed to prevent exposure exceeding the exposure limit values.

(4) The action plan must take into account:

    (a) other working methods;

    (b) choice of appropriate work equipment emitting less artificial optical radiation;

    (c) technical measures to reduce the emission of artificial optical radiation including, where necessary, the use of interlocks, shielding or similar health protection mechanisms;

    (d) appropriate maintenance programmes for work equipment, workplaces and workstation systems;

    (e) the design and layout of workplaces and workstations;

    (f) limitation of the duration and level of the exposure;

    (g) the availability of personal protective equipment;

    (h) the instructions of the manufacturer of the equipment where it is covered by relevant European Union Directives;

    (i) the requirements of employees belonging to particularly sensitive risk groups.

(5) If, despite the measures taken under paragraphs (1) and (3), employees are still exposed to levels of artificial optical radiation that exceed the exposure limit values, the employer must take immediate action to:

    (a) reduce exposure to below the exposure limit values;

    (b) identify the reasons why employees have been exposed to levels which exceed the exposure limit values; and

(c) modify the measures taken in accordance with paragraph (3) to prevent employees being exposed again to levels which exceed the exposure limit values.

(6) and (7) demarcate, limit access to, and provide for appropriate signs in those areas where levels of artificial optical radiation are indicated in the risk assessment as exceeding the exposure limit values.

Information and Training (Reg. 5)

(1) If the risk assessment indicates that employees could be exposed to artificial optical radiation which could cause adverse health effects to the eyes or skin of employees, the employer must provide its employees and representatives with suitable and sufficient information and training relating to the outcome of the risk assessment, and this must include the following:

   (a) the technical and organisational measures taken in order to comply with the requirements of Regulation 4;

   (b) the exposure limit values;

   (c) the significant findings of the risk assessment, including any measurements taken, with an explanation of those findings;

   (d) why and how to detect and report adverse health effects to the eyes or skin;

   (e) the circumstances in which employees are entitled to appropriate health surveillance;

   (f) safe working practices to minimise the risk of adverse health effects to the eyes or skin from exposure to artificial optical radiation; and

   (g) the proper use of personal protective equipment.

(2) The employer must ensure that any person, whether or not that person is an employee, who carries out work in connection with the employer's duties under these Regulations has suitable and sufficient information and training.

Health Surveillance and Medical Examinations (Reg. 6)

(1) If the risk assessment indicates that there is a risk of adverse health effects to the skin of employees as a result of exposure to artificial optical radiation, the employer must ensure that such employees are placed under suitable health surveillance.

(2) Health surveillance pursuant to paragraph (1) must be carried out by a doctor or occupational health professional and the risk assessment must be made available to that doctor or occupational health professional.

(3) The employer must ensure that a health record of each of its employees who undergoes health surveillance pursuant to paragraph (1) is made and maintained and that the record or copy of it is kept available in a suitable form.

(4) The health record must contain a summary of the results of the health surveillance carried out.

(5) The employer must:

   (a) on reasonable notice being given, allow an employee access to his or her personal health record; and

   (b) provide the enforcing authority with copies of such health records as it may require.

(6) An employer must ensure that a medical examination is made available to an employee if:

   (a) the risk assessment indicates that the employee has been exposed to levels of artificial optical radiation which exceed the exposure limit values; or

   (b) as a result of health surveillance the employee is found to have an identifiable disease or adverse health effects to the skin which is considered by a doctor or occupational health professional to be the result of exposure to artificial optical radiation.

(7) Where an examination is carried out under paragraph (6), the employer must:

   (a) ensure that a doctor or suitably qualified person informs the employee of the results of the examination which relate to the employee and provides advice on whether health surveillance may be appropriate;

(b) ensure that it is informed of any significant findings from any further health surveillance of the employee taking into account any medical confidentiality;

(c) review the risk assessment;

(d) review any measures taken to comply with Regulation 4 taking into account any advice given by a doctor or other suitably qualified person or the enforcing authority; and

(e) provide continued health surveillance if appropriate.

CONTROL OF ASBESTOS REGULATIONS 2012 (SI 2012 NO. 632)

Part 1: Preliminary

Part 1 covers commencement, interpretation and application.

Regulation 2: Interpretation

This contains a number of definitions. Of particular note are the following: "asbestos" means the following fibrous silicates:

(a) asbestos actinolite, CAS No. 77536-66-4;

(b) asbestos grunerite (amosite), CAS No. 12172-73-5;

(c) asbestos anthophyllite, CAS No. 77536-67-5;

(d) chrysotile, CAS No. 12001-29-5 or CAS No. 132207-32-0;

(e) crocidolite, CAS No. 12001-28-4; and

(f) asbestos tremolite, CAS No. 77536-68-6.

"The control limit" means a concentration of asbestos in the atmosphere when measured in accordance with the 1997 WHO recommended method, or by a method giving equivalent results to that method approved by the Executive, of 0.1 fibres per cubic centimetre of air averaged over a continuous period of 4 hours.

"Control measure" means a measure taken to prevent or reduce exposure to asbestos (including the provision of systems of work and supervision, the cleaning of workplaces, premises, plant and equipment, and the provision and use of engineering controls and personal protective equipment).

Regulation 3: Application of These Regulations

Of special note is a relaxation of specific regulations in certain cases:

(2) Regulations 9 (notification of work with asbestos), 18(1)(a) (designated areas) and 22 (health records and medical surveillance) do not apply where:

    (a) the exposure to asbestos of employees is sporadic and of low intensity; and

    (b) it is clear from the risk assessment that the exposure to asbestos of any employee will not exceed the control limit; and

    (c) the work involves:

        (i) short, non-continuous maintenance activities in which only non-friable materials are handled; or

        (ii) removal without deterioration of non-degraded materials in which the asbestos fibres are firmly linked in a matrix; or

        (iii) encapsulation or sealing of asbestos-containing materials which are in good condition; or

        (iv) air monitoring and control, and the collection and analysis of samples to ascertain whether a specific material contains asbestos.

Part 2: General Requirements

Regulation 4: Duty to Manage Asbestos in Non-Domestic Premises

(1) In this regulation "the dutyholder" means:

    (a) every person who has, by virtue of a contract or tenancy, an obligation of any extent in relation to the maintenance or repair of non-domestic premises or any means of access thereto or egress therefrom; or

    (b) in relation to any part of non-domestic premises where there is no such contract or tenancy, every person who has, to any extent, control of that part of those non-domestic premises or any means of access thereto or egress therefrom, and where there is more than one such dutyholder, the relative contribution to be made by each such person in complying with the requirements of this regulation will be determined by the nature and extent of the maintenance and repair obligation owed by that person.

(2) Every person must co-operate with the dutyholder so far as is necessary to enable the dutyholder to comply with his duties under this regulation.

(3) In order to enable him to manage the risk from asbestos in non-domestic premises, the dutyholder must ensure that a suitable and sufficient assessment is carried out as to whether asbestos is or is liable to be present in the premises.

(4) In making the assessment:

   (a) such steps as are reasonable in the circumstances must be taken; and

   (b) the condition of any asbestos which is, or has been assumed to be, present in the premises must be considered.

(5) Without prejudice to the generality of paragraph (4), the dutyholder must ensure that:

   (a) account is taken of building plans or other relevant information and of the age of the premises; and

   (b) an inspection is made of those parts of the premises which are reasonably accessible.

(6) The dutyholder must ensure that the assessment is reviewed forthwith if:

   (a) there is reason to suspect that the assessment is no longer valid; or

   (b) there has been a significant change in the premises to which the assessment relates.

(7) The dutyholder must ensure that the conclusions of the assessment and every review are recorded.

(8) Where the assessment shows that asbestos is or is liable to be present in any part of the premises the dutyholder must ensure that:

   (a) a determination of the risk from that asbestos is made;

   (b) a written plan identifying those parts of the premises concerned is prepared; and

   (c) the measures which are to be taken for managing the risk are specified in the written plan.

(9) The measures to be specified in the plan for managing the risk must include adequate measures for:

   (a) monitoring the condition of any asbestos or any substance containing or suspected of containing asbestos;

   (b) ensuring any asbestos or any such substance is properly maintained or where necessary safely removed; and

   (c) ensuring that information about the location and condition of any asbestos or any such substance is:

      (i) provided to every person liable to disturb it; and

      (ii) made available to the emergency services.

(10) The dutyholder must ensure that:

   (a) the plan is reviewed and revised at regular intervals, and forthwith if:

      (i) there is reason to suspect that the plan is no longer valid; or

      (ii) there has been a significant change in the premises to which the plan relates;

   (b) the measures specified in the plan are implemented; and

   (c) the measures taken to implement the plan are recorded.

(11) In this regulation, a reference to:

   (a) "the assessment" is a reference to the assessment required by paragraph (3);

   (b) "the premises" is a reference to the non-domestic premises referred to in paragraph (1); and

   (c) "the plan" is a reference to the plan required by paragraph (8).

Regulation 5: Identification of the Presence of Asbestos

An employer must not undertake work in demolition, maintenance, or any other work which exposes or is liable to expose his employees to asbestos in respect of any premises unless either:

(a) he has carried out a suitable and sufficient assessment as to whether asbestos, what type of asbestos, contained in what material and in what condition is present or is liable to be present in those premises; or

(b) if there is doubt as to whether asbestos is present in those premises he:

   (i) assumes that asbestos is present, and that it is not chrysotile alone; and

   (ii) observes the applicable provisions of these Regulations.

Regulation 6: Assessment of Work Which Exposes Employees to Asbestos

(1) An employer must not carry out work which is liable to expose his employees to asbestos unless he has:

   (a) made a suitable and sufficient assessment of the risk created by that exposure to the health of those employees and of the steps that need to be taken to meet the requirements of these Regulations;

   (b) recorded the significant findings of that risk assessment as soon as is practicable after the risk assessment is made; and

   (c) implemented the steps referred to in sub-paragraph (a).

(2) Without prejudice to the generality of paragraph (1), the risk assessment must:

   (a) subject to regulation 5, identify the type of asbestos to which employees are liable to be exposed;

   (b) determine the nature and degree of exposure which may occur in the course of the work;

   (c) consider the effects of control measures which have been or will be taken in accordance with regulation 11;

   (d) consider the results of monitoring of exposure in accordance with regulation 19;

   (e) set out the steps to be taken to prevent that exposure or reduce it to the lowest level reasonably practicable;

   (f) consider the results of any medical surveillance that is relevant; and

   (g) include such additional information as the employer may need in order to complete the risk assessment.

(3) The risk assessment must be reviewed regularly, and forthwith if:

   (a) there is reason to suspect that the existing risk assessment is no longer valid;

   (b) there is a significant change in the work to which the risk assessment relates; or

   (c) the results of any monitoring carried out pursuant to regulation 19 show it to be necessary;

   and where, as a result of the review, changes to the risk assessment are required, those changes must be made and, where they relate to the significant findings of the risk assessment or are themselves significant, recorded.

(4) Where, in accordance with the requirement in paragraph (2)(b), the risk assessment has determined that the exposure of his employees to asbestos may exceed the control limit, the employer must keep a copy of the significant findings of the risk assessment at those premises at which, and for such time as, the work to which that risk assessment relates is being carried out.

Regulation 7: Plans of Work

(1) An employer must not undertake any work with asbestos unless he has prepared a suitable written plan of work detailing how that work is to be carried out.

(2) The employer shall keep a copy of the plan of work at those premises at which the work to which the plan relates is being carried out for such time as that work continues.

(3) In cases of final demolition or major refurbishment of premises, the plan of work shall, so far as is reasonably practicable, and unless it would cause a greater risk to employees than if the asbestos had been left in place, specify that asbestos shall be removed before any other major works begin.

(4) The plan of work must include in particular details of:

   (a) the nature and probable duration of the work;

   (b) the location of the place where the work is to be carried out;

   (c) the methods to be applied where the work involves the handling of asbestos or materials containing asbestos;

   (d) the characteristics of the equipment to be used for:

      (i) protection and decontamination of those carrying out the work; and

      (ii) protection of other persons on or near the worksite;

   (e) the measures which the employer intends to take in order to comply with the requirements of regulation 11; and

   (f) the measures which the employer intends to take in order to comply with the requirements of regulation 17.

(5) The employer must ensure, so far as is reasonably practicable, that the work to which the plan of work relates is carried out in accordance with that plan and any subsequent written changes to it.

Regulation 8: Licensing of Work with Asbestos

(1) An employer must hold a licence granted under paragraph (2) before undertaking any licensable work with asbestos.

(2) The Executive may grant a licence for work with asbestos if it considers it appropriate to do so and:

   (a) the person who wishes the licence to be granted to him has made application for it on a form approved for the purposes of this regulation by the Executive; and

   (b) the application was made at least 28 days before the date from which the licence is to run, or such shorter period as the Executive may allow.

(3) A licence under this regulation:

   (a) comes into operation on the date specified in the licence, and is valid for any period up to a maximum of three years that the Executive may specify in it; and

   (b) may be granted subject to such conditions as the Executive may consider appropriate.

(4) The Executive may vary the terms of a licence under this regulation if it considers it appropriate to do so and in particular may:

   (a) add further conditions and vary or omit existing ones; and

   (b) reduce the period for which the licence is valid or extend that period up to a maximum of three years from the date on which the licence first came into operation.

(5) The Executive may revoke a licence under this regulation if it considers it appropriate to do so.

(6) The holder of a licence under this regulation must return the licence to the Executive:

   (a) when required by the Executive for any amendment; or

   (b) following its revocation.

Regulation 9: Notification of Work with Asbestos

(1) For licensable work with asbestos, an employer must notify the appropriate enforcing authority of:

   (a) the particulars specified in Schedule 1 in writing at least 14 days (or such shorter time before as the enforcing authority may agree) before undertaking any licensable work with asbestos; and

(b) any material change, which might affect the particulars notified in accordance with (1)(a) (including the cessation of the work), in writing and without delay.

(2) For work with asbestos which is not licensable work with asbestos and is not exempted by regulation 3(2), an employer must notify the appropriate enforcing authority of:

(a) the particulars specified in Schedule 1, before work is commenced; and

(b) any material change, which might affect the particulars notified in accordance with (2)(a), without delay.

Regulation 10: Information, Instruction and Training

(1) Every employer must ensure that adequate information, instruction and training is given to those of his employees:

(a) who are or who are liable to be exposed to asbestos, or who supervise such employees, so that they are aware of:

(i) the properties of asbestos and its effects on health, including its interaction with smoking;

(ii) the types of products or materials likely to contain asbestos;

(iii) the operations which could result in asbestos exposure and the importance of preventive controls to minimise exposure;

(iv) safe work practices, control measures, and protective equipment;

(v) the purpose, choice, limitations, proper use and maintenance of respiratory protective equipment;

(vi) emergency procedures;

(vii) hygiene requirements;

(viii) decontamination procedures;

(ix) waste handling procedures;

(x) medical examination requirements; and

(xi) the control limit and the need for air monitoring;

in order to safeguard themselves and other employees; and

(b) who carry out work in connection with the employer's duties under these Regulations, so that they can carry out that work effectively.

(2) The information, instruction and training required by paragraph (1) must be:

(a) given at regular intervals;

(b) adapted to take account of significant changes in the type of work carried out or methods of work used by the employer; and

(c) provided in a manner appropriate to the nature and degree of exposure identified by the risk assessment, and so that the employees are aware of:

(i) the significant findings of the risk assessment, and

(ii) the results of any air monitoring carried out with an explanation of the findings.

Regulation 11: Prevention or Reduction of Exposure to Asbestos

(1) Every employer must:

(a) prevent the exposure of his employees to asbestos so far as is reasonably practicable;

(b) where it is not reasonably practicable to prevent such exposure:

    (i) take the measures necessary to reduce the exposure of his employees to asbestos to the lowest level reasonably practicable by measures other than the use of respiratory protective equipment; and

    (ii) ensure that the number of his employees who are exposed to asbestos at any one time is as low as is reasonably practicable.

(2) Where it is not reasonably practicable for the employer to prevent the exposure of his employees to asbestos in accordance with paragraph (1)(a), the measures referred to in paragraph (1)(b)(i) must include, in order of priority:

    (a) the design and use of appropriate work processes, systems and engineering controls and the provision and use of suitable work equipment and materials in order to avoid or minimise the release of asbestos; and

    (b) the control of exposure at source, including adequate ventilation systems and appropriate organisational measures;

and the employer must so far as is reasonably practicable provide the employees concerned with suitable respiratory protective equipment in addition to the measures required by sub-paragraphs (a) and (b).

(3) Where it is not reasonably practicable to reduce the exposure of an employee to asbestos to below the control limit by the measures referred to in paragraph (1)(b)(i), then, in addition to taking those measures, the employer must provide that employee with suitable respiratory protective equipment which will reduce the concentration of asbestos in the air inhaled by the employee (after taking account of the effect of that respiratory protective equipment) to a concentration which is:

    (a) below the control limit; and

    (b) as low as is reasonably practicable.

(4) Personal protective equipment provided by an employer in accordance with this regulation or with regulation 14(1) must be suitable for its purpose and:

    (a) comply with any provision of the **Personal Protective Equipment Regulations 2002** which is applicable to that item of personal protective equipment; or

    (b) in the case of respiratory protective equipment, where no provision referred to in sub-paragraph (a) applies, be of a type approved or must conform to a standard approved, in either case, by the Executive.

(5) The employer must:

    (a) ensure that no employee is exposed to asbestos in a concentration in the air inhaled by that worker which exceeds the control limit; or

    (b) if the control limit is exceeded:

        (i) immediately inform any employees concerned and their representatives and ensure that work does not continue in the affected area until adequate measures have been taken to reduce employees' exposure to asbestos to below the control limit;

        (ii) as soon as is reasonably practicable identify the reasons for the control limit being exceeded and take the appropriate measures to prevent it being exceeded again; and

        (iii) check the effectiveness of the measures taken pursuant to sub-paragraph (ii) by carrying out immediate air monitoring.

Regulation 12: Use of Control Measures, etc.

(1) Every employer who provides any control measure, other thing or facility pursuant to these Regulations must take all reasonable steps to ensure that it is properly used or applied as the case may be.

(2) Every employee must make full and proper use of any control measure, other thing or facility provided pursuant to these Regulations and:

   (a) where relevant take all reasonable steps to ensure that it is returned after use to any accommodation provided for it; and

   (b) report any defect discovered without delay to that employee's employer.

Regulation 13: Maintenance of Control Measures, etc.

(1) Every employer who provides any control measure to meet the requirements of these Regulations must ensure that:

   (a) in the case of plant and equipment, including engineering controls and personal protective equipment, it is maintained in an efficient state, in efficient working order, in good repair and in a clean condition; and

   (b) in the case of provision of systems of work and supervision and of any other measure, it is reviewed at suitable intervals and revised if necessary.

(2) Where exhaust ventilation equipment or respiratory protective equipment (except disposable respiratory protective equipment) is provided to meet the requirements of these Regulations, the employer must ensure that thorough examinations and tests of that equipment are carried out at suitable intervals by a competent person.

(3) Every employer must keep a suitable record of the examinations and tests carried out in accordance with paragraph (2) and of repairs carried out as a result of those examinations and tests, and that record or a suitable summary thereof must be kept available for at least 5 years from the date on which it was made.

Regulation 14: Provision and Cleaning of Protective Clothing

(1) Every employer must provide adequate and suitable protective clothing for such of his employees as are exposed or are liable to be exposed to asbestos, unless no significant quantity of asbestos is liable to be deposited on the clothes of the employee while at work.

(2) The employer must ensure that protective clothing provided in pursuance of paragraph (1) is either disposed of as asbestos waste or adequately cleaned at suitable intervals.

(3) The cleaning required by paragraph (2) must be carried out either on the premises where the exposure to asbestos has occurred, where those premises are suitably equipped for such cleaning, or in a suitably equipped laundry.

(4) The employer must ensure that protective clothing which has been used and is to be removed from the premises referred to in paragraph (3) (whether for cleaning, further use or disposal) is packed, before being removed, in a suitable receptacle which must be labelled in accordance with the provisions of Schedule 2 as if it were a product containing asbestos or, in the case of protective clothing intended for disposal as waste, in accordance with regulation 24(3).

(5) Where, as a result of the failure or improper use of the protective clothing provided in pursuance of paragraph (1), a significant quantity of asbestos is deposited on the personal clothing of an employee, then for the purposes of paragraphs (2), (3) and (4) that personal clothing must be treated as if it were protective clothing provided in pursuance of paragraph (1).

Regulation 15: Arrangements to Deal with Accidents, Incidents and Emergencies

(1) In the event of an accident, incident or emergency related to the unplanned release of asbestos at the workplace, the employer must ensure that:

    (a) immediate steps are taken to:

        (i) mitigate the effects of the event;

        (ii) restore the situation to normal; and

        (iii) inform any person who may be affected; and

    (b) only those persons who are responsible for the carrying out of repairs and other necessary work are permitted in the affected area and that such persons are provided with:

        (i) appropriate respiratory protective equipment and protective clothing; and

        (ii) any necessary specialised safety equipment and plant, which must be used until the situation is restored to normal.

(2) The remainder of this regulation applies only to licensable work with asbestos, and is without prejudice to the relevant provisions of the **Management of Health and Safety at Work Regulations 1999**.

(3) Subject to paragraph (5), in order to protect the health of an employer's employees from an accident, incident or emergency related to the use of asbestos in a work process or to the removal or repair of asbestos-containing materials at the workplace, the employer must ensure that:

    (a) procedures, including the provision of relevant safety drills (which must be tested at regular intervals), have been prepared which can be put into effect when such an event occurs;

    (b) information on emergency arrangements is available, including:

        (i) details of relevant work hazards and hazard identification arrangements; and

        (ii) specific hazards likely to arise at the time of an accident, incident or emergency; and

    (c) suitable warning and other communication systems are established to enable an appropriate response, including remedial actions and rescue operations, to be made immediately when such an event occurs.

(4) The employer must ensure that information on the procedures, emergency arrangements and systems required by paragraph (3)(a) and (c) and the information required by paragraph (3)(b) is:

    (a) made available to the relevant accident and emergency services to enable those services, whether internal or external to the workplace, to prepare their own response procedures and precautionary measures; and

    (b) displayed at the workplace, if this is appropriate.

(5) Paragraph (3) does not apply where:

    (a) the results of the risk assessment show that, because of the quantity of asbestos present at the workplace, there is only a slight risk to the health of employees; and

    (b) the measures taken by the employer to comply with the duty under regulation 11(1) are sufficient to control that risk.

Regulation 16: Duty to Prevent or Reduce the Spread of Asbestos

Every employer must prevent or, where this is not reasonably practicable, reduce to the lowest level reasonably practicable the spread of asbestos from any place where work under the employer's control is carried out.

Regulation 17: Cleanliness of Premises and Plant

Every employer who undertakes work which exposes or is liable to expose his employees to asbestos must ensure that:

(a) the premises, or those parts of the premises where that work is carried out, and the plant used in connection with that work are kept in a clean state; and

(b) where such work has been completed, the premises, or those parts of the premises where the work was carried out, are thoroughly cleaned.

Regulation 18: Designated Areas

(1) Every employer must ensure that any area in which work under his control is carried out is designated as:

    (a) an asbestos area, subject to regulation 3(2), where any employee would be liable to be exposed to asbestos in that area;

    (b) a respirator zone where the concentration of asbestos fibres in the air in that area would exceed or would be liable to exceed the control limit.

(2) Asbestos areas and respirator zones must be clearly and separately demarcated and identified by notices indicating:

    (a) that the area is an asbestos area or a respirator zone or both, as the case may be; and

    (b) in the case of a respirator zone, that the exposure of an employee who enters it is liable to exceed the control limit and that respiratory protective equipment must be worn.

(3) The employer must not permit any employee, other than an employee who by reason of his work is required to be in an area designated as an asbestos area or a respirator zone, to enter or remain in any such area and only employees who are so permitted shall enter or remain in any such area.

(4) Every employer must ensure that only competent employees:

    (a) enter a respirator zone; and

    (b) supervise any employees who enter a respirator zone;

and for the purposes of this paragraph a competent employee means an employee who has received adequate information, instruction and training.

(5) Every employer must ensure that:

    (a) his employees do not eat, drink or smoke in an area designated as an asbestos area or a respirator zone; and

    (b) arrangements are made for such employees to eat or drink in some other place.

Regulation 19: Air Monitoring

(1) Subject to paragraph (2), every employer must monitor the exposure of his employees to asbestos by measurement of asbestos fibres present in the air:

    (a) at regular intervals; and

    (b) when a change occurs which may affect that exposure.

(2) Paragraph (1) does not apply where:

    (a) the exposure of an employee is not liable to exceed the control limit; or

    (b) the employer is able to demonstrate by another method of evaluation that the requirements of regulation 11(1) and (5) have been complied with.

(3) The employer must keep a suitable record of:

    (a) monitoring carried out in accordance with paragraph (1); or

    (b) where he decides that monitoring is not required because paragraph 2(b) applies, the reason for that decision.

(4) The record required by paragraph (3), or a suitable summary thereof, must be kept:

   (a) in a case where exposure is such that a health record is required to be kept under regulation 22 for at least 40 years; or

   (b) in any other case, for at least 5 years, from the date of the last entry made in it.

(5) In relation to the record required by paragraph (3), the employer must:

   (a) on reasonable notice being given, allow an employee access to his personal monitoring record;

   (b) provide the Executive with copies of such monitoring records as the Executive may require; and

   (c) if he ceases to trade, notify the Executive forthwith in writing and make available to the Executive all monitoring records kept by him.

Regulation 20: Standards for Air Testing and Site Clearance Certification

(1) In paragraph (4) "site clearance certificate for reoccupation" means a certificate issued to confirm that premises or parts of premises where work with asbestos has been carried out have been thoroughly cleaned upon completion of that work in accordance with regulation 17(b).

(2) Every employer who carries out any measurement of the concentration of asbestos fibres present in the air must ensure that criteria are met which are equivalent to those set out in the paragraphs of ISO 17025 which cover organisation, quality systems, control of records, personnel, accommodation and environmental conditions, test and calibration methods, method validation, equipment, handling of test and calibration items, and reporting results.

(3) Every employer who requests a person to carry out any measurement of the concentration of asbestos fibres present in the air must ensure that that person is accredited by an appropriate body as competent to perform work in compliance with ISO 17025.

(4) Every employer who requests a person to assess whether premises or parts of premises where work with asbestos has been carried out have been thoroughly cleaned upon completion of that work and are suitable for reoccupation such that a site clearance certificate for reoccupation can be issued must ensure that that person is accredited by an appropriate body as competent to perform work in compliance with the paragraphs of ISO 17020 and ISO 17025 which cover organisation, quality systems, control of records, personnel, accommodation and environmental conditions, test and calibration methods, method validation, equipment, handling of test and calibration items, and reporting results.

(5) Paragraphs (2) and (3) do not apply to work carried out in a laboratory for the purposes only of research.

Regulation 21: Standards for Analysis

(1) Every employer who analyses a sample of any material to determine whether it contains asbestos must ensure that criteria equivalent to those set out in the paragraphs of ISO 17025 which cover organisation, quality systems, control of records, personnel, accommodation and environmental conditions, test and calibration methods, method validation, equipment, handling of test and calibration items, and reporting results are met.

(2) Every employer who requests a person to analyse a sample of any material taken to determine whether it contains asbestos must ensure that that person is accredited by an appropriate body as competent to perform work in compliance with ISO 17025.

(3) Paragraphs (1) and (2) do not apply to work carried out in a laboratory for the purposes only of research.

Regulation 22: Health Records and Medical Surveillance

(1) For licensable work with asbestos every employer must ensure that:

   (a) a health record is maintained and contains particulars approved by the Executive for all of that employer's employees who are exposed to asbestos; and

   (b) that record, or a copy of that record is kept available in a suitable form for at least 40 years from the date of the last entry made in it; and

   (c) each employee who is exposed to asbestos is under adequate medical surveillance by a relevant doctor.

(2) The medical surveillance required by paragraph (1)(c) must include:

   (a) a medical examination not more than two years before the beginning of such exposure; and

   (b) periodic medical examinations at intervals of at least once every two years or such shorter time as the relevant doctor may require while such exposure continues;

   and each such medical examination must include a specific examination of the chest.

(3) For work with asbestos, which is not licensable work with asbestos, and is not exempted by regulation 3(2), the requirements in paragraphs (1)(a) to (c) apply and:

   (a) a medical examination in accordance with paragraph (1)(c) and (2)(a) must take place on or before 30 April 2015;

   (b) on or after 1 May 2015, a medical examination in accordance with paragraph (1)(c) and (2)(a) must take place not more than 3 years before the beginning of such exposure; and

   (c) a periodic medical examination in accordance with paragraph (1)(c) and (2)(b) must take place at intervals of at least once every 3 years, or such shorter time as the relevant doctor may require while such exposure continues.

(4) Where an employee has been examined in accordance with paragraph (1)(c), the relevant doctor must issue a certificate to the employer and employee stating:

   (a) that the employee has been so examined; and

   (b) the date of the examination;

   and the employer must keep that certificate, or a copy of that certificate for at least 4 years from the date on which it was issued.

(5) An employee to whom this regulation applies must, when required by that employee's employer and at the cost of that employer, attend during the employee's working hours such examination and undertake such tests as may be required for the purposes of paragraph (1)(c) and must furnish the relevant doctor with such information concerning that employee's health as the relevant doctor may reasonably require.

(6) Where, for the purpose of carrying out functions under these Regulations, a relevant doctor requires to inspect any record kept for the purposes of these Regulations, the employer must permit that doctor to do so.

(7) Where medical surveillance is carried out on the premises of the employer, the employer must ensure that suitable facilities are made available for the purpose.

(8) The employer must:

   (a) on reasonable notice being given, allow an employee access to that employee's personal health record;

   (b) provide the Executive with copies of such personal health records as the Executive may require; and

   (c) if the employer ceases to trade notify the Executive without delay in writing and make available to the Executive all personal health records kept by that employer.

(9) Where, as a result of medical surveillance, an employee is found to have an identifiable disease or adverse health effect which is considered by a relevant doctor to be the result of exposure to asbestos at work, the employer of that employee must:

   (a) ensure that a suitable person informs the employee accordingly and provides the employee with information and advice regarding further medical surveillance;

   (b) review the risk assessment;

   (c) review any measure taken to comply with regulation 11 taking into account any advice given by a relevant doctor or by the Executive;

   (d) consider assigning the employee to alternative work where there is no risk of further exposure to asbestos, taking into account any advice given by a relevant doctor; and

   (e) provide for a review of the health of every other employee who has been similarly exposed, including a medical examination (which must include a specific examination of the chest) where such an examination is recommended by a relevant doctor or by the Executive.

Regulation 23: Washing and Changing Facilities

(1) Every employer must ensure that the following are provided to any of that employer's employees who is exposed to asbestos:

    (a) adequate washing and changing facilities;

    (b) where an employer is required to provide protective clothing, adequate facilities for the storage of:

        (i) that protective clothing; and

        (ii) personal clothing not worn during working hours; and

    (c) where an employer is required to provide respiratory protective equipment, adequate facilities for the storage of that equipment.

(2) The facilities provided under paragraph (1) for the storage of:

    (a) personal protective clothing;

    (b) personal clothing not worn during working hours; and

    (c) respiratory protective equipment;

must be separate from each other.

Regulation 24: Storage, Distribution and Labelling of Raw Asbestos and Asbestos Waste

(1) Every employer who undertakes work with asbestos must ensure that raw asbestos or waste which contains asbestos is not:

    (a) stored;

    (b) received into or despatched from any place of work; or

    (c) distributed within any place of work, except in a totally enclosed distribution system;

unless it is in a sealed receptacle or, where more appropriate, sealed wrapping, clearly marked in accordance with paragraphs (2) and (3) showing that it contains asbestos.

(2) Raw asbestos must be labelled in accordance with the provisions of Schedule 2.

(3) Waste containing asbestos must be labelled:

    (a) where the **Carriage of Dangerous Goods and Use of Transportable Pressure Equipment Regulations 2009** apply, in accordance with those Regulations; and

    (b) **in any other case in accordance with the provisions of Schedule 2.**

Part 3: Prohibitions and Related Provisions

Regulation 25: Interpretation of Prohibitions

(1) In this Part:

"asbestos spraying" means the application by spraying of any material containing asbestos to form a continuous surface coating;

"extraction of asbestos" means the extraction by mining or otherwise of asbestos as the primary product of such extraction, but does not include extraction which produces asbestos as a by-product of the primary activity of extraction; and

"supply" means supply by way of sale, lease, hire, hire-purchase, loan, gift or exchange for a consideration other than money, whether (in all cases) as principal or as agent for another.

(2) Any prohibition imposed on any person by this Part applies only to acts done in the course of a trade, business or other undertaking (whether for profit or not) carried on by that person.

(3) Where in this Part it is stated that asbestos has intentionally been added to a product or is intentionally added, it will be presumed where:

   (a) asbestos is present in any product; and

   (b) asbestos is not a naturally occurring impurity of that product, or of any component or constituent of that product;

   that the asbestos has intentionally been added or is intentionally added, as the case may be, subject to evidence to the contrary being adduced in any proceedings.

Regulation 26: Prohibitions of Exposure to Asbestos

(1) A person must not undertake asbestos spraying or working procedures that involve using low-density (less than $1g/cm^3$) insulating or soundproofing materials which contain asbestos.

(2) Every employer must ensure that no employees are exposed to asbestos during the extraction of asbestos.

(3) Every employer must ensure that no employees are exposed to asbestos during the manufacture of asbestos products or of products containing intentionally added asbestos.

Regulation 27: Labelling of Products Containing Asbestos

(1) Subject to paragraph (2), a person must not supply under an exception in Schedule 3 or an exemption granted pursuant to regulation 29 or regulation 30 a product which contains asbestos unless that product is labelled in accordance with the provisions of Schedule 2.

(2) Where a component of a product contains asbestos, in order to comply with this regulation that component must be labelled in accordance with the provisions of Schedule 2 except that where the size of that component makes it impossible for a label to be fixed to it, neither that component nor the product need be labelled.

Regulation 28: Additional Provisions in the Case of Exceptions and Exemptions

(1) Where under an exception in Schedule 3 or an exemption granted pursuant to regulation 29 or regulation 30 asbestos is used in a work process or is produced by a work process, the employer must ensure that the quantity of asbestos and materials containing asbestos at the premises where the work is carried out is reduced to as low a level as is reasonably practicable.

(2) Subject to paragraph (3), where under an exception in Schedule 3 or an exemption granted pursuant to regulation 29 or regulation 30 a manufacturing process which gives rise to asbestos dust is carried out in a building, the employer must ensure that any part of the building in which the process is carried out is:

   (a) so designed and constructed as to facilitate cleaning; and

   (b) equipped with an adequate and suitable vacuum cleaning system which must, where reasonably practicable, be a fixed system.

(3) Paragraph 2(a) does not apply to a building in which, prior to 1 March 1988, there was carried out a process to which either:

   (a) as then in force, regulation 13 of the **Asbestos Regulations 1969** applied and the process was carried out in compliance with that regulation; or

   (b) that regulation did not apply.

Part 4: Miscellaneous

Regulation 29: Exemption Certificates

(1) Subject to paragraph (3), the Executive may, by a certificate in writing, exempt any person or class of persons or any product containing asbestos or class of such products from all or any of the requirements or prohibitions imposed by regulations 4, 8, 12, 13, 21 and 22(5) and (7) and any such exemption may be granted subject to conditions and to a limit of time and may be varied or revoked by a further certificate in writing at any time.

(2) Subject to paragraph (3), the Executive may exempt emergency services from all or any of the requirements or prohibitions imposed by regulations 7 and 9; and any such exemption may be granted subject to conditions and to a limit of time and may be varied or revoked by a further certificate in writing at any time.

(3) The Executive must not grant any exemption under paragraph (1) or (2) unless having regard to the circumstances of the case and in particular to:

   (a) the conditions, if any, which it proposes to attach to the exemption; and

   (b) any other requirements imposed by or under any enactments which apply to the case;

   it is satisfied that the health or safety of persons who are likely to be affected by the exemption will not be prejudiced in consequence of it.

Regulation 30: Exemptions Relating to the Ministry of Defence

The Secretary of State for Defence may, in the interests of national security, exempt any person or class of persons from the prohibition imposed by Part 3 of these Regulations by a certificate in writing, and any such exemption may be granted subject to conditions and to a limit of time and may be varied or revoked by a further certificate in writing at any time.

Regulation 31: Extension Outside Great Britain

These Regulations apply to any work outside Great Britain to which Sections 1 to 59 and 80 to 82 of the **1974 Act** apply by virtue of the **Health and Safety at Work, etc. Act 1974 (Application Outside Great Britain) Order 2001** as they apply to work in Great Britain.

Regulation 32: Existing Licences and Exemption Certificates

(1) An existing licence granted by the Executive under regulation 8(2) of the **Control of Asbestos Regulations 2006** shall:

   (a) continue to have effect as if it had been granted under regulation 8(2) of these Regulations;

   (b) be of the duration and subject to the conditions specified in it as if that duration and those conditions had been specified under regulation 8(3); and

   (c) be liable to variation and revocation under regulation 8(4) and (5); and any requirement in such a licence concerning notification or any exception to such a requirement has effect as a requirement for notification under regulation 9, or as an exception to such a requirement under regulation 3(2) of these Regulations.

(2) An existing exemption granted by the Executive under regulation 7(1) of the **Asbestos (Licensing) Regulations 1983**, regulation 8(1) of the **Asbestos (Prohibitions) Regulations 1992**, regulation 25(1) of the **Control of Asbestos at Work Regulations 2002** or regulation 32 of the **Control of Asbestos Regulations 2006** continues to have effect and be subject to any limitation of time or any conditions specified in it and liable to revocation as if it had been granted under regulation 29(1) or (2) of these Regulations.

(3) An existing exemption granted by the Secretary of State for Defence under regulation 8(3) of the **Asbestos (Prohibitions) Regulations 1992** or regulation 33 of the **Control of Asbestos Regulations 2006** continues to have effect and be subject to any limitation of time or any conditions specified in it and liable to revocation as if it had been granted under regulation 30 of these Regulations.

Regulation 33: Revocations and Savings

(1) The **Control of Asbestos Regulations 2006** are revoked.

(2) The amendments listed in Schedule 3 will have effect.

(3) Any record or register required to be kept under the Regulations revoked either by paragraph(1), or by any of the Regulations revoked by regulation 36(1) of the **Control of Asbestos Regulations 2006** or by regulation 27(1) of the **Control of Asbestos at Work Regulations 2002** shall, notwithstanding that revocation, be kept in the same manner and for the same period as specified in those Regulations as if these Regulations had not been made, except that the Executive may approve the keeping of records at a place or in a form other than at the place where, or in the form in which, records were required to be kept under the Regulations so revoked.

Regulation 34: Defence

Subject to regulation 21 of the **Management of Health and Safety at Work Regulations 1999** in any proceedings for an offence consisting of a contravention of Part 2 of these Regulations it is a defence for any person to prove that he took all reasonable precautions and exercised all due diligence to avoid the commission of that offence.

CONTROL OF ELECTROMAGNETIC FIELDS AT WORK REGULATIONS 2016 (SI 2016 NO. 588)

Amending Legislation

None as yet.

Summary

These Regulations implement in Great Britain **European Directive 2013/35/EU** on the minimum health and safety requirements regarding the exposure of workers to risks arising from physical agents (electromagnetic fields). They impose duties on employers to take reasonable steps to prevent harm in the workplace arising from exposure to electromagnetic fields (EMFs).

An EMF is produced whenever a piece of electrical or electronic equipment is used. EMFs are static electric, static magnetic and time-varying electric, magnetic and electromagnetic (radio wave) fields with frequencies up to 300 GHz. EMFs are present in virtually all workplaces and if they are of high enough intensity, action may be needed to make sure workers are protected from any adverse effects.

EMFs at different frequencies affect the human body in different ways. Sensory effects can include nausea, vertigo, metallic taste in the mouth and flickering sensations in the peripheral vision. Health effects can include nerve stimulation, effects on the central and peripheral nervous system of the body, tingling, muscle contraction, heart arrhythmia and heating effects leading to a rise in core body temperature or localised limb heating.

To protect persons from possible harmful exposure to EMFs the Regulations require the employer to:

- Assess the levels of EMFs to which employees may be exposed.
- Ensure that exposure is below specified 'Exposure Limit Values' (ELVs).
- If required, devise and implement an action plan to ensure compliance with the exposure limits.
- If necessary, assess the risks of employees' exposure and eliminate or minimise those risks.
- Provide information and training on the particular risks (if any) posed to employees by EMFs in the workplace and details of any measures to remove or control them.
- Take action if employees are exposed to EMFs in excess of the ELVs.
- Provide health surveillance or medical examination, as appropriate.

The Regulations contain a Schedule which introduces limits, explains the effects of EMFs and provides details of safety conditions which must be met. The sensory-effect ELVs are allowed to be exceeded when certain safety conditions stated in the Schedule to the Regulations are met and there are exemptions to the exposure limits allowed under certain circumstances.

The HSE guidance for employers, HSG281 *Electromagnetic fields at work - A guide to the Control of Electromagnetic Fields at Work Regulations 2016* (available on the HSE website) will help decide whether workers are already adequately protected, or whether more should be done. It states that the majority of employers will not need to take any additional action to reduce the risk from EMFs as in most workplaces EMFs are already at safe levels. Where employees may be exposed to higher levels of EMFs, the levels and associated risks should already be assessed and managed under the **Management of Health and Safety at Work Regulations 1999**.

PART 1 - INTRODUCTION

Citation and Commencement (Reg. 1)

The Regulations cited as the **Control of Electromagnetic Fields at Work Regulations 2016** came into force on 1 July 2016.

Interpretation (Reg. 2(1))[Part]

AL means an action level which is set out in detail in Parts 2 and 3 of the Schedule to the Regulations.

Direct biophysical effect means an effect on human body tissue caused by its presence in an electromagnetic field.

Electromagnetic field means a static electric, static magnetic and time-varying electric, magnetic and electromagnetic field with a frequency of up to 300 GHz.

ELV means an exposure limit value which is set out in detail in Part 2 of the Schedule to the Regulations.

Employee at particular risk means:

- an employee who has declared to his or her employer a condition which may lead to a higher susceptibility to the potential effects of exposure to electromagnetic fields; or
- an employee who works in close proximity to electro-explosive devices, explosive materials or flammable atmospheres.

Health effect means a direct biophysical effect which is potentially harmful to human health.

Indirect effect means an effect, caused by the presence of an object or a substance in an electromagnetic field, which may present a safety or health hazard.

Sensory effect means a direct biophysical effect involving a transient disturbance in sensory perception or a minor and temporary change in brain function.

Application (Reg. 3)

The Regulations do not apply to the master or crew of a ship or to the employer of such persons in respect of the normal shipboard activities of a ship's crew which are carried out solely by the crew under the direction of the master and for the purposes of this Regulation **ship** includes every description of vessel used in navigation, other than a ship forming part of Her Majesty's Navy.

PART 2 - EXPOSURE AND RISK

Limitation on Exposure to Electromagnetic Fields (Reg. 4)

1. An employer must ensure that employees are not exposed to electromagnetic field levels in excess of the ELVs.

   However:

   - Exposure may exceed the sensory effect ELVs during work activities if the employer ensures that:
     - they are only exceeded temporarily;
     - protection measures have been adopted which minimise, so far as is reasonably practicable, the sensory effects related to movement in static magnetic fields, including nausea and vertigo;
     - adequate information is provided to the employee on the possibility of those sensory effects;
     - where any of those sensory effects are reported to the employer, the exposure assessment under regulation 5, and the protection measures, are updated where necessary.
   - Paragraph (1) does not apply in relation to:
     - Any activity in respect of which a suitable and sufficient exposure limitation system is in place, where that activity is carried out:
       - by a person acting in the capacity of a member of either Her Majesty's armed forces or a visiting force;
       - by any civilian working with such a person;
       - on any premises or part of premises under the control of the Secretary of State for the purposes of the Ministry of Defence or the service authorities of a visiting force.
     - The development, testing, installation, use and maintenance of, or research related to, magnetic resonance imaging equipment for patients in the health sector, where:
       - the exposure of employees to electromagnetic fields is as low as is reasonably practicable;
       - employees are protected against any health effects and safety risks related to that exposure.

Exposure Assessment (Reg. 5)

(1) The employer must make a suitable and sufficient assessment of the levels of electromagnetic fields to which employees may be exposed.

This can involve:

- the use of calculations and measurements to demonstrate that employees are not exposed to electromagnetic field levels in excess of the ELVs;
- assessment of exposure against the ALs in order to determine that specific ELVs are not exceeded.

(3) The assessment may take into account:

- emission information and other safety-related data provided by the manufacturer or distributor of equipment;
- industry standards and guidelines;
- guidance produced by the European Commission;
- guidance produced by the Health and Safety Executive.

(4) The employer must review the assessment when:

- there is reason to suspect it is no longer valid;
- there has been a significant change in the matters to which it relates;

and make such changes to it as are necessary to ensure it remains suitable and sufficient.

Action Plan (Reg. 7)

(1) Where the most recent exposure assessment demonstrates that employees are exposed to electromagnetic field levels in excess of applicable ELVs, the employer must make and implement a suitable and sufficient action plan to rectify this.

(2) The action plan must include consideration of, where relevant:

- other working methods that entail lower exposure to electromagnetic fields;
- replacement equipment designed to reduce the level of exposure;
- technical measures to reduce the emission of electromagnetic fields, including, where necessary, the use of interlocks, screening or similar health protection mechanisms;
- demarcation and access control measures;
- maintenance programmes for work equipment, workplaces and workstation systems;
- the design and layout of workplaces and workstations;
- limitations on the duration and intensity of exposure;
- the availability of suitable personal protective equipment.

(3) Where, despite the measures taken under paragraph (1), the exposure of employees exceeds any ELV, the employer must, as soon as is reasonably practicable, identify and implement any changes to the action plan which are necessary to rectify this.

Risk Assessment (Reg. 8)

(1) The employer must make a suitable and sufficient assessment of the risks to employees arising from their exposure to electromagnetic fields.

(2) The risk assessment must include consideration of, where relevant:

- the ALs and ELVs;
- the frequency range, level, duration and type of exposure, including its distribution over the employee's body and the workplace;
- direct biophysical effects;
- replacement equipment designed to reduce the level of exposure;
- information obtained from any health surveillance or medical examinations;
- information provided by the manufacturer or distributor of equipment;
- multiple sources of exposure;
- simultaneous exposure to multiple frequency fields;
- indirect effects;
- any effects on employees at particular risk;
- other health-and-safety-related information.

(3) The risks referred to in paragraph (1) do not include the risk of effects:
- caused by contact with live conductors;
- caused by multiple and separate instances of exposure;
- which continue to develop when exposure has ceased.

(4) The employer must review the assessment when:
- there is reason to suspect it is no longer valid;
- there has been a significant change in the matters to which it relates;

and make such changes to it as are necessary to ensure it remains suitable and sufficient.

Obligation to Eliminate or Reduce Risks (Reg. 9)

(1) The employer must ensure that, so far as is reasonably practicable, the risks identified in the most recent risk assessment under regulation 8 are eliminated or reduced to a minimum.

(2) Measures taken under paragraph (1) must:
- Be based on the general principles of prevention set out in Schedule 1 to the **Management of Health and Safety at Work Regulations 1999**.
- Take into account technical progress, the potential to restrict access to parts of the workplace, and the availability of measures to control the production of electromagnetic fields at source.

PART 3 - MISCELLANEOUS

Information and Training (Reg. 10)

(1) The employer must provide relevant information and training to any employees who are likely to be subjected to the risks identified in the most recent risk assessment, including in relation to:
- the measures taken under regulation 9;
- the concepts and values of the ALs and ELVs and the possible risks associated with them;
- the possible indirect effects of exposure;
- the results of the most recent exposure assessment under regulation 5;
- how to detect and report sensory and health effects;
- the circumstances in which employees are entitled to health surveillance and medical examinations under regulation 11;
- safe working practices;
- any additional measures taken in respect of employees at particular risk.

Health Surveillance and Medical Examinations (Reg. 11)

(1) The employer must ensure that health surveillance and medical examinations are provided as appropriate to any employee who:
- is exposed to electromagnetic field levels in excess of the health effect ELVs set out in Part 2 of the Schedule to the Regulations;
- reports experiencing a health effect to that employer.

(2) Any health surveillance or medical examinations must be provided during any reasonable hours chosen by the employee.

(3) The employer must keep a suitable record of any health surveillance and medical examinations provided.

Records (Reg. 12)

(1) An employer who employs five or more employees must:
- record the significant findings of the most recent exposure assessment under regulation 5;
- where required to make them, record:
  - the most recent action plan under regulation 7;
  - the significant findings of the most recent risk assessment under regulation 8.

Exemptions (Reg. 13)

(1) The Health and Safety Executive may by a certificate in writing exempt employers from the requirements of regulations 4(1) and 7 in relation to one or more work activities.

(2) An exemption under paragraph (1) must be limited in time and subject to the conditions that:

- the exposure of employees to electromagnetic fields is as low as is reasonably practicable;
- employees are protected against any health effects and safety risks related to that exposure.

(3) The Health and Safety Executive may amend or revoke an exemption at any time by a further certificate in writing.

CONTROL OF LEAD AT WORK REGULATIONS 2002 (SI 2002 NO. 2676)

Amending Legislation

Minor amendments were made by the **Carriage of Dangerous Goods and Use of Transportable Pressure Equipment Regulations 2004** (subsequently revoked by regulations of the same name in 2007 and then, again, in 2009) and the **Chemicals (Hazard Information and Packaging for Supply) Regulations 2009**. Amendments were also made by the **Control of Substances Hazardous to Health (Amendment) Regulations 2004** and by the **Legislative Reform (Health and Safety Executive) Order 2008**.

Summary

The essential feature of these Regulations is the requirement placed on an employer to undertake a risk assessment in regard to his employees' exposure to lead. There are also requirements for control measures, including personal protective equipment, air monitoring and medical surveillance.

Regulation 1: Citation and Commencement

These Regulations came into force on 21 November 2002.

Regulation 2: Interpretation

"Action level" means a blood concentration of:

- in respect of a woman of reproductive capacity, 25 μg/dl;
- in respect of a young person, 40 μg/dl;
- in respect of any other employee, 50 μg/dl.

"Biological monitoring" includes the measuring of a person's blood-lead concentration or urinary lead concentration by atomic absorption spectroscopy.

"Control measure" means a measure taken to reduce exposure to lead (including the provision of systems of work and supervision, the cleaning of workplaces, premises, plant and equipment, the provision and use of engineering controls and personal protective equipment).

"Lead" means lead (including lead alkyls, lead alloys, any compounds of lead and lead as a constituent of any substance or material) which is liable to be inhaled, ingested or otherwise absorbed by persons except where it is given off from the exhaust system of a vehicle on a road within the meaning of section 192 of the **Road Traffic Act 1988**.

"Medical surveillance" means assessment of the state of health of an employee, as related to exposure to lead, and includes clinical assessment and biological monitoring.

"Occupational exposure limit for lead" means in relation to:

- lead other than lead alkyls, a concentration of lead in the atmosphere to which any employee is exposed of 0.15 mg/m^3;
- lead alkyls, a concentration of lead contained in lead alkyls in the atmosphere to which any employee is exposed of 0.10 mg/m^3,

assessed by reference to the content of the element lead in the concentration, and in relation to an 8-hour time-weighted average reference period when calculated by a method approved by the Health and Safety Executive.

"Relevant doctor" means an appointed doctor or an employment medical adviser.

"Suspension level" means a blood-lead concentration of:

- in respect of a woman of reproductive capacity, 30 μg/dl,
- in respect of a young person, 50 μg/dl, or
- in respect of any other employee, 60 μg/dl; or

a urinary lead concentration of:

- in respect of a woman of reproductive capacity, 25 μg Pb/g creatinine, or
- in respect of any other employee, 110 μ Pb/g creatinine.

"Woman of reproductive capacity" means an employee in respect of whom an entry has been made to that effect in that employee's health record in accordance with regulation 10 by a relevant doctor.

"Young person" means a person who has not attained the age of 18 and who is not a woman of reproductive capacity.

Regulation 3: Duties under these Regulations

Where a duty is placed by these Regulations on an employer in respect of his employees, he shall, so far as is reasonably practicable, be under a like duty in respect of any other person, whether at work or not, who may be affected by the work carried out by the employer except in relation to medical surveillance, monitoring, information and training and dealing with accidents the duty shall not extend to persons who are not his employees. These Regulations shall apply to the self-employed except in respect of air monitoring.

These Regulations shall not apply to the master or crew of a ship or to the employer of such persons in respect of the normal shipboard activities of a ship's crew which are carried out solely by the crew under the direction of the master and are not liable to expose persons other than the master and crew to a risk to their health and safety.

Regulation 4: Prohibitions

No employer shall use a glaze other than a leadless glaze or a low solubility glaze in the manufacture of pottery. No employer shall employ a young person or a woman of reproductive capacity in any activity specified in Schedule 1.

Regulation 5: Assessment of the Risk to Health Created by Work Involving Lead

An employer shall not carry out work which is liable to expose any employees to lead unless he has made a suitable and sufficient assessment of the risk created by that work to the health of those employees and of the steps that need to be taken to meet the requirements of these Regulations and implemented the steps.

The risk assessment shall include consideration of:

- the hazardous properties of the lead;
- information on health effects provided by the supplier, including information contained in any relevant safety data sheet;
- the level, type and duration of exposure;
- the circumstances of the work, including the amount of lead involved;
- activities, such as maintenance, where there is the potential for a high level of exposure;
- any relevant occupational exposure limit, action level and suspension level;
- the effect of preventive and control measures which have been or will be taken in accordance with regulation 6;
- the results of relevant medical surveillance;
- the results of monitoring of exposure in accordance with regulation 9;
- in circumstances where the work will involve exposure to lead and another substance hazardous to health, the risk presented by exposure to those substances in combination;
- whether the exposure of any employee to lead is liable to be significant; and
- such additional information as the employer may need in order to complete the risk assessment.

The risk assessment shall be reviewed regularly and forthwith if:

- there is reason to suspect that the risk assessment is no longer valid;
- there has been a significant change in the work to which the risk assessment relates;
- the results of any monitoring carried out in accordance with regulation 9 show it to be necessary; or
- the blood-lead concentration of any employee under medical surveillance in accordance with regulation 10 equals or exceeds the action level;

and where, as a result of the review, changes to the risk assessment are required, those changes shall be made.

Where the employer employs five or more employees, he shall record the significant findings of the risk assessment as soon as is practicable after the risk assessment is made and the steps which he has taken to meet the requirements of regulation 6.

Regulation 6: Prevention or Control of Exposure to Lead

Every employer shall ensure that the exposure of his employees to lead is either prevented or, where this is not reasonably practicable, adequately controlled.

Substitution shall by preference be undertaken, whereby the employer shall avoid, so far as is reasonably practicable, the use of lead at the workplace by replacing it with a substance or process which, under the conditions of its use, either eliminates or reduces the risk to the health of his employees.

Where it is not reasonably practicable to prevent exposure to lead, the employer shall comply with his duty of control by applying protection measures appropriate to the activity and consistent with the risk assessment, including, in order of priority:

- the design and use of appropriate work processes, systems and engineering controls and the provision and use of suitable work equipment and materials;
- the control of exposure at source, including adequate ventilation systems and appropriate organisational measures; and
- where adequate control of exposure cannot be achieved by other means, the provision of suitable personal protective equipment in addition to the measures required above.

The protection measures referred to above shall include:

- arrangements for the safe handling, storage and transport of lead, and of waste containing lead, at the workplace;
- the adoption of suitable maintenance procedures;
- reducing, to the minimum required for the work concerned the number of employees subject to exposure, the level and duration of exposure, and the quantity of lead present at the workplace;
- the control of the working environment, including appropriate general ventilation; and
- appropriate hygiene measures including adequate washing facilities.

Where, despite the control measures the exposure of an employee to lead is, or is liable to be, significant, the employer shall provide that employee with suitable and sufficient protective clothing.

Where there is exposure to lead, control of that exposure shall, so far as the inhalation of lead is concerned, only be treated as being adequate if:

- the occupational exposure limit for lead is not exceeded; or
- where that occupational exposure limit is exceeded, the employer identifies the reasons for the limit being exceeded and takes immediate steps to remedy the situation.

Personal protective equipment provided by an employer in accordance with this regulation shall be suitable for the purpose and shall comply with any provision in the **Personal Protective Equipment Regulations 2002** or in the case of respiratory protective equipment, be of a type approved or shall conform to a standard approved, in either case, by the Executive.

Every employer who provides any control measure, other thing or facility in accordance with these Regulations shall take all reasonable steps to ensure that it is properly used.

Every employee shall make full and proper use of any control measure etc. provided in accordance with these Regulations and, where relevant, shall:

- take all reasonable steps to ensure it is returned after use to any accommodation provided for it; and
- if he discovers a defect therein, report it forthwith to his employer.

Regulation 7: Eating, Drinking and Smoking

Every employer shall ensure, so far as is reasonably practicable, that his employees do not eat, drink or smoke in any place which is, or is liable to be, contaminated by lead.

An employee shall not eat, drink or smoke in any place which he has reason to believe to be contaminated by lead.

Nothing in this Regulation shall prevent the provision and use of drinking facilities in a place which is liable to be contaminated by lead provided such facilities are not liable to be contaminated by lead and where they are required for the welfare of employees who are exposed to lead.

Regulation 8: Maintenance, Examination and Testing of Control Measures

Every employer shall ensure that any control measure is maintained in an efficient state, in efficient working order, in good repair and in a clean condition.

The employer shall ensure that where engineering controls are provided to meet the requirements of regulation 6, that thorough examination and testing of those controls is carried out:

- in the case of local exhaust ventilation plant, at least once every 14 months; and
- in any other case, at suitable intervals.

Where respiratory protective equipment (other than disposable respiratory protective equipment) is provided the employer shall ensure that thorough examination and, where appropriate, testing of that equipment is carried out at suitable intervals.

Every employer shall keep a suitable record of the examinations and tests carried out and of repairs carried out as a result of those examinations and tests, and that record or a suitable summary thereof shall be kept available for at least five years from the date on which it was made.

Every employer shall ensure that personal protective equipment, including protective clothing, is:

- properly stored in a well-defined place;
- checked at suitable intervals; and
- when discovered to be defective, repaired or replaced before further use.

Personal protective equipment which may be contaminated by lead shall be removed on leaving the working area and kept apart from uncontaminated clothing and equipment. The employer shall ensure that this equipment is subsequently decontaminated and cleaned or, if necessary, destroyed.

Regulation 9: Air Monitoring

Where the risk assessment indicates that any of his employees are liable to receive significant exposure to lead, the employer shall ensure that the concentration of lead in air to which his employees are exposed is measured in accordance with a suitable procedure. The monitoring shall be carried out at least every three months.

Except where the exposure arises wholly or in part from exposure to lead alkyls, the interval between each occasion of monitoring may be increased to a maximum of 12 months where there has been no material change in the work or the conditions of exposure since the last occasion of monitoring and the lead in air concentration for each group of employees or work area has not exceeded 0.10 mg/m^3 on the two previous consecutive occasions on which monitoring was carried out.

The employer shall ensure that a suitable record of monitoring carried out for the purpose of this regulation is made and maintained and that that record is kept available for at least five years from the date of the last entry made in it.

Where an employee is required by regulation 10 to be under medical surveillance, an individual record of any monitoring carried out in accordance with this regulation shall be made, maintained and kept in respect of that employee.

The employer shall on reasonable notice being given, allow an employee access to his personal monitoring record, provide the Executive with copies of such monitoring records as the Executive may require and if he ceases to trade, notify the Executive forthwith in writing and make available to the Executive all monitoring records kept by him.

Regulation 10: Medical Surveillance

Every employer shall ensure that each of his employees who is or is liable to be exposed to lead is under suitable medical surveillance by a relevant doctor where:

- the exposure of the employee to lead is, or is liable to be, significant;
- the blood-lead concentration or urinary lead concentration of the employee is measured and equals or exceeds the levels detailed; or
- a relevant doctor certifies that the employee should be under such medical surveillance, and the technique of investigation is of low risk to the employee.

The levels referred to above are:

- a blood-lead concentration of:
  - in respect of a woman of reproductive capacity, 20 μg/dl, or
  - in respect of any other employee, 35 μg/dl; or
  - a urinary lead concentration of:
    - in respect of a woman of reproductive capacity, 20 μg Pb/g creatinine, or
    - in respect of any other employee, 40 μg Pb/g creatinine.

Medical surveillance required shall so far as is reasonably practicable, be commenced before an employee for the first time commences work giving rise to exposure to lead and in any event within 14 working days of such commencement and subsequently be conducted at intervals of not more than 12 months or such shorter intervals as the relevant doctor may require.

Biological monitoring shall be carried out at intervals not exceeding those set out below:

- in respect of an employee other than a young person or a woman of reproductive capacity, at least every six months, but where the results of the measurements for individuals or for groups of workers have shown on the previous two consecutive occasions on which monitoring was carried out a lead in air exposure greater than 0.075 mg/m^3 but less than 0.100 mg/m^3 and where the blood-lead concentration of any individual employee is less than 30 µg/dl, the frequency of monitoring may be reduced to once a year; or
- in respect of any young person or a woman of reproductive capacity, at such intervals as the relevant doctor shall specify, being not greater than three months.

The employer shall ensure that an adequate health record in respect of each of his employees is made and maintained and that that record is kept available in a suitable form for at least 40 years from the date of the last entry made in it.

The employer shall on reasonable notice being given, allow an employee access to his personal health record, provide the Executive with copies of such health records as the Executive may require and if he ceases to trade, notify the Executive forthwith in writing and make available to the Executive all health records kept by him.

Where the blood-lead concentration for an employee equals or exceeds the appropriate action level, the employer shall take steps to determine the reason or reasons for the high level of lead in blood and shall, so far as is reasonably practicable, give effect to measures designed to reduce the blood-lead concentration of that employee to a level below the appropriate action level.

In any case where the blood-lead concentration or urinary lead concentration of an employee reaches the appropriate suspension level, the employer of that employee shall:

- ensure that an entry is made in the health record of the employee by a relevant doctor certifying whether in the professional opinion of the doctor the employee should be suspended from work which is liable to expose that employee to lead;
- ensure that a relevant doctor informs the employee accordingly and provides the employee with information and advice regarding further medical surveillance;
- review the risk assessment;
- review any measure taken to comply with regulation 6, taking into account any advice given by a relevant doctor or by the Executive; and
- provide for a review of the health of any other employee who has been similarly exposed, including a medical examination where such an examination is recommended by a relevant doctor or by the Executive.

Where in the opinion of the relevant doctor the employee need not be suspended from work the entry made in the health record shall include the reasons for that opinion and the conditions, if any, under which the employee may continue to be employed in such work.

Where a relevant doctor has certified by an entry in the health record of an employee that in his professional opinion that employee should not be engaged in work which exposes the employee to lead or that the employee should only be so engaged under conditions specified

in the record, the employer shall not permit the employee to be engaged in that work except in accordance with the conditions, if any, specified in the health record, unless that entry has been cancelled by a relevant doctor.

Where medical surveillance is carried out on the premises of the employer, the employer shall ensure that suitable facilities are made available for the purpose.

An employee to whom this regulation applies shall, when required by his employer and at the cost of the employer, present himself during his working hours for such medical surveillance procedures as may be required and shall furnish the doctor with such information concerning his health as the doctor may reasonably require.

Where for the purpose of carrying out his functions under these Regulations a relevant doctor requires to inspect any workplace or any record kept for the purposes of these Regulations, the employer shall permit that doctor to do so.

The employer shall ensure that in respect of each female employee whose exposure to lead is or is liable to be significant an entry is made in the health record of that employee by a relevant doctor as to whether or not that employee is of reproductive capacity.

Where an employee or an employer is aggrieved by a decision recorded in the health record by a doctor that an employee should not be engaged in work which exposes that employee to lead (or which imposes conditions on such work) or that a female employee is of reproductive capacity, the employee or employer may, by an application in writing to the Executive within 28 days of the date upon which the decision was notified to the employee or employer as the case may be, apply for that decision to be reviewed and the result of that review shall be notified to the employee and employer and entered in the health record in accordance with the approved procedure.

Regulation 11: Information, Instruction and Training

Every employer who undertakes work which is liable to expose an employee to lead shall provide that employee with suitable and sufficient information, instruction and training.

The information, instruction and training provided under that paragraph shall include:

- details of the form of lead to which the employee is liable to be exposed including:
    - the risk which it presents to health;
    - any relevant occupational exposure limit, action level and suspension level;
    - access to any relevant safety data sheet; and
    - other legislative provisions which concern the hazardous properties of that form of lead;
- the significant findings of the risk assessment;
- the appropriate precautions and actions to be taken by the employee in order to safeguard himself and other employees at the workplace;
- the results of any monitoring of exposure to lead carried out in accordance with regulation 9; and
- the collective results of any medical surveillance undertaken in accordance with regulation 10 in a form calculated to prevent those results from being identified as relating to a particular person.

The information, instruction and training required shall be adapted to take account of significant changes in the type of work carried out or methods of work used by the employer and provided in a manner appropriate to the level, type and duration of exposure identified by the risk assessment.

Every employer shall ensure that any person (whether or not his employee) who carries out work in connection with the employer's duties under these Regulations has suitable and sufficient information, instruction and training.

Where containers and pipes for lead used at work are not marked in accordance with any relevant legislation listed in Schedule 2, the employer shall ensure that the contents of those containers and pipes, together with the nature of those contents and any associated hazards, are clearly identifiable.

Regulation 12: Arrangements to Deal with Accidents, Incidents and Emergencies

To protect the health of his employees from an accident, incident or emergency related to the presence of lead at the workplace, the employer shall ensure that:

- procedures, including the provision of appropriate first-aid facilities and relevant safety drills (which shall be tested at regular intervals), have been prepared which can be put into effect when such an event occurs;
- information on emergency arrangements, including:
    - details of relevant work hazards and hazard identification arrangements, and
    - specific hazards likely to arise at the time of an accident, incident or emergency,

is available; and

- suitable warning and other communication systems are established to enable an appropriate response, including remedial actions and rescue operations, to be made immediately when such an event occurs.

The employer shall ensure that information on the procedures and systems required is made available to relevant accident and emergency services to enable those services, whether internal or external to the workplace, to prepare their own response procedures and precautionary measures and displayed at the workplace, if this is appropriate.

In the event of an accident, incident or emergency related to the presence of lead at the workplace, the employer shall ensure that:

- immediate steps are taken to:
    - mitigate the effects of the event,
    - restore the situation to normal, and
    - inform those of his employees who may be affected; and
- only those persons who are essential for the carrying out of repairs and other necessary work are permitted in the affected area and they are provided with:
    - appropriate personal protective equipment, and
    - any necessary specialised safety equipment and plant, which shall be used until the situation is restored to normal.

CONTROL OF MAJOR ACCIDENT HAZARDS REGULATIONS 2015 (COMAH) (SI 2015 NO. 483)

Summary

The Regulations are lengthy and consist of 34 regulations and 6 schedules. The intention here is to provide an overview of the Regulations, which apply to Great Britain. Limited amendments (the **Health and Safety (Amendment) (EU Exit) Regulations 2018**) have occurred to ensure that laws operate effectively following UK exit from the EU; these have been incorporated below where relevant.

Regulation 1: Citation and Commencement

The Regulations came into force on 1 June 2015 and extend to Great Britain.

Regulation 2: Interpretation

The following definitions are given (see the regulation for a complete list):

- "CAS number" is the number assigned to a substance by the Chemical Abstracts Service;
- "Competent authority" has the meaning given in regulation 4;
- "Dangerous substance" means a substance or mixture as listed in Schedule 1, Part 2, column 1, or in a category listed in column 1 of Part 1 of Schedule 1, including in the form of a raw material, product, by-product, residue or intermediate;
- "Establishment" means the whole location under the control of an operator where a dangerous substance is present in one or more installations, including common or related infrastructures or activities, in a quantity equal to or in excess of the quantity listed in the entry for that substance in column 2 of Part 1 or in column 2 of Part 2 of Schedule 1, where applicable using the rule laid down in note 4 in Part 3 of that Schedule;
- "Hazard" means the intrinsic property of a dangerous substance or physical situation, with a potential for creating damage to human health or the environment;
- "Inspection" means all actions including site visits, checks of internal measures, systems and reports and follow-up documents and any necessary follow-up undertaken by or on behalf of the competent authority to check and promote compliance of establishments with the requirements of these Regulations;
- "Installation" means a technical unit, whether at or below ground level, in which dangerous substances present are, or are intended to be, produced, used, handled or stored and includes:
  - equipment, structures, pipework, machinery and tools;
  - railway sidings, docks and unloading quays serving the unit; and
  - jetties, warehouses or similar structures, whether floating or not.
- "Lower tier establishment" means an establishment where a dangerous substance is present in a quantity equal to or in excess of the quantity listed in the entry for that substance in column 2 of Part 1 or in column 2 of Part 2 of Schedule 1, but less than that listed in the entry for that substance in column 3 of Part 1 or in column 3 of Part 2 of Schedule 1, where applicable using the rule laid down in note 4 of Part 3 of that Schedule;
- "Major accident" means an occurrence (including a major emission, fire or explosion) resulting from uncontrolled developments in the course of the operation of any establishment, and leading to serious danger to human health or the environment, whether immediate or delayed, inside or outside the establishment, and involving one or more dangerous substances;
- "Operator" means a person who is in control of the operation of an establishment or installation;
- "Risk" means the likelihood of a specific effect occurring within a specified period or in specified circumstances;
- "Safety report" is to be construed in accordance with regulation 8;
- "Upper tier establishment" means an establishment where a dangerous substance is present in a quantity equal to or in excess of the quantity listed in the entry for that substance in column 3 of Part 1 or in column 3 of Part 2 of Schedule 1, where applicable using the rule laid down in note 4 of Part 3 of that Schedule.

Regulation 3: Application

These Regulations apply to any establishment which is either a lower tier establishment or an upper tier establishment. These Regulations do not apply to establishments under the control of the Ministry of Defence, hazards created by ionising radiation originating from substances, ionising radiation on a nuclear establishment, mineral extraction and processing, offshore exploration, storage of gas underground, offshore sites, waste landfill sites (including underground waste storage) except for chemical and thermal processing operations and storage or operational tailings disposal facilities including tailing ponds or dams that involve dangerous substances.

Regulation 4: The Competent Authority

The competent authority in relation to a nuclear establishment is the ONR and the appropriate agency acting jointly, or otherwise the HSE and the appropriate agency acting jointly.

Regulation 5: General Duties of Operators

Imposes a duty on every operator to take all measures necessary to prevent major accidents and to limit their consequences, both for human health and for the environment. Operators must demonstrate to the satisfaction of the competent authority that they have taken all measures necessary. Operators must also assist the competent authority to enable the competent authority to perform its functions.

Regulation 6: Notifications

Requires the operator to notify the competent authority of specified matters at specified times. For example, prior to commencing construction of a new establishment the operator must send the competent authority notification containing information such as the operator's name and address, the name and position of the person in charge, information identifying dangerous substances, quantity and form of dangerous substances, activities to be carried out and a description of the immediate environment of the establishment. Operators must also notify the competent authority in advance if there is to be a significant increase or decrease in the quantity of dangerous substances held or a significant change in the nature or physical form of those substances or the processes employing them. Operators must notify any modification of the establishment or installation that could have significant consequences in terms of major accident hazards.

Regulation 7: Major Accident Prevention Policies

Every operator must prepare and retain a written major accident prevention policy. Such policies must:

- be designed to ensure a high level of protection of human health and the environment;
- be proportionate to the major accident hazard;
- set out the operator's overall aims and principles of action; and
- set out the role and responsibility of management, and its commitment towards continuously improving the control of major accident hazards.

Regulation 8: Purposes of Safety Reports

Every operator of an upper tier establishment must prepare a safety report to demonstrate that:

- a major accident prevention policy and safety management system for implementing it have been put in place;
- major accident hazards and possible major accident scenarios have been identified and necessary measures have been taken to prevent such accidents and limit their consequences;
- adequate safety and reliability have been taken into account in the design, construction, operation and maintenance of the facility;
- an emergency plan has been prepared in accordance with regulation 12;
- and to provide sufficient information to the competent authority to enable decisions to be made regarding the siting of new activities or developments around establishments.

Regulation 9: Requirements Relating to the Preparation of Safety Reports

Safety reports must contain as a minimum the data and information specified in Schedule 3 and identify the organisations involved in preparing it. An operator must send a safety report to the competent authority prior to the start of construction of the establishment, prior to the start of operation or when modifications leading to a change in the inventory of dangerous substances occur.

Regulation 10: Review of Safety Reports

A safety report must be reviewed no more than five years after the date on which it was last sent to the competent authority or reviewed by the operator. In any event, a safety report must be reviewed and, where necessary, revised following a major accident, where a review is justified by new facts or by new technological knowledge, where there are developments in knowledge concerning the assessment of hazards, prior to making modifications, or following any change to the safety management system that could have significant consequences for the prevention of major accidents or the limitation of the consequences thereof. In the event that a safety report is reviewed, but not revised, the operator must still inform the competent authority in writing without delay.

Regulation 11: Objectives of Emergency Plans

Internal and external emergency plans must contain and control incidents so as to minimise the consequences and to limit damage to human health, the environment and property. They have the objective of implementing the necessary measures to protect human health and the environment from the consequences of major accidents and are used to communicate information to the public and services or authorities in the area as well as providing for the restoration and clean-up of the environment following a major accident.

Regulation 12: Preparation, Review and Testing of Internal Emergency Plans

Operators of upper tier sites must prepare an internal emergency plan, which must contain the information specified in Part 1 of Schedule 4. At least every three years, an operator must review and, where necessary, revise the internal emergency plan and test it.

Regulation 13: Preparation of External Emergency Plans

This regulation requires a local authority in whose administrative area an upper tier establishment is situated to prepare an external emergency plan specifying the measures to be taken outside the establishment. This must be prepared no later than six months (or up to nine months with written agreement of the competent authority) after receipt of the necessary information from the operator. The external emergency plan must contain the information specified in Part 2 of Schedule 4.

Regulation 14: Review and Testing of External Emergency Plans

The local authority must review and, where necessary, revise and test the plan at least every three years.

Regulation 15: Exemption of Local Authority from Preparing an External Emergency Plan

The local authority may be exempted from the requirement to prepare an external emergency plan where the competent authority is of the opinion that the establishment is incapable of creating a major accident hazard outside the establishment. Exemptions must be in writing and must state reasons for being granted. The competent authority may withdraw exemptions.

Regulation 16: Implementing Emergency Plans

An operator or local authority that has prepared an internal or external emergency plan must take reasonable steps to ensure that it is put into effect without delay following a major accident or following an uncontrolled event that by its nature could reasonably be expected to lead to a major accident.

Regulation 17: Provision of Information to the Public

The competent authority must make certain information available to the public. This includes the name of the operator, the address of the establishment, confirmation that the 2015 Regulations apply to the establishment and that a safety report has been sent to the competent authority, a simple explanation of the activities undertaken, the hazard classification of dangerous substances with a simple indication of their principal dangerous characteristics, general information about how the public will be warned, the date of the last routine inspection and details of where further information can be obtained.

In addition to the above, for upper tier establishments the competent authority must also make available to the public general information on the nature of major accident hazards and their consequences, confirmation that the operator is required to make adequate arrangements to deal with major accidents and minimise the consequences and appropriate information from the external emergency plan.

Regulation 18: Provision of Information to Persons Likely to be Affected by a Major Accident at an Upper Tier Establishment

Operators of upper tier establishments must ensure that clear and intelligible information on safety measures and appropriate behaviour in the event of a major accident is sent automatically to all those who are likely to be in an area within which persons are liable to be affected by a major accident occurring at the establishment, as well as to every school, hospital or other area of public use within that area. This information must be reviewed and, where necessary, revised at least every three years or in the event of any modification of the establishment or an installation which could have significant consequences in terms of major accident hazards.

The above information must be sent to every person and every school, hospital or other area of public use at least every five years or if it is revised following a review.

Regulation 19: Provision of Information Pursuant to a Request

Where an operator is of the opinion that environmental information sent to the competent authority should not be made available on request by reason of an exception in regulation 12 or 13 of the **Environmental Information Regulations 2004** or by reason of an exception in regulation 10 or 11 of the **Environmental Information (Scotland) Regulations 2004**, the operator must inform the competent authority in writing of its opinion and the reason for it. Where the competent authority receives a request for environmental information under the above regulations it must take into account any opinion and reasons provided by the operator.

Regulation 20: Trans-Boundary Consequences

Where a major accident has transboundary consequences, the competent authority must send information to the country so that it can prepare emergency plans or effect land use policies.

Regulation 21: Power of the Competent Authority to Accept Information in Another Document

Allows the competent authority to permit an operator to provide information that is required to be included in a notification, a major accident prevention policy, a safety report, an internal emergency plan or the details of action to be taken following a major accident by making reference to information contained in another document provided pursuant to a requirement imposed under the **Environmental Permitting (England and Wales) Regulations 2016** or the **Pollution Prevention and Control (Scotland) Regulations 2012**.

Regulation 22: Examination of Safety Reports by the Competent Authority

Imposes a duty on the competent authority to communicate the conclusions of its examination of the safety report to an establishment operator within a reasonable period of time following receipt of the safety report.

Regulation 23: Prohibition of Operation

Imposes functions on the competent authority with respect to prohibiting the operation of an establishment.

Regulation 24: Domino Effects and Domino Groups

The competent authority must identify groups of establishments where the risk or consequences of the major accident may be increased because of their geographical position, the proximity of establishments to each other or the inventories of dangerous substances held by establishments. Where a domino group is identified, the competent authority must notify each operator of an establishment in that group. Operators of 'Domino group' establishments must co-operate with each other in putting in place arrangements for the exchange of information, informing neighbouring sites that do not fall within these Regulations of their proximity to a domino group and supplying the local authority with information to enable the preparation of an external emergency plan.

Regulation 25: Inspections and Investigations

Imposes a duty on the competent authority to organise a system of inspections of establishments appropriate to the type of establishment concerned.

Regulation 26: Action to be Taken Following a Major Accident

Following a major accident the operator of an establishment must inform the competent authority and provide information including the circumstances of the accident, the dangerous substances involved, the data available for assessing the consequences of the accident and the emergency measures taken. The operator must also inform the competent authority of the steps needed to mitigate the medium- and long-term consequences and prevent recurrence. This information must be updated if necessary.

The competent authority has a duty to ensure that any necessary urgent, medium- and long-term measures are taken. They must collect information to enable a full analysis of the technical, organisational and managerial aspects of the accident and must take appropriate action to ensure that the operator takes necessary remedial measures. The competent authority must make recommendations on future preventative measures.The competent authority must provide international organisations with specified information regarding a major accident.

Regulation 27: Enforcement and Penalties

Sets out the arrangements for the enforcement of these Regulations together with maximum penalties on summary conviction and on indictment.

Regulation 28: Fees Payable by Operators to the Competent Authority

Sets out the arrangements for the payment by operators of fees to the competent authority for performance of any function conferred on the authority by these Regulations.

Regulation 29: Fees Payable to Local Authorities for the Preparation, Review and Testing of External Emergency Plans

This regulation enables a local authority to charge the operator a fee for preparing, reviewing and testing external emergency plans.

Regulations 30 to 33: these regulations form Part 10 and deal with consequential amendments, revocations, saving and transitional provisions.

Schedules

There are six Schedules to these Regulations, which are as follows:

- Schedule 1: Dangerous substances
    - Part 1: Categories of dangerous substances
    - Part 2: Named dangerous substances
    - Part 3: Notes to Parts 1 and 2
- Schedule 2: Requirements and matters to be addressed by safety management systems
- Schedule 3: Minimum data and information to be included in a safety report
- Schedule 4: Information to be included in internal and external emergency plans
- Schedule 5: This has been revoked by amendment to the Regulations- it formerly covered Criteria for the notification of a major accident to the European Commission.
- Schedule 6: Amendments to secondary legislation

CONTROL OF NOISE AT WORK REGULATIONS 2005 (SI 2005 NO. 1643)

Summary

The intention here is to provide an overview of the Regulations, which apply to Great Britain.

Amending Legislation

Health and Safety (Miscellaneous Amendments and Revocations) Regulations 2009

Health and Safety (Enforcing Authority for Railways and Other Guided Transport Systems) Regulations 2006

Regulation 1: Citation and Commencement

These Regulations came into force on 6 April 2006. (Music and entertainment sectors only - 6 April 2008.)

Regulation 2: Interpretation

"Daily personal noise exposure" means the level of daily personal noise exposure of an employee as ascertained in accordance with Schedule 1 Part 1, taking account of the level of noise and the duration of exposure and covering all noise.

"Enforcing authority" means the Executive, local authority or Office of Rail Regulation, determined in accordance with the provisions of the **Health and Safety (Enforcing Authority) Regulations 1998** and the **Health and Safety (Enforcing Authority for Railways and Other Guided Transport Systems) Regulations 2006**.

"Exposure limit value" means the level of daily or weekly personal noise exposure or of peak sound pressure set out in regulation 4 which must not be exceeded.

"Health surveillance" means assessment of the state of health of an employee, as related to exposure to noise.

"Lower exposure action value" means the lower of the two levels of daily or weekly personal noise exposure or of peak sound pressure set out in regulation 4 which, if reached or exceeded, require specified action to be taken to reduce risk.

"Upper exposure action value" means the higher of the two levels of daily or weekly personal noise exposure or of peak sound pressure set out in regulation 4 which, if reached or exceeded, require specified action to be taken to reduce risk.

"Weekly personal noise exposure" means the level of weekly personal noise exposure as ascertained in accordance with Schedule 1 Part 2, taking account of the level of noise and the duration of exposure and covering all noise.

"Working day" means a daily working period, irrespective of the time of day when it begins or ends, and of whether it begins or ends on the same calendar day.

Regulation 4: Exposure Limit Values and Action Values

(1) The lower exposure action values are:

    (a) a daily or weekly personal noise exposure of 80 dB (A-weighted); and

    (b) a peak sound pressure of 135 dB (C-weighted).

(2) The upper exposure action values are:

    (a) a daily or weekly personal noise exposure of 85 dB (A-weighted); and

    (b) a peak sound pressure of 137 dB (C-weighted).

(3) The exposure limit values are:

    (a) a daily or weekly personal noise exposure of 87 dB (A-weighted); and

    (b) a peak sound pressure of 140 dB (C-weighted).

(4) Where the exposure of an employee to noise varies markedly from day to day, an employer may use weekly personal noise exposure in place of daily personal noise exposure for the purpose of compliance with these Regulations.

(5) In applying the exposure limit values in paragraph (3), but not in applying the lower and upper exposure action values in paragraphs (1) and (2), account shall be taken of the protection given to the employee by any personal hearing protectors provided by the employer in accordance with regulation 7(2).

Regulation 5: Assessment of the Risk to Health and Safety Created by Exposure to Noise at the Workplace

An employer who carries out work which is liable to expose any employees to noise at or above a lower exposure action value shall make a suitable and sufficient assessment of the risk from that noise to the health and safety of those employees, and the risk assessment shall identify the measures which need to be taken to meet the requirements of these Regulations.

In conducting the risk assessment, the employer shall assess the levels of noise to which workers are exposed by means of:

(a) observation of specific working practices;

(b) reference to relevant information on the probable levels of noise corresponding to any equipment used in the particular working conditions; and

(c) if necessary, measurement of the level of noise to which his employees are likely to be exposed;

and the employer shall assess whether any employees are likely to be exposed to noise at or above a lower exposure action value, an upper exposure action value, or an exposure limit value.

The risk assessment shall include consideration of:

(a) The level, type and duration of exposure, including any exposure to peak sound pressure.

(b) The effects of exposure to noise on employees or groups of employees whose health is at particular risk from such exposure.

(c) Any effects on the health and safety of employees resulting from the interaction between noise and the use of ototoxic substances at work, or between noise and vibration.

(d) Any indirect effects on the health and safety of employees resulting from the interaction between noise and audible warning signals or other sounds that need to be audible in order to reduce risk at work.

(e) Any information provided by the manufacturers of work equipment.

(f) The availability of alternative equipment designed to reduce the emission of noise.

(g) Any extension of exposure to noise at the workplace beyond normal working hours, including exposure in rest facilities supervised by the employer.

(h) Appropriate information obtained following health surveillance, including, where possible, published information.

(i) The availability of personal hearing protectors with adequate attenuation characteristics.

The risk assessment should be reviewed regularly and whenever there is reason to suspect that it is no longer valid, or there has been a significant change in the work to which the assessment relates. Changes to the risk assessment shall be made if required by the review.

Employees or their representatives shall be consulted on the risk assessment and the employer shall record the significant findings as soon as practicable after the assessment is made.

Regulation 6: Elimination or Control of Exposure to Noise at the Workplace

The employer shall ensure that risk from the exposure of his employees to noise is either eliminated at source or, where this is not reasonably practicable, reduced to as low a level as is reasonably practicable. If any employee is likely to be exposed to noise at or above an upper exposure action value, the employer shall reduce exposure to as low a level as is reasonably practicable by establishing and implementing a programme of organisational and technical measures, excluding the provision of personal hearing protectors, which is appropriate to the activity.

Control measures shall be based on the general principles of prevention set out in Schedule 1 to the **Management of Health and Safety at Work Regulations 1999** and shall include consideration of:

(a) Other working methods which reduce exposure to noise.

(b) Choice of appropriate work equipment emitting the least possible noise, taking account of the work to be done.

(c) The design and layout of workplaces, workstations and rest facilities.

(d) Suitable and sufficient information and training for employees, such that work equipment may be used correctly, in order to minimise their exposure to noise.

(e) Reduction of noise by technical means.

(f) Appropriate maintenance programmes for work equipment, the workplace and workplace systems.

(g) Limitation of the duration and intensity of exposure to noise.

(h) Appropriate work schedules with adequate rest periods.

The employer must ensure that his employees are not exposed to noise above an exposure limit value; or if an exposure limit value is exceeded forthwith:

(a) Reduce exposure to noise to below the exposure limit value.

(b) Identify the reason for that exposure limit value being exceeded.

(c) Modify the organisational and technical measures in place to prevent it being exceeded again.

Where rest facilities are made available to employees, the employer shall ensure that exposure to noise in these facilities is reduced to a level suitable for their purpose and conditions of use.

The employer shall adapt any measure taken in compliance with the requirements of this regulation to take account of any employee or group of employees whose health is likely to be particularly at risk from exposure to noise, and consult with the employees concerned or their representatives on the measures to be taken to meet the requirements of this regulation.

Regulation 7: Hearing Protection

An employer who carries out work which is likely to expose any employees to noise at or above a lower exposure action value shall make personal hearing protectors available upon request to any employee who is so exposed. If the employer is unable by other means to reduce the levels of noise to which an employee is likely to be exposed to below an upper exposure action value, he shall provide personal hearing protectors to any employee who is so exposed.

If in any area of the workplace under the control of the employer an employee is likely to be exposed to noise at or above an upper exposure action value for any reason the employer shall ensure that:

(a) the area is designated a Hearing Protection Zone;

(b) the area is demarcated and identified by means of an appropriate sign indicating that ear protection must be worn;

(c) access to the area is restricted where this is practicable and the risk from exposure justifies it;

and shall ensure so far as is reasonably practicable that no employee enters that area unless that employee is wearing personal hearing protectors.

Any personal hearing protectors made available or provided shall be selected by the employer:

(a) so as to eliminate the risk to hearing or to reduce the risk to as low a level as is reasonably practicable;

(b) after consultation with the employees concerned or their representatives;

and shall comply with any requirement of the **Personal Protective Equipment Regulations 2002** which is applicable to them.

Regulation 8: Maintenance and Use of Equipment

The employer must ensure that anything provided by him in compliance with his duties under these Regulations is fully and properly used, and maintained in an efficient state, in efficient working order and in good repair.

Every employee shall make full and proper use of personal hearing protectors provided to him and of any other control measures provided by his employer and if he discovers any defect in any personal hearing protectors or other control measures report it to his employer as soon as is practicable.

Regulation 9: Health Surveillance

If the risk assessment indicates that there is a risk to the health of his employees who are, or are liable to be, exposed to noise, the employer shall ensure that such employees are placed under suitable health surveillance, which shall include testing of their hearing. The employer shall ensure that a health record in respect of each of his employees who undergoes health surveillance is made and maintained and that the record or a copy thereof is kept available in a suitable form. The employer shall allow an employee access to his personal health record (on reasonable notice being given) and provide the enforcing authority with copies of such health records as it may require.

Where, as a result of health surveillance, an employee is found to have identifiable hearing damage the employer shall ensure that the employee is examined by a doctor and, if the doctor or any specialist to whom the doctor considers it necessary to refer the employee considers that the damage is likely to be the result of exposure to noise, the employer shall:

(a) Ensure that a suitably qualified person informs the employee accordingly.

(b) Review the risk assessment.

(c) Review any measure taken to comply with regulations 6, 7 and 8, taking into account any advice given by a doctor or occupational health professional, or by the enforcing authority.

(d) Consider assigning the employee to alternative work where there is no risk from further exposure to noise, taking into account any advice given by a doctor or occupational health professional.

(e) Ensure continued health surveillance and provide for a review of the health of any other employee who has been similarly exposed.

An employee to whom this regulation applies shall, when required by his employer and at the cost of his employer, present himself during his working hours for such health surveillance procedures as may be required.

Regulation 10: Information, Instruction and Training

Where his employees are exposed to noise which is likely to be at or above a lower exposure action value, the employer shall provide those employees and their representatives with suitable and sufficient information, instruction and training which should include:

(a) The nature of risks from exposure to noise.

(b) The organisational and technical measures taken in order to comply with the requirements of regulation 6.

(c) The exposure limit values and upper and lower exposure action values set out in regulation 4.

(d) The significant findings of the risk assessment, including any measurements taken, with an explanation of those findings.

(e) The availability and provision of personal hearing protectors under regulation 7 and their correct use in accordance with regulation 8.

(f) Why and how to detect and report signs of hearing damage.

(g) The entitlement to health surveillance under regulation 9 and its purposes.

(h) Safe working practices to minimise exposure to noise.

(i) The collective results of any health surveillance undertaken in accordance with regulation 9 in a form calculated to prevent those results from being identified as relating to a particular person.

The information, instruction and training shall be updated to take account of significant changes in the type of work carried out or the working methods used by the employer and the employer shall ensure that any person, whether or not his employee, who carries out work in connection with the employer's duties under these Regulations has suitable and sufficient information, instruction and training.

Regulation 11: Exemption Certificates from Hearing Protection

The Executive may, by a certificate in writing, exempt certain persons or classes of persons from some of the provisions of regulation 6 and 7 where, because of the nature of the work the full and proper use of personal hearing protectors would be likely to cause greater risk to health or safety than not using such protectors, or in respect of activities carried out by emergency services which could conflict with the requirements of these provisions.

CONTROL OF PESTICIDES REGULATIONS 1986 (SI 1986 NO. 1510)

Summary

These Regulations were made under the **Food and Environment Protection Act 1985**, and implement the provisions of Part III of that Act.

The aim of the Act is to protect the health of human beings, creatures and plants; to safeguard the environment and to secure safe, efficient and humane methods of controlling pests.

Contravention of the provisions in these Regulations and the various conditions is an offence under s.16(12) of the 1985 Act.

The Regulations apply to substances used for protecting plants from harmful organisms, regulating plant growth, giving protection against harmful insects, controlling organisms with harmful effects, such as in buildings, and for protecting animals against, for example, parasites.

Herbicides are classed as "other dangerous chemicals" and fall under the **Control of Substances Hazardous to Health Regulations 2002**. Provision is also made for the release of information on pesticides to the public.

The Regulations provide a range of controls over the advertisement, sale, supply, storage and use of pesticides. The main provisions are outlined below.

Risk Assessment

As with any other hazard, employers and managers must exercise their responsibility to fellow workers, the general public, animals, plants and the environment at large. This process begins with the assessment of the risks posed by pesticides and herbicides. Useful information regarding the risks may be obtained from the labels on the packaging of the substances. In particular, the labels indicate what crops the substance is suitable for; maximum application rates; and minimum harvest intervals. The labels also indicate the type of premises for storage and indicate the category of land that the substances are to be used on.

Initiation of Control Procedures

After assessing the risks it is the duty of management to initiate control procedures. Control is especially important to prevent pesticides and herbicides leaching into water courses and causing pollution. The principal means of control is by ensuring that all persons involved in handling and using the substances are properly trained and suitably qualified. Engineering controls, such as segregation and isolation, will assist in keeping the hazardous substances away from people, animals and plants. As a last resort personal protective equipment, such as gloves and face-masks, should be issued to operatives.

The control of herbicides and pesticides should be regularly monitored for effectiveness and reviewed when necessary.

Regulation 4: Prohibitions

This regulation prohibits the advertisement, sale, supply, storage and use of any pesticide unless ministerial approval and consent is given in respect to the pesticide and its application respectively. Such approvals and consents may be subject to certain conditions, as detailed in the various Schedules to the Regulations.

Regulation 5: Approvals

This deals with the issuing of approvals by the Ministers which may be one of three types:

- Experimental permits, which allow testing and development with a view to providing further health and safety or any other relevant information.
- Provisional approval, which is valid for a stipulated period of time and allows any outstanding data requirements to be satisfied.
- Full approval for an unspecified period of time.

Approvals may be reviewed, revoked or suspended at any time.

Regulation 6: Consents

Ministerial consent is required for:

(a) The advertising of pesticides, subject to the conditions imposed by Schedule 1 of the Regulations.

(b) The sale, supply, and storage of pesticides, subject to the conditions imposed by Schedule 2.

(c) The use of pesticides, subject to the conditions imposed by Schedule 3 (and Schedule 4, for use from aircraft). One of the conditions of consent specified in Schedule 3 regarding the use of pesticides is that any person born later than 31 December 1964 must either obtain a certificate of competence before using an approved pesticide, or must be under the direct and personal supervision of another person who holds such a certificate.

Regulation 7: Seizure, Disposal, etc.

This regulation provides for the seizure and disposal of pesticides in the event of any breaches to the mentioned provisions. Such seizures and disposals may extend to anything treated with the pesticide.

Regulation 8: Release of Information to the Public

This provides for the release/inspection of information relating to pesticides given provisional or full approval.

CONTROL OF SUBSTANCES HAZARDOUS TO HEALTH REGULATIONS 2002

Amending Legislation

The **Control of Substances Hazardous to Health (Amendment) Regulations 2003 (SI 2003 No. 978)** have the effect of adding:

- a definition of mutagen to regulation 2(1) and amending references in regulations 7 and 13 to carcinogen to also include mutagen; and
- 17 polychlorodibenzodioxins and polychlorodibenzofurans to the list of substances in Schedule 1 to which the definition of carcinogen relates.

The **Carriage of Dangerous Goods and Use of Transportable Pressure Equipment Regulations 2007** (subsequently revoked and replaced by Regulations of the same name in 2009) made minor amendments to Schedule 7 of these Regulations referring to the Carriage Regulations and removing references to associated revoked legislation.

The **Control of Substances Hazardous to Health (Amendment) Regulations 2004** replaced the concept of occupational exposure standards and maximum exposure limits with a single new Workplace Exposure Limit (WEL) for substances hazardous to health; also introduced were 'principles of good practice' for the control of exposure to substances hazardous to health, designed to ensure that Workplace Exposure Limits are not exceeded.

Minor amendments have also been made by the **REACH Enforcement Regulations 2008** and the **Chemicals (Hazard Information and Packaging for Supply) Regulations 2009**.

Regulation 1: Citation and Commencement

These Regulations came into force on 21 November 2002.

Regulation 2: Interpretation

In these Regulations:

- "Biological agent" means a micro-organism, cell culture, or human endoparasite, whether or not genetically modified, which may cause infection, allergy, toxicity or otherwise create a hazard to human health.
- "The CHIP Regulations" means the **Chemicals (Hazard Information and Packaging for Supply) Regulations 2009**.
- "The **CLP Regulation**" means **Regulation (EC) No. 1272/2008** of the European Parliament and of the Council on Classification, labelling and packaging of substances and mixtures (as amended by UK law).
- "Control measure" means a measure taken to reduce exposure to a substance hazardous to health (including the provision of systems of work and supervision, the cleaning of workplaces, premises, plant and equipment, the provision and use of engineering controls and personal protective equipment).
- "Hazard", in relation to a substance, means the intrinsic property of that substance, which has the potential to cause harm to the health of a person.
- "Health surveillance" means assessment of the state of health of an employee, as related to exposure to substances hazardous to health, and includes biological monitoring.
- "Inhalable dust" means airborne material, which is capable of entering the nose and mouth during breathing, as defined by BS EN 481:1993.
- "Micro-organism" means a microbiological entity, cellular or non-cellular, which is capable of replication or of transferring genetic material.
- "Respirable dust" means airborne material which is capable of penetrating to the gas exchange region of the lung, as defined by BS EN 481:1993.
- "Risk", in relation to the exposure of an employee to a substance hazardous to health, means the likelihood that the potential for harm to the health of a person will be attained under the conditions of use and exposure and also the extent of that harm.
- A "Safety data sheet" is defined in **REACH (EC Regulation 1907/2006)** as it applies in Great Britain.
- "Substance" means a natural or artificial substance, whether in solid or liquid form or in the form of a gas or vapour (including micro-organisms).

- "Substance hazardous to health" means a substance (including a mixture):
  - Which is listed in Table 3.2 of Part 3 of Annex VI of the **GB CLP Regulation** and for which an indication of danger specified for the substance is very toxic, toxic, harmful, corrosive or irritant.
  - For which the Health and Safety Executive has approved a workplace exposure limit.
  - Which is a biological agent.
  - Which is dust of any kind, except dust which is a substance within the above categories when present at a concentration in air equal to or greater than:
    - 10 mg/m^3, as a time-weighted average over an eight-hour period, of inhalable dust, or
    - 4 mg/m^3, as a time-weighted average over an eight-hour period, of respirable dust.
  - Which, not being a substance falling within the sub-paragraphs above, because of its chemical or toxicological properties and the way it is used or is present at the workplace, creates a risk to health.
- "Workplace Exposure Limit" for a substance hazardous to health means the exposure limit approved by the HSE for the substance in relation to the specific reference period, when calculated by the approved method, as contained in EH40/2005 *Workplace exposure limits*.

Regulation 3: Duties under these Regulations

Where any duty is placed by these Regulations on an employer in respect of his employees, he shall, so far as is reasonably practicable, be under a like duty in respect of any other person, whether at work or not, who may be affected by the work carried on by the employer.

The duty under regulation 11 (health surveillance) shall not extend to non-employees.

The duties under regulations 10 and 12 (monitoring, and information and training) shall not extend to non-employees unless those persons are on the premises where the work is being carried out.

The Regulations, with the exception of regulations 10 and 11, apply to a self-employed person.

The duties imposed by the Regulations do not apply to the master or crew of a sea-going ship, or to the employer of such persons in relation to the normal shipboard activities of a ship's crew, under the direction of the master.

Regulation 4: Prohibitions Relating to Certain Substances

Substances described in Column 1 of Schedule 2 are prohibited to the extent set out in the corresponding entry in Column 2 of that Schedule.

The importation into the United Kingdom of matches made from white phosphorous is prohibited. A person shall not supply, during the course of or for use at work, any of these substances or articles. Contravention of this regulation shall be punishable under the **Customs and Excise Management Act 1979**.

From 1 June 2009, the reference (in paragraphs (2)(a) and (4)) to prohibition on the supply or use of a number of specific substances (e.g. 2-naphthylamine, those containing benzene) is removed as there are now similar restrictions contained within the **REACH Regulation (EC 1907/2006)**. In all, three entries (11, 12 and 13) have been removed from Schedule 2 (prohibitions).

Regulation 5: Application of Regulations 6 to 13

Regulations 6 to 13 shall have effect with a view to protecting persons against a risk to their health, whether immediate or delayed, arising from exposure to substances hazardous to health except:

- Where and to the extent that the following Regulations apply, namely:
  - The **Coal Mines (Control of Inhalable Dust) Regulations 2007**.
  - The **Control of Lead at Work Regulations 2002**.
  - The **Control of Asbestos Regulations 2012**.
- Where the substance is hazardous to health solely by virtue of its radioactive, explosive or flammable properties, or solely because it is at a high or low temperature or a high pressure.
- Where the risk to health is a risk to the health of a person to whom the substance is administered in the course of his medical treatment.

Medical treatment means medical or dental examination or treatment which is conducted by, or under the direction of a registered medical practitioner, registered dentist, or other person who is an appropriate practitioner. This includes any such examination or treatment conducted for the purpose of research.

Regulation 6: Assessment of the Risk to Health Created by Work Involving Substances Hazardous to Health

An employer shall not carry out work which is liable to expose any employees to any substance hazardous to health, unless he has made a suitable and sufficient assessment of the risk created by that work to the health of those employees, and of the steps that need to be taken to meet the requirements of these Regulations, and implemented the steps.

The risk assessment shall include consideration of:

- The hazardous properties of the substance.
- Information on health effects provided by the supplier, including information contained in any relevant safety data sheet.
- The level, type and duration of exposure.
- The circumstances of the work, including the amount of the substance involved.
- Activities, such as maintenance, where there is the potential for a high level of exposure.
- Any relevant workplace exposure limit or similar occupational exposure limit.
- The effect of preventive and control measures, which have been or will be taken in accordance with regulation 7.
- The results of relevant health surveillance.
- The results of the monitoring of exposure, in accordance with regulation 10.
- In circumstances where the work will involve exposure to more than one substance hazardous to health, the risk presented by exposure to such substances in combination.
- The approved classification of any biological agent.
- Such additional information as the employer may need, in order to complete the risk assessment.

The risk assessment shall be reviewed regularly and forthwith if:

- There is reason to suspect that the risk assessment is no longer valid.
- There has been a significant change in the work to which the risk assessment relates.
- The results of any monitoring carried out in accordance with regulation 10 show it to be necessary.

Where, as a result of the review, changes to the risk assessment are required, those changes shall be made.

Where the employer employs five or more employees, he shall record:

- The significant findings of the risk assessment as soon as is practicable, after the risk assessment is made.
- The steps which he has taken to meet the requirements of regulation 7.

Regulation 7: Prevention or Control of Exposure to Substances Hazardous to Health

Every employer shall ensure that the exposure of his employees to substances hazardous to health is either prevented or, where this is not reasonably practicable, adequately controlled. [Paragraph (1)]

In complying with his duty of prevention, substitution shall by preference be undertaken, whereby the employer shall avoid, so far as is reasonably practicable, the use of a substance hazardous to health at the workplace by replacing it with a substance or process which, under the conditions of its use, either eliminates or reduces the risk to the health of his employees.

Where it is not reasonably practicable to prevent exposure to a substance hazardous to health, the employer shall comply with his duty of control by applying protection measures appropriate to the activity and consistent with the risk assessment, including, in order of priority:

- The design and use of appropriate work processes, systems and engineering controls and the provision and use of suitable work equipment and materials.
- The control of exposure at source, including adequate ventilation systems and appropriate organisational measures.
- Where adequate control of exposure cannot be achieved by other means, the provision of suitable personal protective equipment in addition to the measures required above.

The measures referred to above shall include:

- Arrangements for the safe handling, storage and transport of substances hazardous to health, and of waste containing such substances, at the workplace.

- The adoption of suitable maintenance procedures.
- Reducing, to the minimum required for the work concerned:
    - The number of employees subject to exposure.
    - The level and duration of exposure.
    - The quantity of substances hazardous to health present at the workplace.
- The control of the working environment, including appropriate general ventilation.
- Appropriate hygiene measures, including adequate washing facilities.

Where it is not reasonably practicable to prevent exposure to a carcinogen or mutagen, the employer shall apply the following measures in addition to those required above:

- Totally enclosing the process and handling systems, unless this is not reasonably practicable.
- The prohibition of eating, drinking and smoking in areas that may be contaminated by carcinogens or mutagens.
- Cleaning floors, walls and other surfaces at regular intervals and whenever necessary.
- Designating those areas and installations which may be contaminated by carcinogens or mutagens and using suitable and sufficient warning signs.
- Storing, handling and disposing of carcinogens or mutagens safely, including using closed and clearly labelled containers.

Where it is not reasonably practicable to prevent exposure to a biological agent, the employer shall apply the following measures in addition to those required above:

- Displaying suitable and sufficient warning signs, including the biohazard sign shown in Part IV of Schedule 3.
- Specifying appropriate decontamination and disinfection procedures.
- Instituting means for the safe collection, storage and disposal of contaminated waste, including the use of secure and identifiable containers, after suitable treatment where appropriate.
- Testing, where it is necessary and technically possible, for the presence, outside the primary physical confinement, of biological agents used at work.
- Specifying procedures for working with, and transporting at the workplace, a biological agent or material that may contain such an agent.
- Where appropriate, making available effective vaccines for those employees who are not already immune to the biological agent to which they are exposed or are liable to be exposed.
- Instituting hygiene measures compatible with the aim of preventing or reducing the accidental transfer or release of a biological agent from the workplace, including:
    - The provision of appropriate and adequate washing and toilet facilities.
    - Where appropriate, the prohibition of eating, drinking, smoking and the application of cosmetics in working areas where there is a risk of contamination by biological agents.
- Where there are human patients or animals which are, or are suspected of being, infected with a Group 3 or 4 biological agent, the employer shall select the most suitable control and containment measures from those listed in Part II of Schedule 3, with a view to adequately controlling the risk of infection.

Without prejudice to the generality of paragraph (1), where there is exposure to a substance hazardous to health, control of exposure shall only be treated as adequate if:

- The principles of good practice for the control of exposure to substances hazardous to health set out in Schedule 2A are applied.
- Any workplace exposure limit approved for the substance is not exceeded.
- For a substance:
    - which carries the risk phrase R45, R46 or R49, or a substance or process which is listed in Schedule 1,
    - which carries the risk phrase R42 or R42/43, or which is listed in Section C of the HSE publication, *Asthmagen? Critical assessments of the evidence for agents implicated in occupational asthma*, or any other substance which the risk assessment has shown to be a potential cause of occupational asthma;

    exposure is reduced to as low a level as is reasonably practicable.

Personal protective equipment provided by an employer in accordance with this regulation shall be suitable for the purpose and shall comply with any provision in the **Personal Protective Equipment Regulations 2002** which is applicable to that item of personal protective equipment or, in the case of respiratory protective equipment, shall be of a type approved or shall conform to a standard approved, in either case, by the Executive.

Regulation 8: Use of Control Measures, etc.

Every employer who provides any control measure, other thing or facility in accordance with these Regulations shall take all reasonable steps to ensure that it is properly used or applied as the case may be.

Every employee shall make full and proper use of any control measure, other thing or facility provided in accordance with these Regulations and, where relevant, shall:

- take all reasonable steps to ensure it is returned after use to any accommodation provided for it;
- if he discovers a defect therein, report it forthwith to his employer.

Regulation 9: Maintenance, Examination and Testing of Control Measures, etc.

Every employer who provides any control measure to meet the requirements of regulation 7 shall ensure that:

- in the case of plant and equipment, including engineering controls and personal protective equipment, it is maintained in an efficient state, in efficient working order, in good repair and in a clean condition; and
- in the case of the provision of systems of work and supervision and of any other measure, it is reviewed at suitable intervals and revised if necessary.

Where engineering controls are provided to meet the requirements of regulation 7, the employer shall ensure that thorough examination and testing of those controls is carried out in the case of local exhaust ventilation plant, at least once every 14 months, or for local exhaust ventilation plant used in conjunction with a process specified in Column 1 of Schedule 4, at not more than the interval specified in the corresponding entry in Column 2 of that Schedule or in any other case, at suitable intervals.

Where respiratory protective equipment (other than disposable respiratory protective equipment) is provided to meet the requirements of regulation 7, the employer shall ensure that thorough examination and, where appropriate, testing of that equipment is carried out at suitable intervals.

Every employer shall keep a suitable record of the examinations and tests carried out, and of repairs carried out as a result of those examinations and tests, and that record or a suitable summary thereof shall be kept available for at least five years from the date on which it was made.

Every employer shall ensure that personal protective equipment, including protective clothing, is:

- Properly stored in a well-defined place.
- Checked at suitable intervals.
- When discovered to be defective, repaired or replaced before further use.

Personal protective equipment which may be contaminated by a substance hazardous to health shall be removed on leaving the working area and kept apart from uncontaminated clothing and equipment.

The employer shall ensure that the equipment referred to above is subsequently decontaminated and cleaned or, if necessary, destroyed.

Regulation 10: Monitoring Exposure at the Workplace

Where the risk assessment indicates that it is requisite for ensuring the maintenance of adequate control of the exposure of employees to substances hazardous to health; or it is otherwise requisite for protecting the health of employees, the employer shall ensure that the exposure of employees to substances hazardous to health is monitored in accordance with a suitable procedure. This requirement shall not apply where the employer is able to demonstrate by another method of evaluation that the requirements of regulation 7 have been complied with.

The monitoring referred to above shall take place at regular intervals and when any change occurs, which may affect that exposure.

Where a substance or process is specified in Column 1 of Schedule 5, monitoring shall be carried out at least at the frequency specified in the corresponding entry in Column 2 of that Schedule.

The employer shall ensure that a suitable record of monitoring carried out for the purpose of this regulation is made and maintained and that the record is kept available:

- where the record is representative of the personal exposures of identifiable employees, for at least 40 years; or
- in any other case, for at least five years from the date of the last entry made in it.

Where an employee is required by regulation 11 to be under health surveillance, an individual record of any monitoring carried out in accordance with this regulation shall be made, maintained and kept, in respect of that employee.

The employer shall, on reasonable notice being given, allow an employee access to his personal monitoring record, provide the Executive with copies of such monitoring records as the Executive may require and if he ceases to trade, notify the Executive forthwith in writing and make available to the Executive all monitoring records kept by him.

Regulation 11: Health Surveillance

Where it is appropriate for the protection of the health of his employees who are, or are liable to be, exposed to a substance hazardous to health, the employer shall ensure that such employees are under suitable health surveillance.

Health surveillance shall be treated as being appropriate where:

- The employee is exposed to one of the substances specified in Column 1 of Schedule 6 and is engaged in a process specified in Column 2 of that Schedule, and there is a reasonable likelihood that an identifiable disease or adverse health effect will result from that exposure.
- The exposure of the employee to a substance hazardous to health is such that:
  - An identifiable disease or adverse health effect may be related to the exposure.
  - There is a reasonable likelihood that the disease or effect may occur under the particular conditions their work.
  - There are valid techniques for detecting indications of the disease or effect and the technique of investigation is of low risk to the employee.

The employer shall ensure that a health record, in respect of each of his employees for whom the health surveillance is required, is made and maintained and that the record is kept available in a suitable form, for at least 40 years from the date of the last entry made in it.

The employer shall, on reasonable notice being given, allow an employee access to his personal health record, provide the Executive with copies of such health records as the Executive may require and if he ceases to trade, notify the Executive forthwith in writing and make available to the Executive all health records kept by him.

If an employee is exposed to a substance specified in Schedule 6 and is engaged in a process specified, the health surveillance required shall include medical surveillance under the supervision of a relevant doctor, at intervals of not more than 12 months or such shorter intervals as the relevant doctor may require.

Where an employee is subject to medical surveillance and a relevant doctor has certified by an entry in the health record of that employee, that in his professional opinion that employee should not be engaged in work which exposes him to that substance or that he should only be so engaged under conditions specified in the record, the employer shall not permit the employee to be engaged in such work except in accordance with the conditions, if any, specified in the health record, unless that entry has been cancelled by a relevant doctor.

Where an employee is subject to medical surveillance and a relevant doctor has certified by an entry in his health record that medical surveillance should be continued after his exposure to that substance has ceased, the employer shall ensure that the medical surveillance of that employee is continued in accordance with that entry while he is employed by the employer, unless that entry has been cancelled by a relevant doctor.

An employee to whom this regulation applies shall, when required by his employer and at the cost of the employer, present himself during his working hours for such health surveillance procedures as may be required and, in the case of an employee who is subject to medical surveillance, shall furnish the relevant doctor with such information concerning his health as the relevant doctor may reasonably require.

Where, as a result of health surveillance, an employee is found to have an identifiable disease or adverse health effect, which is considered by a relevant doctor or other occupational health professional to be the result of exposure to a substance hazardous to health, the employer of that employee shall:

- Ensure that a suitably qualified person informs the employee accordingly and provides the employee with information and advice regarding further health surveillance.
- Review the risk assessment.

- Review any measure taken to comply with regulation 7, taking into account any advice given by a relevant doctor, occupational health professional or the Executive.
- Consider assigning the employee to alternative work where there is no risk of further exposure to that substance, taking into account any advice given by a relevant doctor or occupational health professional.
- Provide for a review of the health of any other employee who has been similarly exposed, including a medical examination where such an examination is recommended by a relevant doctor, occupational health professional or the Executive.

Where, for the purpose of carrying out his functions under these Regulations, a relevant doctor requires to inspect any workplace or any record kept for the purposes of these Regulations, the employer shall permit him to do so.

Where an employee or an employer is aggrieved by a decision recorded in the health record by a doctor to suspend an employee from work which exposes him to a substance hazardous to health (or to impose conditions on such work), he may, by an application in writing to the Executive, within 28 days of the date on which he was notified of the decision, apply for that decision to be reviewed in accordance with a procedure approved by the HSE, and the result of that review shall be notified to the employee and employer and entered into the health record, in accordance with the approved procedure.

Regulation 12: Information, Instruction and Training for Persons who may be Exposed to Substances Hazardous to Health

Every employer who undertakes work, which is liable to expose an employee to a substance hazardous to health, shall provide that employee with suitable and sufficient information, instruction and training.

The information, instruction and training provided shall include:

- Details of the substances hazardous to health to which the employee is liable to be exposed, including:
    - The names of those substances and the risk which they present to health.
    - Any relevant workplace exposure limit or similar occupational exposure limit.
    - Access to any relevant safety data sheet.
    - Other legislative provisions which concern the hazardous properties of those substances.
- The significant findings of the risk assessment.
- The appropriate precautions and actions to be taken by the employee in order to safeguard himself and other employees at the workplace.
- The results of any monitoring of exposure in accordance with regulation 10 and, in particular, in the case of a substance hazardous to health for which a workplace exposure limit has been approved, the employee or his representatives shall be informed if the results of such monitoring show that the workplace exposure limit has been exceeded.
- The collective results of any health surveillance undertaken in accordance with regulation 11, in a form calculated to prevent those results from being identified as relating to a particular person.
- Where employees are working with a Group 4 biological agent or material that may contain such an agent, the provision of written instructions and, if appropriate, the display of notices which outline the procedures for handling such an agent or material.

The information, instruction and training required shall be adapted to take account of significant changes in the type of work carried out or methods of work used by the employer and provided in a manner appropriate to the level, type and duration of exposure identified by the risk assessment.

Every employer shall ensure that any person (whether or not his employee) who carries out work in connection with the employer's duties under these Regulations, has suitable and sufficient information, instruction and training.

Where containers and pipes for substances hazardous to health used at work are not marked in accordance with any relevant legislation listed in Schedule 7, the employer shall ensure that the contents of those containers and pipes, together with the nature of those contents and any associated hazards, are clearly identifiable.

Regulation 13: Arrangements to Deal with Accidents, Incidents and Emergencies

To protect the health of his employees from an accident, incident or emergency related to the presence of a substance hazardous to health at the workplace, the employer shall ensure that:

- Procedures, including the provision of appropriate first-aid facilities and relevant safety drills (which shall be tested at regular intervals), have been prepared which can be put into effect when such an event occurs.
- Information on emergency arrangements, including details of relevant work hazards and hazard identification arrangements and specific hazards likely to arise at the time of an accident, incident or emergency, is available.
- Suitable warning and other communication systems are established to enable an appropriate response, including remedial actions and rescue operations, to be made immediately when such an event occurs.

The employer shall ensure that information on the procedures and systems required is made available to relevant accident and emergency services to enable those services, whether internal or external to the workplace, to prepare their own response procedures and precautionary measures and is displayed at the workplace, if this is appropriate.

In the event of an accident, incident or emergency related to the presence of a substance hazardous to health at the workplace, the employer shall ensure that:

- Immediate steps are taken to:
  - Mitigate the effects of the event.
  - Restore the situation to normal.
  - Inform those of his employees who may be affected.
- Only those persons who are essential for the carrying out of repairs and other necessary work are permitted in the affected area and they are provided with:
  - Appropriate personal protective equipment.
  - Any necessary specialised safety equipment and plant, which shall be used until the situation is restored to normal.
- In the case of an incident or accident, which has or may have resulted in the release of a biological agent which could cause severe human disease, as soon as practicable thereafter his employees or their representatives are informed of the causes of that incident or accident, and the measures taken or to be taken to rectify the situation.

Provided the substance hazardous to health is not a carcinogen, mutagen or biological agent, these duties shall not apply where:

- The results of the risk assessment show that, because of the quantity of each substance hazardous to health present at the workplace, there is only a slight risk to the health of employees.
- The measures taken by the employer to comply with the duty under regulation 7(1) are sufficient to control that risk.

An employee shall report, to his employer or to any other employee of that employer with specific responsibility for the health and safety of his fellow employees, any accident or incident which has or may have resulted in the release of a biological agent which could cause severe human disease.

Regulation 14: Provisions Relating to Certain Fumigations

An employer shall not undertake fumigation to which this regulation applies, unless he has notified the persons specified in Part I of Schedule 9 of his intention to undertake the fumigation and provided to those persons the information specified in Part II of that Schedule, at least 24 hours in advance, or such shorter time in advance as the persons required to be notified may agree.

An employer who undertakes a fumigation to which this regulation applies shall ensure that, before the fumigant is released, suitable warning notices have been affixed at all points of reasonable access to the premises, or to those parts of the premises in which the fumigation is to be carried out and that after the fumigation has been completed, and the premises are safe to enter, those warning notices are removed.

Regulations 15-20 deal with various administrative provisions including exemption certificates, revocations and savings.

Regulation 21: Defence

Subject to regulation 21 of the **Management of Health and Safety at Work Regulations 1999,** in any proceedings for an offence consisting of a contravention of these Regulations it shall be a defence for any person to prove that he took all reasonable precautions and exercised all due diligence to avoid the commission of that offence.

CONTROL OF VIBRATION AT WORK REGULATIONS 2005 (SI 2005 NO. 1093)

These Regulations transpose into UK law and implement **EC Directive 2002/44/EC** on the minimum health and safety requirements regarding the exposure of workers to the risks arising from physical agents (vibration). The Regulations impose duties on employers to protect employees who may be exposed to risk from exposure to vibration at work, and other persons who might be affected by the work, whether they are at work or not.

The Regulations apply to both hand-arm and whole-body vibration and make provision for action and limit values for daily exposure (regulation 4); for risk assessment (regulation 5); the elimination of or reduction of exposure to vibration to as low a level as is reasonably practicable (regulation 6(1)); a programme of reduction measures to be taken at the action levels (regulation 6(2)); actions to be taken at the limit values, and a prohibition on exceeding the limit values (regulation 6(4)). There are also provisions for weekly averaging of vibration exposure in specified circumstances (regulation 6(5)); health surveillance (regulation 7); and for information, instruction and training (regulation 8).

Regulation 1: Citation and Commencement

These Regulations came into force on 6 July 2005.

Regulation 2: Interpretation

Daily exposure means the quantity of mechanical vibration to which a worker is exposed during a working day, normalised to an eight-hour reference period, which takes account of the magnitude and duration of the vibration.

Enforcing authority means the HSE or local authority or Office of Rail Regulation.

Exposure action value means the level of daily exposure set out in regulation 4 for any worker, which, if breached, requires specified action to be taken to reduce risk.

Exposure limit value means the level of daily exposure set out in regulation 4 for any worker which must not be exceeded, save as set out in regulation 6(5).

Exposure to vibration means the exposure of an employee to mechanical vibration arising out of or in connection with his work.

Hand-arm vibration means mechanical vibration which is transmitted into the hands and arms during a work activity.

Mechanical vibration means vibration occurring in a piece of machinery or equipment or in a vehicle as a result of its operation.

Whole-body vibration means mechanical vibration which is transmitted into the body when seated or standing through the supporting surface, during a work activity or as described in regulation 5(3).

Working day means a daily working period irrespective of the time when it begins or ends, and whether it begins or ends on the same calendar day.

Regulation 3: Application and Transitional Provisions

Under regulation 3(2) there was a transitional period for the exposure limit values up to 6 July 2010. This was designed to allow work activities where the use of older tools, vehicles and machinery (supplied prior to 6 July 2007) could not keep exposures below the exposure limit value to continue in certain circumstances.

Under regulation 3(3) the transitional period was extended to 6 July 2014 in the case of whole-body exposures in the agriculture and forestry sectors, a concession which has been criticised by trade unions and other safety bodies. However, in using such equipment the employer must take into account the latest technical advances and organisational measures to reduce exposure to as low as is reasonably practicable, as based on Schedule 1 to **MHSWR 1999**.

Under regulation 3(4) the duty of the employer also applies to any other person who may be affected by the work carried out by the employer, except that the provisions in respect of health surveillance and information, instruction and training do not extend to non- employees, unless they are on the premises where the work is being carried out. Self-employed persons are also subject to the Regulations under regulation 3(5).

The Regulations do not apply to the master or crew of a ship (which includes every description of vessel used in navigation) or to the employer of such persons in respect of "normal shipboard activities".

Regulation 4: Exposure Limit Values and Action Values

Under regulation 4 (1) values are specified for hand-arm vibration as follows:

- The daily exposure limit value is 5 m/s^2 A(8).
- The daily exposure action value is 2.5 m/s^2 A(8).

The daily exposure is to be ascertained on the basis of Schedule 1, Part 1.

For whole-body vibration:

- The daily exposure limit value is 1.15 m/s^2 A(8).
- The daily exposure action value is 0.5 m/s^2 A(8).

The daily exposure is to be ascertained on the basis of Schedule 2, Part 1.

Regulation 5: Assessment of the Risk to Health Created by Vibration at the Workplace

Regulation 5(1) states the duty of an employer to carry out a suitable and sufficient risk assessment of those employees who are liable to be exposed to vibration risk, and to identify measures necessary to be taken to meet the requirements of the Regulations.

Regulation 5(2) requires the employer to assess daily the exposure to vibration by means of:

- Observation of specific working practices.
- Reference to relevant information on the probable magnitude of vibration corresponding to the equipment used in the particular working conditions.
- If necessary, measure the magnitude of vibration to which his employees are liable to be exposed.

The purpose of 5(2) is to enable the employer to assess whether any employees are likely to be exposed at or above an exposure action value or above an exposure limit value.

Regulation 5(3) specifies that the risk assessment shall include consideration of:

- The magnitude, type and duration of exposure, including any intermittent vibration or repeated shocks.
- The effects of vibration exposure on employees at risk.
- Any effects of vibration on work equipment and the workplace, including handling of controls, indicator reading, structural stability and security of joints.
- Any information provided by work equipment manufacturers.
- Availability of replacement equipment which is designed to reduce vibration exposure.
- Any extension of whole-body vibration exposure beyond normal working hours and in employer-supervised rest facilities.
- Specific working conditions such as low temperatures.
- Appropriate health surveillance information, including published information.

Regulation 5(4) states that the risk assessment must be reviewed regularly, and if:

- There is reason to suspect that the assessment is no longer valid.
- There has been a significant change in the work to which the assessment relates.

Where review changes are made to an assessment:

- The employer must record significant findings as soon as is practicable.
- The measures he has taken and intends to take must be recorded.

Regulation 6: Elimination or Control of Exposure to Vibration at the Workplace

Regulation 6(1) requires that the employer shall ensure that his employees' risk from vibration exposure is either eliminated at source or, where not reasonably practicable, reduced to as low a level as is reasonably practicable.

Regulation 6(2) states that where it is not reasonably practicable to eliminate risk at source and an exposure action value is likely to be reached or exceeded, the employer shall reduce exposure to as low a level as is reasonably practicable by establishing and implementing a programme of organisational and technical measures which is appropriate to the activity.

Regulation 6(3) deals with the measures to be taken by the employer based on the general principles of prevention set out in

MHSWR, Schedule 1, and includes consideration of:

- Other working methods which eliminate or reduce exposure to vibration.
- Choosing ergonomically designed work equipment which for the type of work to be done produces the least possible vibration.
- Provision of auxiliary equipment which reduces the risk of vibration-caused injuries.
- Appropriate maintenance programmes for work equipment, the workplace and workplace systems.
- Design and layout of workplaces, workstations and rest facilities.
- Provision of suitable and sufficient information and training for employees such that work equipment is used correctly and safely in order to minimise vibration exposure.
- Limitation of the duration and magnitude of vibration exposure.
- Provision of appropriate work schedules with adequate rest periods.
- Provision of clothing to protect employees from cold and damp.

Regulation 6(4) states that an employer must:

- Ensure that his employees are not exposed to vibration above an exposure limit value.
- If an exposure limit value is exceeded:
    - Reduce vibration exposure to below the limit value.
    - Identify why the limit was exceeded.
    - Take measures to prevent it from being exceeded again.

Regulation 6(5) covers situations where vibration exposure (as ascertained on the basis of Schedule 1, Part 2 for HAV, and Schedule 2, Part 2, for whole-body vibration) may vary over time from below the action value to exceeding the limit value, and where:

- Any vibration exposure averaged over one week is less than the exposure limit value.
- Risk from the actual pattern of exposure is less than the corresponding risk from constant exposure at the limit value.
- Risk is reduced to as low a level as is reasonably practicable under the circumstances.
- Employees are subject to increased health surveillance as appropriate.

Regulation 6(6) states that the employer shall adapt any compliance measure taken to take account of the employee(s) who are at risk.

Regulation 7: Health Surveillance

Regulation 7(1) states that the employer must place under appropriate health surveillance those employees whom the risk assessment indicates are at risk from, or liable to be exposed to, vibration; and those employees who are likely to be exposed to vibration at or above an exposure action value.

Regulation 7(2) gives the purpose of health surveillance as to prevent or diagnose any vibration exposure health effects, and is appropriate where:

- A link can be established between exposure and an identifiable disease or adverse health effect.
- The disease or effect may occur under the particular conditions of the work.
- There are valid techniques for detecting the disease or effect.

Regulation 7(3) requires the employer to keep health records of employees under health surveillance; and regulation 7(4) entitles employees subject to surveillance to access to their personal records; the enforcing authority must be provided with such records as required.

Regulation 7(5) deals with employees found to have an identifiable disease or adverse health effect which is considered to be the result of vibration exposure. Under such circumstances, the employer shall:

- Ensure that the employee is informed of his condition by a suitably qualified person and provided with information and advice on what should happen next.
- Ensure that he is himself informed of any significant findings from employee health surveillance.

- Review the risk assessment, particularly in relation to measures taken under regulation 6, and advice given by an occupational health professional or enforcing authority.
- Assign the employee to alternative work where there is no further risk of vibration exposure.
- Review the health of any other employee who has been similarly exposed.

Regulation 7(6) requires affected employees to present themselves for health surveillance during working hours, when required by the employer, and at the employer's expense.

Regulation 8: Information, Instruction and Training

Regulation 8(1) requires that where a risk assessment indicates there is a vibration risk to employees, or where employees are likely to be exposed to vibration at or above the action level, the employer shall provide those employees and their representatives with suitable and sufficient information, instruction and training.

Regulation 8(2) states that it shall include the organisational and technical measures taken in order to comply with the requirements of regulation 6; the exposure limit values and action values set out in regulation 4; the significant findings of the risk assessment; why and how to detect and report signs of injury; entitlement to appropriate health surveillance under regulation 7; safe working practices to minimise exposure to vibration; the collective results of any health surveillance undertaken, without identifying it as relating to particular persons. The information, instruction and training shall be updated to take account of significant changes in the type of work or methods used.

Regulations 9 to 11: Exemptions

Subject to certain conditions, exemptions may be granted by the Executive in respect of activities carried out by emergency services; in the case of air transport; and activities carried out in the interests of national security.

Regulation 12: Extension outside Great Britain

These Regulations apply in relation to activities outside Great Britain to which Sections 1 to 59 and 80 to 82 of **HSWA 1974** apply by virtue of the **Health and Safety at Work, etc. Act 1974 (Application outside Great Britain) Order 2013**.

Regulation 13: Amendments

Amendments are made by these Regulations to the **Offshore Installations and Wells (Design and Construction etc.) Regulations 1996**, and to the wording of regulation 12 of the **Provision and Use of Work Equipment Regulations 1998**.

Schedule 1: Hand-Arm Vibration

Part 1 explains the mathematical formula for the calculation of daily exposure to vibration, A(8).

Part 2 details the calculation of exposure to vibration averaged over one week, A(8)week.

The measurement and evaluation of human exposure to hand-transmitted mechanical vibration (Schedule 1) is dealt with in British Standard **BS EN 5349-1:2001**.

Schedule 2: Whole-Body Vibration

Part 1 explains the formula for calculation of daily exposure to vibration, A(8).

Part 2 gives the formula for calculating exposure to vibration averaged over one week, A(8)week.

The measurement and evaluation of human exposure to whole-body mechanical vibration and shock (Schedule 2) is covered by ISO 2631-1:1997.

CORPORATE MANSLAUGHTER AND CORPORATE HOMICIDE ACT 2007

(Selected provisions only)

Section 1: The Offence

(1) An organisation to which this section applies is guilty of an offence if the way in which its activities are managed or organised:

    (a) causes a person's death, and

    (b) amounts to a gross breach of a relevant duty of care owed by the organisation to the deceased.

(2) The organisations to which this section applies are:

    (a) a corporation;

    (b) a department or other body listed in Schedule 1;

    (c) a police force;

    (d) a partnership, or a trade union or employers' association, that is an employer.

(3) An organisation is guilty of an offence under this section only if the way in which its activities are managed or organised by its senior management is a substantial element in the breach referred to in subsection (1).

(4) For the purposes of this Act:

    (a) "relevant duty of care" has the meaning given by section 2, read with sections 3 to 7;

    (b) a breach of a duty of care by an organisation is a "gross" breach if the conduct alleged to amount to a breach of that duty falls far below what can reasonably be expected of the organisation in the circumstances;

    (c) "senior management", in relation to an organisation, means the persons who play significant roles in:

        (i) the making of decisions about how the whole or a substantial part of its activities are to be managed or organised, or

        (ii) the actual managing or organising of the whole or a substantial part of those activities.

(5) The offence under this section is called:

    (a) corporate manslaughter, in so far as it is an offence under the law of England and Wales or Northern Ireland;

    (b) corporate homicide, in so far as it is an offence under the law of Scotland.

(6) An organisation that is guilty of corporate manslaughter or corporate homicide is liable on conviction on indictment to a fine.

(7) The offence of corporate homicide is indictable only in the High Court of Justiciary.

Section 2: Meaning of "Relevant Duty of Care"

(1) A "relevant duty of care", in relation to an organisation, means any of the following duties owed by it under the law of negligence:

    (a) a duty owed to its employees or to other persons working for the organisation or performing services for it;

    (b) a duty owed as occupier of premises;

    (c) a duty owed in connection with:

        (i) the supply by the organisation of goods or services (whether for consideration or not),

        (ii) the carrying on by the organisation of any construction or maintenance operations,

        (iii) the carrying on by the organisation of any other activity on a commercial basis, or

        (iv) the use or keeping by the organisation of any plant, vehicle or other thing;

(d) a duty owed to a person who, by reason of being a person within subsection (2), is someone for whose safety the organisation is responsible.

Section 4: Military Activities

Any duty of care in respect of peacekeeping operations, or operations for dealing with terrorism, civil unrest or serious disorder, together with activities in preparation for the same, as well as training of a hazardous nature and any activities carried on by members of the special forces, will be a 'relevant duty of care'.

Section 5: Policing and Law Enforcement

Any duty of care in respect of operations for dealing with terrorism, civil unrest or serious disorder, preparation for the same or training of a hazardous nature where those operations involve policing or law enforcement where officers come under attack or face the threat of attack or violent resistance, is not a 'relevant duty of care'.

Section 6: Emergencies

Any duty of care owed by a fire and rescue authority/service/board, organisations providing a service of responding to emergency circumstances, relevant NHS bodies, organisations providing ambulance services or transport of organs, organisations providing rescue services, or the armed forces in respect of the way in which it responds to emergency circumstances is not a 'relevant duty of care' unless it is a duty owed to employees or others working for the organisation or performing services for it, or is a duty owed as an occupier of premises.

Section 8: Factors for Jury

(1) This section applies where:

   (a) it is established that an organisation owed a relevant duty of care to a person, and

   (b) it falls to the jury to decide whether there was a gross breach of that duty.

(2) The jury must consider whether the evidence shows that the organisation failed to comply with any health and safety legislation that relates to the alleged breach, and if so:

   (a) how serious that failure was;

   (b) how much of a risk of death it posed.

(3) The jury may also:

   (a) consider the extent to which the evidence shows that there were attitudes, policies, systems or accepted practices within the organisation that were likely to have encouraged any such failure as is mentioned in subsection (2), or to have produced tolerance of it;

   (b) have regard to any health and safety guidance that relates to the alleged breach.

(4) This section does not prevent the jury from having regard to any other matters they consider relevant.

(5) In this section "health and safety guidance" means any code, guidance, manual or similar publication that is concerned with health and safety matters and is made or issued (under a statutory provision or otherwise) by an authority responsible for the enforcement of any health and safety legislation.

Section 9: Power to Order Breach, etc. to be Remedied

(1) A court before which an organisation is convicted of corporate manslaughter or corporate homicide may make an order (a "remedial order") requiring the organisation to take specified steps to remedy:

   (a) the breach mentioned in section 1(1) ("the relevant breach");

   (b) any matter that appears to the court to have resulted from the relevant breach and to have been a cause of the death;

   (c) any deficiency, as regards health and safety matters, in the organisation's policies, systems or practices of which the relevant breach appears to the court to be an indication.

(2) A remedial order may be made only on an application by the prosecution specifying the terms of the proposed order. Any such order must be on such terms (whether those proposed or others) as the court considers appropriate having regard to any representations made, and any evidence adduced, in relation to that matter by the prosecution or on behalf of the organisation.

(3) Before making an application for a remedial order the prosecution must consult such enforcement authority or authorities as it considers appropriate having regard to the nature of the relevant breach.

(4) A remedial order:

   (a) must specify a period within which the steps referred to in subsection (1) are to be taken;

   (b) may require the organisation to supply to an enforcement authority consulted under subsection (3), within a specified period, evidence that those steps have been taken.

   A period specified under this subsection may be extended or further extended by order of the court on an application made before the end of that period or extended period.

(5) An organisation that fails to comply with a remedial order is guilty of an offence, and liable on conviction on indictment to a fine.

Section 10: Power to Order Conviction, etc. to be Publicised

(1) A court before which an organisation is convicted of corporate manslaughter or corporate homicide may make an order (a "publicity order") requiring the organisation to publicise in a specified manner:

   (a) the fact that it has been convicted of the offence;

   (b) specified particulars of the offence;

   (c) the amount of any fine imposed;

   (d) the terms of any remedial order made.

(2) In deciding on the terms of a publicity order that it is proposing to make, the court must:

   (a) ascertain the views of such enforcement authority or authorities (if any) as it considers appropriate, and

   (b) have regard to any representations made by the prosecution or on behalf of the organisation.

(3) A publicity order:

   (a) must specify a period within which the requirements referred to in subsection (1) are to be complied with;

   (b) may require the organisation to supply to any enforcement authority whose views have been ascertained under subsection (2), within a specified period, evidence that those requirements have been complied with.

(4) An organisation that fails to comply with a publicity order is guilty of an offence, and liable on conviction on indictment to a fine.

CRIMINAL LAW ACT 1967

This section of the Act relates to legal requirements for employers to manage work-related violence/aggression.

Section 3: Use of Force in Making Arrest, etc.

(1) A person may use such force as is reasonable in the circumstances in the prevention of crime, or in effecting or assisting in the lawful arrest of offenders or suspected offenders or of persons unlawfully at large.

(2) Subsection (1) above shall replace the rules of the common law on the question when force used for a purpose mentioned in the subsection is justified by that purpose.

Section 3

Case Note - R. v. Morris (Daryl Howard) (2013) EWCA Crim 436, at paragraph 19:

"19. The use of reasonable force in self defence or in defence of another person is lawful. The essence of these defences is the honestly held belief of the defendant as to the facts [...]. In relation to use of force in the prevention of crime (such as to prevent an unlawful attack on another), the defence is afforded by s.3 of the Criminal Law Act 1967. If honest belief affords a defence under s.3 in those circumstances, it must equally do so for a person who claims to have used reasonable force to prevent the commission of a crime other than a crime of violence against another."

DANGEROUS SUBSTANCES AND EXPLOSIVE ATMOSPHERES REGULATIONS 2002 (SI 2002 NO. 2776)

These Regulations repealed the **Highly Flammable Liquids and Liquefied Petroleum Gases Regulations 1972**.

Amending Legislation

Minor amendments were made by the **Carriage of Dangerous Goods and Use of Transportable Pressure Equipment Regulations 2004** (subsequently revoked and replaced by Regulations of the same name in 2007 and then, again, in 2009).

Further minor amendments were made by the **Chemicals (Hazard Information and Packaging for Supply) Regulations 2009 (CHIP)**.

From June 2015, these Regulations also cover substances that are corrosive to metals and gases under pressure to allow for changes in the EU Chemical Agents Directive.

Regulation 1: Citation and Commencement

These Regulations may be cited as the **Dangerous Substances and Explosive Atmospheres Regulations 2002** and were fully in force by 30 June 2003.

Regulation 2: Interpretation

In these Regulations:

- "the **CLP Regulation**" means **Regulation (EC) No. 1272/2008** of the European Parliament and of the Council of 16 December 2008 on classification, labelling and packaging of substances and mixtures;

- "dangerous substance" means:

    (a) a substance or mixture which meets the criteria for classification as hazardous within any physical hazard class laid down in the **CLP Regulation**, whether or not the substance is classified under that Regulation;

    (b) a substance or mixture which because of its physico-chemical or chemical properties and the way it is used or is present at the workplace creates a risk, not being a substance or mixture falling within subparagraph (a); or

    (c) any dust, whether in the form of solid particles or fibrous materials or otherwise, which can form an explosive mixture with air or an explosive atmosphere, not being a substance or mixture falling within subparagraphs (a) or (b) above;

- "explosive atmosphere" means a mixture, under atmospheric conditions, of air and one or more dangerous substances in the form of gases, vapours, mists or dusts in which, after ignition has occurred, combustion spreads to the entire unburned mixture;

- "hazard" means the physico-chemical or chemical property of a dangerous substance which has the potential to give rise to fire, explosion, or other events which can result in harmful physical effects of a kind similar to those which can be caused by fire or explosion, or be corrosive to metals, affecting the safety of a person, and references in these Regulations to "hazardous" shall be construed accordingly;

- "mixture" means a mixture or solution composed of two or more substances;

- "personal protective equipment" means all equipment which is intended to be worn or held by a person at work and which protects that person against one or more risks to his safety, and any addition or accessory designed to meet that objective;

- "risk" means the likelihood of a person's safety being affected by harmful physical effects being caused to him from fire, explosion or other events arising from the hazardous properties of a dangerous substance in connection with work and also the extent of that harm;

- "risk assessment" means the assessment of risks required by regulation 5(1);

- "safety data sheet" means a safety data sheet within the meaning of **Regulation (EC) 1907/2006 (REACH)**;

- "substance" means any natural or artificial substance whether in solid or liquid form or in the form of a gas or vapour;

- "workplace" means any premises or part of premises used for or in connection with work, and includes:

    (a) any place within the premises to which an employee has access while at work; and

    (b) any room, lobby, corridor, staircase, road or other place:

    (iii) used as a means of access to or egress from that place of work, or,

    (iv) where facilities are provided for use in connection with that place of work, other than a public road; and

- "work processes" means all technical aspects of work involving dangerous substances and includes:
  - appropriate technical means of supervision,
  - connecting devices,
  - control and protection systems,
  - engineering controls and solutions,
  - equipment,
  - materials, f machinery, f plant,
  - protective systems, and
  - warning and other communication systems.

Regulation 3: Application

These Regulations, apart from regulations 15, 16 and 17(4) to (5), shall not apply to the master or crew of a ship or to the employer of such persons in respect of the normal ship-board activities of a ship's crew which are carried out solely by the crew under the direction of the master and, for the purposes of this paragraph:

- "ship" includes every description of vessel used in navigation, other than a ship forming part of Her Majesty's Navy or an offshore installation; and
- the reference to the normal ship-board activities of a ship's crew includes the construction, reconstruction or conversion of a ship outside, but not inside, Great Britain; and the repair of a ship save repair when carried out in dry dock.

Regulations 5(4)(c), 7 and 11 shall not apply to:

- Areas used directly for and during the medical treatment of patients.
- The use of gas appliances burning gaseous fuel (that is to say, any fuel which is in a gaseous state at a temperature of 15°C under a pressure of 1 bar) which are used for cooking, heating, hot water production, refrigeration, lighting or washing; and have, where applicable, a normal water temperature not exceeding 105°C including forced draught burners and heating bodies to be equipped with such burners but not including an appliance specifically designed for use in an industrial process carried out on industrial premises.
- Gas fittings within the meaning of the **Gas Safety (Installation and Use) Regulations 1998** located in domestic premises.
- The manufacture, handling, use, storage and transport of explosives or chemically unstable substances.

[Further exceptions apply to mines, quarries, borehole sites and offshore installations.]

Regulation 4: Duties under these Regulations

Where a duty is placed by these Regulations on an employer in respect of his employees, he shall, so far as is reasonably practicable, be under a like duty in respect of any other person, whether at work or not, who may be affected by the work carried on by the employer, except that:

- the duties of the employer under regulations 6(5)(f) and 7(5) (which relate, respectively, to the provision of suitable personal protective equipment and the provision of appropriate work clothing) shall not extend to persons who are not his employees; and
- the duties of the employer under regulations 8 and 9 (which relate, respectively, to dealing with accidents and to provision of information, instruction and training) shall not extend to persons who are not his employees, unless those persons are at the workplace where the work is being carried on and subject to the following, namely, that, in relation to the application of regulation 9 to such persons, regulation 9 shall apply to the extent that is required by the nature and the degree of the risk.

These Regulations shall apply to a self-employed person as they apply to an employer and an employee and as if that self-employed person were both an employer and employee.

Regulation 5: Risk Assessment

Where a dangerous substance is or is liable to be present at the workplace, the employer shall make a suitable and sufficient assessment of the risks to his employees which arise from that substance.

The risk assessment shall include consideration of:

- the hazardous properties of the substance;
- information on safety provided by the supplier, including information contained in any relevant safety data sheet;

- the circumstances of the work including:
    - the work processes and substances used and their possible interactions;
    - the amount of the substance involved;
    - where the work will involve more than one dangerous substance, the risk presented by such substances in combination; and
    - the arrangements for the safe handling, storage and transport of dangerous substances and of waste containing dangerous substances;
- activities, such as maintenance, where there is the potential for a high level of risk;
- the effect of measures which have been or will be taken pursuant to these Regulations;
- the likelihood that an explosive atmosphere will occur and its persistence;
- the likelihood that ignition sources, including electrostatic discharges, will be present and become active and effective;
- the scale of the anticipated effects of a fire or an explosion;
- any places which are or can be connected via openings to places in which explosive atmospheres may occur; and
- such additional safety information as the employer may need in order to complete the risk assessment.

The risk assessment shall be reviewed by the employer regularly so as to keep it up to date and particularly if there is reason to suspect that the risk assessment is no longer valid; or there has been a significant change in the matters to which the risk assessment relates including when the workplace, work processes, or organisation of the work undergoes significant changes, extensions or conversions and where, as a result of the review, changes to the risk assessment are required, those changes shall be made.

Where the employer employs five or more employees, the employer shall record the significant findings of the risk assessment as soon as is practicable after that assessment is made, including in particular:

- the measures which have been or will be taken by him pursuant to these Regulations;
- sufficient information to show that the workplace and work processes are designed, operated and maintained with due regard for safety and that, in accordance with the **Provision and Use of Work Equipment Regulations 1998** adequate arrangements have been made for the safe use of work equipment; and
- where an explosive atmosphere may occur at the workplace and subject to the transitional provisions in regulation 17(1) to (3), sufficient information to show:
    - those places which have been classified into zones pursuant to regulation 7(1);
    - equipment which is required for, or helps to ensure, the safe operation of equipment located in places classified as hazardous pursuant to regulation 7(1);
    - that any verification of overall explosion safety required by regulation 7(4) has been carried out; and
    - the aim of any co-ordination required by regulation 11 and the measures and procedures for implementing it.

No new work activity involving a dangerous substance shall commence unless an assessment has been made and the measures required by these Regulations have been implemented.

Regulation 6: Elimination or Reduction of Risks from Dangerous Substances

Every employer shall ensure that risk is either eliminated or reduced so far as is reasonably practicable.

In complying with this duty, substitution shall by preference be undertaken, whereby the employer shall avoid, so far as is reasonably practicable, the presence or use of a dangerous substance at the workplace by replacing it with a substance or process which either eliminates or reduces the risk.

Where it is not reasonably practicable to eliminate risk, the employer shall, so far as is reasonably practicable, apply measures, consistent with the risk assessment and appropriate to the nature of the activity or operation:

- to control risks, and
- to mitigate the detrimental effects of a fire or explosion or the other harmful physical effects arising from dangerous substances.

The following measures are, in order of priority, those specified for controlling risks:

- the reduction of the quantity of dangerous substances to a minimum;
- the avoidance or minimising of the release of a dangerous substance;
- the control of the release of a dangerous substance at source;
- the prevention of the formation of an explosive atmosphere, including the application of appropriate ventilation;
- ensuring that any release of a dangerous substance which may give rise to risk is suitably collected, safely contained, removed to a safe place, or otherwise rendered safe, as appropriate;
- the avoidance of ignition sources including electrostatic discharges and adverse conditions which could cause dangerous substances to give rise to harmful physical effects; and
- the segregation of incompatible dangerous substances.

The following measures are those specified for mitigating the effects of fire and explosion:

- the reduction to a minimum of the number of employees exposed;
- the avoidance of the propagation of fires or explosions;
- the provision of explosion pressure relief arrangements;
- the provision of explosion suppression equipment;
- the provision of plant which is constructed so as to withstand the pressure likely to be produced by an explosion; and
- the provision of suitable personal protective equipment.

The employer shall arrange for the safe handling, storage and transport of dangerous substances and waste containing dangerous substances.

The employer shall ensure that any conditions necessary pursuant to these Regulations for ensuring the elimination or reduction of risk are maintained.

The employer shall, so far as is reasonably practicable, take the general safety measures specified in Schedule 1, subject to those measures being consistent with the risk assessment and appropriate to the nature of the activity or operation.

Regulation 7: Places Where Explosive Atmospheres May Occur

(1) Every employer shall classify places at the workplace where an explosive atmosphere may occur into hazardous or non-hazardous places in accordance with paragraph 1 of Schedule 2 and shall classify those places so classified as hazardous into zones in accordance with paragraph 2 of that Schedule; and that Schedule shall have effect subject to the notes at the end of that Schedule.

(2) The employer shall ensure that the requirements specified in Schedule 3 are applied to equipment and protective systems in the places classified as hazardous pursuant to paragraph (1).

(3) Where necessary, places classified as hazardous pursuant to paragraph (1) shall be marked by the employer with signs at their points of entry in accordance with Schedule 4.

(4) Before a workplace containing places classified as hazardous pursuant to paragraph (1) is used for the first time, the employer shall ensure that its overall explosion safety is verified by a person who is competent in the field of explosion protection as a result of his experience or any professional training or both.

(5) The employer shall ensure that appropriate work clothing which does not give rise to electrostatic discharges is provided for use in places classified as hazardous pursuant to paragraph (1).

(This regulation is subject to the transitional provisions.)

Regulation 8: Arrangements to Deal with Accidents, Incidents and Emergencies

In order to protect the safety of his employees from an accident, incident or emergency related to the presence of a dangerous substance at the workplace, the employer shall ensure that:

- procedures, including the provision of appropriate first-aid facilities and relevant safety drills (which shall be tested at regular intervals), have been prepared which can be put into effect when such an event occurs;
- information on emergency arrangements, including details of relevant work hazards and hazard identification arrangements, and specific hazards likely to arise at the time of an accident, incident or emergency is available;

- suitable warning and other communication systems are established to enable an appropriate response, including remedial actions and rescue operations, to be made immediately when such an event occurs;
- where necessary, before any explosion conditions are reached, visual, or audible, warnings are given and employees withdrawn; and
- where the risk assessment indicates it is necessary, escape facilities are provided and maintained to ensure that, in the event of danger, employees can leave endangered places promptly and safely.

The employer shall ensure that information on the matters referred to above is made available to relevant accident and emergency services to enable those services, whether internal or external to the workplace, to prepare their own response procedures and precautionary measures and displayed at the workplace, unless the results of the risk assessment make this unnecessary.

In the event of an accident, incident or emergency related to the presence of a dangerous substance at the workplace, the employer shall ensure that:

- immediate steps are taken to mitigate the effects of the event, restore the situation to normal, and inform those of his employees who may be affected; and
- only those persons who are essential for the carrying out of repairs and other necessary work are permitted in the affected area and they are provided with appropriate personal protective equipment and protective clothing and any necessary specialised safety equipment and plant which shall be used until the situation is restored to normal.

These requirements shall not apply where the results of the risk assessment show that, because of the quantity of each dangerous substance at the workplace, there is only a slight risk to employees and the measures taken by the employer to comply with his duty under regulation 6 are sufficient to control that risk.

Regulation 9: Information, Instruction and Training

Where a dangerous substance is present at the workplace, the employer shall provide his employees with:

- suitable and sufficient information, instruction and training on the appropriate precautions and actions to be taken by the employee in order to safeguard himself and other employees at the workplace;
- the details of any such substance including the name of the substance and the risk which it presents, access to any relevant safety data sheet; and legislative provisions which concern the hazardous properties of the substance; and
- the significant findings of the risk assessment.

The information, instruction and training required shall be adapted to take account of significant changes in the type of work carried out or methods of work used by the employer; and provided in a manner appropriate to the risk assessment.

Regulation 10: Identification of Hazardous Contents of Containers and Pipes

Where containers and pipes used at work for dangerous substances are not marked in accordance with relevant requirements of the legislation listed in Schedule 5, the employer shall, subject to any derogations provided for in that legislation, ensure that the contents of those containers and pipes, together with the nature of those contents and any associated hazards, are clearly identifiable.

Regulation 11: Duty of Co-ordination

Where two or more employers share the same workplace (whether on a temporary or a permanent basis) where an explosive atmosphere may occur, the employer responsible for the workplace shall co-ordinate the implementation of all the measures required by these Regulations to be taken to protect employees from any risk from the explosive atmosphere.

Schedule 1

General Safety Measures

The following measures are those specified for the purposes of regulation 6(8).

Workplace and Work Processes

- Ensuring that the workplace is designed, constructed and maintained so as to reduce risk.
- Designing, constructing, assembling, installing, providing and using suitable work processes so as to reduce risk.
- Maintaining work processes in an efficient state, in efficient working order and in good repair.

- Ensuring that equipment and protective systems meet the following requirements:
    - where power failure can give rise to the spread of additional risk, equipment and protective systems shall be able to be maintained in a safe state of operation independently of the rest of the plant in the event of power failure;
    - means for manual override shall be possible, operated by employees competent to do so, for shutting down equipment and protective systems incorporated within automatic processes which deviate from the intended operating conditions, provided that the provision or use of such means does not compromise safety;
    - on operation of emergency shutdown, accumulated energy shall be dissipated as quickly and as safely as possible or isolated so that it no longer constitutes a hazard; and
    - necessary measures shall be taken to prevent confusion between connecting devices.

Organisational Measures

The application of appropriate systems of work including the issuing of written instructions for the carrying out of the work and a system of permits-to-work with such permits being issued by a person with responsibility for this function prior to the commencement of the work concerned where the work is carried out in hazardous places or involves hazardous activities.

Schedule 2

(Which substantially reproduces the provisions of Annex I of **Council Directive 99/92/EC**.)

Classification of Places Where Explosive Atmospheres May Occur

Places where explosive atmospheres may occur.

A place in which an explosive atmosphere may occur in such quantities as to require special precautions to protect the health and safety of the workers concerned is deemed to be hazardous within the meaning of these Regulations.

A place in which an explosive atmosphere is not expected to occur in such quantities as to require special precautions is deemed to be non- hazardous within the meaning of these Regulations.

Classification of Hazardous Places

Hazardous places are classified in terms of zones on the basis of the frequency and duration of the occurrence of an explosive atmosphere.

Zone 0

A place in which an explosive atmosphere consisting of a mixture with air of dangerous substances in the form of gas, vapour or mist is present continuously or for long periods or frequently.

Zone 1

A place in which an explosive atmosphere consisting of a mixture with air of dangerous substances in the form of gas, vapour or mist is likely to occur in normal operation occasionally.

Zone 2

A place in which an explosive atmosphere consisting of a mixture with air of dangerous substances in the form of gas, vapour or mist is not likely to occur in normal operation but, if it does occur, will persist for a short period only.

Zone 20

A place in which an explosive atmosphere in the form of a cloud of combustible dust in air is present continuously, or for long periods or frequently.

Zone 21

A place in which an explosive atmosphere in the form of a cloud of combustible dust in air is likely to occur in normal operation occasionally.

Zone 22

A place in which an explosive atmosphere in the form of a cloud of combustible dust in air is not likely to occur in normal operation but, if it does occur, will persist for a short period only.

Schedule 3

Criteria for The Selection of Equipment and Protective Systems

Equipment and protective systems for all places in which explosive atmospheres may occur shall be selected on the basis of the requirements set out in the **Equipment and Protective Systems Intended for Use in Potentially Explosive Atmospheres Regulations 2016** unless the risk assessment finds otherwise.

In particular, the following categories of equipment shall be used in the zones indicated, provided they are suitable for gases, vapours, mists, dusts or mists and dusts, as appropriate:

- in zone 0 or zone 20, category 1 equipment,
- in zone 1 or zone 21, category 1 or 2 equipment,
- in zone 2 or zone 22, category 1, 2 or 3 equipment.

For the purposes of this Schedule and regulations 7(2) and 17(1):

(a) "equipment" means machines, apparatus, fixed or mobile devices, control components and instrumentation thereof and detection or prevention systems which, separately or jointly, are intended for the generation, transfer, storage, measurement, control and conversion of energy and the processing of material, as the case may be, and which are capable of causing an explosion through their own potential sources of ignition;

(b) "protective systems" means devices other than components of equipment which are intended to halt incipient explosions immediately or limit the effective range of an explosion or both, as the case may be, and which systems are separately placed on the market for use as autonomous systems;

(c) "devices" means safety devices, controlling devices and regulating devices intended for use outside potentially explosive atmospheres but required for or contributing to the safe functioning of equipment and protective systems with respect to the risks of explosion;

(d) "component" means any item essential to the safe functioning of equipment and protective systems but with no autonomous function; and

(e) "potentially explosive atmosphere" means an atmosphere which could become explosive due to local and operational conditions.

Schedule 4

(which substantially reproduces the provisions of Annex III of **Council Directive 99/92/EC.**)

Warning Sign for Places Where Explosive Atmospheres May Occur

Distinctive features:

(a) triangular shape;

(b) black letters on a yellow background with black edging (the yellow part to take up at least 50% of the area of the sign).

Schedule 5

Legislation Concerned with The Marking of Containers and Pipes The **Health and Safety (Safety Signs and Signals) Regulations 1996 (SI 1996/341)**. The **Good Laboratory Practice Regulations 1999 (SI 1999/3106)**.

The **CLP Regulation**.

The Carriage of Dangerous Goods and Use of Transportable Pressure Equipment Regulations 2009 (SI 2009/1348).

Schedule 6

Amendments

Paragraphs 1, 7 and 8 feature amendments to other legislation. The remaining paragraphs have been revoked.

Schedule 7

Repeal and Revocation

DANGEROUS SUBSTANCES (NOTIFICATION AND MARKING OF SITES) REGULATIONS 1990 (SI 1990 NO. 304)

Amending Legislation

The original regulations relied on a definition in the **Classification, Packaging and Labelling of Dangerous Substances Regulations 1984**. Subsequently these have been replaced on several occasions, and the relevant definition of "dangerous substance" is any substance that is classified as dangerous for conveyance in the **Carriage of Dangerous Goods and Use of Transportable Pressure Equipment Regulations 2007 (CDG 2007)**.

The **Health and Safety (Miscellaneous Repeals, Revocations and Amendments) Regulations 2013** have amended these Regulations to include a legal requirement to notify the fire and rescue service about any site storing 150 tonnes or more of ammonium nitrate and mixtures containing ammonium nitrate where the nitrogen content exceeds certain levels.

Regulation 1: Citation and Commencement

These Regulations came into force on 1 September 1990.

Regulation 2: Interpretation

"CDG 2007" means the **Carriage of Dangerous Goods and Use of Transportable Pressure Equipment Regulations 2007**. "The Safety Signs Regulations" means the **Health and Safety (Safety Signs and Signals) Regulations 1996**.

"Classification" in relation to a dangerous substance means the classification for that substance ascertained in accordance with regulation 47 of **CDG 2007**.

"Dangerous substance" means any substance which falls within the definition of "dangerous goods" in regulation 2(1) of **CDG 2007** and any reference to "dangerous substances" includes a reference to one dangerous substance.

"The Executive" means the Health and Safety Executive.

"Fire Authority" in relation to any site means the relevant authority (as defined in section 6 of the **Fire (Scotland) Act 2005**) for the area in which the site is situated or, in England and Wales, the fire and rescue authority under the **Fire and Rescue Services Act 2004** for the area in which the site is situated.

"Relevant ammonium nitrate mixtures" means ammonium nitrate and mixtures containing ammonium nitrate where the nitrogen content exceeds 15.75% of the mixture by weight.

"Site" means:

- the whole of an area of land under the control of a person and includes a pier, jetty or similar structure whether floating or not; or
- a structure, whether floating or not, which is within the inland waters of Great Britain and which is under the control of a person.

In the definitions of "classification" and "dangerous substance" the references to **CDG 2007** shall apply as if the substances in question were being carried by road.

Any reference to the person in control of a site is a reference to the person having such control in connection with the carrying on by him of a trade, business or other undertaking (whether for profit or not).

In determining the total quantity of dangerous substances or relevant ammonium nitrate mixtures present at a site account shall be taken of any quantity of dangerous substances or relevant ammonium nitrate mixtures which are in any vehicle, vessel, aircraft or hovercraft under the control of the person in control of the site which is used for storage purposes at the site; but no account shall be taken of any dangerous substances or relevant ammonium nitrate mixtures which are in a vehicle, vessel, aircraft or hovercraft used for transporting them or in the fuel tank of a vehicle, vessel, aircraft or hovercraft.

Regulation 3: Exceptions

The provisions of Schedule 1 (which sets out exceptions to the Regulations) shall have effect.

Regulation 4: Notification

The person in control of a site shall ensure that there is not present on site at any one time, a total quantity of 25 tonnes or more of dangerous substances, or a total quantity of 150 tonnes or more of relevant ammonium nitrate mixtures, unless the particulars specified in Part I of Schedule 2 have been notified in writing to the fire authority and the enforcing authority.

Where a notification has been made and a change specified in Part II of Schedule 2 takes place, the person in control of the site shall forthwith notify that change in writing to the fire authority and the enforcing authority.

Where a specified change has been notified, any resumption in the presence of a total quantity of 25 tonnes or more of dangerous substances at the site shall be subject to a fresh notification.

Regulation 5: Access Marking

The person in control of a site shall ensure that there is not present on site at any one time a total quantity of 25 tonnes or more of dangerous substances unless safety signs are displayed to give adequate warning to firemen before entering the site in an emergency that dangerous substances are present.

The safety signs referred to shall be warning signs as defined by the Safety Signs Regulations bearing the hazard warning symbol (but not the text) shown in Schedule 3 to these Regulations; and all such signs shall comply with respect to colours and layout.

Regulation 6: Location Marking

An inspector may give directions to the person in control of a site requiring him to display, at all times when a total quantity of 25 tonnes or more of dangerous substances is present at the site, safety signs at such locations within the site as are specified in the directions.

Directions may only be given where the inspector is satisfied on reasonable grounds that there is, or is liable to be present at any one time on site, a total quantity of 25 tonnes or more of dangerous substances and the display of safety signs at the locations is necessary in order to warn firemen in an emergency that dangerous substances are present.

The safety signs referred to shall be warning signs as defined with respect to colours and layout.

The warning signs and supplementary signs shall bear the hazard warning symbol and hazard warning text respectively. The hazard warning symbol and hazard warning text shall be:

- In the case where there is one dangerous substance or there are two or more dangerous substances with the same classification at the location where the signs are displayed, that specified in Schedule 3 appropriate to the classification of such substance or substances as specified.
- In the case where there are two or more dangerous substances with different classifications at the location where the signs are displayed, that specified for "mixed hazards".

Directions may be given by an inspector under this regulation in any such reasonable manner as he may think fit, and may be withdrawn by him at any time.

The person to whom directions are given shall comply with those directions, but safety signs need not be displayed at a location specified in the directions at a time when dangerous substances are not present at that location.

Any reference in this regulation to the presence of dangerous substances at a location is a reference to the presence of dangerous substances at or within the vicinity of that location.

Regulation 7: Signs to be Kept Clean, etc.

The person in control of the site shall, so far as is reasonably practicable, ensure that any safety signs displayed at the site are kept clean and free from obstruction.

Regulation 8: Enforcing Authority

In England and Wales, the enforcing authority for these Regulations shall be the fire authority except that:

- the enforcing authority for regulation 4 shall be ascertained in accordance with the **Health and Safety (Enforcing Authority) Regulations 1989**; and
- the enforcing authority for regulations 5 to 7 in relation to a site occupied by a body specified in regulation 4(3) of the said 1989 Regulations shall be the Executive.

In Scotland, the enforcing authority for these Regulations shall be the Scottish Fire and Rescue Service except that:

- the enforcing authority for regulation 4 shall be ascertained in accordance with the **Health and Safety (Enforcing Authority) Regulations 1989**; and
- the enforcing authority for regulations 5 to 7 in relation to a site occupied by a body specified in regulation 4(3) of the said 1989 Regulations shall be the Executive.

Regulation 9: Exemption Certificates

The Executive may, by certificate in writing, exempt any person or class of persons, or any activity or class of activities, from any requirement imposed by these Regulations. Any such exemption may be granted subject to conditions and to a time limit and may be revoked by a certificate in writing at any time. The Executive shall not grant exemption unless, having regard to the circumstances of the case, and in particular to the conditions, if any, which it proposes to attach to the exemption, and any other requirements imposed by or under any enactment which apply to the case, it is satisfied that the health and safety of persons who are likely to be affected by the exemption will not be prejudiced because of it.

There are four schedules to these Regulations:

- Schedule 1: Exceptions
- Schedule 2: Matters to be Notified
- Schedule 3: Table of Classifications and Hazard Warnings
- Schedule 4: Repeals and Enabling Powers

DATA PROTECTION ACT 2018

This is a lengthy piece of legislation, comprising 7 Parts, with 215 sections and 20 schedules. Accordingly, only an overview is provided here; full details should be obtained by reading the Act itself.

The **Data Protection Act 2018** makes provision for:

- the regulation of the processing of information relating to individuals;
- the Information Commissioner's functions under certain regulations relating to information;
- a direct marketing code of practice; and
- connected purposes.

This Act applies to the processing of personal data by a Controller or Processor who is based in the UK, regardless of whether the actual processing of the personal data takes place inside or outside the UK.

PART 1

Section 1 - Overview

- This Act makes provision about the processing of personal data.
- Most processing of personal data is subject to the **General Data Protection Regulation (GDPR)**.
- **Part 1** provides an overview of the Act, deals with the protection of personal data and gives definitions of key terms.
- **Part 2** supplements the **GDPR** (see Chapter 2) and applies a broadly equivalent regime to certain types of processing to which the **GDPR** does not apply (see Chapter 3).
- **Part 3** makes provision about the processing of personal data by competent authorities for law enforcement purposes and implements the **Law Enforcement Directive**.
- **Part 4** makes provision about the processing of personal data by the intelligence services.
- **Part 5** makes provision about the Information Commissioner.
- **Part 6** makes provision about the enforcement of the data protection legislation.
- **Part 7** makes supplementary provision, including provision about the application of this Act to the Crown and to Parliament.

Section 2 - Protection of Personal Data

(1) The **GDPR**, the applied **GDPR** and this Act protect individuals with regard to the processing of personal data, in particular by:
   (a) requiring personal data to be processed lawfully and fairly, on the basis of the 'data subject's' consent or another specified basis,
   (b) conferring rights on the 'data subject' to obtain information about the processing of personal data and to require inaccurate personal data to be rectified, and
   (c) conferring functions on the Commissioner, giving the holder of that office responsibility for monitoring and enforcing their provisions.
(2) When carrying out functions under the **GDPR**, the applied **GDPR** and this Act, the Commissioner must have regard to the importance of securing an appropriate level of protection for personal data, taking account of the interests of 'data subjects', controllers and others and matters of general public interest.

Section 3 (in part) - Terms Relating to the Processing of Personal Data

"Personal data" means any information relating to an identified or identifiable living individual where the **GDPR** does or does not apply, or where a competent authority or intelligence service processes personal data either automatically or as part of a filing system.

"Processing", in relation to information, means an operation or set of operations which is performed on information, or on sets of information, such as:

- collection, recording, organisation, structuring or storage,
- adaptation or alteration,

- retrieval, consultation or use,
- disclosure by transmission, dissemination or otherwise making available,
- alignment or combination, or
- restriction, erasure or destruction.

"Data subject" means the identified or identifiable living individual to whom personal data relates.

"Controller" and **"processor"**, in relation to the processing of personal data to which Chapter 2 or 3 of Part 2, Part 3 or Part 4 applies, have the same meaning as in that Chapter or Part.

"The data protection legislation" means:

- the **GDPR**,
- the applied **GDPR**,
- this Act,
- regulations made under this Act, and
- regulations made under section 2(2) of the **European Communities Act 1972** which relate to the **GDPR** or the **Law Enforcement Directive**.

PART 2

Sections 6 and 7 give the meanings of further terms such as "controller", "public body" and "public authority".

Sections 8 and 9 are concerned with the lawfulness of processing personal data.

Sections 10 and 11 deal with special categories of personal data.

The rights of the "data subject" are given in sections 12 to 14, whilst restrictions on the "data subject's" rights are detailed in sections 15 and 16.

Sections 22 to 28 deal with the application of the **GDPR** and relevant exemptions, including on grounds of national security and for the purposes of defence.

PART 3

The six "Data protection principles" are set out at sections 35 to 40.

Section 35 - The first data protection principle is that the processing of personal data for any of the law enforcement purposes must be lawful and fair.

Section 36 - The second data protection principle is that (a) the law enforcement purpose for which personal data is collected on any occasion must be specified, explicit and legitimate, and (b) personal data so collected must not be processed in a manner that is incompatible with the purpose for which it was collected.

Section 37 - The third data protection principle is that personal data processed for any of the law enforcement purposes must be adequate, relevant and not excessive in relation to the purpose for which it is processed.

Section 38 - The fourth data protection principle is that (a) personal data processed for any of the law enforcement purposes must be accurate and, where necessary, kept up to date, and (b) every reasonable step must be taken to ensure that personal data that is inaccurate, having regard to the law enforcement purpose for which it is processed, is erased or rectified without delay.

Section 39 - The fifth data protection principle is that personal data processed for any of the law enforcement purposes must be kept for no longer than is necessary for the purpose for which it is processed.

Section 40 - The sixth data protection principle is that personal data processed for any of the law enforcement purposes must be so processed in a manner that ensures appropriate security of the personal data, using appropriate technical or organisational measures (and, in this principle, "appropriate security" includes protection against unauthorised or unlawful processing and against accidental loss, destruction or damage).

Further provision the rights of the "data subject" are given at sections 43 to 54.

Sections 55 to 71 deal with the general obligations of data controllers and processors, including the duty to notify without undue delay a personal data breach to the Commissioner (section 67) and to the 'data subject' (section 68).

Transfers of personal data to third countries is covered in sections 72 to 78.

PART 4

Sections 82 to 113 are concerned with the processing of personal data by the intelligence services. The data protection principles as they apply to processing by the intelligence services are reiterated at sections 86 to 91. Rights of the 'data subject', including the right to information and the right to access personal data, are given in sections 92 to 100.

The obligations of controllers and processors regarding personal data are set out in sections 101 to 108.

PART 5

Sections 114 to 141 provide detail on the Information Commissioner's role, including general functions under the **GDPR** and safeguards and the international role of the Information Commissioner. Codes of practice on data sharing (section 121), direct marketing (section 122) and data protection and journalism (section 124) are included, as are the power to conduct consensual audits of compliance with good practice, records of national security certificates, and information provided to the Commissioner (including confidentiality). Arrangements for fees and charges, and for making reports to Parliament, are also included.

PART 6

Arrangements for enforcement are included at sections 142 to 181. This Part covers the issuing of "Information", "Assessment" and "Enforcement" notices. Powers of entry and inspection are laid out at section 154. Penalties are detailed at sections 155 to 159. The right to appeal is set out in section 162.

Sections 170 to 173 set out the offences relating to personal data, with relevant defences.

Section 170 - Unlawful Obtaining etc. of Personal Data

(1) It is an offence for a person knowingly or recklessly:
  (a) to obtain or disclose personal data without the consent of the controller,
  (b) to procure the disclosure of personal data to another person without the consent of the controller, or
  (c) after obtaining personal data, to retain it without the consent of the person who was the controller in relation to the personal data when it was obtained.

(2) It is a defence for a person charged with an offence under subsection (1) to prove that the obtaining, disclosing, procuring or retaining:
  (a) was necessary for the purposes of preventing or detecting crime,
  (b) was required or authorised by an enactment, by a rule of law or by the order of a court or tribunal, or
  (c) in the particular circumstances, was justified as being in the public interest.

(3) It is also a defence for a person charged with an offence under subsection (1) to prove that:
  (a) the person acted in the reasonable belief that the person had a legal right to do the obtaining, disclosing, procuring or retaining,
  (b) the person acted in the reasonable belief that the person would have had the consent of the controller if the controller had known about the obtaining, disclosing, procuring or retaining and the circumstances of it, or
  (c) the person acted:
    (i) for the special purposes,
    (ii) with a view to the publication by a person of any journalistic, academic, artistic or literary material, and
    (iii) in the reasonable belief that in the particular circumstances the obtaining, disclosing, procuring or retaining was justified as being in the public interest.

(4) It is an offence for a person to sell personal data if the person obtained the data in circumstances in which an offence under subsection (1) was committed.

(5) It is an offence for a person to offer to sell personal data if the person:
  (a) has obtained the data in circumstances in which an offence under subsection (1) was committed, or
  (b) subsequently obtains the data in such circumstances.

Section 171 - Re-identification of De-identified Personal Data

(1) It is an offence for a person knowingly or recklessly to re-identify information that is de-identified personal data without the consent of the controller responsible for de-identifying the personal data.

(2) For the purposes of this section and section 172 [Re-identification: effectiveness testing conditions]:
   (a) personal data is "de-identified" if it has been processed in such a manner that it can no longer be attributed, without more, to a specific 'data subject';
   (b) a person "re-identifies" information if the person takes steps which result in the information no longer being de-identified within the meaning of paragraph (a).

(3) It is a defence for a person charged with an offence under subsection (1) to prove that the re-identification:
   (a) was necessary for the purposes of preventing or detecting crime,
   (b) was required or authorised by an enactment, by a rule of law or by the order of a court or tribunal, or
   (c) in the particular circumstances, was justified as being in the public interest.

(4) It is also a defence for a person charged with an offence under subsection (1) to prove that:
   (a) the person acted in the reasonable belief that the person:
      (i) is the 'data subject' to whom the information relates,
      (ii) had the consent of that 'data subject', or
      (iii) would have had such consent if the 'data subject' had known about the re-identification and the circumstances of it,
   (b) the person acted in the reasonable belief that the person:
      (i) is the controller responsible for de-identifying the personal data,
      (ii) had the consent of that controller, or
      (iii) would have had such consent if that controller had known about the re-identification and the circumstances of it,
   (c) the person acted:
      (i) for the special purposes,
      (ii) with a view to the publication by a person of any journalistic, academic, artistic or literary material, and
      (iii) in the reasonable belief that in the particular circumstances the re-identification was justified as being in the public interest, or
   (d) the effectiveness testing conditions were met (see section 172).

(5) It is an offence for a person knowingly or recklessly to process personal data that is information that has been re-identified where the person does so:
   (a) without the consent of the controller responsible for de-identifying the personal data, and
   (b) in circumstances in which the re-identification was an offence under subsection (1).

(6) It is a defence for a person charged with an offence under subsection (5) to prove that the processing:
   (a) was necessary for the purposes of preventing or detecting crime,
   (b) was required or authorised by an enactment, by a rule of law or by the order of a court or tribunal, or
   (c) in the particular circumstances, was justified as being in the public interest.

(7) It is also a defence for a person charged with an offence under subsection (5) to prove that:
   (a) the person acted in the reasonable belief that the processing was lawful,
   (b) the person acted in the reasonable belief that the person:
      (i) had the consent of the controller responsible for de-identifying the personal data, or
      (ii) would have had such consent if that controller had known about the processing and the circumstances of it, or
   (c) the person acted:
      (i) for the special purposes,
      (ii) with a view to the publication by a person of any journalistic, academic, artistic or literary material, and
      (iii) in the reasonable belief that in the particular circumstances the processing was justified as being in the public interest.

DEREGULATION ACT 2015

Introduction

This Act introduced a number of provisions of relevance to health and safety at work, including an exemption of some self-employed persons from the application of section 3(2) of the 1974 Act.

Section 1 of the **Deregulation Act 2015** is a deregulatory provision because it will exempt from section 3(2) of the 1974 Act those self- employed persons who do not conduct a "prescribed undertaking".

Section 1 amends section 3 of the **Health and Safety at Work, etc. Act 1974** (general duty of employers and self-employed to persons other than their employees). An amendment to section 3(2) of the 1974 Act has the effect of limiting the scope of the general duty under that section so that only self-employed persons who conduct an "undertaking of a prescribed description" have an obligation to conduct their undertaking in such a way as to ensure that, so far as is reasonably practicable, they themselves and other persons who may be affected thereby are not exposed to risks to their health and safety. This exemption arose from the government-commissioned 2011 Löfstedt report, *Reclaiming health and safety for all*, which recommended that self-employed persons be exempt from health and safety law where they pose no potential risk of harm to others through their work activity. The underlying policy is that self-employed people will retain duties under section 3(2) only if their undertaking involves carrying out an activity which is specified within 'the regulations' (i.e. the **Health and Safety at Work, etc. Act 1974 (General Duties of Self-Employed Persons) (Prescribed Undertakings) Regulations 2015** - see the entry elsewhere in this guide).

A new subsection (2A) has been inserted into section 3 of the 1974 Act. This new subsection sets out ways in which undertakings may be described in regulations made under section 3(2) (as amended).

Section 1: Health and Safety at Work: General Duty of Self-Employed Persons

(1) Section 3 of the **Health and Safety at Work, etc. Act 1974** (general duty of employers and self-employed to persons other than their employees) is amended in accordance with subsections (2) and (3).

(2) In subsection (2) (which imposes a general duty with respect to health and safety on self-employed persons):

 (a) after "self-employed person" insert "who conducts an undertaking of a prescribed description";

 (b) for "his undertaking" substitute "the undertaking".

(3) After subsection (2) insert:

 "(2A) A description of undertaking included in regulations under subsection (2) may be framed by reference to:

 (a) the type of activities carried out by the undertaking, where those activities are carried out or any other feature of the undertaking;

 (b) whether persons who may be affected by the conduct of the undertaking, other than the self-employed person (or his employees), may thereby be exposed to risks to their health or safety." [...]

Section 6 of the **Deregulation Act 2015** amends section 11 of the **Employment Act 1989** (exemption of Sikhs from requirements to wear safety helmets on construction sites). The amendment extends the scope of the exemption in section 11 of the 1989 Act so that turban- wearing Sikhs will be exempt from legal requirements to wear a safety helmet in all workplaces, either as workers or visitors, subject to certain exclusions. This amendment does not remove the requirement for an employer to assess the risk to his employees, nor to make available any protective equipment, including head protection, considered to be necessary following the risk assessment. The decision not to wear appropriate head protection is to be made by the turban-wearing Sikh individual.

The exclusions referred to above apply to limited circumstances where the Sikh individual is:

- providing, or is training to provide, an urgent response to hazardous situations, such as fire or riots, where the wearing of a safety helmet is considered necessary to protect the Sikh from a risk of injury; or

- a member of, or a person providing support to, Her Majesty's Forces and is taking part in, or is training in how to take part in, a military operation where the wearing of a safety helmet is necessary to protect the Sikh from a risk of injury.

Section 7 provides for a similar exemption to section 6, except that this applies to article 13 of the **Employment (Miscellaneous Provisions) (Northern Ireland) Order 1990**, which applies in Northern Ireland only.

Section 108 imposes a duty on persons exercising certain regulatory functions (potentially health and safety inspectors) to have regard (in the exercise of those functions) to the desirability of promoting economic growth. In carrying out this duty, the person must, in particular, consider the importance of ensuring that any regulatory action they take is necessary and proportionate. This measure has been introduced following the post-implementation review of the Regulators' Compliance Code which found that regulators had a tendency to regard the promotion of economic growth as subsidiary to their statutory duties.

ELECTRICITY AT WORK REGULATIONS 1989 (SI 1989 NO. 635)

Summary

These Regulations impose health and safety requirements with respect to electricity at work.

The Regulations impose duties upon employers, self-employed persons, managers of mines and quarries and employees (regulation 3). The duties imposed by the Regulations do not, however, extend to the master or crew of a sea-going ship or to their employer in relation to the normal ship-board activities of a ship's crew under the direction of the master (regulation 32(a)); nor do those duties extend to any person in relation to any aircraft or hovercraft which is moving under its own power (regulation 32(b)).

These Regulations came into force on 1 April 1990. They do not contain voltage thresholds. Aside from the exceptions outlined above, they apply to all places of work.

"Danger" is defined as "risk of injury" and "injury" is defined as:

> "death or personal injury from electrical causes, fire or explosion associated with the generation, provision, transmission, transformation, rectification, conversion, conduction, distribution, control, storage, measurement or use of electrical energy".

The Regulations deal with the construction and maintenance of electrical systems; overloads; adverse or hazardous environments; insulation; protection and earthing; prohibition on switching the neutral conductor; joints to be mechanically sound; excess current protection; provision to cut off supply; prevention of re-energisation of equipment rendered dead; need to challenge need for live working; adequate lighting; need for employees to have the technical knowledge and experience to prevent danger.

The Regulations are supported by a **Memorandum of Guidance on the Electricity at Work Regulations** and two ACoPs relating to mines and quarries. The memorandum mentions the 16th edition (now superseded by the 17th edition) of the Institution of Electrical Engineers (now 'IET') Regulations as a "source of advice", although it has no legal status.

The **Low Voltage Electrical Equipment (Safety) Regulations 1989** implemented **Council Directive 73/23/EEC** on 1 June 1989 relating to all electrical equipment designed for use within the following ranges:

- Alternating current 50 to 1,000 volts.
- Direct current 75 to 1,500 volts.

Construction of equipment must comply with EU engineering practice to ensure safety when connected to the electricity supply and provide an acceptable level of protection against electrical shock.

The Regulations

The requirements are outlined in brief here.

- Regulations 1 and 2 name the Regulations and define the terms used.
- Regulation 3 outlines the dutyholders and mentions employers, self-employed, mine operators, quarry operators and employees. All dutyholders are required to comply with the Regulations. In addition, employees must also co-operate with their employer.
- Regulation 4 requires systems to be constructed to prevent danger and to be maintained to prevent danger. Work activities, such as operation, use and maintenance of a system shall be carried out so as not to give rise to danger, and suitable protective equipment shall be provided and maintained.
- Regulation 5 requires that no electrical equipment be put into use where its strength and capability may be exceeded in such a way as may give rise to danger.
- Regulation 6 deals with electrical equipment that may be exposed to adverse hazardous environments and requires the construction or protection to be sufficient to prevent danger from arising.
- Regulation 7 requires all conductors in a system which may give rise to danger to be either suitably covered with insulating material and protected, or to have suitable precautions taken, including being suitably placed, to prevent danger.
- Regulation 8 deals with earthing, or other suitable means, to prevent danger arising when any conductor, other than the circuit conductor, may become charged as a result of either use of the system or a fault developing in the system.
- Regulation 9 deals with the integrity of referenced conductors, while regulation 10 stipulates that where necessary to prevent danger, every joint and connection in a system shall be mechanically and electrically suitable for use.

- Regulation 11 covers the provision of efficient means to protect every part of the system from excess current and regulation 12 requires suitable means for cutting off the supply of electrical equipment and of isolating that equipment.
- Regulation 13 is an important regulation requiring that adequate precautions are taken to prevent electrical equipment which has been made dead, in order to prevent danger while work is carried out on or near that equipment, from becoming electrically charged if danger may arise. Regulation 14 prevents working on or near live conductors where danger may arise, unless it is unreasonable for them to be dead, and it is reasonable to work on or near to them while live, and suitable precautions are taken to prevent injury.
- Regulation 15 requires that adequate working space, access and lighting be provided at all electrical equipment on which, and near which, work is carried out, and which may give rise to danger.
- Regulation 16 is very important and concerns the competence of the persons carrying out electrical work. The Memorandum requires them to have the technical knowledge and experience to avoid danger when carrying out the specific work undertaken. Blanket competence is not considered to be sufficient. In addition, where the employer does not have the expertise required by the Regulations in-house, then external services may have to be brought in to ensure compliance.

NB: Regulations 17 to 28 were concerned only with mines but were revoked on 6 April 2015 by the **Mines Regulations 2014**.

- Lastly, regulation 29 deals with the defences available under the Regulations to persons charged with offences in criminal proceedings. It stipulates that, with regard to contraventions of certain regulations, it shall be a defence to prove that the dutyholder took all reasonable steps and "exercised all due diligence" to avoid the commission of an offence.

The "due diligence" defence relies, in essence, upon demonstrating that however much care was taken the injury would still have occurred.

The Memorandum to the Regulations contains a wealth of technical detail aimed at clarifying the Regulations. It is also worth remembering that "electricity" is classed as a product for the purposes of the **Consumer Protection Act 1987** and this means that, where a defect occurs in an electrical installation or system that results in injury, damage or death, liability is strict.

ELECTRICITY SAFETY, QUALITY AND CONTINUITY REGULATIONS 2002 (SI 2002 NO. 2665)

The Electricity Safety, Quality and Continuity Regulations 2002 replace the **Electricity Supply Regulations 1988** and all subsequent amendments. They impose requirements regarding the installation and use of electrical networks and equipment owned or operated by generators, distributors (which include, in these Regulations, transmitters), and meter operators, and the participation of suppliers in providing electricity to consumers (all such persons are collectively referred to as "dutyholders" in this note). Agents, contractors and sub-contractors of duty holders also have duties under these Regulations. These Regulations were notified in draft to the European Commission in accordance with **Council Directive 98/34/EC** (O.J. No. L 204, 21.7.1998, p. 37) as amended by **Council Directive 98/48/EC** (O.J. No. L 217, 5.8.1998, p. 18).

Part I (Regulations 1-5)

Contains introductory provisions.

Regulation 1 contains defined terms; because these Regulations are targeted at technical and safety requirements, some of the defined terms have a different meaning from those used in the **Electricity Act 1989** and in the **Utilities Act 2000**.

"High voltage" means any voltage exceeding low voltage.

"Low voltage" means:

- in relation to alternating current, a voltage exceeding 50 volts but not exceeding 1,000 volts; and
- in relation to direct current, a voltage exceeding 120 volts but not exceeding 1,500 volts.

Regulation 2 contains time-limited exemptions for continued use of old equipment not complying with the requirements of the Regulations (e.g. pre-1937 cut-outs) and for the phased introduction of several new requirements (e.g. risk assessment of substations).

Regulation 3 contains general duties relating to the safe use and operation of equipment, and requires risk registers to be maintained for substations and overhead lines.

Regulation 4 requires duty holders to co-operate as necessary in order that they may each comply with these Regulations.

Regulation 5 imposes requirements on dutyholders to inspect their equipment and to maintain certain records for at least 10 years.

Part II (Regulations 6-10)

Contains provisions relating to electrical protection and earthing.

Regulation 6 imposes a requirement for generators and distributors to install adequate protective devices in their networks. Regulation 7 requires generators and distributors to ensure continuity of the supply neutral conductor.

Regulation 8 imposes certain requirements for connections with earth for all systems, and also for high voltage networks and for low voltage networks in particular.

Regulation 9 contains requirements for distributors operating protective multiple earthing systems, including the circumstances in which earthing terminals of consumers' installations should not be connected to the distributor's combined neutral and protective conductor.

Regulation 10 contains requirements for earthing of metalwork.

Part III (Regulation 11)

Contains provisions relating to substations, specifically requirements for enclosures, safety and other signs (see Schedule 1), and fire precautions.

Part IV (Regulations 12-15)

Contains provisions relating to underground cables and associated equipment. Regulation 12 imposes restrictions on the use of underground cables.

Regulation 13 imposes requirements for mechanical protection of such equipment and regulation 14 contains requirements regarding the depth and manner of installation.

Regulation 14 states:

(1) Every conductor below ground shall be placed at such depth or be otherwise protected as to avoid, so far as is reasonably practicable, any damage or danger by reason of such uses of the land which can reasonably be expected when the conductor is placed below ground.

(2) In addition to satisfying the requirements of paragraph (1), an underground cable containing conductors not connected with earth shall be protected, marked or otherwise indicated so as to ensure, so far as is reasonably practicable, that any person excavating the ground above the conductor will receive a warning of its presence.

(3) The protection, marking or indication required by paragraph (2) shall be made by placing the cable in a pipe or duct or by overlaying the cable at a suitable distance with protective tiles or warning tape or by the provision of such other protective or warning device, mark or indication, or by a suitable combination of such measures, as will be likely to provide an appropriate warning.

Regulation 15 requires generators and distributors to maintain maps of underground cables and equipment and to permit inspection by, and to provide copies to, specified persons.

(1) This regulation applies in respect of any network or part thereof, owned or operated by a generator or distributor which is below ground on land which is not under his control.

(2) Every generator or distributor shall have and, so far as is reasonably practicable, keep up to date, a map or series of maps indicating the position and depth below surface level of all networks or parts thereof which he owns or operates.

(3) The generator or distributor shall make a copy of the whole or the relevant part of any map prepared or kept for the purposes of paragraph (2) available for inspection by any of:

   (a) the Secretary of State;

   (b) the local planning authority, or, in Scotland, the planning authority, for the area where the network or part thereof is situated; and

   (c) any other person who can show reasonable cause for requiring to inspect any part of the map, and shall, on request, provide a copy of such map or part of the map.

(4) The generator or distributor may, at his discretion, require payment of a reasonable fee for the inspection or copying of the map or part thereof referred to in paragraph (3).

(5) Any map prepared for the purposes of paragraph (2) may be prepared and kept by electronic means provided that that means has the capability of reproducing such map in printed form.

(6) Nothing in this regulation shall require the inclusion, on a map prepared or kept for the purposes of paragraph (2), of information relating to the position and depth below surface level of networks or parts thereof which were placed below ground before 1 October 1988 where it would not be reasonably practicable to obtain such information.

Part V (Regulations 16-20)

Contains provisions relating to overhead lines.

Regulation 16 specifies the equipment affected by this Part and imposes a limit on nominal voltage.

Regulation 17 imposes minimum heights for overhead electric lines and other cables (with further requirements in Schedule 2).

(1) Subject to paragraph (3), the height above ground of any overhead line, at the maximum likely temperature of that line, shall not be less than that specified by paragraph (2).

(2) In relation to an overhead line used, or intended to be used, at a voltage specified in column 1 of Schedule 2 the height referred to in paragraph (1) shall be:

   (a) at any point where that line is over a road accessible to vehicular traffic, the height specified in column 2 of Schedule 2 as appropriate to that voltage; and

   (b) at any other point, the height specified in column 3 of Schedule 2 as appropriate to that voltage.

(3) Paragraph (2) does not apply to any overhead line at a point where it is not over a road accessible to vehicular traffic and which:

    (a) is surrounded by insulation; or

    (b) is not surrounded by insulation and is at least 4.3 metres above ground and connects equipment mounted on a support to any overhead line; or

    (c) is connected with earth.

(4) The height above ground of any wire or cable which is attached to a support carrying any overhead line shall not be less than 5.8 metres at any point where it is over any road accessible to vehicular traffic.

Regulation 18 contains requirements relating to insulation and protection of such lines.

(1) Any part of an overhead line which is not connected with earth and which is not ordinarily accessible shall be supported on insulators or surrounded by insulation.

(2) Any part of an overhead line which is not connected with earth and which is ordinarily accessible shall be:

    (a) made dead; or

    (b) so insulated that it is protected, so far as is reasonably practicable, against mechanical damage or interference; or

    (c) adequately protected to prevent danger.

(3) Any person responsible for erecting a building or structure which will cause any part of an overhead line which is not connected with earth to become ordinarily accessible shall give reasonable notice to the generator or distributor who owns or operates the overhead line of his intention to erect that building or structure.

(4) Any bare conductor not connected with earth shall be situated, throughout its length, vertically above a bare electric line which is connected with earth.

(5) No overhead line shall, so far as is reasonably practicable, come so close to any building, tree or structure as to cause danger.

(6) In this regulation the expression "ordinarily accessible" means the overhead line could be reached by hand if any scaffolding, ladder or other construction was erected or placed on, in, against or near to a building or structure.

Regulation 19 imposes requirements to prevent access to high voltage overhead conductors and to fix safety signs to supports for overhead lines (see Schedule 1).

(1) Every support carrying a high voltage overhead line shall, if the circumstances reasonably require, be fitted with devices to prevent, so far as is reasonably practicable, any unauthorised person from reaching a position at which any such line would be a source of danger.

(2) Every support carrying a high voltage overhead line, and every support carrying a low voltage overhead line incorporating bare phase conductors, shall have attached to it sufficient safety signs complying with Schedule 1 of such size and placed in such positions as are necessary to give due warning of such danger as is reasonably foreseeable in the circumstances.

Regulation 20 relates to fitting insulators to stay wires for supports carrying overhead lines.

Part VA (Regulation 20A)

The single regulation in this Part relates to avoidance of interference with, or interruption of, supply caused by trees.

Part VI (Regulations 21 and 22)

Contains provisions relating to generation.

Regulation 21 requires persons to ensure switched alternative sources of energy remain isolated from a distributor's network.

Regulation 22 imposes requirements on persons intending to operate a source of energy in parallel with a distributor's network.

Part VII (Regulations 23-29)

Contains general requirements relating to the provision of electricity to consumers' installations and other networks.

Regulation 23 requires distributors to take precautions against supply failure.

Regulation 24 contains provisions relating to distributors' and meter operators' equipment on consumers' premises, including electrical protection, security and connections to consumers' earthing terminals.

Regulation 25 specifies requirements for persons connecting new installations or new networks to a distributor's network, with provision for settling disputes arising from a distributor's delay in giving or refusal to give consent for connections.

Regulation 26 specifies the procedure if a distributor considers that an installation is unsafe or is causing interference and the procedure to challenge the distributor's refusal to give or continue a supply.

Regulation 27 imposes requirements to give information relating to a supply and to maintain the quality of supply within certain tolerance limits.

Regulation 28 requires other information affecting a consumer to be provided on request.

Regulation 29 permits distributors to discontinue a supply for such period as may be necessary under certain circumstances.

Part VIII (Regulations 30-36)

Contains miscellaneous provisions.

Regulation 30 entitles inspectors appointed by the Secretary of State to the provision of facilities and information where an inspection of a generator's or distributor's network or equipment is being carried out.

Regulation 31 and Schedule 3 contain a requirement on generators, distributors and meter operators to give particulars to the Secretary of State relating to accidents and other events involving their networks and equipment and domestic consumers' installations.

Regulation 32 and Schedule 4 contain a requirement on a distributor to give notice to the Secretary of State of specified interruptions of supply to consumers.

Regulation 33 permits the Secretary of State to grant exemptions from the Regulations, and regulation 34 enables the Secretary of State to prohibit the use of networks or equipment owned or operated by duty holders or of a consumer's installation in specified circumstances, with provision for settling disputes.

Regulation 35 provides that specified persons who fail to comply with specified provisions of the Regulations commit an offence under section 29 of the **Electricity Act 1989**.

Regulation 36 and Schedule 5 specify Regulations (the **Electricity Supply Regulations 1988** and subsequent amendments) which are revoked by these Regulations.

SCHEDULE 1

Regulations 11(c)(i) and 19(2)

DESIGN, COLOURS AND PROPORTIONS OF THE SAFETY SIGN

1. A safety sign shall be of the design, and shall have the proportions, shown in the diagram below, except that the height of the text may be increased to a maximum of $0.12 \times L$.

2. The triangle, symbol and text shall be shown in black on a yellow background.

3. The symbol shall not occupy more than 50% of the area within the triangle.

4. A safety sign may include additional text but any such text:

    (a) shall be in black; and

    (b) shall be the same size as the text used on the safety sign,

and no part of any additional text shall appear on the sign higher than the base of the triangle.

SCHEDULE 2

Regulation 17(2)

MINIMUM HEIGHT ABOVE GROUND OF OVERHEAD LINES

Column 1	Column 2	Column 3
NOMINAL VOLTAGES	**Over Roads**	**Other Locations**
Not exceeding 33,000 volts	5.8 metres	5.2 metres
Exceeding 33,000 volts but not exceeding 66,000 volts	6 metres	6 metres
Exceeding 66,000 volts but not exceeding 132,000 volts	6.7 metres	6.7 metres
Exceeding 132,000 volts but not exceeding 275,000 volts	7 metres	7 metres
Exceeding 275,000 volts but not exceeding 440,000 volts	7.3 metres	7.3 metres

EMPLOYERS' HEALTH AND SAFETY POLICY STATEMENTS (EXCEPTION) REGULATIONS 1975 (SI 1975 NO. 1584)

These Regulations came into operation on 1 November 1975 and provide an exemption for very small businesses from the requirement to have a written statement of general health and safety policy.

Exception from Provisions Relating to Employers' Health and Safety Policy Statements

Regulation 2:

Any employer who carries on an undertaking in which for the time being he employs less than five employees is hereby excepted as respects that undertaking from the provisions of subsection (3) of section 2 of the **Health and Safety at Work, etc. Act 1974** (which subsection requires employers to bring to the notice of their employees a written statement of their general policy with respect to the health and safety at work of their employees and the organisation and arrangements for the time being in force for carrying out that policy).

EMPLOYERS' LIABILITY (COMPULSORY INSURANCE) ACT 1969

Amending Legislation

The **Employers' Liability (Compulsory Insurance) Regulations 1998** consolidated with amendments the **Employers' Liability (Compulsory Insurance) General Regulations 1971** and subsequent amending regulations made under the **Employers' Liability (Compulsory Insurance) Act 1969**.

The principal changes made by the regulations were to raise the sum to be insured from not less than £2 million to not less than £5 million.

Section 1: Insurance Against Liability for Employees

The following are important points.

(1) Every employer carrying on any business in Great Britain shall insure, and maintain insurance, under one or more approved policies with an authorised insurer or insurers against liability for bodily injury or disease sustained by his employees, and arising out of and in the course of their employment in Great Britain in that business, but except in so far as regulations otherwise provide not including injury or disease suffered or contracted outside Great Britain.

(2) Regulations may provide that the amount for which an employer is required by this Act to insure and maintain insurance shall, either generally or in such cases or classes of case as may be prescribed by the regulations, be limited in such manner as may be so prescribed.

(3) For the purposes of this Act:

- "Approved" policy means a policy of insurance not subject to any conditions or exceptions prohibited for those purposes by regulations.
- "Authorised Insurer" means a person or body of persons lawfully carrying on in the United Kingdom insurance business of a class specified in the **Insurance Companies Act 1982**, or, being an insurance company the head office of which is in a member State, lawfully carrying on in a member State other than the United Kingdom insurance business of a corresponding class, and issuing the policy or policies in the course thereof.
- "Business" includes a trade or profession, and includes any activity carried on by a body of persons, whether corporate or unincorporated.

Except as otherwise provided by regulations, an employer not having a place of business in Great Britain shall be deemed not to carry on business there.

Section 2: Employees to be Covered

The term "Employee" means an individual who has entered into or works under a contract of service or apprenticeship with an employer whether by way of manual labour, clerical work or otherwise, whether such contract is expressed or implied, oral or in writing.

This Act shall not require an employer to insure:

- in respect of an employee of whom the employer is the husband, wife, civil partner, father, mother, grandfather, grandmother, stepfather, stepmother, son, daughter, grandson, granddaughter, stepson, stepdaughter, brother, sister, half-brother or half-sister; or
- except as otherwise provided by regulations, in respect of employees not ordinarily resident in Great Britain.

Section 3: Employers Exempted from Insurance

This Act shall not require any insurance to be effected by:

- Any body corporate established by or under any enactment for the carrying on of any industry or part of an industry, or of any undertaking, under national ownership or control.
- In relation to any such cases as may be specified in the regulations, any employer exempted by regulations.
- Any of the following authorities:
  - a health service body, as defined in section 60(7) of the **National Health Service and Community Care Act 1990**;
  - the National Health Service Commissioning Board, a clinical commissioning group established under section 14D of the **National Health Service Act 2006**;
  - a National Health Service trust established under section 25 of the **National Health Service Act 2006**, section 18 of the **National Health Service (Wales) Act 2006** or the **National Health Service (Scotland) Act 1978**, an NHS foundation trust and a Local Health Board established under section 11 of the **National Health Service (Wales) Act 2006**;

- the Common Council of the City of London;
- the council of a London borough;
- the council of a county or county district in England;
- the council of a county or county borough in Wales;
- the Broads Authority;
- a National Park authority;
- a council constituted under section 2 of the **Local Government etc. (Scotland) Act 1994** in Scotland;
- any joint board or joint committee in England and Wales or joint committee in Scotland which is so constituted as to include among its members representatives of any such council;
- the Strathclyde Passenger Transport Authority;
- any joint authority established by Part IV of the **Local Government Act 1985**;
- an economic prosperity board established under section 88 of the **Local Democracy, Economic Development and Construction Act 2009**;
- a combined authority established under section 103 of that Act;
- an authority established for an area in England by an order under section 207 of the **Local Government and Public Involvement in Health Act 2007** (joint waste authorities);
- the London Fire and Emergency Planning Authority;
- any local policing body;
- any chief constable established under section 2 of the **Police Reform and Social Responsibility Act 2011**;
- the Commissioner of Police of the Metropolis;
- the Scottish Police Authority and the Scottish Fire and Rescue Service;
- the Commission for Equality and Human Rights.

Section 4: Certificates of Insurance

Provision may be made by regulations for securing that certificates of insurance in such form and containing such particulars as may be prescribed by the regulations, are issued by insurers to employers entering into contracts of insurance in accordance with the requirements of this Act and for the surrender in such circumstances as may be so prescribed of certificates so issued.

Where a certificate of insurance is required to be issued to an employer in accordance with regulations, the employer (subject to any provision made by the regulations as to the surrender of the certificate) shall during the currency of the insurance and such further period (if any) as may be provided by regulations:

- comply with any regulations requiring him to display copies of the certificate of insurance for the information of his employees;
- produce the certificate of insurance or a copy thereof on demand to any inspector duly authorised by the Secretary of State for the purposes of this Act and produce or send the certificate or a copy thereof to such other persons, at such place and in such circumstances as may be prescribed by regulations;
- permit the policy of insurance or a copy thereof to be inspected by such persons and in such circumstances as may be so prescribed.

A person who fails to comply with a requirement imposed by or under this section shall be liable on summary conviction to a fine not exceeding level 3 on the standard scale.

Section 5: Penalty for Failure to Insure

An employer who on any day is not insured in accordance with this Act when required to be so shall be guilty of an offence and shall be liable on summary conviction to a fine not exceeding level 4 on the standard scale. Where an offence under this section committed by a corporation has been committed with the consent or connivance of, or facilitated by any neglect on the part of, any director, manager, secretary or other officer of the corporation, he, as well as the corporation shall be deemed to be guilty of that offence and shall be liable to be proceeded against and punished accordingly.

EMPLOYER'S LIABILITY (DEFECTIVE EQUIPMENT) ACT 1969

Section 1: Extension of Employer's Liability for Defective Equipment

(1) Where:

- an employee suffers personal injury in the course of his employment in consequence of a defect in equipment provided by his employer for the purposes of the employer's business; and the defect is attributable wholly or partly to the fault of a third party (whether identified or not), the injury shall be deemed to be also attributable to negligence on the part of the employer (whether or not he is liable in respect of the injury apart from this subsection) but without prejudice to the law relating to contributory negligence and to any remedy by way of contribution or in contract or otherwise which is available to the employer in respect of the injury.

(2) In so far as any agreement intends to exclude or limit any liability of an employer arising under the above subsection, the agreement shall be void.

(3) In this section:

- "business" includes the activities carried on by any public body;
- "employee" means a person who is employed by another person under a contract of service or apprenticeship and is so employed for the purposes of a business carried on by that other person: and
- "employer" shall be construed accordingly;
- "equipment" includes any plant and machinery, vehicle, aircraft and clothing;
- "fault" means negligence, breach of statutory duty or other act or omission which gives rise to liability in tort in England and Wales or which is wrongful and gives rise to liability in damages in Scotland;
- "personal injury" includes loss of life, any impairment of a person's physical or mental condition and any disease.

(4) This section binds the Crown, and persons in the service of the Crown shall accordingly be treated as employees of the Crown.

This Act does not extend to Northern Ireland.

EMPLOYMENT RIGHTS ACT 1996

[In part]

Amending Legislation

The **Employment Relations Act 1999** (ERA 99) amended the **Employment Rights Act 1996** by removing existing monetary limits to compensation in cases where employees are dismissed or victimised in some way as a result of exposing a danger to health and safety at work, thus resulting in parity with the provisions of the **Public Interest Disclosure Act 1998**. The ERA 99, section 37, removed the financial limit for compensatory awards in cases of unfair dismissal for health and safety reasons.

Minor and consequential amendments have been made by the **Employment Act 2002**. Further amendments have been made by the **Enterprise and Regulatory Reform Act 2013**, the **Employment Rights (Employment Particulars and Paid Annual Leave) (Amendment) Regulations 2018** and the **Employment Rights (Miscellaneous Amendments) Regulations 2019**, the **Employment Rights (Employment Particulars and Paid Annual Leave) (Amendment) Regulations 2018** and the **Employment Rights (Miscellaneous Amendments) Regulations 2019**.

The Act

The Act has 245 sections and 3 schedules, only a few of which have any direct bearing on health and safety at work. They are summarised here.

Section 1: Statement of Initial Employment Particulars

Where a worker begins employment with an employer, the employer shall give the worker a written statement of particulars of employment. An amendment introduced by the **Employment Rights (Employment Particulars and Paid Annual Leave) (Amendment) Regulations 2018** gives workers who have started employment on or after 6 April 2020 the right to receive the bulk of the 'Statement of particulars' on their first day of employment. Employers can decide to give particulars **Rights (Employment Particulars and Paid Annual Leave) (Amendment) Regulations 2018** gives workers who have started employment on or after 6 April 2020 the right to receive the bulk of the 'Statement of particulars' on their first day of employment. Employers can decide to give particulars in instalments provided all are given within two months and the majority are given on day 1.

The statement shall contain particulars of:

- the names of the employer and worker;
- the date when the employment began; and
- in the case of a statement given to an employee, the date on which the employee's period of continuous employment began, taking into account any employment with a previous employer which counts towards that period.

The statement shall also contain particulars of:

- the scale or rate of remuneration or the method of calculating remuneration;
- the intervals at which remuneration is paid- weekly, monthly or other specified intervals;
- any terms and conditions relating to hours of work including any terms and conditions relating to normal working hours, the days of the week the worker is required to work, and whether or not such hours or days may be variable, and if they may be how they vary or how that variation is to be determined;
- any terms and conditions relating to entitlement to holidays (including public holidays and holiday pay), incapacity for work due to sickness or injury, including any provision for sick pay, any other paid leave, and pensions and pension schemes (see **Note (1)** below); (see **Note (1)** below);
- any other benefits provided by the employer that do not fall within another paragraph of this subsection;
-
- the length of notice which the worker is obliged to give and entitled to receive to terminate his contract of employment or other worker's contract or other worker's contract;
- the title of the job which the worker is employed to do or a brief description of the work for which he is employed;
- where the employment is not intended to be permanent, the period for which it is expected to continue or, if it is for a fixed term, the date when it is to end;
- any probationary period, including any conditions and its duration (see **Note (2)** below);
- any probationary period, including any conditions and its duration (see **Note (2)** below);

- either the place of work or, where the worker is required or permitted to work at various places, an indication of that and of the address of the employer;
- any collective agreements which directly affect the terms and conditions of the employment including, where the employer is not a party, the persons by whom they were made; and
- where the worker is required to work outside the United Kingdom for a period of more than one month:
  - the period for which he is to work outside the United Kingdom;
  - the currency in which remuneration is to be paid while he is working outside the United Kingdom and any additional remuneration and any benefits payable to him, by reason of his being required to work outside the United Kingdom; and
  - any terms and conditions relating to his return to the United Kingdom;
- any training entitlement provided by the employer;
- any part of that training entitlement which the employer requires the worker to complete; and
- any other training which the employer requires the worker to complete and which the employer will not bear the cost of.

Notes:

- The requirement for the statement to contain particulars of the terms and conditions of pensions and pension schemes does not apply to a worker of a body or authority if the worker's pension rights depend on the terms of a pension scheme established under any provision contained in or having effect under an Act, and any such provision requires the body or authority to give to a new worker information concerning the worker's pension rights or the determination of questions affecting those rights.
- A 'probationary period' means a temporary period specified in the contract of employment or other worker's contract between a worker and an employer that commences at the beginning of the employment and is intended to enable the employer to assess the worker's suitability for the employment.

If there is a change in any of the particulars, the employer is required to give the worker a written statement containing particulars of the change.

- any training entitlement provided by the employer;
- any part of that training entitlement which the employer requires the worker to complete; and
- any other training which the employer requires the worker to complete and which the employer will not bear the cost of.

Notes:

(1) The requirement for the statement to contain particulars of the terms and conditions of pensions and pension schemes does not apply to a worker of a body or authority if the worker's pension rights depend on the terms of a pension scheme established under any provision contained in or having effect under an Act, and any such provision requires the body or authority to give to a new worker information concerning the worker's pension rights or the determination of questions affecting those rights.

(2) A 'probationary period' means a temporary period specified in the contract of employment or other worker's contract between a worker and an employer that commences at the beginning of the employment and is intended to enable the employer to assess the worker's suitability for the employment.

If there is a change in any of the particulars, the employer is required to give the worker a written statement containing particulars of the change.

Section 11: References to Employment Tribunals

workerworkerWhere a statement under section 1 or section 4 (a statement of changes to the particulars required by section 1), or a pay statement or a standing statement of fixed deductions has been given to a worker, and a question arises as to the particulars which ought to have been included or referred to in the statement, either the employer or the worker may require the question to be referred to and determined by an employment tribunal.

An employment tribunal shall not consider a reference under this section in a case where the employment to which the reference relates has ceased unless an application was made before the end of the period of three months beginning with the date on which the employment ceased, or within such further period as the tribunal considers reasonable.

A further subsection (subsection (6)) was added by the **Enterprise and Regulatory Reform Act 2013**. This new subsection relates to the extension of time limits to facilitate conciliation before institution of proceedings.

Section 43B: Disclosures Qualifying for Protection

A "qualifying disclosure" means any disclosure of information which, in the reasonable belief of the worker making the disclosure is made in the public interest and tends to show one or more of the following:

- that a criminal offence has been committed, is being committed or is likely to be committed;
- that a person has failed, is failing or is likely to fail to comply with any legal obligation to which he is subject;
- that a miscarriage of justice has occurred, is occurring or is likely to occur;
- that the health or safety of any individual has been, is being or is likely to be endangered;
- that the environment has been, is being or is likely to be damaged; or
- that information tending to show any of the above matters has been, or is likely to be deliberately concealed.

It is immaterial whether the relevant failure occurred, occurs or would occur in the United Kingdom or elsewhere, and whether the law applying to it is that of the United Kingdom or of any other country or territory.

A disclosure of information is not a qualifying disclosure if the person making the disclosure commits an offence by making it.

A disclosure of information in respect of which a claim to legal professional privilege could be maintained in legal proceedings is not a qualifying disclosure if it is made by a person to whom the information had been disclosed in the course of obtaining legal advice.

Section 43C: Disclosure to Employer or Other Responsible Person

A qualifying disclosure is made in accordance with this section if the worker makes the disclosure in good faith:

- to his employer, or
- where the worker reasonably believes that the relevant failure relates solely or mainly to the conduct of a person other than his employer, or any other matter for which a person other than his employer has legal responsibility, to that other person.

A worker who, in accordance with a procedure whose use by him is authorised by his employer, makes a qualifying disclosure to a person other than his employer, is to be treated as making the qualifying disclosure to his employer.

Section 43D: Disclosure to Legal Adviser

A qualifying disclosure is made in accordance with this section if it is made in the course of obtaining legal advice.

Section 44: Health and Safety Cases

This and following sections deal with protection from suffering detriment in employment.

An employee has the right not to be subjected to any detriment by any act, or any deliberate failure to act, by his employer done on the ground that:

- having been designated by the employer to carry out activities in connection with preventing or reducing risks to health and safety at work, the employee carried out (or proposed to carry out) any such activities;
- being a representative of workers on matters of health and safety at work or member of a safety committee the employee performed (or proposed to perform) any functions as such a representative or a member of such a committee.

An employee has the right not to be subjected to detriment by any act or deliberate failure to act by his employer done on the ground that:

- The employee took part (or proposed to take part) in consultation with the employer pursuant to the **Health and Safety (Consultation with Employees) Regulations 1996** or in an election of representatives of employee safety within the meaning of those Regulations (whether a candidate or otherwise).
- Being an employee at a place where there was no such representative or safety committee, or there was such a representative or safety committee but it was not reasonably practicable for the employee to raise the matter by those means, he brought to his employer's attention, by reasonable means, circumstances connected with his work which he reasonably believed were harmful or potentially harmful to health or safety.

An employee has the right not to be subjected to detriment by an act or deliberate failure to act by his employer done on the ground that:

- in circumstances of danger which the employee reasonably believed to be serious and imminent and which he could not reasonably have expected to avert, he left (or proposed to leave) or (while the danger persisted) refused to return to his place of work or any dangerous part of his place of work, or
- in circumstances of danger which the employee reasonably believed to be serious and imminent, he took (or proposed to take) appropriate steps to protect himself or other persons from the danger.

For the purposes of the latter point, whether steps which the employee took (or proposed to take) were appropriate is to be judged by reference to all the circumstances including, in particular, his knowledge and the facilities and advice available to him at the time.

An employee is not to be regarded as having been subjected to a detriment on the ground specified above if the employer shows that it was (or would have been) so negligent for the employee to take the steps which he took (or proposed to take) that a reasonable employer might have treated him as the employer did.

Section 47: Employee Representatives

An employee has the right not to be subjected to any detriment by any act, or any deliberate failure to act, by his employer done on the ground that, being an employee representative or a candidate in an election in which any person elected will be such an employee representative, he performed (or proposed to perform) any functions or activities as such an employee representative or candidate.

An employee has the right not to be subjected to any detriment by any act, or by any deliberate failure to act, by his employer done on the ground of his participation in an election of employee representatives.

Section 47B: Protected Disclosures

A worker has the right not to be subjected to any detriment by any act or any deliberate failure to act by his employer, by another worker in the course of that worker's employment, or by an agent of the worker's employer with the employer's authority, on the ground that the worker has made a protected disclosure.

Where a worker is subjected to detriment by anything done by another worker or by an agent of the worker's employer, that thing is treated as also done by the worker's employer. It is immaterial whether the thing is done with the knowledge or approval of the worker's employer.

The worker's employer has a defence that the employer took all reasonable steps to prevent the other worker from doing that thing, or from doing anything of that description.

Section 48: Complaints to Employment Tribunals

An employee may present a complaint to an employment tribunal that he has been subjected to a detriment.

On such a complaint it is for the employer to show the ground on which any act, or deliberate failure to act, was done.

An employment tribunal shall not consider a complaint under this section unless it is presented before the end of the period of three months beginning with the date of the act or failure to act to which the complaint relates or, where that act or failure is part of a series of similar acts or failures, the last of them, or within such further period as the tribunal considers reasonable.

Section 49: Remedies

Where an employment tribunal finds a complaint under section 48 well-founded, the tribunal shall make a declaration to that effect, and may make an award of compensation to be paid by the employer to the complainant in respect of the act or failure to act.

The amount of compensation awarded shall be such as the tribunal considers just and equitable in all the circumstances having regard to the infringement to which the complaint relates, and any loss which is attributable to the act, or failure to act, which infringed the complainant's right.

The loss shall be taken to include any expenses reasonably incurred by the complainant in consequence of the act, or failure to act, and loss of any benefit which he might reasonably be expected to have had but for that act or failure to act.

In ascertaining the loss the tribunal shall apply the same rule concerning the duty of a person to mitigate his loss as applies to damages recoverable under the common law of England and Wales or (as the case may be) Scotland.

Where the tribunal finds that the act, or failure to act, was to any extent caused or contributed to by action of the complainant, it shall reduce the amount of the compensation by such proportion as it considers just and equitable having regard to that finding.

Where the complaint is made under section 48(1A) (for having made a protected disclosure) and it appears to the tribunal that the protected disclosure was not made in good faith, the tribunal may, if it considers it just and equitable in all the circumstances to do so, reduce any award it makes to the worker by no more than 25%.

Section 61: Right to Time Off for Employee Representatives

An employee who is an employee representative or a candidate in an election in which any person elected will, on being elected, be such an employee representative, is entitled to be permitted by his employer to take reasonable time off during the employee's working hours in order to perform his functions as such an employee representative or candidate or in order to undergo training to perform such functions.

The working hours of an employee shall be taken to be any time when, in accordance with his contract of employment, the employee is required to be at work.

Section 62: Right to Remuneration for Time Off under Section 61

An employee who is permitted to take time off under section 61 is entitled to be paid remuneration by his employer for the time taken off at the appropriate hourly rate. The appropriate hourly rate is the amount of one week's pay divided by the number of normal working hours in a week for that employee when employed under the contract of employment in force on the day when the time off is taken. Where the number of normal working hours differs from week to week or over a longer period, the amount of one week's pay shall be divided instead by the average number of normal working hours calculated by dividing by 12 the total number of the employee's normal working hours during the period of 12 weeks ending with the last complete week before the day on which the time off is taken.

Where the employee has not been employed for a sufficient period to enable this calculation to be made, the amount of one week's pay shall be divided by a number which fairly represents the number of normal working hours in a week as are appropriate in the circumstances.

The considerations referred to are:

- the average number of normal working hours in a week which the employee could expect in accordance with the terms of his contract, and
- the average number of normal working hours of other employees engaged in relevant comparable employment with the same employer.

A right to any amount under the above does not affect any right of an employee in relation to remuneration under his contract of employment ("contractual remuneration").

Any contractual remuneration paid to an employee in respect of a period of time off under section 61 goes towards discharging any liability of the employer to pay remuneration in respect of that period, and, conversely, any payment of remuneration in respect of a period goes towards discharging any liability of the employer to pay contractual remuneration in respect of that period.

Section 63: Complaints to Employment Tribunals

An employee may present a complaint to an employment tribunal where his employer has unreasonably refused to permit him to take time off under section 61 or failed to make any payments to which the employee is entitled under section 62. The complaint must be presented to the employment tribunal before the end of the period of three months beginning with the day on which the time off was taken or on which it is alleged that time off should have been permitted, or within such further period as the tribunal considers reasonable.

Section 86: Rights of Employer and Employee to Minimum Notice

The notice required to be given by an employer to terminate the contract of employment of a person who has been continuously employed for one month or more is not less than:

- one week's notice if his period of continuous employment is less than two years;
- one week's notice for each year of continuous employment if his period of continuous employment is two years or more but less than 12 years; and
- 12 weeks' notice if his period of continuous employment is 12 years or more.

The notice required to be given by an employee who has been continuously employed for one month or more to terminate his contract of employment is not less than one week.

Any provision for shorter notice in any contract of employment with a person who has been continuously employed for one month or more has effect but this does not prevent either party from waiving his right to notice on any occasion or from accepting a payment in lieu of notice.

Any contract of employment of a person who has been continuously employed for three months or more which is a contract for a term certain of one month or less shall have effect as if it were for an indefinite period and accordingly, the above periods of notice apply to the contract. They do not apply to a contract made in contemplation of the performance of a specific task which is not expected to last for more than three months unless the employee has been continuously employed for a period of more than three months. This does not affect any right of either party to a contract of employment to treat the contract as terminable without notice by reason of the conduct of the other party.

Section 92: Right to Written Statement of Reasons for Dismissal

An employee is entitled to be provided by his employer with a written statement giving particulars of the reasons for the employee's dismissal:

- if the employee is given by the employer notice of termination of his contract of employment,
- if the employee's contract of employment is terminated by the employer without notice, or
- if the employee is employed under a limited-term contract and the contract terminates by virtue of the limiting event without being renewed under the same contract.

An employee is entitled to a written statement only if he makes a request for one and if so a statement shall be provided within 14 days of such a request.

An employee is not entitled to a written statement unless on the effective date of termination he has been, or will have been, continuously employed for a period of not less than two years ending with that date.

An employee is entitled to a written statement without having to request it and irrespective of whether she has been continuously employed for any period if she is dismissed:

- at any time while she is pregnant, or
- after childbirth in circumstances in which her ordinary or additional maternity leave period ends by reason of the dismissal.

An employee who is dismissed while absent from work during an ordinary or additional adoption leave period is entitled to a written statement under this section without having to request it and irrespective of whether he has been continuously employed for any period if he is dismissed in circumstances in which that period ends by reason of the dismissal.

A written statement is admissible in evidence in any proceedings.

'The effective date of termination' means:

- in relation to an employee whose contract of employment is terminated by notice, the date on which the notice expires;
- in relation to an employee whose contract of employment is terminated without notice, the date on which the termination takes effect; and
- in relation to an employee who is employed under a limited-term contract which terminates by virtue of the limiting event without being renewed under the same contract, the date on which the termination takes effect.

Where the contract of employment is terminated by the employer, and the required notice to be given by an employer would, if duly given on the material date, expire on a date later than the effective date of termination, the later date is the effective date of termination.

'The material date' means the date when notice of termination was given by the employer, or where no notice was given, the date when the contract of employment was terminated by the employer.

Section 94: The Right Not to be Unfairly Dismissed

An employee has the right not to be unfairly dismissed by his employer.

Section 95: Circumstances in which an Employee is Dismissed

An employee is dismissed by his employer if:

- the contract under which he is employed is terminated by the employer (whether with or without notice),
- he is employed under a limited-term contract and that contract terminates by virtue of the limiting event without being renewed under the same contract, or
- the employee terminates the contract under which he is employed (with or without notice) in circumstances in which he is entitled to terminate it without notice by reason of the employer's conduct.

An employee shall be taken to be dismissed by his employer if:

- the employer gives notice to the employee to terminate his contract of employment, and
- at a time within the period of that notice the employee gives notice to the employer to terminate the contract of employment on a date earlier than the date on which the employer's notice is due to expire; and
- the reason for the dismissal is to be taken to be the reason for which the employer's notice is given.

Section 98: General

This and following sections deal with fairness.

In determining whether the dismissal of an employee is fair or unfair, it is for the employer to show the reason (or, if more than one, the principal reason) for the dismissal and that it is either a reason given below or some other substantial reason of a kind such as to justify dismissal of an employee holding the position which the employee held.

The potentially fair reasons are that the dismissal:

- relates to the capability or qualifications of the employee for performing work of the kind which he was employed to do;
- relates to the conduct of the employee;
- is for the reason that the employee was redundant; or

- is for the reason that the employee could not continue to work in the position which he held without contravention (either on his part or on that of his employer) of a duty or restriction imposed by or under an enactment.

"Capability", in relation to an employee, means his capability assessed by reference to skill, aptitude, health or any other physical or mental quality.

"Qualifications", in relation to an employee, means any degree, diploma or other academic, technical or professional qualification relevant to the position which he held.

Where the employer has fulfilled the above requirements, the determination of the question whether the dismissal is fair or unfair depends on whether in the circumstances (including the size and administrative resources of the employer's undertaking) the employer acted reasonably or unreasonably in treating it as a sufficient reason for dismissing the employee, and shall be determined in accordance with equity and the substantial merits of the case.

Section 100: Health and Safety Cases

An employee who is dismissed shall be regarded as unfairly dismissed if the reason (or, if more than one, the principal reason) for the dismissal is that having been designated by the employer to carry out activities in connection with preventing or reducing risks to health and safety at work, the employee carried out (or proposed to carry out) any such activities; or being a representative of workers on matters of health and safety at work or member of a safety committee, the employee performed (or proposed to perform) any functions as such a representative or a member of such a committee.

An employee who is dismissed shall be regarded as unfairly dismissed where:

- being an employee at a place where there was no such representative or safety committee, or there was such a representative or safety committee but it was not reasonably practicable for the employee to raise the matter by those means, he brought to his employer's attention, by reasonable means, circumstances connected with his work which he reasonably believed were harmful or potentially harmful to health or safety;

- in circumstances of danger which the employee reasonably believed to be serious and imminent and which he could not reasonably have been expected to avert, he left (or proposed to leave) or (while the danger persisted) refused to return to his place of work or any dangerous part of his place of work; or

- in circumstances of danger which the employee reasonably believed to be serious and imminent, he took (or proposed to take) appropriate steps to protect himself or other persons from the danger.

For the purposes of the above, whether steps which an employee took (or proposed to take) were appropriate is to be judged by reference to all the circumstances including, in particular, his knowledge and the facilities and advice available to him at the time.

An employee shall not be regarded as unfairly dismissed if the employer shows that it was (or would have been) so negligent for the employee to take the steps which he took (or proposed to take) that a reasonable employer might have dismissed him for taking (or proposing to take) them.

Section 101A: Working Time Cases

An employee who is dismissed shall be regarded as unfairly dismissed if the reason (or, if more than one, the principal reason) for the dismissal is that the employee:

- refused (or proposed to refuse) to comply with a requirement which the employer imposed (or proposed to impose) in contravention of the **Working Time Regulations 1998**;

- refused (or proposed to refuse) to forgo a right conferred on him by those Regulations;

- failed to sign a workforce agreement for the purposes of those Regulations, or to enter into, or agree to vary or extend, any other agreement with his employer which is provided for in those Regulations; or

- being a representative of members of the workforce or a candidate in an election in which any person elected will, on being elected, be such a representative, performed (or proposed to perform) any functions or activities as such a representative or candidate.

Section 103: Employee Representatives

An employee who is dismissed shall be regarded as unfairly dismissed if the reason (or, if more than one, the principal reason) for the dismissal is that the employee, being an employee representative, or a candidate in an election in which any person elected will, on being elected, be such an employee representative, performed (or proposed to perform) any functions or activities as such an employee representative or candidate.

An employee who is dismissed shall be regarded as unfairly dismissed if the reason (or, if more than one, the principal reason) for the dismissal is that the employee took part in an election of employee representatives.

Section 111: Complaints to Employment Tribunal

A complaint may be presented to an employment tribunal against an employer by any person that he was unfairly dismissed by the employer. An employment tribunal shall not consider a complaint under this section unless it is presented to the tribunal:

- before the end of the period of three months beginning with the effective date of termination, or
- within such further period as the tribunal considers reasonable in a case where it is satisfied that it was not reasonably practicable for the complaint to be presented before the end of that period of three months.

The time period can be extended because of mediation in certain cross-border disputes (see section 207A). In such cases, the time limit expires instead at the end of four weeks after mediation ends.

Where a dismissal is with notice, an employment tribunal shall consider a complaint under this section if it is presented after the notice is given but before the effective date of termination.

In relation to a complaint which is presented as mentioned above, the provisions of this Act, so far as they relate to unfair dismissal, have effect as if:

- references to a complaint by a person that he was unfairly dismissed by his employer included references to a complaint by a person that his employer has given him notice in such circumstances that he will be unfairly dismissed when the notice expires;
- references to reinstatement included references to the withdrawal of the notice by the employer;
- references to the effective date of termination included references to the date which would be the effective date of termination on the expiry of the notice; and
- references to an employee ceasing to be employed included references to an employee having been given notice of dismissal.

Where the dismissal is alleged to be unfair by virtue of section 104F (blacklists), an employment tribunal may consider a complaint that is otherwise out of time if, in all the circumstances of the case, it considers that it is just and equitable to do so.

Section 112: The Remedies: Orders and Compensation

This section applies where, on a complaint under section 111, an employment tribunal finds that the grounds of the complaint are well-founded.

The tribunal shall explain to the complainant what orders may be made under section 113 (i.e. an order for reinstatement or re-engagement), and in what circumstances they may be made, and ask him whether he wishes the tribunal to make such an order.

If the complainant expresses such a wish, the tribunal may make an order under section 113.

If no order is made, the tribunal shall make an award of compensation for unfair dismissal to be paid by the employer to the employee.

ENTERPRISE AND REGULATORY REFORM ACT 2013

This Act came into force in October 2013 and makes a wide range of provisions for the reduction of legislative burdens. Of primary relevance in the field of health and safety are the changes concerning protected disclosures (sections 17-20) and the changes to civil liability for breach of health and safety duties (section 69).

Relevant changes to the **Employment Rights Act 1996** have been included in the coverage of that Act elsewhere in this document. The purposes of the Act include:

- To make provision about employment law.
- To establish and make provision about the Competition and Markets Authority.
- To abolish the Competition Commission and the Office of Fair Trading.
- To make provision for the reduction of legislative burdens.
- To make provision about copyright.
- To amend section 9(5) of the **Equality Act 2010**.

The Act:

- Creates a better employment tribunal system by encouraging parties to come together to settle their dispute before an employment tribunal claim is lodged, through Advisory, Conciliation and Arbitration Services' (ACAS) early conciliation and greater use of settlement agreements.
- Takes forward a number of measures announced through the Government's Red Tape Challenge, including changes so that in future civil claims for breach of health and safety duties can only be brought where it can be proved that an employer has been negligent.
- It also establishes the principle that an employer should always have the opportunity, even where a strict duty applies, to defend themselves on the basis of having taken all reasonable steps to protect their employees. In this regard, section 69 amends section 47 of the **Health and Safety at Work, etc. Act 1974** (civil liability). The effect of this change is to remove the option to bring a claim for breach of statutory duty in the majority of circumstances. The revised version of section 47 may be found within the coverage of the 1974 Act elsewhere in this document.
- Simplifies regulation through reduced inspection burdens.
- Repeals unnecessary laws and time-limits new laws so that there are only ever relevant and necessary laws in place.
- Extends the Primary Authority Scheme to provide consistent regulatory advice to thousands more small firms.
- Makes amendments to the composition of the Employment Appeal Tribunal (with effect from 25 June 2013).
- Has also been a vehicle for a wide range of repeals and reforms to existing law.

Most provisions came into force in October 2013 or April 2014.

ENVIRONMENTAL DAMAGE (PREVENTION AND REMEDIATION) (ENGLAND) REGULATIONS 2015 (SI 2015 NO. 810)

These Regulations came into force on 19 July 2015 and replace the **Environmental Damage (Prevention and Remediation) Regulations 2009**. There are 36 regulations followed by six schedules. The following text concentrates on relevant sections and requirements.

Minor amendments were introduced by the **Environmental Damage (Prevention and Remediation) (England) (Amendment) Regulations 2015** and the **Environmental Damage (Prevention and Remediation) (England) (Amendment) Regulations 2017 and 2019**.

Part 1: Introductory Provisions

Regulation 2: Interpretation

"Activity" means any economic activity, whether public or private and whether or not carried out for profit.

"Baselines" means the baselines from which the breadth of the territorial sea is measured for the purposes of the **Territorial Sea Act 1987**.

"Marine waters" means waters classified as marine waters pursuant to **Directive 2008/56/EC** of the European Parliament and of the Council establishing a framework for Community action in the field of marine environmental policy.

"Natural habitat" means habitats of species that are protected and listed, for example those that are defined in the **Conservation of Wild Birds Directive** whose natural range includes any part of the UK's territory.

"Natural resource" means:

(a) protected species;

(b) natural habitats;

(c) species or habitats on a Site of Special Scientific Interest (SSSI);

(d) water; and

(e) land.

"Operator" means the person who operates or controls an activity, including the holder of the permit or authorisation relating to that activity, or the person registering or notifying an activity for the purposes of any enactment.

"Protected species" means the species mentioned in **Directive 2009/147/EC** or **Directive 92/43/EEC** whose natural range includes any part of the UK's territory.

Powers are provided to the Welsh Ministers in relation to environmental damage in Wales, except where the damage is caused by certain specified operations regulated on a UK-wide basis.

Regulation 4: Meaning of "Environmental Damage"

These Regulations aim to prevent and remediate environmental damage which is defined as including damage to a protected species or natural habitat, a site of special scientific interest, surface water or groundwater, marine waters or land.

Regulation 5: Environmental Damage to which these Regulations Apply

These Regulations apply to environmental damage if it is caused by an activity mentioned in Schedule 2. For environmental damage to a protected species, natural habitat or a site of special scientific interest, these Regulations will also apply in relation to environmental damage caused by any other activity if the operator intended to cause environmental damage or was negligent as to whether environmental damage would be caused.

Regulation 6: Areas of Application

These Regulations apply in England and all waters up to one nautical mile seaward from the baselines in England and up to 12 nautical miles from the baselines in Wales and Northern Ireland.

Regulation 7: Other Legislation

These Regulations do not override any other legislation concerning damage to the environment.

Regulation 8: Exemptions

These Regulations do not apply to:

- Damage before 1 March 2009.
- Damage that occurred after 1 March 2009, or is or was threatened after that date, but is caused by an incident, event or emission that took place before that date.
- Damage caused by an incident, event or emission that takes or took place after that date if it derives from an activity that took place and finished before that date.
- Environmental damage caused by:
    - an act of terrorism;
    - an exceptional natural phenomenon;
    - activities the sole purpose of which is to protect against natural disasters;
    - an incident in respect of which liability or compensation falls within the scope of various International Conventions;
    - activities the main purpose of which is to serve national defence or international security;
    - radioactivity from an activity covered by the Treaty establishing the European Atomic Energy Community or caused by an incident or activity in respect of which liability falls within the scope of the Paris Convention on Third Party Liability in the Field of Nuclear Energy and the Brussels Supplementary Convention;
    - any activity carried out in the course of commercial sea fishing if all legislation relating to that fishing was complied with;
    - pollution of a diffuse character where it is not possible to establish a causal link between the damage and specific activities.

Regulation 9: Exclusion from Damage to Water

Subject to certain conditions being satisfied, damage to water does not include damage caused by new modifications to the physical characteristics of a surface water body, an alteration to the level of a body of groundwater pursuant to **Directive 2000/60/EC** or deterioration from high status to good status of a body of surface water resulting from new sustainable human development activities where article 4 (7) of that Directive is complied with.

Regulation 10: Enforcing Authorities Under the Environmental Permitting (England and Wales) Regulations 2016

These Regulations are enforced in accordance with this regulation if damage is caused by an activity that requires a permit or registration under the **Environmental Permitting (England and Wales) Regulations 2016**.

If either the Environment Agency or Natural Resources Wales is responsible for granting the permit, and the damage is to marine waters in the Welsh zone, or to a natural habitat or protected species or an SSSI in those waters, it is to be enforced by the Welsh Ministers. In all other cases the Environment Agency is the regulator.

If the local authority grants the permit, Part 2 is enforced by the local authority; Part 3 is enforced by the local authority if the damage is to land, by the Environment Agency if the damage is to water or by Natural England if the damage is to natural habitats or protected species or an SSSI. If a local authority in Wales is responsible for granting a permit, the Regulations are to be enforced by the Welsh Ministers if the damage is to marine waters in the Welsh zone, or to a natural habitat or protected species or an SSSI in those waters. In any other case the Environment Agency is the enforcement body.

Regulation 11: Enforcing Authorities in Other Cases

If the damage is caused by an activity that does not require a permit or registration under the **Environmental Permitting (England and Wales) Regulations 2016**, the Regulations are enforced as below:

- Damage to water - Environment Agency.
- Damage to surface water or groundwater - Environment Agency.
- Damage to marine waters - Marine Management Organisation.
- Damage to natural habitats, protected species or SSSIs on land - Natural England.
- Damage to natural habitats, protected species or SSSIs in water - Environment Agency.

Regulation 12: Enforcement

These Regulations can be enforced by any or all of the enforcing authorities in cases where there is more than one type of environmental damage. An enforcing authority may appoint any other enforcing authority to act on its behalf.

Part 2: Preventing Environmental Damage

Regulations 13 and 14: Preventing Environmental Damage/Preventing Further Environmental Damage

An operator of an activity that causes an imminent threat of environmental damage or has caused environmental damage must take all practicable steps to prevent that/further damage and notify the enforcing authority. The enforcing authority may serve a notice on the operator that describes the threat, specifies measures required to prevent danger and requires the operator to take those measures or measures equivalent to them, within a specified period.

Regulation 15: Action by the Enforcing Authority

Any duty in Part 2 placed on the operator of an activity may be carried out by the enforcing authority in an emergency, if the operator cannot be ascertained or if the operator fails to comply with a notice under regulation 13(2) or 14(2).

Regulation 16: Following Instructions from a Public Authority

When an operator acts in accordance with the instructions of a public authority and, as a result, causes or threatens to cause environmental damage and action is subsequently taken under regulations 13, 14 or 15, the operator may recover the costs of those actions from the public authority unless the instructions related to an emission or incident caused by the operator's own activities.

Part 3: Remediation

Regulation 17: Assessment of Damage

The enforcing authority must establish whether or not there has been environmental damage.

Regulation 18: Determining Liability to Remediate

If the enforcing authority establishes that the damage is environmental damage, it must notify the responsible operator of that fact and that the operator's activity was the cause of the damage. The enforcing authority must also notify the operator to submit proposals, within a specified timeframe, for measures that will achieve remediation of the damage in accordance with Schedule 3. The operator has a right to appeal. The enforcing authority may withdraw the notification if it is satisfied that it should not have been served or that an appeal is likely to succeed.

If an enforcing authority serves a notice to a responsible operator for remediation of environmental damage then the enforcing authority must as soon as is reasonably practicable notify the Secretary of State.

If an enforcing authority serves a notice to a responsible operator for remediation of environmental damage then the enforcing authority must as soon as is reasonably practicable notify the Secretary of State.

Regulation 19: Appeals Against Liability to Remediate

A person served with a notice under regulation 18 can appeal by giving notice to the Secretary of State. Notice of appeal must be served within 28 days of service of the notification under regulation 18 unless the time limit is extended by the Secretary of State.

Grounds for appeal are:

(a) the operator's activity was not a cause of the environmental damage;

(b) the enforcing authority has acted unreasonably in deciding that the damage is environmental damage;

(c) the environmental damage resulted from compliance with an instruction from a public authority;

(d) the operator was not at fault or negligent and the damage was caused by an emission or event expressly authorised by, and fully in accordance with, the conditions of a permit listed in Schedule 4;

(e) the operator was not at fault or negligent and the damage was caused by an emission or activity or any manner of using a product in the course of an activity, that the operator demonstrates was not considered likely to cause environmental damage according to the state of scientific and technical knowledge at the time when the emission was released or the activity took place; or

(f) the damage was the result of an act of a third party and occurred despite the fact that the operator had taken all appropriate safety measures.

Procedures for appeal are contained in Schedule 5. The result of an appeal may be that the notice is confirmed or quashed.

Regulation 20: Remediation Notices

On receipt of proposals from the operator, the enforcing authority must, so far as is practicable, consult any person who has notified an enforcing authority under regulation 29 and any person on whose land the remedial measures will be carried out. The enforcing authority may consult any other person appearing to it to be necessary. Following consultation, the enforcing authority must serve a notice on the operator that specifies the damage, remediation measures (together with reasons), the period within which those measures must be taken, any additional monitoring or investigative measures that the operator must carry out during remediation, and the right of appeal against the notice.

Where a responsible operator has received a notice from the enforcing authority under regulation 18, it is required to identify potential remedial measures (in compliance with Schedule 3) and submit them in writing to the enforcing authority for approval.

Regulation 21: Appeal Against a Remediation Notice

The operator may appeal on the grounds that the contents of the notice are unreasonable; notice of appeal must be given to the Secretary of State. Notice of appeal must be served within 28 days of service of the remediation notice unless the time limit is extended by the Secretary of State. The notice may be confirmed, varied or quashed. The Secretary of State must give written notification of the final decision and the reasons for it and may, if appropriate, add further compensatory remediation requirements necessitated by the lapse of time since the remediation notice was served. A remediation notice need not be complied with pending determination of an appeal unless the person hearing the appeal directs otherwise.

Regulation 22: Further Provisions on Remediation Notices

Further remediation notices may be served at any time while remediation is being carried out or, if remediation has not been achieved, at the end of the remediation period.

Regulation 23: Action by the Enforcing Authority

Once the enforcing authority has established that, in its opinion, the damage is environmental damage, it may carry out any reasonable works at any time if the responsible operator cannot be identified, if the responsible operator fails to comply with the remedial notice (whether or not an appeal is pending) or if the responsible operator is not required to carry out remediation under the Regulations.

Part 4: Administration, Enforcement and Review

Regulation 24: Costs when the Enforcing Authority Acts Instead of the Operator

An operator who is liable to carry out works under Part 2 is liable for the reasonable costs incurred by the enforcing authority in taking any reasonable action under regulation 15. The responsible operator is liable for the reasonable costs of the enforcing authority for any action taken under regulation 23(a) or (b).

Regulation 25: Costs Concerned with Administration

An operator who is liable to carry out works under Part 2 is liable for reasonable costs incurred by the enforcing authority in preparing any notice under Part 2, or in ensuring compliance with Part 2.

The responsible operator is liable for the costs incurred by the enforcing authority under Part 3 of:

- assessing whether damage is environmental damage;
- establishing who is the responsible operator;
- establishing appropriate remediation;
- carrying out necessary consultation; and
- monitoring the remediation, both during and after the work.

Regulation 26: Proceedings for Costs by an Enforcing Authority

The enforcing authority cannot commence proceedings for the recovery of costs under these Regulations after a period of five years since the completion of the measures to which the proceedings relate or the identification of the operator liable to carry out the measures, whichever is the later.

Regulation 27: Costs Recoverable from Owner to be a Charge on Premises

Where costs are recoverable under these Regulations from an owner of premises and the enforcing authority serves a notice on that person under this regulation, the costs will carry interest at such reasonable rate as the authority may determine from the date of service of the notice until the whole amount is paid, and the costs and accrued interest are a charge on the premises.

A notice served under this regulation must specify the amount of the costs that the enforcing authority claims is recoverable, that costs carry interest and that costs and accrued interest are a charge on the premises with effect from a period of 21 days beginning with the date of service of the notice or, where an appeal is brought, as from the final determination or withdrawal of the appeal. A person served with a notice under this regulation has 21 days from the date of service to appeal to the County Court.

The Court may confirm the notice without modification, order that the notice is to have effect with the substitution of a different amount for the amount originally specified in it, or order that the notice is to be of no effect.

Regulation 28: Recovery of Costs from Other Persons

Operators who incur liability under these Regulations may recover all or part of their costs from any other person who also caused the damage.

Regulation 29: Requests for Action by Interested Parties

Any person who is affected or likely to be affected by environmental damage, or who otherwise has a sufficient interest, may notify the appropriate enforcing authority of any environmental damage which is being, or has been caused, or of which there is an imminent threat.

The enforcing authority must consider the notification and inform the notifier of the action, if any, that it intends to take. If practicable, and before taking any decision, the enforcing authority must notify the operator concerned of the notification and invite the operator to submit comments.

The enforcing authority does not have to consider the notification, notify the operator or invite the operator to comment if, in the opinion of the enforcing authority, the notifier is not likely to be affected or does not have a sufficient interest, or the information provided does not disclose any environmental damage or threat thereof, or as a result of the urgency of the situation it is not practicable to comply.

Regulation 30: Grant of, and Compensation for, Rights of Entry etc

Any person whose consent is required before any works required by these Regulations may be carried out must grant such rights in relation to any land or water as will enable the operator or their representative to carry out that work. A person who grants rights is, upon application, entitled to compensation from the operator determined in accordance with Schedule 6.

Regulation 31: Powers of Authorised Persons

Enforcing authorities may authorise persons for the purposes of enforcing these Regulations. The powers in section 108 of the **Environment Act 1995** apply in relation to these Regulations. Additional powers are granted to a person authorised by the Secretary of State in relation to the sea.

Regulation 32: Provision of Information to the Enforcing Authority

An enforcing authority may require an operator to provide such information as it may reasonably require for the purpose of enabling the enforcing authority to carry out its functions under these Regulations. Failure to provide such information is an offence.

Regulation 33: Enforcement

Enforcement action cannot be taken after 30 years from the date of the emission, event or incident concerned.

Regulation 34: Penalties

A person guilty of an offence is liable on summary conviction to a fine or imprisonment for up to 3 months or both. Upon conviction on indictment, a person is liable to a fine or to imprisonment not exceeding two years or both.

Where a body corporate is guilty of an offence that is proved to have been committed with the consent or connivance of, or to have been attributable to any neglect on the part of any director, manager, secretary or other similar person of the body corporate, or on the part of any person who was purporting to act in any such capacity, that person is guilty of the offence as well as the body corporate.

Regulation 35: Review

The Secretary of State must from time to time carry out a review of these Regulations and set out the conclusions of the review in a published report. The report must set out the objectives to be achieved by the regulatory system established in these Regulations, assess the extent to which those objectives have been achieved and must assess whether those objectives remain appropriate and, if so, the extent to which they could be achieved with a system that imposes less regulation.

The Schedules

There are six schedules to these Regulations:

- Schedule 1: Damage to Protected Species, Natural Habitats and Sites of Special Scientific Interest
- Schedule 2: Activities Causing Damage
- Schedule 3: Remediation
- Schedule 4: Permits, etc.
- Schedule 5: Procedures for Appeals
- Schedule 6: Compensation

ENVIRONMENTAL DAMAGE (PREVENTION AND REMEDIATION) (WALES) REGULATIONS 2009 (SI 2009 NO. 995)

These Regulations came into force on 6 May 2009 and apply in relation to Wales. There are 34 regulations followed by six schedules. The text below concentrates on relevant sections and requirements.

A number of amendments were made to the Regulations by the **Environmental Damage (Prevention and Remediation) (Amendment) (Wales) Regulations 2015 (SI 2015 No. 1394)**: and the **Environmental Damage (Prevention and Remediation) (Wales) (Amendment) (No.2) Regulations 2015 (SI 2015 No. 1937)**.

Part 1: Introductory Provisions

Regulation 2: Interpretation

"Activity" means any economic activity, whether public or private and whether or not carried out for profit.

"Baseline" means the baselines from which the breadth of the territorial sea is measured for the purposes of the **Territorial Sea Act 1987**.

"Groundwater" means all water that is below the surface of the ground in the saturation zone and in direct contact with the ground or subsoil.

"Marine waters" means waters classified as marine waters pursuant to **Directive 2008/56/EC** of the European Parliament and of the Council establishing a framework for Community action in the field of marine environmental policy.

"Natural habitat" means:

(a) the habitats of species mentioned in article 4 (2) of, or Annex I to, **Council Directive 2009/147/EC** on the conservation of wild birds or listed in Annex II to **Council Directive 92/43/EEC** on the conservation of natural habitats and of wild fauna and flora;

(b) the natural habitats listed in Annex I to **Council Directive 92/43/EEC**; and

(c) the breeding sites or resting places of the species listed in Annex IV to **Council Directive 92/43/EEC**.

"Natural resource" means:

(a) protected species;

(b) natural habitats;

(c) species or habitats on a site of special scientific interest for which the site has been notified under section 28 of the **Wildlife and Countryside Act 1981**;

(d) water; and

(e) land.

"Operator" means the person who operates or controls an activity, the holder of a permit or authorisation relating to that activity or the person registering or notifying such an activity.

"Protected species" means a species of a kind mentioned in article 4(2) of **Council Directive 2009/147/EC** or listed in Annex I to that Directive or Annexes II and IV to **Council Directive 92/43/EEC**.

"Services" means the functions performed by a natural resource for the benefit of another natural resource or the public.
"Wales" has the meaning given under section 158 of the **Government of Wales Act 2006**.

In relation to the deliberate release and placing on the market of genetically modified organisms, "operator" and "responsible operator" includes:

(a) the holder of a relevant consent issued under **Directive 2001/18/EC** of the European Parliament and of the Council on the deliberate release into the environment of genetically modified organisms;

(b) the holder of a relevant consent for the deliberate release of genetically modified organisms granted by the Welsh Ministers under section 111(1) of the **Environmental Protection Act 1990**; or

(c) the holder of a relevant authorisation issued under **Regulation (EC) No. 1829/2003** of the European Parliament and of the Council on genetically modified food and feed.

Regulation 4: Meaning of "Environmental Damage"

These Regulations aim to prevent and remediate environmental damage which is defined as including damage to protected species or natural habitats, a site of special scientific interest, surface water or groundwater, marine waters or land.

Environmental damage to groundwater means any damage to a body of groundwater such that its conductivity, level or concentration of pollutants changes sufficiently to lower its status pursuant to **Directive 2000/60/EC** of the European Parliament and of the Council (and for pollutants **Directive 2006/118/EC** of the European Parliament and of the Council on the protection of groundwater against pollution and deterioration) (whether or not the body of groundwater is in fact reclassified as being of lower status).

Environmental damage to marine waters means damage to marine waters such that their environmental status is significantly adversely affected.

Environmental damage to land means contamination of land by substances, preparations, organisms or micro-organisms that results in a significant risk of adverse effects on human health.

Regulation 5: Environmental Damage to which these Regulations Apply

These Regulations apply to environmental damage if it is caused by an activity mentioned in Schedule 2. For environmental damage to protected species, natural habitats or a site of special scientific interest, the Regulations also apply in relation to environmental damage caused by any other activity if the operator intended to cause environmental damage or was negligent as to whether environmental damage would be caused.

Regulation 6: Areas of Application

These Regulations apply in Wales and all waters up to one nautical mile seaward from the baselines in Wales.

Regulation 7: Other Legislation

These Regulations do not override any other legislation concerning damage to the environment.

Regulation 8: Exemptions

These Regulations do not apply to:

- Damage before these Regulations came into force.
- Damage that occurred after these Regulations came into force, or is or was threatened after that date, but is caused by an incident, event or emission that took place before that date.
- Damage caused by an incident, event or emission that takes or took place after that date if it derives from an activity that took place and finished before that date.
- Environmental damage caused by:
    - an act of terrorism;
    - an exceptional natural phenomenon;
    - activities the sole purpose of which is to protect against natural disasters;
    - an incident in respect of which liability or compensation falls within the scope of various International Conventions;
    - activities the main purpose of which is to serve national defence or international security;
    - radioactivity from an activity covered by the Treaty establishing the European Atomic Energy Community or caused by an incident or activity in respect of which liability falls within the scope of the Paris Convention on Third Party Liability in the Field of Nuclear Energy and the Brussels Supplementary Convention;
    - damage caused in the course of commercial sea fishing if all legislation relating to that fishing was complied with;
    - pollution of a diffuse character where it is not possible to establish a causal link between the damage and specific activities.

Regulation 9: Exemption from Damage to Water

Subject to certain conditions being satisfied, damage to water does not include damage caused by new modifications to the physical characteristics of a surface water body, an alteration to the level of a body of groundwater pursuant to **Directive 2000/60/EC** or deterioration from high status to good status of a body of surface water resulting from new sustainable human development activities pursuant to that Directive.

Regulation 10: Enforcing Authorities under the Environmental Permitting (England and Wales) Regulations 2016

These Regulations will be enforced in accordance with the 2016 Regulations if the damage is caused by an activity that requires a permit or registration under the 2016 Regulations.

If either the Environment Agency or Natural Resources Wales is responsible for granting the permit, these Regulations will be enforced by Natural Resources Wales in all cases. If the local authority is responsible for granting the permit then Part 2 is to be enforced by the local authority and Part 3 will be enforced by the local authority (where damage is to land), Natural Resources Wales (if damage is to water), the Welsh Ministers (if damage is to marine waters), and Natural Resources Wales (if damage is to natural habitats or protected species or a site of special scientific interest).

Regulation 11 identifies enforcing authorities in other cases.

Regulation 12: Enforcement

These Regulations can be enforced by any or all of the enforcing authorities in cases where there is more than one type of environmental damage. An enforcing authority may appoint any other enforcing authority to act on its behalf.

Part 2: Preventing Environmental Damage

Regulations 13 and 14: Preventing Environmental Damage/Preventing Further Environmental Damage

An operator of an activity that causes an imminent threat of environmental damage or has caused environmental damage must take all practicable steps to prevent that/further damage and notify the enforcing authority. The enforcing authority may serve a notice on the operator that describes the threat, specifies measures required to prevent danger and requires the operator to take those measures or measures equivalent to them, within a specified period.

Regulation 15: Action by the Enforcing Authority

Any duty in Part 2 placed on the operator of an activity may be carried out by the enforcing authority in an emergency, if the operator cannot be ascertained or if the operator fails to comply with a notice.

Regulation 16: Following Instructions from a Public Authority

When an operator acts in accordance with the instructions of a public authority and, as a result, causes or threatens to cause environmental damage and action is subsequently taken under regulations 13, 14 or 15, the operator may recover the costs of those actions from the public authority unless the instructions related to an emission or incident caused by the operator's own activities.

Part 3: Remediation

Regulation 17: Assessment of Damage

The enforcing authority must establish whether or not there has been environmental damage.

Regulation 18: Determining Liability to Remediate

If the enforcing authority establishes that the damage is environmental damage, it must notify the responsible operator of any activity or activities that caused the damage that the damage is environmental damage and that the responsible operator's activity was a cause of the environmental damage. The enforcing authority must also notify the operator to submit proposals, within a specified timeframe, for measures that will achieve remediation of the damage in accordance with Schedule 4. The operator has a right to appeal. The enforcing authority may withdraw the notification if it is satisfied that it should not have been served or that an appeal is likely to succeed.

Regulation 19: Appeals against Liability to Remediate

A person served with a notice under regulation 18 can appeal by giving notice to the Welsh Ministers. Notice of appeal must be served within 28 days of service of the notification under regulation 18 unless the time limit is extended by the Welsh Ministers.

Grounds for appeal are:

(a) the operator's activity was not a cause of the environmental damage;

(b) the enforcing authority has acted unreasonably in deciding that the damage is environmental damage;

(c) the environmental damage resulted from compliance with an instruction from a public authority;

(d) the operator was not at fault or negligent and the environmental damage was caused by an emission or event expressly authorised by, and fully in accordance with, the conditions of a permit listed in Schedule 3;

(e) the operator was not at fault or negligent and the damage was caused by an emission or activity or any manner of using a product in the course of an activity, that the operator demonstrates was not considered likely to cause environmental damage according to the state of scientific and technical knowledge at the time when the emission was released or the activity took place; or

(f) the damage was the result of an act of a third party and occurred despite the fact that the operator had taken all appropriate safety measures.

Procedures for appeal are contained in Schedule 5. The result of an appeal may be that the notice is confirmed or quashed.

Regulation 20: Remediation Notices

On receipt of proposals from the operator, the enforcing authority must, so far as is practicable, consult any person who has notified an enforcing authority under regulation 29 and any person on whose land the remedial measures will be carried out. The enforcing authority may consult any other person appearing to it to be necessary. Following consultation, the enforcing authority must serve a notice on the operator that specifies the damage, remediation measures (together with reasons), the period within which those measures must be taken, any additional monitoring or investigative measures that the operator must carry out during remediation, and the right of appeal against the notice. The enforcing authority may withdraw or vary the remediation notice if it is satisfied that the notice should not have been served or that an appeal is likely to succeed. Failure to comply with a remediation notice is an offence.

Regulation 21: Appeal Against a Remediation Notice

The operator may appeal on the grounds that the contents of the notice are unreasonable; notice of appeal must be given to the Welsh Ministers. Notice of appeal must be served on the Welsh Ministers within 28 days of service of the remediation notice unless the time limit is extended by the Welsh Ministers. The notice may be confirmed, varied or quashed. The Welsh Ministers must give written notification of the final decision and the reasons for it and may, if appropriate, add further compensatory remediation requirements necessitated by the lapse of time since the remediation notice was served. A remediation notice need not be complied with pending determination of an appeal unless the person hearing the appeal directs otherwise.

Regulation 22: Further Provisions on Remediation Notices

Further remediation notices may be served at any time while remediation is being carried out or, if remediation has not been achieved, at the end of the remediation period.

Regulation 23: Action by the Enforcing Authority

Once the enforcing authority has established that, in its opinion, the damage is environmental damage, it may carry out any reasonable works at any time if the responsible operator cannot be identified, if the responsible operator fails to comply with the remedial notice (whether or not an appeal is pending) or if the responsible operator is not required to carry out remediation under the Regulations.

Part 4: Administration and Enforcement

Regulation 24: Costs when the Enforcing Authority Acts Instead of the Operator

An operator who is liable to carry out works under Part 2 is liable for the reasonable costs incurred by the enforcing authority in taking any reasonable action under regulation 15. The responsible operator is liable for the reasonable costs of the enforcing authority for any action taken under regulation 23 unless the responsible operator was not liable for the action taken.

Regulation 25: Costs Concerned with Administration

An operator who is liable to carry out works under Part 2 is liable for reasonable costs incurred by the enforcing authority in preparing any notice under Part 2, or in ensuring compliance with Part 2.

The responsible operator is liable for the costs incurred by the enforcing authority under Part 3 of:

- assessing whether damage is environmental damage;
- establishing who is the responsible operator;
- establishing appropriate remediation;
- carrying out necessary consultation; and
- monitoring the remediation, both during and after the work.

Regulation 26: Proceedings for Costs by an Enforcing Authority

The enforcing authority cannot commence proceedings for the recovery of costs under these Regulations after a period of 5 years since the completion of the measures to which the proceedings relate or the identification of the operator liable to carry out the measures, whichever is the later.

Regulation 27: Costs Recoverable from Owner to be a Charge on Premises

Where costs are recoverable under these Regulations from an owner of premises and the enforcing authority serves a notice on that person under this regulation, the costs will carry interest at such reasonable rate as the authority may determine from the date of service of the notice until the whole amount is paid, and the costs and accrued interest are a charge on the premises.

A notice served under this regulation must specify the amount of the costs that the enforcing authority claims is recoverable, that costs carry interest and that costs and accrued interest are a charge on the premises with effect from a period of 21 days beginning with the date of service of the notice or, where an appeal is brought, as from the final determination or withdrawal of the appeal. A person served with a notice under this regulation has 21 days from the date of service to appeal to the County Court.

The Court may confirm the notice without modification, order that the notice is to have effect with the substitution of a different amount for the amount originally specified in it, or order that the notice is to be of no effect.

Regulation 28: Recovery of Costs from Other Persons

Operators who incur liability under these Regulations may recover all or part of their costs from any other person who also caused the damage.

Regulation 29: Requests for Action by Interested Parties

Any person who is affected or likely to be affected by environmental damage, or who otherwise has a sufficient interest, may notify the appropriate enforcing authority of any environmental damage which is being, or has been caused, or of which there is an imminent threat.

The enforcing authority must consider the notification and inform the notifier of the action, if any, that it intends to take. If practicable, and before taking any decision, the enforcing authority must notify the operator concerned of the notification and invite the operator to submit comments.

The enforcing authority does not have to consider the notification, notify the operator or invite the operator to comment if, in the opinion of the enforcing authority, the notifier is not likely to be affected or does not have a sufficient interest, or the information provided does not disclose any environmental damage or threat thereof, or as a result of the urgency of the situation it is not practicable to comply.

Regulation 30: Grant of, and Compensation for, Rights of Entry, etc.

Any person whose consent is required before any works required by these Regulations may be carried out must grant such rights in relation to any land or water as will enable the operator or their representative to carry out that work. A person who grants rights is, upon application, entitled to compensation from the operator determined in accordance with Schedule 6.

Regulation 31: Powers of Authorised Persons

Enforcing authorities may authorise persons for the purposes of enforcing these Regulations. The powers in section 108 of the **Environment Act 1995** apply in relation to these Regulations. Additional powers are granted to a person authorised by the Welsh Ministers in relation to the sea.

Regulation 32: Provision of Information to the Enforcing Authority

An enforcing authority may require an operator to provide such information as it may reasonably require for the purpose of enabling the enforcing authority to carry out its functions under these Regulations. Failure to provide such information is an offence.

Regulation 33: Enforcement

Enforcement action cannot be taken after 30 years from the date of the emission, event or incident concerned.

Regulation 34: Penalties

A person guilty of an offence under these Regulations is liable on summary conviction to a fine or to imprisonment for up to 3 months or both. Upon conviction on indictment, a person is liable to a fine or to imprisonment not exceeding two years or both.

Where a body corporate is guilty of an offence that is proved to have been committed with the consent or connivance of, or to have been attributable to any neglect on the part of any director, manager, secretary or other similar person of the body corporate, or on the part of any person who was purporting to act in any such capacity, that person is guilty of the offence as well as the body corporate.

The Schedules

There are six schedules to these Regulations:

- Schedule 1: Damage to Protected Species and Natural Habitats
- Schedule 2: Activities Causing Damage
- Schedule 3: Permits, etc.
- Schedule 4: Remediation
- Schedule 5: Appeals
- Schedule 6: Compensation

ENVIRONMENTAL LIABILITY (SCOTLAND) REGULATIONS 2009 (SI 2009 NO. 266)

These Regulations came into force on 24 June 2009 and have been amended by the **Environmental Liability (Scotland) Amendment Regulations 2015**, with effect from July 19 2015. There are 22 regulations, supplemented by 4 schedules. An overview of the Regulations is given below. The Regulations extend to Scotland only.

Regulation 2: Interpretation

"Activity" means any activity carried out in the course of an economic activity, a business or an undertaking, irrespectively of its private or public, profit or non-profit character.

"Enactment" has the meaning assigned to it in section 126(1) (interpretation) of the **Scotland Act 1998**. "Environmental damage" means damage falling within regulation 4.

"Genetically modified organisms" has the meaning assigned to it by **Directive 2001/18/EC**. "Marine waters" means waters classified as marine waters pursuant to **Directive 2008/56/EC**. "Protected species and natural habitats" means:

(a) the species mentioned in article 4(2) of **Directive 2009/147/EC** or listed in Annex I to that Directive or the species listed in Annexes II and IV to **Directive 92/43/EEC**; and

(b) the habitats of species mentioned in article 4(2) of **Directive 2009/147/EC** or listed in Annex I to that Directive or the habitats of species listed in Annex II to **Directive 92/43/EEC** or the natural habitats listed in Annex I to **Directive 92/43/EEC** and the breeding sites or resting places of the species listed in Annex IV to **Directive 92/43/EEC**.

"The water environment" has the meaning assigned to it by section 3(2) of the **Water Environment and Water Services (Scotland) Act 2003**.

Regulation 4: Application

These Regulations apply in relation to damage to protected species and natural habitats if it has significant adverse effects on reaching or maintaining the favourable conservation status of the protected species or natural habitat and it is caused by an activity listed in Schedule 1 or by the fault or negligence of an operator whilst carrying on any other activity. The Regulations also apply to water or land damage caused by an activity listed in Schedule 1.

Regulation 5: Exemptions

These Regulations do not apply to:

- in relation to damage to protected species and natural habitats, previously identified adverse effects resulting from an act by an operator which was expressly authorised by the relevant authorities;

- environmental damage or imminent threat of such damage caused by:
  - an act of armed conflict, hostilities, civil war or insurrection;
  - a natural phenomenon of exceptional, inevitable and irresistible character; or
  - pollution of a diffuse character where it is not possible to establish a causal link between the damage and the activities of individual operators;

- environmental damage or an imminent threat of such damage arising from an incident in respect of which liability or compensation falls within the scope of various International Conventions;

- radioactivity from an activity covered by the Treaty establishing the European Atomic Energy Community or caused by an incident or activity in respect of which liability or compensation falls within the scope of the Paris Convention on Third Party Liability in the Field of Nuclear Energy and the Brussels Supplementary Convention;

- activities, the main purpose of which is to serve national defence or international security or the sole purpose of which is to protect from natural disasters;

- damage caused by an emission, event or incident that took place before the coming into force of these Regulations;

- environmental damage of the type defined in regulation 4(1)(b)(ii) to marine waters caused by an emission, event or incident that took place before 19 July 2015;

- damage caused by an emission, event or incident that occurs after the coming into force of these Regulations which results from a specific activity that took place and finished before that date;

- damage resulting from the release of genetically modified organisms if more than 75 years have passed since the release; or
- damage not falling within the above paragraph if more than 30 years have passed since the emission, event or incident occurred which resulted in the damage.

Regulation 6: Other Legislation

These Regulations do not affect the right of a responsible operator to limit liability in accordance with the **Convention on Limitation of Liability for Maritime Claims 1976** and are without prejudice to any other enactment concerning damage to the environment.

Regulation 7: Competent Authority

The competent authority in relation to instances of environmental damage or an imminent threat of such damage:

- to protected species or natural habitats in the territorial sea or coastal water is the Scottish Ministers;
- to protected species or natural habitats in any other place, is Scottish Natural Heritage;
- to land or, in relation to environmental damage of the type defined in regulation 4(1)(b)(i), to the water environment, is the Scottish Environment Protection Agency; and
- to marine waters, in relation to environmental damage of the type defined in regulation 4(1)(b)(ii), is the Scottish Ministers.

In relation to environmental damage of the type defined in regulation 4(1)(a), the competent authority shall decide whether or not the damage has occurred or will occur as a result of the fault or negligence of an operator.

Where more than one instance of environmental damage has occurred and the competent authority is unable to ensure the remedial measures are taken at the same time, the competent authority shall determine which instance of environmental damage is to be remedied first.

When determining which incidence of environmental damage is to be remedied first, the competent authority shall have regard to the following matters:

(a) the nature, extent and gravity of the instances of environmental damage concerned;

(b) the possibility of natural recovery; and

(c) any risk to human health.

Before determining which incidence of environmental damage is to be remedied first, the competent authority shall, if practicable, consult any interested person and the owner or occupier of the land upon which, or any part of the water environment or any marine waters in respect of which, remedial measures are to be taken.

A person who is consulted may make representations to the competent authority within such time limit as specified by the authority and the competent authority shall take into account any representations in making its determination.

Any decision taken by a competent authority under these Regulations which imposes requirements as to preventive or remedial measures on an operator shall be notified to the relevant operator, state the grounds on which it is based, and advise the operator of any available appeal and any time limit to which such an appeal is subject.

Regulation 8: Assistance by Public Bodies

A competent authority may impose a requirement on a public body to take preventive or remedial measures where it appears to the competent authority that those measures need to be taken as a matter of urgency and the public body is better able to take the measures. Such decisions will be made known to the relevant public body and state the grounds on which they are based. Costs of compliance are to be met by the competent authority.

When requested, a public body must provide a competent authority with any advice or information that would assist the competent authority in carrying out its functions under these Regulations.

Regulation 9: Powers of Entry and Inspection

Any person authorised in writing by a competent authority for the purpose of carrying out its functions under these Regulations may exercise the following powers:

- to enter at any reasonable time or, in an emergency, if need be by force;
- to be accompanied by any other person duly authorised by the competent authority as well as by a police constable if the authorised person has reasonable cause to expect serious obstruction in the execution of their duty;

- to take with them any equipment or materials needed for their duty;
- to make examinations and investigations;
- to direct that the premises, or anything in them, shall be left undisturbed for as long as is reasonably necessary for the purpose of any examination or investigations;
- to take measurements, photographs and recordings;
- to take samples of any articles or substances and of the air, water or land in, on, or in the vicinity of, the premises;
- to cause any article or substance to be dismantled or subjected to any process or test (but not so as to damage or destroy it unless necessary);
- to take possession of any article or substance and detain it for the purposes of examination, to ensure that it is not tampered with before examination is completed and to ensure that it is available for use as evidence in any proceedings for an offence under these Regulations;
- to require any person to answer such questions as the authorised person thinks fit to ask and to sign a declaration of truth;
- to require the production of records and to inspect and take copies of the same;
- to carry out experimental borings or other works on the premises and to install, keep or maintain monitoring and other apparatus on the premises;
- to require such facilities and assistance as are necessary.

Regulation 10: Preventive Measures

In the event of an imminent threat of environmental damage caused by an activity, the operator must without delay take the necessary preventive measures. If, notwithstanding the preventive measures, an imminent threat of environmental damage remains, the operator must notify the competent authority of the circumstances as soon as practicable. In the absence of such notification, if a competent authority has reasonable grounds for believing that there is an imminent threat of environmental damage it may require an operator to provide information about the threat.

Where the operator fails to comply with the above requirements, or cannot be identified or is not required to pay the costs in accordance with these Regulations, the competent authority instead of the operator may itself take preventive measures. Failure by an operator to comply without reasonable excuse is an offence.

Regulation 11: Identification and Determination of Remedial Measures

This regulation applies where environmental damage has occurred and requires the relevant operator to identify, in accordance with Schedule 3, potential remedial measures and to submit them without delay to the competent authority for approval unless the competent authority has taken action. If an operator fails to submit potential remedial measures then the competent authority shall require them to do so.

As soon as practicable after receipt of the potential remedial measures and before approving them, the competent authority shall, if practicable, consult any interested person and the owner or occupier of the land upon which, or any part of the water environment or any marine waters in respect of which, the potential remedial measures are to be carried out. A person who is consulted may make representations to the competent authority within a set time limit; the competent authority shall take these representations into account when making its determination. Following consultation, the competent authority shall determine which remedial measures shall be implemented and will inform the operator accordingly.

Failure by an operator to comply with these requirements without reasonable excuse is an offence.

Regulation 12: Operator to Take Remedial Action

In the event of environmental damage, an operator must:

- immediately notify the competent authority of the circumstances;
- take all practicable steps to control, contain, remove or otherwise manage any contaminants or any other damage factors in order to limit or prevent further environmental damage and adverse effects on human health or further impairment of services; and
- on approval being given by the competent authority, take the necessary remedial measures.

In the absence of a notification by an operator, if a competent authority has reasonable grounds for believing that environmental damage has occurred, it may require the operator to provide information about the damage.

The competent authority may, at any time:

- require an operator to provide supplementary information on environmental damage;
- take, or require an operator to take, all practicable steps to immediately control, contain, remove or otherwise manage any contaminants and any other damage factors in order to limit or prevent further environmental damage and adverse effects on human health or further impairment of services;
- require an operator to take the necessary remedial measures.

Where an operator fails to comply with the above requirements, cannot be identified or is not required to pay the costs in accordance with these Regulations, the competent authority may itself take the necessary remedial measures but only as a means of last resort.

Failure by an operator to comply with the requirements of this regulation without reasonable excuse is an offence.

Regulation 13: Appeals and Interim Measures

The operator has a right to appeal to the Sheriff on questions of fact and law, such appeal being by way of summary application. Appeals must be brought within 28 days from the date after the date of intimation of the decision containing the requirement that the operator wishes to appeal. The Sheriff may confirm the decision of the competent authority, quash the decision and order the competent authority to reimburse any costs incurred (where the Sheriff considers that the competent authority has acted unreasonably), remit the decision to the competent authority for re-determination or make such other order as the Sheriff thinks fit.

Regulation 14: Request for Action and Review

Any person who is affected or is likely to be affected by environmental damage or otherwise has a sufficient interest or is a non-governmental organisation promoting environmental protection may submit any observations to the competent authority in relation to an instance of environmental damage or an imminent threat of such damage and request the competent authority to take action. Requests must be made in writing and must be accompanied by relevant information and data in support of the observation.

Provided the competent authority is satisfied that the request plausibly demonstrates the existence of environmental damage or an imminent threat of such damage, the competent authority will notify the operator of the request, provide it with a copy of the accompanying information and invite the operator to respond. Having considered representations from the operator, the competent authority shall notify both the person who made the request and the operator of its decision regarding the request and provide reasons for it.

Regulation 15: Co-operation between Competent Authorities

Where, in the opinion of the competent authority, an instance of environmental damage or an imminent threat of such damage arises from an activity carried on in Scotland which is likely to affect another Member State or another part of the UK, the competent authority will co-operate with the relevant competent authority of that Member State or part of the UK. The competent authority will provide such information as may be required by the competent authority of the Member State or part of the UK and will consider using its powers under regulations 10(5) or 12(4) in the event that preventive or remedial measures are not taken by the operator. The Scottish Ministers will also be notified.

Regulation 16: Grant of, and Compensation for, Rights of Entry

Any person whose consent is required before any measures required by these Regulations may be carried out must grant such rights in relation to any land, any part of the water environment or any marine waters as will enable the relevant person to carry out such measures. Before requiring any such consent, the relevant person shall reasonably endeavour to consult every person who appears to be the owner or occupier of the land, any part of the water environment or any marine waters, and who appears to be a person who might be required to grant any rights.

Provided a person who grants or who joins in granting the above rights gives the relevant person notice of a claim stating the grounds of the claim and the amount claimed in accordance with Schedule 4, the relevant person shall compensate that person where they sustain damage as a consequence of granting the rights.

Regulation 17: Costs

The competent authority can recover from the operator who has caused damage or the imminent threat of damage, the costs that it has incurred in relation to preventive or remedial measures taken under these Regulations and any costs incurred by it under regulation 8(3) or 15(1).

An operator will not be required to bear the cost of preventive or remedial measures if it demonstrates that the environmental damage or the imminent threat of such damage:

- was caused by a third party despite the fact that appropriate safety measures were in place; or
- resulted from compliance with an order or instruction from a public authority other than one arising from an emission or incident caused by the operator's own activities.

An operator is not required to pay the cost of remedial measures if it demonstrates that it was not at fault or negligent and that the environmental damage was caused by:

- an emission or event expressly authorised by, and fully in accordance with the conditions of, an authorisation granted in relation to an activity in Schedule 1; or
- an emission or activity or any manner of using a product in the course of an activity which the operator demonstrates was not considered likely to cause environmental damage according to the state of scientific and technical knowledge at the time of the emission or activity.

The competent authority has up to five years to initiate proceedings for the recovery of costs. The five years is taken from the later of:

- the date on which the competent authority completed any relevant measures taken under these Regulations; or
- the date on which the competent authority identified the responsible operator.

Regulation 18: Allocation of Costs

Where the activities of more than one operator have resulted in environmental damage or an imminent threat thereof, the competent authority will determine the operator's responsibility for the costs of the environmental damage. Responsibility for costs will be decided:

- by considering the percentage split of each operator;
- on a joint and several basis;
- with reference to a particular area or period of time; or
- in such other manner as the competent authority deems appropriate.

The competent authority may require the operators to provide information for the purposes of determining their responsibility for costs; a failure to comply with this requirement without reasonable excuse is an offence.

Regulation 19: Penalties

Summary conviction may result in a fine not exceeding the statutory maximum, or a prison sentence of up to 12 months, or both. Conviction on indictment may result in a fine or imprisonment for up to two years, or both.

Regulation 20: Offences by Bodies Corporate

Where a body corporate is guilty of an offence that is proved to have been committed with the consent or connivance of, or to have been attributable to any neglect on the part of any director, manager, secretary or other similar person of the body corporate, or on the part of any person who was purporting to act in any such capacity, that person is guilty of the offence as well as the body corporate.

Regulation 21: Offences by Scottish Partnerships

Where an offence is committed by a Scottish partnership (other than a limited liability partnership) and is proved to have been committed with the consent or connivance of, or to be attributable to any neglect on the part of, a partner, that partner as well as the partnership is to be deemed guilty of that offence and is liable to be proceeded against and punished accordingly.

Regulation 22: Offences by Limited Liability Partnerships

Where an offence under these Regulations is committed by a limited liability partnership and is proved to have been committed with the consent or connivance of, or to be attributable to any neglect on the part of, any member of that partnership or person who was purporting to act as such, that member or person as well as the limited liability partnership, is to be deemed guilty of that offence and is liable to be proceeded against and punished accordingly.

The Schedules

There are four schedules to these Regulations:

- Schedule 1: Activities for the Purposes of Regulation 4(1)
- Schedule 2: Supplementary Provisions in Respect of Powers of Entry and Inspection
- Schedule 3: Remediation of Environmental Damage
- Schedule 4: Compensation

ENVIRONMENTAL PERMITTING (ENGLAND AND WALES) REGULATIONS 2016 (SI 2016 NO. 1154)

Introduction

These Regulations are made under the **Pollution Prevention and Control Act 1999** and the **Water Act 2014** and came into force on 1 January 2017. They provide a consolidated system of environmental permitting and replace the main requirements of the **Environmental Permitting (England and Wales) Regulations 2010** and associated amendments, which established a single 'environmental permitting' system in England and Wales. The Regulations have been amended (by the **Environmental Permitting (England and Wales) (Amendment) (EU Exit) Regulations 2019**) to ensure that they operate effectively after UK exit from the EU.

The 2016 Regulations now incorporate a system for permitting:

- Waste operations, mining waste operations, mobile plant and installations.
- Water discharges.
- Groundwater discharges.
- Radioactive substances.
- Small waste incineration plant (England only).
- Solvent emission activity (England only).
- Flood risk activity.
- Medium combustion plant.
- Specified generator.

The Regulations transpose permitting requirements of many European Directives.

The **Environmental Permitting (England and Wales) (Amendment) Regulations 2018** add provision to the principal Regulations inserting requirements of the **Medium Combustion Plant Directive (2015/2193)** (as amended by the **Environmental Permitting (England and Wales) (Amendment) (EU Exit) Regulations 2019**). They control emissions from Medium Combustion Plants (MCPs) and specified generators. MCPs are classed as being combustion plants that have a net thermal input that is equal to or greater than 1 megawatt but less than 50 megawatts.

The requirements of the Amendment Regulations include:

- MCPs that are brought into operation after 20 December 2018 cannot operate without a permit.
- MCPs already in operation with a net rated thermal input of above 5 megawatts and 1 to 5 megawatts will be brought into the permitting regime by 1 January 2024 and 1 January 2029 respectively.
- MCPs must comply with emission limit values for sulphur dioxide, nitrogen dioxide and dust (exceptions include interruptions in the supply of low sulphur fuel or gas).

Generators having a net thermal rated input that is equal to or greater than 1 megawatt but less than 50 megawatts (subject to exclusions) are classed as specified generators. These will also require a permit that will set emission limits to atmosphere. As with MCPs the regime will be phased in over several years.

The **Environmental Protection (Miscellaneous Amendments) (England and Wales) Regulations 2018** amend the regulations by introducing certain waste operations and provisions that apply to flood risk activities and radioactive substance activities. Provisions regarding the production and review of a written management system for waste operations and materials facilities, where not already within a permit, are also included. A condition is also provided for waste operations for the operator to demonstrate to the regulator their compliance with a specified scheme of technical competence.

The **Environmental Protection (Miscellaneous Amendments) (England and Wales) Regulations 2018** amend the regulations by introducing certain waste operations and provisions that apply to flood risk activities and radioactive substance activities. Provisions regarding the production and review of a written management system for waste operations and materials facilities, where not already within a permit, are also included. A condition is also provided for waste operations for the operator to demonstrate to the regulator their compliance with a specified scheme of technical competence.

Part 1: General

Interpretation

The following selected definitions are reproduced from the **Environmental Permitting (England and Wales) Regulations 2016** under the Open Government Licence.

"Installation" means:

(a) a stationary technical unit where one or more activities are carried on, and

(b) any other location on the same site where any other directly associated activities are carried on,

and references to an installation include references to part of an installation.

"Mobile plant" means either Part B mobile plant or waste mobile plant.

"Pollution", in relation to a water discharge activity or groundwater activity, means the direct or indirect introduction, as a result of human activity, of substances or heat into the air, water or land which may be harmful to human health or the quality of aquatic ecosystems or terrestrial ecosystems directly depending on aquatic ecosystems; result in damage to material property; or impair or interfere with amenities or other legitimate uses of the environment.

"Pollution", other than in relation to a water discharge activity or groundwater activity, means any emission as a result of human activity which may:

(a) be harmful to human health or the quality of the environment,

(b) cause offence to a human sense,

(c) result in damage to material property, or

(d) impair or interfere with amenities and other legitimate uses of the environment.

"Excluded waste operation" means any part of a waste operation not carried on at an installation or by means of Part B mobile plant that:

(a) requires a marine licence under the **Marine and Coastal Access Act 2009**, or

(b) relates to waste described in regulation 3(2) of the **Controlled Waste (England and Wales) Regulations 2012**.

"Exempt facility" means:

(a) an exempt waste operation,

(b) an exempt water discharge activity,

(c) an exempt groundwater activity, or

(d) an exempt flood risk activity.

"Exempt waste operation" means a waste operation:

(a) that is not carried on at an installation, and

(b) that meets the requirements of paragraph 4(1) of Schedule 2.

"Operate a regulated facility" means:

(a) operate an installation or mobile plant, or

(b) arry on a waste operation, mining waste operation, radioactive substances activity, water discharge activity, groundwater activity, small waste incineration plant operation, solvent emission activity or flood risk activity.

"Operator" means:

(a) the person who has control over the operation of a regulated facility;

(b) if a regulated facility has not yet been put into operation, the person who will have control over the facility when it is put into operation; or

(c) if a regulated facility has ceased to be in operation, the person who holds the environmental permit which authorised the operation of the facility.

"Regulated facility" means any of the following:

(a) an installation,

(b) mobile plant,

(c) a waste operation,

(d) a mining waste operation,

(e) a radioactive substances activity,

(f) a water discharge activity,

(g) a groundwater activity,

(h) a small waste incineration plant,

(i) a solvent emission activity,

(j) a flood risk activity,

(k) a medium combustion plant,

(l) a specified generator.

But the following are not regulated facilities:

(a) an exempt facility,

(b) an excluded waste operation,

(c) the disposal or recovery of household waste from a domestic property within the curtilage of that property by a person other than an establishment or undertaking,

(d) an excluded flood risk activity.

Part 2: Environmental Permits

Chapter 1: Application to the Crown and Requirement for an Environmental Permit

Regulation 11: Application to the Crown

The Regulations are binding on Crown premises although they are not criminally liable for offences under reg. 38 (offences) and no proceedings can be taken under reg. 42 (High Court proceedings). (The High Court can, however, on application of a regulator, declare a contravention of these Regulations.) Schedule 4 to the Regulations specifies further provisions in relation to Crown premises.

Regulation 12: Requirement for an Environmental Permit (extracts)

"(1) A person must not, except under and to the extent authorised by an environmental permit:

(a) operate a regulated facility; or

(b) cause or knowingly permit a water discharge activity or groundwater activity.

(2) Paragraph (1)(b) does not apply if the water discharge activity or groundwater activity is an exempt facility.

(3) In respect of a radioactive substances activity, paragraph (1) does not apply to a person to whom a radioactive substances exemption applies for that activity."

"(1A) Paragraph (1)(a) does not apply in relation to the operation of a medium combustion plant, mobile medium combustion plant or a specified generator comprising:

(a) a new medium combustion plant, before 20 December 2018;

(b) an existing medium combustion plant with a rated thermal input greater than 5 megawatts, before 1 January 2024;

(c) an existing medium combustion plant with a rated thermal input of less than or equal to 5 megawatts, before 1 January 2029;

(d) a specified generator, before the permitting date."

Chapter 2: Grant of an Environmental Permit

Regulations 13 to 19 and Schedule 5

An application for a permit should be made by the operator of the regulated facility. (Note: where two or more operators run different parts of the same regulated facility they each need to make an application for their part and will need to meet their own permit conditions.)

Regulation 14 sets out the content and form of an environmental permit.

Where a permit requires the operator to undertake works to land which they have no right to, the person who is entitled must give consent to the operator.

Where a permitted mobile plant is operating on the site of another permitted regulated facility, the regulated facility permit will prevail if there are inconsistencies between the two permits.

The regulator can authorise several operations by the same operator under a single site permit. This is the case where the operator operates:

- More than one regulated facility on the same site (with some exceptions).
- More than one mobile plant.
- More than one standard facility.
- More than one radioactive substances activity where all such activities are in respect of the use or potential use of the same premises for underground disposal.

The regulator can also consolidate existing permits into a single permit under similar circumstances.

Environmental permits, once granted, remain in force until they are revoked, surrendered, replaced with a consolidated permit or they cease to have effect.

Chapter 3: Variation, Transfer, Revocation and Surrender of an Environmental Permit

Regulations 20 to 25

Permits can be varied either by the regulator or on an application made by the operator. As a general rule, however, the regulator cannot, on its own initiative and without the agreement of the operator, vary a permit for a stand-alone water discharge activity if it has been granted or varied within the last four years (some exceptions).

Permits can be transferred from one operator to another in part or as a whole:

- if the operator is one individual (A) and the regulator is satisfied that A cannot be found, on the application of the proposed transferee only; or
- if the operator is two or more individuals (A and B) and the regulator is satisfied that A cannot be found, on the joint application of B and the proposed transferee; or
- otherwise on the joint application of the operator and the proposed transferee.

Operators of Part B installations (except waste operations), mobile plant, a solvent emission activity, a stand-alone water discharge activity, a stand-alone groundwater activity or a stand-alone flood risk activity may surrender their permit by notifying the regulator. The permit ceases to have effect on the date specified, which must not be less than 20 working days after notification.

An application to surrender a permit may be made by the operator. This must be accepted by the regulator if they are satisfied that the site has been returned to a satisfactory state and there is no risk of pollution. In the case of a Part B installation (except waste operations), mobile plant, a solvent emission activity, stand-alone water discharge activities or stand-alone groundwater activities, the process is one of 'notification' rather than 'application'. This removes the requirement for the regulator to 'accept' and the permit will cease to have effect on the date of notification.

Chapter 4: Standard Rules

Regulations 26 to 30

Any "rule-making authority" (Secretary of State, Welsh Ministers or the Environment Agency/Natural Resources Wales) can publish "standard rules". Standard rules specify the conditions to be met by a "class of facilities" and can be used instead of site-specific conditions.

The operator may decide whether they wish to operate under a "standard permit" applying standard rules. Where standard rules apply there will be generic assessments of risk for the "standard facilities" which will be available to the operator.

Chapter 5: Appeals in Relation to Environmental Permits

Regulation 31

There is a right of appeal to the appropriate authority. Appeals can be made in a number of instances, e.g. against enforcement notice served by the regulator, refusal of a permit, and rejection of application for transfer, etc.

There is no right of appeal against a Direction issued by the Secretary of State/Welsh Ministers. This is also the case where an application for grant or variation of a permit for certain mining waste facilities has been refused.

Part 3: Discharge of Functions in Relation to a Regulated Facility

Regulation 32: Discharge of Functions

Functions in relation to a regulated facility that is or will be operated in England are exercisable by the EA. Functions in relation to a regulated facility that is or will be operated in Wales are exercisable by NRW.

In relation to waste mobile plant, if the principal place of business of the operator is in England, functions are exercisable by the EA, whereas if the principal place of business of the operator is in Wales, then the functions are exercisable by NRW. If the principal place of business is not in England or Wales, then the functions are exercisable by the appropriate agency that granted the environmental permit, or, where no permit was granted, the appropriate agency in whose area waste mobile plant is first intended to be operated.

Functions in relation to a regulated facility of the following description or class are exercisable by the local authority in whose area the regulated facility is or will be operated:

(a) a Part A(2) installation;

(b) a Part B installation or Part B mobile plant, but not in respect of any of the following regulated facilities carried on at the installation or by means of mobile plant:

 (i) a waste operation (unless it is a Part B activity);

 (ii) a mining waste operation;

 (iii) a water discharge activity;

 (iv) a groundwater activity;

(c) a small waste incineration plant;

(d) a solvent emission activity.

If the principal place of business of the operator of Part B mobile plant is in England and Wales, functions in relation to that regulated facility are exercisable by the local authority in whose area the place of business is.

If the principal place of business of the operator of Part B mobile plant is not in England and Wales, functions in relation to that regulated facility are exercisable by:

(a) the local authority which granted the environmental permit authorising the operation of the regulated facility; or

(b) if no permit has been granted, the local authority in whose area the regulated facility is first operated, or is intended to be first operated.

Regulation 33: Direction to a Regulator: Discharge of Functions by a Different Regulator

An appropriate authority may direct the appropriate agency to exercise such local authority functions as are, and for such period as is, specified in the direction; or a local authority to exercise such appropriate agency functions as are, and for such period as is, specified in the direction.

A local authority may only be directed to exercise appropriate agency functions in respect of an installation, but not in respect of a mining waste operation carried on at an installation; or mobile plant.

When giving a direction under this regulation the appropriate authority must notify (in cases where the appropriate authority is the Secretary of State) the EA; where the appropriate authority is the Welsh Ministers, the NRW, and any local authority or other person whom the appropriate authority considers is affected by the direction.

Regulation 34 requires regulators to make periodic reviews of permits and to undertake periodic inspections of regulated facilities.

Regulation 35 states that Schedules 7 to 25 have effect in relation to the description or class of regulated facilities.

Part 4: Enforcement and Offences

Regulations 36 and 37

A notice can be served by the regulator if an operator is not complying with, or is likely to contravene, a permit or its conditions. The notice must:

- state the regulator's view that the operator has contravened, is contravening, or is likely to contravene an environmental permit condition;
- specify:
    - the matters constituting the contravention;
    - the steps that must be taken to remedy the contravention;
    - the time period in which steps must be taken to remedy the contravention.

Suspension notices can be served under regulation 37 where there is a serious risk of pollution or a contravention of a permit condition has occurred and there is a risk of pollution. While this remains in force, the operation is no longer authorised under a permit.

Regulation 38: Main Offences

It is an offence to:

- Operate a regulated facility, or cause or knowingly permit a water discharge activity or groundwater activity except under and to the extent authorised by an environmental permit.
- Fail to comply with or to contravene an environmental permit condition.
- Fail to comply with a suspension notice, enforcement notice, prohibition notice, landfill closure notice, mining waste facility closure notice, flood risk emergency works notice or flood risk activity remediation notice.
- Fail to comply with a notice requiring the provision of information, without reasonable excuse.
- Make a false or misleading statement.
- Intentionally make a false entry in a record required under an environmental permit condition.
- With intent to deceive, forge or use a document issued or authorised to be issued or required for any purpose under an environmental permit condition.

If an offence committed by a person under regulation 38 is due to the act or default of some other person, that other person is also guilty of the offence and liable to be proceeded against and punished accordingly, whether or not proceedings for the offence are taken against the first mentioned person.

Regulation 39: Penalties

- On summary conviction: a fine and/or six months' imprisonment.
- On conviction on indictment: a fine and/or up to five years' imprisonment.

Regulation 40: Defences

It is a defence to prove that the acts that caused the contravention were done in an emergency to avoid danger to human health. This is not an absolute defence - the operator must also have taken reasonably practicable steps to minimise pollution and must have notified the regulator as soon as was reasonably practicable.

A person who knowingly permits a water or groundwater discharge activity from an abandoned mine (or part) is not guilty of an offence unless:

- the person is the owner or former operator, and
- the mine was abandoned after 31 December 1999.

Regulation 41: Offences by a Body Corporate

If an offence is committed by a body corporate but is shown to be as a result of the consent or connivance of an officer or attributable to their neglect, the individual can be held liable in addition to the body corporate.

Regulation 42: Enforcement by the High Court

The regulator may take proceedings in the High Court for the purpose of securing compliance with an enforcement notice, suspension notice, prohibition notice, landfill closure notice or mining waste facility closure notice, flood risk emergency works notice or flood risk activity notice.

Regulation 44: Power of Court to Order Remediation

In addition to or instead of penalties imposed under regulation 39, the court may order steps to be taken to remedy those matters relating to the conviction.

Part 5: Public Registers

Regulations 45 to 56

Regulators must maintain a public register of information concerning the regulated facilities they have responsibility for. The register should be available to the public free of charge although a reasonable charge can be made for copies. Local authorities must also keep copies of information relating to those regulated facilities under the control of the Environment Agency/Natural Resources Wales.

Information does not have to be included if it is in the interests of national security not to do so.

Information can be withheld from the register for reasons of commercial or industrial confidentiality but a note to that effect must appear on the register.

Part 6: Powers and Functions of the Regulator and the Appropriate Authority

Regulations 57 to 69

Where there is considered to be a risk of serious pollution from a regulated facility under an environmental permit, the regulator may take steps to remove the risk and charge back the costs to the operator. Costs are not recoverable if the operator shows that there was no risk of serious pollution or that the costs were unnecessary.

Part 7: Miscellaneous Provisions

Regulations 70 to 80

New applications are not required for existing permits. Existing permits and licences automatically become environmental permits from the date these Regulations come into force. There are also a number of transitional provisions made. Where there is an outstanding application on the date these Regulations came into force they will continue to be determined under the old regime. Once granted, the permit will become an environmental permit at the end of the appeal period.

Any outstanding enforcement action will continue to be valid.

Schedules

Schedule 1 - Activities, Installations and Mobile Plant

This Schedule is lengthy with lists of the activities that require a permit and exemptions to that requirement. Part 2 of this Schedule details which activities are Part A(1), A(2) and B and refers to certain emissions to air, discharges to water and to certain substances. The specific emissions, discharges and substances are listed in Part 1 of this Schedule.

Schedule 1A has been inserted by the **Environmental Permitting (England and Wales) (Amendment) (EU Exit) Regulations 2019**. It covers changes to various European directives that are relevant to permitting to ensure that they operate effectively following UK exit from the EU.

Schedule 2 - Exempt Facilities: General

Some operations that are considered to be of low risk may be exempt from a permit; they must, however, be registered as exempt by the regulator. A register of the exemptions must be kept.

Subject to the descriptions and conditions given in Schedule 3, some waste operations, water discharge activities, groundwater activities and flood risk activities may be exempt.

Exempt waste operations must be inspected periodically.

Schedule 3 - Exempt Facilities: Descriptions and Conditions

This Schedule lists the detailed descriptions and conditions for the exempt waste, water discharge, groundwater activities and flood risk activities.

Schedule 4 - Application to the Crown

Gives further details on the application of these Regulations to the Crown.

Schedule 5 - Environmental Permits

Specifies the procedures associated with the grant, variation, transfer and surrender of environmental permits. This Schedule also details the requirements regarding compensation in relation to conditions which affect certain interests in land.

Schedule 6 - Appeals to the Appropriate Authority

Specifies the procedures for appeals.

Schedules 7 to 25

These Schedules contain specific details on the application of these Regulations to specific activities and installations. For example, Schedule 25A identifies a medium combustion plant as being combustion plant that has a net thermal input that is equal to or greater than 1 megawatt but less than 50 megawatts (subject to date restrictions). Schedule 25B identifies a specified generator as having a net thermal rated input that is equal to or greater than 1 megawatt but less than 50 megawatts (subject to exclusions).

Schedules 26 to 29

These cover enforcement undertakings, public registers, revocations and consequential amendments.

ENVIRONMENTAL PROTECTION ACT 1990

Introduction

This is a voluminous and detailed framework Act. The 1990 Act consists of over 164 sections and 16 schedules. The following text concentrates on relevant sections and requirements.

Amendments

EPA 1990 has been amended on many occasions by, amongst others, the **Environment Act 1995**, the **Clean Neighbourhoods and Environment Act 2005**, the **Hazardous Waste (England and Wales) Regulations 2005**, the **Waste Management (England and Wales) Regulations 2006**, the **Waste (Household Waste Duty of Care) (England and Wales) Regulations 2005**, the **Pollution Prevention and Control Act 1999**, the **Local Government (Scotland) Act 1994**, the **Noise and Statutory Nuisance Act 1993** and the **Environmental Permitting Regulations**.

More recently the **Hazardous Waste (Miscellaneous Amendments) Regulations 2015** (regulation 2) have amended section 62A of this Act (lists of waste displaying hazardous properties) and the Unauthorised Deposit of Waste (Fixed Penalties) Regulations 2016 introduce the issue of fixed penalty notices for fly-tipping offences.

The **Environmental Protection (Miscellaneous Amendments) (England and Wales) Regulations 2018** introduce in England a fixed penalty notice for breaches of the duty of care for household waste.

Where appropriate, amendments have been incorporated into the text below.

Interpretation - EPA 1990

Environment consists of all, or any, of the following media, namely, the air, water and land, and the medium of air includes the air within buildings and the air within other natural or man-made structures above or below ground.

Pollution of the environment is due to the release (into any environmental medium) from any process of substances, which are capable of causing harm to man or any other living organisms supported by the environment.

Harm means harm to the health of living organisms or other interference with the ecological systems of which they form part and, in the case of man, includes offence caused to any of his senses or harm to his property.

Process means any activities carried on in Great Britain, whether on premises or by means of mobile plant, which are capable of causing pollution of the environment.

Activities means industrial or commercial activities or activities of any other nature whatsoever.

Great Britain includes so much of the adjacent territorial sea as is, or is treated as, relevant territorial waters. Mobile plant means plant which is designed to move or to be moved, whether on roads or otherwise.

Enforcing Authority, in relation to England and Wales, is the Environment Agency or the local authority. In relation to Scotland, references to the 'enforcing authority' and a 'local enforcing authority' are references to the Scottish Environment Protection Agency (SEPA).

Authorisation means an authorisation for a process whether on premises or by means of mobile plant.

A substance is 'released' into any environmental medium, whenever it is released directly into that medium, whether it is released into it within or outside Great Britain, and release includes:

- In relation to air, any emission of the substance into the air.
- In relation to water, any entry (including any discharge) of the substance into water.
- In relation to land, any deposit, keeping or disposal of the substance in or on land.

Part I - Integrated Pollution Control and Air Pollution Control by Local Authorities

Part I of the EPA (i.e. sections 1-28) has been repealed by the **Pollution Prevention and Control Act 1999** and the **Environmental Permitting Regulations 2016** in England and Wales and equivalent legislation in other parts of the UK.

Part II - Waste on Land

This part of the Act, as amended, applies to the disposal of all controlled waste. It now includes agricultural, mines and quarries waste and covers hazardous waste.

Section 33: Prohibition on Unauthorised or Harmful Depositing, Treatment or Disposal of Waste

(1) A person shall not:

    (a) Deposit controlled waste or extractive waste, or knowingly cause or permit controlled waste or extractive waste to be deposited in or on any land, unless an environmental permit, authorising the deposit, is in force and the deposit is in accordance with the permit.

    (b) Submit controlled waste, or knowingly cause or knowingly permit controlled waste to be submitted, to any listed operation (other than an operation listed within subsection (1)(a)) that:

        (i) is carried out in or on any land, or by means of any mobile plant, and

        (ii) is not carried out under and in accordance with an environmental permit.

    (c) Keep or manage controlled waste or extractive waste in a manner likely to cause pollution of the environment or harm to human health.

The above does not apply to:

- An exempt waste operation.
- A waste operation which is, or forms part of, an operation which:
  - is the subject of a licence under Part 2 of the **Food and Environment Protection Act 1985** or
  - by virtue of an order under section 7 of that Act, does not require a licence.
- Household waste from a domestic property which is treated, kept or disposed of within the curtilage of the property.

Cases prescribed in Regulations made by the Secretary of State and the Regulations may make different exceptions for different areas.

The Secretary of State, in exercising the above power, shall have regard in particular to the expediency of excluding from the prohibitions in subsection (1) any deposits which are small enough or of such a temporary nature that they may be so excluded; any means of treatment or disposal which are innocuous enough to be so excluded; and cases for which adequate controls are provided by another enactment than this section.

Where controlled waste is carried in and deposited from a motor vehicle, the person who controls or is in a position to control the use of the vehicle shall be treated as knowingly causing the waste to be deposited whether or not he gave any instructions for this to be done.

A person who contravenes the above commits an offence.

It shall be a defence for a person charged with an offence under this section to prove:

- That he took all reasonable precautions and exercised all due diligence to avoid the commission of the offence.
- That the acts alleged to constitute the contravention were done in an emergency in order to avoid danger to human health in a case where:
  - he took all such steps as were reasonably practicable in the circumstances for minimising pollution of the environment and harm to human health; and
  - particulars of the acts were furnished to the waste regulation authority as soon as reasonably practicable after they were done.

Note: the **Clean Neighbourhoods and Environment Act 2005 (CN&E Act 2005)** removed the defence of acting under the instructions of an employer.

A person (other than an establishment or undertaking) who commits a relevant offence shall be liable on summary conviction to a fine not exceeding the statutory maximum and on conviction on indictment, to a fine.

Note: Section 33 also contains analogous provisions for Scotland.

Section 33A: Investigation and Enforcement Costs

Inserted by the **CN&E Act 2005**.

The courts can order convicted offenders to pay costs to the regulatory authority in respect of investigations and seizure of vehicles. Fixed penalty notices may be issued in Scotland.

Section 33B: Clean-Up Costs

Inserted by the **CN&E Act 2005**.

This section addresses the payment of clean-up costs back to the relevant person, for example, the Environment Agency or the occupier of the land.

Section 33C: Forfeiture of Vehicles

The courts can make an order to deprive the offender of his rights in the vehicle (including its fuel) at the time of his conviction and to vest those rights in the relevant enforcing authority.

Section 34: Duty of Care, etc. as Respects Waste

Implemented through the **Waste (England and Wales) Regulations 2011** and **Waste (Household Waste Duty of Care) (England and Wales) Regulations 2005**.

It shall be the duty of any person who imports, produces, carries, keeps, treats or disposes of controlled waste or, as a dealer or broker, has control of such waste, to take all such measures applicable to him in that capacity as are reasonable in the circumstances:

- To prevent any contravention by any other person of section 33 of this Act.

- To prevent any contravention by any other person of regulation 12 of the **Environmental Permitting Regulations** or of a condition of an environmental permit.

- To prevent the escape of the waste from his control or that of any other person.

- On the transfer of the waste, to secure that the transfer is only to an authorised person or to a person for authorised transport purposes, and that there is transferred such a written description of the waste, as will enable other persons to avoid a contravention of that section and to comply with the duty under this subsection, as respects the escape of waste.

The above duty does not apply to an occupier of domestic property as respects the household waste produced on the property. However, the **Waste (Household Waste Duty of Care) (England and Wales) Regulations 2005** have inserted section 2A into the EPA which states:

"It shall be the duty of the occupier of any domestic property in England or Wales to take all such measures available to him as are reasonable in the circumstances to secure that any transfer by him of household waste produced on the property is only to an authorised person or to a person for authorised transport purposes."

The following are authorised persons:

- Any authority which is a waste collection authority for the purposes of this Part.

- Any person who is the holder of an environmental permit in relation to a waste operation.

- Any person who is carrying on an exempt waste operation.

- Any person to whom section 33(1) does not apply by virtue of Regulations made by the Secretary of State or by virtue of Regulations under section 2 of the **Pollution Prevention and Control Act 1999**.

- Any person registered as a carrier of controlled waste.

- Any person who is not required to be so registered by virtue of Regulations under that Act.

- A waste disposal authority in Scotland.

The following are authorised transport purposes:

- Transport of controlled waste within the same premises between different places in those premises.
- Transport to a place in Great Britain of controlled waste which has been brought from a country or territory outside Great Britain, not having been landed in Great Britain until it arrives at that place.
- Transport by air or sea of controlled waste from a place in Great Britain to a place outside Great Britain.

A transfer of waste in stages shall be treated as taking place when the first stage of the transfer takes place, and a series of transfers between the same parties of waste of the same description shall be treated as a single transfer taking place, when the first of the transfers in the series takes place.

The Secretary of State may, by Regulations, make provision imposing requirements on any person who is subject to the duty imposed above, as respects the making and retention of documents and the furnishing of documents or copies of documents.

Section 34A: Fixed Penalty Notices

Inserted by the **CN&E Act 2005**.

Fixed penalty notices of £300 may be served where a person has failed to comply with a duty to furnish documents. Once the fixed penalty has been accepted, proceedings cannot be instigated for prosecution.

Section 34B: Power to Search and Seize Vehicles, etc.

(England and Wales only) An authorised officer, or constable, in certain circumstances can stop, search and seize vehicles or enter any premises for the purpose of searching a vehicle. Only uniformed constables can stop a vehicle on the road. It is an offence to not give assistance, required information, or to give false or misleading information.

Section 34C: Seizure of Vehicles: Supplementary

Addresses procedures, administration, etc. in relation to seized vehicles.

Waste Management Licences

In England and Wales, sections 35 to 43 have now been repealed by the **Environmental Permitting Regulations**. The duties in sections 35 to 43 remain in force in Scotland.

Section 35: Waste Management Licences: General

A waste management licence is a licence granted by a waste regulation authority authorising the treatment, keeping or disposal of any specified description of controlled waste in or on specified land or the treatment or disposal of any specified description of controlled waste by means of specified mobile plant.

A licence relating to treatment, keeping or disposal of waste in or on land shall be granted to the person who is in occupation of the land. A licence relating to the treatment or disposal of waste by means of mobile plant shall be granted to the plant operator.

A licence shall be granted on such terms and subject to such conditions as appear to the waste regulation authority to be appropriate and the conditions may relate:

- To the activities which the licence authorises.
- To the precautions to be taken and works to be carried out in connection with or in consequence of those activities.
- To the location of the boundaries of the specified land.

Conditions may require the holder of a licence to carry out works or do other things notwithstanding that he is not entitled to carry out the works or do the thing and any person whose consent would be required shall grant, or join in granting, the holder of the licence such rights in relation to the land as will enable the holder of the licence to comply with any requirements imposed on him by the licence.

This section also makes provision for penalties for the offence of making a false entry in a record required to be kept as a condition of the licence, or forging a licence with intent to deceive.

Sections 35A to 43

Section 35A provides for compensation to be paid to any person who has granted, or joined in granting, the rights under section 35 or section 38.

Section 36 makes provision for the grant of licences, while section 36A requires the waste regulation authority to consult with certain parties before the grant of certain licences.

Section 37 makes provision for the variation of licences, with section 37A requiring consultation before some variations.

Section 38 sets out the conditions and arrangements for revocation and suspension of licences, while section 39 deals with the surrender of licences and section 40 with the arrangements for transfer of licences.

Section 40A was inserted by the **Waste (Scotland) Regulations 2011** and makes provision for consolidated licences. This allows the authority to replace the licence or licences with a consolidated licence in cases where:

- a licence has been varied, or affected by a partial revocation, surrender and transfer;
- there is more than one site licence held by the same person and applying to the same site; or
- there is more than one mobile plant licence held by the same person.

Section 41, on fees and charges for licences, was repealed in England, Wales and Scotland by the **Environment Act 1995**.

Section 42 applies in Scotland only and deals with supervision of licensed activities. The waste regulation authority that granted the licence has a duty to take the steps needed for the purposes of ensuring that the activities authorised by the licence do not cause pollution of the environment or harm to human health or become seriously detrimental to the amenities of the locality affected by the activities. The authority must also take steps needed for the purpose of ensuring that the conditions of the licence are complied with.

Section 43 makes provision for appeals to the Secretary of State from decisions with respect to licences.

Section 44

Section 44 deals with offences of making false or misleading statements or false entries and sets out the penalties to be applied in such cases.

Sections 44ZA to 44ZD

These sections apply only in Scotland and were added by the **Local Government in Scotland Act 2003**. The current version came into force on 23 March 2007.

The local authority is given a duty to prepare an integrated waste management plan and to submit it to the Scottish Ministers for approval. Ministers may approve the integrated waste management plan without modification, they can approve it with modifications that they consider to be appropriate, or they can refuse to approve the plan.

It shall be the duty of a local authority to endeavour to carry out its waste management functions in accordance with its approved integrated waste management plan. A local authority may, from time to time, or if requested by the Scottish Ministers, modify its integrated waste management plan. If it does so, the local authority must submit the modified integrated waste management plan to the Scottish Ministers for approval.

Sections 44A to B

Section 44A was inserted by the **Environment Act 1995**. It was subsequently repealed by the **Waste (England and Wales) Regulations 2011**. Section 44B (National waste strategy: Scotland) was repealed by the **National Waste Management Plan for Scotland Regulations 2007**.

Sections 45 to 48 and 51 to 61: Collection, Disposal or Treatment of Controlled Waste

Note: sections 49 (waste recycling plans by collection authorities), 50 (waste disposal plans of waste regulation authorities), 54 (special provisions for land occupied by disposal authorities: Scotland) and 61 (duty of waste regulation authorities as respects closed landfills) have been repealed. Sections 45, 52 and 57 are part repealed. Sections 47ZA, 47ZB, 59ZA and 59A apply in England and Wales only.

These sections deal with the collection, disposal and treatment of controlled waste, particularly in relation to waste collection and disposal authorities. These sections address the duties and functions of waste collection and disposal authorities, receptacles for waste collection, powers for recycling and the payment of recycling credits. Of particular importance is section 59.

Section 59: Powers to Require Removal of Waste Unlawfully Deposited

If any controlled waste or extractive waste is deposited in or on any land, in the area of a waste regulation authority or waste collection authority, in contravention of section 33(1), or regulation 12 of the **Environmental Permitting Regulations**, the authority may, by notice served on him, require the occupier to do either or both of the following:

- To remove the waste from the land within a specified period not less than a period of 21 days, beginning with the service of the notice.
- To take within such a period, specified steps with a view to eliminating or reducing the consequences of the deposit of the waste.

Section 62: Special Provision with Respect to Certain Dangerous or Intractable Waste

This section only applies in Scotland. In England and Wales, this section was repealed by the **Hazardous Waste (England and Wales) Regulations 2005**.

If the Secretary of State considers that controlled waste of any kind is, or may be so dangerous or difficult to treat, keep or dispose of that special provision is required for dealing with it, he shall make provision by Regulations for the treatment, keeping or disposal of waste of that kind ("special waste").

Section 62A: Lists of Waste Displaying Hazardous Properties

The Secretary of State (in England) or the National Assembly for Wales can make regulations listing any controlled waste in England/Wales which is not listed as a hazardous waste in the Hazardous Waste List.

Section 75: Meaning of Waste, etc.

"Waste" is anything that is any substance or object which the holder discards or intends or is required to discard. For the purposes of this definition, "holder" means the waste producer or the natural or legal person who is in possession of the waste.

"Waste producer" means any person whose activities produce waste or any person who carries out pre-processing, mixing or other operations resulting in a change in the nature or composition of this waste.

"Controlled waste" means household, industrial and commercial waste, or any such waste.

"Household waste" means waste from domestic property, that is to say a building or self-contained part of a building, which is used wholly for the purposes of living accommodation; a caravan, which usually and for the time being, is situated on a caravan site, a residential home, premises forming part of a university or school or other educational establishment and premises forming part of a hospital or nursing home.

"Industrial waste" means waste from any of the following premises:

- Any factory, any premises used for the purposes of, or in connection with, the provision to the public of transport services by land, water or air.
- Any premises used for the purposes of or in connection with, the supply to the public of gas, water or electricity or the provision of sewerage services.
- Any premises used for the purposes of, or in connection with, the provision to the public of postal or telecommunications services.
- Any mine or quarry or any premises used for agriculture within the meaning of the **Agriculture Act 1947**.

"Commercial waste" means waste from premises used wholly or mainly for the purposes of a trade or business, or the purposes of sport, recreation or entertainment excluding household waste, industrial waste, waste from any mine or quarry and waste from premises used for agriculture within the meaning of the **Agriculture Act 1947** or, in Scotland, the **Agriculture (Scotland) Act 1948**; and waste of any other description prescribed by Regulations made by the Secretary of State.

"Hazardous waste" means any waste which is a hazardous waste for the purposes of the **Hazardous Waste (England and Wales) Regulations 2005**. This definition does not apply in Scotland.

Part IIA - Contaminated Land

Inserted by the **Environment Act 1995**.

Sections 78A to 78YC of the Act, together with the **Contaminated Land (England) Regulations 2006**, contain the framework for identifying and dealing with contaminated land.

Sections 78A to 78D: Identification of Contaminated Land and Special Sites

Local authorities have a duty to inspect their land to identify whether any is contaminated and whether any should be designated as a 'special site' because of the nature of the contamination. Local authorities are required to draw up a contaminated land strategy and must follow guidance from the Secretary of State.

"Contaminated land" is defined as land which appears to be in such a condition, by reason of substances, in, on or under the land, that:

- Significant harm is being caused or there is a significant possibility of such harm being caused.
- Significant pollution of controlled waters is being, or is likely to be, caused.

Following identification, the local authority should then notify the appropriate agency, the owner of the land, the occupiers of any part of the land and any other appropriate person. The site may be designated as 'special'.

Sections 78E to 78G: Remediation

Following designation of a site as contaminated, the enforcing authority should serve a remediation notice on the appropriate person. The appropriate person is normally the person(s) who knowingly caused or permitted the contamination. If they cannot be found, it is usually the current occupier or owner. It is an offence not to comply with the requirements of a remediation notice (see section 78M(3) and (4)). Failure to comply with a remediation notice carries, on summary conviction an unlimited fine plus a further fine of one-tenth of the greater of **£5,000** or level 4 on the standard scale (currently **£2,500**) for each day the offence continues.

Section 78H: Restrictions and Prohibitions on Serving Remediation Notices

Paragraph (5) requires that a remediation notice is not served in the following circumstances:

- Where it appears to the enforcing authority that there is nothing by way of remediation that could be specified in a remediation notice. (Must publish a Remediation Declaration.)
- If appropriate things are being or will be done by way of remediation without the service of a remediation notice.
- If the appropriate person is the enforcing authority itself.
- If the enforcing authority is to carry out the remediation itself.

Appeals are available under section 78L. The **Contaminated Land (England) Regulations 2006** detail the grounds for appeal.

Sections 78N and 78P: Power of Enforcing Authority to Carry out Remediation

The enforcing authority may carry out the remediation work itself, in certain circumstances. For example, in the case of serious harm or where a remediation notice is not complied with.

Section 78Q: Special Sites

The **Contaminated Land (England) Regulations 2006** specify those sites which may be 'special'. The **CN&E Act 2005** has been amended so that radioactive contamination is now included. In the case of Special Sites, the appropriate Agency adopts the remediation notice once it has been served.

A further section, 78QA, dealing with land no longer considered to be contaminated was added by the **Regulatory Reform (Scotland) Act 2014** and applies in Scotland only. Equivalent provisions for England and Wales are not yet in force (as of October 2017).

Sections 78R to 78T: Public Registers

Each enforcing authority is required to maintain a register containing particulars relating to contaminated land and special sites.

Part III - Statutory Nuisances and Clean Air

Section 79: Statutory Nuisances and Inspections

Section 79(1), as amended, defines the following statutory nuisances:

- Any premises in such a state as to be prejudicial to health or a nuisance.
- Smoke emitted from premises so as to be prejudicial to health or a nuisance.
- Fumes or gases emitted from premises so as to be prejudicial to health or a nuisance (private dwellings only).
- Any dust, steam, smell or other effluvia arising on industrial, trade or business premises and being prejudicial to health or a nuisance.
- Any accumulation or deposit which is prejudicial to health or a nuisance.
- Any animal kept in such a manner or place as to be prejudicial to health or a nuisance.
- Any insects emanating from relevant industrial, trade or business premises and being prejudicial to health or a nuisance (from April 2006, inserted by **CN&E Act 2005**).
- Artificial light emitted from premises so as to be prejudicial to health or a nuisance (from April 2006, inserted by **CN&E Act 2005**).
- Noise emitted from premises so as to be prejudicial to health or a nuisance.
- Noise that is prejudicial to health or a nuisance and is emitted from or caused by a vehicle, machinery or equipment in a street (inserted by the **Noise and Statutory Nuisance Act 1993**).
- Any other matter declared by any enactment to be a statutory nuisance (e.g. the **Public Health Act 1936**, regarding ponds and watercourses).

Local authorities have a duty to inspect their areas from time to time to detect whether a nuisance exists, or is likely to occur or recur.

Section 80: Summary Proceedings

Where the local authority is satisfied that a statutory nuisance exists, it must serve an abatement notice on the person responsible, or if they cannot be found, the owner or occupier. (**CN&E Act 2005** allows the abatement notice to be deferred for seven days while efforts are made to persuade the person responsible to stop the nuisance.) Procedures for noise from vehicles, machinery and equipment in the street, allow a notice to be affixed.

Failure to comply with the terms of the abatement notice may result in:

- A fine not exceeding level 5 on the standard scale plus a daily fine of up to one-tenth of the greater of £5,000 or level 4 on the standard scale (currently £2,500) for each day that the offence continues after conviction.
- For offences on industrial, trade or business premises, an unlimited fine (£40,000 in Scotland).

Section 81: Supplementary Provisions

Where a statutory nuisance which exists or has occurred within the area of a local authority, or which has affected any part of that area, appears to the local authority to be wholly or partly caused by some act or default committed or taking place outside the area, the local authority may act under section 80 above as if the act or default were wholly within that area, except that any appeal shall be heard by a magistrates' court, or in Scotland, the Sheriff having jurisdiction where the act or default is alleged to have taken place.

Where an abatement notice has not been complied with the local authority may, whether or not they take proceedings for an offence or, in Scotland, whether or not proceedings have been taken for an offence, under section 80(4) above, abate the nuisance and do whatever may be necessary in execution of the notice.

Expenses reasonably incurred by a local authority in abating, or preventing the recurrence of the statutory nuisance may be recovered from the person by whose act or default the nuisance was caused.

If the local authority feels that proceedings for an offence under section 80(4) would afford an inadequate remedy in the case of any statutory nuisance, they may take proceedings in the High Court or, in Scotland, in any court of competent jurisdiction in order to secure the abatement, prohibition or restriction of the nuisance.

Section 82: Summary Proceedings by Persons Aggrieved by Statutory Nuisances

Action to abate a nuisance may also be taken by an individual through the magistrates' court (Sheriff Court in Scotland).

Part IV - Litter, etc.

Creates an offence of leaving litter and allows for fixed penalty notices to be served. Also allows the designation of litter control areas. Abandoned trolleys are also addressed under this part.

Part V - Radioactive Substances

Now repealed and replaced mainly by the **Environmental Permitting Regulations**.

Part VI - Genetically Modified Organisms

Part VII - Nature Conservation

This part (sections 128-138) has been repealed.

Part VIII - Miscellaneous

Addresses pollution at sea, control of dogs, and straw and stubble burning.

EQUALITY ACT 2010

This became law in April 2010, with most of the provisions effective from 1 October 2010. It repealed the **Disability Discrimination Act 1995**, the **Race Relations Act 1976** and the **Sex Discrimination Act 1975**. (Note: It did not replace the **Equality Act 2006** which covers other provisions.)

It is a vast piece of legislation, comprising 16 Parts and 28 Schedules. Only the most relevant content is included here.

Part 1: Socio-Economic Inequalities

This part is not yet in force.

Part 2: Key Concepts

The protected characteristics are age; disability; gender reassignment; marriage and civil partnership; pregnancy and maternity; race; religion or belief; sex; sexual orientation.

Prohibited conduct includes the following.

Direct Discrimination (Section 13)

(1) A person (A) discriminates against another (B) if, because of a protected characteristic, A treats B less favourably than A treats or would treat others.

(2) If the protected characteristic is age, A does not discriminate against B if A can show A's treatment of B to be a proportionate means of achieving a legitimate aim.

(3) If the protected characteristic is disability, and B is not a disabled person, A does not discriminate against B only because A treats or would treat disabled persons more favourably than A treats B.

(5) If the protected characteristic is race, less favourable treatment includes segregating B from others.

(6) If the protected characteristic is sex:

   (a) less favourable treatment of a woman includes less favourable treatment of her because she is breast-feeding;

   (b) in a case where B is a man, no account is to be taken of special treatment afforded to a woman in connection with pregnancy or childbirth.

Discrimination Arising from Disability (Section 15)

(1) A person (A) discriminates against a disabled person (B) if:

   (a) A treats B unfavourably because of something arising in consequence of B's disability; and

   (b) A cannot show that the treatment is a proportionate means of achieving a legitimate aim.

Pregnancy and Maternity Discrimination: Work Cases (Section 18)

(1) This section has effect for the purposes of the application of Part 5 (work) to the protected characteristic of pregnancy and maternity.

(2) A person (A) discriminates against a woman if, in the protected period in relation to a pregnancy of hers, A treats her unfavourably because of the pregnancy, or because of illness suffered by her as a result of it.

(3) A person (A) discriminates against a woman if A treats her unfavourably because she is on compulsory maternity leave.

(4) A person (A) discriminates against a woman if A treats her unfavourably because she is exercising or seeking to exercise, or has exercised or sought to exercise, the right to ordinary or additional maternity leave.

(5) For the purposes of subsection (2), if the treatment of a woman is in implementation of a decision taken in the protected period, the treatment is to be regarded as occurring in that period (even if the implementation is not until after the end of that period).

(6) The protected period, in relation to a woman's pregnancy, begins when the pregnancy begins, and ends:

(a) if she has the right to ordinary and additional maternity leave, at the end of the additional maternity leave period or (if earlier) when she returns to work after the pregnancy;

(b) if she does not have that right, at the end of the period of two weeks beginning with the end of the pregnancy.

Indirect Discrimination (Section 19)

(1) A person (A) discriminates against another (B) if A applies to B a provision, criterion or practice which is discriminatory in relation to a relevant protected characteristic of B's.

(2) For the purposes of subsection (1), a provision, criterion or practice is discriminatory in relation to a relevant protected characteristic of B's if:

   (a) A applies, or would apply, it to persons with whom B does not share the characteristic,

   (b) it puts, or would put, persons with whom B shares the characteristic at a particular disadvantage when compared with persons with whom B does not share it,

   (c) it puts, or would put, B at that disadvantage, and

   (d) A cannot show it to be a proportionate means of achieving a legitimate aim.

Duty to Make Adjustments for Disabled Persons (Section 20)

The duty comprises the following three requirements:

(3) The first requirement is a requirement, where a provision, criterion or practice of A's puts a disabled person at a substantial disadvantage in relation to a relevant matter in comparison with persons who are not disabled, to take such steps as it is reasonable to have to take to avoid the disadvantage.

(4) The second requirement is a requirement, where a physical feature puts a disabled person at a substantial disadvantage in relation to a relevant matter in comparison with persons who are not disabled, to take such steps as it is reasonable to have to take to avoid the disadvantage.

(5) The third requirement is a requirement, where a disabled person would, but for the provision of an auxiliary aid, be put at a substantial disadvantage in relation to a relevant matter in comparison with persons who are not disabled, to take such steps as it is reasonable to have to take to provide the auxiliary aid.

Part 5: Work

Employees and Applicants (Section 39)

(1) An employer (A) must not discriminate against a person (B):

   (a) in the arrangements A makes for deciding to whom to offer employment;

   (b) as to the terms on which A offers B employment;

   (c) by not offering B employment.

(2) An employer (A) must not discriminate against an employee of A's (B):

   (a) as to B's terms of employment;

   (b) in the way A affords B access, or by not affording B access, to opportunities for promotion, transfer or training or for receiving any other benefit, facility or service;

   (c) by dismissing B;

   (d) by subjecting B to any other detriment.

(3) An employer (A) must not victimise a person (B):

    (a) in the arrangements A makes for deciding to whom to offer employment;

    (b) as to the terms on which A offers B employment;

    (c) by not offering B employment.

(4) An employer (A) must not victimise an employee of A's (B):

    (a) as to B's terms of employment;

    (b) in the way A affords B access, or by not affording B access, to opportunities for promotion, transfer or training or for any other benefit, facility or service;

    (c) by dismissing B;

    (d) by subjecting B to any other detriment.

(5) A duty to make reasonable adjustments applies to an employer.

Enquiries about Disability and Health (Section 60)

A person (A) to whom an application for work is made must not ask about the health of the applicant (B):

(a) before offering work to B; or

(b) where A is not in a position to offer work to B, before including B in a pool of applicants from whom A intends (when in a position to do so) to select a person to whom to offer work.

A does not contravene a relevant disability provision merely by asking about B's health; but A's conduct in reliance on information given in response may be a contravention of a relevant disability provision.

Sex Equality (Sections 64 to 71)

Relevant Types of Work (Section 64)

(1) Sections 66 to 70 apply where:

    (a) a person (A) is employed on work that is equal to the work that a comparator of the opposite sex (B) does;

    (b) a person (A) holding a personal or public office does work that is equal to the work that a comparator of the opposite sex (B) does.

(2) The references in subsection (1) to the work that B does are not restricted to work done contemporaneously with the work done by A.

Equal Work (Section 65)

(1) For the purposes of this Chapter, A's work is equal to that of B if it is:

    (a) like B's work;

    (b) rated as equivalent to B's work; or

    (c) of equal value to B's work.

(2) A's work is like B's work if:

    (a) A's work and B's work are the same or broadly similar; and

    (b) such differences as there are between their work are not of practical importance in relation to the terms of their work.

(3) So on a comparison of one person's work with another's for the purposes of subsection (2), it is necessary to have regard to:

   (a) the frequency with which differences between their work occur in practice; and

   (b) the nature and extent of the differences.

(4) A's work is rated as equivalent to B's work if a job evaluation study:

   (a) gives an equal value to A's job and B's job in terms of the demands made on a worker; or

   (b) would give an equal value to A's job and B's job in those terms were the evaluation not made on a sex-specific system.

(5) A system is sex-specific if, for the purposes of one or more of the demands made on a worker, it sets values for men different from those it sets for women.

(6) A's work is of equal value to B's work if it is:

   (a) neither like B's work nor rated as equivalent to B's work; but

   (b) nevertheless equal to B's work in terms of the demands made on A by reference to factors such as effort, skill and decision-making.

Part 9: Enforcement

An employment tribunal has jurisdiction to determine a complaint relating to a contravention of Part 5 (work); see section 120.

Schedule 1 Part 1 - Determination of Disability

Schedule 7 Part 1 - Terms of Work

Schedule 8 - Work: Reasonable Adjustments

Schedule 9 - Work: Exceptions

EUROPEAN UNION (WITHDRAWAL AGREEMENT) ACT 2020

Note

The following draws heavily on the explanatory notes that accompany the text of the **European Union (Withdrawal Agreement) Act 2020**. Material within the Act that is considered to be of little direct relevance to health, safety and environmental management has been excluded for the sake of brevity.

The Act has 42 sections, arranged in five parts, with five schedules. What follows is a summary of some key provisions of this Act.

Overview

The **European Union (Withdrawal Agreement) Act 2020** ('The Act') implements the 'Withdrawal Agreement', as agreed between the UK and the EU. The Withdrawal Agreement sets out the arrangements for the United Kingdom's withdrawal from the EU. The Act amends the **European Union (Withdrawal) Act 2018** (see Appendix below) to ensure it reflects the terms of the Withdrawal Agreement.

The Act also creates powers to make secondary legislation, where appropriate, to enable the Withdrawal Agreement to be implemented domestically.

There will be an implementation period, which will last until 11.00 pm on 31 December 2020 ('IP completion day'). During the implementation period, existing EU law will continue to apply to the UK. New pieces of EU law introduced during the implementation period will also apply in the UK.

Relationship to EU Law

On 31 January 2020 ('Exit day'), the **European Union (Withdrawal) Act 2018** repealed the **European Communities Act 1972**. As of 'Exit day', the UK ceased to be an EU Member State. That being the case, the UK's relationship with EU law will be in accordance with the Withdrawal Agreement, rather than as a Member State.

The Act will make sure that existing legislation continues to operate properly during the implementation period, despite the fact that the UK is no longer a Member State.

On IP completion day, existing EU law that is applicable in the UK will be converted into 'Retained EU law' and historic European Court of Justice decisions will be domesticated. After IP completion day, it will be possible to decide whether to depart from any retained EU law.

Governance, Enforcement and Safeguards

The European Court of Justice's jurisdiction in the UK will come to an end on IP completion day. The European Court's continued jurisdiction until IP completion day will ensure that EU rules are interpreted and applied consistently in both the UK and the EU for the duration of the implementation period. The UK will retain the ability to challenge the application of EU law throughout the implementation period.

Citizens' Rights

The Act establishes an independent body to monitor the implementation and application of the citizens' rights part of the Withdrawal Agreement.

The Act makes provision for citizens' rights by legislating for:

- rights in relation to entry and residence (**Sections 7 to 11**);
- recognition of professional qualifications (**Section 12**);
- co-ordination of social security systems (**Section 13**);
- non-discrimination and equal treatment (**Section 14**); and
- monitoring of citizens' rights through the establishment of an Independent Monitoring Authority (the IMA) (**Section 15**).

All EU citizens, EEA EFTA and Swiss nationals, and their family members, resident in the UK will be eligible to apply for leave under the EU Settlement Scheme.

(See Appendix below for further details.)

Other Separation Issues

Sections 18 and 19 provide the technical basis for the winding down of ongoing processes and arrangements so as to ensure an orderly withdrawal from the EU and provide legal certainty for individuals and businesses. For example, goods placed on the UK or EU market under EU law before the end of the implementation period may continue to circulate freely between the UK and the EU until they reach their end users.

New arrangements may be needed to ensure the future economic and security relationship between the UK and the EU after the implementation period.

Main Financial Provision

Section 20 addresses the financial settlement arrangements for payments to be made by the UK to the EU, and vice versa. This does not include other costs arising as a consequence of the UK exiting the EU, e.g. the costs of new administrative arrangements.

Northern Ireland

The Northern Ireland protocol is set out at **Sections 21 to 24**. This ensures that the UK (including Northern Ireland) does not remain in a customs union with the European Union and makes arrangements that seek to ensure that there are no checks and controls conducted at or near the border between Northern Ireland and Ireland.

Parliamentary Oversight

There will be parliamentary scrutiny over any EU legislation made during the implementation period that affects the UK's vital national interests.

Parliamentary Sovereignty

Section 38 recognises the sovereignty of the UK Parliament, which subsists notwithstanding directly applicable or directly effective EU law continuing to be recognised and available in domestic law.

Appendix

European Union (Withdrawal) Act 2018

The **European Union (Withdrawal) Act 2018** repealed the **European Communities Act 1972**, converts EU law that was effective on 'Exit day' into domestic law, and preserves laws made in the UK to implement EU obligations. It also creates temporary powers to make secondary legislation to enable corrections to be made to the laws that would otherwise no longer operate appropriately once the UK has left the EU, so that the domestic legal system continues to function correctly outside the EU.

Notes on Citizens' Rights

Free movement rights for EU citizens, European Economic Area (EEA), European Free Trade Association (EFTA) nationals, and Swiss nationals are implemented domestically mainly through the **Immigration (European Economic Area) Regulations 2016** (the '**EEA Regulations**').

Free movement covers four broad areas:

- the right to enter the UK;
- the right to reside;
- the right to work; and
- rights to access benefits and services, and to equal treatment.

As free movement ends, the UK will move away from the EU law framework of rights. The **EEA Regulations** will be revoked at the end of the implementation period. In place of the EU law framework of residence, a domestic law framework for residence will be established based on the skills people can contribute to the UK.

EU citizens, EEA EFTA nationals, and Swiss nationals, and their family members, resident in the UK before the end of the implementation period are already able to apply for residence status under the EU Settlement Scheme.

EU citizens, EEA EFTA nationals, and Swiss nationals, and their family members who have been continuously resident in the UK for five years are eligible for settled status, also known as 'indefinite leave to remain'. Those who have been continuously resident in the UK for less than five years are eligible for 'pre-settled status', also known as 'limited leave to remain'. Those with either settled status or pre-settled status will continue to be entitled to work, study, and access public services and benefits on the same basis as they do now. These entitlements will be subject to future domestic policy changes which apply to UK nationals.

Notes on Professional Qualifications

A number of EU Directives provide for the recognition of professional qualifications (such as those for Chartered Safety and Health Practitioners, Chartered Environmental Health Practitioners, and Environmental Health Officers). These Directives are implemented into UK law by, for example, the **European Union (Recognition of Professional Qualifications) Regulations 2015** and the **Medical Act 1983**.

EU citizens and EEA EFTA nationals and their family members residing or working in the UK at the end of the implementation period with recognitions under these Directives will continue to have qualifications recognised under the Withdrawal Agreement and the EEA EFTA Separation Agreement.

Swiss nationals with recognised qualifications will continue to have qualifications recognised under the Swiss Citizens' Rights Agreement. Lawyers will, for five years after the end of the implementation period, be able to use their qualifications to provide services if certain conditions are met.

During the implementation period, individuals may continue to apply for recognition of their professional qualifications. For those in scope of the residence parts of the Withdrawal Agreement and EEA EFTA Separation Agreement, any qualifications recognised, or in the process of recognition, by the end of the implementation period will continue to be recognised. Decisions on recognition of qualifications sought after the end of the implementation period will be subject to the outcome of future relationship negotiations.

For those covered by the Swiss Citizens' Rights Agreement, any qualifications recognised, or in the process of recognition, by the end of the implementation period will continue to be recognised. Any Swiss or UK national who has a qualification, or is in the process of obtaining one when the implementation period ends, will have up to four years from the end of the implementation period to apply for recognition.

FATAL ACCIDENTS ACT 1976

Section 1: Right of Action for Wrongful Act Causing Death

(1) If death is caused by any wrongful act, neglect or default which would (if death had not ensued) have entitled the person injured to maintain an action and recover damages in respect thereof, the person who would have been liable if death had not ensued shall be liable to an action for damages, notwithstanding the death of the person injured.

(2) Subject to section IA(2) below, every such action shall be for the benefit of the dependants of the person ("the deceased") whose death has been so caused.

(3) In this Act "dependant" means:

   (a) the wife or husband or former wife or husband of the deceased;

   (b) the civil partner or former civil partner of the deceased;

   (c) any person who was living with the deceased in the same household immediately before the date of the death; and had been living with the deceased in the same household for at least two years before that date; and was living during the whole of that period as the husband or wife of the deceased;

   (d) any parent or other ascendant of the deceased;

   (e) any person who was treated by the deceased as his parent;

   (f) any child or other descendant of the deceased;

   (g) any person (not being a child of the deceased) who, in the case of any marriage to which the deceased was at any time a party, was treated by the deceased as a child of the family in relation to that marriage;

   (h) any person (not being a child of the deceased) who, in the case of any civil partnership in which the deceased was at any time a civil partner, was treated by the deceased as a child of the family in relation to that civil partnership;

   (i) any person who is, or is the issue of, a brother, sister, uncle or aunt of the deceased.

(4) The reference to the former wife or husband of the deceased in subsection (3)(a) above includes a reference to a person whose marriage to the deceased has been annulled or declared void as well as a person whose marriage to the deceased has been dissolved. A similar provision exists in the case of a civil partnership.

(5) In deducing any relationship for the purposes of subsection (3) above:

   - any relationship of affinity shall be treated as a relationship by consanguinity, any relationship of the half blood as a relationship of the whole blood, and the stepchild of any person as his child, and

   - an illegitimate person shall be treated as the legitimate child of his mother and reputed father.

(6) Any reference in this Act to injury includes any disease and any impairment of a person's physical or mental condition.

Section 1A: Bereavement

(1) An action under this Act may consist of or include a claim for damages for bereavement.

(2) A claim for damages for bereavement shall only be for the benefit:

   - of the wife or husband or civil partner of the deceased; and

   - where the deceased was a minor who was never married or a civil partner:

     – of his parents, if he was legitimate; and

     – of his mother, if he was illegitimate.

(3) Subject to (5) below, the sum to be awarded as damages under this section shall be £12,980.

(4) Where there is a claim for damages under this section for the benefit of both the parents of the deceased, the sum awarded shall be divided equally between them (subject to any deduction failing to be made in respect of costs not recovered from the defendant).

(5) The Lord Chancellor may by order made by statutory instrument, subject to annulment in pursuance of a resolution of either House of Parliament, amend this section by varying the sum for the time being specified in subsection (3) above.

Section 2: Persons Entitled to Bring the Action

(1) The action shall be brought by and in the name of the executor or administrator of the deceased.

- If there is no executor or administrator of the deceased, or
- If no action is brought within six months after the death by and in the name of an executor or administrator of the deceased,

the action may be brought by and in the name of all or any of the persons for whose benefit an executor or administrator could have brought it.

(2) Not more than one action shall lie for and in respect of the same subject matter of complaint.

(3) The plaintiff in the action shall be required to deliver to the defendant or his solicitor full particulars of the persons for whom and on whose behalf the action is brought and of the nature of the claim in respect of which damages are sought to be recovered.

Section 3: Assessment of Damages

(1) In the action such damages, other than damages for bereavement, may be awarded as are proportional to the injury resulting from the death to the dependants respectively.

(2) After deducting the costs not recovered from the defendant any amount recovered otherwise than as damages for bereavement shall be divided among the dependants in such shares as may be directed.

(3) In an action under this Act where there fall to be assessed damages payable to a widow in respect of the death of her husband there shall not be taken account the remarriage of the widow or her prospects of remarriage.

(4) In an action under this Act where there fall to be assessed damages payable to a person who is a dependant by virtue of section 1(3)(b) above in respect of the death of the person with whom the dependant was living as husband or wife or civil partner there shall be taken into account (together with any other matter that appears to the court to be relevant to the action) the fact that the dependant had no enforceable right to financial support by the deceased as a result of their living together.

(5) If the dependants have incurred funeral expenses in respect of the deceased, damages may be awarded in respect of those expenses.

(6) Money paid into court in satisfaction of a cause of action under this Act may be in one sum without specifying any person's share.

Section 4: Assessment of Damages: Disregard of Benefits

In assessing damages in respect of a person's death in an action under this Act, benefits which have accrued or will or may accrue to any person from his estate or otherwise as a result of his death shall be disregarded.

Section 5: Contributory Negligence

Where any person dies as the result partly of his own fault and partly of the fault of any other person or persons, and accordingly if an action were brought for the benefit of the estate under the **Law Reform (Miscellaneous Provisions) Act 1934**, as the damages recoverable would be reduced under section 1(1) of the **Law Reform (Contributory Negligence) Act 1945**, so any damages recoverable in an action under this Act shall be reduced to a proportionate extent.

FIRE SAFETY (SCOTLAND) REGULATIONS 2006 (SI 2006 NO. 456)

These Regulations came into force on 1 October 2006.

Note: References here to the sections of the Act refer to the **Fire (Scotland) Act 2005**.

Regulation 3: Duty to Review

A review of an assessment under section 53 or 54 must be carried out regularly so as to keep it up to date. A review of an assessment under section 53 or 54 must be carried out if:

(a) there is reason to suspect that it is no longer valid; or

(b) there has been a significant change in the matters to which it relates including when the relevant premises, special, technical and organisational measures or organisation of the work undergo significant changes.

Regulation 4: Duty in Respect of Young Persons

An employer must not employ a young person unless he or she has, in relation to risks to young persons, carried out or reviewed an assessment in accordance with his or her duties under section 53 or 54 and these Regulations.

Regulation 5: Assessment and Review Duty in Respect of Young Persons

In carrying out or reviewing an assessment under section 53 an employer, before employing a young person, must take particular account of the following in respect of harm caused by fire:

(a) the inexperience, lack of awareness of risks and immaturity of young persons;

(b) the fitting-out and layout of the relevant premises;

(c) the nature, degree and duration of exposure to physical and chemical agents;

(d) the form, range, and use of work equipment, and the way in which it is handled;

(e) the organisation of processes and activities;

(f) the extent of the fire safety training provided or to be provided to young persons; and

(g) risks from agents, processes and work listed in the Annex to **Council Directive 94/33/EC** on the protection of young people at work.

Regulation 6: Assessment and Review Duty in Respect of Dangerous Substances

Where a dangerous substance is or is liable to be present in the relevant premises, the matters which must be taken into account when a person carries out an assessment or a review under section 53 or 54 are:

(a) the hazardous properties of the substance;

(b) information on safety provided by the supplier, including information contained in any relevant safety data sheet;

(c) the circumstances of the work including:

　(i) the special, technical and organisational measures and the substances used and their possible interactions;

　(ii) the amount of the substance involved;

　(iii) where the work will involve more than one dangerous substance, the risk presented by such substances in combination; and

　(iv) the arrangements for the safe handling, storage and transport of dangerous substances and of waste containing dangerous substances;

(d) activities, such as maintenance, where there is the potential for a high level of risk;

(e) the effect of measures which have been or will be taken pursuant to the 2005 Act and to these Regulations;

(f) the likelihood that an explosive atmosphere will occur and its persistence;

(g) the likelihood that ignition sources, including electrostatic discharges, will be present and become active and effective;

(h) the scale of the anticipated effects;

(i) any places which are, or can be connected via openings to, places in which explosive atmospheres may occur; and

(j) such additional safety information as the person with duties under section 53 or 54 may need in order to complete the assessment or review.

Regulation 7: New Work Activities where Dangerous Substances are Present

No new work activity involving a dangerous substance may commence unless the person with duties under section 53 or 54 has fulfilled their Chapter 1 duties in respect of the dangerous substances.

Regulation 8: Duty to Record Information

As soon as practicable after an assessment has been carried out or reviewed, the person with duties under section 53 or 54 must record the information specified in regulation 9 where:

(a) he or she employs five or more employees; or

(b) a licence or registration under an enactment is required in relation to the relevant premises; or

(c) an alterations notice requiring this by virtue of section 65(6)(a) is in force in relation to the relevant premises.

Regulation 9: Specified Information

The specified information is:

(a) the significant findings of the assessment, including the measures which have been or will be taken by the person having duties under section 53 or 54 pursuant to Part 3 of the 2005 Act and these Regulations; and

(b) any relevant person or group of relevant persons identified by the assessment as being especially at risk from fire.

Regulation 10: Fire Safety Arrangements

(1) In carrying out duties to which a person is subject by virtue of section 53(2)(b), 53(3)(b), 54(2)(b) or 54(5)(b), a person must make and give effect to such arrangements as are appropriate, having regard to the size of his or her undertaking and the nature of its activities, for the effective planning, organisation, control, monitoring and review of the fire safety measures within the meaning of Schedule 2 to the 2005 Act.

(2) That person must record the arrangements referred to in paragraph (1) where:

(a) he or she employs five or more employees; or

(b) a licence or registration under an enactment is required in relation to the relevant premises; or

(c) an alterations notice requiring this by virtue of section 65(6)(b) is in force in relation to the relevant premises.

Regulation 11: Elimination or Reduction of Risks from Dangerous Substances

(1) Where a dangerous substance is present in relevant premises, a person having duties under section 53 or 54 must ensure that risk to relevant persons related to the presence of the substance is either eliminated or reduced so far as is reasonably practicable.

(2) In complying with the duty under paragraph (1), a person must, so far as is reasonably practicable, replace a dangerous substance, or the use of a dangerous substance, with a substance or process which either eliminates or reduces the risk to relevant persons.

(3) Where it is not reasonably practicable to eliminate risk pursuant to paragraphs (1) and (2), a person must, so far as is reasonably practicable, apply measures consistent with the assessment under section 53 or 54 and appropriate to the nature of the activity or operation, including the measures specified in the Schedule to:

(a) control the risk; and

(b) mitigate the detrimental effects of fire.

(4) The person with duties under section 53 or 54 must also:

(a) arrange for the safe handling, storage and transport of dangerous substances and waste containing dangerous substances; and

(b) ensure that any conditions necessary pursuant to these Regulations and the 2005 Act for ensuring the elimination or reduction of risk are maintained.

Regulation 12: Means for Fighting Fire and Means for Giving Warning in the Event of Fire

(1) Where necessary (whether due to the features of the relevant premises, the activity carried on there, any hazard present or any other relevant circumstances) in order to ensure the safety of relevant persons in respect of harm caused by fire, a person with duties under section 53 or 54 must ensure that:

(a) the relevant premises are, to the extent that it is appropriate, equipped with appropriate means for fighting fire and means for giving warning in the event of fire; and

(b) any non-automatic fire-fighting equipment so provided is easily accessible, simple to use and indicated by signs.

(2) For the purposes of paragraph (1), what is appropriate is to be determined having regard to the dimensions and use of the relevant premises, the equipment contained in the relevant premises, the physical and chemical properties of the substances likely to be present and the maximum number of persons who may be present at any one time.

(3) The person with duties under section 53 or 54 must, where necessary:

   (a) take measures for fighting fire in the relevant premises, adapted to the nature of the activities carried on there and the size of the undertaking and of the relevant premises concerned;

   (b) nominate competent persons to implement those measures and ensure that the number of such persons, their training and the equipment available to them are adequate, taking into account the size of, and the specific hazards involved in, the relevant premises concerned; and

   (c) arrange any necessary contacts with external emergency services, particularly as regards fire-fighting and rescue work.

Regulation 13: Means of Escape

(1) Where necessary in order to ensure the safety of relevant persons in respect of harm caused by fire, the person with duties under section 53 or 54 must ensure that routes to emergency exits from relevant premises and the exits themselves are kept free from obstruction at all times.

(2) The following requirements must be complied with in respect of relevant premises where necessary (whether due to the features of the relevant premises, the activity carried on there, any hazard present or any other relevant circumstances) in order to ensure the safety of relevant persons in respect of harm caused by fire:

   (a) emergency routes and exits must lead as directly as possible to a safe area beyond the relevant premises;

   (b) in the event of danger from fire, it must be possible for persons to evacuate the relevant premises as quickly and as safely as possible;

   (c) the number, distribution and dimensions of emergency routes and exits must be adequate having regard to the use of, equipment contained in, and the dimensions of the relevant premises and the maximum number of persons who may be present there at any one time;

   (d) doors on the emergency route shall open in the direction of escape;

   (e) sliding or revolving doors must not be used for exits specifically intended as emergency exits;

   (f) doors on the emergency route must not be so locked or fastened that they cannot be easily and immediately opened by any person who may require to use them in an emergency;

   (g) emergency routes and exits must be indicated by signs; and

   (h) emergency routes and exits requiring illumination must be provided with emergency lighting of adequate intensity in the case of failure of their normal lighting.

Regulation 14: Procedures for Serious and Imminent Danger from Fire and for Danger Areas

(1) A person with duties under section 53 or 54 must:

   (a) establish and, where necessary, give effect to appropriate procedures, including fire safety drills, to be followed in relevant premises in the event of serious and imminent danger to relevant persons from fire;

   (b) nominate a sufficient number of competent persons to implement those procedures in so far as they relate to the evacuation of relevant persons from the relevant premises; and

   (c) ensure that no relevant person has access to any area to which it is necessary to restrict access on grounds of safety in respect of harm caused by fire, unless the person concerned has received adequate safety instruction.

(2) Without prejudice to the generality of paragraph (1)(a), the procedures referred to in that sub-paragraph must:

   (a) so far as is practicable, require any relevant persons who are exposed to serious and imminent danger from fire to be informed of the nature of the hazard and of the steps taken or to be taken to protect them from it;

   (b) enable the relevant persons concerned (if necessary by taking appropriate steps in the absence of guidance or instruction and in the light of their knowledge and the technical means at their disposal) to stop work and immediately proceed to a safe area beyond the relevant premises in the event of their being exposed to serious, imminent and unavoidable danger from fire; and

   (c) save in exceptional cases for reasons duly substantiated (which cases and reasons must be specified in those procedures), require the relevant persons concerned to be prevented from resuming work in any situation where there is still a serious and imminent danger from fire.

Regulation 15: Additional Emergency Measures in Respect of Dangerous Substances

(1) Subject to paragraph (4), in order to ensure the safety in respect of harm caused by fire of relevant persons arising from an accident, incident or emergency related to the presence of a dangerous substance in the relevant premises, the person with duties under section 53 or 54 must ensure that:

    (a) information on emergency arrangements is available, including:

        (i) details of relevant work hazards and hazard identification arrangements; and

        (ii) specific hazards likely to arise at the time of an accident, incident or emergency;

    (b) suitable warning and other communication systems are established to enable an appropriate response, including remedial actions and rescue operations, to be made immediately when such an event occurs;

    (c) where necessary, before any explosion conditions are reached, visual or audible warnings are given and relevant persons withdrawn; and

    (d) where the assessment indicates it is necessary, escape facilities are provided and maintained to ensure that, in the event of danger, relevant persons can leave endangered places promptly and safely.

(2) Subject to paragraph (4), the person with duties under section 53 or 54 must ensure that the information required by regulation 14(1)(a) and paragraph (1)(a) of this regulation, together with information on the matters referred to in paragraphs (1)(b) and (d) is:

    (a) made available to relevant accident and emergency services to enable those services, whether internal or external to the relevant premises, to prepare their own response procedures and precautionary measures; and

    (b) displayed at the relevant premises, unless the results of the assessment make this unnecessary.

(3) Subject to paragraph (4), in the event of a fire arising from an accident, incident or emergency related to the presence of a dangerous substance in the relevant premises, the person with duties under section 53 or 54 must ensure that:

    (a) immediate steps are taken to:

        (i) mitigate the effects of the fire;

        (ii) estore the situation to normal; and

        (iii) inform those relevant persons who may be affected; and

    (b) only those persons who are essential for the carrying out of repairs and other necessary work are permitted in the affected area and they are provided with:

        (i) appropriate personal protective equipment and protective clothing; and

        (ii) any necessary specialised safety equipment and plant,

        (iii) which must be used until the situation is restored to normal.

(4) Paragraphs (1) to (3) do not apply where:

    (a) the results of the assessment show that, because of the quantity of each dangerous substance in the premises, there is only a slight risk to relevant persons; and

    (b) the measures taken by the person with duties under section 53 or 54 to comply with his or her duty under regulation 11 are sufficient to control that risk.

Regulation 16: Maintenance

(1) Where necessary in order to ensure the safety of relevant persons in respect of harm caused by fire the person with duties under section 53 or 54 must ensure that the relevant premises and any facilities, equipment and devices provided in respect of the relevant premises under these Regulations or, subject to paragraph (5), under any other enactment, including any enactment repealed or revoked by, under, or by virtue of the 2005 Act, are subject to a suitable system of maintenance and are maintained in an efficient state, in efficient working order and in good repair.

(2) Where the relevant premises form part of a building, the person with duties under section 53 or 54 may make arrangements with the occupier of any premises forming part of the building for the purpose of ensuring that the requirements of paragraph (1) are met.

(3) Paragraph (2) applies even if the other premises are not relevant premises.

(4) Where the occupier of the other premises is not also the owner of those premises, the reference to the occupier in paragraph (2) is taken to be a reference to both the occupier and the owner.

(5) Paragraph (1) only applies to facilities, equipment and devices provided under other enactments where they are provided in connection with fire safety measures.

Regulation 17: Safety Assistance

(1) The person with duties under section 53 or 54 must, subject to paragraphs (5) and (6), nominate one or more competent persons to assist him or her in undertaking the measures necessary to comply with the Chapter 1 duties.

(2) Where the person with duties under section 53 or 54 nominates persons in accordance with paragraph (1), he or she must make arrangements for ensuring adequate co-operation between them.

(3) The person with duties under section 53 or 54 must ensure that the number of persons nominated under paragraph (1), the time available for them to fulfil their functions and the means at their disposal are adequate having regard to the size of the premises, the risks to which relevant persons are exposed and the distribution of those risks throughout the relevant premises.

(4) The person with duties under section 53 or 54 must ensure that:

  (a) any person nominated by him or her in accordance with paragraph (1) who is not in his or her employment:

   (i) is informed of the factors known or suspected by him or her to affect the safety in respect of harm caused by fire of any other person who may be affected by the carrying on by him or her (whether for profit or not) of an undertaking; and

   (ii) where regulation 18(3) applies, has access to the information referred to in regulation 18(3); and

  (b) any person nominated by him or her in accordance with paragraph (1) is given such information about any person working in his or her undertaking who is:

   (i) employed by him or her under a fixed-term contract of employment, or

   (ii) employed in an employment business,

   as is necessary to enable that person properly to carry out the function specified in that paragraph.

(5) Paragraph (1) does not apply to a self-employed person who is not in partnership with any other person, where he or she has sufficient training and experience or knowledge and other qualities properly to undertake the fire safety measures.

(6) Paragraph (1) does not apply to individuals who are together carrying on business in partnership, where at least one of the individuals concerned has sufficient training and experience or knowledge and other qualities:

  (a) properly to undertake the fire safety measures; and

  (b) properly to assist his or her fellow partners in undertaking those measures.

(7) Where there is a competent person in the employment of a person with duties under section 53 or 54, that competent person must be nominated for the purposes of paragraph (1) in preference to a competent person not in his or her employment.

Regulation 18: Provision of Information to Employees

(1) An employer must provide his or her employees with comprehensible and relevant information on:

  (a) the risks to them identified by the assessment carried out or reviewed under section 53 and these Regulations;

  (b) the fire safety measures taken in accordance with section 53(2)(b) or section 53(3)(b);

  (c) the procedures referred to in regulation 14(1)(a);

  (d) the identities of those persons nominated by him or her in accordance with regulation 12(3)(b) or nominated in accordance with regulation 14(1)(b); and

  (e) the risks notified to him or her in accordance with regulation 21(1)(c).

(2) An employer must, before employing a child, provide a parent of the child with comprehensible and relevant information on:

  (a) the risks to that child identified by the assessment carried out or reviewed under section 53 and these Regulations;

  (b) the fire safety measures taken in accordance with section 53(2)(b) or section 53(3)(b); and

  (c) the risks notified to him or her in accordance with regulation 21(1)(c);

  and for the purposes of this paragraph, "parent of the child" includes a person with parental responsibilities, within the meaning of section 1(3) of the **Children (Scotland) Act 1995**, in relation to the child.

(3) Where a dangerous substance is present in the relevant premises, an employer must, in addition to the information provided under paragraph (1) provide his or her employees with:

  (a) the details of any such substance including:

(i) the name of the substance and the risk which it presents;

(ii) access to any relevant safety data sheet; and

(iii) legislative provisions (concerning the hazardous properties of any such substance) which apply to the substance; and

(b) the significant findings of the assessment carried out or reviewed under section 53 and these Regulations.

(4) The information required by paragraph (3) must be:

(a) adapted to take account of significant changes in the activity carried out or methods of work used by the employer; and

(b) provided in a manner appropriate to the risk identified by the assessment carried out or reviewed under section 53 and these Regulations.

Regulation 19: Provision of Information to Employers and the Self-Employed from Outside Undertakings

(1) A person with duties under section 53 or 54 must ensure that the employer of any employees from an outside undertaking who are working in the relevant premises is provided with comprehensible and relevant information on:

(a) the risks to those employees; and

(b) the fire safety measures taken by the person with duties under section 53 or 54.

(2) A person with duties under section 53 or 54 must ensure that any person working in his or her undertaking who is not his or her employee is provided with appropriate instructions and comprehensible and relevant information regarding any risks to that person.

(3) A person with duties under section 53 or 54 must:

(a) ensure that the employer of any employees from an outside undertaking who are working in the relevant premises is provided with sufficient information to enable that employer to identify any person nominated by the person with duties under section 53 or 54 in accordance with regulation 14(1)(b) to implement evacuation procedures as far as those employees are concerned; and

(b) take all reasonable steps to ensure that any person from an outside undertaking who is working in the relevant premises receives sufficient information to enable that person to identify any person nominated by the person with duties under section 53 or 54 in accordance with regulation 14(1)(b) to implement evacuation procedures as far as they are concerned.

Regulation 20: Training

(1) An employer with duties under section 53 must ensure that his or her employees are provided with adequate fire safety training:

(a) at the time when they are first employed; and

(b) on their being exposed to new or increased risks because of:

(i) their being transferred or given a change of responsibilities within the employer's undertaking; or

(ii) the introduction of new work equipment into, or a change respecting work equipment already in use within, the employer's undertaking; or

(iii) the introduction of new technology into the employer's undertaking; or

(iv) the introduction of a new system of work into, or a change respecting a system of work already in use within, the employer's undertaking.

(2) The training referred to in paragraph (1) must:

(a) include sufficient instruction and training on the appropriate precautions and actions to be taken by the employee in order to safeguard himself or herself and other relevant persons on the premises;

(b) be repeated periodically when appropriate;

(c) be adapted to take account of any new or changed risks;

(d) be provided in a manner appropriate to the risk identified by the assessment carried out or reviewed under section 53; and

(e) take place during working hours.

Regulation 20A: Capabilities [added by the Fire Safety (Scotland) Amendment Regulations 2010]

An employer with duties under section 53 must, when entrusting tasks to an employee, take into consideration the employee's capabilities as regards health and safety, so far as those capabilities relate to fire and are relevant to those tasks.

Regulation 21: Co-operation and Co-ordination

(1) Where two or more persons with duties under section 53 or 54 share, or have duties in respect of, relevant premises (whether on a temporary or a permanent basis) each such person must:

   (a) co-operate with the other persons concerned so far as is necessary to enable them to comply with the requirements and prohibitions imposed on them by or under these Regulations and the 2005 Act;

   (b) (taking into account the nature of his or her activities) take all reasonable steps to co-ordinate the measures he or she takes to comply with the requirements and prohibitions imposed on him or her by or under these Regulations and the 2005 Act with the measures the other persons are taking to comply with the requirements and prohibitions imposed on them by or under these Regulations and the 2005 Act; and

   (c) take all reasonable steps to inform the other persons with duties under section 53 or 54 concerned of the risks to relevant persons arising out of or in connection with the conduct by him or her of his or her undertaking.

(2) Where two or more persons with duties under section 53 or 54 share relevant premises (whether on a temporary or a permanent basis) where an explosive atmosphere may occur, the person with such duties who has overall responsibility for the relevant premises must co-ordinate the implementation of all the measures required by the Chapter 1 duties to be taken to protect relevant persons from any risk from the explosive atmosphere.

Regulation 22: Duties of Employees

Each employee must, while at work, inform his or her employer or any other employee with specific responsibility for the safety in respect of harm caused by fire of his or her fellow employees:

(a) of any work situation which a person with the first-mentioned employee's training and instruction would reasonably consider represented a serious and immediate danger to safety in respect of harm caused by fire; and

(b) of any matter which a person with the first-mentioned employee's training and instruction would reasonably consider represented a shortcoming in the employer's protection arrangements for safety in respect of harm caused by fire;

in so far as that situation or matter either affects the safety in respect of harm caused by fire of that first-mentioned employee or arises out of or in connection with his or her own activities at work, and has not previously been reported to his or her employer or to any other employee of that employer in accordance with this regulation.

Regulation 23: Maintenance of Measures Provided in Relevant Premises for Protection of Fire-Fighters

(1) Where necessary in order to secure the safety of fire-fighters (whether employees of the Scottish Fire and Rescue Service or otherwise) in the event of a fire in relevant premises, the person with duties under section 53 or 54 must ensure that the relevant premises and any facilities, equipment and devices provided in respect of the relevant premises for the use by or protection of fire-fighters under these Regulations, the 2005 Act or under any other enactment, including any enactment repealed or revoked by, under, or by virtue of, the 2005 Act, are subject to a suitable system of maintenance and are maintained in an efficient state, in efficient working order and in good repair.

(2) Where the relevant premises form part of a building, the person with duties under section 53 or 54 may make arrangements with the occupier of any premises forming part of the building for the purpose of ensuring that the requirements of paragraph (1) are met.

(3) Paragraph (2) applies even if the other premises are not relevant premises.

(4) Where the occupier of the other premises is not also the owner of those premises, the reference to the occupier in paragraph (2) is taken to be a reference to both the occupier and the owner.

Regulation 24: Maintenance of Measures Provided in the Common Areas of Private Dwellings for Protection of Fire-Fighters

(1) Regulation 23 shall apply to the common areas of private dwellings as if they were relevant premises, with the modifications specified in paragraphs (2) and (3).

(2) The duty imposed by paragraph (1) shall apply to:

   (a) a person who has control to any extent of the common areas of private dwellings, to that extent; and

(b) if a person falls within sub-paragraph (a) other than by virtue of:

   (i) having control to any extent of the common areas of private dwellings in connection with the carrying on by the person (whether for profit or not) of an undertaking; or

   (ii) owning the common areas of private dwellings;

the person or persons who own the common areas of private dwellings shall also comply with the duty.

FIRE (SCOTLAND) ACT 2005

This is a lengthy piece of legislation, made up of some 91 sections (although some have been repealed) and 4 schedules, the most relevant of which are covered here.

Part 1, section 1A establishes the Scottish Fire and Rescue Service. Sections 2 to 7 (Joint fire and rescue boards, the meaning of "relevant authority" and provision for the appointment of a Chief Officer) have all been repealed.

Chapter 2 (sections 8-11) deals with principal fire and rescue functions.

Chapter 3 (sections 13-16A) covers ancillary functions such as the power to respond to other eventualities, the provision of other services, charging, etc.

Chapter 4 (sections 17-24A) deals with the supply and use of water, and with fire hydrants. Chapter 5 (sections 25-32) sets out the powers of employees and constables.

Section 25: Powers of Authorised Employees in Relation to Emergencies

(1) An employee of the Scottish Fire and Rescue Service who is authorised in writing by the Scottish Fire and Rescue Service for the purposes of this section (an "authorised employee") and on duty may:

    (a) if the employee reasonably believes that a fire has broken out, do anything the employee reasonably believes to be necessary for the purpose of:

        (i) extinguishing the fire; or

        (ii) protecting life or property;

    (b) if the employee reasonably believes that a road traffic accident has occurred, do anything the employee reasonably believes to be necessary for the purpose of:

        (i) rescuing people; or

        (ii) protecting them from serious harm;

    (c) if the employee reasonably believes that an emergency other than a fire or road traffic accident has occurred, do anything the employee reasonably believes to be necessary for the purpose of carrying out any function conferred on the authority in relation to the emergency; and

    (d) do anything the employee reasonably believes to be necessary for the purpose of preventing or limiting damage to property resulting from action taken as mentioned in paragraph (a), (b) or (c).

(2) An authorised employee may in particular under subsection (1):

    (a) enter premises or a place (by force if necessary);

    (b) move a vehicle without the consent of its owner;

    (c) force open and enter a lockfast vehicle;

    (d) close a road;

    (e) stop and regulate traffic;

    (f) restrict the access of persons to premises or a place.

Section 26 sets out powers of constables in relation to fires. These are similar to sections 25(1)(a) and (d). Particular powers are set out in section 26(2) and include:

(a) enter (by force if necessary) premises or a place;

(b) move a vehicle without the consent of its owner;

(c) force open and enter a lockfast vehicle;

(d) restrict the access of persons to premises or a place.

Section 27: Powers of Authorised Employees in Relation to Obtaining Information

(1) Subject to subsection (2) an employee of the Scottish Fire and Rescue Service who is authorised in writing by the Scottish Fire and Rescue Service for the purposes of this section (an "authorised employee") may at any reasonable time enter premises for the purpose of obtaining information needed for the carrying out of the Scottish Fire and Rescue Service's functions under section 9, 10 or 11.

(2) An authorised employee may not under subsection (1):

   (a) enter premises by force; or

   (b) demand admission to premises occupied as a private dwelling unless 24 hours' notice in writing has first been given to the occupier of the dwelling.

(3) If, on the application of an authorised employee, a sheriff or justice of the peace is satisfied:

   (a) that:

      (i) it is necessary for the employee to enter premises for the purposes of subsection (1); and

      (ii) the employee is unable to do so, or is likely to be unable to do so, otherwise than by force,

   the sheriff or justice may issue a warrant authorising the employee to enter the premises by force at any reasonable time; or

   (b) that it is necessary for the employee to enter premises for the purposes of subsection (1) without giving notice as required by subsection (2)(b), the sheriff or justice may issue a warrant authorising the employee to enter the premises at any time (by force if necessary).

(4) If an authorised employee exercises a power of entry by virtue of this section, the employee may:

   (a) take onto the premises:

      (i) such other persons, and

      (ii) such equipment,

   as the employee considers necessary; and

   (b) require any person present on the premises to provide the employee with any:

      (i) facilities, information, documents or records, or

      (ii) other assistance,

   that the employee may reasonably request.

(5) An authorised employee exercising a power of entry by virtue of this section shall, if so required, produce the items mentioned in subsection (6):

   (a) before entering the premises; or

   (b) at any time before leaving the premises.

(6) Those items are:

   (a) evidence of the employee's authorisation for the purpose of this section; and

   (b) any warrant under subsection (3)(a) or (b).

Section 53: Duties of Employers to Employees

(1) Each employer shall ensure, so far as is reasonably practicable, the safety of the employer's employees in respect of harm caused by fire in the workplace.

(2) Each employer shall:

   (a) carry out an assessment of the workplace for the purpose of identifying any risks to the safety of the employer's employees in respect of harm caused by fire in the workplace;

(b) take in relation to the workplace such of the fire safety measures as are necessary to enable the employer to comply with the duty imposed by subsection (1).

(3) Where under subsection (2)(a) an employer carries out an assessment, the employer shall:

(a) in accordance with regulations under section 57, review the assessment; and

(b) take in relation to the workplace such of the fire safety measures as are necessary to enable the employer to comply with the duty imposed by subsection (1).

(4) Schedule 2 makes provision as to the fire safety measures.

Section 54: Duties in Relation to Relevant Premises

(1) Where a person has control to any extent of relevant premises the person shall, to that extent, comply with subsection (2).

(2) The person shall:

(a) carry out an assessment of the relevant premises for the purpose of identifying any risks to the safety of relevant persons in respect of harm caused by fire in the relevant premises; and

(b) take in relation to the relevant premises such of the fire safety measures as in all the circumstances it is reasonable for a person in his position to take to ensure the safety of relevant persons in respect of harm caused by fire in the relevant premises.

(3) If a person falls within subsection (1) other than by virtue of:

(a) having control to any extent of relevant premises in connection with the carrying on by the person (whether for profit or not) of an undertaking; or

(b) owning relevant premises;

the person who owns the relevant premises shall also comply with subsection (2).

(4) A person who has, by virtue of a contract or tenancy, an obligation of any extent in relation to:

(a) the maintenance or repair of:

(i) relevant premises; or

(ii) anything in relevant premises; or

(b) safety in respect of harm caused by fire in relevant premises;

shall also comply, to the extent of the obligation, with subsection (2).

(5) Where under subsection (2)(a) a person carries out an assessment, the person shall:

(a) in accordance with regulations under section 57, review the assessment; and

(b) take in relation to the relevant premises such of the fire safety measures as in all the circumstances it is reasonable for a person in his position to take to ensure the safety of relevant persons in respect of harm caused by fire in the relevant premises.

Section 55: Taking of Measures under Section 53 or 54: Considerations

(1) Subsection (2) applies where under section 53(2)(b) or (3)(b) or 54(2)(b) or (5)(b) a person is required to take any fire safety measures.

(2) The person shall implement the fire safety measures on the basis of the considerations mentioned in subsection (3).

(3) Those considerations are:

(a) avoiding risks;

(b) evaluating risks which cannot be avoided;

(c) combating risks at source;

(d) adapting to technical progress;

(e) replacing the dangerous with the non-dangerous or the less dangerous;

(f) developing a coherent overall fire prevention policy which covers technology, organisation of work and the influence of factors relating to the working environment;

(g) giving collective fire safety protective measures priority over individual measures; and

(h) giving appropriate instructions to employees.

Section 56: Duties of Employees

Each employee shall while at work:

(a) take reasonable care for the safety in respect of harm caused by fire of:

  (i) the employee; and

  (ii) any other relevant person who may be affected by acts or omissions of the employee; and

(b) in relation to any requirement imposed by virtue of this Part on the employee's employer, co-operate with the employer in so far as is necessary for the purpose of enabling the employer to comply with the requirement.

Section 57: Risk Assessments: Power to Make Regulations

(1) The Scottish Ministers may make Regulations about the carrying out of assessments and reviews under sections 53 and 54.

(2) Regulations under subsection (1) may in particular make provision for or in connection with:

  (a) specifying matters which persons must take into account when carrying out assessments and reviews in relation to substances specified in the Regulations;

  (b) specifying other matters which persons must take into account when carrying out assessments and reviews;

  (c) requiring persons to carry out assessments and reviews before employing persons of a description so specified;

  (d) requiring persons in such circumstances as may be so specified to keep records of such information as may be so specified; and

  (e) specifying circumstances in which reviews must be carried out.

Section 62: Powers of Enforcement Officers

(1) An enforcement officer may do anything necessary for the purpose mentioned in section 61(3).

[Section 61 deals with Enforcing Authorities. Section 61(1) states that each enforcing authority shall enforce the Chapter 1 duties (see below). Section 61(3) states that the enforcing authority may appoint enforcement officers to enforce the Chapter 1 duties.]

(2) An enforcement officer may in particular under subsection (1):

  (a) at any reasonable time (or, in a situation which in the opinion of the officer is or may be dangerous, at any time), enter relevant premises and inspect the whole or part of the relevant premises and anything in them;

  (b) take onto the relevant premises:

    (i) such other persons, and

    (ii) such equipment,

    as the officer considers necessary;

  (c) require a person on the relevant premises who is subject to any of the Chapter 1 duties to provide the officer with any:

    (i) facilities, information, documents or records, or

    (ii) other assistance,

    which relate to those duties and which the officer may reasonably request;

    ['Chapter 1 duties' are the 'Fire safety duties', which are set out in sections 53 to 60 inclusive. Sections 53 to 57 have been included above. Section 58 gives Scottish Ministers the power to make regulations about fire safety; section 59 empowers Scottish Ministers to make further provision for the protection of fire-fighters; and section 60 allows for the temporary suspension of Chapter 1 duties in cases where Chapter 1 duties would prevent a member of the armed forces, or of visiting armed forces, or a police constable or others that the Scottish Ministers may prescribe, from carrying out their operational duties.]

  (d) inspect and copy any documents or records on the relevant premises or remove them from the relevant premises;

  (e) carry out any inspections, measurements and tests in relation to:

    (i) the relevant premises, or

    (ii) an article or substance found on the relevant premises,

    that the officer considers necessary;

(f) take samples of an article or substance found on the relevant premises for the purpose of ascertaining its fire resistance or flammability;

(g) if an article found on the relevant premises appears to the officer to have caused or to be likely to cause danger to the safety of a relevant person in respect of harm caused by fire, dismantle the article (but not so as to destroy it or damage it unless it is necessary to do so for the purpose of the inspection); and

(h) take possession of an article or substance found in the relevant premises and retain it for as long as is necessary for the purpose of:

  (i) examining it and doing anything the officer has power to do under paragraph (e) or (g);

  (ii) ensuring that it is not tampered with before the officer's examination of it is completed;

  (iii) ensuring that it is available for use as evidence in proceedings for an offence relevant to the inspection.

(3) An enforcement officer exercising the power mentioned in subsection (2)(a) shall, if so required, produce evidence of the officer's authority to do so:

  (a) before entering the premises; or at any time before leaving the premises.

(4) If an enforcement officer exercises the power in subsection (2)(f), the officer shall:

  (a) leave a notice at the relevant premises with a person who is subject to any of the Chapter 1 duties in relation to the relevant premises (or, if that is impracticable, fix the notice in a prominent position at the relevant premises) giving particulars of the article or substance and stating that the officer has taken a sample of it; and

  (b) if it is practicable to do so, give such a person at the relevant premises a portion of the sample marked in a manner sufficient to identify it.

(5) Before exercising the power mentioned in subsection (2)(g), an enforcement officer shall consult such persons as appear to the officer to be appropriate for the purpose of ascertaining what dangers, if any, there may be in doing anything which the officer proposes to do under that power.

(6) If requested to do so by a person present in the relevant premises who is subject to any of the Chapter 1 duties in relation to the relevant premises, an enforcement officer shall cause:

  (a) anything which the officer proposes to do on the relevant premises under the power mentioned in paragraph (d) or (e) of subsection (2), or

  (b) anything which the officer proposes to do under the power mentioned in paragraph (g) of that subsection,

  to be done in the presence of that person.

(7) If an enforcement officer exercises the power in subsection (2)(h), the officer shall leave a notice at the relevant premises with a person who is subject to any of the Chapter 1 duties in relation to the relevant premises (or, if that is impracticable, fix the notice in a prominent position at the relevant premises) giving particulars of the article or substance and stating that the officer has taken possession of it.

(8) An enforcement officer who, by virtue of this section, enters relevant premises:

  (a) which are unoccupied, or

  (b) from which the occupier is temporarily absent,

  shall on departure leave the relevant premises as effectively secured against unauthorised entry as the officer found them.

Section 63: Prohibition Notices

(1) Where subsection (2) applies in relation to relevant premises, an enforcing authority may serve a prohibition notice on the occupier of the relevant premises.

(2) This subsection applies where having regard in particular to the matter mentioned in subsection (3), the enforcing authority considers that use of the relevant premises involves or will involve a risk to relevant persons so serious that use of the relevant premises ought to be prohibited or restricted.

(3) The matter is anything affecting relevant persons' escape from the relevant premises in the event of fire.

(4) A prohibition notice is a notice:

  (a) stating that the enforcing authority considers that subsection (2) applies;

(b) specifying the matters which the enforcing authority considers give rise or, as the case may be, will give rise to the risk;

(c) directing that until those matters have been remedied the use to which the prohibition notice relates is:

(i) prohibited; or

(ii) restricted to such extent as may be specified in the notice; and

(d) subject to subsection (5), specifying when the notice shall take effect.

(5) An enforcing authority may specify that a notice shall take effect on service of the notice only if the authority considers that, in consequence of the matters specified under subsection (4)(b), there is or, as the case may be, will be an imminent risk of serious personal injury to relevant persons.

(6) A prohibition notice may specify steps which may be taken to remedy the matters specified in the notice.

(7) If relevant premises fall within paragraph (a) of subsection (5) of section 78 (premises not falling within the definition of 'domestic premises'), the enforcing authority shall, before serving the prohibition notice and if it is practicable to do so, notify the local authority in whose area the relevant premises are situated of:

(a) the enforcing authority's intention to serve a prohibition notice; and

(b) the use which it is intended to prohibit or, as the case may be, restrict.

(8) Where an enforcing authority serves a prohibition notice on the occupier of relevant premises, the authority may, by notice in writing to the occupier, withdraw the prohibition notice.

Section 64: Enforcement Notices

(1) Where an enforcing authority considers that a person has failed to comply with any of the Chapter 1 duties, the authority may serve an enforcement notice on the person.

(2) An enforcement notice is a notice:

(a) stating that the enforcing authority considers that the person on whom the notice is served has failed to comply with the Chapter 1 duty specified in the notice;

(b) specifying why the authority considers that the person has failed to comply with the duty in question; and

(c) requiring the person, before the expiry of the period specified in the notice (being a period of at least 28 days), to take the action so specified.

(3) Where:

(a) an enforcing authority (the "first enforcing authority") proposes to serve an enforcement notice on a person; and

(b) the first enforcing authority considers that the person has failed to comply with any of the Chapter 1 duties in relation to:

(i) a workplace in relation to which some other authority is the enforcing authority, or

(ii) employees who work in such a workplace,

any enforcement notice served by the first enforcing authority may include requirements relating to that workplace or those employees.

(4) Before serving an enforcement notice including a requirement such as is mentioned in subsection (3) the first enforcing authority shall consult the other enforcing authority.

(5) Before serving an enforcement notice including a requirement to make an alteration to relevant premises, the enforcing authority shall consult:

(a) subject to subsection (6), the person appointed under section 7(1) of the **Building (Scotland) Act 2003** as verifier in relation to those premises;

(b) if the notice relates to a workplace in relation to which the authority responsible to any extent for enforcing Part I of the **Health and Safety at Work, etc. Act 1974** and the existing statutory provisions is:

(i) the Health and Safety Executive; or

(ii) by virtue of Part I of that Act or the existing statutory provisions, any other authority;

the Executive or, as the case may be, that other authority; and

(c) any other person whose consent to the alteration would be required by virtue of any enactment.

(6) If the local authority in whose area the relevant premises are situated is also in relation to those premises:

(a) the enforcing authority; and

(b) the person appointed under section 7(1) of the **Building (Scotland) Act 2003** as verifier;

the enforcing authority need not consult the local authority.

(7) Failure to comply with subsection (4) or (5) shall not affect the validity of an enforcement notice.

(8) Where an enforcing authority serves an enforcement notice on a person, the authority may:

(a) before the expiry of the period specified in the notice, by notice in writing to the person withdraw the enforcement notice;

(b) except where an application under section 66 has been made and not determined, extend, or further extend, the period specified in the enforcement notice.

[Section 66 deals with Appeals against notices and sets out that the Sheriff may revoke the notice, vary the notice or confirm the notice. Section 66 also provides that appeals must be brought within 21 days from the date of service of the notice. Section 66 also states that enforcement and alterations notices shall, once an appeal is lodged, be suspended pending the appeal hearing.]

(9) In subsection (5)(b), "existing statutory provisions" has the meaning given by section 53(1) of the **Health and Safety at Work, etc. Act 1974**.

(10) For the purposes of this section, "Chapter 1 duties" does not include the duty imposed by section 56.

FOOD SAFETY ACT 1990

The **Food Safety Act 1990** is enabling legislation, analogous to **HSWA**, and more specific regulations may be passed under its umbrella.

Local Authorities are designated as "Food Authorities" and have the power to appoint "Authorised Officers" to act in matters relating to food safety which arise under the Act. The officers are normally the Environmental Health Officers of the local authority and have the power to inspect or seize suspect food and to serve improvement or prohibition notices.

Under the Act it is an offence to render food so as to be injurious to health, or to sell food which does not comply with food safety requirements.

GAS SAFETY (MANAGEMENT) REGULATIONS 1996 (SI 1996 NO. 551)

These Regulations came into force on 1 April 1996 (Regulation 8 with effect from 31 October 1996) and provide for the preparation and acceptance of safety cases in respect of the conveyance of gas in a network and impose requirements in respect of gas escapes and the composition and pressure of gas.

Regulation 2 defines a "safety case" as a document containing the particulars specified in the Schedule referred to in the provision of the Regulations under which the safety case is prepared. (Schedule 1 details the particulars to be included in the safety case of a person conveying gas; Schedule 2 details the particulars to be included in a safety case of a network emergency co-ordinator.)

Regulation 2 also defines a "network" as a connected network of pipes used for the conveyance of gas from a gas processing facility, a storage facility or an interconnector, except a connected network of pipes used exclusively for supplying gas to non-domestic premises.

Regulation 3 prohibits a person from conveying gas in a network unless he has prepared a safety case which has been accepted by the Health and Safety Executive and, where others convey gas in the network, a person (referred to in the Regulations as a "network emergency co-ordinator") has prepared a safety case which has been similarly accepted.

Regulation 4 requires a safety case to be revised as often as may be appropriate; it also requires a safety case to be revised at least every three years.

Regulation 5 requires that any procedures or arrangements described in a safety case are followed and provides for specified defences for contravention of the requirement. The specified defences are:

- that it was not in the best interests of health and safety to follow the procedures or arrangements concerned and there was insufficient time to revise the safety case, or
- the commission of the offence was due to a contravention by another person and the accused had taken all reasonable precautions and exercised all due diligence to ensure that the procedures or arrangements were followed.

Regulation 6 imposes requirements on specified persons to co-operate with a person conveying gas in a network and with a network emergency co-ordinator to enable them to comply with the provisions of the Regulations. Regulation 6 also empowers a person conveying gas in a network to direct persons not to consume gas where this is necessary to prevent a "supply emergency". It also requires a person conveying gas to provide, on request to persons proposing to carry out work to gas fittings, information about operating pressures of the gas at the outlet of a service pipe.

Regulation 7 requires British Gas plc to provide a continuously manned telephone service for receiving reports of gas escapes, and requires such reports to be passed on to the persons made responsible under the regulation for preventing the escapes. The regulation also imposes specified duties on occupiers of premises and others with respect to gas escapes. The regulation imposes specified duties with respect to the investigation of incidents on persons conveying or supplying gas.

Regulation 8 and **Schedule 3** impose requirements with respect to the characteristics and testing of gas.

HAZARDOUS WASTE (ENGLAND AND WALES) REGULATIONS 2005 (SI 2005 NO. 894)

Amendments

Numerous amendments have been made to the Regulations since they were introduced, these requirements including those of the **Waste (Miscellaneous Amendments) (EU Exit) (No. 2) Regulations 2019**.

These amendments, where relevant, have been incorporated in the text below.

The **Hazardous Waste Regulations** repeal the **Special Waste Regulations 1996** and replace the term 'special waste' with 'hazardous waste'. The Regulations implement the **Hazardous Waste Directive (91/689/EEC)** and impose additional requirements.

Scotland chose to amend the **Special Waste Regulations** with the **Special Waste Amendment (Scotland) Regulations 2005**. Scotland therefore retains the term 'special' and also keeps the 72-hour pre-notification requirements. Northern Ireland has a similar system to Scotland but uses the term 'hazardous waste'.

Regulation 1: Citation and Commencement

These Regulations came into force in two phases, on 16 April 2005 and 16 July 2005.

The Regulations extend to England and Wales only.

Regulations 2 to 5 cover general definitions such as the meaning of 'waste', the list of wastes and general interpretation of terms used in the Regulations.

Regulation 6: Hazardous Waste

A waste is hazardous if it is listed as a hazardous waste in the List of Wastes, is listed in regulations made under section 62A(1) of the **Environmental Protection Act 1990**, or is a specific batch of waste which is determined pursuant to regulation 8 to be hazardous waste. The "List of Wastes" is set out in the **List of Wastes Decision (2000/532/EC)**.

Regulation 7: Non-Hazardous Waste

A waste is non-hazardous waste if it is a waste which is not a hazardous waste pursuant to regulation 6, or if it is a specific batch of waste which is determined pursuant to regulation 9 to be a non-hazardous waste.

Regulations 8, 9 and 10: Specific Waste to be Treated as Hazardous or Non-Hazardous

Regulations 8 and 9 give the Secretary of State (England) or the Welsh Assembly Government (Wales) powers, in certain circumstances, to designate waste as hazardous or non-hazardous waste. However, the Secretary of State must not decide to treat waste as non-hazardous if it has been diluted or mixed with the aim of lowering the initial concentrations of hazardous substances to a level below the threshold for defining waste as hazardous.

The Secretary of State may revoke a determination made under regulation 8 or 9.

Regulations 12, 13 and 14: General Application, Asbestos Waste and Separately Collected Fractions

There is an exclusion from these controls for domestic waste which displays hazardous properties but not if it comprises asbestos waste or is collected separately. In both cases, the Regulations do not impose obligations directly on householders (see for example regulation 13(2)).

Regulation 14A states that hazardous waste produced at shop premises by customers of the occupier shall be treated as being produced by the occupier for the purposes of these Regulations.

Regulation 15: Radioactive Waste

Where a radioactive substance activity does not require an environmental permit by virtue of a radioactive substances exemption and has one or more hazardous properties arising other than from its radioactive nature, it is subject to the requirements of the **Hazardous Waste Regulations**. Exemptions are mentioned in the **Environmental Permitting (England and Wales) Regulations 2016**.

Regulations 16 and 17: Agricultural and Mines and Quarries Wastes

These regulations did not apply to agricultural or mines and quarries waste before 15 May 2007.

Regulation 18: Meaning of Mixing of Hazardous Waste

Hazardous waste of any description shall be considered to have been mixed if it has been mixed with:

(a) A different category of hazardous waste.

(b) In the case of hazardous waste comprising waste oil, waste oil of different characteristics.

(c) A non-hazardous waste.

(d) Any other substance or material.

Regulation 19: Prohibition on Mixing Hazardous Waste Without a Permit

Any establishment or undertaking which carries out the disposal or recovery of hazardous waste, or which produces, collects or transports hazardous waste is prohibited from the mixing of hazardous waste unless it is permitted as part of a disposal or recovery operation and is authorised by, and is conducted in accordance with, the requirements of a waste permit.

The prohibition applies to mixing of waste oil only to the extent that the prohibition is technically feasible and economically viable and only where such mixing would impede the treatment of the waste oil.

Regulation 20: Duty to Separate Mixed Wastes

This regulation imposes a duty, where the hazardous waste has been mixed other than in accordance with a permit/exemption, on the holder to separate different categories of Hazardous Waste, where technically and economically feasible and necessary to comply with the Waste Directive conditions. (This applies to the holder whether mixing was carried out by the holder or a previous holder.)

Regulations 21 to 32: Notification of Premises

Revoked by the **Hazardous Waste (England and Wales) (Amendment) Regulations 2016** (SI 2016/336) regulation 2(3), 1 April 2016.

Regulations 33 to 41: Movement of Hazardous Waste

Requires documents (consignment notes) to be completed whenever hazardous waste is removed from premises (which includes removal from ships and removal by pipeline). The various types of form are set out in Schedules 4 to 7.

The Environment Agency must maintain a coding standard that makes provision for the composition of consignment notes. The coding standard must enable each consignment of hazardous waste to be given a unique consignment code.

Producers, holders, carriers, consignors and consignees are all required to complete various parts of the forms. If the consignee rejects the waste, suitable alternative arrangements must be made (see also regulation 42).

Where more than one carrier transports the consignment a schedule of carriers must also be completed. Regulation 38 (Multiple collections) was revoked by the **Waste (England and Wales) Regulations 2011**.

Regulations 42 to 43: Duty of Consignee Not Accepting Delivery

These regulations specify the duties placed on the consignee if he does not accept delivery of a consignment whether wholly or partly. Having been rejected and before the consignment is removed from the original place for delivery, the hazardous waste producer or holder identified in the relevant part of the original consignment note shall ensure that a copy of a new consignment note is prepared in respect of the rejected consignment.

Regulation 44 (Procedure for rejected multiple collection consignments) was revoked by the **Waste (England and Wales) Regulations 2011**.

Regulation 45: Duty to Deliver Consignment Promptly

It is the duty of the carrier to deliver the consignment to the consignee promptly and without undue delay.

Regulation 46: Cross-Border Movement of Hazardous Waste

Schedule 7 deals with cross-border transfers within the United Kingdom and Gibraltar.

Regulations 47 to 55: Records and Returns

Any person who discharges, disposes or recovers hazardous waste in or on land, or receives hazardous waste from a transfer station shall record and identify the waste. Records must be kept in a register, which must be updated within 24 hours of receipt or deposit of the waste and must be kept on site. Records must be retained for three years or, if there is a waste permit, until that permit is surrendered or revoked.

If the person required to make or retain a register has a waste permit pursuant to which the site is operated, consignment notes must be kept for five years after the deposit of the waste, or if the permit authorises disposal of waste in a landfill, until the permit is surrendered or revoked.

Producers, holders, consignors, brokers of, or dealers in hazardous waste shall keep a record of the quantity, nature, origin and, where relevant, the destination, frequency of collection, mode of transport and treatment method of the waste. Records must be preserved for three years. Carriers of hazardous waste must keep records for at least 12 months commencing on the date of delivery of the waste to its destination.

Previous holders of the waste have a right to be supplied with documentary evidence that the disposal or recovery operation concerned has been carried out.

Consignees are obliged to make quarterly returns to the regulator. They must also send to the producer, holder or consignor, a return showing acceptance of the waste and a copy of the consignment note together with a description of the methods of disposal or recovery. This must be done within one month of the end of the quarter in which the waste was accepted.

Those who are required to retain records may be required to produce them to the regulator or emergency services on request.

Regulations 56 to 60: The Agency's Functions

Part 8 sets out the Agency's functions. In particular, the Agency is required to inspect producers of hazardous waste periodically and to keep any records sent to it pursuant to Part 7 for a minimum of 3 years. The Agency must also retain registers.

Note that regulation 57 (Inspections of collection and transport operations) was revoked by the **Waste (England and Wales) Regulations 2011**.

Regulations 61, 62 and 63: Emergencies and Grave Danger

Regulations 61 and 62 impose duties on holders of hazardous waste and the regulator in the event of an emergency or grave danger which arises from hazardous waste. Specifically, a holder is required to take all lawful and reasonable steps to avert (or mitigate where not reasonably practicable) the emergency or grave danger and to notify the regulator as soon as reasonably practicable in the circumstances.

The regulator will exercise its functions in order to take all reasonably practicable steps to avert or mitigate an emergency or grave danger.

Regulation 65: Offences

These Regulations are enforced by the Environment Agency (regulation 64).

It is an offence to fail to comply with the requirements of these Regulations. The maximum penalty is an unlimited fine.

Regulation 65A was added by the **Environmental Civil Sanctions (Miscellaneous Amendments) (England) Regulations 2010** and applies only in England. This regulation provides that the Environment Agency may impose a variable monetary penalty, restoration notice, compliance notice or stop notice, or accept an enforcement undertaking, in relation to an offence under regulation 68 (false and misleading information) or under regulation 65 for a failure to comply with provisions set out within this regulation.

Regulation 66: Defences

The following defences apply:

- he was not reasonably able to comply with the provision in question by reason of an emergency or grave danger and that he took all steps that were reasonably practicable in the circumstances for:
    - minimising any threat to the public or the environment; and
    - ensuring that the provision in question was complied with as soon as reasonably practicable after the event; or
- if there is no emergency or grave danger he took all reasonable precautions and exercised due diligence to avoid the commission of the offence.

HAZARDOUS WASTE (MISCELLANEOUS AMENDMENTS) REGULATIONS 2015 (SI 2015 NO. 1360)

These Regulations came into force on 1 July 2015 and amend a number of pieces of environmental legislation. Where legislation that has been amended appears in this guide, the amendments made by these Regulations have been incorporated.

The legislation that is covered in this guide and which has been affected by these Regulations includes:

- The **Environmental Protection Act 1990** (amended by regulation 2).
- The **Hazardous Waste (England and Wales) Regulations 2005** (amended by regulation 3).

HEALTH ACT 2006

This is the enabling Act that banned smoking in workplaces in England and Wales. Reference is made to this Act by the **Smoke-Free (Premises and Enforcement) Regulations 2006** and the **Smoke-Free Premises, etc. (Wales) Regulations 2007**.

The equivalent Act for Scotland is the **Smoking, Health and Social Care (Scotland) Act 2005**.

Section 2: Smoke-Free Premises

(1) Premises are smoke-free if they are open to the public.

But unless the premises also fall within subsection (2), they are smoke-free only when open to the public.

(2) Premises are smoke-free if they are used as a place of work:

   (a) by more than one person (even if the persons who work there do so at different times, or only intermittently); or

   (b) where members of the public might attend for the purpose of seeking or receiving goods or services from the person or persons working there (even if members of the public are not always present).

   They are smoke-free all the time.

(3) If only part of the premises is open to the public or (as the case may be) used as a place of work mentioned in subsection (2), the premises are smoke-free only to that extent.

(4) In any case, premises are smoke-free only in those areas which are enclosed or substantially enclosed.

(5) The appropriate national authority may specify in Regulations what "enclosed" and "substantially enclosed" mean.

(6) Section 3 provides for some premises, or areas of premises, not to be smoke-free despite this section.

(7) Premises are "open to the public" if the public or a section of the public has access to them, whether by invitation or not, and whether on payment or not.

(8) "Work", in subsection (2), includes voluntary work.

Section 3: Smoke-Free Premises: Exemptions

(1) The appropriate national authority may make Regulations providing for specified descriptions of premises, or specified areas within specified descriptions of premises, not to be smoke-free despite section 2.

(2) Descriptions of premises which may be specified under subsection (1) include, in particular, any premises where a person has his home, or is living whether permanently or temporarily (including hotels, care homes, and prisons and other places where a person may be detained).

(3) The power to make Regulations under subsection (1) is not exercisable so as to specify any description of:

   (a) premises in respect of which a premises licence under the **Licensing Act 2003** authorising the sale by retail of alcohol for consumption on the premises has effect;

   (b) premises in respect of which a club premises certificate (within the meaning of section 60 of that Act) has effect.

(4) But subsection (3) does not prevent the exercise of that power so as to specify any area, within a specified description of premises mentioned in subsection (3), where a person has his home, or is living whether permanently or temporarily.

(5) For the purpose of making provision for those participating as performers in a performance, or in a performance of a specified description, not to be prevented from smoking if the artistic integrity of the performance makes it appropriate for them to smoke:

   (a) the power in subsection (1) also includes power to provide for specified descriptions of premises or specified areas within such premises not to be smoke-free in relation only to such performers; and

   (b) subsection (3) does not prevent the exercise of that power as so extended.

(6) The Regulations may provide, in relation to any description of premises or areas of premises specified in the Regulations, that the premises or areas are not smoke-free:

   (a) in specified circumstances;

   (b) if specified conditions are satisfied; or

(c) at specified times;

or any combination of those.

(7) The conditions may include conditions requiring the designation in accordance with the Regulations, by the person in charge of the premises, of any rooms in which smoking is to be permitted.

(8) For the purposes of subsection (5), the references to a performance:

    (a) include, for example, the performance of a play, or a performance given in connection with the making of a film or television programme; and

    (b) if the Regulations so provide, include a rehearsal.

HEALTH AND SAFETY AND NUCLEAR (FEES) REGULATIONS 2021 (SI 2021 NO. 33)

The **Health and Safety and Nuclear (Fees) Regulations 2021** revoke and replace the **Health and Safety and Nuclear (Fees) Regulations 2016 (SI 2016/253)**. They introduce fee increases for fees that were prescribed by the 2016 Regulations.

Regulations 23-24 - Fees for Intervention

Regulation 23: If a person is contravening or has contravened one or more of the relevant statutory provisions for which the Executive is the enforcing authority and an inspector is of the opinion that that person is doing so or has done so, and notifies that person in writing of that opinion, a fee is payable by that person to the Executive for its performance of the following functions:

- the performance by the Executive of any function conferred on it by the relevant statutory provisions, in consequence of any contravention referred to in the opinion notified to that person;
- the performance by the Executive, during a site visit, of any function conferred on it by the relevant statutory provisions for which no fee is payable by virtue of the above.

An inspector of the opinion that a person is contravening or has contravened one or more of the relevant statutory provisions must have regard, when deciding whether to notify that person in writing of that opinion, to the guidance entitled *HSE 47 - Guidance on the application of Fee for Intervention*.

A written notification must:

(a) specify the provision or provisions to which that inspector's opinion relates;

(b) give particulars of the reasons for that opinion; and

(c) inform the person to whom it is given that fee for intervention is payable to the Executive in accordance with **Regulation 24**.

Fee for intervention is payable by a person in respect of functions performed by the Executive during a site visit only to the extent that the performance of any such function by the Executive is reasonably attributable to that person.

Supplementary provisions on fees for intervention, such as limits to fees, time scale for payment and circumstances where no fee for intervention is payable are included in **Regulation 24**.

Regulation 25 deals with repayments and disputes. If a person is charged with, but not convicted of, one or more criminal offences or has been served with one or more enforcement notices that is/are subsequently cancelled, the Executive must repay such part of any fee for intervention paid as is wholly and exclusively attributable to the performance by the Executive of functions relating only to the offence for which the person was not convicted or, as the case may be, the enforcement notice/s that was/were cancelled. The Executive must repay fees paid in error.

Regulation 26 requires the Secretary of State to review the operation and effect of these Regulations and to publish a report within five years after the Regulations come into force.

HEALTH AND SAFETY AT WORK ETC. ACT 1974

Introduction

Prior to 1974, health and safety legislation was reactive, dealing with problems in particular industries, or particular premises- factories, mines, shops, offices and railway premises. This left large sections of the working population unaffected and unprotected by any safety Regulations. In 1970, a Government Committee was set up, under the Chairmanship of Lord Robens, whose objective was:

"To review the provisions made for the safety and health of persons in the course of their employment and to consider whether any changes are needed..."

The Committee produced the Robens Report which led in turn to the **Health and Safety at Work, etc. Act 1974**. For the first time, the Act covered employers and employees rather than premises and brought a further 7- 8 million new workers within the ambit of safety legislation.

Amendments

In recent years, the most significant changes to this Act have been to the offences and penalties set out in section 33 (see the **Health and Safety (Offences) Act 2008** elsewhere in this document), and to the provisions for civil liability as set out in section 47, which were effectively reversed by the action of section 69 of the **Enterprise and Regulatory Reform Act 2013**.

The **Deregulation Act 2015** has amended section 3(2) to limit the scope of application of section 3 (General duties of self-employed persons to persons other than their employees) to those who conduct "an undertaking of a prescribed description", thus exempting large numbers of self-employed people from the requirements of the 1974 Act.

Section 2: General Duties of Employers to their Employees

(1) It shall be the duty of every employer to ensure, so far as is reasonably practicable, the health, safety and welfare at work of all his employees.

(2) Without prejudice to the generality of an employer's duty under the preceding subsection, the matters to which that duty extends include in particular:

 (a) the provision and maintenance of plant and systems of work that are, so far as is reasonably practicable, safe and without risks to health;

 (b) arrangements for ensuring, so far as is reasonably practicable, safety and absence of risks to health in connection with the use, handling, storage and transport of articles and substances;

 (c) the provision of such information, instruction, training and supervision as is necessary to ensure, so far as is reasonably practicable, the health and safety at work of his employees;

 (d) so far as is reasonably practicable, as regards any place of work under the employer's control, the maintenance of it in a condition that is safe and entrance to and egress from it that are safe and without such risks;

 (e) the provision and maintenance of a working environment for his employees that is, so far as is reasonably practicable, safe, without risks to health, and adequate as regards facilities and arrangements for their welfare at work.

(3) Except in such cases as may be prescribed, it shall be the duty of every employer to prepare and as often as may be appropriate revise a written statement of his general policy with respect to the health and safety at work of his employees and the organisation and arrangements for the time being in force for carrying out that policy, and to bring the statement and any revision of it to the notice of all his employees.

 *NB: The **Employers' Health and Safety Policy Statements (Exception) Regulations 1975** exempt employers who have fewer than 5 employees from having to comply with this subsection.*

(4) Regulations made by the Secretary of State may provide for the election in prescribed cases by recognised trade unions (within the meaning of the Regulations) of safety representatives from amongst the employees, and those representatives shall represent the employees in consultations with the employers under subsection (6) below and shall have such other functions as may be prescribed.

(5) [Repealed by the **Employment Protection Act 1975**].

(6) It shall be the duty of every employer to consult any such representatives with a view to the making and maintenance of arrangements which will enable him and his employees to co-operate effectively in promoting and developing measures to ensure the health and safety at work of the employees, and in checking the effectiveness of such measures.

(7) In such cases as may be prescribed it shall be the duty of every employer, if requested to do so by the safety representatives mentioned in subsection (4) above to establish, in accordance with Regulations made by the Secretary of State, a safety committee having the function of keeping under review the measures taken to ensure the health and safety at work of his employees and such other functions as may be prescribed.

Section 3: General Duties of Employers and Self-Employed to Persons other than Employees

(1) It shall be the duty of every employer to conduct his undertaking in such a way as to ensure, so far as is reasonably practicable, that persons not in his employment who may be affected thereby are not thereby exposed to risks to their health or safety.

(2) It shall be the duty of every self-employed person who conducts an undertaking of a prescribed description to conduct the undertaking in such a way as to ensure, so far as is reasonably practicable, that he and other persons (not being his employees) who may be affected thereby are not thereby exposed to risks to their health or safety.

(2A) A description of undertaking included in regulations under subsection (2) may be framed by reference to:

(a) the type of activities carried out by the undertaking, where those activities are carried out or any other feature of the undertaking;

(b) whether persons who may be affected by the conduct of the undertaking, other than the self-employed person (or his employees), may thereby be exposed to risks to their health or safety.

(3) In such cases as may be prescribed, it shall be the duty of every employer and every self-employed person, in the prescribed circumstances and in the prescribed manner, to give to persons (not being his employees) who may be affected by the way in which he conducts his undertaking the prescribed information about such aspects of the way in which he conducts his undertaking as might affect their health or safety.

Note that the **Deregulation Act 2015** makes amendments to Section 3 to limit the scope of this duty to self-employed persons who conduct an "undertaking of a prescribed description", i.e. one specifically prescribed by regulations made by the Secretary of State.

Section 4: Duties of Persons Concerned with Premises to Persons other than their Employees

(1) This section has effect for imposing on persons duties in relation to those who:

(a) are not their employees; but

(b) use non-domestic premises made available to them as a place of work or as a place where they may use plant or substances provided for their use there and applies to premises so made available and other non-domestic premises used in connection with them.

(2) It shall be the duty of each person who has, to any extent, control of premises to which this section applies or of the means of access thereto or egress therefrom or of any plant or substance in such premises to take such measures as it is reasonable for a person in his position to take to ensure, so far as is reasonably practicable, that the premises, all means of access thereto or egress therefrom available for use by persons using the premises and any plant or substance in the premises or, as the case may be, provided for use there, is or are safe and without risks to health.

(3) Where a person has, by virtue of any contract or tenancy, an obligation of any extent in relation to:

(a) the maintenance or repair of any premises to which this section applies or any means of access thereto or egress therefrom; or

(b) the safety of or the absence of risks to health arising from plant or substances in any such premises;

that person shall be treated, for the purposes of subsection (2) above, as being a person who has control of the matters to which his obligation extends.

(4) Any reference in this section to a person having control of any premises or matter is a reference to a person having control of the premises or matter in connection with the carrying on by him of a trade, business or other undertaking (whether for profit or not).

The language of this section is rather long-winded but it deals with the general duties of persons concerned with premises towards persons who are not their employees and recognises that in relation to premises there may be more than one person exercising a degree of control. For example, in a multi-storey building containing several companies or organisations who rent space from a landlord, the individual companies exercise control over their accommodation and must maintain good access to and egress from their parts of the premises. On the other hand, the landlord of the building would be responsible for maintaining access to and egress from the common areas of the premises, lift lobbies, external fire-exits, and plant rooms. Briefly, anyone who has partial control of premises must ensure the safety of any person who enters the premises to carry out work.

Section 5: Duty of Persons in Control of Premises in Relation to Harmful Emissions into the Atmosphere

This section has been repealed and its requirements are now contained in the **Environmental Protection Act 1990**.

Section 6: General Duties of Manufacturers, etc. as Regards Articles and Substances for Use at Work

NB: s6 was amended by the **Consumer Protection Act 1987**.

Articles for Use at Work

(1) Any person who designs, manufactures, imports or supplies any article for use at work (or any article of fairground equipment) shall:

   (a) ensure, so far as is reasonably practicable, that the article is so designed and constructed that it will be safe and without risks to health at all times when it is being set, used, cleaned or maintained by a person at work;

   (b) carry out or arrange for the carrying out of such testing and examination as may be necessary for the performance of the duty in (a) above;

   (c) take such steps as are necessary to secure that persons supplied by that person with the article are provided with adequate information about the use for which the article is designed or has been tested and about any conditions necessary to ensure that it will be safe and without risks to health at all such times of setting, using, cleaning, maintaining and when being dismantled, or disposed of; and

   (d) take such steps as are necessary to secure, so far as is reasonably practicable, that persons so supplied are provided with all such revisions of information provided to them by virtue of the preceding paragraph as are necessary by reason of its becoming known that anything gives rise to a serious risk to health or safety.

(1A) It shall be the duty of any person who designs, manufactures, imports or supplies any article of fairground equipment:

   (a) to ensure, so far as is reasonably practicable, that the article is so designed and constructed that it will be safe and without risks to health at all times when it is being used for or in connection with the entertainment of members of the public;

   (b) to carry out or arrange for the carrying out of such testing and examination as may be necessary for the performance of the duty imposed on him by the preceding paragraph;

   (c) to take such steps as are necessary to secure that persons supplied by that person with the article are provided with adequate information about the use for which the article is designed or has been tested and about any conditions necessary to ensure that it will be safe and without risks to health at all times when it is being used for or in connection with the entertainment of members of the public; and

   (d) to take such steps as are necessary to secure, so far as is reasonably practicable, that persons so supplied are provided with all such revisions of information provided to them by virtue of the preceding paragraph as are necessary by reason of its becoming known that anything gives rise to a serious risk to health or safety.

Duty on Designers and Manufacturers to Carry Out Research

(2) It shall be the duty of any person who undertakes the design or manufacture of any article for use at work or of any article of fairground equipment to carry out or arrange for the carrying out of any necessary research with a view to the discovery and, so far as is reasonably practicable, the elimination or minimisation of risks to health or safety to which the design or article may give rise.

Duties on Installers of Articles for Use at Work

(3) It shall be the duty of any person who erects or installs any article for use at work in any premises where the article is to be used by persons at work or who erects or installs any article of fairground equipment to ensure, so far as is reasonably practicable, that nothing about the way in which the article is erected or installed makes it unsafe or a risk to health at any time when it is being set, used, cleaned, or maintained by someone at work.

Substances for Use at Work

(4) Every person who manufactures, imports or supplies any substance shall:

- ensure, so far as is reasonably practicable, that the substance will be safe and without risks to health at all times when it is being used, handled, processed, stored, or transported by any person at work or in premises to which s4 applies;
- carry out or arrange for the carrying out of such testing and examination as may be necessary for the performance of the above duties;
- take such steps as are necessary to secure that a person supplied by that person with the substance is provided with adequate information about:
    - any risks to health or safety to which the inherent properties of the substance may give rise;
    - the results of any relevant tests which have been carried out on or in connection with the substance;
    - any conditions necessary to ensure that the substance will be safe and without risk to health at all times when it is being used, handled, processed, stored, transported and disposed of; and
- take such steps as are necessary to secure, so far as is reasonably practicable, that persons so supplied are provided with all such revisions of information as are necessary by reason of it becoming known that anything gives rise to a serious risk to health or safety.

(5) Any person who manufactures any substance must carry out, or arrange for the carrying out of, any necessary research with a view to the discovery and, so far as is reasonably practicable, the elimination or minimisation of any health and safety risks at all times when the substances are being used, handled, processed, stored, or transported by someone at work.

NB: There is no duty on suppliers of industrial articles and substances to research.

(6) Nothing in the preceding provisions of this section shall be taken to require a person to repeat any testing, examination or research which has been carried out otherwise than by him or at his instance in so far as it is reasonable to rely on the results thereof for the purposes of those provisions.

(7) Any duty imposed on any person by any of the preceding provisions of this section shall extend only to things done in the course of a trade, business or other undertaking carried on by him (whether for profit or not) and to matters within his control.

Custom-Built Articles

(8) Where a person designs, manufactures, imports or supplies an article for use at work or an article of fairground equipment and does so for or to another [person] on the basis of a written undertaking by that other [person] to take specified steps sufficient to ensure, so far as is reasonably practicable, that the article will be safe and without risks to health at all times when being set, used, cleaned, or maintained by persons at work, the undertaking shall have the effect of relieving the designer or manufacturer etc. from the duty specified in section 6(1)(a), to such extent as is reasonable, having regard to the terms of the undertaking.

Importers Liable for Offences of Foreign Manufacturers and Designers

In order to give added protection to industrial users from unsafe imported products this new subsection has been introduced which in effect makes importers of unsafe products liable for the acts or omissions of foreign designers and manufacturers.

(8A) Nothing in subsection (7) or (8) above shall relieve any person who imports any article or substance from any duty in respect of anything which:

   (a) in the case of an article designed outside the United Kingdom, was done by and in the course of any trade, profession or other undertaking carried on by, or was within the control of, the person who designed the article; or

   (b) in the case of an article or substance manufactured outside the United Kingdom, was done by and in the course of any trade, profession or other undertaking carried on by, or was within the control of, the person who manufactured the article or substance.

(9) Where a person ("the ostensible supplier") supplies any article or substance for use at work to another ("the customer") under a hire-purchase agreement, conditional sale agreement or credit-sale agreement, and the ostensible supplier:

  (a) carries on the business of financing the acquisition of goods by others by means of such agreements; and

  (b) in the course of that business acquired his interest in the article or substance supplied to the customer as a means of financing its acquisition by the customer from a third person (the effective supplier),

  the effective supplier and not the ostensible supplier shall be treated for the purposes of this section, as supplying the article or substance to the customer, and any duty imposed by the preceding provisions of this section on suppliers shall accordingly fall on the effective supplier and not on the ostensible supplier.

(10) For the purposes of this section an absence of safety or a risk to health shall be disregarded insofar as it can be shown that the absence of safety or risk to health was not reasonably foreseeable.

In determining whether any duty is owed under subsections (1), (1A) or (4) above, regard will be had to any relevant information or advice which has been provided to any person by the designer, manufacturer, importer or supplier.

Note: Section 6 is a very long section later amended by the **Consumer Protection Act 1987**. Looking at the requirements of the section, one can see that responsibility for safety goes right back to the drawing board stage. Where a designer is negligent in his design of a machine or other article for use at work, he can be held liable at criminal law under **HSWA**. Manufacturers, importers and suppliers are in exactly the same position. They have a definite duty to ensure that, whatever they are dealing with, they must carry out the necessary research with a view to discovering and, so far as is reasonably practicable, eliminating or minimising any risk to health or safety to which any manufactured article or substance might give rise.

There is provision in the section for the transfer of liability by written undertaking which simply means that the responsibility placed on a supplier or manufacturer etc. to ensure that an article or substance is safe may be shifted to another person provided there is a clear written agreement to that effect. This covers situations where an article has been ordered to a customer's own specification or is to become a component part of another article. Installers and erectors of equipment and machinery for use at work must ensure, so far as is reasonably practicable, that no health and safety hazards arise from the method of erection or installation.

Section 7: Employees' Duties

It shall be the duty of every employee while at work:

(a) to take reasonable care for the health and safety of himself and of other persons who may be affected by his acts or omissions at work; and

(b) as regards any duty or requirement imposed on his employer or any other person by or under any of the relevant statutory provisions, to co-operate with him so far as is necessary to enable that duty or requirement to be performed or complied with.

Note: Both acts and omissions are included. Thus, failure of an employee to wear protective clothing, for example, or failure to check machinery which he/she is responsible for checking, would render him/her liable to prosecution under this section. Similarly, skylarking, horseplay and taking unsafe shortcuts in his work would leave an employee open to prosecution. "Work" and "at work" are worthy of explanation. '"Work" means work as an employee or as a self-employed person. Employees are "at work" throughout the time when they are doing something which is part of their employment. This may include, for example, travelling between different sites or buildings. Self-employed persons are at work throughout the time they devote to work as a self-employed person. The definition of work has been extended to include training provided under government and other schemes by the **Health and Safety (Training for Employment) Regulations 1989**.

Section 8: Duty Not to Interfere With or Misuse Things Provided Pursuant to Certain Provisions

No person shall intentionally or recklessly interfere with or misuse anything provided in the interests of health, safety or welfare in pursuance of any of the relevant statutory provisions.

Note: The term "no person" implies that the duty is not limited to employees. **Any** person so interfering could be liable under this section. Interference with fire-fighting or first-aid equipment would fall into this category.

Section 9: Duty Not to Charge Employees for Things Done or Provided Pursuant to Certain Specific Requirements

No employer shall levy or permit to be levied on any employee of his any charge in respect of anything done or provided in pursuance of any specific requirement of the relevant statutory provisions.

Note: For example, this covers such matters as provision of PPE at the employer's expense.

Section 15: Health and Safety Regulations and Approved Codes of Practice

(1) Subject to the provisions of section 50, the Secretary of State shall have power to make Regulations under this section for any of the general purposes of this Part (and Regulations so made are in this Part referred to as "health and safety regulations").

[Section 50 deals with Regulations made under the relevant statutory provisions, stating that the Secretary of State's power to make Regulations may be exercisable so as to give effect to proposals submitted by the Executive (HSE) or independently of such proposals provided the Secretary of State has consulted the Executive, the Office for Nuclear Regulation and other bodies that may appear to the Secretary of State to be appropriate.]

(1A) In subsection (1), the reference to the general purposes of this Part does not include a reference to any of the following:

   (a) the nuclear safety purposes;

   (b) the nuclear security purposes;

   (c) the nuclear safeguards purposes;

   (d) the radioactive material transport purposes.

(1B) Subsection (1A) does not preclude health and safety regulations from including provision merely because the provision could be made for any of the purposes mentioned in paragraphs (a) to (d) of that subsection.

[Subsections (1A) and (1B) were added by the **Energy Act 2013**.]

(2) Without prejudice to the generality of subsection (1), health and safety regulations may for any of the general purposes of this Part make provision for any of the purposes mentioned in Schedule 3.

(3) Health and safety regulations:

   (a) may repeal or modify any of the existing statutory provisions;

   (b) may exclude or modify in relation to any specified class of case any of the provisions of sections 2 to 9 or any of the existing statutory provisions;

   (c) may make a specified authority or class of authorities responsible, to such an extent as may be specified, for the enforcement of any of the relevant statutory provisions.

Section 19: Appointment of Inspectors

This section empowers enforcing authorities to appoint inspectors. Inspectors are entitled to exercise the powers specified in their written instrument of appointment. Inspectors may, when seeking to exercise their powers, be required to produce their instrument of appointment (i.e. the letter, etc. that shows they are an enforcing authority inspector).

Section 20: Powers of Inspectors

(1) Subject to the provisions of section 19 and this section, an inspector may, for the purpose of carrying into effect any of the relevant statutory provisions within the field of responsibility of the enforcing authority which appointed him, exercise the powers set out in subsection (2) below.

(2) The powers of an inspector referred to in the preceding subsection are the following, namely:

   (a) At any reasonable time (or, in a situation which in his opinion is or may be dangerous, at any time) to enter any premises which he has reason to believe it is necessary for him to enter for the purpose mentioned in subsection (1) above.

(b) To take with him a constable if he has reasonable cause to apprehend any serious obstruction in the execution of his duty.

(c) Without prejudice to the preceding paragraph, on entering any premises by virtue of paragraph (a) above to take with him:

   (i) any other person duly authorised by his (the inspector's) enforcing authority; and

   (ii) any equipment or materials required for any purpose for which the power of entry is being exercised.

(d) To make such examination and investigation as may in any circumstances be necessary for the purpose mentioned in subsection (1) above.

(e) As regards any premises which he has power to enter, to direct that those premises or any part of them, or anything therein, shall be left undisturbed (whether generally or in particular respects) for so long as is reasonably necessary for the purpose of any examination or investigation under paragraph (d) above.

(f) To take such measurements and photographs and make such recordings as he considers necessary for the purpose of any examination or investigation under paragraph (d) above.

(g) To take samples of any articles or substances found in any premises which he has power to enter, and of the atmosphere in or in the vicinity of any such premises.

(h) In the case of any article or substance found in any premises which he has power to enter, being an article or substance which appears to him to have caused or to be likely to cause danger to health or safety, to cause it to be dismantled or subjected to any process or test (but not so as to damage or destroy it unless this is in the circumstances necessary for the purpose mentioned in subsection (1) above).

(i) In the case of any such article or substance as is mentioned in the preceding paragraph, to take possession of it and retain it for so long as is necessary for all or any of the following purposes, namely:

   (i) to examine it and do to it anything which he has power to do under that paragraph;

   (ii) to ensure that it is not tampered with before his examination of it is completed;

   (iii) to ensure that it is available for use as evidence in any proceedings for an offence under any of the relevant statutory provisions or any proceedings relating to a notice under section 21 or 22.

(j) To require any person whom he has reasonable cause to believe to be able to give any information relevant to any examination or investigation under paragraph (d) above to answer (in the absence of persons other than a person nominated by him to be present and any persons whom the inspector may allow to be present) such questions as the inspector thinks fit to ask and to sign a declaration of the truth of his answers.

(k) To require the production of, inspect, and take copies of or of any entry in:

   (i) any books or documents which by virtue of any of the relevant statutory provisions are required to be kept; and

   (ii) any other books or documents which it is necessary for him to see for the purposes of any examination or investigation under paragraph (d) above.

(l) To require any person to afford him such facilities and assistance with respect to any matter or things within that person's control or in relation to which that person has responsibilities as are necessary to enable the inspector to exercise any of the powers conferred on him by this section.

(m) Any other power which is necessary for that purpose mentioned in subsection (1) above.

(3) The Secretary of State may by Regulations make provision as to the procedure to be followed in connection with the taking of samples under subsection (2)(g) above (including provision as to the way in which samples that have been so taken are to be dealt with).

(4) Where an inspector proposes to exercise the power conferred by subsection (2)(h) above in the case of an article or substance found in any premises, he shall, if so requested by a person who at the time is present in and has responsibilities in relation to those premises, cause anything which is to be done by virtue of that power to be done in the presence of that person unless the inspector considers that its being done in that person's presence would be prejudicial to the safety of the State.

(5) Before exercising the power conferred by subsection (2)(h) above in the case of any article or substance, an inspector shall consult such persons as appear to him appropriate for the purpose of ascertaining what dangers, if any, there may be in doing anything which he proposes to do under that power.

(6) Where under the power conferred by subsection(2)(i) above an inspector takes possession of any article or substance found in any premises, he shall leave there, either with a responsible person or, if that is impracticable, fixed in a conspicuous position, a notice giving particulars of that article or substance sufficient to identify it and stating that he has taken possession of it under that power; and before taking possession of any such substance under that power an inspector shall, if it is practicable for him to do so, take a sample thereof and give to a responsible person at the premises a portion of the sample marked in a manner sufficient to identify it.

(7) No answer given by a person in pursuance of a requirement imposed under subsection (2)(j) above shall be admissible in evidence against that person or the spouse or civil partner of that person in any proceedings.

(8) Nothing in this section shall be taken to compel the production by any person of a document of which he would on grounds of legal or professional privilege be entitled to withhold production on an order for discovery in an action in the High Court or, as the case may be, for the production of documents in an action in the Court of Session.

Section 21: Improvement Notices

If an inspector is of the opinion that a person:

(a) is contravening one or more of the relevant statutory provisions; or

(b) has contravened one or more of those provisions in circumstances that make it likely that the contravention will continue or be repeated,

he may serve on him a notice (in this Part referred to as an "improvement notice") stating that he is of that opinion, specifying the provision or provisions as to which he is of that opinion, giving particulars of the reasons why he is of that opinion, and requiring that person to remedy the contravention or, as the case may be, the matters occasioning it within such period (ending not earlier than the period within which an appeal against the notice can be brought under section 24) as may be specified in the notice.

Section 22: Prohibition Notices

(1) This section applies to any activities which are being or are about to be carried on by or under the control of any person, being activities to or in relation to which any of the relevant statutory provisions apply or will, if the activities as so carried on, apply.

(2) If as regards any activities to which this section applies an inspector is of the opinion that, as carried on or likely to be carried on by or under the control of the person in question, the activities involve or, as the case may be, will involve a risk of serious personal injury, the inspector may serve on that person a notice (in this Part referred to as a "prohibition notice").

(3) A prohibition notice shall:

   (a) state that the inspector is of the said opinion;

   (b) specify the matters which in his opinion give or, as the case may be, will give rise to the said risk;

   (c) where in his opinion any of those matters involves or, as the case may be, will involve a contravention of any of the relevant statutory provisions, state that he is of that opinion, specify the provision or provisions as to which he is of that opinion, and give particulars of the reasons why he is of that opinion; and

   (d) direct that the activities to which the notice relates shall not be carried on by or under the control of the person on whom the notice is served unless the matters specified in the notice in pursuance of paragraph (b) above and any associated contraventions of provisions so specified in pursuance of paragraph (c) above have been remedied.

(4) A direction contained in a prohibition notice in pursuance of subsection (3)(d) above shall take effect:

   (a) at the end of the period specified in the notice; or

   (b) if the notice so declares, immediately.

Section 23: Supplementary Provisions to Sections 21 and 22

(1) In this section "a notice" means an improvement notice or a prohibition notice.

(2) The notice may (but need not) include directions as to the measures to be taken to remedy any contravention or matter to which the notice relates; and any such directions:

   (a) may be framed to any extent by reference to any approved code of practice; and

   (b) may be framed so as to afford the person on whom the notice is served a choice between different ways of remedying the contravention or matter.

(3) Where any of the relevant statutory provisions apply to a building or any matter connected with a building and an inspector proposes to serve an improvement notice relating to a contravention of that provision in connection with that building or matter, the notice shall not direct any measures to be taken to remedy the contravention of that provision which are more onerous than those necessary to secure conformity with the requirements of any building regulations for the time being in force to which that building or matter would be required to conform if the relevant building were being newly erected unless the provision in question imposes specific requirements more onerous than the requirements of any such building regulations to which the building or matter would be required to conform as aforesaid.

In this subsection " the relevant building", in the case of a building, means the building, and, in the case of a matter connected with the building, means the building with which the matter is connected.

(4) Before an inspector serves in connection with any premises used or about to be used as a place of work a notice requiring or likely to lead to the taking of measures affecting the means of escape in case of fire with which the premises are or ought to be provided, he shall consult the fire and rescue authority.

In this subsection "fire and rescue authority", in relation to premises, means:

   (a) where **RRFSO** applies, the enforcing authority within the meaning given by Article 25 of that Order;

   (b) in any other case, the fire and rescue authority under the **Fire and Rescue Services Act 2004** for the area where the premises are (or are to be) situated.

(5) Where an improvement notice or a prohibition notice which is not to take immediate effect has been served:

   (a) the notice may be withdrawn by the inspector at any time before the end of the period specified therein in pursuance of section 21 or section 22(4) as the case may be; and

   (b) the periods so specified may be extended or further extended by an inspector at any time when an appeal against the notice is not pending.

Section 23 contains parallel, but separate, provisions for Scotland and for Wales.

Section 24: Appeal Against Improvement or Prohibition Notice

(1) In this section "a notice" means an improvement notice or a prohibition notice.

(2) A person on whom a notice is served may within such period from the date of its service as may be prescribed appeal to an employment tribunal; and on such an appeal the tribunal may either cancel or affirm the notice and, if it affirms it, may do so either in its original form or with such modifications as the tribunal may in the circumstances think fit.

(3) Where an appeal under this section is brought against a notice within the period allowed under the preceding subsection, then:

   (a) in the case of an improvement notice, the bringing of the appeal shall have the effect of suspending the operation of the notice until the appeal is finally disposed of or, if the appeal is withdrawn, until the withdrawal of the appeal;

   (b) in the case of a prohibition notice, the bringing of the appeal shall have the like effect if, but only if, on the application of the appellant the tribunal so directs (and then only from the giving of the direction).

(4) One or more assessors may be appointed for the purposes of any proceedings brought before an employment tribunal under this section.

Section 25: Power to Deal with Cause of Imminent Danger

(1) Where, in the case of any article or substance found by him in any premises which he has power to enter, an inspector has reasonable cause to believe that, in the circumstances in which he finds it, the article or substance is a cause of imminent danger of serious personal injury, he may seize it and cause it to be rendered harmless (whether by destruction or otherwise).

(2) Before there is rendered harmless under this section:

   (a) any article that forms part of a batch of similar articles; or

   (b) any substance,

the inspector shall, if it is practicable for him to do so, take a sample thereof and give to a responsible person at the premises where the article or substance was found by him, a portion of the sample marked in a manner sufficient to identify it.

(3) As soon as may be after any article or substance has been seized and rendered harmless under this section, the inspector shall prepare and sign a written report giving particulars of the circumstances in which the article or substance was seized and so dealt with by him, and shall:

 (a) give a signed copy of the report to a responsible person at the premises where the article or substance was found by him; and

 (b) unless that person is the owner of the article or substance, also serve a signed copy of the report on the owner;

and if, where paragraph (b) above applies, the inspector cannot after reasonable enquiry ascertain the name or address of the owner, the copy may be served on him by giving it to the person to whom a copy was given under the preceding paragraph.

Section 28: Restrictions on the Disclosure of Information

(1) In this and the two following subsections:

 (a) "relevant information" means information obtained by a person under section 27(1) or furnished to any person under section 27A, by virtue of section 43A(6) or in pursuance of a requirement imposed by any of the relevant statutory provisions; and

 (b) "the recipient" in relation to any relevant information, means the person by whom that information was so obtained or to whom that information was so furnished, as the case may be.

[Section 27 deals with obtaining of information by the Executive or enforcing authorities, authorising the Executive to serve a notice requiring a person to furnish such information about such matters as may be specified in the notice within such time period as may be specified.

Section 27A enables the Commissioners for HM Revenue and Customs to disclose information to enforcing authority inspectors if they feel it appropriate to do so for the purposes of facilitating the exercise of the enforcing authority inspector's powers.

Section 43A enables the Secretary of State to make Regulations requiring persons who provide railway services to pay a railway safety levy.]

(2) Subject to the following subsection, no relevant information shall be disclosed without the consent of the person by whom it was furnished.

(3) The preceding subsection shall not apply to:

 (a) disclosure of information to the Executive, the Office for Nuclear Regulation, the Environment Agency, Natural Resources Wales, the Scottish Environment Protection Agency, a government department or any enforcing authority;

 (b) without prejudice to paragraph (a) above, disclosure by the recipient of information to any person for the purpose of any function conferred on the recipient by or under any of the relevant statutory provisions;

 (c) without prejudice to paragraph (a) above, disclosure by the recipient of information to:

  (i) an officer of a local authority who is authorised by that local authority to receive it;

  (ii) an officer of a water undertaker, sewerage undertaker, water authority or water development board who is authorised by that undertaker, authority or board to receive it;

  (iii) [deleted];

  (iv) a constable authorised by a chief officer of police to receive it;

 (d) disclosure by the recipient of information in a form calculated to prevent it from being identified as relating to a particular person or case;

 (e) disclosure of information for the purposes of any legal proceedings or any investigation or enquiry held by virtue of section 14(2) or (2A), or for the purposes of a report of any such proceedings or inquiry or of a special report made by virtue of section 14(2) or (2A).

 (f) any other disclosure of information by the recipient if:

  (i) the recipient is, or is acting on behalf of a person who is, a public authority for the purposes of the **Freedom of Information Act 2000**, and

  (ii) the information is not held by the authority on behalf of another person.

(4) In the preceding subsection, any reference to the Executive, the Office for Nuclear Regulation, the Environment Agency,

Natural Resources Wales, the Scottish Environment Protection Agency, a government department or an enforcing authority includes respectively a reference to an officer of that body or authority (including, in the case of an enforcing authority, any inspector appointed by it), and also, in the case of a reference to the Executive or the Office for Nuclear Regulation, includes a reference to:

(a) a person performing any functions of the Executive or Office for Nuclear Regulation on its behalf by virtue of section 13(3) of this Act or, as the case may be, section 95 of the **Energy Act 2013**;

(b) an officer of a body which is so performing any such functions; and

(c) an adviser appointed under section 13(7) or, in the case of the Office for Nuclear Regulation, a person providing advice to that body.

(5) A person to whom information is disclosed in pursuance of any of paragraphs (a) to (e) of subsection (3) above shall not use the information for a purpose other than:

(a) in a case falling within paragraph (a) of that subsection, a purpose of the Executive, of the Office for Nuclear Regulation or of the Environment Agency or of Natural Resources Wales or of the Scottish Environment Protection Agency or of the government department in question, or the purposes of the enforcing authority in question in connection with the relevant statutory provisions, as the case may be;

(b) in the case of information given to an officer of a body which is a local authority, a water undertaker, a sewerage undertaker, a water authority, a river purification board or a water development board, the purposes of the body in connection with the relevant statutory provisions or any enactment whatsoever relating to public health, public safety or the protection of the environment;

(c) in the case of information given to a constable, the purposes of the police in connection with the relevant statutory provisions or any enactment whatsoever relating to public health, public safety or the safety of the State.

(6) References in subsections (3) and (5) above to a local authority include the Inner London Education Authority and a joint authority established by Part IV of the **Local Government Act 1985**, an economic prosperity board established under section 88 of the **Local Democracy, Economic Development and Construction Act 2009**, a combined authority established under section 103 of that Act and the London Fire and Emergency Planning Authority.

(7) A person shall not disclose any information obtained by him as a result of the exercise of any power conferred by section 14(4)(a) or 20 (including, in particular, any information with respect to any trade secret obtained by him in any premises entered by him by virtue of any such power) except:

(a) for the purposes of his functions; or

(b) for the purposes of any legal proceedings or any investigation or inquiry held by virtue of section 14(2) or (2A) or for the purposes of a report of any such proceedings or inquiry or of a special report made by virtue of section 14(2) or (2A); or

(c) with the relevant consent.

In this subsection "the relevant consent" means, in the case of information furnished in pursuance of a requirement imposed under section 20, the consent of the person who furnished it, and, in any other case, the consent of a person having responsibilities in relation to the premises where the information was obtained.

(8) Notwithstanding anything in the preceding subsection an inspector shall, in circumstances in which it is necessary to do so for the purposes of assisting in keeping persons (or the representatives of persons) employed at any premises adequately informed about matters affecting their health, safety and welfare, give to such persons or their representatives the following descriptions of information, that is to say:

(a) factual information obtained by him as mentioned in that subsection which relates to those premises or anything which was or is therein or was or is being done therein; and

(b) information with respect to any action which he has taken or proposes to take in or in connection with those premises in the performance of his functions, and, where an inspector does as aforesaid, he shall give the like information to the employer of the first-mentioned persons.

(9) Notwithstanding anything in subsection (7) above, a person who has obtained such information as is referred to in that subsection may furnish to a person who appears to him to be likely to be a party to any civil proceedings arising out of any accident, occurrence, situation or other matter, a written statement of relevant facts observed by him in the course of exercising any of the powers referred to in that subsection.

(9A) Subsection (7) above does not apply if:

(a) the person who has obtained any such information as is referred to in that subsection is, or is acting on behalf of a person who is, a public authority for the purposes of the **Freedom of Information Act 2000**; and

(b) the information is not held by the authority on behalf of another person.

(10) The Broads Authority and every National Park authority shall be deemed to be local authorities for the purposes of this section.

Notes:

In reading section 28, references are made to the following sections and subsections:

- Section 27(1): "a person under section 27(1)" is a person on whom a notice has been served by the Executive requiring him/her to furnish such information as is specified in the notice.
- Section 14(2): "any investigation or inquiry held by virtue of section 14(2)" is a reference to the Executive's power to investigate and make a special report (or authorise another person to do so) or to direct that an enquiry be held.
- Section 14(2)(A): "The Executive may at any time, with the consent of the Secretary of State, direct an inquiry to be held into any matter to which this section applies."
- Section 13(3) refers to the Executive's power to make agreements with any government department or other person for that department or person to perform any of the functions of the Executive, with or without payment.
- Section 13(7) refers to the Executive's power to appoint persons or committees to provide advice to the Executive on any of its functions and to pay appropriate remuneration for such service.
- Section 14(4)(a) refers to the Executive's power to confer on persons making inquiries on their behalf powers of entry and inspection.
- Section 20 refers to the powers of inspectors (see above).

Sections 29 to 32: Special Provisions Relating to Agriculture

[Repealed by the **Employment Protection Act 1975**.]

Section 33: Offences

Note: References to "a person" in this section should be read as either a natural or a legal person (e.g. a company).

(1) It is an offence for a person:

   (a) to fail to discharge a duty to which he is subject by virtue of sections 2 to 7;

   (b) to contravene section 8 or 9;

   (c) to contravene any health and safety regulations or any requirement or prohibition imposed under any such regulations (including any requirement or prohibition to which he is subject by virtue of the terms of any condition or restriction attached to any licence, approval, exemption or other authority issued, given or granted under the regulations);

   (d) to contravene any requirement imposed by or under regulations under section 14 or intentionally to obstruct any person in the exercise of his powers under that section; (*NB: section 14 - Power of the Executive to direct investigations and inquiries*);

   (e) to contravene any requirement imposed by an inspector under section 20 or 25 (*NB: section 20 - Powers of inspectors; section 25 - Inspectors' powers to deal with cause of imminent danger*);

   (f) to prevent or attempt to prevent any other person from appearing before an inspector or from answering any question to which the inspector may by virtue of section 20(2) require an answer;

   (g) to contravene any requirement or prohibition imposed by an improvement notice or a prohibition notice (including any such notice as modified on appeal);

   (h) intentionally to obstruct an inspector in the exercise or performance of his powers or duties or to obstruct a customs officer in the exercise of his powers under section 25A;

   (i) to contravene any requirement imposed by a notice under section 27(1) (*NB: section 27(1) - Obtaining of information by the Executive*);

   (j) to use or disclose any information in contravention of section 27(4) or 28 (*NB: section 27 - Obtaining of information by the Executive; section 28 - Restrictions on disclosure of information*);

   (k) to make a statement which he knows to be false or recklessly to make a statement which is false where the statement is made:

(i) in purported compliance with a requirement to furnish information imposed by or under any of the relevant statutory provisions; or

(ii) for the purpose of obtaining the issue of a document under any of the relevant statutory provisions to himself or another person;

(iii) intentionally to make a false entry in any register, book, notice or other document required by or under any of the relevant statutory provisions to be kept, served or given or, with intent to deceive, to make use of any such entry which he knows to be false;

(l) with intent to deceive, to forge or use a document issued or authorised to be issued under any of the relevant statutory provisions or required for any purpose thereunder or to make or have in his possession a document so closely resembling any such document as to be calculated to deceive;

(m) falsely pretending to be an inspector;

(n) to fail to comply with an order made by a court under section 42 (*NB: section 42 - Power of court to order cause of offence to be remedied or forfeiture*).

Subsections (1A), (2), (3) and (4) have been replaced with Schedule 3A- see the **Health and Safety (Offences) Act 2008**.

Section 36: Offences Due to Fault of Other Person

(1) Where the commission by any person of an offence under any of the relevant statutory provisions is due to the act or default of some other person, that other person shall be guilty of the offence, and a person may be charged with and convicted of the offence by virtue of this subsection whether or not proceedings are taken against the first-mentioned person.

(2) Where there would be or have been the commission of an offence under section 33 by the Crown but for the circumstance that that section does not bind the Crown, and that fact is due to the act or default of a person other than the Crown, that person shall be guilty of the offence which, but for the circumstance, the Crown would be committing or would have committed and may be charged with and convicted of that offence accordingly.

(3) The preceding provisions of this section are subject to any provision made by virtue of section 15(6) (*NB: section 15(6) deals with making of health and safety regulations*).

Section 37: Offences by Bodies Corporate

(1) Where an offence under any of the relevant statutory provisions committed by a body corporate is proved to have been committed with the consent or connivance of, or to have been attributable to any neglect on the part of, any director, manager, secretary or other similar officer of the body corporate or a person who was purporting to act in any such capacity, he as well as the body corporate shall be guilty of that offence and shall be liable to be proceeded against and punished accordingly.

(2) Where the affairs of a body corporate are managed by its members, the preceding subsection shall apply in relation to the acts and defaults of a member in connection with his functions of management as if he were a director of the body corporate.

Section 39: Prosecution by Inspectors

An inspector authorised by the enforcing authority which appointed him may, although not being a barrister or solicitor, prosecute before a magistrates' court proceedings for an offence under any of the relevant statutory provisions.

This does not apply in Scotland.

Section 40: Onus of Proof

In any proceedings for an offence under any of the relevant statutory provisions involving a failure to comply with a duty or requirement:

- to do something so far as is practicable,
- to do something so far as is reasonably practicable, or
- to use the best means to do something,

it shall be for the accused to prove that it was not practicable or not reasonably practicable to do more than was in fact done to satisfy the duty or requirement, or that there was no better practicable means than was in fact used to satisfy the duty or requirement.

Section 47: Civil Liability

Note: This section was amended by the **Enterprise and Regulatory Reform Act 2013**, the main effect of which in this context is to limit the ability to bring claims for a breach of statutory duty.

(1) Nothing in this Part shall be construed:

    (a) as conferring a right of action in any civil proceedings in respect of any failure to comply with any duty imposed by sections 2 to 7 or any contravention of section 8; or

    (b) as affecting the operation of section 12 of the **Nuclear Installations Act 1965** (right to compensation by virtue of certain provisions of that Act).

(2) Breach of a duty imposed by a statutory instrument containing (whether alone or with other provision) health and safety regulations shall not be actionable except to the extent that regulations under this section so provide.

(2A) Breach of a duty imposed by an existing statutory provision shall not be actionable except to the extent that regulations under this section so provide (including by modifying any of the existing statutory provisions).

(2B) Regulations under this section may include provision for:

    (a) a defence to be available in any action for breach of the duty mentioned in subsection (2) or (2A);

    (b) any term of an agreement which purports to exclude or restrict any liability for such a breach to be void.

(3) No provision made by virtue of section 15(6)(b) shall afford a defence in any civil proceedings.

(4) Subsections (1)(a), (2) and (2A) above are without prejudice to any right of action which exists apart from the provisions of this Act, and subsection (2B)(a) above is without prejudice to any defence which may be available apart from the provisions of the regulations there mentioned.

[Subsections (5) and (6) repealed by the **Enterprise and Regulatory Reform Act 2013**]

(7) The power to make regulations under this section shall be exercisable by the Secretary of State.

HEALTH AND SAFETY AT WORK, ETC. ACT 1974 (CIVIL LIABILITY) (EXCEPTIONS) REGULATIONS 2013 (SI 2013 NO. 1667)

These Regulations came into force on 1 October 2013 and made amendments to the **Employment Rights Act** and the **Management of Health and Safety at Work Regulations 1999**. The controversial amendments provide for an exception that allows new or expectant mothers to bring claims for damages for personal injury where others cannot.

Regulation 2: Exception Relating to Compulsory Maternity Leave

(1) Breach of a duty imposed by section 72(1) of the **Employment Rights Act 1996** (which by virtue of section 72(4) of that Act is for these purposes treated as imposed by health and safety regulations) shall, so far as it causes damage, be actionable.

(2) Any term of an agreement which purports to exclude or restrict any liability for such a breach is void.

Regulation 3: Exception Relating to the Management of Health and Safety at Work Regulations 1999

In the **Management of Health and Safety at Work Regulations 1999** for regulation 22 substitute: "22.

(1) Breach of a duty imposed by regulation 16, 16A, 17 or 17A shall, so far as it causes damage, be actionable by the new or expectant mother.

(2) Any term of an agreement which purports to exclude or restrict any liability for such a breach is void."

Regulation 4: Revocations

The **Management of Health and Safety at Work (Amendment) Regulations 2006** are revoked.

HEALTH AND SAFETY AT WORK, ETC. ACT 1974 (GENERAL DUTIES OF SELF-EMPLOYED PERSONS) (PRESCRIBED UNDERTAKINGS) REGULATIONS 2015 (SI 2015 NO. 1583)

Introduction

These Regulations have effect from 1 October 2015 and specify the circumstances in which self-employed persons will be required to comply with their duty under section 3(2) of the **Health and Safety at Work, etc. Act 1974** ("the 1974 Act") to conduct their undertakings in such a way as to ensure, so far as reasonably practicable, that they themselves and other persons (not being their employees) who may be affected by their work activities are not exposed to risks to their health and safety. Every self-employed person continues to hold a duty in respect of their employees under section 2 of the 1974 Act.

Regulation 2 identifies which undertakings are of a prescribed description for the purposes of section 3(2) of the 1974 Act. Regulation 2(a) introduces the Schedule, which prescribes an undertaking if it involves the carrying out of one or more of the activities specified. If an undertaking is not prescribed in the Schedule, regulation 2(b) also prescribes those undertakings which involve any activity that poses risks to the health and safety of another person, other than the person conducting it or their employees.

Regulation 3 requires the Secretary of State to review the operation and effect of these Regulations and publish a report within five years after they come into force and within every five years after that. Following a review it will fall to the Secretary of State to consider whether the Regulations should remain as they are, or be revoked or be amended.

Regulation 2: Prescribed Descriptions of Undertakings

An undertaking is of a prescribed description for the purposes of section 3 (2) of the **Health and Safety at Work, etc. Act 1974** if it involves the carrying out of any activity which:

(a) is listed in the Schedule; or

(b) where not listed in the Schedule, may pose a risk to the health and safety of another person (other than the self-employed person carrying it out or their employees).

Schedule - Activities

Agriculture (including Forestry)

1. Any work which is an agricultural activity (which is to be read in accordance with regulation 2(1) of the **Health and Safety (Enforcing Authority) Regulations 1998**).

Asbestos

2. (1) Any work with asbestos.

    (2) Any work which:

    (a) involves sampling activity; but

    (b) is not work with asbestos.

    (3) Any activity carried out by a dutyholder under regulation 4 of the **Control of Asbestos Regulations 2012** (duty to manage asbestos in non-domestic premises).

    (4) In this paragraph:

    (a) "asbestos" has the meaning given in regulation 2 of the 2012 Regulations;

    (b) "dutyholder" has the meaning given in regulation 4(1) of the 2012 Regulations;

    (c) "sampling activity" means:

    (i) air monitoring;

    (ii) the collection of air samples; or

    (iii) the analysis of air samples,

    to ascertain whether asbestos fibres are present in the air, or to measure the concentration of such fibres; and

    (d) "work with asbestos" is to be read in accordance with regulation 2(2) of the 2012 Regulations.

Construction

3. (1) Any work which is carried out on a construction site.

   (2) Any work in relation to a project carried out by a designer, a client, a contractor, the principal contractor or a principal designer which gives rise to a duty under the **Construction (Design and Management) Regulations 2015**.

   (3) In this paragraph:

   (a) "client", "contractor", "designer", "principal contractor", "principal designer" and "project" have the meanings given in regulation 2(1) of the 2015 Regulations; and

   (b) "construction site" is to be read in accordance with that regulation.

Gas

4. Any activity to which the **Gas Safety (Installation and Use) Regulations 1998** apply.

Genetically Modified Organisms

5. Contained use within the meaning of regulation 2(1) of the **Genetically Modified Organisms (Contained Use) Regulations 2014**.

Railways

6. The operation of a railway (which is to be read in accordance with regulation 2 of the **Health and Safety (Enforcing Authority for railways and Other Guided Transport Systems) Regulations 2006**.

HEALTH AND SAFETY (CONSULTATION WITH EMPLOYEES) REGULATIONS 1996 (SI 1996 NO. 1513)

Summary

The Regulations became effective on 1 October 1996. They implemented provisions made by the **Management of Health and Safety at Work Regulations (MHSWR) 1992** requiring employers to consult with safety representatives, in good time, on various matters; they were later subject to minor amendment by **MHSWR 99**.

You should note that these Regulations extend consultation to non-union representatives of employee safety.

Regulation 3: Duty of Employer to Consult

Where there are employees who are not represented by safety representatives under the 1977 Regulations, the employer shall consult those employees in good time on matters relating to their health and safety at work in particular with regard to:

- The introduction of any measure at the workplace affecting the health and safety of the employees concerned.
- His arrangements for appointing or nominating persons in accordance with regulations 7 and 8 of the **Management of Health and Safety at Work Regulations 1999** or article 13 of the **Regulatory Reform (Fire Safety) Order 2005** (in Scotland, regulation 12 of the **Fire Safety (Scotland) Regulations 2006**).
- Any health and safety information the employer is required to provide to the employees by or under the relevant statutory provisions.
- The planning and organisation of any health and safety training he is required to provide to those employees by or under the relevant statutory provisions.
- The health and safety consequences of the planning and introduction of new technologies in the workplace.

Regulation 4: Employees to be Consulted

Employers may consult:

- Employees directly.
- In respect of any group of employees, one or more persons in that group who were elected, by the employees in that group at the time of the election, to represent that group for the purposes of such consultation. Any such persons elected are referred to in these Regulations as representatives of employee safety.

Where consultation is through such employee representatives, the employer must inform the employees of the names of those representatives, and the group of employees they represent.

An employer shall not consult such a representative when:

- the employee representative has informed the employer that he no longer intends to represent his group of employees in health and safety consultations;
- the employee representative no longer works in the group of employees he represents;
- the period of election has expired without that employee representative being re-elected;
- that employee representative has become incapacitated from performing the duties required under these Regulations;

and where in accordance with the above the employer discontinues consultation with that person he shall inform the employees in the group concerned accordingly.

Employees and their representatives must be informed by the employer if he decides to change from consulting with the employee representatives to consulting with the employees directly.

Regulation 5: Duty of Employer to Provide Information

The following provisions must be made:

- Where consultation is direct, an employer must provide all information, within his knowledge, the employees will require in order to participate fully in the consultation.
- The same applies to employee representatives, who must be given all necessary information to enable them to participate fully and effectively in consultation and in the carrying out of their functions.

- In addition, these employee representatives must also be provided with information associated with the records to be kept under the **Reporting of Injuries, Diseases and Dangerous Occurrences Regulations 2013 (RIDDOR)** where the information relates to the workplace or the group of the employees they represent.
- The employer is not obliged to disclose information that:
    - is against the interests of national security;
    - would contravene any prohibition imposed under any legislation;
    - does not relate to health and safety;
    - relates specifically to an individual (unless that individual has given his or her consent);
    - would damage the employer's undertaking, or the undertaking of another person where that other person supplied the information; or
    - has been obtained by the employer for the purpose of any legal proceedings.

Regulation 6: Functions of Representatives of Employee Safety

Employee representatives may make representation to the employer:

- On any potential hazards and dangerous occurrences in the workplace which may affect the health and safety of the employees they represent.
- On any general health and safety matters and particularly in relation to the matters on which employers are obliged to consult.
- In representing their group of employees in consultations at the workplace with enforcing authority inspectors.

Regulation 7: Training, Time Off and Provision of Facilities, etc.

Employers must provide representatives with appropriate training and other relevant facilities so as to enable the representatives to carry out their duties efficiently. Employers must also meet all reasonable costs associated with the training, including travel and subsistence. In addition, the employee representatives must be given paid time off to perform their safety duties and to attend relevant training courses. Paid time off must also be provided for candidates standing for election as employee representatives to allow them to perform their duties as candidates.

If employers refuse to allow employee representatives time off with pay to fulfil their duties, the representatives may complain to an employment tribunal.

In addition, an employer shall provide such other facilities and assistance as a representative of employee safety may reasonably require for the purpose of carrying out his functions under these Regulations.

Regulation 8: Amendment to Employment Rights Act 1996

The **Employment Rights Act 1996** has been amended to protect employees who participate in consultation with employers, from suffering any detriment for a breach of duty under these Regulations.

Regulation 9: Exclusion of Civil Liability

Breach of a duty imposed by these Regulations shall, subject to regulation 7 and Schedule 2, not confer any right of action in any civil proceedings.

Regulation 10: Application of Health and Safety Legislation

Any references to health and safety Regulations or to the relevant statutory provisions in certain sections of the 1974 Act, the **Health and Safety (Enforcing Authority) Regulations 1989**, and the **Health and Safety (Training for Employment) Regulations 1990**, shall apply as if they included references to these Regulations.

Regulation 11: Application to the Crown and Armed Forces

Section 48 of the 1974 Act shall apply in respect of these Regulations.

The Regulations shall apply in respect of members of the armed forces with regard to consultation with representatives of employee safety except that such persons are appointed by the employer- not elected.

Regulation 12: Disapplication to Sea-Going Ships

These Regulations shall not apply to or in relation to a master or crew of a sea-going ship or to the employer of such persons in respect of the normal ship-board activities of a ship's crew under the direction of the master.

Regulation 13: Amendment of 1977 Regulations

This amendment deletes certain words from regulation 3 of the 1977 Regulations in relation to employees employed in a coal mine.

HEALTH AND SAFETY (DISPLAY SCREEN EQUIPMENT) REGULATIONS 1992 (SI 1992 NO. 2792)

Summary Note

Note from the date of the Regulations that they became law before the widespread use of the mouse, scanner and laser printer, and other computer peripherals commonly used today. Although not specifically mentioned here, there remains an obligation to undertake a risk assessment on such equipment if it is used in the work environment, under the risk assessment obligation under **MHSWR**, as amended.

The guidance *Work with display screen equipment*, L26, was updated in 2003 to take into account the amendments to the Regulations, and modern work equipment.

The Regulations

The Regulations came into force on 1 January 1993. They were amended in 2002.

Regulation 1: Definitions

The following definitions are given:

"Display Screen Equipment": Any alphanumeric or graphic display screen, regardless of the display process involved.
"Operator": A self-employed person who habitually uses display screen equipment as a significant part of his normal work.
"Use" means use for or in connection with work.

"User" means an employee who habitually uses display screen equipment as a significant part of his normal work.

"Workstation": An assembly comprising:

- display screen equipment (whether provided with software determining the interface between the equipment and its operator or user or any other input device),
- any optional accessories to the display screen equipment,
- any disk drive, telephone, modem, printer, document holder, work chair, desk, work surface or other item peripheral to the display screen equipment, and
- the immediate work environment around the display screen equipment.

Exemptions: Nothing in these Regulations shall apply to, or in relation to:

- drivers' cabs or control cabs for vehicles or machinery;
- display screen equipment on board a means of transport;
- display screen equipment mainly intended for public operation;
- portable systems not in prolonged use;
- calculators, cash registers or any equipment having a small data or measurement display required for direct use of the equipment;
- window typewriters.

Regulation 2: Analysis of Workstations

Every employer shall, for the purpose of assessing the health and safety risks to which persons are exposed, perform a suitable and sufficient analysis of those workstations which, regardless of who has provided them, are used, for the purposes of his undertaking by users, or have been provided by him and are used for the purposes of his undertaking by operators.

Any assessment made by an employer in pursuance of the above paragraph shall be reviewed by him if there is reason to suspect that it is no longer valid, or there has been a significant change in the matters to which it relates. Where as a result of any such review changes to an assessment are required, the employer concerned shall make them.

The employer shall reduce the risks identified in consequence of an assessment to the lowest extent reasonably practicable.

Regulation 3: Requirements for Workstations

Every employer shall ensure that any workstation which may be used for the purposes of his undertaking meets the requirements laid down in the Schedule to these Regulations, to the extent specified in paragraph 1 thereof.

Regulation 4: Daily Work Routine of Users

Every employer shall so plan the activities of users at work in his undertaking that their work on display screen equipment is periodically interrupted by such breaks or changes of activity as reduce their workload at that equipment.

Regulation 5: Eye and Eyesight Testing

(1) Where a person:

    (a) is a user in the undertaking in which he is employed; or

    (b) is to become a user in the undertaking in which he is, or is to become, employed,

the employer who carries on the undertaking shall, if requested by that person, ensure that an appropriate eye and eyesight test is carried out on him by a competent person within the time specified in paragraph (2).

(2) The time referred to in paragraph (1) is:

- in the case of a person mentioned in paragraph (1)(a), as soon as practicable after the request; and
- in the case of a person mentioned in paragraph (1)(b), before he becomes a user.

Frequency of testing: At regular intervals after an employee has been provided with an eye and eyesight test, his employer shall ensure that he is provided with a further eye and eyesight test of an appropriate nature, any such test to be carried out by a competent person.

Where a user experiences visual difficulties which may reasonably be considered to be caused by work on display screen equipment, his employer shall ensure that he is provided at his request with an appropriate eye and eyesight test, any such test to be carried out by a competent person as soon as practicable after being requested.

Provision of glasses: Every employer shall ensure that each user employed by him is provided with special corrective appliances appropriate for the work being done by the user concerned where normal corrective appliances cannot be used, and the result of any eye and eyesight test which the user has been given shows provision to be necessary.

Regulation 6: Provision of Training

Where a person is a user in the undertaking in which he is employed, or is to become a user in the undertaking in which he is, or is to become, employed, the employer shall ensure that he is provided with adequate health and safety training in the use of any workstation upon which he may be required to work.

Every employer shall ensure that each user at work in his undertaking is provided with adequate health and safety training whenever the organisation of any workstation in that undertaking upon which he may be required to work is substantially modified.

Regulation 7: Provision of Information

Every employer shall ensure that operators and users at work in his undertaking are provided with adequate information about all aspects of health and safety relating to their workstations, and such measures taken by him in compliance with his duties under the Regulations.

Regulation 8: Exemption Certificates

This regulation empowers the Secretary of State for Defence in the interests of national security to exempt any of the home or visiting forces from any of the requirements of these Regulations.

Regulation 9: Extension Outside Great Britain

This regulation extends the provisions of the Regulations to certain premises and activities outside Great Britain.

HEALTH AND SAFETY (ENFORCING AUTHORITY) REGULATIONS 1998 (SI 1998 NO. 494)

These Regulations re-enacted earlier legislation dated 1977 which made provision with respect to the enforcement of **HSWA** by local authorities. The HSE was made the enforcing authority of relevant statutory provisions, except where some other authority is responsible for their enforcement.

In practice, this means that "construction", "industrial" or "storage"- type workplaces or those places where large numbers of people might be gathered together are the responsibility of the HSE, whereas "office" or "retail"- type workplaces fall under the local authority. Thus the same organisation, for example a service-based publishing company with a printing workshop, might fall within the responsibility of different enforcing authorities in different departments of the company. Where there is uncertainty, the Regulations permit the enforcing authorities to agree on joint responsibility.

HEALTH AND SAFETY (FIRST-AID) REGULATIONS 1981 (SI 1981 NO. 917)

Amending Legislation

Changes to the Regulations were made by the **Offshore Installations and Pipeline Works (First-Aid) Regulations 1989**, the **Management and Administration of Safety and Health at Mines Regulations 1993**, the **Diving at Work Regulations 1997**, the **Management of Health and Safety at Work Regulations 1999**, and the **Health and Safety (Fees) Regulations 2001**; none of which involve material alteration to the substance of the 1981 Regulations. Reg. 3(5) was added by the **Health and Safety (Miscellaneous Amendments) Regulations 2002**.

Most recently, the Regulations have been amended to remove the requirement for first-aid training providers to be approved by the HSE. This change came into force on 1 October 2013.

The Regulations

The Approved Code of Practice states that an employer should make an assessment of first-aid needs appropriate to the circumstances (hazards and risks) of each workplace.

The Regulations were innovative in a number of ways. The most important aspect was the shift away from the previously rigid specifications covering the number of first aiders and the number and content of first-aid boxes, towards a greater consideration for the training of first aiders and their suitability to deal with their respective workplace situations.

There are no fixed ratios of first aiders to the total number of people employed, contained in the new Regulations. The Approved Code of Practice does recommend minimum numbers of first aiders to be provided, but more importantly the Regulations place the onus on the employer to assess how many first aiders are required, bearing in mind not only the total number of employees but also:

- The nature of the work and the workforce.
- The size of the organisation and the distribution of employees.
- The location of the establishment.
- Work patterns, including shift work and the needs of travelling, remote and lone workers.
- Annual leave and first-aid provision for non-employees.
- The distance from outside medical services.
- The organisation's history of accidents.

Similarly, the detailed requirements in the old Regulations on the number and the content of first-aid boxes have been replaced by general recommendations contained in the Guidance Notes.

The greater part of the ACoP is an amplification of the key regulation 3, in particular the meaning of the phrase "adequate and appropriate" which applies to both the provision of "suitable persons" and the provision of first-aid "equipment and facilities". The Guidance Notes deal largely with the contents of first-aid boxes and rooms and the content of training programmes for first aiders. As mentioned above, following an amendment introduced by the **Health and Safety (Miscellaneous Revocations and Amendments) Regulations 2013**, there is no longer a requirement for first aiders to undergo HSE-approved training. The HSE will continue to set the standards for existing training- the one-day Emergency First-Aid at Work (EFAW) and three-day First-Aid at Work (FAW) courses- which will continue to be the building blocks in all cases where a first-aid needs assessment shows that training is necessary. Employers will still have to ensure that they have an adequate number of trained first aiders as identified in their needs assessment. The HSE has published a revised ACoP (L74), available on the HSE website.

In terms of personnel, the number of suitable persons is dependent on the risk. The ACoP (para. 52 and Appendix 3) suggests that, where 25 or more people are employed, even in low-hazard environments, at least one EFAW-trained first aider should be provided. Where there are more than 50 people at work in higher hazard workplaces, at least one FAW-trained first aider should be provided for every 50 employees. However, the ACoP also makes clear that there are no hard and fast rules on exact numbers since employers will need to take into account all the relevant circumstances of their workplace. The employer will also need to ensure adequate coverage for holiday and sickness absence and, where a company works shifts, at least one first aider per shift should be appointed.

Should an assessment show that a first-aider is not required, the minimum requirement is for an 'Appointed Person' to take charge of first-aid arrangements, including looking after supplies and calling the emergency services when required.

Employers should ensure that first aiders have undertaken suitable training, have an appropriate first-aid qualification and remain competent to perform their role. Typically, first aiders will hold a valid certificate of competence in either Emergency First Aid at Work (EFAW), which covers provision of emergency first aid only, or First Aid at Work (FAW), which includes EFAW and also equips the first aider to apply first aid to a range of specific injuries and illnesses.

Regulation 3: General Duty of the Employer to Make Provision for First Aid

The following provisions are to be made:

(1) An employer shall provide, or ensure that there are provided, such equipment and facilities as are adequate and appropriate in the circumstances for enabling first aid to be rendered to employees if they are injured or become ill at work.

(2) Subject to paragraphs (3) and (4), an employer shall provide or ensure that there is provided, such number of suitable persons as is adequate and appropriate in the circumstances for rendering first aid to his employees if they are injured or become ill at work; and for this purpose a person shall not be suitable unless he has undergone such training and has such qualifications as may be appropriate in the circumstances of that case.

(3) Where a person provided under paragraph (2) is absent in temporary and exceptional circumstances it shall be sufficient compliance with that paragraph if the employer appoints a person, or ensures that a person is appointed, to take charge of:

   (a) the situation relating to an injured or ill employee who will need help from a medical practitioner or nurse, and

   (b) the equipment and facilities provided under paragraph (1),

   throughout the period of any such absence.

(4) Where having regard to:

   (a) the nature of the undertaking, and

   (b) the number of employees at work, and

   (c) the location of the establishment,

   it would be adequate and appropriate if, instead of a person for rendering first aid, there was a person appointed to take charge, as in paragraph (3) (a) and (b), then instead of complying with paragraph (2) the employer may appoint such a person, or ensure that such a person is appointed.

(5) Any first-aid room provided pursuant to this regulation shall be easily accessible to stretchers and to any other equipment needed to convey patients to and from the room and be signposted, such sign to comply with regulation 4 of the **Health and Safety (Safety Signs and Signals) Regulations 1996**.

Size of Establishment, Location of Workers

[From the ACoP]

Generally, the larger the workforce, the greater the first-aid provision that is required. The employer should consider how the size of the premises could affect quick access to first-aid facilities, such as whether additional first-aid provision is needed on sites with more than one building or in a multi-floor building.

The employer remains responsible for adequate first-aid provision for travelling, remote or lone workers. Those who travel long distances or who are continuously mobile should carry a personal first-aid kit. Where employees work in remote areas, the employer should consider issuing personal communicators and providing additional training. For lone workers, other means of summoning help (e.g. a mobile phone) may be useful. Where a site is remote from emergency medical services, employers may need to make special arrangements to ensure appropriate transport is available. Employers should inform the emergency services, in writing, of their location and any particular circumstances, including specific hazards.

First-Aid Box Contents

[From the ACoP]

Paragraph 37 of the ACoP states that:

"First-aid containers should be easily accessible and preferably placed near to hand-washing facilities. They should only be stocked with items useful for giving first aid and should be protected from dust and damp."

Paragraph 38 goes on to say that:

"The contents of first-aid containers should be examined frequently and restocked soon after use. Sufficient supplies should be held in stock on site. Care should be taken to dispose of items safely once they reach their expiry date."

The risk assessment may indicate that additional materials and equipment are required, including such things as foil blankets, aprons, hypoallergenic tape, calcium gluconate for hydrofluoric acid burns, etc.

The ACoP (para. 42) recommends that "tablets and medicines should not be kept in the first-aid container" although it does note an exception, which is the use of aspirin that can be administered in cases of suspected heart attack in accordance with currently accepted first-aid practice.

If a defibrillator is provided, those who may need to use it should be trained.

Appendix 2 provides guidance on the contents of first-aid kits. The minimum content in a low risk environment would be:

- A leaflet giving general advice on first aid.
- 20 individually wrapped, sterile plasters (assorted sizes - hypoallergenic if necessary).
- Two sterile eye pads.
- Two individually wrapped, triangular bandages, preferably sterile.
- Six safety pins.
- Two large sterile, individually wrapped, unmedicated wound dressings.
- Six medium-sized, sterile, individually wrapped, unmedicated wound dressings.
- At least three pairs of disposable gloves.

Travelling first-aid kit contents might typically include:

- A leaflet giving general guidance on first aid.
- Six individually wrapped, sterile plasters (hypoallergenic if necessary).
- Two individually wrapped, triangular bandages, preferably sterile.
- Two safety pins.
- One large sterile, unmedicated dressing.
- Individually wrapped, moist cleansing wipes.
- Two pairs of disposable gloves.

Regulation 4: Duty of Employer to Inform his Employees of the Arrangements Made in Connection with First Aid

An employer shall inform his employees of the arrangements that have been made in connection with the provision of first aid, including the location of equipment, facilities and personnel.

Regulation 5: Duty of Self-Employed Person to Provide First-Aid Equipment

A self-employed person shall provide, or ensure that there is provided, such equipment, if any, as is adequate and appropriate in the circumstances to enable him to render first aid to himself while he is at work.

Checklist for Assessment of First-Aid Needs

[From the ACoP]

Factor to consider	Space for notes	Impact on first-aid provision
Hazards (use the findings of your general risk assessment and take account of any parts of your workplace that have different work activities/hazards which may require different levels of first-aid provision)		
Does your workplace have low-level hazards such as those that might be found in offices and shops?		The minimum provision is: an appointed person to take charge of first-aid arrangements; a suitably stocked first-aid box.
Does your workplace have higher-level hazards such as chemicals or dangerous machinery?		You should consider: • providing first- aiders; • providing additional training for first- aiders to deal with injuries resulting from special hazards; • providing a suitably stocked first-aid box; • providing additional first-aid equipment; • precise location of first-aid equipment; providing a first-aid room; informing the emergency services of specific hazards, etc. in advance.
Do your work activities involve special hazards such as hydrofluoric acid or confined spaces?		You should consider: • providing first aiders; • additional training for first aiders to deal with injuries resulting from special hazards; • additional first-aid equipment; • precise location of first-aid equipment; • providing a first-aid room; • informing the emergency services of specific hazards, etc. in advance.
Employees		
How many people are employed on site?		Where there are small numbers of employees, the minimum provision is: • an appointed person to take charge of first-aid arrangements; • a suitably stocked first-aid box. • Where there are large numbers of employees, ie.e. more than 25, even in low-hazard environments, you should consider providing: • first- aiders; • additional first-aid equipment; • a first-aid room.
Are there inexperienced workers on site, or employees with disabilities or particular health problems?		You should consider: • additional training for first- aiders; • additional first-aid equipment; • local siting of first-aid equipment. Your first-aid provision should cover any work experience trainees. • a first-aid room.

(Continued)

Factor to consider	Space for notes	Impact on first-aid provision
Does your workplace have low-level hazards such as those that might be found in offices and shops?		The minimum provision is: an appointed person to take charge of first-aid arrangements; a suitably stocked first-aid box.
Does your workplace have higher-level hazards such as chemicals or dangerous machinery?		You should consider: • providing first aiders; • providing additional training for first aiders to deal with injuries resulting from special hazards; • providing a suitably stocked first-aid box; • providing additional first-aid equipment; • precise location of first-aid equipment; providing a first-aid room; informing the emergency services of specific hazards, etc. in advance.
Do your work activities involve special hazards such as hydrofluoric acid or confined spaces?		You should consider: • providing first aiders; • additional training for first aiders to deal with injuries resulting from special hazards; • additional first-aid equipment; • precise location of first-aid equipment; • providing a first-aid room; • informing the emergency services of specific hazards, etc. in advance.
How many people are employed on site?		Where there are small numbers of employees, the minimum provision is: • an appointed person to take charge of first-aid arrangements; • a suitably stocked first-aid box. • Where there are large numbers of employees, i.e. more than 25, even in low-hazard environments, you should consider providing: • first aiders; • additional first-aid equipment; • a first-aid room.
Are there inexperienced workers on site, or employees with disabilities or particular health problems?		You should consider: • additional training for first aiders; • additional first-aid equipment; • local siting of first-aid equipment. Your first-aid provision should cover any work experience trainees. • a first-aid room.
Accidents and ill-health record		
What is your record of accidents and ill health? What injuries and illness have occurred and where did they happen?		Ensure your first-aid provision will cater for the types of injuries and illnesses that have occurred in your workplace. Monitor accidents and ill health and review your first-aid provision as appropriate.
Working arrangements		
Do you have employees who travel a lot, work remotely or work alone?		You should consider: • issuing personal first-aid kits; • issuing personal communicators/mobile phones to employees.

Do any of your employees work shifts or out-of-hours?		You should ensure there is adequate first-aid provision at all times people are at work.
Are the premises spread out, e.g. are there several buildings on the site or multi-floor buildings?		You should consider the need for provision in each building or on each floor.
Is your workplace remote from emergency medical services?		You should: • inform the emergency services of your location; • consider special arrangements with the emergency services; • consider emergency transport requirements.
Do any of your employees work at sites occupied by other employers?		You should make arrangements with other site occupiers to ensure adequate provision of first aid. A written agreement between employers is strongly recommended.
Do you have sufficient provision to cover absences of first aiders or appointed persons?		You should consider: • what cover is needed for annual leave and other planned absences; • what cover is needed for unplanned and exceptional absences.
Non-employees		
Do members of the public or non-employees visit your premises?		Under the **Health and Safety (First-Aid) Regulations 1981**, you have no legal duty to provide first aid for non-employees but HSE strongly recommends that you include them in your first-aid provision.

Suggested numbers of first-aid personnel to be available at all times people are at work:

[From the ACoP]

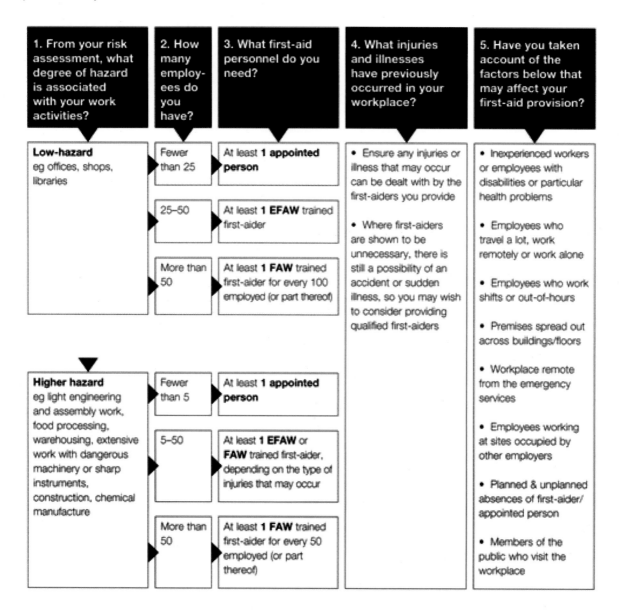

NB: First aiders and appointed persons take holidays and are often absent from premises for other reasons. Sufficient people must be appointed to cover these absences to enable first-aid personnel to be available at all times when people are at work.

HEALTH AND SAFETY INFORMATION FOR EMPLOYEES REGULATIONS 1989 (SI 1989 NO. 682)

Amending Legislation

The **Health and Safety Information for Employees (Modifications and Repeals) Regulations 1995** revoked a number of statutory requirements to display health and safety information, in particular those made with reference to specific industrial processes under the **Factories Act 1961**. They also allowed an employer to dispense with the standard Health and Safety Law poster and, subject to HSE approval, use or display a more work-environment-related poster or leaflet.

The **Health and Safety Information for Employees (Amendment) Regulations 2009** make further minor changes. Specifically, they have made provision for an alternative, modern, HSE-approved poster which doesn't show the contact details of HSE or EMAS (the details can be provided separately to employees).

Regulation 1: Citation and Commencement

These Regulations came into force on 18 October 1989.

Regulation 2: Interpretation and Application

"The 1974 Act" means the **Health and Safety at Work, etc. Act 1974**.

"The approved poster" and "the approved leaflet" have the meanings assigned by regulation 3.

"Employment medical advisory service" means the employment medical advisory service referred to in section 55 of the 1974 Act. "Ship" has the meaning assigned to it by section 742 of the **Merchant Shipping Act 1894**.

The Regulations shall have effect for the purpose of providing information to employees relating to health, safety and welfare but they shall not apply in relation to the master and crew of a sea-going ship.

Regulation 3: Meaning of and Revisions to the Approved Poster and Leaflet

"The approved poster" or "the approved leaflet" means, respectively, a poster or leaflet in the form approved and published for the purposes of these Regulations by the Health and Safety Executive, as revised from time to time in accordance with the following paragraph.

The Health and Safety Executive may approve a revision (in whole or in part) to the form of poster or leaflet; and where it does so it shall publish the revised form of poster or leaflet and issue a notice in writing specifying the date the revision was approved.

Any revision shall not take effect until five years after the date of its approval. During that time the employer may use the approved poster or the approved leaflet incorporating the revision.

The Health and Safety Executive may approve a particular form of poster or leaflet for use in relation to a particular employment or class of employment and where any such form has been approved the Executive shall publish it and issue a notice in writing specifying the date that form was approved and the particular employment or class of employment in respect of which it is approved.

An employer may, in respect of employment for which a particular poster or leaflet has been approved, comply with the requirements by displaying that particular form of poster or giving that particular form of leaflet.

Regulation 4: Provision of Poster or Leaflet

An employer shall, in relation to each of his employees:

- ensure that the approved poster is kept displayed in a readable condition:
    - at a place which is reasonably accessible to the employee while he is at work, and
    - in such a position in that place as to be easily seen and read by that employee; or
- give the employee the approved leaflet.

An employer shall be treated as having complied with the duty to give the employee the approved leaflet from the date the employee commences employment with him if he gives the employee the approved leaflet as soon as is reasonably practicable after that date.

Where the form of poster or leaflet is revised then on or before the date the revision takes effect:

- An employer who chooses to display a poster and keep it in readable condition shall ensure that the approved poster displayed is the one as revised.
- An employer who chooses to provide an approved leaflet shall either give to the employees concerned fresh approved leaflets (as revised) or bring the revision to their notice in writing.

Regulation 5: Provision of Further Information

An employer who chooses to display an approved poster shall ensure that the following information is clearly and indelibly written on the poster in the appropriate space:

- the name of the enforcing authority for the premises where the poster is displayed and the address of the office of that authority for the area in which those premises are situated; and
- the address of the office of the employment medical advisory service for the area in which those premises are situated;

or information as to how any of his employees may obtain the information referred to.

Where there is a change in any of the matters referred to in the above paragraph it shall be sufficient compliance with that paragraph for the corresponding amendment to the poster to be made within six months from the date thereof.

An employer who gives his employee an approved leaflet shall give with the leaflet a written notice containing:

- the name of the enforcing authority for the premises where the employee works, and the address of the office of that authority for the area in which those premises are situated; and
- the address of the office of the employment medical advisory service for the area in which those premises are situated;

or information as to how any of his employees may obtain the information referred to above.

Where the employee works in more than one location he shall be treated as working at the premises from which his work is administered, and if his work is administered from two or more premises, the employer may choose any one of them for the purpose of complying.

Where an employer chooses to provide an approved leaflet and there is a change in any of the matters referred to above, the employer shall within six months of the date thereof give to the employee a written notice specifying the change.

Regulation 6: Exemption Certificates

The Health and Safety Executive may, by a certificate in writing, exempt any person or class of persons from all or any of the requirements imposed by these Regulations and any such exemption may be granted subject to conditions and to a limit of time and may be revoked in writing at any time. An exemption may not be granted unless, having regard to the circumstances of the case, and in particular to:

- the conditions if any, which it proposes to attach to the exemption; and
- any other requirements imposed by or under any enactment which apply to the case,

it is satisfied that the health, safety and welfare of persons who are likely to be affected by the exemption will not be prejudiced in consequence of it.

Regulation 7: Defence

In any proceedings for an offence for a contravention of these Regulations it shall be a defence for the accused to prove that he took all reasonable precautions and exercised all due diligence to avoid the commission of that offence.

HEALTH AND SAFETY (MISCELLANEOUS AMENDMENTS) REGULATIONS 2002 (SI 2002 NO. 2174)

These came into force on 17 September 2002.

The following amendments were introduced as a result of these Regulations:

Health and Safety (First-Aid) Regulations 1981

Regulation 3 is amended by adding the following paragraph:

- Any first-aid room provided [...] shall be easily accessible to stretchers and to any other equipment needed to convey patients to and from the room and be signposted, such sign to comply with regulation 4 of the **Health and Safety (Safety Signs and Signals) Regulations 1996** [...].

Health and Safety (Display Screen Equipment) Regulations 1992

- **Regulation 3** was substituted to make clear that every employer shall ensure that any workstation which may be used for the purposes of his undertaking meets the requirements laid down in the schedule to the **DSE Regulations**.
- Paragraphs (1) and (2) of **regulation 5** were substituted to clarify the arrangements for provision of eye and eyesight tests to users, or to those who are to become users.
- Paragraph (1) of **regulation 6** was substituted to clarify the duty to provide users or those who are to become users with adequate health and safety training in the use of any workstation.

Manual Handling Operations Regulations 1992

Regulation 4 of the **Manual Handling Operations Regulations 1992** is amended by adding the following paragraph:

- In determining for the purposes of this regulation whether manual handling operations at work involve a risk of injury and in determining the appropriate steps to reduce that risk regard shall be had in particular to:
    - the physical suitability of the employee to carry out the operations;
    - the clothing, footwear or other personal effects he is wearing;
    - his knowledge and training;
    - the results of any relevant risk assessment carried out pursuant to regulation 3 of the **Management of Health and Safety at Work Regulations 1999**;
    - the employee is within a group of employees identified by that assessment as being especially at risk; and
    - the results of any health surveillance provided pursuant to regulation 6 of the **Management of Health and Safety at Work Regulations 1999**.

Personal Protective Equipment at Work Regulations 1992

Regulation 4 originally stated:

(a) It is appropriate for the risk or risks involved and the conditions at the place where exposure to the risk may occur.

(b) It takes account of ergonomic requirements and the state of health of the person or persons who may wear it.

The above is replaced with the following:

(a) It is appropriate for the risk or risks involved, the conditions at the place where exposure to the risk may occur, and the period for which it is worn.

(b) It takes account of ergonomic requirements and the state of health of the person or persons who may wear it, and of the characteristics of the workstation of each such person.

An additional paragraph has also been added to **regulation 4** as follows:

- Where it is necessary to ensure that personal protective equipment is hygienic and otherwise free of risk to health, every employer and every self-employed person shall ensure that personal protective equipment provided under this regulation is provided to a person for use only by him.

An addition to **regulation 6** under inclusions in the assessment is as follows:

(d) an assessment as to whether the personal protective equipment is compatible with other personal protective equipment which is in use and which an employee would be required to wear simultaneously.

In **regulation 9** after the points that the employer should ensure that the employee knows, the following has been added:

- and shall ensure that such information is kept available to employees.

At the end of **regulation 9** the following has been added:

- The employer shall, where appropriate, and at suitable intervals, organise demonstrations in the wearing of personal protective equipment.

Workplace (Health, Safety and Welfare) Regulations 1992

The definition of '"Workplace" was amended and a new **regulation 4A** inserted as follows:

Regulation 4A: Stability and Solidity

Where a workplace is in a building, the building shall have a stability and solidity appropriate to the nature of the use of the workplace. A new paragraph was inserted into **regulation 7**, as follows:

(a) a workplace shall be adequately thermally insulated where it is necessary, having regard to the type of work carried out and the physical activity of the persons carrying out the work; and

(b) excessive effects of sunlight on temperature shall be avoided.

Paragraph 3 of **regulation 25** was substituted with the following:

Rest rooms and rest areas shall:

(a) include suitable arrangements to protect non-smokers from discomfort caused by tobacco smoke; and

(b) be equipped with:

    (i) an adequate number of tables and adequate seating with backs for the number of persons at work likely to use them at any one time; and

    (ii) seating which is adequate for the number of disabled persons at work and suitable for them.

A new **regulation 25A** was inserted as follows:

Regulation 25A: Disabled Persons

Where necessary, those parts of the workplace (including in particular doors, passageways, stairs, showers, washbasins, lavatories and workstations) used or occupied directly by disabled persons at work shall be organised to take account of such persons.

Other minor amendments were made to **regulations 5(3) and 24(2)**. **Regulation 6(3)** was deleted.

Provision and Use of Work Equipment Regulations 1998

Paragraphs (1) and (2) of **regulation 10** were substituted with the following:

(1) Every employer shall ensure that an item of work equipment conforms at all times with any essential requirements, other than requirements which, at the time of its being first supplied or put into service in any place in which these Regulations apply, did not apply to work equipment of its type.

(2) In this regulation "essential requirements", in relation to an item of work equipment, means requirements relating to the design and construction of work equipment of its type in any of the instruments listed in Schedule 1 (being instruments which give effect to Community directives concerning the safety of products).

Paragraph (2) of **regulation 11** was substituted with the following:

The measures required by paragraph (1) shall consist of:

(a) the provision of fixed guards enclosing every dangerous part or rotating stock-bar where and to the extent that it is practicable to do so, but where or to the extent that it is not, then

(b) the provision of other guards or protection devices where and to the extent that it is practicable to do so, but where or to the extent that it is not, then

(c) the provision of jigs, holders, push-sticks or similar protection appliances used in conjunction with the machinery where and to the extent that it is practicable to do so,

and the provision of such information, instruction, training and supervision as is necessary.

Paragraph (1) of **regulation 18** was substituted as follows:

Every employer shall ensure, so far as is reasonably practicable, that all control systems of work equipment:

(a) are safe; and

(b) are chosen making due allowance for the failures, faults and constraints to be expected in the planned circumstances of use.

Minor amendments were made to **regulation 35**.

Lifting Operations and Lifting Equipment Regulations 1998

Minor amendments were made to the definition of "accessory for lifting" and to **regulation 3(4)**.

HEALTH AND SAFETY (OFFENCES) ACT 2008

This Act received Royal Assent on 16 October 2008 and came into force in January 2009. The Act amends Section 33 of the **Health and Safety at Work, etc. Act 1974 (HSWA)**. It replaces the penalty provisions of section 33(1A) to (4) of the 1974 Act by inserting a new Schedule 3A to the 1974 Act. This Schedule sets out the mode of trial and maximum penalties for the health and safety offences set out in section 33(1)(a) to (o) and for offences under the "existing statutory provisions" (i.e. pre-dating the 1974 Act) where no other penalty is specified.

The effect of the Act is to:

- make imprisonment an option for more health and safety offences in both the lower and higher courts;
- make certain offences, which were previously triable only in the lower courts, triable in either the lower or higher courts.

It extends to the whole of the United Kingdom.

Section 1: Health and Safety Offences: Mode of Trial and Maximum Penalty

This section amends section 33 of the 1974 Act and Article 31 of the **Health and Safety at Work (Northern Ireland) Order 1978**. It gives effect to a new Schedule 3A, which is inserted into both the 1974 Act and the 1978 Order. The content of the new Schedule 3A is given in the table below.

Offence	Mode of Trial	Penalty on Summary Conviction	Penalty on Conviction on Indictment
An offence under section 33(1)(a) consisting of a failure to discharge a duty to which a person is subject by virtue of sections 2 to 6.	Summarily or on indictment.	Imprisonment for a term not exceeding 12 months, or a fine, or both.	Imprisonment for a term not exceeding two years, or a fine, or both.
An offence under section 33(1)(a) consisting of a failure to discharge a duty to which a person is subject by virtue of section 7.	Summarily or on indictment.	Imprisonment for a term not exceeding 12 months, or a fine, or both.	Imprisonment for a term not exceeding two years, or a fine, or both.
An offence under section 33(1)(b) consisting of a contravention of section 8.	Summarily or on indictment.	Imprisonment for a term not exceeding 12 months, or a fine, or both.	Imprisonment for a term not exceeding two years, or a fine, or both.
An offence under section 33(1)(b) consisting of a contravention of section 9.	Summarily or on indictment.	A fine.	A fine.
An offence under section 33(1)(c).	Summarily or on indictment.	Imprisonment for a term not exceeding 12 months, or a fine, or both.	Imprisonment for a term not exceeding two years, or a fine, or both.
An offence under section 33(1)(d).	Summarily only.	A fine.	
An offence under section 33(1)(e), (f) or (g).	Summarily or on indictment.	Imprisonment for a term not exceeding 12 months, or a fine, or both.	Imprisonment for a term not exceeding two years, or a fine, or both.
An offence under section 33(1)(h).	Summarily only.	Imprisonment for a term not exceeding 51 weeks (in England and Wales) or 12 months (in Scotland), or a fine, or both.	
An offence under section 33(1)(i).	Summarily or on indictment.	A fine.	A fine.
An offence under section 33(1)(j).	Summarily or on indictment.	Imprisonment for a term not exceeding 12 months, or a fine, or both.	Imprisonment for a term not exceeding two years, or a fine, or both.

Offence	Mode of Trial	Penalty on Summary Conviction	Penalty on Conviction on Indictment
An offence under section 33(1)(k), (l) or (m).	Summarily or on indictment.	Imprisonment for a term not exceeding 12 months, or a fine, or both.	Imprisonment for a term not exceeding two years, or a fine, or both.
An offence under section 33(1)(n).	Summarily only.	A fine.	
An offence under section 33(1)(o).	Summarily or on indictment.	Imprisonment for a term not exceeding 12 months, or a fine, or both.	Imprisonment for a term not exceeding two years, or a fine, or both.
An offence under the existing statutory provisions for which no other penalty is specified.	Summarily or on indictment.	Imprisonment for a term not exceeding 12 months, or a fine, or both.	Imprisonment for a term not exceeding two years, or a fine, or both.

Notes

Where the table refers to imprisonment for a term not exceeding 12 months, this is to be read as a reference to a term not exceeding 6 months until the coming into force of section 154(1) of the **Criminal Justice Act 2003**. Section 154(1), which has not yet been brought into force, will increase from six months to 12 months the maximum term of imprisonment that may be imposed, on summary conviction, for an offence triable either summarily or on indictment.

Similarly, where the table refers to imprisonment for a term not exceeding 51 weeks, until section 281(5) of the **Criminal Justice Act 2003** is brought into force this should be read as a reference to a term not exceeding six months. This provision will have the effect of increasing the maximum term of imprisonment that may be imposed on conviction of a summary-only offence from six months to 51 weeks.

These provisions of the **Criminal Justice Act 2003** extend only to England and Wales. Therefore, the penalties that may be imposed by the Scottish courts are as stated in the table.

In Northern Ireland, the maximum prison sentence that may be handed down on summary conviction remains at sixsixmonths. This is stated in the new Schedule 3A to the **Health and Safety at Work (Northern Ireland) Order 1978**, which is to be found at Schedule 2 of the 2008 Act.

HEALTH AND SAFETY (SAFETY SIGNS AND SIGNALS) REGULATIONS 1996 (SI 1996 NO. 341)

Amending Legislation

Minor amendments to these Regulations were made by **MHSWR 99**.

Summary

These Regulations came into force on 1 April 1996 and are aimed at standardising safety signs throughout EU member states. They require employers to provide safety signs where other methods cannot satisfactorily deal with the problems identified by the risk assessments made by the employer under **MHSWR**. The Regulations deal with both traditional safety signs and other means of communication, such as hand signals, acoustic signals and verbal communications.

The Regulations

Regulation 2: Interpretation

The following are some of the definitions that are given of safety signs and signals:

"Acoustic signal" means a coded sound signal which is released and transmitted by a device designed for that purpose, without the use of a human or artificial voice.

"Emergency escape or first-aid sign" means a sign giving information on escape routes or emergency exits or first-aid or rescue facilities.

"Fire safety sign" means a sign (including an illuminated sign or an acoustic signal) which provides information on escape routes and emergency exits in case of fire; provides information on the identification or location of fire-fighting equipment; or gives warning in case of fire.

"Hand signal" means a movement or position of the arms or hands or combination thereof, in coded form, for guiding persons who are carrying out manoeuvres which create a risk to the health or safety of persons at work.

"Illuminated sign" means a sign produced by a device made of transparent or translucent materials which are illuminated from the inside or the rear in such a way as to give the appearance of a luminous surface (e.g. many emergency exit signs).

"Safety colour" means a colour to which a meaning is assigned (E.g. yellow means 'be careful' or 'take precautions').

"Safety sign" means a sign referring to a specific object, activity or situation and providing information or instructions about health or safety at work by means of a signboard, a safety colour, an illuminated sign, an acoustic signal, a verbal communication or a hand signal.

"Signboard" means a sign which provides information or instructions by a combination of geometric shape, colour and a symbol or pictogram which is rendered visible by lighting of sufficient intensity. [In practice many signboards may be accompanied by supplementary text (e.g. 'Fire exit' alongside the symbol of a moving person).]

"Symbol or pictogram" means a figure which describes a situation or prescribes behaviour and which is used on a signboard or illuminated surface. [Standard symbols appear in Schedule 1 of the Regulations, although some variation in detail is acceptable provided the meaning is the same. They are for use on a signboard or illuminated sign (e.g. the trefoil ionising radiation warning sign).]

"Verbal communication" means a predetermined spoken message communicated by a human or artificial voice.

Regulation 3: Application

These Regulations do not apply to signs used in connection with the supply of any hazardous substance, mixture, product or equipment. They do not apply to dangerous goods during the course of their transport by road, rail, inland waterway, sea or air, nor do they apply to signs used for regulating road, rail, inland waterway, sea or air traffic. There is also the usual disapplication to the master or crew of a sea-going ship.

These Regulations apply in Great Britain, but do not extend to Northern Ireland.

Regulation 4: Provision and Maintenance of Safety Signs

Safety signs must be provided and maintained if the risk assessment made under Regulation 3 of **MHSWR** indicates that the employer, having adopted all appropriate techniques for collective protection, and measures, methods or procedures used in the organisation of work, cannot avoid or adequately reduce risks to employees except by the provision of appropriate safety signs to warn or instruct, or both, of the nature of those risks and the measures to be taken to protect against them.

Regulation 5: Information, Instruction and Training

Every employer shall ensure that comprehensible and relevant information on the measures to be taken in connection with safety signs is provided to each of his employees.

Every employer shall ensure that each of his employees receives suitable and sufficient instruction and training in the meaning of safety signs and the measures to be taken in connection with safety signs.

HEALTH AND SAFETY (SHARP INSTRUMENTS IN HEALTHCARE) REGULATIONS 2013 (SI 2013 NO. 645)

These Regulations came into force on 11 May 2013 and impose duties on employers in the healthcare sector to protect employees from injuries caused by medical sharps, thus implementing **Council Directive 2010/32/EU**.

Regulation 2: Interpretation

"Healthcare contractor" means an employer whose main activity is not the management, organisation or provision of healthcare, but who provides services under contract to a healthcare employer.

"Healthcare employer" means an employer whose main activity is the management, organisation and provision of healthcare. "Injury" includes infection.

"Medical sharp" means an object or instrument necessary for the exercise of specific healthcare activities, which is able to cut, prick or cause injury.

"Safer sharp" means a medical sharp that is designed and constructed to incorporate a feature or mechanism which prevents or minimises the risk of accidental injury from cutting or pricking the skin.

Regulation 3: Application of Requirements to Employers

The Regulations apply to:

- Healthcare employers.
- Healthcare contractors whose employees, or other persons who work under their supervision and direction, are exposed to a risk of injury from medical sharps in relation to the provision of services to a healthcare employer.

Regulation 4: Application of Requirements to Healthcare Contractors

The requirements of the Regulations on a healthcare contractor apply:

- only in relation to work:
    - on a healthcare employer's premises or
    - under the authority of a healthcare employer;
- only to the extent that the healthcare contractor controls:
    - a person who uses, supervises or manages the use or disposal of medical sharps;
    - the activities which give rise to the risk of injury from medical sharps.

Regulation 5: Use and Disposal of Medical Sharps

An employer must ensure that:

- The use of medical sharps at work is avoided so far as is reasonably practicable.
- When medical sharps are used at work, safer sharps are used so far as is reasonably practicable.
- Needles that are medical sharps are not capped after use at work unless:
    - It is required to control a risk identified by a risk assessment carried out under the **Management of Health and Safety at Work Regulations 1999**.
    - The risk of injury to employees is effectively controlled by the use of a suitable appliance, tool or other equipment.
- In relation to the safe disposal of medical sharps that are not designed for re-use:
    - written instructions for employees and
    - clearly marked and secure containers

    are located close to areas where medical sharps are used at work.
- The policies and procedures in place to meet the above requirements are reviewed at suitable intervals to ensure that they remain up to date and effective.

Regulation 6: Information and Training

- An employer must provide employees exposed to a risk of injury at work from medical sharps with information on:
    - The risk of injury from medical sharps.
    - Legislative requirements relating to the protection of persons at work from the risks to health and safety from medical sharps, including duties on employers and employees.
    - Good practice in preventing injury from medical sharps.
    - The benefits and drawbacks of vaccination and non-vaccination in respect of blood-borne diseases.
    - The support provided by the employer to an employee who is injured at work by a medical sharp.
- This information should be developed and promoted with co-operation from worker representatives in the employer's undertaking (i.e. safety representatives within the meaning of the **Safety Representatives and Safety Committees Regulations 1977** or representatives of employee safety within the meaning of the **Health and Safety (Consultation with Employees) Regulations 1996**).
- An employer must provide employees who are exposed to a risk of injury at work from medical sharps with training on:
    - the safe use and disposal of medical sharps;
    - the correct use of safer sharps;
    - what employees should do if they are injured at work by a medical sharp;
    - the health surveillance and other procedures to be conducted by the employer where an employee is injured by a medical sharp;

    to the extent that those matters are relevant to the type of work carried out by that employee.

Regulation 7: Arrangements in the Event of Injury

- Where an employer is notified of any incident at work in which an employee has suffered an injury from a medical sharp, the employer must:
    - record the incident;
    - investigate the circumstances and cause of the incident;
    - take any necessary action to prevent a recurrence.
- Additionally, where an employer is notified of any incident at work in which an employee has suffered an injury caused by a medical sharp that exposed, or may have exposed, the employee to a biological agent, the employer must:
    - take immediate steps to ensure that the employee receives medical advice;
    - ensure that any treatment advised by a registered medical practitioner, including post-exposure prophylaxis (i.e. treatment to prevent infection or development of disease), is made available to the employee;
    - consider providing the employee with counselling.

Regulation 8: Notification of Injuries

- Employees, or persons working under the supervision and direction of a healthcare employer or a healthcare contractor, who suffer an injury from a medical sharp must:
    - notify the employer or a responsible person of the incident;
    - provide, when requested, sufficient information as to the circumstances of the incident to enable the employer to comply with Regulation 7.
- For employees or persons working under the supervision and direction of a healthcare contractor, this regulation only applies to incidents which take place:
    - on a healthcare employer's premises; or
    - under the authority of a healthcare employer.

Regulation 9: Extension Outside Great Britain

These Regulations apply to and in relation to the premises and activities outside Great Britain to which Sections 1 to 59 and 80 to 82 of the **Health and Safety at Work, etc. Act 1974** apply by virtue of the **Health and Safety at Work, etc. Act 1974 (Application Outside Great Britain) Order 2013** as they apply within Great Britain.

IONISING RADIATION (MEDICAL EXPOSURE) REGULATIONS 2017 (SI 2017 NO. 1322) (AS AMENDED)

NB: Similar provisions apply in Northern Ireland (the **Ionising Radiation (Medical Exposure) Regulations (Northern Ireland) 2018**).

These Regulations implement, as respects Great Britain, some of the provisions of **Council Directive 2013/59/Euratom** laying down basic safety standards for protection against the dangers from exposure to ionising radiation. The Directive repeals **Directives 89/618/Euratom, 90/641/Euratom, 96/29/Euratom, 97/43/Euratom** and **2003/122/Euratom**.

In particular, these Regulations transpose Directive requirements relating to dangers arising from ionising radiation in relation to medical exposure. They impose duties on employers and those with responsibilities for administering ionising radiation to protect persons undergoing medical exposures whether as part of their own medical diagnosis or treatment, as part of research, as asymptomatic individuals, as those undergoing non-medical imaging using medical radiological equipment or as carers and comforters of persons undergoing medical exposures.

These Regulations revoke other Regulations relating to medical exposures and prior-authorisation for the administration of radioactive substances for the purposes of diagnosis, treatment and research.

Regulation 2 is an interpretation provision.

Regulation 3 states that these Regulations apply in England, Wales and Scotland, and sets out the medical exposures to which the Regulations apply, namely:

- to patients as part of their own medical diagnosis or treatment;
- to individuals as part of health screening programmes;
- to patients or other persons voluntarily participating in medical or biomedical, diagnostic or therapeutic, research programmes;
- to carers and comforters;
- to asymptomatic individuals;
- to individuals undergoing non-medical imaging using medical radiological equipment.

Regulation 4 sets out conditions under which the Licensing Authority may issue a licence for the administration of radioactive substances. Further provisions relating to the application for and the issuing of such licences are contained in Schedule 1.

Regulation 5 requires the employer and the practitioner who wish to administer radioactive substances to hold a valid licence issued by the Licensing Authority. Such licences will specify the radiological installation and purposes as appropriate.

Regulation 6 requires the employer to establish a framework of general procedures, protocols and quality assurance programmes. The procedures must cover the matters set out in Schedule 2 as a minimum. Written protocols, where appropriate, must be in place for standard radiological practices. The employer must:

- establish recommendations regarding referral guidelines;
- establish quality assurance programmes for standard operating procedures;
- review and make available diagnostic reference levels;
- establish dose constraints where appropriate; and
- raise awareness of the effects of ionising radiation amongst individuals capable of childbearing or breastfeeding.

Regulation 7 requires the employer's procedures to include provision for clinical audit to be carried out.

Regulation 8 sets out the duties of the employer in relation to accidental or unintended medical exposures including provisions for:

- providing information about clinically significant exposures;
- quality assurance programmes for radiotherapy;
- analysis and recording of events involving or potentially involving accidental or unintended exposures; and
- processes for investigating and notifying the relevant enforcing authority when significant events have occurred.

Regulation 9 sets out the duties of the enforcing authority with regard to timely dissemination of information relating to significant accidental or unintended exposures.

Regulation 10 sets out the respective responsibilities of practitioners, operators and referrers. Practitioners and operators are required to follow the framework of procedures provided by the employer. The practitioner is responsible for the justification of a medical exposure. Authorisation of exposures is addressed here and in regulation 11. The operator is responsible for each practical aspect he or she carries out. The referrer must provide medical data as required by the practitioner in order that appropriate justification can take place.

Regulation 11 prohibits any medical exposure which has not been justified and authorised and sets out matters to be taken into account for justification. These include requirements relating to licensing and approval by an expert advisory committee, in the case of research, for exposures involving administration of radioactive substances. Justification of the exposure of carers and comforters is also required and recommendations or guidelines should be considered as part of justification of the exposure of asymptomatic individuals.

Regulation 12 provides for the optimisation process, and specifies the elements that are the responsibilities of the operator and the practitioner, depending on their involvement. Specific requirements are included for exposures in research, for carers and comforters and for exposures involving radioactive substances. Particular regard should be given to the exposures of children, exposures involving high doses, exposures of individuals involved in health screening programmes and pregnant or potentially pregnant or breastfeeding individuals. Regulation 12 also requires the employer to take steps to ensure that a clinical evaluation is recorded of each medical exposure.

Regulation 13 requires employers to provide when requested, to the Secretary of State, data relating to dose estimates from diagnostic and interventional medical exposures.

Regulation 14 provides for suitable medical physics experts to be appointed and involved in relation to medical exposures.

Regulation 15 sets out general duties of the employer with respect to medical radiological equipment. These include requirements for quality assurance programmes, appropriate testing of equipment, performance criteria and actions to be taken when equipment does not perform appropriately.

Regulation 16 sets out additional requirements for equipment installed when the Regulations come into force (6 February 2018) including the transfer of information relating to patient dose where appropriate.

Regulation 17 prohibits a practitioner or operator from carrying out a medical exposure without having been adequately trained, except if supervised appropriately for practical aspects when undergoing training. The employer must keep and make available training records during inspections undertaken by the relevant enforcing authority. Further information regarding adequate training is set out in Schedule 3.

Regulation 18 provides that the Regulations are made enforceable as health and safety regulations under the **Health and Safety at Work, etc. Act 1974**.

Regulation 19 provides that there is a defence of due diligence to proceedings for an offence under the Regulations that all reasonable steps were taken and due diligence exercised.

Regulation 20 revokes the **Ionising Radiation (Medical Exposure) Regulations 2000** and, subject to transitional provisions relating to existing certificates, the **Medicines (Administration of Radioactive Substances) Regulations 1978** and the **Medicines (Radioactive Substances) Order 1978**.

Regulation 21 and Schedule 4 make provision consequential on the coming into force of these Regulations.

Regulation 22 makes provision for the review of these Regulations at the end of the period of five years beginning with the date on which they come into force.

IONISING RADIATIONS REGULATIONS 2017 (SI 2017 NO. 1075)

The **Ionising Radiations Regulations 2017 (IRR17)** came into force on 1 January 2018 and replaced the **Ionising Radiations Regulations 1999 (IRR99)**. The main changes to **IRR99** are:

- The dose limit for exposure to the lens of the eye has been reduced from 150 mSv to 20 mSv in a year.
- A new system of authorisation for work with ionising radiation has been implemented; the higher the radiation protection risk, the greater the requirements. A three-tier system of regulatory control (notification, registration and consent) has replaced the previous requirement for notification and prior authorisation.
- The requirement for notification has been changed to a lower level of activity than in **IRR99**.
- The definition of an "outside worker" has been broadened so that it includes both classified and non-classified workers.
- There is now a requirement to put procedures in place to estimate doses to members of the public.
- Guidance has been clarified regarding the duties of employees to co-operate with employers in meeting the requirements of these Regulations.
- Medical appeals by an employee are made to the HSE within 28 days of the employee being notified of the appointed doctor's decision.

The following text is an extract from the Interpretation section (reproduced under the terms of the Open Government Licence) and a brief explanation of the requirements of the legislation.

Regulation 2: Interpretation

(1) In these Regulations:

"Accelerator" means an apparatus or installation in which particles are accelerated and which emits ionising radiation with an energy higher than 1MeV.

"Appointed doctor" means a registered medical practitioner who meets such recognition criteria as may from time to time be specified in writing by the Executive.

"Approved" means approved for the time being in writing for the purposes of these Regulations by the Executive or the ONR (as the case may be) and published in such form as that body considers appropriate.

"Approved dosimetry service" means a dosimetry service approved in accordance with regulation 36.

"Authorised defence site" has the meaning given by regulation 2(1) of the **Health and Safety (Enforcing Authority) Regulations 1998**.

"Calendar year" means a period of 12 months beginning with the 1 January.

"Classified outside worker" means a classified person who carries out services in the controlled area of any employer (other than the controlled area of their own employer).

"Classified person" means:

(a) a person designated as such pursuant to regulation 21(1); and

(b) in the case of a classified outside worker employed by an undertaking in Northern Ireland or in another member State, a person who has been designated as a category A exposed worker within the meaning of Article 40 of the Directive.

"Carers and comforters" means individuals knowingly and willingly incurring an exposure to ionising radiation by helping, other than as part of their occupation, in the support and comfort of individuals undergoing or having undergone medical exposure.

"Contamination" means the unintended or undesirable presence of radioactive substances on surfaces or within solids, liquids or gases or on the human body, and "contaminated" is to be construed accordingly.

"Controlled area" means:

(a) in the case of an area situated in Great Britain, an area which has been so designated in accordance with regulation 17(1); and

(b) in the case of an area situated in Northern Ireland or in another member State, an area subject to special rules for the purposes of protection against ionising radiation and to which access is controlled as specified in Article 37 of the Directive.

"The Directive" means **Council Directive 2013/59/Euratom** laying down basic safety standards for protection against the dangers arising from exposure to ionising radiation, and repealing **Directives 89/618/Euratom, 90/641/Euratom, 96/29/Euratom, 97/43/Euratom** and **2003/122/Euratom**.

"Dose" means, in relation to ionising radiation, any dose quantity or sum of dose quantities mentioned in Schedule 3.

"Dose assessment" means the dose assessment made and recorded by an approved dosimetry service in accordance with regulation 22.

"Dose constraint" means a constraint set on the prospective doses of individuals which may result from a given radiation source.

"Dose limit" means, in relation to persons of a specified class, the limit on effective dose or equivalent dose specified in Schedule 3 in relation to a person of that class.

"Dose rate" means, in relation to a place, the rate at which a person or part of a person would receive a dose of ionising radiation from external radiation if that person were at that place, being a dose rate at that place averaged over one minute.

"Dose record" means, in relation to a person, the record of the doses received by that person as a result of that person's exposure to ionising radiation, being the record made and maintained on behalf of their employer by the approved dosimetry service in accordance with regulation 22.

"Employment medical adviser" means an employment medical adviser appointed under section 56 of the 1974 Act.

"External radiation" means, in relation to a person, ionising radiation coming from outside the body of that person.

"Extremities" means a person's hands, forearms, feet and ankles.

"Health record" means, in relation to an employee, the record of medical surveillance of that employee maintained by the employer in accordance with regulation 25(3).

"High-activity sealed source" means a sealed source for which the quantity of the radionuclide is equal to or exceeds the relevant quantity value set out in Part 4 of Schedule 7.

"Industrial irradiation" means the use of ionising radiation to sterilise, process or alter the structure of products or materials.

"Industrial radiography" means the use of ionising radiation for non-destructive testing purposes where an image of the item under test is formed (but excluding any such testing which is carried out in a cabinet which a person cannot enter).

"Internal radiation" means, in relation to a person, ionising radiation coming from inside the body of that person.

"Ionising radiation" means the transfer of energy in the form of particles or electromagnetic waves of a wavelength of 100 nanometres or less or a frequency of 3×10^{15} hertz or more capable of producing ions directly or indirectly.

"Local rules" means rules made pursuant to regulation 18(1).

"Maintained", where the reference is to maintaining plant, apparatus, equipment or facilities, means maintained in an efficient state, in efficient working order and good repair.

"Medical exposure" means the exposure to ionising radiation of:

(a) patients and asymptomatic individuals as part of their own medical diagnosis or treatment;

(b) individuals as part of health screening programmes;

(c) patients or other persons voluntarily participating in medical or biomedical, diagnostic or therapeutic, research programmes;

(d) individuals undergoing non-medical imaging using medical radiological equipment.

"Member State" means a member State of the European Union.

"New nuclear build site" has the meaning given by regulation 2A of the **Health and Safety (Enforcing Authority) Regulations 1998**.

"Non-classified outside worker" means a person who is not a classified person who carries out services in the supervised or, pursuant to regulation 19(3)(c), controlled area of any employer (other than the supervised or controlled area of their own employer).

"Nuclear premises" means premises which are or are on:

(a) a GB nuclear site (within the meaning given by section 68 of the **Energy Act 2013**);

(b) ban authorised defence site;

(c) a new nuclear build site; or

(d) a nuclear warship site.

"Nuclear warship site" has the meaning given by regulation 2B of the **Health and Safety (Enforcing Authority) Regulations 1998**.

"The ONR" means the Office for Nuclear Regulation.

"Outside worker" means a classified outside worker and a non-classified outside worker.

"Overexposure" means any exposure of a person to ionising radiation to the extent that the dose received by that person causes a dose limit relevant to that person to be exceeded or, in relation to regulation 27(2), causes a proportion of a dose limit relevant to any employee to be exceeded.

"Practice" means work involving:

(a) the production, processing, handling, disposal, use, storage, holding or transport of radioactive substances; or

(b) the operation of any electrical equipment emitting ionising radiation and containing components operating at a potential difference of more than 5kV,

which can increase the exposure of individuals to ionising radiation.

"Radiation accident" means an accident where immediate action would be required to prevent or reduce the exposure to ionising radiation of employees or any other persons.

"Radiation generator" means a device capable of generating ionising radiation such as X-rays, neutrons, electrons or other charged particles.

"Radiation passbook" means:

(a) in the case of a classified outside worker employed by an employer in Great Britain:

   (i) a passbook approved by the Executive for the purpose of these Regulations; or

   (ii) a passbook to which paragraph 9 of Schedule 8 (transitional provisions) applies; and

(b) in the case of a classified outside worker employed by an employer in Northern Ireland or in another member State, a passbook authorised by the competent authority for Northern Ireland or that member State, as the case may be.

"Radiation protection adviser" means an individual who, or a body which, meets such criteria of competence as may from time to time be specified in writing by the Executive.

"Radioactive material" means material incorporating radioactive substances.

"Radioactive source" means an entity incorporating a radioactive substance (or substances) for the purpose of utilising the radioactivity of that substance (or substances).

"Radioactive substance" means any substance which contains one or more radionuclides whose activity cannot be disregarded for the purposes of radiation protection.

"Relevant doctor" means an appointed doctor or an employment medical adviser.

"Sealed source" means a radioactive source whose structure is such as to prevent, under normal conditions of use, any dispersion of radioactive substances into the environment, but it does not include any radioactive substance inside a nuclear reactor or any nuclear fuel element.

"Supervised area" means an area which has been so designated by the employer in accordance with regulation 17(3).

"Trainee" means a person aged 16 years or over (including a student) who is undergoing instruction or training which involves operations which would, in the case of an employee, be work with ionising radiation.

"Transport" means, in relation to a radioactive substance, carriage of that substance on a road within the meaning of, in relation to England and Wales, section 192 of the **Road Traffic Act 1988** and, in relation to Scotland, section 151 of the **Roads (Scotland) Act 1984** or through another public place (whether on a conveyance or not), or by rail, inland waterway, sea or air and, in the case of transport on a conveyance, a substance is deemed as being transported from the time that it is loaded onto the conveyance for the purpose of transporting it until it is unloaded from that conveyance, but a substance is not to be considered as being transported if:

(a) it is transported by means of a pipeline or similar means; or

(b) it forms an integral part of a conveyance and is used in connection with the operation of that conveyance.

"Work with ionising radiation" means work to which these Regulations apply by virtue of regulation 3(1).

(2) In these Regulations any reference to:

   (a) an employer includes a reference to a self-employed person and any duty imposed by these Regulations on an employer in respect of that employer's employee extends to a self-employed person in respect of themselves;

   (b) an employee includes a reference to:

      (i) a self-employed person, and

      (ii) a trainee who but for the operation of this sub-paragraph and paragraph (3) would not be classed as an employee;

   (c) exposure to ionising radiation is a reference to exposure to ionising radiation arising from work with ionising radiation;

   (d) a person entering, remaining in or working in a controlled or supervised area includes a reference to any part of a person entering, remaining in or working in any such area.

(3) For the purposes of these Regulations and Part I of the 1974 Act:

   (a) the word "work" is extended to include any instruction or training which a person undergoes as a trainee and the meaning of "at work" is extended accordingly; and

   (b) a trainee, while undergoing instruction or training in respect of work with ionising radiation, is to be treated as the employee of the person whose undertaking (whether for profit or not) is providing that instruction or training and that person is to be treated as the employer of that trainee except that the duties to the trainee imposed upon the person providing instruction or training will only extend to matters under the control of that person.

(4) In these Regulations, where reference is made to a quantity or concentration specified in Schedule 7, that quantity or concentration is to be treated as being exceeded if:

   (a) where only one radionuclide is involved:

      (i) the quantity of that radionuclide exceeds the quantity specified in the appropriate entry in Parts 1, 2 or 4 of Schedule 7; or

      (ii) the concentration of that radionuclide exceeds the concentration specified in the appropriate entry in Parts 1 or 2 of Schedule 7; or

   (b) where more than one radionuclide is involved, the quantity or concentration ratio calculated in accordance with Part 3 of Schedule 7 exceeds one.

(5) Nothing in these Regulations is to be construed as preventing a person from entering or remaining in a controlled area or a supervised area where that person enters or remains in any such area:

   (a) in the due exercise of a power of entry conferred on that person by or under any enactment; or

   (b) for the purpose of undergoing a medical exposure.

(6) In these Regulations:

   (a) any reference to an effective dose means the sum of the effective dose to the whole body from external radiation and the committed effective dose from internal radiation; and

   (b) any reference to equivalent dose to a human tissue or organ includes the committed equivalent dose to that tissue or organ from internal radiation.

Brief Explanation of the Regulations

These Regulations revoke and supersede the **Ionising Radiations Regulations 1999**.

The Regulations impose duties on employers to protect employees and other persons against ionising radiation arising from work with radioactive substances and other sources of ionising radiation. The Regulations also impose certain duties on employees.

The Regulations are divided into seven Parts; there are 43 regulations and 9 Schedules.

For the purposes of the Regulations, an employer includes a self-employed person and an employee includes a self-employed person and a trainee.

Generally, the Regulations apply to any practice (as defined, and which encompasses various types of work), and to any other work carried out in an atmosphere of radon above a particular concentration. In the Regulations, work with ionising radiation means work to which the Regulations apply.

Regulation 5 requires certain work with ionising radiation to be notified to the appropriate authority (either the Health and Safety Executive ("the Executive") or, where the work relates to particular nuclear-related sites, the Office for Nuclear Regulation ("the ONR")). The work which requires notification is a residual category of work; amongst other exclusions, work which arises from practices which require registration under regulation 6 or require a consent under regulation 7 do not require notification.

Regulation 6 requires all practices to be registered with the appropriate authority other than those excluded from registration by regulation 6(2). Amongst other exclusions, practices consisting of work which is excluded from notification because the work falls within Schedule 1, are excluded from registration. Practices which require a consent under regulation 7, and practices which involve moderate amounts of radioactive material (not exceeding 1,000kg) where the activity concentration value of that material is less than the values in column 4 of Part 1 of Schedule 7, are also excluded from registration.

Regulation 7 requires an employer to obtain a consent from the appropriate authority to carry out certain practices.

The Regulations:

- Require employers to make a prior assessment of the risks arising from their work with ionising radiation, to make an assessment of the hazards likely to arise from that work and to prevent and limit the consequences of identifiable radiation accidents.

- Require employers to take all reasonable steps to restrict as far as is reasonably practicable the extent to which employees and other persons are exposed to ionising radiation.

- Require respiratory protective equipment used in work with ionising radiation to conform with agreed standards and require all personal protective equipment and other controls to be regularly examined and properly maintained.

- Impose limits (specified in Schedule 3) on the doses of ionising radiation which employees and other persons may receive.

- Require in certain circumstances the preparation of contingency plans for radiation accidents which are reasonably foreseeable.

The Regulations require that employers consult radiation protection advisers in respect of matters specified in Schedule 4 and that employers ensure that adequate information, instruction and training is given to employees and other persons. Employers are required to co-operate by exchanging information to enable compliance by others with requirements to limit the exposure of employees to ionising radiation.

The Regulations further:

- Provide that areas in which persons need to follow special procedures to restrict exposure or in which persons are likely to receive more than specified doses of ionising radiation be designated as controlled or supervised areas.

- Restrict entry into controlled areas to specified persons and circumstances.

- Require radiation employers to set out appropriate local rules for controlled or supervised areas and to appoint radiation protection supervisors for the purpose of securing compliance with the Regulations.

- Impose specified duties upon employers in relation to outside workers.

- Require radiation levels to be monitored in controlled or supervised areas and provide for the maintenance and testing of monitoring equipment.

The Regulations require that employees who are likely to receive more than specified doses of ionising radiation be designated as classified persons, that doses received by classified persons be assessed by one or more dosimetry services approved by the Executive and that records of such doses are made and kept for each such person.

The Regulations also provide for:

- Certain employees to be subject to medical surveillance.

- Any cases in which an employee has received an overexposure to be investigated and notified to the appropriate authority.

- Investigations to be made where employees are exposed above specified levels.
- Modified dose limits for employees who have received an overexposure.

The Regulations:

- Require that where a radioactive substance is to be used as a source of ionising radiation, it should, whenever reasonably practicable, be in the form of a sealed source and that any articles embodying or containing radioactive substances are suitably designed, constructed, maintained and tested.
- Cover the accounting for, keeping and moving of radioactive substances and require that incidents in which more than specified quantities of radioactive substances escape or are lost or stolen be notified to the appropriate authority.
- Impose duties on manufacturers, etc. and installers of articles for use in work with ionising radiation to ensure that such articles are designed, constructed and installed so as to restrict, so far as is reasonably practicable, exposure to ionising radiation.
- Impose similar duties upon employers in relation to equipment used for medical exposures together with additional duties in relation to the testing and safe operation of such equipment.
- Require employers to investigate any defect in medical equipment which may have resulted in a person receiving a dose of ionising radiation much greater than was intended and to notify the appropriate authority of such incidents.
- Prohibit interference with sources of ionising radiation.

The Regulations impose duties upon employees engaged in carrying out work with ionising radiation. The Regulations also:

- provide for the approval of dosimetry services by the Executive;
- provide for a defence on contravention of certain regulations;
- provide for exemptions to be granted by the appropriate authority;
- extend the provision of the Regulations outside Great Britain;
- contain transitional provisions and savings; and
- introduce modifications relating to the Ministry of Defence and visiting forces.

The Regulations make consequential and other modifications to the enactments specified in Schedule 9. In particular:

- The **Health and Safety (Enforcing Authority) Regulations 1998** and the **Health and Safety (Enforcing Authority for Railways and Other Guided Transport Systems) Regulations 2006** are modified to transfer enforcement responsibility for these Regulations in relation to road, rail and inland waterway to the ONR.
- The **Health and Safety and Nuclear (Fees) Regulations 2016** are modified to include an application fee of £25 for a registration under regulation 6 or a consent to carry out specified practices under regulation 7.

LIFTING OPERATIONS AND LIFTING EQUIPMENT REGULATIONS 1998 (SI 1998 NO. 2307)

Introduction

Minor amendments of little consequence were made by the **Health and Safety (Miscellaneous Amendments) Regulations 2002**.

The Regulations, which came into force on 5 December 1998, set out the health and safety requirements for lifting equipment and made provision with respect to the following matters:

- the strength and stability of lifting equipment (regulation 4);
- the safety of lifting equipment for lifting persons (regulation 5);
- the way lifting equipment is positioned and installed (regulation 6);
- the marking of machinery and accessories for lifting, and lifting equipment which is designed for lifting persons or which might so be used in error (regulation 7);
- the organisation of lifting operations (regulation 8);
- the thorough examination and inspection of lifting equipment in specified circumstances (regulation 9);
- the evidence of examination to accompany it outside the undertaking (regulation 9);
- the exception for winding apparatus at mines from regulation 9;
- transitional arrangements relating to regulation 9 and the making of reports of thorough examinations and records of inspections (regulation 10 and Schedule 1);
- the keeping of information in the reports and records (regulation 11).

Before looking at the main requirements of the Regulations in detail, we should take note of some definitions.

"Lifting Equipment" is work equipment for lifting or lowering loads and includes its attachments for anchoring, fixing or supporting it. "Work Equipment" means any machinery, appliance, apparatus, tool or installation for use at work.

"Load" includes a person.

"Thorough Examination" means a thorough examination by a competent person.

The Regulations govern the minimum requirements for the use of work equipment by workers at work and under regulation 3 impose duties in respect of those requirements on:

- employers;
- the self-employed;
- persons having control of lifting equipment;
- persons who use, supervise or manage the use of lifting equipment.

The Regulations only have limited application to ships.

Regulation 4: Strength and Stability

Every employer must ensure that lifting equipment is of adequate strength and stability for each load, having regard in particular to the stress induced at its mounting or fixing point. He must also ensure that every part of a load and anything attached to it and used in lifting it is of adequate strength.

Regulation 5: Lifting Equipment for Lifting Persons

Every employer must ensure that lifting equipment for lifting persons:

- is such as to prevent a person using it being crushed, trapped or struck or falling from the carrier;
- is such as to prevent, so far as is reasonably practicable, a person using it while carrying out activities from the carrier, being crushed, trapped or struck or falling from the carrier;
- has suitable devices to prevent the risk of a carrier falling;
- is such that a person trapped in any carrier is not thereby exposed to danger and can be freed.

Every employer must ensure that if the above risks cannot be prevented for reasons inherent in the site and height differences, the carrier has an enhanced safety co-efficient suspension rope or chain and the rope or chain is inspected by a competent person every working day.

Regulation 6: Positioning and Installation

Every employer must ensure that lifting equipment is positioned or installed in such a way as to reduce, to as low as is reasonably practicable, the risk of the equipment or a load striking a person or from a load drifting, falling freely, or being released unintentionally; and is otherwise safe. The employer must also ensure that there are suitable devices to prevent a person from falling down a shaft or hoistway.

Regulation 7: Marking of Lifting Equipment

Every employer must ensure that machinery and accessories for lifting loads are clearly marked to indicate their safe working loads.

Where the safe working load of machinery for lifting loads depends on its configuration the machinery must be clearly marked to indicate its safe working load for each configuration, or information which clearly indicates its safe working load for each configuration must be kept with the machinery.

Any accessories for lifting must also be marked in such a way that it is possible to identify the characteristics necessary for their safe use. Lifting equipment which is designed for lifting persons must be appropriately and clearly marked to this effect.

Lifting equipment which is not so designed but which might be so used in error must be appropriately and clearly marked to the effect that it is not designed for lifting persons.

Regulation 8: Organisation of Lifting Operations

Every employer must ensure that every lifting operation involving lifting equipment is:

- properly planned by a competent person;
- appropriately supervised;
- carried out in a safe manner.

Regulation 9: Thorough Examination and Inspection

Every employer must ensure that before lifting equipment is put into service for the first time by him it is thoroughly examined for any defect unless either:

- new equipment (never before used) and which has a recent certificate of conformity (because the conformity process is deemed to have been a thorough examination and test); or
- other equipment which you have received from another undertaking (e.g. hired out, second-hand, etc.) and which has physical evidence (e.g. a test certificate) of a recent thorough examination being carried out.

Every employer must ensure that, where the safety of lifting equipment depends on the installation conditions, it is thoroughly examined to ensure that it has been installed correctly and is safe to operate:

- after installation and before being put into service for the first time;
- after assembly and before being put into service at a new site or in a new location.

Every employer must ensure that lifting equipment which is exposed to conditions causing deterioration which is liable to result in dangerous situations is thoroughly examined:

- in the case of lifting equipment for lifting persons or an accessory for lifting, at least every six months;
- in the case of other lifting equipment, at least every 12 months; or
- in either case, in accordance with an examination scheme; and
- each time that exceptional circumstances which are liable to jeopardise the safety of the lifting equipment have occurred; and
- furthermore, if appropriate for the purpose, such lifting equipment is inspected by a competent person at suitable intervals between thorough examinations to ensure that health and safety conditions are maintained and that any deterioration can be detected and remedied in good time.

Every employer must ensure that no lifting equipment:

- leaves his undertaking; or
- if obtained from the undertaking of another person, is used in his undertaking,

unless it is accompanied by physical evidence that the last thorough examination required to be carried out under this regulation has been carried out.

This regulation does not apply to winding apparatus to which the **Mines (Shafts and Winding) Regulations 1993** apply.

Regulation 10: Reports and Defects

A person making a thorough examination for an employer under regulation 9 must notify the employer forthwith of any defect in the lifting equipment which in his opinion is, or could become, a danger to persons. As soon as is practicable, he must make a report of the thorough examination in writing and authenticated by him or on his behalf by signature to the employer and any person from whom the lifting equipment has been hired or leased. Where there is, in his opinion, a defect in the lifting equipment involving an existing or imminent risk of serious personal injury he must send a copy of the report as soon as is practicable to the relevant enforcing authority.

A person making an inspection for an employer under regulation 9 must notify the employer forthwith of any defect in the lifting equipment which in his opinion is or could become a danger to persons and as soon as is practicable make a record of the inspection in writing.

Every employer who has been notified of any defect must ensure that the lifting equipment is not used before the defect is rectified or, in a case where a defect could become a danger, after a time specified and before the defect is rectified.

NB: In this regulation "relevant enforcing authority" means:

- where the defective lifting equipment has been hired or leased by the employer, the Executive; and
- otherwise, the enforcing authority for the premises in which the defective lifting equipment was thoroughly examined.

Regulation 11: Keeping of Information

Where an employer obtaining lifting equipment to which these Regulations apply receives an EC declaration of conformity relating to it, he must keep the declaration for so long as he operates the lifting equipment.

The employer must ensure that the information contained in every report made to him is kept available for inspection:

- in the case of a thorough examination of lifting equipment not used before, other than an accessory for lifting, until he ceases to use the lifting equipment;
- in the case of a thorough examination of an accessory for lifting not used before, for two years after the report is made;
- in the case of a thorough examination of lifting equipment where safety depends on installation conditions, until he ceases to use the lifting equipment at the place it was installed or assembled;
- in the case of a thorough examination of lifting equipment which is exposed to conditions causing deterioration, until the next report is made or the expiration of two years, whichever is later.

Every record made under regulation 10 must be kept available until the next such record is made.

The accompanying Schedule to the Regulations sets out in detail the following information that must be included in a Report of a Thorough Examination:

- The name and address of the employer for whom the thorough examination was made.
- The address of the premises at which the thorough examination was made.
- Particulars sufficient to identify the lifting equipment including, where known, its date of manufacture.
- The date of the last thorough examination.
- The safe working load of the lifting equipment or (where its safe working load depends on the configuration of the lifting equipment) its safe working load for the last configuration in which it was thoroughly examined.
- In relation to the first thorough examination of lifting equipment after installation or after assembly at a new site or in a new location:
  - that it is such thorough examination;
  - (if such be the case) that it has been installed correctly and would be safe to operate.

- In relation to a thorough examination of lifting equipment which is exposed to conditions causing deterioration:
    - whether it is a thorough examination:
        - within an interval of six months;
        - within an interval of 12 months;
        - in accordance with an examination scheme; or
        - after the occurrence of exceptional circumstances;
        - (if such be the case) that the lifting equipment would be safe to operate.
- In relation to every thorough examination of lifting equipment:
    - Identification of any part found to have a defect which is or could become a danger to persons, and a description of the defect;
    - particulars of any repair, renewal or alteration required to remedy a defect found to be a danger to persons;
    - in the case of a defect which is not yet but could become a danger to persons:
        - the time by which it could become such danger;
        - particulars of any repair, renewal or alteration required to remedy it;
    - the latest date by which the next thorough examination must be carried out;
    - where the thorough examination included testing, particulars of any test;
    - the date of the thorough examination.
- The name, address and qualifications of the person making the report, that he is self-employed or, if employed, the name and address of his employer.
- The name and address of a person signing or authenticating the report on behalf of its author.
- The date of the report.

LIMITATION ACT 1980

Section 1: Time Limits

This part of the Act gives the ordinary time limits for bringing actions of the various classes mentioned in the following provisions of this part. The ordinary time limits given in this part are subject to extension or exclusion in accordance with the later provisions of the Act.

(Only the sections of the Act concerned with personal injury torts are included here.)

Section 2: Time Limit for Actions Founded on Tort

An action founded on tort shall not be brought after the expiration of six years from the date on which the cause of action accrued.

Section 5: Time Limit for Actions Founded on Simple Contract

An action founded on simple contract shall not be brought after the expiration of six years from the date on which the cause of action accrued.

Section 11: Special Time Limit for Actions in Respect of Personal Injuries

(1) This section applies to any action for damages for negligence, nuisance or breach of duty (whether the duty exists by virtue of a contract or of provision made by or under a statute or independently of any contract or any such provision) where the damages claimed by the claimant for the negligence, nuisance or breach of duty consist of or include damages in respect of personal injuries to the claimant or any other person.

(1A) This section does not apply to any action brought for damages under section 3 of the **Protection from Harassment Act 1997**.

(2) None of the time limits given in the preceding provisions of this Act shall apply to an action to which this section applies.

(3) An action to which this section applies shall not be brought after the expiration of the period applicable in accordance with subsection (4) or (5) below.

(4) Except where subsection (5) below applies, the period applicable is three years from:

- the date on which the cause of action accrued; or
- the date of knowledge (if later) of the person injured.

(5) If the person injured dies before the expiration of the period mentioned in subsection (4) above, the period applicable as respects the cause of action surviving for the benefit of his estate by virtue of section 1 of the **Law Reform (Miscellaneous Provisions) Act 1934** shall be three years from:

  (a) the date of death; or

  (b) the date of the personal representative's knowledge;

  whichever is the later.

(6) For the purposes of this section "personal representative" includes any person who is or has been a personal representative of the deceased, including an executor who has not proved the will (whether or not he has renounced probate) but not anyone appointed only as a special personal representative in relation to settled land; and regard shall be had to any knowledge acquired by any such person while a personal representative or previously.

(7) If there is more than one personal representative, and their dates of knowledge are different, subsection (5)(b) above shall be read as referring to the earliest of those dates.

Section 11A: Actions in Respect of Defective Products

(1) This section shall apply to an action for damages by virtue of any provision of Part 1 of the **Consumer Protection Act 1987**.

(2) None of the time limits given in the preceding provisions of this Act shall apply to an action to which this section applies.

(3) An action to which this section applies shall not be brought after the expiration of the period of 10 years from the relevant time, within the meaning of section 4 of the said Act of 1987; and this subsection shall operate to extinguish a right of action and shall do so whether or not that right of action had accrued, or time under the following provisions of this Act had begun to run, at the end of the said period of 10 years.

(4) Subject to subsection (5) below, an action to which this section applies in which the damages claimed by the claimant consist of or include damages in respect of personal injuries to the claimant or any other person or loss of or damage to any property, shall not be brought after the expiration of the period of three years from whichever is the later of:

- the date on which the cause of action accrued; and
- the date of knowledge of the injured person or, in the case of loss or damage to property, the date of knowledge of the claimant or (if earlier) of any person in whom his cause of action was previously vested.

(5) If in a case where the damages claimed by the claimant consist of or include damages in respect of personal injuries to the claimant or any other person the injured person died before the expiration of the period mentioned in subsection (4) above, that subsection shall have effect as respects the cause of action surviving for the benefit of his estate by virtue of section 1 of the **Law Reform (Miscellaneous Provisions) Act 1934** as if for the reference to that period there were substituted a reference to the period of three years from whichever is the later of:

- the date of death; and
- the date of the personal representative's knowledge.

(6) For the purposes of this section "personal representative" includes any person who is or has been a personal representative of the deceased, including an executor who has not proved the will (whether or not he has renounced probate) but not anyone appointed only as a special personal representative in relation to settled land; and regard shall be had to any knowledge acquired by any such person while a personal representative or previously.

(7) If there is more than one personal representative and their dates of knowledge are different, subsection (5)(b) above shall be read as referring to the earliest of those dates.

Section 12: Special Time Limit for Actions under Fatal Accidents Legislation

(1) An action under the **Fatal Accidents Act 1976** shall not be brought if the death occurred when the person injured could no longer maintain an action and recover damages in respect of the injury (whether because of a time limit in this Act or in any other Act, or for any other reason).

Where any such action by the injured person would have been barred by the time limit in section 11 or 11A of this Act, no account shall be taken of the possibility of that time limit being overridden under section 33 of this Act [Discretionary exclusion of time limit for actions in respect of personal injuries or death].

(2) None of the time limits given in the preceding provisions of this Act shall apply to an action under the **Fatal Accidents Act 1976** but no such action shall be brought after the expiration of three years from:

- the date of death; or
- the date of knowledge of the person for whose benefit the action is brought; whichever is the later.

Section 13: Operation of Time Limit under Section 12 in Relation to Different Dependants

(1) Where there is more than one person for whose benefit an action under the **Fatal Accidents Act 1976** is brought, section 12(2)(b) of this Act shall be applied separately to each of them.

(2) Subject to subsection (3) below, if by virtue of subsection (1) above the action would be outside the time limit given by section 12(2) as regards one or more, but not all, of the persons for whose benefit it is brought, the court shall direct that any person as regards whom the action would be outside that limit shall be excluded from those for whom the action is brought.

(3) The court shall not give such a direction if it is shown that if the action were brought exclusively for the benefit of the person in question it would not be defeated by a defence of limitation (whether in consequence of section 28 of this Act or an agreement between the parties not to raise the defence, or otherwise).

Section 14: Definition of Date of Knowledge for Purposes of Sections 11 and 12

(1) Subject to subsection (1A) below, in sections 11 and 12 of this Act references to a person's date of knowledge are references to the date on which he first had knowledge of the following facts:

- that the injury in question was significant; and
- that the injury was attributable in whole or in part to the act or omission which is alleged to constitute negligence, nuisance or breach of duty; and
- the identity of the defendant; and
- if it is alleged that the act or omission was that of a person other than the defendant, the identity of that person and the additional facts supporting the bringing of an action against the defendant;

and knowledge that any acts or omissions did or did not, as a matter of law, involve negligence, nuisance or breach of duty is irrelevant.

(1A) In section 11A and 12 of this Act so far as that section applies to an action by virtue of section 6(1)(a) of the **Consumer Protection Act 1987** (death caused by defective product) references to a person's date of knowledge are references to the date on which he first had knowledge of the following facts:

- such facts about the damage caused by the defect as would lead a reasonable person who had suffered such damage to consider it sufficiently serious to justify his instituting proceedings for damages against a defendant who did not dispute liability and was able to satisfy a judgment; and
- that the damage was wholly or partly attributable to the facts and circumstances alleged to constitute the defect; and
- the identity of the defendant;

but, in determining the date on which a person first had such knowledge there shall be disregarded both the extent (if any) of that person's knowledge on any date of whether particular facts or circumstances would or would not, as a matter of law, constitute a defect and, in a case relating to loss of or damage to property, any knowledge which that person had on a date on which he had no right of action by virtue of Part 1 of that Act in respect of the loss or damage.

(2) For the purposes of this section an injury is significant if the person whose date of knowledge is in question would reasonably have considered it sufficiently serious to justify his instituting proceedings for damages against a defendant who did not dispute liability and was able to satisfy a judgment.

(3) For the purposes of this section a person's knowledge includes knowledge which he might reasonably have been expected to acquire:

- from facts observable or ascertainable by him; or
- from facts ascertainable by him with the help of medical or other appropriate expert advice which it is reasonable for him to seek;

but a person shall not be fixed under this subsection with knowledge of a fact ascertainable only with the help of expert advice so long as he has taken all reasonable steps to obtain (and, where appropriate, to act on) that advice.

Section 14A: Special Time Limit for Negligence Actions Where Facts Relevant to Cause of Action are Not Known at Date of Accrual

(1) This section applies to any action for damages for negligence, other than one to which section 11 of this Act applies, where the starting date for reckoning the period of limitation under subsection (4)(b) below falls after the date on which the cause of action accrued.

(2) Section 2 of this Act shall not apply to an action to which this section applies.

(3) An action to which this section applies shall not be brought after the expiration of the period applicable in accordance with subsection (4) below.

(4) That period is either:

   (a) six years from the date on which the cause of action accrued; or

   (b) three years from the starting date as defined by subsection (5) below, if that period expires later than the period mentioned in paragraph (a) above.

(5) For the purposes of this section, the starting date for reckoning the period of limitation under subsection (4)(b) above is the earliest date on which the claimant or any person in whom the cause of action was vested before him first had both the knowledge required for bringing an action for damages in respect of the relevant damage and a right to bring such an action.

(6) In subsection (5) above "the knowledge required for bringing an action for damages in respect of the relevant damage" means knowledge both:

    (a) of the material facts about the damage in respect of which damages are claimed; and

    (b) of the other facts relevant to the current action mentioned in subsection (8) below.

(7) For the purposes of subsection (6)(a) above, the material facts about the damage are such facts as would lead a reasonable person who had suffered such damage to consider it sufficiently serious to justify his instituting proceedings for damages against a defendant who did not dispute liability and was able to satisfy a judgment.

(8) The other facts referred to in subsection (6)(b) above are:

- that the damage was attributable in whole or in part to the act or omission which is alleged to constitute negligence; and
- the identity of the defendant; and
- if it is alleged that the act or omission was that of a person other than the defendant, the identity of that person and the additional facts supporting the bringing of an action against the defendant.

(9) Knowledge that any acts or omissions did or did not, as a matter of law, involve negligence is irrelevant for the purposes of subsection (5) above.

(10) For the purposes of this section a person's knowledge includes knowledge which he might reasonably have been expected to acquire:

- from facts observable or ascertainable by him; or
- from facts ascertainable by him with the help of appropriate expert advice which it is reasonable for him to seek;

but a person shall not be taken by virtue of this subsection to have knowledge of a fact ascertainable only with the help of expert advice so long as he has taken all reasonable steps to obtain (and, where appropriate, to act on) that advice.

MANAGEMENT OF HEALTH AND SAFETY AT WORK REGULATIONS 1999 (SI 1999 NO. 3242)

Introduction

European Directives introduced prior to 1992 were assimilated into UK legislation in the form of Regulations. The main Directive at that time was **Directive 89/391/EEC** also known as the Framework Directive which later became the **Management of Health and Safety at Work Regulations 1992**. The 1999 version of these Regulations came into force on 29 December 1999.

Regulation 2: Disapplication

Other than to activities on board ship, there are certain exemptions for occasional or short-term work involving work regarded as not being harmful, damaging or dangerous to young people in a family undertaking.

Regulation 3: Risk Assessment

Risk assessment covers the following points:

- Every employer must make a suitable and sufficient assessment of the risks to the health and safety of his employees whilst they are at work.
- Every employer must make a suitable and sufficient assessment of the risks to the health and safety of persons not in his employment arising out of or in connection with the conduct by him of his undertaking.
- Every self-employed person will make a suitable and sufficient assessment of risks to his own health and safety whilst at work and to the health and safety of other persons not in his employment arising out of his conduct of his undertaking.
- The purpose of assessment is to identify the measures necessary to comply with the requirements and prohibitions imposed by the relevant statutory provisions.
- The assessment must be reviewed if it is no longer valid or there has been a significant change in the matters to which it relates. Any changes required by any subsequent review must be implemented.
- An employer shall not employ a young person unless he has made a risk assessment in relation to that young person.
- The young person's risk assessment shall take account of:
    - his/her inexperience, lack of awareness of risks, and immaturity;
    - the fitting-out and layout of the workplace and workstation;
    - the nature, degree and duration of exposure to physical, biological and chemical agents;
    - the form, range, and use of work equipment and the way in which it is handled;
    - the organisation of processes and activities;
    - the extent of health and safety training provided to the young person;
    - the risks from certain agents, processes and work.
- Employers with five or more employees must record the assessment.
    - The record must include the significant findings and identify any group of employees particularly at risk.

Regulation 4: Principles of Prevention to be Applied

Any preventive and protective measures implemented by an employer must be based on principles specified in Schedule 1 to the Regulations.

Regulation 5: Health and Safety Arrangements

Every employer shall make and give effect to such arrangements as are appropriate for the effective planning, organisation, control, monitoring and review of the necessary preventive and protective measures having regard to the nature of his activities and the size of his undertaking. Employers with five or more employees shall record these arrangements.

Regulation 6: Health Surveillance

Every employer should ensure that his employees are provided with such health surveillance as is appropriate, having regard to the risks to their health and safety which are identified by the assessment.

Regulation 7: Health and Safety Assistance

This is a long regulation with 8 paragraphs. The main points are as follows:

- Every employer shall [...] appoint one or more competent persons to assist him in undertaking the measures he needs to take to comply with the requirements and prohibitions imposed upon him by or under the relevant statutory provisions.
- A person shall be regarded as competent where he has sufficient training and experience or knowledge and other qualities properly to undertake the measures referred to.
- Where more than one competent person is appointed the employer shall make arrangements to ensure co-operation between them and also ensure that they are given sufficient time and adequate means to fulfil their functions.
- Where there is a competent person in the employer's employment he shall be appointed as a competent person in preference to a competent person not in his employment.
- Where the competent person appointed is not in the employer's employment, the employer shall ensure that he is provided with any information affecting the health and safety of any other person who may be affected by the conduct of his undertaking.

Regulation 8: Procedure for Serious and Imminent Danger and for Danger Areas

This deals with the employer's need to:

- Devise appropriate procedures to be followed in the event of serious and imminent danger to persons at work in his undertaking.
- Nominate a sufficient number of competent persons to implement those procedures where they relate to the evacuation from premises of people at work.
- Restrict employee access to dangerous areas on grounds of health and safety unless the employee has received appropriate training.
- So far as is reasonably practicable, inform employees of the nature of any hazards and the procedures to be adopted in order to avoid them.
- Enable the employee to stop work immediately and go to a place of safety.
- Prevent employees from resuming work until the danger has passed.

Regulation 9: Contacts with External Services

Every employer shall ensure that any necessary contacts with external services are arranged with regard to first-aid, emergency medical care and rescue work.

Regulation 10: Information for Employees

Employers must provide employees with the following information:

- Risks to their health and safety.
- Preventive and protective measures.
- The procedures for dealing with and reacting to emergencies as outlined in regulation 8.
- The identity of the competent person(s) nominated in regulation 8.
- The nature of risk notified to him by any other employers sharing the workplace.
- Before employing a child, an employer must provide the parent of the child with comprehensible and relevant information on the risks to the child's health and safety identified in the assessment; the preventive and protective measures, and the risks notified to him in accordance with regulation 11.

Regulation 11: Co-operation and Co-ordination

Where two or more employers share a workplace each employer has a duty to co-operate and co-ordinate measures in order to ensure compliance with all statutory duties. Each employer shall take all reasonable steps to inform other employers and self-employed persons of such arrangements.

Regulation 12: Persons Working in Host Employers' or Self-Employed Persons' Undertakings

This regulation applies where employees of employer A carry out work in the undertakings of employer B.

Employees of employer A could be working for employer B under a service contract for cleaning, repair, maintenance, etc. or employees in temporary employment business could be working under A's control.

The important principle is the fact that such persons (employees of A) [and the employer of such persons (A)] who visit another employer's premises to carry out work must be provided with appropriate information and instructions by B regarding the relevant risks to their health and safety arising out of B's undertaking and sufficient information to identify the person responsible for carrying out any evacuation of the premises and also comprehensible information as to those arrangements for evacuation.

Regulation 13: Capabilities and Training

Every employer shall take into account his employees' capabilities as regards health and safety when entrusting them with any tasks. The employer shall ensure the provision of adequate health and safety training for employees:

- on joining the company, on being transferred or given new responsibilities;
- on being exposed to new or increased risks as a result of:
    - being transferred or given a change of responsibilities;
    - the introduction of new work equipment;
    - the introduction of new technology;
    - the introduction of a new system of work or a change to the existing system of work.

All health and safety training shall be repeated periodically where appropriate, and shall be adapted to take account of any new or changed risks to health and safety. Training shall take place during working hours.

Regulation 14: Employee's Duties

Employees shall use any equipment, dangerous substance, transport equipment, means of production or safety device provided by their employer in accordance with any training or instructions given by the employer. In addition employees must inform their employer or work colleagues of any work situation which they reasonably consider represents a serious and immediate danger to health and safety and also inform them of any matter which reasonably presents a shortcoming in the employer's health and safety arrangements.

Regulation 15: Temporary Workers

Every employer must provide any temporary worker with comprehensible information on any special occupational qualifications or skills required to carry out his work safely and any health surveillance required to be provided under any of the relevant statutory provisions. The information must be provided prior to the commencement of any work.

Every employer and every self-employed person shall provide any person employed in an employment business who is to carry out work in his undertaking with comprehensible information on any special occupational qualifications and skills required to be held by the employee if he is to carry out this work safely and on health surveillance required to be provided to the employee by or under any of the relevant statutory provisions. Employers and self-employed persons must also ensure that those carrying on an employment business whose employees are to carry out work in their undertaking receive similar comprehensible information and that this information is provided by those carrying on the employment business to the said employees.

Note: This regulation helps to ensure that temporary workers receive the information outlined above both from the host employer and from the 'employment business'.

Regulation 16: Risk Assessment in Respect of New or Expectant Mothers

(1) Where persons working in an undertaking include women of child-bearing age and the work is of a kind which could involve risk by reason of her condition to the health and safety of a new or expectant mother, or to that of her baby, from any processes or working conditions, or certain physical, biological or chemical agents the assessment required under regulation 3 shall include an assessment of such risk.

(2) In relation to an individual employee where the risk cannot be avoided, the employer shall, if it is reasonable to do so, change her hours of work or alter her working conditions.

(3) Where it is not reasonable to do so, the employer shall suspend the employee from work so long as it is necessary to avoid such risk.

(4) References to risk in relation to any infectious or contagious disease are references to a level of risk at work which is in addition to the level of risk to which a new or expectant mother may be expected to be exposed outside the workplace.

Regulation 16A: Alteration of Working Conditions in Respect of New or Expectant Mothers (Agency Workers)

(1) Where, in the case of an individual agency worker, the taking of any other action the hirer is required to take under the relevant statutory provisions would not avoid the risk referred to in regulation 16(1) the hirer shall, if it is reasonable to do so, and would avoid such risks, alter her working conditions or hours of work.

(2) If it is not reasonable to alter the working conditions or hours of work, or if it would not avoid such risk, the hirer shall without delay inform the temporary work agency, who shall then end the supply of that agency worker to the hirer.

(3) In paragraphs (1) and (2) references to risk, in relation to risk from any infectious or contagious disease, are references to a level of risk at work which is in addition to the level to which a new or expectant mother may be expected to be exposed outside the workplace.

Regulation 17: Certificate from Registered Medical Practitioner in Respect of New or Expectant Mothers

Where a new or expectant mother works at night and she obtains from a registered medical practitioner a certificate to the effect that for health and safety reasons she should not be at work for any period identified in the certificate, the employer shall suspend her from work for so long as is necessary for her health or safety.

Regulation 17A: Certificate from Registered Medical Practitioner in Respect of New or Expectant Mothers (Agency Workers)

Where a new or expectant mother works at night and a certificate from a registered medical practitioner or a registered midwife shows that it is necessary for her health or safety that she should not be at work for any period of such work identified in the certificate, the hirer shall without delay inform the temporary work agency, who shall then end the supply of that agency worker to the hirer.

Regulation 18: Notification by New or Expectant Mothers

An employer shall not be required to take any of the actions in regulations 16 or 17 in relation to a new or expectant mother until she has notified him in writing that she is pregnant, has given birth within the previous six months, or is breastfeeding. Where she has notified her employer of her pregnancy but has failed, within a reasonable time of being requested in writing, to produce a certificate from a registered medical practitioner or a registered midwife showing that she is pregnant, the employer need not take any of the actions referred to above. This also applies where the employer knows that she is no longer a new or expectant mother or if the employer cannot establish whether she remains a new or expectant mother.

Regulation 18A: Notification by New or Expectant Mothers (Agency Workers)

(1) Nothing in regulation 16A(1) or (2) shall require the hirer to take any action in relation to an agency worker until she has notified the hirer in writing that she is pregnant, has given birth within the previous six months, or is breastfeeding.

(2) Nothing in regulation 16A(2) shall require the temporary work agency to end the supply of the agency worker until she has notified the temporary work agency in writing that she is pregnant, has given birth within the previous six months, or is breastfeeding.

(3) Nothing in regulation 16A(1) shall require the hirer to maintain action taken in relation to an agency worker:

   (a) in a case:

      (i) to which regulation 16A(1) relates; and

      (ii) where the agency worker has notified the hirer, that she is pregnant, where she has failed, within a reasonable time of being requested to do so in writing by the hirer, to produce for the hirer's inspection a certificate from a registered medical practitioner or a registered midwife showing that she is pregnant; or

      (iii) once the hirer knows that she is no longer a new or expectant mother; or

   (b) if the hirer cannot establish whether she remains a new or expectant mother.

   Note: The **Agency Workers Regulations 2010** added one further regulation, reg. 18AB, which states that regulations 16A, 17A and 18A will not apply where the agency worker has not completed the qualifying period or is no longer entitled to certain rights conferred by the **Agency Workers Regulations 2010**. Regulation 18AB also states that "*nothing in regulations 16A or 17A imposes a duty on the hirer or temporary work agency beyond the original intended duration, or likely duration of the assignment, whichever is longer.*"

Regulation 19: Protection of Young Persons

Every employer shall ensure that young persons employed by him are protected at work from any risks to their health or safety due to their lack of experience, absence of awareness of existing or potential risks, or immaturity. Except where a young person is undergoing necessary training or being supervised by a competent person and any risk will be reduced to the lowest reasonably practicable level, no employer shall employ a young person for work:

- which is beyond his physical or psychological capacity;
- which involves harmful exposure to agents which are toxic, carcinogenic, cause heritable genetic damage or harm to the unborn child or which in any other way chronically affect human health;
- which involves harmful exposure to radiation;
- which involves the risk of accidents which it may be reasonably assumed cannot be recognised or avoided by the young persons owing to their insufficient attention to safety or lack of experience or training;
- in which there is a risk to health from:
    - extreme cold or heat,
    - noise, or
    - vibration.

In determining whether work will involve any of the above harm or risks regard shall be paid to the assessment required under regulation 3.

Regulation 20: Exemption Certificates

This regulation enables the Secretary of State for Defence in the interests of national security to exempt home and visiting forces from the requirements of the Regulations except in relation to those concerning new or expectant mothers.

Regulation 21: Provisions as to Liability

Nothing in the relevant statutory provisions shall operate so as to afford an employer a defence in any criminal proceedings for a contravention of those provisions by reason of any act or default of an employee or a person appointed by him under regulation 7.

Regulation 22: Exclusion of Civil Liability

(1) Breach of a duty imposed by regulation 16, 16A, 17 or 17A shall, so far as it causes damage, be actionable by the new or expectant mother.

(2) Any term of an agreement which purports to exclude or restrict any liability for such a breach is void.

Note: This revised wording was substituted by the **Health and Safety at Work, etc. Act 1974 (Civil Liability)(Exceptions) Regulations 2013**, which are referred to elsewhere in this guide.

Regulations 23 to 26; 29 and 30

These deal with extension of the Regulations outside Great Britain, amendments and revocations to other Regulations and transitional provisions. Regulations 27 and 28 have been revoked.

Schedule 1

This schedule contains the principles of prevention referred to in regulation 4 which in turn are the General Principles of Prevention contained in Article 6(2) of **Council Directive 89/391/EEC**:

- avoiding risks;
- evaluating the risks which cannot be avoided;
- combating the risks at source;
- adapting the work to the individual, especially as regards the design of workplaces, the choice of work equipment and the choice of working and production methods, with a view, in particular, to alleviating monotonous work and work at a predetermined work-rate and to reducing their effect on health;
- adapting to technical progress;
- replacing the dangerous with the non-dangerous or the less dangerous;

- developing a coherent overall prevention policy which covers technology, organisation of work, working conditions, social relationships and the influence of factors relating to the working environment;
- giving collective protective measures priority over individual protective measures; and
- giving appropriate instructions to employees.

Schedule 2

This schedule contains consequential amendments to many other Regulations.

MANUAL HANDLING OPERATIONS REGULATIONS 1992 (SI 1992 NO. 2793)

Manual Handling

The Regulations are designed to ensure that employees are not put at risk of injury from the manual handling of loads at work. What is an injury? What is manual handling? What is a load? These are defined in the Regulations.

Manual Handling or Mechanisation

The Regulations require the employer to take appropriate organisational measures, or appropriate means, in particular mechanisation, in order to avoid the need for manual handling of loads. In other words, only expect the manual handling of loads where they cannot be handled by mechanical equipment. Where manual handling cannot be avoided, the employer must use the appropriate means to reduce the risk involved. This is a simple two-step procedure:

- reduce the need for manual handling to essentials;
- reduce the residual risks involved in the handling through:
    - training,
    - organisational measures, and
    - improved workplace conditions.

The employer is required to assess the health and safety conditions of the type of work involved and, in particular, the characteristics of loads. Requirements also relate to worker information, training, consultation and participation, with precise information being given, where possible, on the weight of the load and the centre of gravity of the heaviest side when a package is eccentrically loaded. Consultation and participation must take into account the individual risk factors of each worker and may include:

- physical suitability to carry out the task in question;
- the wearing of suitable clothing, footwear or other personal effects; and
- possession of adequate or appropriate knowledge or training.

Here again, as in PPE requirements, we have an example of an assessment having to be made before it can be determined how best to satisfy the requirements in individual and specific workplace circumstances.

Summary of Manual Handling Regulations

There are only eight regulations to be considered but they are comprehensive in their approach to the problem of eliminating or minimising the risk of injury.

Regulation 1 deals with "citation and exclusions"; regulations 6, 7 and 8 deal with "exemption certificates, extension outside Great Britain, and repeals and revocations". These are unlikely to figure in an examination. The remaining main regulations are as follows:

Regulation 2: Interpretation

"Injury" does not include injury caused by any toxic or corrosive substance which:

- has leaked or spilled from a load;
- is present on the surface of a load but has not leaked or spilled from it; or
- is a constituent part of a load;

and "injured" shall be construed accordingly.

"Load" includes any person and any animal.

"Manual handling operations" means any transporting or supporting of a load (including the lifting, putting down, pushing, pulling, carrying or moving thereof) by hand or by bodily force.

Regulation 3: Disapplication of Regulations

The Regulations do not apply to or in relation to the master or crew of any sea-going ship or to the employer of such persons in respect of the normal ship-board activities of a ship's crew under the direction of the master.

Regulation 4: Duties of Employers

Each employer shall, so far as is reasonably practicable, avoid the need for his employees to undertake any manual handling operations which involve a risk of their being injured; or where it is not reasonably practicable to avoid the need for his employees to undertake any manual handling operations which involve a risk of their being injured:

- make a suitable and sufficient assessment of all such manual handling operations to be undertaken by them;
- take appropriate steps to reduce the risk of injury to those employees arising out of their undertaking any such manual handling operations to the lowest level reasonably practicable; and
- take appropriate steps to provide any of those employees who are undertaking any such manual handling operations with general indications and, where it is reasonably practicable to do so, precise information on:
    - the weight of each load, and
    - the heaviest side of any load whose centre of gravity is not positioned centrally.

In determining for the purposes of this regulation whether manual handling operations at work involve a risk of injury and in determining the appropriate steps to reduce that risk regard shall be had in particular to:

- the physical suitability of the employee to carry out the operations;
- the clothing, footwear or other personal effects he is wearing;
- his knowledge and training;
- the results of any relevant risk assessment carried out pursuant to regulation 3 of the **Management of Health and Safety at Work Regulations 1999**;
- whether the employee is within a group of employees identified by that assessment as being especially at risk; and
- the results of any health surveillance provided pursuant to regulation 6 of the **Management of Health and Safety at Work Regulations 1999**.

Regulation 5: Duties of Employees

Each employee while at work shall make full and proper use of any system of work provided for his use by his employer in compliance with these Regulations.

The Code of Practice accompanying the Regulations contains guidance and advice on the Regulations and method of assessment.

Schedule 1: Factors for Manual Handling Assessments

The Schedule of factors to be considered by the employer when making his manual handling assessment is as follows:

Factors and Questions

The tasks

Do they involve:

- Holding or manipulating loads at distance from trunk?
- Unsatisfactory bodily movement or posture, especially:
    - Twisting the trunk?
    - Stooping?
    - Reaching upwards?
- Excessive movement of loads, especially:
    - Excessive lifting or lowering distances?
    - Excessive carrying distances?
- Excessive pushing or pulling of loads?
- Risk of sudden movement of loads?
- Frequent or prolonged physical effort?
- Insufficient rest or recovery periods?
- A rate of work imposed by a process?

The loads	Are they: • Heavy? • Bulky or unwieldy? • Difficult to grasp? • Unstable, or with contents likely to shift? • Sharp, hot or otherwise potentially damaging?
The working environment	Are there: • Space constraints preventing good posture? • Uneven, slippery or unstable floors? • Variations in level of floors or work surfaces? • Extremes of temperature or humidity? • Conditions causing ventilation problems or gusts of wind? • Poor lighting conditions?
Individual capability	Does the job: • Require unusual strength, height, etc.? • Create a hazard to those who might reasonably be considered to be pregnant or to have a health problem? • Require special information or training for its safe performance?
Other factors	Is movement or posture hindered by PPE or by clothing?

NEW ROADS AND STREET WORKS ACT 1991

Part III: Street Works in England and Wales

Sections 65 to 69 contain general requirements as to the execution of street works. They include provision for the proper guarding, lighting and signing of works in progress and the avoidance of unnecessary obstruction of the street. They impose requirements on undertakers executing street works to employ properly qualified supervisors and operatives, to afford facilities to street authorities to inspect works, and to inform others whose apparatus in the street may be affected by the works.

NITRATE POLLUTION PREVENTION REGULATIONS 2015 (SI 2015 NO. 668)

These Regulations came into force on 1 May 2015 and apply in England only. They implement **Directive 91/676/EEC** concerning the protection of waters against pollution by nitrates from agricultural sources.

There are 44 regulations, arranged over 11 Parts and supported by 4 Schedules.

These Regulations revoke a number of consolidated provisions (see Part 11) including the **Nitrate Pollution Prevention Regulations 2008**. **Part 1** is concerned with introductory provisions and includes a definition of polluted water.

Water is polluted if:

- it is freshwater and contains a concentration of nitrates greater than 50 mg/l, or could do so if these Regulations were not to apply there, or
- it is eutrophic or may in the near future become eutrophic if these Regulations were not to apply there.

Part 2 covers the designation of nitrate vulnerable zones (regulation 3). Regulation 4 makes provision for the review of nitrate vulnerable zones, requiring the Secretary of State to keep under review the eutrophic state of fresh surface waters, as well as estuarial and coastal waters. Regulation 6 makes provision for appeals and for bringing proceedings before a First-tier Tribunal.

Part 3 consists of two regulations limiting the application of organic manure.

Part 4 deals with crop requirements, including an exclusion for crops in greenhouses, the planning and spreading of nitrogen fertiliser, recording of information, total nitrogen spread, grass grown for dehydration or for chlorophyll production and calculating the amount of nitrogen available for crop uptake from organic manure.

Part 5 deals with methods to control the spreading of nitrogen fertiliser. The regulations in this part cover risk maps, when to spread fertiliser, spreading near surface water, boreholes, springs and wells and requirements for controlling how nitrogen fertiliser is spread (using spreading equipment with a spreading trajectory of less than 4 metres from the ground per regulation 18), as well as how organic manure is incorporated into the ground. This Part also contains regulations on closed periods for spreading organic manure and provides for certain exemptions for organic holdings, which provisions were formerly contained in Part 6 of the 2008 Regulations of the same name.

Part 6 covers the storage of organic manure.

Part 7 deals with calculations and records. This Part makes provision for keeping records relating to the storage of manure, of nitrogen produced by animals on the holding, of livestock manure brought onto or sent off the holding, sampling and analysis, records of crops sown and records of spreading nitrogen fertiliser. Reference is also made to a requirement for the occupier of the holding to keep a copy of advice obtained from a FACTS adviser.

Part 8 consists of three regulations covering the application by the occupier of a holding for a derogation in a case where 80% or more of the agricultural area is sown with grass. Arrangements are also set out for how the application will be determined and for appeals.

Part 9 deals with review by the Secretary of State of the effectiveness of the restrictions in nitrate vulnerable zones imposed as a means of reducing or preventing water pollution caused by nitrates from agricultural sources. This is to be done at least every four years and, if necessary, the restrictions are to be revised.

Part 10 deals with enforcement. Any person who breaches these Regulations may be liable on summary conviction to a fine not exceeding the statutory maximum, or on indictment to an unlimited fine. Where the offence has been committed by a body corporate and that offence is proved to have been committed with the consent, connivance or due to the neglect of any director, manager, secretary, etc., then that person, as well as the body corporate, is liable to be proceeded against and punished accordingly.

NITRATE POLLUTION PREVENTION (WALES) REGULATIONS 2013 (SI 2013 NO. 2506)

These Regulations came into force on 25 October 2013. They revoke the **Nitrate Pollution Prevention (Wales) Regulations 2008**. The new Regulations continue to implement **Directive 91/676/EEC** concerning the protection of waters against pollution by nitrates from agricultural sources.

There are 51 regulations, arranged over 10 Parts and supported by 5 Schedules.

Part 1 is concerned with introductory provisions and includes a definition of "Polluted water", which is as follows:

Water is polluted if:

(a) it is freshwater and contains a concentration of nitrates greater than 50 mg/l, or could do so if these Regulations were not to apply there, or

(b) it is eutrophic or may in the near future become eutrophic if these Regulations were not to apply there.

Part 2 covers the designation of nitrate vulnerable zones and makes provision for appeals and for bringing proceedings before the appointed person. Effects of determinations made by the appointed person are dealt with at regulation 10. Regulation 11 makes provision for the review of nitrate vulnerable zones, requiring the Welsh Ministers to keep under review the eutrophic state of fresh surface waters, as well as estuarial and coastal waters.

Part 3 consists of two regulations limiting the application of organic manure.

Part 3A was added by the **Nitrate Pollution Prevention (Wales) (Amendment) Regulations 2015** (SI 2015/2020). This Part consists of three regulations dealing with derogations. An occupier of any holding (or someone acting on their behalf) may apply to Natural Resources Wales for a derogation where 80% or more of the agricultural area is sown with grass. Arrangements for appeals against refusal of a derogation application are set out at regulation 13B.

Part 4 deals with crop requirements, including the planning and spreading of nitrogen fertiliser, recording of information, total nitrogen spread and maximum nitrogen limits by crop.

Part 5 deals with methods to control the spreading of nitrogen fertiliser. The regulations in this part cover risk maps, when to spread fertiliser, spreading near surface water, boreholes, springs and wells and requirements for controlling how nitrogen fertiliser is spread (using spreading equipment with a spreading trajectory of less than 4 metres from the ground), as well as how organic manure is incorporated into the ground.

Part 6 is concerned with closed periods for spreading nitrogen fertiliser and provides for certain exemptions, such as crops sown before 15 September and for organic holdings.

Part 7 covers the storage of organic manure.

Part 8 deals with calculations and records. This Part makes provision for recording the size of the holding and keeping records relating to the storage of manure, of nitrogen produced by animals on the holding, of livestock manure brought onto or sent off the holding, sampling and analysis, records of crops sown and records of spreading nitrogen fertiliser.

Part 9 deals with monitoring and review by the Welsh Ministers of the effectiveness of the restrictions in nitrate vulnerable zones imposed by these Regulations.

Part 10 deals with enforcement. Any person who breaches these Regulations may be liable on summary conviction to a fine not exceeding the statutory maximum, or on indictment to an unlimited fine. Where the offence has been committed by a body corporate and that offence is proved to have been committed with the consent, connivance or due to the neglect of any director, manager, secretary, etc., then that person, as well as the body corporate, is liable to be proceeded against and punished accordingly.

OCCUPIERS' LIABILITY ACT 1957

This Act came into force on 1 January 1958 and rationalised and replaced the old common law rules on occupiers' liability. In so doing, this Act created a "common duty of care", applicable to all those who lawfully enter premises.

Section 1: Preliminary

The following are key points:

(1) The rules enacted by the two next following sections shall have effect, in place of the rules of the common law, to regulate the duty which an occupier of premises owes to his visitors in respect of dangers due to the state of the premises or to things done or omitted to be done on them.

(2) The rules shall regulate the nature of the duty imposed by law in consequence of a person's occupation or control of premises and of any invitation or permission he gives to another to enter or use the premises, but they shall not alter the rules of the common law as to the persons on whom a duty is so imposed or to whom it is owed; and accordingly the persons who are to be treated as an occupier and as his visitors are the same as the persons who would at common law be treated as an occupier and as his invitees or licensees.

(3) The rules in relation to an occupier of premises and his visitors shall also apply in like manner as the common law principles would apply to an occupier of premises and his invitees or licensees, to regulate:

- the obligations of a person occupying or having control over any fixed or moveable structure, including any vessel, vehicle or aircraft; and
- the obligations of a person occupying or having control over any premises or structure in respect of damage to property, including the property of persons who are not themselves his visitors.

(4) A person entering any premises in exercise of rights conferred by virtue of:

(a) section 2(1) of the **Countryside and Rights of Way Act 2000**, or

(b) an access agreement or order under the **National Parks and Access to the Countryside Act 1949**,

is not, for the purposes of this Act, a visitor of the occupier of the premises.

Note: Subsection (4) was substituted by the **Countryside and Rights of Way Act 2000**.

Section 2: Extent of Occupiers' Ordinary Duty

This deals with the following duties:

(1) An occupier of premises owes the same duty, the "common duty of care", to all his visitors, except in so far as he is free to and does extend, restrict, modify or exclude his duty to any visitor or visitors by agreement or otherwise.

(2) The common duty of care is a duty to take such care as in all the circumstances of the case is reasonable to see that the visitor will be reasonably safe in using the premises for the purposes for which he is invited or permitted by the occupier to be there.

(3) The circumstances relevant for the present purpose include the degree of care, and of want of care, which would ordinarily be looked for in such a visitor, so that (for example) in proper cases:

- an occupier must be prepared for children to be less careful than adults; and
- an occupier may expect that a person, in the exercise of his calling, will appreciate and guard against any special risks ordinarily incident to it, so far as the occupier leaves him free to do so.

(4) In determining whether the occupier of premises has discharged the common duty of care to a visitor, regard is to be had to all the circumstances, so that (for example):

- where damage is caused to a visitor by a danger of which he had been warned by the occupier, the warning is not to be treated without more as absolving the occupier from liability, unless in all the circumstances it was enough to enable the visitor to be reasonably safe; and
- where damage is caused to a visitor by a danger due to the faulty execution of any work of construction, maintenance or repair by an independent contractor employed by the occupier, the occupier is not to be treated without more as answerable for the danger if in all the circumstances he had acted reasonably in entrusting the work to an independent contractor and had taken such steps (if any) as he reasonably ought in order to satisfy himself that the contractor was competent and that the work had been properly done.

(5) The common duty of care does not impose on an occupier any obligation to a visitor in respect of risks willingly accepted as his by the visitor (the question whether a risk was so accepted to be decided on the same principles as in other cases in which one person owes a duty of care to another).

(6) For the purposes of this section, persons who enter premises for any purpose in the exercise of a right conferred by law are to be treated as permitted by the occupier to be there for that purpose, whether they in fact have his permission or not.

Section 3: Effect of Contract on Occupier's Liability to Third Party

Several points are of note:

(1) Where an occupier of premises is bound by contract to permit persons who are strangers to the contract to enter or use the premises, the duty of care which he owes to them as his visitors cannot be restricted or excluded by that contract, but (subject to any provision of the contract to the contrary) shall include the duty to perform his obligations under the contract, whether undertaken for their protection or not, in so far as those obligations go beyond the obligations otherwise involved in that duty.

(2) A contract shall not by virtue of this section have the effect, unless it expressly so provides, of making an occupier who has taken all reasonable care answerable to strangers to the contract for dangers due to the faulty execution of any work of construction, maintenance or repair or other like operation by persons other than himself, his servants and persons acting under his direction and control.

(3) In this section "stranger to the contract" means a person not for the time being entitled to the benefit of the contract as a party to it or as the successor by assignment or otherwise of a party to it, and accordingly includes a party to the contract who has ceased to be so entitled.

(4) Where by the terms or conditions governing any tenancy (including a statutory tenancy which does not in law amount to a tenancy) either the landlord or the tenant is bound, though not by contract, to permit persons to enter or use premises of which he is the occupier, this section shall apply as if the tenancy were a contract between the landlord and the tenant.

(5) This section, in so far as it prevents the common duty of care from being restricted or excluded, applies to contracts entered into and tenancies created before the commencement of this Act, as well as to those entered into or created after its commencement; but, in so far as it enlarges the duty owed by an occupier beyond the common duty of care, it shall have effect only in relation to obligations which are undertaken after that commencement or which are renewed by agreement (whether express or implied) after that commencement.

Section 4: Repealed by the Defective Premises Act 1972

Section 5: Implied Term in Contracts

(1) Where persons enter or use, or bring or send goods to, any premises in exercise of a right conferred by contract with a person occupying or having control of the premises, the duty he owes them in respect of dangers due to the state of the premises or to things done or omitted to be done on them, in so far as the duty depends on a term to be implied in the contract by reason of its conferring that right, shall be the common duty of care.

(2) The foregoing subsection shall apply to fixed and moveable structures as it applies to premises.

(3) This section does not affect the obligations imposed on a person by or by virtue of any contract for the hire of, or for the carriage for reward of persons or goods in, any vehicle, vessel, aircraft or other means of transport, or by or by virtue of any contract of bailment.

(4) This section does not apply to contracts entered into before the commencement of this Act.

Section 6: Application to Crown

This Act shall bind the Crown, but as regards the Crown's liability in tort shall not bind the Crown further than the Crown is made liable in tort by the **Crown Proceedings Act 1947**, and that Act and in particular section 2 of it shall apply in relation to duties under sections 2 and 3 of this Act as statutory duties.

OCCUPIERS' LIABILITY ACT 1984

Introduction

This was an Act to amend the law of England and Wales as to the liability of persons as occupiers of premises for injury suffered by persons other than their visitors; and, by virtue of section 2, to amend the **Unfair Contract Terms Act 1977** as it applied to England and Wales, in relation to persons obtaining access to premises for recreational or educational purposes.

New subsections 1(6A), (6B) and (6C) and a new section 1A were added by the **Countryside and Rights of Way Act 2000**. These additional subsections limit the liability on landowners to those exercising their 'right to roam'. Subsection 1(6AA) was added by the **Marine and Coastal Access Act 2009**.

Section 1: Duty of Occupier to Persons other than his Visitors

(1) The rules enacted by this section have effect, in place of the rules of the common law, to determine:

- whether any duty is owed by a person as occupier of premises to persons other than his visitors in respect of any risk of their suffering injury on the premises by reason of any danger due to the state of the premises or to things done or omitted to be done on them; and
- if so, what that duty is.

(2) For the purposes of this section, the persons who are to be treated respectively as an occupier of any premises (which, for those purposes, include any fixed or movable structure) and as his visitors are:

- any person who owes in relation to the premises the duty referred to in section 2 of the **Occupiers' Liability Act 1957** (the common duty of care), and
- those who are his visitors for the purposes of that duty.

(3) An occupier of premises owes a duty to another (not being his visitor) in respect of any such risk as is referred to in subsection (1) above if:

- he is aware of the danger or has reasonable grounds to believe that it exists;
- he knows or has reasonable grounds to believe that the other is in the vicinity of the danger concerned or that he may come into the vicinity of the danger (in either case, whether the other has lawful authority for being in that vicinity or not); and
- the risk is one against which, in all the circumstances of the case, he may reasonably be expected to offer the other some protection.

(4) Where, by virtue of this section, an occupier of premises owes a duty to another in respect of such a risk, the duty is to take such care as is reasonable in all the circumstances of the case to see that he does not suffer injury on the premises by reason of the danger concerned.

(5) Any duty owed by virtue of this section in respect of a risk may, in an appropriate case, be discharged by taking such steps as are reasonable in all the circumstances of the case to give warning of the danger concerned or to discourage persons from incurring the risk.

(6) No duty is owed by virtue of this section to any person in respect of risks willingly accepted as his by that person (the question whether a risk was so accepted to be decided on the same principles as in other cases in which one person owes a duty of care to another).

(6A) At any time when the right conferred by section 2(1) of the **Countryside and Rights of Way Act 2000** is exercisable in relation to land which is access land for the purposes of Part I of that Act, an occupier of the land owes (subject to subsection (6C) below) no duty by virtue of this section to any person in respect of:

 (a) a risk resulting from the existence of any natural feature of the landscape, or any river, stream, ditch or pond whether or not a natural feature, or

 (b) a risk of that person suffering injury when passing over, under or through any wall, fence or gate, except by proper use of the gate or of a stile.

(6AA) Where the land is coastal margin for the purposes of Part 1 of that Act (including any land treated as coastal margin by virtue of section 16 of that Act), subsection (6A) has effect as if for paragraphs (a) and (b) of that subsection there were substituted "*a risk resulting from the existence of any physical feature (whether of the landscape or otherwise).*"

(6B) For the purposes of subsection (6A) above, any plant, shrub or tree, of whatever origin, is to be regarded as a natural feature of the landscape.

(6C) Subsection (6A) does not prevent an occupier from owing a duty by virtue of this section in respect of any risk where the danger concerned is due to anything done by the occupier:

(a) with the intention of creating that risk, or

(b) being reckless as to whether that risk is created.

(7) No duty is owed by virtue of this section to persons using the highway, and this section does not affect any duty owed to such persons.

(8) Where a person owes a duty by virtue of this section, he does not, by reason of any breach of the duty, incur any liability in respect of any loss of or damage to property.

(9) In this section:

- "Highway" means any part of a highway other than a fen or waterway.
- "Injury" means anything resulting in death or personal injury, including any disease and any impairment of physical or mental condition.
- "Movable structure" includes any vessel, vehicle or aircraft.

Section 1A: Special Considerations Relating to Access Land

In determining whether any, and if so what, duty is owed by virtue of section 1 by an occupier of land at any time when the right conferred by section 2(1) of the **Countryside and Rights of Way Act 2000** is exercisable in relation to the land, regard is to be had, in particular, to:

(a) the fact that the existence of that right ought not to place an undue burden (whether financial or otherwise) on the occupier,

(b) the importance of maintaining the character of the countryside, including features of historic, traditional or archaeological interest, and

(c) any relevant guidance given under section 20 of that Act.

Section 3: Application to Crown

Section 1 of this Act shall bind the Crown, but as regards the Crown's liability in tort shall not bind the Crown further than the Crown is made liable in tort by the **Crown Proceedings Act 1947**.

OCCUPIERS' LIABILITY (SCOTLAND) ACT 1960

The obligations and the person who has the duty of care remains broadly the same as the English 1957 and 1984 **Occupiers' Liability Acts**. However, there are some notable differences, namely:

Distinction Between Lawful Visitors and Trespassers

The **Occupiers' Liability (Scotland) Act 1960** does not distinguish between lawful visitors and trespassers; the status of the visitor is irrelevant. There is only therefore this single Act to cover all situations.

Trespassers

In English legislation, the 1984 Act places responsibility as an occupier, to trespassers where three conditions are met:

- he is aware of the danger or has reasonable grounds to believe it exists;
- he knows or has reasonable grounds to believe that the other is in the vicinity of the danger concerned or that he may come into the vicinity of the danger; and
- the risk is one against which, in all the circumstance of the case, he may reasonably be expected to offer the other some protection.

The Scottish 1960 Act does not contain these three conditions. Section 2 requires an occupier to take such steps as are reasonable in the circumstances to see that the trespasser will be reasonably safe.

Extent of Liability

In England, occupiers' liability is limited to death and personal injury. In Scotland, liability extends to the loss of or damage to property as well as to death and personal injury.

Section 2: Extent of Occupier's Duty to Show Care

(1) The care which an occupier of premises is required, by reason of his occupation or control of the premises, to show towards a person entering thereon in respect of dangers which are due to the state of the premises or to anything done or omitted to be done on them and for which the occupier is in law responsible shall, except in so far as he is entitled to and does extend, restrict, modify or exclude by agreement his obligations towards that person, be such care as in all the circumstances of the case is reasonable to see that that person will not suffer injury or damage by reason of any such danger.

(2) Nothing in the foregoing subsection shall relieve an occupier of premises of any duty to show in any particular case any higher standard of care which in that case is incumbent on him by virtue of any enactment or rule of law imposing special standards of care on particular classes of persons.

(3) Nothing in the foregoing provisions of this Act shall be held to impose on an occupier any obligation to a person entering on his premises in respect of risks which that person has willingly accepted as his; and any question whether a risk was so accepted shall be decided on the same principles as in other cases in which one person owes to another a duty to show care.

PERSONAL PROTECTIVE EQUIPMENT (PPE) AT WORK REGULATIONS 1992 (SI 1992 NO. 2966)

Note

As amended by the **Health and Safety (Miscellaneous Amendments) Regulations 2002 (SI 2002 No. 2174)**.

NB: Do not confuse these Regulations with the **Personal Protective Equipment Regulations 2002**, or the previous **PPE (EC Directive) Regulations 1992** as amended 1993, 1994 and 1996, made under consumer protection legislation, which are concerned with the standards to which PPE is to be manufactured.

The **Health and Safety (Miscellaneous Repeals, Revocations and Amendments) Regulations 2013** have amended these Regulations so that they now apply to the provision and use of head protection on construction sites.

Summary

These Regulations revoked much of the older more specific PPE-related Regulations. They cover all protective equipment for use at work from that designed for adverse weather conditions through protective clothing such as aprons, gloves, footwear, helmets, jackets, eye protection, safety harnesses and respirators to life jackets where employees work on or near water.

They do not apply where there is a more comprehensive requirement for provision and use of PPE, as mentioned below.

You should note specifically that the Regulations require employers to provide PPE but only as a last resort after they have taken all measures to attempt to remove or control the risk, although they can use PPE as an interim measure while carrying out remedial action.

Regulation 2: Interpretation

In the Regulations, Personal Protective Equipment (PPE) is defined as:

"all equipment (including clothing affording protection against the weather) which is intended to be worn or held by a person at work and which protects him against one or more risks to his health or safety, and any addition or accessory designed to meet that objective".

Definition and Application:

PPE includes both the following, when they are worn for protection of health and safety:

- protective clothing such as aprons, protective clothing for adverse weather conditions, gloves, safety footwear, safety helmets, high visibility waistcoats, and
- protective equipment such as eye protectors, life jackets, respirators, underwater breathing apparatus and safety harnesses.

Regulation 3: Disapplication of These Regulations

PPE does not include the following:

- Ordinary working clothes and uniforms which do not specifically protect the health and safety of the wearer.
- An offensive weapon within the meaning of section 1(4) of the **Prevention of Crime Act 1953** used as self-defence or as deterrent equipment.
- Portable devices for detecting and signalling risks and nuisances.
- PPE used for protection while travelling on a road within the meaning (in England and Wales) of section 192(1) of the **Road Traffic Act 1988** and (in Scotland) of section 151 of the **Roads (Scotland) Act 1984**.
- Equipment used during the playing of competitive games.

Regulations 4 and 6 to 12 shall not apply where any of the following Regulations apply and in respect of any risk to a person's health or safety for which any of them require the provision or use of PPE, namely:

- **Control of Lead at Work Regulations 2002**.
- **Ionising Radiations Regulations 2017**.
- **Control of Asbestos Regulations 2012**.
- **Control of Substances Hazardous to Health Regulations 2002**.
- **Control of Noise at Work Regulations 2005**.

Regulation 4: Provision of Personal Protective Equipment

(1) Subject to paragraph (1A) every employer shall ensure that suitable PPE is provided for his employees who may be exposed to a risk to their health or safety while at work, except where and to the extent that such risk has been adequately controlled by other means which are equally or more effective.

(1A) Where the characteristics of any policing activity are such that compliance by the relevant officer with the requirement in paragraph (1) would lead to an inevitable conflict with the exercise of police powers or performance of police duties, that requirement shall be complied with so far as is reasonably practicable.

(2) Every self-employed person shall ensure that he is provided with suitable PPE where he may be exposed to a risk to his health or safety while at work except where and to the extent that such risk has been adequately controlled by other means which are equally or more effective.

(3) PPE shall not be suitable unless:

　(a) it is appropriate for the risk or risks involved, the conditions at the place where exposure to the risk may occur, and the period for which it is worn.

　(b) It takes account of ergonomic requirements and the state of health of the person or persons who may wear it, and of the characteristics of the workstation of each such person.

　(c) It is capable of fitting the wearer correctly, if necessary after adjustments within the range for which it is designed.

　(d) So far as is practicable, it is effective to prevent or adequately control the risk or risks involved without increasing overall risk.

　(e) It complies with any enactment (whether in an Act or instrument) which implements in Great Britain any provision on design or manufacture with respect to health or safety in any of the relevant EU directives which is applicable to that item of personal protective equipment.

(4) Where it is necessary to ensure that personal protective equipment is hygienic and otherwise free of risk to health, every employer and every self-employed person shall ensure that personal protective equipment provided under this regulation is provided to a person for use only by him.

Regulation 5: Compatibility of Personal Protective Equipment

Every employer shall ensure that where the presence of more than one risk to health or safety makes it necessary for his employee to wear or use simultaneously more than one item of personal protective equipment, such equipment is compatible and continues to be effective against the risks in question.

This applies equally to a self-employed person in respect of equipment worn by himself.

Regulation 6: Assessment of Personal Protective Equipment

Before choosing any PPE, an employer or self-employed person shall ensure that an assessment is made to determine whether the PPE he intends to provide is suitable.

The assessment shall include:

- an assessment of any risks to health or safety which have not been avoided by other means;
- the definition of the characteristics which PPE must have in order to be effective against the risks referred to taking into account any risks which the equipment itself may create;
- comparison of the characteristics of the PPE available with the characteristics referred to above;
- an assessment as to whether the PPE is compatible with other PPE which is in use and which an employee would be required to wear simultaneously.

Every employer or self-employed person who is required to make an assessment shall ensure that any such assessment is reviewed if:

- there is reason to suspect it is no longer valid; or
- there has been a significant change in the matters to which it relates.

Where as a result of any such review changes in the assessment are required, the relevant employer or self-employed person shall ensure that they are made.

Regulation 7: Maintenance and Replacement of PPE

Every employer shall ensure that any PPE provided to his employees is maintained (including replaced or cleaned as appropriate) in an efficient state, in efficient working order and in good repair.

This applies equally to a self-employed person.

Regulation 8: Accommodation of PPE

Where PPE is provided, the employer will ensure the provision of appropriate accommodation for its storage when not in use.

Regulation 9: Information, Instruction and Training

Where an employer is required to ensure that PPE is provided to an employee, the employer shall also ensure that the employee is provided with such information, instruction and training as is adequate and appropriate to enable the employee to know:

- the risks which the PPE will avoid or limit;
- the purpose for which and the manner in which PPE is to be used;
- any action to be taken by the employee to ensure that the PPE remains in an efficient state, in efficient working order and in good repair;

and shall ensure that such information is kept available to employees.

The information and instruction provided must be comprehensible to the persons to whom it is provided.

The employer shall, where appropriate, and at suitable intervals, organise demonstrations in the wearing of PPE.

Regulation 10: Use of PPE

Every employer shall take all reasonable steps to ensure that any PPE provided to his employees is properly used.

Every employee shall use any PPE provided to him in accordance both with any training in the use of the PPE concerned which has been received by him and the instructions respecting that use which have been provided to him under regulation 9. This applies equally to self- employed persons.

Every employee and self-employed person shall take all reasonable steps to ensure that PPE is returned to the accommodation provided for it after use.

Regulation 11: Reporting Loss or Defect

Every employee who has been provided with PPE shall forthwith report to his employer any loss of or obvious defect in that PPE. The remaining regulations 12, 13 and 14 cover exemption certificates, extension outside Great Britain and repeals and modifications.

PRESSURE EQUIPMENT (SAFETY) REGULATIONS 2016 (SI 2016 NO. 1105)

These Regulations transpose **Directive 2014/68/EU** dated 15 May 2014 on the harmonisation of the laws of Member States relating to the making available on the market of pressure equipment.

The Directive repeals and replaces **Directive 1997/23/EC** dated 29 May 1997 relating to pressure equipment, which was implemented in the UK by the **Pressure Equipment Regulations 1999 (SI 1999 No. 2001) (as amended)**. These Regulations revoke and replace **SI 1999 No. 2001**.

Article 13 of the Directive (classification of pressure equipment) was required to be implemented by 28 February 2015 and was transposed by the **Pressure Equipment (Amendment) Regulations 2015 (SI 2015 No. 399)** which amended **SI 1999 No. 2001**. That amendment has been incorporated into these Regulations.

There are 91 regulations arranged over 6 Parts, supported by 12 schedules. A summary of these regulations follows.

Part 1: Preliminary

Regulation 3 sets out the application of the Regulations to pressure equipment and assemblies as defined in **Regulation 2**.

Regulation 4 introduces **Schedule 1** which sets out exceptions to the application of the Regulations for certain types of equipment and for equipment covered by certain other EU legislation.

Regulation 5 sets out an exception for the showing of pressure equipment at trade fairs, exhibitions and demonstrations.

Regulations 6 and 7 detail the types of pressure equipment and assemblies of pressure equipment which must comply with the essential safety requirements of the Directive, and **regulation 8** details the pressure equipment and assemblies, generally for lower temperatures or pressures, which must comply with sound engineering practice.

Part 2: Obligations of Economic Operators

Manufacturers

Regulations 9 to 19 set out the obligations that are specific to manufacturers.

Manufacturers must ensure that pressure equipment or assemblies coming within **regulation 6 or 7** comply with the essential safety requirements of the Directive set out in **Schedule 2**, and must classify the equipment and carry out the relevant conformity assessment procedure before the vessel is placed on the market, affixing the CE marking, labelling the equipment and ensuring it is accompanied by instructions and safety information. More limited obligations apply to pressure equipment and assemblies coming within regulation 8. Manufacturers must also monitor pressure equipment and assemblies and take corrective action if it is found not to be in conformity with the requirements of these Regulations.

Regulation 19 refers to authorised representatives who may be appointed by manufacturers to perform certain tasks on their behalf.

Importers

Regulations 20 to 29 set out the obligations that are specific to importers.

These obligations include ensuring that they are not placing on the market pressure equipment or assemblies which are not in conformity with the essential safety requirements, checking that the manufacturer has carried out a relevant conformity assessment procedure and labelled the equipment correctly and indicating on the equipment the name and address of the importer.

Distributors

Regulations 30 to 36 set out the obligations that are specific to distributors.

These obligations include acting with due care to ensure that pressure equipment and assemblies are in conformity with Part 2 and checking that the equipment bears the CE marking and is labelled correctly. They also include an obligation to ensure that, while it is the distributor's responsibility, the storage and transport of pressure equipment does not jeopardise its conformity with the essential safety requirements.

All Economic Operators

Regulations 37 to 39 set out obligations which apply to all economic operators.

These obligations include making sure, before making pressure equipment or assemblies available on the market, that the EU declaration of conformity is in English. They also include an obligation to identify other economic operators in the supply chain, and a prohibition on the improper use of the CE marking.

Part 3: Conformity Assessment

Part 3 sets out provisions concerning the conformity assessment procedure, declaration of conformity and CE marking for pressure equipment and assemblies coming within **regulation 6 or 7**. It also sets out provisions for the issuing of European approval for materials.

Part 4: Notification of Conformity Assessment Bodies

Part 4 sets out provisions concerning notification and monitoring of the bodies which carry out conformity assessment procedures under the Regulations.

Part 5: Market Surveillance and Enforcement

Regulation 66 identifies the market surveillance authority which has an obligation to enforce the Regulations.

Regulation 68 and **Schedules 7 to 9** provide for the enforcement powers which the enforcing authorities are to have.

Regulation 76 provides for the contravention of certain provisions of these Regulations to be an offence.

Regulation 77 sets out the penalties that are to apply for offences under these Regulations.

Regulation 84 sets out provision for appeals against notices served under these Regulations.

Part 6: Miscellaneous

Part 6 sets out a review provision, transitional provisions, revocations and savings and introduces **Schedule 12** (consequential amendments).

PRESSURE SYSTEMS SAFETY REGULATIONS 2000 (SI 2000 NO. 128)

Summary

Most liquids and gases become hazardous when they are under a pressure greater than atmospheric.

The **Pressure Systems Safety Regulations 2000** are concerned with the risks created by a release of stored energy through system failure. With the exception of the scalding effects of steam, the Regulations do not consider the hazardous properties of the contents released following system failure.

The Regulations

These Regulations have replaced the **Pressure Systems and Transportable Gas Containers Regulations 1989** and came into force on 21 February 2000. Transportable gas containers were removed from the scope of PSTGCR by the **Carriage of Dangerous Goods (Classification, Packaging and Labelling) and Use of Transportable Pressure Receptacles Regulations 1996 (CDGCPL2) (SI 1996 No. 2092)** as a consequence of the **Pressure Equipment Directive**.

Interpretation

"Competent Person" means a competent individual person (other than an employee) or a competent body of persons corporate or unincorporate; and accordingly any reference in these Regulations to a competent person performing a function includes a reference to his performing it through his employees.

"Danger" in relation to a pressure system means reasonably foreseeable danger to persons from system failure, but (except in the case of steam) it does not mean danger from the hazardous characteristics of the relevant fluid other than from its pressure.

"Examination" means a careful and critical scrutiny of a pressure system or part of a pressure system, in or out of service as appropriate, using suitable techniques, including testing, where appropriate to assess its actual condition and whether, for the period up to the next examination, it will not cause danger when properly used if normal maintenance is carried out. For this purpose "normal maintenance" means such maintenance as it is reasonable to expect the user (in the case of an installed system) or owner (in the case of a mobile system) to ensure is carried out independently of any advice from the competent person making the examination.

"The Executive" means the Health and Safety Executive.

"Installed System" means a pressure system other than a mobile system.

"Maximum Allowable Pressure" and "Minimum Allowable Pressure" mean the maximum pressure and minimum pressure respectively for which a pressure vessel is designed.

"Mobile System" means a pressure system which can be readily moved between and used in different locations but it does not include a pressure system of a locomotive.

"Owner" in relation to a pressure system means the employer or self-employed person who owns the pressure system or, if he does not have a place of business in Great Britain, his agent in Great Britain or, if there is no such agent, the user.

"Pipeline" means a pipe or system of pipes used for the conveyance of relevant fluid across the boundaries of premises, together with any apparatus for inducing or facilitating the flow of relevant fluid through, or through a part of, the pipe or system, and any valves, valve chambers, pumps, compressors and similar works which are annexed to, or incorporated in the course of, the pipe or system.

"Pipework" means a pipe or system of pipes together with associated valves, pumps, compressors and other pressure-containing components and includes a hose or bellows but does not include a pipeline or any protective devices.

"Pressure Receptacle" has the meaning in regulation 2(1) of **CDG 2007**, except that it includes any permanent fitting to a pressure receptacle, and regulation 2(1) shall apply as if the receptacle were being carried by road.

"Pressure System" means:

- a system comprising one or more pressure vessels of rigid construction, any associated pipework and protective devices;
- the pipework with its protective devices to which a pressure receptacle, an old pressure receptacle, or transportable pressure equipment is, or is intended to be, connected; or
- a pipeline and its protective devices,

which contains or is liable to contain a relevant fluid, but does not include a pressure receptacle, an old pressure receptacle or transportable pressure equipment.

"Protective Devices" means devices designed to protect the pressure system against system failure and devices designed to give warning that system failure might occur, and includes bursting discs.

"Relevant Fluid" means:

- steam;
- any fluid or mixture of fluids which is at a pressure greater than 0.5 bar above atmospheric pressure, and which fluid or mixture of fluids is a gas; or a liquid which would have a vapour pressure greater than 0.5 bar above atmospheric pressure when in equilibrium with its vapour at either the actual temperature of the liquid or 17.5 degrees Celsius; or
- a gas dissolved under pressure in a solvent contained in a porous substance at ambient temperature and which could be released from the solvent without the application of heat.

"Safe Operating Limits" means the operating limits (incorporating a suitable margin of safety) beyond which system failure is liable to occur. "Scheme of Examination" means the written scheme referred to in regulation 8.

"System Failure" means the unintentional release of stored energy (other than from a pressure relief system) from a pressure system.

"Transportable Pressure Equipment" has the same meaning as in regulation 2(1) of **CDG 2007** except that it shall exclude a tank within the meaning of those Regulations.

"User" in relation to a pressure system or a vessel means the employer or self-employed person who has control of the operation of the pressure system or such a vessel or, in the case of a pressure system or such a vessel at or in a mine, it means the manager for the time being of that mine or, in the case of a quarry, it means the operator for the time being of that quarry.

Any reference in these Regulations to anything being in writing or written shall include reference to a form in which it can be reproduced as a written copy when required and which is secure from loss or unauthorised interference.

Regulation 3: Application and Duties

These Regulations shall apply to or in relation to pressure systems which are used or intended to be used at work. Any requirement or prohibition imposed by the Regulations on an employer in respect of the activities of his employees shall also extend to a self-employed person in respect of his own activities at work.

Any requirement or prohibition imposed by the Regulations on a person who designs or manufactures, imports or supplies any pressure system, or any article which is intended to be a component part of any pressure system, shall extend only to such a system or article designed, manufactured, imported or supplied in the course of a trade, business or other undertaking carried on by him whether for profit or not. Requirements and prohibitions imposed on a person extend only to matters within his control.

Regulation 4: Design and Construction

Any person who designs, manufactures, imports or supplies any pressure system or any article which is intended to be a component part of any pressure system shall ensure that the pressure system or article shall be properly designed and properly constructed from suitable material, so as to prevent danger and to enable all necessary examinations for preventing danger to be carried out. Where the pressure system has any means of access to its interior, it must be so designed and constructed as to ensure, so far as practicable, that access can be gained without danger. The pressure system must be provided with such protective devices as may be necessary for preventing danger. Any such device designed to release contents must do so safely, so far as is practicable.

Regulation 5: Provision of Information and Marking

(1) Any person who designs for another any pressure system or any article which is intended to be a component part thereof or supplies (whether as manufacturer, importer or in any other capacity) any pressure system or any such article, shall provide sufficient written information concerning its design, construction, examination, operation and maintenance as may reasonably foreseeably be needed to enable the provisions of these Regulations to be complied with.

(2) The employer of a person who modifies or repairs any pressure system shall provide sufficient written information concerning the modification or repair as may reasonably foreseeably be needed to enable the provisions of these Regulations to be complied with.

(4) Any person who manufactures a pressure vessel shall ensure that before it is supplied by him the information specified in Schedule 3 is marked on the vessel, or on a plate attached to it, in a visible, legible and indelible form; and no person shall import a pressure vessel unless it is so marked.

(5) The mark or plate must not be falsified or removed.

Regulation 6: Installation

The employer of a person who installs a pressure system at work shall ensure that nothing about the way in which it is installed gives rise to danger or otherwise impairs the operation of any protective device or inspection facility.

Regulation 7: Safe Operating Limits

The user of an installed system and owner of a mobile system shall not operate the system or allow it to be operated unless he has established the safe operating limits of that system. The owner of a mobile system shall, if he is not also the user of it, supply the user with a written statement specifying the safe operating limits of that system or ensure that the system is legibly and durably marked with such safe operating limits and that the mark is clearly visible.

Regulation 8: Written Scheme of Examination

The user of an installed system and owner of a mobile system shall not operate the system or allow it to be operated unless he has a written scheme for the periodic examination, by a competent person, of all protective devices, every pressure vessel and pipeline in which a defect may give rise to danger, and those parts of the pipework in which a defect may give rise to danger. Any such parts must be identified in the scheme.

The user or owner must ensure that the scheme has been drawn up or certified as being suitable by a competent person and that the content of the scheme is reviewed at appropriate intervals by a competent person for the purpose of determining whether it is suitable in current conditions of use of the system. The content of the scheme must be modified in accordance with any recommendations made by the competent person arising out of the review.

No person shall draw up or certify a scheme of examination unless the scheme is suitable and specifies the nature and frequency of examination and any measures necessary to prepare the pressure system for safe examination other than those it would be reasonable to expect the user (in the case of an installed system) or owner (in the case of a mobile system) to take without specialist advice. Where appropriate the scheme must provide for an examination to be carried out before the pressure system is used for the first time.

Regulation 9: Examination in Accordance with the Written Scheme

The user of an installed system and the owner of a mobile system must ensure that those parts of the pressure system included in the scheme of examination are examined by a competent person within the intervals specified in the scheme and, where the scheme so provides, before the system is used for the first time. The user must also, before each examination, take all appropriate safety measures to prepare the system for examination.

Where a competent person has carried out an examination he must make a written report of the examination, sign it or add his name to it, date it and send it to the user or owner. The report must be sent as soon as is practicable after completing the examination and in any event to arrive within 28 days of the completion of the examination (or, in the case of integrated installed systems where the examination is part of a series, within 28 days of the completion of the last examination in that series).

Where the competent person is the user or owner the requirement to send the report to the user or owner shall not apply.

The required report must:

- state which parts of the pressure system have been examined, the condition of those parts and the results of the examination;
- specify any repairs or modifications to, or changes in the established safe operating limits of, the parts examined which, in the opinion of the competent person, are necessary to prevent danger or to ensure the continued effective working of the protective devices;
- specify the date by which any such repairs or modifications must be completed or any such changes to the safe operating limits must be made;
- specify the date within the limits set by the scheme of examination after which the pressure system may not be operated without a further examination under the scheme of examination; and
- state whether in the opinion of the competent person the scheme of examination is suitable (for the purpose of preventing danger from those parts of the pressure system included in it) or should be modified, and if the latter state the reasons.

The user of an installed system and the owner of a mobile system which has been examined under this regulation shall ensure that the system is not operated, and no person shall supply such a mobile system for operation, after the dates specified under the above paragraph (in each case). The dates may be postponed by written agreement where this does not give rise to danger and must be notified by the user or owner to the enforcing authority before the date specified in the report.

Where the competent person is the user or owner the reference to an agreement in writing shall not apply, but there shall be included in the notification a declaration that the postponement will not give rise to danger.

The owner of a mobile system shall ensure that the specified date is visibly, legibly and durably marked on the mobile system.

Regulation 10: Action in Case of Imminent Danger

If the competent person carrying out an examination is of the opinion that the pressure system or part of the pressure system will give rise to imminent danger unless certain repairs or modifications have been carried out or unless suitable changes to the operating conditions have been made, he shall forthwith make a written report to that effect identifying the system and specifying the repairs, modifications or changes concerned. The report must be given:

- in the case of an installed system, to the user;
- in the case of a mobile system, to the owner and to the user, if any,

and the competent person must within 14 days of the completion of the examination send a written report containing the same particulars to the enforcing authority for the premises at which the pressure system is situated.

Where the report is given to the user of a pressure system he must ensure that the system (or, if the report only affects a discrete part of the system, that part) is not operated. Where the report is given to the owner of a mobile system, he must take all reasonably practicable steps to ensure that the system (or, if the report only affects a discrete part of the system, that part) is not operated until the repairs, modifications or changes have been carried out or made.

Where the competent person is the user or owner the requirement to give the report to the user or owner shall not apply.

Regulation 11: Operation

The user of an installed system and the owner of a mobile system must provide for any person operating the system adequate and suitable instructions for the safe operation of the system and any necessary emergency action to be taken. The user of a pressure system must ensure that it is operated only in accordance with the instructions provided.

Regulation 12: Maintenance

The user of an installed system and the owner of a mobile system shall ensure that the system is properly maintained in good repair, so as to prevent danger.

Regulation 13: Modification and Repair

The employer of a person who modifies or repairs a pressure system at work shall ensure that nothing about the way in which it is modified or repaired gives rise to danger or otherwise impairs the operation of any protective device or inspection facility.

Regulation 14: Keeping of Records, etc.

The user of an installed system and the owner of a mobile system must keep the last competent person's report relating to the system and any previous reports if they contain information relevant to assessing whether:

- the system is safe to operate, or
- any repairs or modifications to the system can be safely carried out.

They must also keep:

- instructions specified in paragraph 30 of Schedule 2 to the **Pressure Equipment (Safety) Regulations 2016** and provided pursuant to regulation 14 or 24 of those Regulations; and
- any agreement made pursuant to regulation 9(7) and, in a case to which regulation 9(8) applies, a copy of the notification referred to in regulation 9(7)(c) until a further examination has been carried out since that agreement or notification under the scheme of examination.

Anything required to be kept by this regulation shall be kept:

- In the case of an installed system, at the premises where the system is installed, or at other premises approved for the purposes of this sub-paragraph by the enforcing authority responsible for enforcing these Regulations at the premises where the system is installed.
- In the case of a mobile system, at the premises in Great Britain from which the deployment of the system is controlled.
- In a case to which regulation 2(2) applies, by means whereby it is capable of being reproduced as required by regulation 2(2)(a) at the premises referred to or as appropriate.

Where the user or owner of a pressure system or part thereof changes, the previous user or owner shall as soon as is practicable give to the new user or owner in writing anything kept by him under this regulation.

Regulation 15: Precautions to Prevent Pressurisation of Certain Vessels

The user of a vessel to which this paragraph applies shall ensure that the outlet referred to below is at all times kept open and free from obstruction when the vessel is in use.

This applies to a vessel:

- which is constructed with a permanent outlet to the atmosphere or to a space where the pressure does not exceed atmospheric pressure;
- which could become a pressure vessel if that outlet were obstructed.

Regulation 16: Defence

In any proceedings for an offence for a contravention of any of the provisions of these Regulations it shall be a defence for the person charged to prove:

- that the commission of the offence was due to the act or default of another person not being one of his employees (hereinafter called "the other person"); and
- that he took all reasonable precautions and exercised all due diligence to avoid the commission of the offence.

The person charged cannot use the defence without the leave of the court unless, within seven clear days before the hearing to determine the mode of trial, he has served on the prosecutor a notice in writing giving such information identifying or assisting in the identification of the other person as was then in his possession.

Where a contravention of these Regulations by any person is due to the act or default of the other person, that other person shall be guilty of the offence which would, but for the above defence, be constituted by the act or default.

Regulation 17: Power to Grant Exemptions

The Executive may, by a certificate in writing, exempt any person or class of persons or any type or class of pressure system from the application of any of the requirements or prohibitions imposed by these Regulations, subject to conditions and to a limit of time. The exemption may be revoked by a certificate in writing at any time.

The Executive shall not grant an exemption unless, having regard to the conditions and requirements it proposes to attach to the exemption, it is satisfied that the health and safety of persons who are likely to be affected by the exemption will not be prejudiced in consequence of it.

Regulations 18 and 19 deal with repeals, revocations and transitional provisions. Schedule 1 deals with pressure systems which are exempted from all regulations.

Schedule 2 deals with modifications of duties in respect of leasing, hiring or other arrangements.

Schedule 3: Regulation 5(4) and (5), Marking of Pressure Vessels

The information referred to in regulation 5(4) is as follows:

- The manufacturer's name.
- A serial number to identify the vessel.
- The date of manufacture of the vessel.
- The standard to which the vessel was built.
- The maximum allowable pressure of the vessel.
- The minimum allowable pressure of the vessel where it is other than atmospheric.
- The design temperature.

PROHIBITION OF SMOKING IN CERTAIN PREMISES (SCOTLAND) REGULATIONS 2006 (SI 2006 NO. 90)

Reference to "the Act" means the **Smoking, Health and Social Care (Scotland) Act 2005**.

Regulation 2: Display of No-Smoking Notices

(1) At least one no-smoking notice displayed in no-smoking premises that are not a vehicle shall:

   (a) be a minimum size of 230mm by 160mm;

   (b) display the international 'no smoking' symbol, consisting of a graphic representation of a burning cigarette enclosed in a red circle with a red bar across it, at least 85mm in diameter; and

   (c) display the name of the person to whom a complaint may be made by any person who observes another person smoke in the no-smoking premises in question and state that a complaint may be so made.

(2) The remainder of no-smoking notices displayed in no-smoking premises that are not a vehicle and any no-smoking notices displayed on or near no-smoking premises that are not a vehicle shall display the international 'no smoking' symbol, consisting of a graphic representation of a burning cigarette enclosed in a red circle with a red bar across it, at least 85mm in diameter.

(3) A no-smoking notice displayed in no-smoking premises that are a vehicle shall:

   (a) display the international 'no smoking' symbol, consisting of a graphic representation of a burning cigarette enclosed in a red circle with a red bar across it; and

   (b) display the holder of a particular post to whom a complaint may be made by any person who observes another person smoke in the no-smoking premises in question and state that a complaint may be so made.

(4) A no-smoking notice shall be displayed by the person having the management or control of the no-smoking premises in such a manner that it is protected from tampering, damage, removal or concealment.

(5) The requirements in paragraphs (1) to (4) as to the manner of display, form and content of no-smoking notices are to be treated for the purposes of section 3(1) of the Act as if incorporated in it.

Regulation 3: "No-Smoking Premises"

(1) The premises or classes of premises prescribed under section 4(2) of the Act as being "no-smoking premises" for the purposes of Part 1 of the Act are the premises or classes of premises specified in Schedule 1 to these Regulations, being premises or classes of premises which are wholly or substantially enclosed.

(2) The premises or parts of premises or classes of premises or parts of premises prescribed under section 4(2) of the Act which are excluded from the definition of "no-smoking premises" are the premises or parts of premises or classes of premises or parts of premises specified in Schedule 2 to these Regulations.

(3) For the purposes of section 4(2) of the Act:

   (a) "premises" includes:

      (i) any building or part of a building;

      (ii) any structure or part of a structure, whether moveable or otherwise;

      (iii) any installation on land (including the foreshore and other land intermittently covered by water), any offshore installation, and any other installation (whether floating, or resting on the seabed or the subsoil thereof, or resting on other land covered with water or the subsoil thereof);

      (iv) any tent, marquee or stall; and

      (v) any vehicle;

   (b) "wholly enclosed" means:

      (i) for premises other than a vehicle or part of a vehicle, having a ceiling or roof and, except for doors, windows and passageways, wholly enclosed, whether permanently or temporarily; or

      (ii) for premises that are a vehicle, or part of a vehicle, having a top or roof and, except for doors, windows or exits, wholly enclosed, whether permanently or temporarily;

   (c) "substantially enclosed" means:

      (i) for premises other than a vehicle or part of a vehicle, having a ceiling or roof and, except for doors, windows and passageways, substantially enclosed, whether permanently or temporarily; or

      (ii) for premises that are a vehicle, or part of a vehicle, having a top or roof and, except for doors, windows or exits, substantially enclosed, whether permanently or temporarily;

and in determining whether premises are "substantially enclosed", no account is to be taken of openings in which there are doors, windows or other fittings that can be opened or shut;

(d) premises shall be taken to be "substantially enclosed" if:

    (i) the opening in the premises has an area, or

    (ii) if there is more than one, both or all those openings have an aggregate area,

which is less than half of the area of the walls, including any other structures serving the purpose of walls, which constitute the perimeter of the premises;

(e) where an opening is in, or consists of the absence of, such walls or other structures or a part of them, their area shall be measured for the purposes of paragraph (d) as if it included the area of the opening; and

(f) "has access" means has access whether on payment or otherwise, and whether as of right or by virtue of express or implied permission.

Regulations 4 and 5 relate to the imposition and payment of fixed penalties.

PROVISION AND USE OF WORK EQUIPMENT REGULATIONS 1998 (SI 1998 NO. 2306)

Amending Legislation

These Regulations were modified by the **Health and Safety (Miscellaneous Amendments) Regulations 2002**, the **Construction (Design and Management) Regulations 2007**, the **Supply of Machinery (Safety) Regulations 2008**, the **Health and Safety (Miscellaneous Repeals, Revocations and Amendments) Regulations 2013**, the **Construction Projects Regulations 2013**, the **Mines Regulations 2014**, the **Deregulation Act 2015** and the **Deregulation Act 2015 (Health and Safety at Work) (General Duties of Self-Employed Persons) (Consequential Amendments) Order 2015**.

There are also amendments of little consequence in the **Police (Health and Safety) Regulations 1999**, the **Pressure Equipment Regulations 1999**, and the **Noise Emission in the Environment by Equipment for Use Outdoors Regulations 2001**.

PUWER 98, in shorthand terms, has replaced the original **PUWER 1992** which was one of the original 'Six-pack'. It has also revoked a number of statutory instruments dealing with dangerous and unfenced machinery such as power presses, woodworking machinery and abrasive wheels.

The Regulations

The Regulations follow.

Definitions

Inspection	Such visual or rigorous inspection by a competent person as is appropriate for the purpose. The purpose is to identify whether the equipment can be operated, adjusted and maintained safely and that any deterioration, defect, or damage can be detected and remedied.
Thorough examination	A thorough examination by a competent person and includes testing, the nature and extent of which are appropriate for the purpose described.
Use	Any activity involving work equipment including starting, stopping, programming, setting, transporting, repairing, modifying, maintaining, servicing and cleaning.
Work equipment	Any machinery, appliance, apparatus, tool or installation for use at work. This is a very wide definition and according to the accompanying ACoP includes: • "Tool box tools"- hammers, knives, handsaws, meat cleavers, etc. • Single machines such as drilling machines, circular saws, photocopiers, combine harvesters, dumper trucks, etc. • Apparatus such as laboratory apparatus (Bunsen burners, etc.). • Lifting equipment such as hoists, lift trucks, elevating work platforms, lifting slings, etc. • Other equipment such as ladders, pressure water cleaners, etc. • An installation such as a series of machines connected together, e.g. a paper-making line or enclosure for providing sound insulation or scaffolding or similar access equipment.

Regulations 1 to 3

These deal with citation, interpretation and application.

Regulation 4: Suitability of Work Equipment

Under this regulation, the employer must ensure that work equipment is so constructed or adapted as to be suitable for the purpose for which it is used or provided. In selecting work equipment, he must have regard to the working conditions and to the risks to the health and safety of persons which exist in the premises or undertaking in which the work equipment is to be used and any additional risk posed by the use of the work equipment.

The employer must ensure that work equipment is used only for operations for which, and under conditions for which, it is suitable. This means suitable in any respect which it is reasonably foreseeable will affect the health or safety of any person.

Regulation 5: Maintenance

The employer must ensure that work equipment is maintained in an efficient state, in efficient working order, in good repair, and where any machinery has a maintenance log, the log is kept up to date.

Regulation 6: Inspection

The employer must ensure that, where the safety of work equipment depends on the installation conditions, it is inspected after installation and before being put into service for the first time, or after assembly at a new site or in a new location, to ensure that it has been installed correctly and is safe to operate.

The employer must ensure that work equipment exposed to conditions causing deterioration which is liable to result in dangerous situations is inspected to ensure that health and safety conditions are maintained and that any deterioration can be detected and remedied in good time. The inspections must take place:

- at suitable intervals;
- each time that exceptional circumstances which are liable to jeopardise the safety of the work equipment have occurred.

Every employer shall ensure that the result of an inspection made under this regulation is recorded and kept until the next inspection under this regulation is recorded.

Every employer shall ensure that no work equipment leaves his undertaking, or if obtained from the undertaking of another person, is used in his undertaking, unless it is accompanied by physical evidence that the last inspection required to be carried out under this regulation has been carried out.

This regulation does not apply to certain power presses and ancillary equipment, work equipment for lifting loads including persons, winding apparatus under the **Mines Regulations**, and work equipment required to be inspected by regulations 22(4) or 23(2) of the **Construction (Design and Management) Regulations 2015**, nor does it apply to work equipment to which regulation 12 of the **Work at Height Regulations 2005** applies.

Regulation 7: Specific Risks

Where a specific risk to health or safety is involved, the employer must ensure that the use of the work equipment is restricted to those persons given the task of using it. Any repairs, modifications, maintenance or servicing of the work equipment must be restricted to persons specifically designated to carry out such work. The employer must ensure that the persons so designated have received adequate training in repairing, modifying, maintaining and servicing work equipment.

Regulation 8: Information and Instructions

The employer must ensure that all persons who use work equipment have available to them adequate health and safety information and, where appropriate, written instructions pertaining to the use of the work equipment.

The employer must ensure that any of his employees who supervises or manages the use of work equipment has available to him adequate health and safety information and where appropriate, written instructions pertaining to the use of the work equipment.

The information and instructions must include information and, where appropriate, written instructions on:

- the conditions in which, and the methods by which, the work equipment may be used;
- foreseeable abnormal situations and the action to be taken if such a situation were to occur; and
- any conclusions to be drawn from experience in using the work equipment.

The information and instructions required must be readily comprehensible to those concerned.

Regulation 9: Training

The employer must ensure that all persons who use work equipment have received adequate training for purposes of health and safety, including training in the methods which may be adopted when using the work equipment, any risks which such may entail and precautions to be taken.

The employer must ensure that any of his employees who supervises or manages the use of work equipment has received adequate training for purposes of health and safety, including training in the methods which may be adopted when using the work equipment, any risks which such use may entail and any precautions to be taken.

Regulation 10: Conformity with Community Requirements

The employer must ensure that any item of work equipment conforms at all times with any essential requirements other than those which did not apply to work equipment of its type when it was first supplied or put into service.

For the purposes of this regulation, "essential requirements" means those requirements relating to the design and construction of work equipment in any of the instruments that give effect to Community directives concerning the safety of products.

Regulation 11: Dangerous Parts of Machinery

The employer must ensure that effective measures are taken to prevent access to any dangerous part of machinery or to any rotating stock-bar; or to stop the movement of any dangerous part of the machinery or rotating stock-bar before any part of a person enters a danger zone.

The measures required are:

- the provision of fixed guards enclosing every dangerous part or rotating stock-bar where and to the extent that it is practicable to do so, but where or to the extent that it is not, then,
- the provision of other guards or protection devices where and to the extent that it is practicable to do so, but where or to the extent that it is not, then,
- the provision of jigs, holders, push-sticks or similar protection appliances used in conjunction with the machinery where and to the extent that it is practicable to do so, but where or to the extent that it is not, then,
- the provision of information, instruction, training and supervision.

All guards and protection devices provided must:

- be suitable for the purpose for which they are provided;
- be of good construction, sound material and adequate strength;
- be maintained in an efficient state, in efficient working order and in good repair;
- not give rise to any increased risk to health or safety;
- not be easily bypassed or disabled;
- be situated at sufficient distance from the danger zone;
- not unduly restrict the view of the operating cycle of the machinery, where such a view is necessary;
- be so constructed or adapted that they allow operations necessary to fit or replace parts and for maintenance work, restricting access so that it is allowed only to the area where the work is to be carried out and, if possible, without having to dismantle the guard or protection device.

In this regulation, "Danger Zone" means any zone in or around machinery in which a person is exposed to a risk to health or safety from contact with a dangerous part of machinery or a rotating stock-bar.

"Stock-Bar" means any part of a stock-bar which projects beyond the head-stock of a lathe.

Regulation 12: Protection Against Specified Hazard

The employer must take measures to ensure that the exposure of a person using work equipment to any risk to his health or safety from certain hazards (see under) is either prevented or, where that is not reasonably practicable, adequately controlled.

The measures referred to must be measures other than the provision of personal protective equipment or of information, instruction, training and supervision, so far as is reasonably practicable. They must include, where appropriate, measures to minimise the effects of the hazard as well as to reduce the likelihood of the hazard occurring.

The hazards referred to above are:

- any article or substance falling or being ejected from work equipment;
- rupture or disintegration of parts of work equipment;
- work equipment catching fire or overheating;
- the unintended or premature discharge of any article or of any gas, dust, liquid, vapour or other substance which, in each case, is produced, used or stored in the work equipment;
- the unintended or premature explosion of the work equipment or any article or substance produced, used or stored in it.

For the purposes of this regulation, "adequately" means adequately having regard only to the nature of the hazard and the nature and degree of exposure to the risk.

This regulation does not apply where certain Regulations already require measures to be taken to prevent or control such risk, namely:

- the **Ionising Radiations Regulations 1999**;
- the **Control of Asbestos Regulations 2012**;
- the **Control of Substances Hazardous to Health Regulations 2002**;
- the **Control of Noise at Work Regulations 2005**;
- the **Control of Lead at Work Regulations 2002**;
- the **Control of Vibration at Work Regulations 2005**.

Regulation 13: High or Very Low Temperature

The employer must ensure that work equipment, parts of work equipment and any article or substance produced, used or stored in work equipment which, in each case, is at a high or very low temperature must have protection where appropriate so as to prevent injury to any person by burn, scald or sear.

Regulation 14: Controls for Starting or Making a Significant Change in Operating Conditions

The employer must ensure that, where appropriate, work equipment is provided with one or more controls for the purposes of starting the work equipment (including re-starting after a stoppage for any reason); or controlling any change in the speed, pressure or other operating conditions of the work equipment where such conditions after the change result in risk to health and safety which is greater than or of a different nature from such risks before the change.

The employer must ensure that, where a control is required, it shall not be possible to perform any of the above operations except by a deliberate action on such control.

This does not apply to re-starting or changing operating conditions as a result of the normal operating cycle of an automatic device.

Regulation 15: Stop Controls

The employer must ensure that, where appropriate, work equipment is provided with one or more readily accessible controls, the operation of which will bring the work equipment to a safe condition in a safe manner. Such controls must bring the work equipment to a complete stop where necessary for reasons of health and safety. Controls must also switch off all sources of energy after stopping the functioning of the work equipment and must operate in priority to any control that starts or changes the operating conditions of the work equipment.

Regulation 16: Emergency Stop Controls

The employer must ensure that, where appropriate, work equipment is provided with one or more readily accessible emergency stop controls unless it is not necessary by reason of the nature of the hazards and the time taken for the work equipment to come to a complete stop as a result of the action of any stop control.

Regulation 17: Controls

The employer must ensure that all controls for work equipment are clearly visible and identifiable by appropriate marking where necessary.

Except where necessary, the employer must ensure that no control for work equipment is in a position where any person operating the control is exposed to a risk to his health or safety.

The employer must ensure where appropriate:

- that, so far as is reasonably practicable, the operator of any control is able to ensure from the position of that control that no person is in a place where he would be exposed to a risk to his health or safety as a result of the operation of that control, but where or to the extent that it is not reasonably practicable,
- that, so far as is reasonably practicable, systems of work are effective to ensure that, when work equipment is about to start, no person is in a place where he would be exposed to a risk to his health or safety as a result of the work equipment starting, but where neither of these is reasonably practicable,
- that an audible, visible or other suitable warning is given whenever work equipment is about to start.

Every employer shall take appropriate measures to ensure that any person who is in a place where he would be exposed to a risk to his health or safety as a result of the starting or stopping of work equipment has sufficient time and suitable means to avoid that risk.

Regulation 18: Control Systems

The employer must ensure, so far as is reasonably practicable, that all control systems of work equipment are safe; and are chosen making due allowance for the failures, faults and constraints to be expected in the planned circumstances of use.

A control system will not be safe unless:

- its operation does not create any increased risk to health and safety;
- it ensures, so far as is reasonably practicable, that any fault in, or damage to, any part of the control system or the loss of supply of any source of energy cannot result in additional or increased risk to health and safety;
- it does not impede the operation of any control required by regulations 15 or 16.

Regulation 19: Isolation from Sources of Energy

The employer must ensure that where appropriate work equipment is provided with suitable means to isolate it from all its sources of energy. Those means shall not be suitable unless they are clearly identifiable and readily accessible.

The employer must take appropriate measures to ensure that re-connection of any energy source to work equipment does not expose any person using the work equipment to any risk to his health or safety.

Regulation 20: Stability

The employer must ensure that work equipment or any part of work equipment is stabilised by clamping or otherwise where necessary for purposes of health or safety.

Regulation 21: Lighting

The employer must ensure that suitable and sufficient lighting, which takes account of the operations to be carried out, is provided at any place where a person uses work equipment.

Regulation 22: Maintenance Operations

The employer must take appropriate measures to ensure that work equipment is so constructed or adapted that, so far as is reasonably practicable, maintenance operations which involve a risk to health or safety can be carried out while the work equipment is shut down, or in other cases:

- maintenance operations can be carried out without exposing the person carrying them out to risk to his health or safety; or
- appropriate measures can be taken for the protection of any person carrying out maintenance operations which involve a risk to his health or safety.

Regulation 23: Markings

The employer must ensure that work equipment is marked in a clearly visible manner with any marking appropriate for reasons of health and safety, e.g. safe working load, stop and start controls, colour marking of gas cylinders, colour coding of pipes for services, etc.

Regulation 24: Warnings

The employer must ensure that work equipment incorporates any warnings or warning devices which are appropriate for reasons of health and safety. Such warnings shall not be appropriate unless they are unambiguous, easily perceived and easily understood, e.g. Hard hats must be worn, Do not heat above 60°C, etc. This also includes audible warnings.

Regulation 25: Employees Carried on Mobile Work Equipment

The employer must ensure that no employee is carried by mobile work equipment unless:

- it is suitable for carrying persons; and
- it incorporates features for reducing, to as low as is reasonably practicable, risks to their safety, including risks from wheels or tracks.

Regulation 26: Rolling Over of Mobile Work Equipment

The employer must ensure that where there is a risk to an employee riding on mobile work equipment from its rolling over, it is minimised by:

- stabilising the work equipment;
- a structure which ensures that the work equipment does no more than fall on its side;
- a structure giving sufficient clearance to anyone being carried if it overturns further than that; or
- a device giving comparable protection.

Where there is a risk of anyone being carried by mobile work equipment being crushed by its rolling over, the employer shall ensure that it has a suitable restraining system for him. Compliance with this regulation is not required where:

- it would increase the overall risk to safety;
- it would not be reasonably practicable to operate the mobile work equipment in consequence; or
- in relation to an item of work equipment provided for use in the undertaking or establishment before 5 December 1998 it would not be reasonably practicable.

Regulation 27: Overturning of Forklift Trucks

The employer must ensure that a forklift truck to which regulation 26(3) refers (one which can overturn 180° and which carries an employee), is adapted or equipped to reduce to as low as is reasonably practicable the risk to safety from its overturning.

Regulation 28: Self-Propelled Work Equipment

The employer must ensure that, where self-propelled work equipment may, while in motion, involve risk to the safety of persons:

- it has facilities for preventing its being started by an unauthorised person;
- it has appropriate facilities for minimising the consequences of a collision where there is more than one item of rail-mounted work equipment in motion at the same time;
- it has a device for braking and stopping;
- where safety constraints so require, emergency facilities operated by readily accessible controls or automatic systems are available for braking and stopping the work equipment in the event of failure of the main facility;
- where the driver's direct field of vision is inadequate to ensure safety, there are adequate devices for improving his vision so far as is reasonably practicable;
- if provided for use at night or in dark places:
    - it is equipped with lighting appropriate to the work to be carried out, and
    - is otherwise sufficiently safe for such use;
- if it, or anything carried or towed by it, constitutes a fire hazard and is liable to endanger employees, it carries appropriate fire-fighting equipment, unless such equipment is kept sufficiently close to it.

Regulation 29: Remote-Controlled, Self-Propelled Work Equipment

The employer must ensure that where remote-controlled self-propelled work equipment involves a risk to safety while in motion:

- it stops automatically once it leaves its control range; and
- where the risk is of crushing or impact it incorporates features to guard against such risk unless other appropriate devices are able to do so.

Regulation 30: Drive Shafts

Where the seizure of the drive shaft between mobile work equipment and its accessories or anything towed is likely to involve a risk to safety, the employer must ensure that the work equipment has a means of preventing such seizure. Where this cannot be avoided, every possible measure must be taken to avoid an adverse effect on the safety of an employee.

Where mobile work equipment has a shaft for the transmission of energy between it and other mobile work equipment which could become soiled or damaged by contact with the ground while uncoupled, the employer must ensure that there is a system for safeguarding the shaft.

Regulation 31: Power Presses to which Part IV Does Not Apply

This regulation states that regulations 32 to 35 shall not apply to a power press of a kind which is described in Schedule 2.

The **PUWER Regulations** revoked the **Power Presses Regulations 1965 and 1972** but they were then re-enacted by the following regulations 32 to 36 and Schedules 2 and 3.

First of all another definition:

"Power press" means a press or press brake for the working of metal by means of tools, or for die proving, which is power driven and which embodies a flywheel and clutch.

Regulation 32: Thorough Examination of Power Presses, Guards and Protection Devices

(1) Every employer shall ensure that a power press is not put into service for the first time after installation or after assembly at a new site or in a new location unless:

 (a) it has been thoroughly examined to ensure that it:

  (i) has been installed correctly; and

  (ii) would be safe to operate; and

 (b) any defect has been remedied.

(2) Every employer shall ensure that a guard, other than one to which paragraph (3) relates, or protection device is not put into service for the first time on a power press unless:

 (a) it has been thoroughly examined when in position on that power press to ensure that it is effective for its purpose; and

 (b) any defect has been remedied.

(3) Every employer shall ensure that that part of a closed tool which acts as a fixed guard is not used on a power press unless:

 (a) it has been thoroughly examined when in position on any power press in the premises to ensure that it is effective for its purpose; and

 (b) any defect has been remedied.

(4) For the purpose of ensuring that health and safety conditions are maintained, and that any deterioration can be detected and remedied in good time, every employer shall ensure that:

 (a) every power press is thoroughly examined, and its guards and protection devices are thoroughly examined when in position on that power press:

  (i) at least every 12 months, where it has fixed guards only; or

  (ii) at least every 6 months, in other cases;

  (iii) each time that exceptional circumstances have occurred which are liable to jeopardise the safety of the power press or its guards or protection devices; and

 (b) any defect is remedied before the power press is used again.

(5) Where a power press, guard or protection device was before the coming into force of these Regulations required to be thoroughly examined by regulation 5(2) of the Power Presses Regulations 1965 the first thorough examination under paragraph (4) shall be made before the date by which a thorough examination would have been required by regulation 5(2) had it remained in force.

(6) Paragraph (4) shall not apply to that part of a closed tool which acts as a fixed guard.

(7) In this regulation "defect" means a defect notified under regulation 34 other than a defect which has not yet become a danger to persons.

Regulation 33: Inspection of Guards and Protection Devices

The following duties are placed on the employer:

(1) Every employer shall ensure that a power press is not used after the setting, re-setting or adjustment of its tools, save in trying out its tools or save in die proving, unless:

- its every guard and protection device has been inspected and tested while in position on the power press by a person appointed in writing by the employer who is:
  - competent; or
  - undergoing training for that purpose and acting under the immediate supervision of a competent person, and who has signed a certificate which complies with paragraph (3); or
- the guards and protection devices have not been altered or disturbed in the course of the adjustment of its tools.

(2) Every employer shall ensure that a power press is not used after the expiration of the fourth hour of a working period unless its every guard and protection device has been inspected and tested while in position on the power press by a person appointed in writing by the employer who is:

- competent; or
- undergoing training for that purpose and acting under the immediate supervision of a competent person, and who has signed a certificate which complies with paragraph (3).

(3) A certificate referred to in this regulation shall:

- contain sufficient particulars to identify every guard and protection device inspected and tested and the power press on which it was positioned at the time of the inspection and test;
- state the date and time of the inspection and test, and
- state that every guard and protection device on the power press is in position and effective for its purpose.

(4) In this regulation "working period', in relation to a power press, means:

- the period in which the day's or night's work is done; or
- in premises where a shift system is in operation, a shift.

Regulation 34: Reports

This deals with making reports and notification:

(1) A person making a thorough examination for an employer under regulation 32 shall:

(a) notify the employer forthwith of any defect in a power press or its guard or protection device which in his opinion is or could become a danger to persons;

(b) as soon as is practicable make a report of the thorough examination to the employer in writing authenticated by him or on his behalf by signature or equally secure means and containing the information specified in Schedule 3; and

(c) where there is in his opinion a defect in a power press or its guard or protection device which is or could become a danger to persons, send a copy of the report as soon as is practicable to the enforcing authority for the premises in which the power press is situated.

(2) A person making an inspection and test for an employer under regulation 33 shall forthwith notify the employer of any defect in a guard or protection device which in his opinion is or could become a danger to persons and the reason for his opinion.

Regulation 35: Keeping of Information

(1) Every employer shall ensure that the information in every report made pursuant to regulation 34(1) is kept available for inspection for two years after it is made.

(2) Every employer shall ensure that a certificate under regulation 33 is kept available for inspection at or near the power press to which it relates:

- until superseded by a later certificate; and
- after that, until six months have passed since it was signed.

Regulation 36: Exemption for the Armed Forces

The Secretary of State for Defence may, in the interests of national security, by a certificate in writing exempt any of the home forces, any visiting force or any headquarters from any requirement or prohibition imposed by these Regulations and any such exemption may be granted subject to conditions and to a limit of time and may be revoked by the said Secretary of State by a certificate in writing at any time.

Schedule 2

Power presses to which regulations 32 to 35 do not apply:

- A power press for the working of hot metal.
- A power press not capable of a stroke greater than 6 millimetres.
- A guillotine.
- A combination punching and shearing machine, turret punch press or similar machine for punching, shearing or cropping.
- A machine, other than a press brake, for bending steel sections.
- A straightening machine.
- An upsetting machine.
- A heading machine.
- A riveting machine.
- An eyeleting machine.
- A press-stud attaching machine.
- A zip fastener bottom stop attaching machine.
- A stapling machine.
- A wire stitching machine.
- A power press for the compacting of metal powders.

Schedule 3

Information to be contained in a report of a thorough examination of a power press, guard or protection device:

1. The name of the employer for whom the thorough examination was made.
2. The address of the premises at which the thorough examination was made.
3. In relation to each item examined:
   - that it is a power press, interlocking guard, fixed guard or other type of guard or protection device;
   - where known its make, type and year of manufacture;
   - the identifying mark of:
     - the manufacture;
     - the employer.
4. In relation to the first thorough examination of a power press after installation or after assembly at a new site or in a new location:
   - that it is such thorough examination;
   - either that it has been installed correctly and would be safe to operate or the respects in which it has not been installed correctly or would not be safe to operate;
   - identification of any part found to have a defect, and a description of the defect.
5. In relation to a thorough examination of a power press other than one to which paragraph 4 relates:
   - that it is such other thorough examination;
   - either that the power press would be safe to operate or the respects in which it would not be safe to operate;
   - identification of any part found to have a defect which is or could become a danger to persons, and a description of the defect.
6. In relation to a thorough examination of a guard or protection device:
   - either that it is effective for its purpose or the respects in which it is not effective for its purpose;
   - identification of any part found to have a defect which is or could become a danger to persons, and a description of the defect.
7. Any repair, renewal or alteration required to remedy a defect found to be a danger to persons.

8. In the case of a defect which is not yet but could become a danger to persons:
    - the time by which it could become such danger;
    - any repair, renewal or alteration required to remedy it.
9. Any other defect which requires remedy.
10. Any repair, renewal or alteration referred to in paragraph 7 which has already been effected.
11. The date on which any defect referred to in paragraph 8 was notified to the employer under regulation 34(1)(a).
12. The qualification and address of the person making the report; that he is self-employed or if employed, the name and address of his employer.
13. The date of the thorough examination.
14. The date of the report.
15. The name of the person making the report and where different the name of the person signing or otherwise authenticating it.

PUBLIC INTEREST DISCLOSURE ACT 1998

Introduction

This Act is designed to protect individuals who make certain disclosures of information in the public interest and to allow them to bring action in respect of victimisation. The sections of the Act given below are to be inserted into the relevant sections of the **Employment Rights Act 1996**.

Section 1: Protected Disclosures

The meaning of the term "Protected Disclosure" is given at section 1 of the **Public Interest Disclosure Act**. It is to be inserted after Part IV of the **Employment Rights Act 1996** ("the 1996 Act") as follows:

"Part IVA - Protected Disclosures

Section 43A: Meaning of "Protected Disclosure"

In this Act a "protected disclosure" means a qualifying disclosure as defined by the following section 43B which is made by a worker in accordance with any of sections 43C to 43H.

Section 43B: Disclosures Qualifying for Protection

(1) In this Part a "qualifying disclosure" means any disclosure of information which, in the reasonable belief of the worker making the disclosure, tends to show one or more of the following:

   (a) *a criminal offence has been committed, is being committed or is likely to be committed;*

   (b) *a person has failed, is failing or is likely to fail to comply with any legal obligation to which he is subject;*

   (c) *a miscarriage of justice has occurred, is occurring or is likely to occur;*

   (d) *the health or safety of any individual has been, is being or is likely to be endangered;*

   (e) *the environment has been, is being or is likely to be damaged; or*

   (f) *information tending to show any matter falling within any one of the preceding paragraphs has been, or is likely to be deliberately concealed.*

It is immaterial whether the relevant failure occurred, occurs or would occur in the United Kingdom or elsewhere, and whether the law applying to it is that of the United Kingdom or of any other country or territory.

A disclosure of information is not a qualifying disclosure if the person making it commits an offence in the process.

A disclosure of information in respect of which a claim to legal professional privilege could be maintained in legal proceedings is not a qualifying disclosure when made by a person to whom the information had been disclosed in the course of obtaining legal advice.

Section 43C: Disclosure to Employer or Other Responsible Person

A qualifying disclosure is made if the worker makes the disclosure in good faith:

- to his employer, or
- where the worker reasonably believes that the relevant failure relates solely or mainly to the conduct of a person other than his employer, or any other matter for which a person other than his employer has legal responsibility, to that other person.

A worker who, in accordance with an employer's authorised procedure, makes a qualifying disclosure to a person other than his employer, is to be treated for the purposes of this Part as making the qualifying disclosure to his employer.

Section 43D: Disclosure to Legal Adviser

A qualifying disclosure is made in accordance with this section if it is made in the course of obtaining legal advice.

Section 43E: Disclosure to Minister of the Crown

A qualifying disclosure is made in accordance with this section if:

- the worker's employer is an individual appointed under any enactment by a Minister of the Crown, or a body any of whose members are so appointed, and
- the disclosure is made in good faith to a Minister of the Crown.

Section 43F: Disclosure to Prescribed Person

A qualifying disclosure is made in accordance with this section if the worker:

- makes the disclosure in good faith to a person prescribed by an order made by the Secretary of State for the purposes of this section, and
- reasonably believes that the relevant failure falls within any description of matters in respect of which that person is so prescribed, and that the information disclosed, and any allegation contained in it, are substantially true.

An order prescribing persons for the purposes of this section may specify persons or descriptions of persons, and shall specify the descriptions of matters in respect of which each person, or persons of each description, is or are prescribed.

Section 43G: Disclosure in Other Cases

A qualifying disclosure is made in accordance with this section if:

- the worker makes the disclosure in good faith;
- he reasonably believes that the information disclosed, and any allegation contained in it, are substantially true;
- he does not make the disclosure for purposes of personal gain;
- any of the conditions in the following subsection is met; and
- in all the circumstances of the case, it is reasonable for him to make the disclosure.

The conditions referred to above are:

- that, at the time he makes the disclosure, the worker reasonably believes that he will be subjected to a detriment by his employer if he makes a disclosure to him or in accordance with section 43F;
- that, in a case where no person is prescribed for the purposes of section 43F in relation to the relevant failure, the worker reasonably believes that it is likely that evidence relating to the relevant failure will be concealed or destroyed if he makes a disclosure to his employer; or
- that the worker has previously made a disclosure of substantially the same information to his employer, or in accordance with section 43F.

In deciding whether it is reasonable for the worker to make the disclosure, regard must be given to:

- the identity of the person to whom the disclosure is made;
- the seriousness of the relevant failure;
- whether the relevant failure is continuing or is likely to occur in the future;
- whether the disclosure is made in breach of a duty of confidentiality owed by the employer to any other person;
- any action which the employer or the person to whom the previous disclosure in accordance with section 43F was made has taken or might reasonably be expected to have taken as a result of the previous disclosure; and
- whether in making the disclosure to the employer the worker complied with any procedure whose use by him was authorised by the employer.

For the purposes of this section, a subsequent disclosure may be regarded as a disclosure of substantially the same information as that disclosed by a previous disclosure even though the subsequent disclosure extends to information about action taken or not taken by any person as a result of the previous disclosure.

Section 43H: Disclosure of Exceptionally Serious Failure

A qualifying disclosure is made in accordance with this section if:

- the worker makes the disclosure in good faith;
- he reasonably believes that the information disclosed, and any allegation contained in it, are substantially true;
- he does not make the disclosure for purposes of personal gain;
- the relevant failure is of an exceptionally serious nature; and
- in all the circumstances of the case, it is reasonable for him to make the disclosure.

In determining whether it is reasonable for the worker to make the disclosure, regard shall be had, in particular, to the identity of the person to whom the disclosure is made.

Section 43J: Contractual Duties of Confidentiality

Any provision in an agreement to which this section applies is void in so far as it purports to preclude the worker from making a protected disclosure.

This section applies to any agreement between a worker and his employer (whether a worker's contract or not), including an agreement to refrain from instituting or continuing any proceedings under this Act or any proceedings for breach of contract."

Section 2: Right Not to Suffer Detriment

After section 47A of the 1996 Act there is inserted:

"47B Protected disclosures

(1) *A worker has the right not to be subjected to any detriment by any act, or any deliberate failure to act, by his employer done on the ground that the worker has made a protected disclosure.*

(2) *Except where the worker is an employee who is dismissed in circumstances in which, by virtue of section 197, Part X does not apply to the dismissal, this section does not apply where:*

   (a) *the worker is an employee, and*

   (b) *the detriment in question amounts to dismissal (within the meaning of that Part).*

(3) *For the purposes of this section, and of sections 48 and 49 so far as relating to this section, 'worker', 'worker's contract', 'employment' and 'employer' have the extended meaning given by section 43K."*

Section 3: Complaints to Employment Tribunal

In section 48 of the 1996 Act (Complaints to employment tribunals) after subsection (1) there is inserted:

"(1A) A worker may present a complaint to an employment tribunal that he has been subjected to a detriment in contravention of section 47B."

Section 5: Unfair Dismissal

After section 103 of the 1996 Act there is inserted:

"103A Protected disclosure

An employee who is dismissed shall be regarded for the purposes of this Part as unfairly dismissed if the reason (or, if more than one, the principal reason) for the dismissal is that the employee made a protected disclosure."

PUBLIC ORDER ACT 1986

This Act is relevant in respect of work-related violence or harassment. It defines offences such as "riot", "violent disorder" and "affray". However, only sections 4 and 5 are directly relevant to work-related violence or harassment. Only key extracts from these sections have been given; you should refer to the Act itself for the complete provisions.

Section 4: Fear or Provocation of Violence

(1) A person is guilty of an offence if he:

    (a) uses towards another person threatening, abusive or insulting words or behaviour, or

    (b) distributes or displays to another person any writing, sign or other visible representation which is threatening, abusive or insulting,

with intent to cause that person to believe that immediate unlawful violence will be used against him or another by any person, or to provoke the immediate use of unlawful violence by that person or another, or whereby that person is likely to believe that such violence will be used or it is likely that such violence will be provoked.

Section 4A: Intentional Harassment, Alarm or Distress

(1) A person is guilty of an offence if, with intent to cause a person harassment, alarm or distress, he:

    (a) uses threatening, abusive or insulting words or behaviour, or disorderly behaviour, or

    (b) displays any writing, sign or other visible representation which is threatening, abusive or insulting, thereby causing that or another person harassment, alarm or distress.

Section 5: Harassment, Alarm or Distress

(1) A person is guilty of an offence if he:

    (a) uses threatening or abusive words or behaviour, or disorderly behaviour, or

    (b) displays any writing, sign or other visible representation which is threatening or abusive,

within the hearing or sight of a person likely to be caused harassment, alarm or distress thereby.

Offences under sections 4, 4A and 5 may be committed in a public or a private place, except that no offence is committed where the words or behaviour are used, or the writing, sign or other visible representation is displayed, by a person inside a dwelling and the other person is also inside that or another dwelling.

REGULATORY REFORM (FIRE SAFETY) ORDER 2005 (RRFSO) (SI 2005 NO. 1541)

The **Regulatory Reform (Fire Safety) Order 2005 (RRFSO)** was approved by Parliament in June 2005 and was due to come into force on 1 April 2006, but was actually delayed until 1 October 2006 to give businesses more time to prepare. The legislation applies to England and Wales only. The equivalent legislation in Scotland is the **Fire (Scotland) Act 2005** (Part 3) and the Regulations made under the Act, the **Fire Safety (Scotland) Regulations 2006**. Northern Ireland also has separate legislation.

The **RRFSO** replaces and consolidates a good deal of previous legislation. On introduction of the **RRFSO** the **Fire Precautions Act 1971** was repealed and the **Fire Precautions (Workplace) Regulations 1997** were revoked, although many of the duties, including the requirement for fire risk assessment, were carried forward to the **RRFSO**.

The **RRFSO** simplified and reformed much of the previous legislation relating to fire safety in non-domestic premises, and placed a greater emphasis on fire prevention. The Order introduces significant changes in practice and affects both employers and fire authorities.

In essence, responsibility for fire safety inspection and risk assessment has passed from the fire service to the individual employer or responsible person (or persons), who must comply with the Order. There is a greater emphasis on fire prevention in all non-domestic premises, including the voluntary sector and self-employed people with premises separate from their homes.

One of the most significant changes brought about by the introduction of the new legislation was the abolition of fire certification; fire certificates no longer have legal status. This represented a clear shift in responsibility for fire safety in the workplace away from the Fire and Rescue Services and onto employers and other persons in control of premises.

The duties that have been imposed on persons in control of premises as a result of, and in support of, this change include:

- The general duty to ensure, so far as is reasonably practicable, the safety of employees.
- The general duty in relation to non-employees to make such fire precautions as may reasonably be required in the circumstances to ensure that premises are safe.
- The duty to carry out a fire risk assessment.

Although this does involve a major shift of responsibility, the previous **Fire Precautions (Workplace) Regulations** already provided for a risk assessment-based approach to fire safety in virtually all workplaces; and in premises where people are not employed to work, under existing health and safety legislation there are already duties of care which require safety risks to be assessed, including the assessment of risk from fire. Hence the operator or owner of premises should already be carrying out risk assessments, which include fire risks.

The Order makes a distinction between "general" fire precautions as required under the Order and "special" precautions which are necessary directly in connection with an industrial process and which fall under the scope of health and safety. The Order only covers general fire precautions and other fire safety duties which are necessary to protect relevant persons in case of fire in and around most premises. The Order requires fire precautions to be put in place where necessary and to the extent that it is reasonable and practicable in the circumstances of the case.

Responsibility for complying with the **RRFSO** rests with the responsible person, i.e. the employer in a workplace and any other person who may have control of any part of the premises, e.g. the occupier or owner. In all other premises the person or people in control of the premises will be responsible. If there is more than one responsible person in any type of premises, all must take all reasonable steps to work with each other. The responsible person(s) must be identified.

Key requirements that must be addressed by all "responsible persons" include:

- The provision of general fire precautions to reduce the risk of fire and the risk of spread of fire (Article 8).
- A suitable and sufficient fire risk assessment that addresses the risk of fire, and the risk of spread of fire, must be conducted. One must pay particular attention to those at special risk such as the disabled, and must include consideration of any dangerous substances likely to be on the premises. The fire risk assessment is intended to identify risks which can be eliminated or reduced and to decide the nature and extent of the general fire precautions required to protect people against the remaining fire risks. All significant findings must be recorded where five or more persons are employed (Article 9).
- Principles of prevention (Article 10)- when implementing any preventive and protective measures the following principles should be adopted:
    - Avoid risk.
    - Evaluate risks which cannot be avoided.

- Combat risks at source.
- Adapt to technical progress.
- Replace the dangerous by the non-, or less, dangerous.
- Develop an overall prevention policy.
- Give priority to collective protective measures.
- Provide appropriate instruction for employees.

- The provision of fire safety arrangements (Article 11) - appropriate arrangements for the planning, organisation, control, monitoring and review of all fire safety arrangements must be developed and implemented.
- Elimination or reduction of risks from dangerous substances (Article 12) - to ensure that risks are either eliminated, or reduced so far as is reasonably practicable.
- Fire-fighting and fire detection (Article 13) - to ensure that, where necessary, appropriate equipment for detecting fire, raising the alarm and fighting fire is provided.
- Emergency routes and exits (Article 14) - to ensure, where necessary, that:
  - Emergency routes and exits are kept clear at all times.
  - Emergency routes lead directly to a place of safety.
  - The number, distribution and dimensions of emergency routes and exits are adequate.
  - Emergency doors open in the direction of escape, and can be opened easily by anyone in the event of an emergency.
  - Emergency routes and exits are indicated by appropriate signs.
  - Emergency routes and exits are provided with adequate emergency lighting.
- Establish procedures for serious and imminent danger, and nominate a sufficient number of competent people to help evacuate everyone from the premises (Article 15). Article 16 deals with additional emergency measures in respect of dangerous substances.
- Maintenance (Article 17) - to ensure that the premises and any facilities or fire-safety equipment, etc. are adequately maintained, in efficient working order and good repair. All precautions provided must be subject to maintenance and must be installed and maintained by a competent person, who again must be identified. The precautions to be maintained include those provided for the use of the fire service in the event of fire, e.g. dry risers, etc.
- The provision of safety assistance (Article 18) - by the appointment of one or more competent persons to assist in the implementation of the fire safety arrangements. Where an employer recognises that he may not have sufficient expertise to assess the risk in his premises, the fire service may be approached to provide suitable training. A contentious point at present is that the fire authorities have a duty to provide fire safety advice to employers, but under the **RRFSO** they will be enforcing risk management in the same business in which they sell advice or training.
- Articles 19 and 20 cover the provision of information to employees, and the employers of any other persons working on the premises, with regard to the fire risks, the preventive and protective measures in force, and the emergency procedures.
- Provision of training to employees on precautions and actions to be taken in order to safeguard themselves and others. Training to be given when first employed and also when exposed to new or increased risk. Refresher training at suitable intervals (Article 21).
- Co-operation and Co-ordination (Article 22). Where two or more responsible persons share, or have duties in respect of, premises they must take reasonable measures to:
  - Co-operate, as far as is necessary, to enable compliance with the requirements of the **RRFSO**.
  - Co-ordinate the preventive and protective measures they take.
  - Inform the other responsible persons of the risks to relevant persons arising out of, or in connection with, their work activities.
- General duties of employees at work are set out in Article 23. These include:
  - the duty to take reasonable care of himself and others who might be affected by his acts or omissions;
  - to co-operate with the employer to enable compliance with duties on the employer;
  - to inform the employer or employer's representative of work situations that pose a serious and immediate danger to safety; and
  - to inform the employer of shortcomings in fire safety arrangements.
- Article 24 gives the Secretary of State the power to make Regulations about fire precautions.

- The enforcing authorities for the **RRFSO** are listed in Article 25. They are:
  - The Fire and Rescue Authority - for the majority of workplaces and premises.
  - The Health and Safety Executive:
    - For ships, whilst under construction or repair.
    - For construction sites.
  - The Local Authority - for sports grounds, large sports stadia and stands at sports grounds.
  - The Office for Nuclear Regulation for nuclear licensed sites.
  - The fire service maintained by the Secretary of State for Defence in relation to premises occupied solely for the purposes of the armed forces, visiting forces, international headquarters or defence organizations.
  - A fire inspector or any person authorised by the Secretary of State to act for the purposes of this Order in relation to some premises owned or occupied by the Crown or premises in relation to which the UK Atomic Energy Authority is the responsible person.
- Article 27 provides for powers of inspectors. These powers include:
  - To enter and inspect premises.
  - To make enquiries to ascertain whether the requirements of the **RRFSO** have been complied with and to identify the responsible person.
  - To require the production of records (including plans) that are required to be kept by the **RRFSO** or which it is necessary for the inspector to see.
  - To inspect and take copies of records.
  - To require necessary facilities and assistance.
  - To take samples of articles or substances for the purpose of ascertaining their fire resistance or flammability.
  - To cause articles or substances that appear to the inspector to have caused or be likely to cause danger to be dismantled or subjected to any process or test.
- Article 29: Alterations Notices - the enforcing authority may serve on the responsible person an 'alterations notice' if they are of the opinion that the premises constitute a serious risk to relevant persons, or may constitute such a risk if a change is made to them or to the use to which they are put. Where such a notice has been served, the responsible person must, before making the changes, notify the enforcing authority.
- Article 30: Enforcement Notices - if the enforcing authority is of the opinion that the responsible person or others have failed to comply with any provision of the **RRFSO** or regulations made under it, the authority may serve an 'enforcement notice'. This type of notice may include directions as to the measures that the enforcing authority considers are necessary to remedy the failure. The enforcing authority must carry out consultation before serving a notice that would oblige a person to make alterations to premises.
- Article 31: Prohibition Notices - if the enforcing authority is of the opinion that use of premises involves or will involve a risk to relevant persons so serious that the use of the premises ought to be prohibited or restricted, the authority may serve a 'prohibition notice'. This type of notice may include directions as to the measures which will have to be taken to remedy the matters specified in the notice.
- Prohibitions or restrictions take effect immediately the notice is served if the authority is of the opinion that the risk of personal injury is or will be imminent. In other cases, the notice takes effect at the end of the period specified in the notice.
- Article 32 sets out the offences under the Order. Article 33 provides for the defence that a person took all reasonable steps and exercised all due diligence to avoid commission of the offence.
- Article 34 states that "*In any proceedings for an offence under this Order consisting of a failure to comply with a duty or requirement so far as is practicable or so far as is reasonably practicable, it is for the accused to prove that it was not practicable or reasonably practicable to do more than was in fact done to satisfy the duty or requirement.*"
- Article 35: Appeals - those served with an alterations notice, enforcement notice or prohibition notice may appeal to the Magistrates' Court within 21 days of the notice being served. The court may cancel or affirm the notice, or make modifications to it. Appeals against alterations or enforcement notices will have the effect of suspending the operation of the notice until the appeal is heard or withdrawn; appeals against prohibition notices will not suspend the notice unless the court so directs.

In summary the main duties of an employer are to carry out a fire safety risk assessment; to take steps to remove or reduce identified risks; to meet requirements on the means of escape and fire-fighting equipment, including the maintenance of common fire protection systems; and to take measures to mitigate the spread of fire.

REPORTING OF INJURIES, DISEASES AND DANGEROUS OCCURRENCES REGULATIONS 2013 (RIDDOR) (SI 2013 NO. 1471)

These Regulations replaced **RIDDOR 1995** and came into force on 1 October 2013. The revised Regulations aim to clarify and simplify the reporting requirements, while seeking to ensure that the data collected gives an accurate picture of workplace incidents. Key changes from the 1995 Regulations include:

- The old list of major injuries has been replaced with a shorter list of 'specified injuries'.
- The schedule of industrial diseases was replaced with one showing eight categories of reportable work-related illness.
- The list of dangerous occurrences has been shortened, requiring fewer of these types of event to be reported.

The new Regulations made no significant changes to the reporting requirements for fatal accidents, accidents to members of the public or "over-7-day" injuries.

Acts of suicide that occur on, or in the course of operation of, a relevant transport system are no longer reportable. Reporting and recording certain types of incident remains a legal requirement; failure to do so is a criminal offence.

The Regulations

Regulation 2

This regulation deals with the interpretation of terms. It is lengthy, so only the more important terms are defined here. "Accident" includes an act of non-consensual physical violence done to a person at work.

"Approved manner" means published in a form considered appropriate and approved for the time being for the purposes of these Regulations by the Executive or the Office of Rail Regulation (ORR).

"Biological agent" has the meaning assigned by the **COSHH Regulations**.

"Construction site" has the meaning given by the **Construction (Design and Management) Regulations 2015**.

"Dangerous occurrence" means an occurrence which arises out of or in connection with work and is of a class specified in any of Parts 1 to 6 of Schedule 2.

"Disease" includes a medical condition.

"Passenger train" means a train carrying passengers or made available for that purpose.

"Relevant transport system" means a railway, tramway, trolley vehicle system or guided transport system, except at a factory, dock, construction site, mine or quarry, and does not include a guided bus system as defined by the **Railways and Other Guided Transport Systems (Safety) Regulations 2006**.

"Reportable incident" means an incident giving rise to a notification or reporting requirement under these Regulations.

"Reporting procedure" means, in relation to:

- an injury, death or dangerous occurrence (except at a mine or quarry), the procedure described in paragraph 1 of Part 1 of Schedule 1;
- an occupational disease or a disease offshore, the procedure described in paragraph 2 of Part 1 of Schedule 1;
- exposure to a carcinogen, mutagen or biological agent, the procedure described in paragraph 3 of Part 1 of Schedule 1; or
- an injury, death or dangerous occurrence at a mine or quarry, the procedure described in paragraph 4 of Part 1 of Schedule 1.

"Responsible person" means the person identified in accordance with regulation 3.

"Road vehicle" means any vehicle on a road, other than a train.

"Running line" means any line which is not a siding and is ordinarily used for the passage of trains. "Specified injury" means any injury or condition specified in regulation 4(1) (a) to (h).

"Train" includes a locomotive, tramcar or other power unit and any vehicle used on a relevant transport system. "Well" includes any structures or devices on top of a well.

"Work-related accident" means an accident arising out of or in connection with work.

Regulation 3: Responsible Person

The "responsible person" is:

- in relation to an injury, death or dangerous occurrence reportable under regulation 4, 5, 6 or 7 or recordable under regulation 12(1)(b) involving:
    - an employee, that employee's employer; or
    - a person not at work or a self-employed person, or in relation to any other dangerous occurrence, the person who by means of their carrying on any undertaking was in control of the premises where the reportable or recordable incident happened, at the time it happened; or
- in relation to a diagnosis reportable under regulation 8, 9 or 10 in respect of:
    - an employee, that employee's employer; or
    - a self-employed person, that self-employed person.

Further examples of 'responsible persons' are given for mines, closed tips, quarries, pipelines, wells and offshore installations.

Regulation 4: Non-Fatal Injuries to Workers

Where any person at work, as a result of a work-related accident, suffers:

- any bone fracture diagnosed by a registered medical practitioner, other than to a finger, thumb or toe;
- amputation of an arm, hand, finger, thumb, leg, foot or toe;
- any injury diagnosed by a registered medical practitioner as being likely to cause permanent blinding or reduction in sight in one or both eyes;
- any crush injury to the head or torso causing damage to the brain or internal organs in the chest or abdomen;
- any burn injury (including scalding) which:
    - covers more than 10% of the whole body's total surface area; or
    - causes significant damage to the eyes, respiratory system or other vital organs;
- any degree of scalping requiring hospital treatment;
- loss of consciousness caused by head injury or asphyxia; or
- any other injury arising from working in an enclosed space which:
    - leads to hypothermia or heat-induced illness; or
    - requires resuscitation or admittance to hospital for more than 24 hours,

the responsible person must follow the reporting procedure.

Where any person at work is incapacitated for routine work for more than seven consecutive days (excluding the day of the accident) because of an injury resulting from an accident arising out of or in connection with that work, the responsible person must send a report to the relevant enforcing authority in an approved manner as soon as practicable and in any event within 15 days of the accident.

Regulation 5: Non-Fatal Injuries to Non-Workers

Where any person not at work, as a result of a work-related accident, suffers an injury, and that person is taken from the site of the accident to a hospital for treatment in respect of that injury; or suffers a specified injury on hospital premises; the responsible person must follow the reporting procedure, subject to regulations 14 and 15.

Regulation 6: Work-Related Fatalities

Where any person dies as a result of a work-related accident, the responsible person must follow the reporting procedure.

Where any person dies as a result of occupational exposure to a biological agent, the responsible person must follow the reporting procedure.

Where an employee has suffered an injury reportable under regulation 4 which is a cause of his death within one year of the date of the accident, the employer must notify the relevant enforcing authority of the death in an approved manner without delay, whether or not the injury has been reported under regulation 4.

This regulation is subject to regulations 14 and 15, and does not apply to a self-employed person who suffers a fatal accident or fatal exposure on premises controlled by that self-employed person.

Regulation 7: Dangerous Occurrences

Where there is a dangerous occurrence, the responsible person must follow the reporting procedure, subject to regulations 14 and 15.

Regulation 8: Occupational Diseases

Where, in relation to a person at work, the responsible person receives a diagnosis of:

(a) Carpal Tunnel Syndrome, where the person's work involves regular use of percussive or vibrating tools;

(b) cramp in the hand or forearm, where the person's work involves prolonged periods of repetitive movement of the fingers, hand or arm;

(c) occupational dermatitis, where the person's work involves significant or regular exposure to a known skin sensitiser or irritant;

(d) Hand-Arm Vibration Syndrome, where the person's work involves regular use of percussive or vibrating tools, or the holding of materials which are subject to percussive processes, or processes causing vibration;

(e) occupational asthma, where the person's work involves significant or regular exposure to a known respiratory sensitiser; or

(f) tendonitis or tenosynovitis in the hand or forearm, where the person's work is physically demanding and involves frequent, repetitive movements,

the responsible person must follow the reporting procedure, subject to regulations 14 and 15.

Regulation 9: Exposure to Carcinogens, Mutagens and Biological Agents

Where, in relation to a person at work, the responsible person receives a diagnosis of:

(a) any cancer attributed to an occupational exposure to a known human carcinogen or mutagen (including ionising radiation); or

(b) any disease attributed to an occupational exposure to a biological agent,

the responsible person must follow the reporting procedure, subject to regulations 14 and 15.

Regulation 10: Diseases Offshore

Where, in relation to a person at an offshore workplace, the responsible person receives a diagnosis of any of the diseases listed in Schedule 3, the responsible person must follow the reporting procedure, subject to regulations 14 and 15.

Regulation 11: Gas-Related Injuries and Hazards

(1) Where a conveyor of flammable gas through a fixed pipe distribution system, or a filler, importer or supplier (except by retail) of a refillable container containing liquefied petroleum gas, receives notification of the death, loss of consciousness or taking to hospital of a person because of an injury arising in connection with that gas, that person must:

   (a) notify the Executive of the incident without delay; and

   (b) send a report of the incident to the Executive in an approved manner within 14 days of the incident.

(2) Where an approved person has sufficient information to decide that the design, construction, manner of installation, modification or servicing of a gas fitting is or could have been likely to cause the death, loss of consciousness or taking to hospital of a person because of:

   (a) the accidental leakage of gas;

   (b) the incomplete combustion of gas; or

   (c) the inadequate removal of the products of combustion of gas,

   the approved person must send a report of that information to the Executive in an approved manner within 14 days of acquiring that information.

(3) Nothing is reportable:

   (a) under this regulation, if it is notifiable or reportable elsewhere in these Regulations;

   (b) under paragraph (2), in relation to any gas fitting undergoing testing or examination at a place set aside for that purpose; or

   (c) under paragraph (2), if the approved person has previously reported that information.

(4) In this regulation:

- "approved person" means an employer or self-employed person who is a member of a class of persons approved by the Executive for the purposes of regulation 3(3) of the **Gas Safety (Installation and Use) Regulations 1998**;
- "gas fitting" means a gas fitting defined in those Regulations or any flue or ventilation used in connection with that fitting; and
- "liquefied petroleum gas" means commercial butane (that is, a hydrocarbon mixture consisting predominantly of butane, butylene or any mixture of them) or commercial propane (that is, a hydrocarbon mixture consisting predominantly of propane, propylene or any mixture of them) or any mixture of commercial butane and commercial propane.

Regulation 12: Recording and Record-Keeping

The responsible person must keep a record of any reportable incident under regulation 4, 5, 6 or 7; diagnosis reportable under regulation 8, 9 or 10; injury to a person at work resulting from an accident arising out of or in connection with that work, incapacitating that person for routine work for more than three consecutive days (excluding the day of the accident); and other particulars approved by the Executive or the ORR for demonstrating compliance with the approved manner of reporting under Part 1 of Schedule 1.

Records must be kept for at least three years from the date on which they were made. The records must be kept at the place where the work to which they relate is carried on, or at the usual place of business of the responsible person.

The responsible person must send the relevant enforcing authority such extracts from records as that enforcing authority may require.

Regulation 13 relates to reportable incidents and dangerous occurrences at mines, quarries and offshore workplaces.

Regulation 14 restricts the application of the Regulations such that reporting requirements for injury or death caused by medical treatment or by movement of vehicles on a road do not apply unless the specific circumstances referred to in regulation 14 are met. Similarly, the requirements of regulations 4, 6, 8, 9, 10 or 12(1)(b) do not apply in cases of injury, death or diagnosis of members of the armed forces (or visiting forces) on duty at the time.

Regulation 15 provides that, in cases where there is more than one requirement to make a notification under these Regulations, only one notification will be needed if:

- the facts giving rise to each requirement are identical;
- the information required to be provided by each requirement is provided;
- where the requirements have different time limits, the shortest time limit is complied with; and
- in the case of a mine or quarry, all steps referred to in paragraph 4 of Part 1 of Schedule 1 are complied with. In such cases, only one record needs to be kept.

Regulation 16: Defence

In proceedings against any person for failing to comply with a requirement of these Regulations, it is a defence for that person to prove that they were not aware of the circumstances which gave rise to that requirement, so long as that person had taken all reasonable steps to be made aware, in sufficient time, of such circumstances.

Schedule 1, Part 1: Reporting Procedure

Injuries, Fatalities and Dangerous Occurrences

Where required to follow the reporting procedure by regulation 4, 5, 6 or 7 (except in relation to a mine or quarry), the responsible person must:

- notify the relevant enforcing authority of the reportable incident by the quickest practicable means without delay (this does not apply to a self-employed person who is injured at premises that they own or occupy); and
- send a report of that incident in an approved manner to the relevant enforcing authority within 10 days of the incident (self-employed persons may get someone else to send the report).

Diseases

Where required to follow the reporting procedure by regulation 8 or 10, the responsible person must send a report of the diagnosis in an approved manner to the relevant enforcing authority without delay (a self-employed person may make arrangements for the report to be sent by some other person).

Carcinogens, Mutagens and Biological Agents

Where required to follow the reporting procedure by regulation 9, the responsible person must notify the relevant enforcing authority in an approved manner.

RESTRICTION OF THE USE OF CERTAIN HAZARDOUS SUBSTANCES IN ELECTRICAL AND ELECTRONIC EQUIPMENT REGULATIONS 2012 (SI 2012 NO. 3032)

Introduction

Following UK exit from the EU, these Regulations apply to Great Britain; they apply differently in Northern Ireland.

Application

Regulation 5: EEE to which these Regulations Apply

Regulation 5 refers to Parts 1 and 3 of Schedule 1 to the Regulations, which identify the electrical and electronic equipment (EEE) that the Regulations apply to:

- Large household appliances.
- Small household appliances.
- IT and telecommunications equipment.
- Consumer equipment.
- Lighting equipment.
- Electrical and electronic tools (except large-scale stationary industrial tools).
- Toys, leisure and sports equipment.
- Medical devices (for in vitro diagnostic medical devices from 22 July 2016 and from 22 July 2014 for others).
- Monitoring and control instruments (from 22 July 2017 for industrial monitoring and control instruments and from 22 July 2014 for others).
- Automatic dispensers.
- Other EEE not covered by the above.

Partial list of exclusions to which the Regulations do not apply (under Part 2 of Schedule 1):

- Equipment for the protection of national security.
- Equipment designed to be sent into space.
- Large-scale stationary industrial tools.
- Large-scale fixed installations.
- Means of transport for persons or goods excluding two-wheel non-type-approved vehicles.
- Non-road mobile machinery for professional use.
- Active implantable medical devices.
- Photovoltaic panels.
- Equipment specifically designed for research and development.

Partial list of exclusions to which the Regulations do not apply (under Part 2 of Schedule 1):

- Equipment for the protection of national security.
- Equipment designed to be sent into space.
- Large-scale stationary industrial tools.
- Large-scale fixed installations.
- Means of transport for persons or goods excluding two-wheel non-type-approved vehicles.
- Non-road mobile machinery for professional use.
- Active implantable medical devices.
- Photovoltaic panels.
- Equipment specifically designed for research and development.

Regulation 10: Prohibitions on Placing EEE on the Market (Manufacturers and their Authorised Representatives)

Producers have an obligation to not place new EEE on the market if it contains lead, mercury, hexavalent chromium, polybrominated biphenyls, polybrominated diphenyl ethers, Bis (2-ethylhexyl) phthalate (DEHP), Butyl benzyl phthalate (BBP), Dibutyl phthalate (DBP) or Diisobutyl phthalate (DIBP) in greater concentrations than 0.1% by weight in homogeneous materials or 0.01% by weight for homogeneous materials for cadmium.

Producers must prepare technical documentation supporting that the above requirements have been met (Regulation 12). They must also develop a procedure to demonstrate conformity with the Regulations. If compliance has been demonstrated by the procedure then a UKCA mark should be affixed (Regulation 13).

Producers must hold the documentation for 10 years from placing the EEE on the market (Regulation 15).

Regulation 23: Prohibition on Placing EEE on the Market (Importers)

An importer must not put EEE on the market unless the EEE complies with the restrictions stated above.

Enforcement

The enforcing authority is the Secretary of State ('The Market Surveillance Authority') (**reg. 35**).

Powers are available to allow the Market Surveillance Authority (**reg. 36**) to make test purchases, to enter premises and serve warrants, etc. They may also issue compliance, enforcement and recall notices.

Enforcement officers have powers available to them under Schedule 2:

- Powers of entry at any reasonable time (not a person's residence).
- Power to inspect, seize and detain EEE.
- Power to take measurements, photographs and make recordings.

Compliance Notice (Reg. 36(b))

The Secretary of State has the power to serve a compliance notice where there are reasonable grounds to believe that goods placed on the market or supplied are "infringing goods".

Enforcement Notice (Reg. 36(b))

Where a producer does not comply with the requirements of a Compliance Notice within the specified time period, an Enforcement Notice may be served. This notice may require a number of things, including requiring modifications to the goods, requiring other compliance actions, restricting or prohibiting the marketing of goods and/or requiring the goods to be withdrawn from the market. Details are set out in Schedule 3 to the Regulations.

SAFETY REPRESENTATIVES AND SAFETY COMMITTEES REGULATIONS 1977 (SI 1977 NO. 500)

Amending Legislation

The Regulations were amended by the **Management of Health and Safety at Work Regulations 1999**, but only in terms of citation of the **Offshore Installations and Pipeline Works (First-Aid) Regulations 1989**, the **Diving at Work Regulations 1997**, and the **Health and Safety (Fees) Regulations 2001**.

Safety Representatives: Appointments, Powers and Duties

Under section 2(4) of **HSWA**, safety representatives may be appointed, under Regulations made by the Secretary of State, by recognised trade unions; these Regulations are the **Safety Representatives and Safety Committees Regulations 1977**.

The Regulations are accompanied by an Approved Code of Practice and Guidance Notes.

In addition, there is a separate Approved Code of Practice on Time Off for the Training of Safety Representatives. It is worth noting that the **Offshore Installations (Safety Representatives and Safety Committees) Regulations 1989** allow for the appointment of non-union safety representatives on offshore installations.

The representatives are chosen from the employees. They are usually selected from persons who have at least two years' experience with their employer or in similar employment, but this is not mandatory. The employer must give the representative time off with pay for the purpose of carrying out his functions as a safety representative, and for training.

A duty lies on the employer under section 2(6) of **HSWA** to consult the representative(s):

"with a view to the making and maintenance of arrangements which will enable him and his employees to co-operate effectively in promoting and developing measures to ensure the health and safety at work of the employees, and in checking the effectiveness of such measures".

Note that this requirement is not optional, the duty is an absolute one.

Regulation 3: Appointment of Safety Representatives

A safety representative may be appointed only by a recognised, independent trade union if he is to receive the legal rights given under the **Safety Representatives and Safety Committees Regulations (SR & SC Regs)**. To be an independent trade union, it must be on the list held by the Certification Officer and have applied for, and received, the Certificate of Independence from him.

To be recognised, the trade union must be acknowledged by the employer for negotiating purposes.

The trade union must notify the employer in writing of the appointment of a safety representative in order that that representative may receive his legal rights.

The Regulations specify that a safety representative shall cease to be one in the following circumstances:

- when the trade union notifies the employer in writing that the appointment has ceased;
- when he ceases to be employed at the workplace;
- when he resigns.

A person appointed as a safety representative must, so far as is reasonably practicable, have been employed for at least two years by his employer or have at least two years' experience in similar employment.

Regulation 4: Functions of Safety Representatives

The main function of a safety representative is to represent the employees in consultations with the employer. Other functions include:

- the right to carry out inspections of the workplace:
    - to look at the causes of accidents;
    - to investigate potential hazards and dangerous occurrences;
- to investigate complaints from employees they represent concerning health and safety matters at work;
- to make representations to employers on any of the above matters;
- to make representations to employers on general health and safety matters;

- to consult with, and receive information from, health and safety inspectors;
- to attend meetings of the safety committee as safety representatives.

An employer must permit a safety representative time off, during working hours, with pay to perform his functions and to undergo such necessary training as may be reasonable.

Regulation 4A: Employer's Duty to Consult and Provide Facilities and Assistance

The revised content of this regulation was inserted by the **Regulatory Reform (Fire Safety) Order 2005**. Every employer shall consult safety representatives in good time with regard to:

- the introduction of any measure at the workplace which may substantially affect the health and safety of the employees the safety representatives concerned represent;
- his arrangements for appointing or nominating competent persons;
- any health and safety information he is required to provide to employees;
- the planning and organisation of any health and safety training that the employer is required to provide to employees; and
- the health and safety consequences of the introduction of new technologies into the workplace.

Every employer must provide such facilities and assistance as safety representatives may reasonably require for the purpose of carrying out their functions.

Similar provisions apply to Scotland.

Regulation 5: Inspections of the Workplace

Safety representatives are entitled to inspect the workplace, or part of it:

- if they have given the employer reasonable notice in writing and have not inspected the workplace within the previous three months;
- where there has been a substantial change in the conditions of work;
- where new information concerning hazards relevant to the workplace has been issued by the HSE since the last inspection- this applies whether or not three months have elapsed since the last inspection.

The employer shall provide such facilities and assistance, including facilities for independent investigation and private discussion, as the safety representatives may reasonably require.

Regulation 6: Inspections following Notifiable Accidents, Occurrences and Diseases

After an over-three-day injury (as defined in **RIDDOR 2013**), a notifiable accident, a dangerous occurrence or notifiable disease, as specified in **RIDDOR** the safety representative may carry out an inspection of the workplace concerned where it is in the interests of the employees whom he represents. Such inspection shall be carried out where it is safe to do so.

The employer shall provide such facilities and assistance, including facilities for independent investigation and private discussion, as the safety representative may reasonably require.

Regulation 7: Inspection of Documents and Provision of Information

On reasonable notice being given to the employer, safety representatives are entitled to inspect and take copies of any document relevant to the workplace or to the employees whom they represent and which the employer is required to keep by virtue of any relevant statutory provision.

Safety representatives are entitled to receive information within the employer's knowledge which is necessary to enable the safety representatives to perform their functions. This has been extended by the **Management of Health and Safety at Work Regulations** which now require the employer to consult safety representatives in good time with regard to the introduction of any measure at the workplace which may substantially affect the health and safety of those employees whom the safety representatives represent. The employer must also inform the safety representatives of the name(s) of the person(s) nominated to act in an emergency; provide any health and safety information on the planning and organisation of health and safety; and any information concerning health and safety training and the health and safety consequences of new technology.

The employer need not disclose information which:

- is against the interests of national security;
- would contravene a prohibition imposed by, or under, an enactment;
- relates specifically to an individual, unless he consents to its disclosure;

- other than for its effects on health and safety, would cause substantial injury to the undertaking;
- has been obtained by the employer for the purposes of bringing, or defending, any legal proceedings.

Regulation 8: Cases where Safety Representatives Need Not be Employees

Members of the British Actors Equity Association and the Musicians Union may be safety representatives although not employees of the employer concerned.

Regulation 9: Safety Committees

A duty is placed on the employer, when so requested in writing by at least two safety representatives, to establish a safety committee.

- The committee shall be established within three months following the request.
- Consultation with those representatives who made the request and with representatives of recognised trade unions shall be made by the employer.
- The employer shall place in a conspicuous place a notice stating:
    - the composition of the committee, and
    - the workplace(s) to be covered by it.

Regulation 11: Provisions as to Employment Tribunals

A safety representative may complain to an employment tribunal that:

- The employer has not permitted him time off for the purpose of carrying out his functions or receiving training.
- The employer has failed to pay him for his time off.

Complaints must normally be presented to the tribunal within three months of the date when the failure occurred. Where a tribunal finds a complaint to be well-founded, they will make a declaration to that effect and they may make an award of compensation, the amount of which being what the tribunal considers to be just and equitable in all the circumstances.

SIMPLE PRESSURE VESSELS (SAFETY) REGULATIONS 2016 (SI 2016 NO. 1092)

These Regulations transpose **Directive 2014/29/EU** of 26 February 2014 on the harmonisation of the laws of Member States relating to the making available on the market of simple pressure vessels.

The Directive repeals and replaces **Directive 2009/105/EC** relating to simple pressure vessels, which was implemented in the UK by the **Simple Pressure Vessels (Safety) Regulations 1991 (SI 1991 No. 2749) (as amended)**. These Regulations revoke and replace **SI 1991 No. 2749**.

The Regulations place duties on manufacturers, importers and distributors and establish requirements for conformity, notification of conformity assessment bodies, market surveillance and enforcement. Essential Safety Requirements are given in **Schedule 1**.

Part 1

Interpretation (Regulation 2)

For the purposes of these Regulations, "vessel" means a simple pressure vessel manufactured in series with the following characteristics:

- welded, and intended to contain air or nitrogen at a gauge pressure greater than 0.5 bar, and not intended to be fired;
- made of certain types of steel or aluminium;
- cylindrical with outwardly dished or flat ends, or spherical;
- having a maximum working pressure not exceeding 30 bar, with the product of pressure and volume not exceeding 10,000 bar.litres; and
- having a minimum working temperature no lower than -50°C, with a maximum working temperature no higher than 300°C if constructed of steel or 100°C if constructed of aluminium or aluminium alloy.

Application

Regulation 3 sets out the application of the Regulations to vessels as defined in **Regulation 2**, which are divided into two categories:

Category A vessels, which are vessels of which the product of PSxV exceeds 50 bar.L, and

Category B vessels, being vessels of which the product of PSxV is 50 bar.L or less.

It also sets out exceptions to the application of the Regulations for certain vessels designed or intended for nuclear use, the propulsion of ships or aircraft, and for fire extinguishers.

Part 2: Obligations of Economic Operators

Manufacturers

Regulations 4 to 16 set out the obligations that are specific to manufacturers.

Category A vessels must undergo a conformity assessment to demonstrate compliance with the essential safety requirements of the Regulations, and Category B vessels (of a lower capacity and pressure and therefore a lower risk than Category A) must be designed and manufactured in accordance with sound engineering practice. Obligations include ensuring that a Category A vessel has been designed and manufactured in accordance with the essential safety requirements set out in Schedule 1, having a relevant conformity assessment procedure carried out before the vessel is placed on the market, affixing the CE marking and labelling the vessel.

Regulations 15 and 16 refer to authorised representatives who may be appointed by manufacturers to perform certain tasks on their behalf.

Importers

Regulations 17 to 27 set out the obligations that are specific to importers.

These obligations include ensuring that they are not placing on the market vessels which are not in conformity with the essential safety requirements, checking that the manufacturer has carried out a relevant conformity assessment procedure and labelled the vessels correctly and indicating on the vessel the name and address of the importer.

Distributors

Regulations 28 to 34 set out the obligations that are specific to distributors.

These obligations include acting with due care to ensure that vessels are in conformity with **Part 2** and checking that the vessels bear the CE marking and are labelled correctly. They also include an obligation to ensure that, while it is the distributor's responsibility, the storage and transport of a Category A vessel does not jeopardise its conformity with the essential safety requirements.

All Economic Operators

Regulations 35 to 38 set out obligations which apply to all economic operators.

These obligations include making sure, before making a Category A vessel available on the market, that the EU declaration of conformity is in English. They also include an obligation to identify other economic operators in the supply chain, and a prohibition on the improper use of the CE marking.

Part 3: Conformity of Category A Vessels

Part 3 sets out provisions concerning the conformity assessment procedure, declarations of conformity and CE marking for Category A vessels.

Part 4: Notification of Conformity Assessment Bodies

Part 4 sets out provisions concerning the bodies which carry out conformity assessment procedures under the Regulations.

Part 5: Market Surveillance and Enforcement

Part 5 sets out provisions for market surveillance and enforcement of these Regulations.

Regulation 54 identifies the market surveillance authority which has an obligation to enforce the Regulations. **Regulation 56** and **Schedules 5 to 8** provide for the enforcement powers which the enforcing authorities are to have. **Regulation 64** provides for the contravention of certain provisions of these Regulations to be an offence.

Regulation 65 sets out the penalties that are to apply for offences under these Regulations.

Part 6: Miscellaneous

Part 6 sets out a review provision and transitional provisions and consequential amendments.

A certificate issued under certain provisions of the **Simple Pressure Vessels (Safety) Regulations 1991 (as amended)** will be valid under these Regulations, and those Regulations will continue to apply to vessels placed on the market before the commencement date.

Regulation 78 makes consequential amendments.

SMOKE-FREE (PREMISES AND ENFORCEMENT) REGULATIONS 2006 (SI 2006 NO. 3368)

These Regulations came into force on 1 July 2007 and apply in England only. In these Regulations, references to "the Act" refer to the Health Act 2006.

Regulation 2: Enclosed and Substantially Enclosed Premises

(1) For the purposes of section 2 of the Act, premises are enclosed if they:

    (a) have a ceiling or roof; and

    (b) except for doors, windows and passageways, are wholly enclosed either permanently or temporarily.

(2) For the purposes of section 2 of the Act, premises are substantially enclosed if they have a ceiling or roof but there is:

    (a) an opening in the walls, or

    (b) an aggregate area of openings in the walls,

which is less than half of the area of the walls, including other structures that serve the purpose of walls and constitute the perimeter of the premises.

(3) In determining the area of an opening or an aggregate area of openings for the purposes of paragraph (2), no account is to be taken of openings in which there are doors, windows or other fittings that can be opened or shut.

(4) In this regulation "roof" includes any fixed or moveable structure or device which is capable of covering all or part of the premises as a roof, including, for example, a canvas awning.

Regulation 3: Enforcement

(1) Each of the following authorities is designated as an enforcement authority for the purposes of Chapter 1 of Part 1 of the Act:

    (a) a unitary authority;

    (b) a district council in so far as it is not a unitary authority;

    (c) a London borough council;

    (d) a port health authority;

    (e) the Common Council of the City of London;

    (f) the Sub-Treasurer of the Inner Temple and the Under Treasurer of the Middle Temple; and

    (g) the Council of the Isles of Scilly.

SMOKE-FREE PREMISES, ETC. (WALES) REGULATIONS 2007 (SI 2007 NO. 787)

These Regulations came into force at 6am on 2 April 2007 and apply only in relation to Wales. In these Regulations, references to "the Act" refer to the **Health Act 2006**.

Regulation 2: Meaning of "Enclosed" and "Substantially Enclosed" Premises

(1) For the purposes of section 2 of the Act, premises are enclosed if they have a ceiling or roof and, except for doors, windows and passageways, they are wholly enclosed either permanently or temporarily.

(2) For the purposes of section 2 of the Act, premises are substantially enclosed if they have a ceiling or roof and any openings in the walls have a total area which is less than half of the area of the walls, including other structures which serve the purpose of walls.

(3) In determining the area of openings for the purposes of paragraph (2), no account is to be taken of openings in which there are doors, windows or other fittings which can be opened or shut.

(4) In this regulation "roof" includes any fixed or moveable structure or device.

Regulation 3: Exemptions for Smoke-Free Premises

(1) A private dwelling is not smoke-free except for any part of it which is:

    (a) shared with other premises (including any other private dwelling), or

    (b) used solely as a place of work other than work which is excluded by paragraphs (2) or (3).

(2) Work undertaken in part of a dwelling which is used solely as a place of work is excluded from paragraph (1)(b) if no person (other than a person who lives in the dwelling) works in that part or is invited to attend that part in connection with the work.

(3) There is excluded from paragraph (1)(b) all work which is undertaken solely:

    (i) to provide personal or health care for a person living in the dwelling;

    (ii) to assist with the domestic work of the household in the dwelling;

    (iii) to maintain the structure or fabric of the dwelling;

    (iv) to install, inspect, maintain or remove any service provided to the dwelling for the benefit of persons living in it.

(4) Subject to paragraphs (5) and (6) the following descriptions of premises are not smoke-free:

    (a) designated rooms for use by those aged 18 years or more in:

        (i) a care home;

        (ii) an adult hospice;

        (iii) a mental health unit which provides residential accommodation for patients;

    (b) designated rooms in a research or testing facility;

    (c) designated bedrooms in a hotel, guesthouse, inn, hostel or members' club.

(5) For the purposes of paragraph (4) a "designated room" or a "designated bedroom" as the case may be, means a room which:

    (a) has been designated by the person in charge of the establishment concerned as a room in which smoking is permitted;

    (b) has a ceiling and, except for doors and windows, is completely enclosed on all sides by solid floor to ceiling walls;

    (c) does not have a ventilation system that ventilates into any other part of the premises (except any other designated rooms or designated bedrooms, as the case may be);

    (d) does not have any door which opens on to smoke-free premises that is not mechanically closed immediately after use; and

    (e) is clearly marked as a room in which smoking is permitted.

(6) A designated room in a research or testing facility is not smoke-free whilst it is being used for any research or tests which relate to:

    (a) emissions from tobacco and other products used for smoking;

    (b) development of products for smoking with lower fire hazard or the fire safety testing of materials involving products for smoking;

(c) development of smoking or pharmaceutical products that could result in the manufacture of less dangerous products for smoking; or

(d) smoking cessation programmes.

Regulation 3A: Temporary Exemption for Prisons

This short-lived provision was added by the **Smoke-Free Premises, etc. (Wales)(Amendment) Regulations 2016** and allowed smoking in cells. It ceased to have effect on 5 April 2017.

Regulation 4: Smoke-Free Vehicles

Subject to the following paragraphs of this regulation, a vehicle shall be smoke-free if it is used:

(a) for the transport of members of the public or a section of the public (whether or not for reward or hire); or

(b) for work purposes by more than one person (even if the persons who use it for such purposes do so at different times, or only intermittently).

This regulation applies to vehicles and parts of vehicles which are enclosed.

A vehicle or part of a vehicle is enclosed for the purposes of paragraph (2) where it has doors or windows which may be opened but it is not enclosed unless it is wholly or partly covered by a roof.

This regulation applies to all vehicles other than:

(a) aircraft;

(b) ships or hovercraft in respect of which regulations could be made under section 85 of the **Merchant Shipping Act 1995** (safety and health on ships), including that section as applied by any Order in Council under section 1(1)(h) of the **Hovercraft Act 1968** or to persons on any such ship or hovercraft; or

(c) private vehicles.

In this regulation "roof" does not include any roof which is completely stowed away so that it does not cover any part of a compartment in which persons may travel.

Regulation 4A: Private Vehicles with Children Present

Added by the **Smoke-Free Premises, etc. (Wales) (Amendment) Regulations 2015**. A private vehicle or part thereof is smoke-free if:

it is enclosed;

there is more than one person present in the vehicle; and

a person under the age of 18 is present in the vehicle.

Regulation 5: No-Smoking Signs: Smoke-Free Premises

For the purposes of section 6 of the Act, any person who occupies or is concerned in the management of smoke-free premises must make sure that no-smoking signs meeting the requirements specified in paragraph (2) are displayed in those premises in accordance with the requirements contained in paragraph (3).

A no-smoking sign must:

(a) be flat and rectangular and at least 160 millimetres by 230 millimetres;

(b) contain a graphic representation of a burning cigarette enclosed in a red circle at least 85 millimetres in diameter with a red bar across the circle which crosses the cigarette symbol;

(c) contain the following words — "*Mae ysmygu yn y fangre hon yn erbyn y gyfraith / It is against the law to smoke in these premises*".

A no-smoking sign complying with the requirements of paragraph (2) must be displayed in a prominent position at or near each entrance to smoke-free premises.

Regulation 6: No-Smoking Signs: Smoke-Free Vehicles

The relevant person in relation to a vehicle which is smoke-free by virtue of regulation 4 must make sure that no-smoking signs meeting the requirements specified in paragraph (2) are displayed on the vehicle in accordance with the requirements contained in paragraph (3).

A no-smoking sign must contain a graphic representation of a burning cigarette enclosed in a red circle at least 75 millimetres in diameter with a red bar across the circle which crosses the cigarette symbol.

(3) A no-smoking sign complying with the requirements of paragraph (2) must be displayed in a prominent position in each compartment of the vehicle, which is wholly or partly covered by a roof, including a driver's compartment.

(4) In paragraph (3) "roof" does not include a roof which is completely stowed away so that it does not cover any part of a compartment in which persons may travel.

(5) For the purpose of this regulation and regulation 7, a "relevant person" in relation to a smoke-free vehicle means:

   (a) the operator;

   (b) the driver; and

   (c) any person on a vehicle who is responsible for order or safety on it.

Regulation 7: Duty to Prevent Smoking in Smoke-Free Vehicles

It is the duty of the relevant person in relation to a vehicle which is smoke-free by virtue of regulation 4 to cause a person smoking in the vehicle to stop smoking.

Regulation 7A: Duty to Prevent Smoking in Smoke-Free Private Vehicles

The driver of a vehicle that is smoke-free by virtue of regulation 4A is under a duty to cause any person who is smoking in the vehicle to stop smoking.

Regulation 7B: Fixed Penalties

An authorised officer of an enforcement authority who has reason to believe that a person has committed an offence under section 8(4) of the Act in relation to a vehicle that is smoke-free by virtue of regulation 4A, may give that person a penalty notice in respect of the offence.

Regulation 8: Enforcement: Designation of Enforcement Authorities

(1) County councils and county borough councils in Wales are designated as enforcement authorities for the purposes of Chapter 1 of Part 1 of the Act.

(2) Subject to paragraph (3), each enforcement authority has enforcement functions in relation to the premises and vehicles which are within its area.

(3) Where more than one enforcement authority is investigating the same person under powers conferred by Chapter 1 of Part 1 of the Act, the authorities concerned may by agreement transfer enforcement functions to one of them or to any other enforcement authority.

(4) The Chief Officer of each police force is designated as an enforcement authority for the purposes of Chapter 1 of Part 1 of the Act.

(5) An enforcement authority designated under paragraph (4) has enforcement functions in relation to vehicles that:

   (a) are smoke-free by virtue of regulation 4A; and

   (b) are within the police area for which the police force in question is maintained.

Regulation 9: Enforcement: Penalty Notice

(1) The penalty notice forms set out in the Schedule to these Regulations are specified in relation to the offences described in them.

(2) Where there is a change to the amount of a fixed penalty or a discounted amount or to a level on the standard scale, the relevant specified form must be varied to reflect that change.

(3) An enforcement authority may include information on penalty notice forms as to the method of payment or to facilitate financial and administrative processing of the forms and may include on the forms coats of arms, logos or other devices to represent the authority.

SMOKING, HEALTH AND SOCIAL CARE (SCOTLAND) ACT 2005

This Act of the Scottish Parliament received Royal Assent on 5 August 2005. The Act intends, amongst other things, to prohibit smoking in certain wholly or substantially enclosed places and to make provision for penalties to be imposed.

Part 1 - Smoking: Prohibition and Control

Section 1: Offence of Permitting Others to Smoke in No-Smoking Premises

(1) A person who, having the management or control of no-smoking premises, knowingly permits another to smoke there commits an offence.

(2) A person accused of an offence under this section is to be regarded as having knowingly permitted another to smoke in no-smoking premises if that person ought to have known that the other person was smoking there.

(3) It is a defence for an accused charged with an offence under this section to prove:

   (a) that the accused (or any employee or agent of the accused) took all reasonable precautions and exercised all due diligence not to commit the offence; or

   (b) that there were no lawful and reasonably practicable means by which the accused could prevent the other person from smoking in the no-smoking premises.

(4) A person guilty of an offence under this section is liable, on summary conviction, to a fine not exceeding level 4 on the standard scale.

Section 2: Offence of Smoking in No-Smoking Premises

(1) A person who smokes in no-smoking premises commits an offence.

(2) It is a defence for an accused charged with an offence under this section to prove that the accused did not know, and could not reasonably be expected to have known, that the place in which it is alleged that the accused was smoking was no-smoking premises.

(3) A person guilty of an offence under this section is liable, on summary conviction, to a fine not exceeding level 3 on the standard scale.

Section 3: Display of Warning Notices In and On No-Smoking Premises

(1) If notices are not conspicuously displayed:

   (a) in, on or near no-smoking premises so as to be visible to and legible by persons in and persons approaching the premises; and

   (b) stating:

      (i) that the premises are no-smoking premises; and

      (ii) that it is an offence to smoke there or knowingly to permit smoking there;

   the person having the management or control of the premises commits an offence.

(2) It is a defence for an accused charged with an offence under this section to prove that the accused (or any employee or agent of the accused) took all reasonable precautions and exercised all due diligence not to commit the offence.

(3) The Scottish Ministers may, after consulting such persons as they consider appropriate, by regulations provide further as to the manner of display, form and content of the notices referred to in subsection (1) and that any such provision is to be treated, for the purposes of that subsection, as if incorporated in it.

(4) A person guilty of an offence under this section is liable, on summary conviction, to a fine not exceeding level 3 on the standard scale.

Section 4: Meaning of "Smoke" and "No-Smoking Premises"

(1) In this Part, "smoke" means smoke tobacco, any substance or mixture which includes it or any other substance or mixture; and a person is to be taken as smoking if the person is holding or otherwise in possession or control of lit tobacco, of any lit substance or mixture which includes tobacco or of any other lit substance or mixture which is in a form or in a receptacle in which it can be smoked.

(2) In this Part, "no-smoking premises" means such premises or such classes of premises, being premises of a kind mentioned in subsection (4), as are prescribed by regulations made by the Scottish Ministers after consulting such persons as they consider appropriate on a draft of the regulations.

(3) Regulations under subsection (2) may prescribe premises or parts of premises or classes of premises or parts of premises which are excluded from the definition of "no-smoking premises".

(4) The kind of premises referred to in subsection (2) is premises which are wholly or substantially enclosed and:

   (a) to which the public or a section of the public has access;

   (b) which are being used wholly or mainly as a place of work;

   (c) which are being used by and for the purposes of a club or other unincorporated association; or

   (d) which are being used wholly or mainly for the provision of education or of health or care services.

(5) In subsection (4)(b), the reference to work includes work undertaken for no financial advantage.

(6) Regulations under subsection (2) may, for the purposes of that subsection, define or elaborate the meaning of any of the expressions:

   (a) "premises";

   (b) "wholly or substantially enclosed";

   (c) "the public"; and

   (d) "has access".

(7) Regulations under subsection (2) may define or elaborate the meaning of "premises":

   (a) by reference to the person or class of person who owns or occupies them;

   (b) so as to include vehicles, vessels, trains and other means of transport (except aircraft), or such, or such classes, of them as are specified in the regulations.

(8) The Scottish Ministers may, by regulations, after consulting such persons as they consider appropriate on a draft of the regulations, modify subsection (4) so as:

   (a) to add a kind of premises to, or

   (b) remove a kind of premises (but not the kind referred to in paragraph (a) of that subsection) from, those in that subsection.

(9) Regulations made by virtue of subsection (7)(b) may provide as to how the statement referred to in section 3(1)(b) is to be expressed in the case of each of the means of transport referred to in the regulations and that any such provision is to be treated, for the purposes of that section, as if incorporated in it.

Section 6: Fixed Penalties

Gives effect to Schedule 1, which lays down fixed penalties for offences under this Act.

Section 7: Powers to Enter and Require Identification

Authorised officers may enter (by force if necessary) and search any no-smoking premises to ascertain whether an offence has been or is being committed there.

SOCIAL ACTION, RESPONSIBILITY AND HEROISM ACT 2015

Introduction

This Act came into force on 13 April 2015 and sets out the issues to which a court must have regard in determining a claim in negligence or breach of statutory duty.

Section 1: When this Act Applies

This Act applies when a court, in considering a claim that a person was negligent or in breach of statutory duty, is determining the steps that the person was required to take to meet a standard of care.

Section 2: Social Action

The court must have regard to whether the alleged negligence or breach of statutory duty occurred when the person was acting for the benefit of society or any of its members.

Section 3: Responsibility

The court must have regard to whether the person, in carrying out the activity in the course of which the alleged negligence or breach of statutory duty occurred, demonstrated a predominantly responsible approach towards protecting the safety or other interests of others.

Section 4: Heroism

The court must have regard to whether the alleged negligence or breach of statutory duty occurred when the person was acting heroically by intervening in an emergency to assist an individual in danger.

SOCIAL SECURITY ADMINISTRATION ACT 1992

This Act consolidated much of the Social Security legislation. Of interest here is the power to make Regulations concerning the reporting of accidents.

Section 8: Notification of Accidents, etc.

Regulations may provide:

- for requiring the prescribed notice of an accident in respect of which industrial injuries benefit may be payable to be given within the prescribed time by the employed earner to the earner's employer or other prescribed person;
- for requiring employers:
    - to make reports, to such person and in such form and within such time as may be prescribed, of accidents in respect of which industrial injuries benefit may be payable;
    - to furnish to the prescribed person any information required for the determination of claims, or of questions arising in connection with claims or awards;
    - to take such other steps as may be prescribed to facilitate the giving notice of accidents, the making of claims and the determination of claims and of questions so arising.

SOCIAL SECURITY (CLAIMS AND PAYMENTS) REGULATIONS 1979 (SI 1979 NO. 628)

Introduction

Much of this piece of legislation (notably Part 2, 'Claims', Part 3, 'Payments' and most of Part 5, 'Miscellaneous Provisions', together with Schedules 1, 2, 3 and 5) has been repealed. For your purposes, the main areas of interest relate to the recording of industrial accidents, as set out in regulations 25 and 26.

Background

These Regulations were made solely for the purpose of consolidation of the **Social Security (Claims and Payments) Regulations 1975** and subsequent amending Regulations.

They mainly provide for the manner in which claims for and payments of benefits under the **Social Security Act** are to be made. For your purposes, only Part IV (Special Provisions Relating to Industrial Injuries Benefit) is applicable.

Regulation 24: Notice of Accidents

Every employed earner who suffers personal injury by accident in respect of which benefit may be payable shall give notice of such accident either in writing or orally as soon as is practicable after the happening thereof. Provided that any such notice required to be given by an employed earner may be given by some other person acting on his behalf.

Every such notice shall be given to the employer, or (if there is more than one employer) to one of such employers, or to any foreman or other official under whose supervision the employed earner is employed at the time of the accident, or to any person designated for the purpose by the employer, and shall give the appropriate particulars.

Any entry of the appropriate particulars of an accident made in a book kept for that purpose in accordance with the provisions of regulation 25 shall, if made as soon as practicable after the happening of an accident by the employed earner or by some other person acting on his behalf, be sufficient notice of the accident for the purposes of this regulation.

In this regulation:

- "Employer" means, in relation to any person, the employer of that person at the time of the accident and 'employers' shall be construed accordingly.
- "Employed earner" means a person who is, or is treated as, an employed earner for the purposes of industrial injuries benefit.

In this regulation and regulation 25, "appropriate particulars" means the particulars indicated in Schedule 4 to these Regulations.

Regulation 25: Obligations of Employers

(1) Every employer shall take reasonable steps to investigate the circumstances of every accident of which notice is given to him or to his servant or his agent in accordance with the provision of regulation 24 and, if there appear to him to be any discrepancies between the circumstances found by him as a result of his investigation and the circumstances appearing from the notice so given, he shall record the circumstances so found.

(2) Every employer who is required to do so by the Secretary of State shall furnish to an officer of the Department within such reasonable period as may be required, such information and particulars as shall be required.

(3) Every owner or occupier (being an employer) of any factory, mine or quarry or of any premises to which any provisions of the **Health and Safety at Work, etc. Act 1974** apply, shall, subject to the following provisions of this paragraph:

   (a) keep readily accessible a book or books (or by electronic means) in a form approved by the Secretary of State in which the appropriate particulars (as defined in regulation 24) of any accident causing personal injury to a person employed by the employer may be entered by that person or by some other person acting on his behalf; and

   (b) preserve every such book, when it is filled, for the period of 3 years beginning with the date of the last entry therein.

Regulation 26: Obligations of Claimants for, and Beneficiaries in Receipt of, Disablement Benefit

(1) Every claimant for, and every beneficiary in receipt of, disablement benefit shall comply with every notice given to him by the Secretary of State which requires him either:

   (a) to submit himself to a medical examination by a health care professional approved by the Secretary of State who has experience in the issues specified in regulation 12(1) of the **Social Security and Child Support (Decisions and Appeals) Regulations 1999** for the purpose of determining the effects of the relevant accident or the treatment appropriate to the relevant injury or loss of faculty; or

(b) to submit himself to such medical treatment for the said injury or loss of faculty as is considered appropriate in his case by the medical practitioner in charge of the case.

(2) Every notice given to a claimant or beneficiary requiring him to submit himself to medical examination shall be given in writing and shall specify the time and place for examination and shall not require the claimant or beneficiary to submit himself to examination before the expiration of the period of 6 days beginning with the date of the notice or such shorter period as may be reasonable in the circumstances.

(3) Every claimant and every beneficiary who, in accordance with the foregoing provisions of this regulation, is required to submit himself to a medical examination or to medical treatment:

(4) shall attend at every such place and at every such time as may be required; and

(a) may, in the discretion of the Secretary of State, be paid such travelling and other allowances (including compensation for loss of remunerative time) as the Secretary of State may with the consent of the Minister for the Civil Service determine.

Schedule 4: Particulars to be Given of Accidents

- Full name, address and occupation of injured person.
- Date and time of accident.
- Place where the accident happened.
- Cause and nature of injury.
- Name, address and occupation of person giving notice, if other than the injured person.

SUPPLY OF MACHINERY (SAFETY) REGULATIONS 2008 (SI 2008 NO. 1597)

The Regulations

The legislation came into force on 29 December 2009 and transposes the **Machinery Directive (2006/42/EC)**. It consists of 28 regulations (in 7 Parts) and 7 schedules. Schedule 2 reproduces *verbatim* 11 annexes from the **Machinery Directive**. Like many Directives of this kind, the **Machinery Directive** aims to remove barriers to trade by harmonising safety requirements. The following extracts concentrate on certain key areas.

Regulations 2 and 4 to 6

As always, definitions and disapplications are crucial to an understanding of any new legislation and these are contained throughout but especially in regulations 2 and 4 to 6. Some of the more important definitions are listed below:

"CE marking" means a mark consisting of the symbol "CE" set out in the form shown in Annex III (Part 3 of Schedule 2).

"Essential health and safety requirements" means the requirements in Annex I (Part 1 of Schedule 2), being requirements relating to the design and construction of the products to which these Regulations apply, ensure a high level of protection of the health and safety of persons and, where appropriate, of domestic animals and property and, in the case of machinery referred to in section 2.4 of Annex I, of the environment.

"Harmonised standard" means a non-binding technical specification adopted by the European Committee for Standardisation (CEN) or the European Committee for Electrotechnical Standardisation (CENELEC) or the European Telecommunications Standards Institute (ETSI) on the basis of a remit issued by the European Commission.

"Machinery"- this is extensively defined in regulation 4(3) and includes assemblies fitted with drive systems (like circular saws), interchangeable equipment (such as is used with a tractor), safety components, lifting accessories (like slings). Some machinery (listed in Schedule 3) is specifically excluded. Also excluded is machinery wholly covered by more specific requirements of other Directives (see reg. 5).

"Partly completed machinery"- defined in regulation 6, this is essentially machinery which cannot perform a specific application and which is only intended to be incorporated into other machinery.

"Responsible person" means, in relation to machinery or partly completed machinery:

- the manufacturer;
- the manufacturer's authorised representative.

"Safe" means, in relation to machinery, that, when the machinery is properly installed and maintained and used for the purposes for which it is intended, or under conditions which can reasonably be foreseen, it does not:

(a) endanger the health of, or result in death or injury to, any person; or

(b) where appropriate:

(c) endanger the health of, or result in death or injury to, domestic animals; or

(d) endanger property;

(e) in the case of machinery referred to in section 2.4 of Annex I (Part 1 of Schedule 2), endanger the environment.

Regulation 7: Supply of Machinery: General Obligations and Prohibitions

(1) No responsible person shall place machinery on the market or put it into service unless it is safe.

(2) Before placing machinery on the market or putting it into service, the responsible person must:

    (a) Ensure that the machine satisfies the relevant essential health and safety requirements.

    (b) Ensure that the technical file is compiled and made available.

    (c) Provide information necessary to operate the machine safely.

    (d) Follow the appropriate conformity assessment procedure (outlined in regs 10, 11 and 12).

    (e) Draw up the EC declaration of conformity (a copy must accompany the machinery and the original be retained), prescribed in Annex II.

    (f) Affix the 'CE' marking to the machinery (visible, legible, and indelible), prescribed in Annex III.

(3) The responsible person must carry out (or arrange to be carried out) all necessary research and testing to comply with (1) and (2).

(4) There is a presumption of conformity with the Essential Health and Safety Requirements if a machine is manufactured in accordance with a published harmonised standard ('published' here meaning a standard whose reference has been published in the Official Journal of the European Union). This of course is only to the extent to which that standard covers the essential health and safety requirements.

(5) & (6) For certain procedures covered by regs 11 and 12 there may be ongoing obligations, as prescribed in Annexes IX and X (these are related to EC Type-examination and full quality assurance options, respectively).

Regulation 8: Supply of Partly Completed Machinery: General Obligations and Prohibitions

Before partly completed machinery is placed on the market, the responsible person must:

(a) Prepare and make available the relevant technical documentation (described in Annex VII).

(b) Prepare assembly instructions (Annex VI).

(c) Draw up a declaration of incorporation.

The assembly instructions and declaration of incorporation are supplied with the partly completed machinery. Once incorporated into a machine, the assembly instructions and declaration of incorporation form part of that machine's technical file (discussed later). Once again all necessary research and tests must be conducted.

Regulation 9: Putting into Service

This regulation was revoked by the **Supply of Machinery (Safety) (Amendment) Regulations 2011 (SI 2011 No. 2157)**.

Regulation 10: Machinery Not Referred To in Annex IV

Annex IV refers to categories of machinery which are considered more dangerous (e.g. circular saws, chainsaws). This regulation applies to those which do not appear in that list (i.e. most other general machinery). For these cases, the conformity assessment procedure prescribed in Annex VIII (i.e. reproduced in Schedule 2, Part 8) should be followed. This involves the responsible person drawing up a technical file and ensuring that the manufacturing process is checked to make sure it produces products that comply. This procedure is commonly called 'self-assessment'.

Regulation 11: Annex IV Machinery Manufactured Fully in Accordance with Published Harmonised Standards and Fully Covered by those Standards

If the machinery is identified in Annex IV **and** it is manufactured wholly in accordance with one or more published harmonised standards **and** those standards fully cover that machine then the responsible person has a choice of three conformity assessment procedures. These are prescribed in Annexes VIII, IX and X, respectively. The Annex VIII ('self-assessment') procedure has already been outlined.

The Annex IX ('EC Type-Examination') procedure involves submission of a representative sample of the machine and also the technical file to a 'notified body'. The notified body carries out the conformity assessment and issues an EC Type-Examination Certificate if it complies.

The Annex X ('Full Quality Assurance') procedure requires the responsible person to produce the machine under an approved quality management system (which must cover design, manufacture, inspection and testing). A notified body assesses and approves the quality management system. The technical file is also assessed as part of this.

Regulation 12: Annex IV Machinery Not Manufactured Fully in Accordance with Published Harmonised Standards or Not Fully Covered by those Standards

A reduced choice is available to Annex IV machinery not fully covered by published harmonised standards. This might be because no published harmonised standards exist for the machine in question. In these cases, the responsible person can follow either Annex IX or X procedures (i.e. EC Type-examination or full quality assurance).

Regulation 13: CE-Marked Machinery Taken to Comply with the Regulations

Unless there is evidence to the contrary, enforcement authorities, courts and the Secretary of State are obliged to presume that a 'CE'-marked machine accompanied by a valid EC declaration of conformity complies in all respects with these Regulations. Failure to provide a copy of the technical file when requested by an enforcement authority provides reasonable grounds for suspicion.

Regulation 14: Machinery Covered by More than One Directive

Where more than one Directive applies to a machine, the application of the 'CE' mark signifies that all applicable requirements of all relevant Directives are satisfied (there may be exceptions to this if allowed by the other Directive).

Regulation 15: Protection of CE Marking

CE marks must not be applied to machinery which does not comply with these Regulations. Neither must anyone affix a marking that is likely to be confused with a CE mark or impair the CE mark or mislead people as to the meaning of the CE mark.

Regulations 16 to 19: Designation and Monitoring of Notified Bodies

These regulations cover the designation, monitoring, term, functions and fee levying of notified bodies. These are third parties designated by the Secretary of State to carry out certain functions (like EC Type-examination and assessment and approval of Quality Systems under the conformity procedures mentioned earlier). The 'notified' refers to the fact that they are notified by the Secretary of State to the European Commission.

Regulations 20 to 24: Enforcement

The powers of the enforcement authorities are detailed in Schedule 5. There are the usual offences and penalties. A statutory defence of due diligence is also available for the accused.

Selected Schedules

Schedule 2, Part 2 (Annex II of the Directive): EC Declaration of Conformity and Declaration of Incorporation

We shall only describe the EC declaration of conformity here, which should:

- State the business name and full address of the responsible person and, where that person is not the manufacturer, of the manufacturer.
- State the name and address of the person authorised to compile the technical file.
- Contain a description and identification of the machinery including, in particular its make; generic denomination, function, model, type; commercial name and serial number.
- Contain a sentence expressly declaring that the machinery fulfils all the relevant requirements of the Directive (and similar sentences for all other Directives that apply).
- State, where appropriate, the name, address and identification number of the notified body which carried out the EC type-examination and the number of the EC type-examination certificate (as per Annex IX procedure).
- State, where appropriate, the name, address and identification number of the notified body which approved the full quality assurance system (as per Annex X procedure).
- Specify (as appropriate) the published harmonised standards used.
- Specify (as appropriate) other technical standards and specifications used.
- Specify place and date of the declaration.
- Disclose the identity and contain the signature of the person empowered to draw up the declaration on behalf of the responsible person.

Schedule 2, Part 3 (Annex III of the Directive): CE Marking

This part of the schedule gives the specification of the CE mark itself.

Where an Annex X conformity procedure has been followed (i.e. full quality assurance), the mark is followed by the identification number of the notified body. Note that the CE marking is not the only marking that may be required. Annex I (Schedule 2, Part 1) identifies a number of items that may also need to be included as part of compliance with the essential health and safety requirements (1.7.3), namely:

- Name and address of the manufacturer.
- Designation of machinery.
- Designation of series or type.
- Serial number, if any.
- Year of construction (i.e. when it was actually completed).
- If designed for such, information regarding its use in an explosive atmosphere.
- Any safety-related information regarding the machinery in use (e.g. maximum speed of rotating parts).

- Mass of any part where it must be handled by lifting equipment during use.

Schedule 2, Part 7 (Annex VII of the Directive): Technical Files

We will only describe the technical file for machinery here (that for partly completed machinery is similar but slightly different in the details).

The technical file for machinery consists of:

- A general description of the machine.
- Drawings of the machine.
- Drawings of the control circuitry.
- Details of tests carried out to check conformity against essential health and safety requirements.
- List of applicable essential health and safety requirements.
- Description of methods adopted to eliminate hazards.
- The standards and other technical specifications used (indicate the essential health and safety requirements covered by these standards).
- Any technical reports/certificate giving the results of tests.
- A copy of the instructions for the machinery.
- Where appropriate, the declaration of incorporation for included partly completed machinery.
- Where appropriate, the EC declaration of conformity of machinery/products incorporated into the machine.
- A copy of the EC declaration of conformity.
- For series manufacture, the internal measures to be taken to ensure that production machinery is to the same standard (i.e. quality assurance and quality control).

TRADE UNION AND LABOUR RELATIONS (CONSOLIDATION) ACT 1992 AS AMENDED

Introduction

This Act consolidates the law in relation to trade unions, employers' associations, trade disputes, collective bargaining, industrial action, ACAS, and a host of relevant administrative functions and procedures. It is contained in 303 sections and 3 Schedules.

Amending Legislation

The **Employment Relations Act 1999** and **Trade Union Reform and Employment Rights Act 1993**. More recently, the **Trade Union and Labour Relations (Consolidation) Act 1992 (Amendment) Order 2013/763** made amendments to section 188 (reducing the period between the beginning of consultation and the first dismissal taking effect from 90 days to 45 days); to section 193 (reducing the period between notifying the Secretary of State and the first dismissal taking effect from 90 days to 45 days); and replaced section 282 (short-term employment) with a new section 282 entitled "fixed term employment".

Only extracts relevant to disciplinary procedures and dismissal are included here.

Section 1: Meaning of Trade Union

"Trade union" means an organisation which consists wholly or mainly of:

- workers of one or more descriptions and whose principal purposes include the regulation of relations between workers of that description and employers or employers' associations, or
- constituent or affiliated organisations which fulfil the above conditions, or
- representatives of such constituent or affiliated organisations.

Section 5: Meaning of "Independent Trade Union"

An "independent trade union" means a trade union which is not under the domination or control of an employer or group of employers or of one or more employers' associations and is not liable to interference from any such group or association arising out of the provision of financial or material support tending towards such control.

Section 10: Quasi-Corporate Status of Trade Unions

A trade union is not a body corporate but is capable of:

- making contracts;
- suing and being sued in its own name in proceedings relating to property or founded on contract or tort or any other cause of action.

Proceedings for an offence alleged to have been committed by it or on its behalf may be brought against it in its own name.

A trade union shall not be registered as if it were a corporate body, nor shall it be registered as a company under the **Companies Act 2006**, or under the terms of the **Friendly Societies Act 1974 or the Co-operative and Community Benefit Societies Act 2014**.

Section 137: Refusal of Employment on Grounds Related to Union Membership

It is unlawful to refuse a person employment because:

- He is, or is not, a member of a trade union.
- He is unwilling to accept a requirement:
    - To become or cease to be, or to remain or not to become, a member of a trade union.
    - To make payments or suffer deductions in the event of his not being a member of a trade union.

A person thus unlawfully refused employment has a right of complaint to an employment tribunal. Where an advertisement is published which indicates, or might reasonably be understood as indicating:

(a) that employment to which the advertisement relates is open only to a person who is, or is not, a member of a trade union, or

(b) that any such requirement as is mentioned above will be imposed in relation to employment to which the advertisement relates, a person who does not satisfy that condition or, as the case may be, is unwilling to accept that requirement, and who seeks and is refused employment to which the advertisement relates, shall be conclusively presumed to have been refused employment for that reason.

Where there is an arrangement or practice under which employment is offered only to persons put forward or approved by a trade union, and the trade union puts forward or approves only persons who are members of the union, a person who is not a member of the union and who is refused employment in pursuance of the arrangement or practice shall be taken to have been refused employment because he is not a member of the trade union.

A person shall be taken to be refused employment if he seeks employment of any description with a person and that person:

(a) refuses or deliberately omits to entertain and process his application or enquiry, or

(b) causes him to withdraw or cease to pursue his application or enquiry, or

(c) refuses or deliberately omits to offer him employment of that description, or

(d) makes him an offer of such employment the terms of which are such as no reasonable employer who wished to fill the post would offer and which is not accepted, or

(e) makes him an offer of such employment but withdraws it or causes him not to accept it.

Where a person is offered employment on terms which include a requirement that he is, or is not, a member of a trade union, or any such requirement as is mentioned above and he does not accept the offer because he does not satisfy or, as the case may be, is unwilling to accept the requirement, he shall be treated as having been refused employment for that reason.

Where a person may not be considered for appointment or election to an office in a trade union unless he is a member of the union, or of a particular branch or section of the union or of one of a number of particular branches or sections of the union, nothing in this section applies to anything done for the purpose of securing compliance with that condition although as holder of the office he would be employed by the union.

For this purpose an "office" means any position by virtue of which the holder is an official of the union.

The provisions of this section apply in relation to an employment agency acting, or purporting to act, on behalf of an employer as in relation to an employer.

Section 138: Refusal of Service of Employment Agency on Grounds Related to Union Membership

This section is similar to section 137 where refusal of its services by an employment agency to a person on grounds related to trade union membership is unlawful.

A person who is unlawfully refused any service of an employment agency has a right of complaint to an employment tribunal.

Section 146: Detriment on Grounds Related to Union Membership or Activities

A worker has the right not to be subjected to any detriment as an individual by any act, or any deliberate failure to act by his employer, if the act or failure takes place for the sole or main purpose of:

- preventing or deterring him from being or seeking to become a member of an independent trade union, or penalising him for doing so;

- preventing or deterring him from taking part in the activities of an independent trade union at an appropriate time, or penalising him for doing so;

- preventing or deterring him from making use of trade union services at an appropriate time, or penalising him for doing so; or

- compelling him to be or become a member of any trade union or of a particular trade union or of one of a number of particular trade unions.

"An appropriate time" means a time outside the worker's working hours or a time within his working hours at which in accordance with agreed arrangements or consent given by his employer, it is permissible for him to take part in trade union activities or (as the case may be) make use of trade union services.

"Working hours" in relation to a worker, means in accordance with his contract of employment (or other contract personally to do work or perform services), he is required to be at work.

A worker or former worker may present a complaint to an employment tribunal that he has been subjected to a detriment by his employer in contravention of this section.

This section does not apply when the worker is an employee and the detriment in question amounts to dismissal.

Section 147: Time Limit for Proceedings

An employment tribunal shall not consider a complaint under section 146 unless it is presented before the end of the period of three months beginning with the date of the act or failure to which the complaint relates or, where that act or failure is part of a series of similar acts or failures (or both), the last of them. Where the tribunal is satisfied that it was not reasonably practicable for the complaint to be presented within this time, it may be presented within such further period as it deems reasonable.

Section 149: Remedies

Where the tribunal finds a complaint under section 146 is well-founded, it shall declare to that effect and may make an award of compensation in respect of the complaint. The amount of compensation awarded shall be such as the tribunal considers to be just and equitable in all the circumstances having regard to the infringement complained of and to any loss sustained by the complainant which is attributable to the act or failure that infringed his right.

Section 152: Dismissal of Employee on Grounds Related to Trade Union Membership or Activities

The dismissal of an employee shall be regarded as unfair if the reason (or, if more than one, the principal reason) for it was that the employee:

- Was or proposed to become a member of an independent trade union.
- Had taken part or proposed to take part in the activities of an independent trade union at an appropriate time.
- Had made use, or proposed to make use, of trade union services at an appropriate time.
- Had failed to accept an offer made in contravention of section 145A or 145B (inducements relating to union membership or activities, or to collective bargaining).
- Was not a member of any trade union or had refused, or proposed to refuse, to become or remain a member.

Section 153: Selection for Redundancy on Grounds Related to Union Membership or Activities

Where an employee's dismissal was that he was redundant but it is shown that the circumstances relating to his redundancy applied equally to one or more other employees, similarly employed in the same undertaking, and who have not been dismissed, and that the reason for his selection for redundancy was one of those specified in section 152, the dismissal shall be regarded as unfair.

Section 156: Minimum Basic Award

Where a dismissal is unfair by virtue of section 152 or 153, the basic minimum award, before any reduction is made under section 122 of the **Employment Rights Act 1996**, shall be not less than £6,634562.

Note: this figure is correct as of 6 April 202120. Compensation limits are varied annually; this figure is found in the Schedule to the **Employment Rights (Increase of Limits) Order 202120**.

Section 237: Dismissal of Those Taking Part in Unofficial Industrial Action

An employee has no right to complain of unfair dismissal if at the time of dismissal he was taking part in an unofficial strike or other unofficial industrial action.

This does not apply to the dismissal of the employee if it is shown that the reason (or, if more than one, the principal reason) for the dismissal or, in a redundancy case, for selecting the employee for dismissal was for reasons such as jury service, family, health and safety, working time, employee representative, protected disclosure, flexible working, pension scheme membership and study and training cases.

A strike or other industrial action is unofficial in relation to an employee unless:

- he is a member of a trade union and the action is authorised or endorsed by that union;
- he is not a member of a trade union but there are among those taking part in the industrial action members of a trade union by which the action has been authorised or endorsed;

provided that a strike or other industrial action shall not be regarded as unofficial if none of those taking part in it are members of a trade union.

The provisions of section 20(2) apply for the purpose of determining whether industrial action is to be taken to have been authorised or endorsed by a trade union.

The question whether industrial action is to be so taken in any case shall be determined by reference to the facts as at the time of dismissal. Provided that, where an act is repudiated as mentioned in section 21, industrial action shall not thereby be treated as unofficial before the end of the next working day after the day on which the repudiation takes place.

In this section the "time of dismissal" means:

(a) where the employee's contract of employment is terminated by notice, when the notice is given;

(b) where the employee's contract of employment is terminated without notice, when the termination takes effect; and

(c) where the employee is employed under a contract for a fixed term which expires without being renewed under the same contract, when that term expires.

"Working day" means any day which is not a Saturday or Sunday, Christmas Day, Good Friday or a bank holiday under the **Banking and Financial Dealings Act 1971**.

For the purposes of this section membership of a trade union for purposes unconnected with the employment in question shall be disregarded; but an employee who was a member of a trade union when he began to take part in industrial action shall continue to be treated as a member for the purpose of determining whether that action is unofficial in relation to him or another notwithstanding that he may in fact have ceased to be a member.

Section 238: Dismissals in Connection with Other Industrial Action

(1) This section applies in relation to an employee who has a right to complain of unfair dismissal (the "complainant") and who claims to have been unfairly dismissed, where at the date of the dismissal:

    (a) the employer was conducting or instituting a lock-out, or

    (b) the complainant was taking part in a strike or other industrial action.

(2) In such a case, an employment tribunal shall not determine whether the dismissal was fair or unfair unless it is shown that one or more of the relevant employees of the same employer have not been dismissed or that a relevant employee has, before the expiry of the period of three months since the date of dismissal, been offered re-engagement, and the complainant has not been so offered.

(2A) Subsection (2) does not apply to the dismissal of the employee if it is shown that the reason, or principal reason for the dismissal or, in a redundancy case for selecting the employee for dismissal was one of the following:

- Dismissal in jury service.
- Family reasons.
- Health and safety cases.
- Working time cases.
- Employee representative cases.
- Flexible working cases.
- Pension scheme membership cases.
- Study and training cases.

(2B) Subsection (2) does not apply in relation to an employee who is regarded as unfairly dismissed by virtue of section 238A below.

(5) In this section "date of dismissal" means:

    (a) where the employee's contract of employment was terminated by notice, the date on which the employer's notice was given, and

    (b) in any other case, the effective date of termination.

Section 238A: Participation in Official Industrial Action

(1) For the purposes of this section an employee takes protected industrial action if he commits an act which, or a series of acts each of which, he is induced to commit by an act which by virtue of section 219 is not actionable in tort.

(2) An employee who is dismissed shall be regarded for the purposes of Part X of the **Employment Rights Act 1996** (unfair dismissal) as unfairly dismissed if:

   (a) the reason (or, if more than one, the principal reason) for the dismissal is that the employee took protected industrial action, and

   (b) subsection (3), (4) or (5) applies to the dismissal.

(3) This subsection applies to a dismissal if the date of the dismissal is within the protected period (i.e. the sum of the basic period and any extension period in relation to that employee).

(4) This subsection applies to a dismissal if:

   (a) the date of the dismissal is after the end of that period, and

   (b) the employee had stopped taking protected industrial action before the end of that period.

(5) This subsection applies to a dismissal if:

   (a) the date of the dismissal is after the end of that period,

   (b) the employee had not stopped taking protected industrial action before the end of that period, and

   (c) the employer had not taken such procedural steps as would have been reasonable for the purposes of resolving the dispute to which the protected industrial action relates.

(6) In determining whether an employer has taken those steps regard shall be had, in particular, to:

   (a) whether the employer or a union had complied with procedures established by any applicable collective or other agreement;

   (b) whether the employer or a union offered or agreed to commence or resume negotiations after the start of the protected industrial action;

   (c) whether the employer or a union unreasonably refused, after the start of the protected industrial action, a request that conciliation services be used;

   (d) whether the employer or a union unreasonably refused, after the start of the protected industrial action, a request that mediation services be used in relation to procedures to be adopted for the purposes of resolving the dispute.

   (e) where there was agreement to use either of the services mentioned in paragraphs (c) and (d), the matters specified in section 238B.

(7) In determining whether an employer has taken those steps no regard shall be had to the merits of the dispute.

(7A) For the purposes of this section "the protected period", in relation to the dismissal of an employee, is the sum of the basic period and any extension period in relation to that employee.

(7B) The basic period is 12 weeks beginning with the first day of protected industrial action.

(7C) An extension period in relation to an employee is a period equal to the number of days falling on or after the first day of protected industrial action (but before the protected period ends) during the whole or any part of which the employee is locked out by his employer.

(7D) In subsections (7B) and (7C), the "first day of protected industrial action" means the day on which the employee starts to take protected industrial action (even if on that day he is locked out by his employer).

(8) For the purposes of this section no account shall be taken of the repudiation of any act by a trade union as mentioned in section 21 in relation to anything which occurs before the end of the next working day (within the meaning of section 237) after the day on which the repudiation takes place.

(9) In this section "date of dismissal" has the meaning given by section 238(5) [i.e. where the employee's contract of employment was terminated by notice, the date on which the employer's notice was given, and in any other case, the effective date of termination].

TREATY ON THE FUNCTIONING OF THE EUROPEAN UNION

A treaty is a document which binds two or more countries to do something together.

Only three Articles, which are relevant to health and safety, are recorded here- harmonisation of essential technical requirements (Article 114); improvement in standards of health and safety (Article 153) and the 'Ordinary legislative procedure' (Article 294). The full text of the Treaty may be found at **http://eur-lex.europa.eu/**

Article 114 (formerly Article 95 of the Treaty of Rome)

NB: This Article seeks to achieve harmonisation of standards across the EU. Of particular relevance to health and safety practitioners is paragraph 3.

1. Save where otherwise provided in the Treaties, the following provisions shall apply for the achievement of the objectives set out in Article 26. The European Parliament and the Council shall, acting in accordance with the ordinary legislative procedure and after consulting the Economic and Social Committee, adopt the measures for the approximation of the provisions laid down by law, regulation or administrative action in Member States which have as their object the establishment and functioning of the internal market.

2. Paragraph 1 shall not apply to fiscal provisions, to those relating to the free movement of persons nor to those relating to the rights and interests of employed persons.

3. The Commission, in its proposals envisaged in paragraph 1 concerning health, safety, environmental protection and consumer protection, will take as a base a high level of protection, taking account in particular of any new development based on scientific facts. Within their respective powers, the European Parliament and the Council will also seek to achieve this objective.

4. If, after the adoption of a harmonisation measure by the European Parliament and the Council, by the Council or by the Commission, a Member State deems it necessary to maintain national provisions on grounds of major needs referred to in Article 36, or relating to the protection of the environment or the working environment, it shall notify the Commission of these provisions as well as the grounds for maintaining them.

5. Moreover, without prejudice to paragraph 4, if, after the adoption of a harmonisation measure by the European Parliament and the Council, by the Council or by the Commission, a Member State deems it necessary to introduce national provisions based on new scientific evidence relating to the protection of the environment or the working environment on grounds of a problem specific to that Member State arising after the adoption of the harmonisation measure, it shall notify the Commission of the envisaged provisions as well as the grounds for introducing them.

6. The Commission shall, within six months of the notifications as referred to in paragraphs 4 and 5, approve or reject the national provisions involved after having verified whether or not they are a means of arbitrary discrimination or a disguised restriction on trade between Member States and whether or not they shall constitute an obstacle to the functioning of the internal market.

   In the absence of a decision by the Commission within this period the national provisions referred to in paragraphs 4 and 5 shall be deemed to have been approved.

   When justified by the complexity of the matter and in the absence of danger for human health, the Commission may notify the Member State concerned that the period referred to in this paragraph may be extended for a further period of up to six months.

7. When, pursuant to paragraph 6, a Member State is authorised to maintain or introduce national provisions derogating from a harmonisation measure, the Commission shall immediately examine whether to propose an adaptation to that measure.

8. When a Member State raises a specific problem on public health in a field which has been the subject of prior harmonisation measures, it shall bring it to the attention of the Commission which shall immediately examine whether to propose appropriate measures to the Council.

9. By way of derogation from the procedure laid down in Articles 258 and 259, the Commission and any Member State may bring the matter directly before the Court of Justice of the European Union if it considers that another Member State is making improper use of the powers provided for in this Article.

10. The harmonisation measures referred to above shall, in appropriate cases, include a safeguard clause authorising the Member States to take, for one or more of the non-economic reasons referred to in Article 36, provisional measures subject to a Union control procedure.

Article 153 (formerly Article 137 of the Treaty of Rome)

NB: This Article seeks to ensure minimum standards of health and safety across the EU and encourages Member States to improve standards. Member States may put in place measures in excess of the requirements of a European Directive, but only insofar as those measures do not harm the growth and development of small and medium-sized enterprises. The key provisions in this Article, which relate to health and safety at work are to be found in paragraphs 1(a), 1(b), 1(e), 2(a) and 2(b).

1. With a view to achieving the objectives of Article 151, the Union shall support and complement the activities of the Member States in the following fields:

    (a) improvement in particular of the working environment to protect workers' health and safety;

    (b) working conditions;

    (c) social security and social protection of workers;

    (d) protection of workers where their employment contract is terminated;

    (e) the information and consultation of workers;

    (f) representation and collective defence of the interests of workers and employers, including co-determination, subject to paragraph 5;

    (g) conditions of employment for third-country nationals legally residing in Union territory;

    (h) the integration of persons excluded from the labour market, without prejudice to Article 166;

    (i) equality between men and women with regard to labour market opportunities and treatment at work;

    (j) the combating of social exclusion;

    (k) the modernisation of social protection systems without prejudice to point (c).

2. To this end, the European Parliament and the Council:

    (a) may adopt measures designed to encourage co-operation between Member States through initiatives aimed at improving knowledge, developing exchanges of information and best practices, promoting innovative approaches and evaluating experiences, excluding any harmonisation of the laws and regulations of the Member States;

    (b) may adopt, in the fields referred to in paragraph 1(a) to (i), by means of directives, minimum requirements for gradual implementation, having regard to the conditions and technical rules obtaining in each of the Member States. Such directives shall avoid imposing administrative, financial and legal constraints in a way which would hold back the creation and development of small and medium-sized undertakings.

    The European Parliament and the Council shall act in accordance with the ordinary legislative procedure after consulting the Economic and Social Committee and the Committee of the Regions.

    In the fields referred to in paragraph 1(c), (d), (f) and (g), the Council shall act unanimously, in accordance with a special legislative procedure, after consulting the European Parliament and the said Committees.

    The Council, acting unanimously on a proposal from the Commission, after consulting the European Parliament, may decide to render the ordinary legislative procedure applicable to paragraph 1(d), (f) and (g).

3. A Member State may entrust management and labour, at their joint request, with the implementation of directives adopted pursuant to paragraph 2, or, where appropriate, with the implementation of a Council decision adopted in accordance with Article 155.

    In this case, it shall ensure that, no later than the date on which a directive or a decision must be transposed or implemented, management and labour have introduced the necessary measures by agreement, the Member State concerned being required to take any necessary measure enabling it at any time to be in a position to guarantee the results imposed by that directive or that decision.

4. The provisions adopted pursuant to this Article:

    - shall not affect the right of Member States to define the fundamental principles of their social security systems and must not significantly affect the financial equilibrium thereof;

    - shall not prevent any Member State from maintaining or introducing more stringent protective measures compatible with the Treaties.

5. The provisions of this Article shall not apply to pay, the right of association, the right to strike or the right to impose lock-outs.

Article 294 (formerly Article 251 of the Treaty of Rome) - The Ordinary Legislative Procedure

NB: This procedure used to be known as the 'Co-decision procedure' and is now the main procedure by which EU regulations, directives or decisions are adopted by the European Parliament and the Council following a proposal from the Commission.

1. Where reference is made in the Treaties to the ordinary legislative procedure for the adoption of an act, the following procedure shall apply.
2. The Commission shall submit a proposal to the European Parliament and the Council.

First reading

3. The European Parliament shall adopt its position at first reading and communicate it to the Council.
4. If the Council approves the European Parliament's position, the act concerned shall be adopted in the wording which corresponds to the position of the European Parliament.
5. If the Council does not approve the European Parliament's position, it shall adopt its position at first reading and communicate it to the European Parliament.
6. The Council shall inform the European Parliament fully of the reasons which led it to adopt its position at first reading. The Commission shall inform the European Parliament fully of its position.

Second reading

7. If, within three months of such communication, the European Parliament:
   (a) approves the Council's position at first reading or has not taken a decision, the act concerned shall be deemed to have been adopted in the wording which corresponds to the position of the Council;
   (b) rejects, by a majority of its component members, the Council's position at first reading, the proposed act shall be deemed not to have been adopted;
   (c) proposes, by a majority of its component members, amendments to the Council's position at first reading, the text thus amended shall be forwarded to the Council and to the Commission, which shall deliver an opinion on those amendments.
8. If, within three months of receiving the European Parliament's amendments, the Council, acting by a qualified majority:
   (a) approves all those amendments, the act in question shall be deemed to have been adopted;
   (b) does not approve all the amendments, the President of the Council, in agreement with the President of the European Parliament, shall within six weeks convene a meeting of the Conciliation Committee.
9. The Council shall act unanimously on the amendments on which the Commission has delivered a negative opinion.

Conciliation

10. The Conciliation Committee, which shall be composed of the members of the Council or their representatives and an equal number of members representing the European Parliament, shall have the task of reaching agreement on a joint text, by a qualified majority of the members of the Council or their representatives and by a majority of the members representing the European Parliament within six weeks of its being convened, on the basis of the positions of the European Parliament and the Council at second reading.
11. The Commission shall take part in the Conciliation Committee's proceedings and shall take all necessary initiatives with a view to reconciling the positions of the European Parliament and the Council.
12. If, within six weeks of its being convened, the Conciliation Committee does not approve the joint text, the proposed act shall be deemed not to have been adopted.

Third reading

13. If, within that period, the Conciliation Committee approves a joint text, the European Parliament, acting by a majority of the votes cast, and the Council, acting by a qualified majority, shall each have a period of six weeks from that approval in which to adopt the act in question in accordance with the joint text. If they fail to do so, the proposed act shall be deemed not to have been adopted.
14. The periods of three months and six weeks referred to in this Article shall be extended by a maximum of one month and two weeks respectively at the initiative of the European Parliament or the Council.

Special provisions

15. Where, in the cases provided for in the Treaties, a legislative act is submitted to the ordinary legislative procedure on the initiative of a group of Member States, on a recommendation by the European Central Bank, or at the request of the Court of Justice, paragraph 2, the second sentence of paragraph 6, and paragraph 9 shall not apply.

    In such cases, the European Parliament and the Council shall communicate the proposed act to the Commission with their positions at first and second readings. The European Parliament or the Council may request the opinion of the Commission throughout the procedure, which the Commission may also deliver on its own initiative. It may also, if it deems it necessary, take part in the Conciliation Committee in accordance with paragraph 11.

UK REACH

UK REACH is a rather large piece of legislation, with considerable detail and limited application in the core syllabuses. As a result, we have only provided a broad overview of the Regulation here. **REACH** is short for **Registration, Evaluation, Authorisation and Restriction of Chemicals**. It came into force on 1 June 2007. Following the UK's exit from the EU it has been retained with changes made so that it operates effectively after UK exit and as such is now known as **UK REACH** rather than **REACH**.

Some of the main points are:

- If someone manufactures or imports into Great Britain any chemical substance in quantities of 1 tonne or more per annum, that someone must register it. Chemical substances can occur on their own, within mixtures or within articles. During registration the registrant submits a technical dossier to the Health and Safety Executive (HSE). A Chemical Safety Report (CSR) may also be required (for a substance manufactured/imported in quantities of 10 tonnes or more). Relevant information is also required to be passed down the supply chain (to downstream users and distributors), largely through safety data sheets and appended Chemical Safety Assessments (CSAs). But this works both ways; downstream users pass relevant information up the supply chain too.

- Dossiers are evaluated by the HSE for quality in terms of compliance and also in relation to any proposals from the manufacturer/importer for further testing that may be needed. There may be several possible outcomes at this stage. It is envisaged that, for most substances, no further action will be needed after registration. In some cases, however, more information may be requested from the registrant to satisfy any suspicions of risk that may arise during the evaluation process. It may also be decided that the substance needs to be subject to tighter regulation- such as authorisation or restriction.

- Authorisation and restriction are two different regimes for controlling widespread use of certain categories of substances. Authorisation is reserved for substances of very high concern (carcinogens, mutagens, reproductive toxins and compounds which are persistent and bio-accumulative). This means that they cannot be used without specific authorisation to do so. In essence, if something is subject to authorisation and it is not authorised for a particular use, it cannot be used. Restriction is a mechanism used to control marketing and use for substances that are found to pose unacceptable risks. It can take the form of managing the risks (with appropriate controls), restricting to certain uses only or banning the substance altogether. In contrast to authorisation, if something is not restricted then the presumption is that it is free to be used (unless of course it is subject to authorisation!). It is worth noting that substances do not have to have gone through the Registration/Evaluation process to be authorised or restricted. They may have been flagged up for this treatment already by independent routes.

An outline of the content of a safety data sheet is provided. Under **UK REACH** a safety data sheet must contain the following sections:

Section 1: Identification of substances/mixtures and of the company/undertaking.

Section 2: Hazards identification.

Section 3: Composition/information on ingredients.

Section 4: First-aid measures.

Section 5: Fire-fighting measures.

Section 6: Accidental release measures.

Section 7: Handling and storage.

Section 8: Exposure controls/personal protection.

Section 9: Physical and chemical properties.

Section 10: Stability and reactivity.

Section 11: Toxicological information.

Section 12: Ecological information.

Section 13: Disposal considerations.

Section 14: Transport information.

Section 15: Regulatory information.

Section 16: Other information.

UNFAIR CONTRACT TERMS ACT 1977

Amending Legislation

This Act has been updated a number of times, most recently by the **Consumer Rights Act 2015**, Schedule 4, which came into effect on 1 October 2015.

Summary

This extract from the Act deals only with Part I (amendment of law for England and Wales and Northern Ireland), Part II (amendment of law for Scotland) and Schedule 2.

Part I - Amendment of Law for England and Wales and Northern Ireland

Section 1: Scope of Part 1

(1) For the purposes of this Part of this Act, "negligence" means the breach:

   (a) of any obligation, arising from the express or implied terms of a contract, to take reasonable care or exercise reasonable skill in the performance of the contract;

   (b) of any common law duty to take reasonable care or exercise reasonable skill (but not any stricter duty);

   (c) of the common duty of care imposed by the **Occupiers' Liability Act 1957** or the **Occupiers' Liability Act (Northern Ireland) 1957**.

(2) This Part of this Act is subject to Part III and in relation to contracts, the operation of sections 2, 3 and 7 is subject to the exceptions made by Schedule 1.

(3) In the case of both contract and tort, sections 2 to 7 apply (except where the contrary is stated in section 6(4)) only to business liability, that is liability for breach of obligations or duties arising:

   (a) from things done or to be done by a person in the course of a business (whether his own business or another's) or

   (b) from the occupation of premises used for business purposes of the occupier,

   and references to liability are to be read accordingly but liability of an occupier of premises for breach of an obligation or duty towards a person obtaining access to the premises for recreational or educational purposes, being liability for loss or damage suffered by reason of the dangerous state of the premises, is not a business liability of the occupier unless granting that person such access for the purposes concerned falls within the business purposes of the occupier.

(4) In relation to any breach of duty or obligation, it is immaterial for any purpose of this Part of this Act whether the breach was inadvertent or intentional, or whether liability for it arises directly or vicariously.

Section 2: Negligence Liability

(1) A person cannot by reference to any contract term or to a notice given to persons generally or to particular persons exclude or restrict his liability for death or personal injury resulting from negligence.

(2) In the case of other loss or damage, a person cannot so exclude or restrict his liability for negligence except in so far as the term or notice satisfies the requirement of reasonableness.

(3) Where a contract term or notice purports to exclude or restrict liability for negligence a person's agreement to or awareness of it is not of itself to be taken as indicating his voluntary acceptance of any risk.

This section does not apply to a term in a consumer contract or to a notice to the extent that it is a consumer notice.

Section 3: Liability Arising in Contract

The following points are important:

(1) This section applies as between contracting parties where one of them deals on the other's written standard terms of business.

(2) As against that party, the other cannot by reference to any contract term:

   (a) when himself in breach of contract, exclude or restrict any liability of his in respect of the breach; or

   (b) claim to be entitled:

      (i) to render a contractual performance substantially different from that which was reasonably expected of him, or

(ii) in respect of the whole or any part of his contractual obligation, to render no performance at all,

except in so far as (in any of the cases mentioned above in this subsection) the contract term satisfies the requirement of reasonableness.

Subject to the qualification given in section 62 of the **Consumer Rights Act 2015**, this section does not apply to a term in a consumer contract.

Section 4: Unreasonable Indemnity Clauses

This section was repealed by the **Consumer Rights Act 2015**.

Section 5: "Guarantee" of Consumer Goods

This section was repealed by the **Consumer Rights Act 2015**.

Section 6: Sale and Hire-Purchase

(1) Liability for breach of the obligations arising from:

    (a) section 12 of the **Sale of Goods Act 1979** (seller's implied undertakings as to title, etc.);

    (b) section 8 of the **Supply of Goods (Implied Terms) Act 1973** (the corresponding thing in relation to hire-purchase),

cannot be excluded or restricted by reference to any contract term.

(1A) Liability for breach of the obligations arising from:

    (a) section 13, 14 or 15 of the 1979 Act (seller's implied undertakings as to conformity of goods with description or sample, or as to their quality or fitness for a particular purpose);

    (b) section 9, 10 or 11 of the 1973 Act (the corresponding things in relation to hire purchase),

cannot be excluded or restricted by reference to a contract term except in so far as the term satisfies the requirement of reasonableness.

(4) The liabilities referred to in this section are not only the business liabilities defined by section 1(3), but include those arising under any contract of sale of goods or hire-purchase agreement.

Subject to the provision made in section 31 of the **Consumer Rights Act 2015**, this section does not apply to a consumer contract.

Section 7: Miscellaneous Contracts under which Goods Pass

(1) Where the possession or ownership of goods passes under or in pursuance of a contract not governed by the law of sale of goods or hire-purchase, subsections (2) to (4) below apply as regards the effect (if any) to be given to contract terms excluding or restricting liability for breach of obligation arising by implication of law from the nature of the contract.

(1A) Liability in respect of the goods' correspondence with description or sample, or their quality or fitness for any particular purpose, cannot be excluded or restricted by reference to such a term except in so far as the term satisfies the requirement of reasonableness.

(3A) Liability for breach of the obligations arising under section 2 of the **Supply of Goods and Services Act 1982** (implied terms about title, etc. in certain contracts for the transfer of the property in goods) cannot be excluded or restricted by reference to any such term.

(4) Liability in respect of:

    (a) the right to transfer ownership of the goods, or give possession; or

    (b) the assurance of quiet possession to a person taking goods in pursuance of the contract,

cannot (in a case to which subsection (3A) above does not apply) be excluded or restricted by reference to any such term except in so far as the term satisfies the requirement of reasonableness.

Subject to section 31 of the **Consumer Rights Act 2015**, this section does not apply to a consumer contract.

Section 8: Misrepresentation

This section makes an amendment to section 3 of the **Misrepresentation Act 1967** (Avoidance of provision excluding liability for misrepresentation).

Section 9: Effect of Breach

This section was repealed by the **Consumer Rights Act 2015**.

Section 10: Evasion by Means of Secondary Contract

A person is not bound by any contract term prejudicing or taking away his rights which arise under, or in connection with the performance of, another contract, so far as those rights extend to the enforcement of another's liability which this Part of this Act prevents that other from excluding or restricting.

Section 11: The "Reasonableness" Test

(1) In relation to a contract term, the requirement of reasonableness for the purposes of this Part of this Act, section 3 of the **Misrepresentation Act 1967** and section 3 of the **Misrepresentation Act (Northern Ireland) 1967** is that the term shall have been a fair and reasonable one to be included having regard to the circumstances which were, or ought reasonably to have been, known to, or in the contemplation of, the parties when the contract was made.

(2) In determining for the purposes of section 6 or 7 above whether a contract term satisfies the requirement of reasonableness, regard shall be had in particular to the matters specified in Schedule 2 to this Act; but this subsection does not prevent the court or arbitrator from holding, in accordance with any rule of law, that a term which purports to exclude or restrict any relevant liability is not a term of the contract.

(3) In relation to a notice (not being a notice having contractual effect), the requirement of reasonableness under this Act is that it should be fair and reasonable to allow reliance on it, having regard to all the circumstances obtaining when the liability arose or (but for the notice) would have arisen.

(4) Where by reference to a contract term or notice a person seeks to restrict liability to a specified sum of money, and the question arises (under this or any other Act) whether the term or notice satisfies the requirement of reasonableness, regard shall be had in particular (but without prejudice to subsection (2) above in the case of contract terms) to:

   (a) the resources which he could expect to be available to him for the purpose of meeting the liability should it arise; and

   (b) how far it was open to him to cover himself by insurance.

(5) It is for those claiming that a contract term or notice satisfies the requirement of reasonableness to show that it does.

Section 12: "Dealing as Consumer"

This section was repealed by the **Consumer Rights Act 2015**.

Section 13: Varieties of Exemption Clause

(1) To the extent that this Part of the Act prevents the exclusion or restriction of any liability it also prevents:

   (a) making the liability or its enforcement subject to restrictive or onerous conditions;

   (b) excluding or restricting any right or remedy in respect of the liability or subjecting a person to any prejudice in consequence of his pursuing any such right or remedy;

   (c) excluding or restricting rules of evidence or procedure;

   and (to that extent) sections 2, 6 and 7 also prevent excluding or restricting liability by reference to terms and notices which exclude or restrict the relevant obligation or duty.

(2) But an agreement in writing to submit present or future differences to arbitration is not to be treated under this Part of this Act as excluding or restricting any liability.

Section 14: Interpretation of Part I

In this Part of the Act:

- "business" includes a profession and the activities of any government department or local or public authority;
- "consumer contract" has the same meaning as in the **Consumer Rights Act 2015** (see section 61);
- "consumer notice" has the same meaning as in the **Consumer Rights Act 2015** (see section 61);
- "goods" has the same meaning as in the **Sale of Goods Act 1979**;
- "purchase Agreement" has the same meaning as in the **Consumer Credit Act 1974**;

- "negligence" has the meaning given by section 1(1);
- "notice" includes an announcement, whether or not in writing, and any other communication or pretended communication; and
- "personal Injury" includes any disease and any impairment of physical or mental condition.

Part II - Amendment of Law for Scotland

Section 15: Scope of Part II

(1) This Part of this Act is subject to Part III of this Act and does not affect the validity of any discharge or indemnity given by a person in consideration of the receipt by him of compensation in settlement of any claim which he has.

(2) Subject to the next subsection, sections 16 and 17 of this Act apply to any contract only to the extent that the contract:

   (a) relates to the transfer of the ownership or possession of goods from one person to another (with or without work having been done on them);

   (b) constitutes a contract of service or apprenticeship;

   (c) relates to services of whatever kind, including (without prejudice to the foregoing generality) carriage, deposit and pledge, care and custody, mandate, agency, loan and services relating to the use of land;

   (d) relates to the liability of an occupier of land to persons entering upon or using that land;

   (e) relates to a grant of any right or permission to enter upon or use land not amounting to an estate or interest in the land.

(3) Notwithstanding anything in the previous subsection, sections 16 and 17:

   - do not apply to any contract to the extent that the contract:
     - is a contract of insurance (including a contract to pay an annuity on human life);
     - relates to the formation, constitution or dissolution of any body corporate or unincorporated association or partnership;
   - apply to:
     - a contract of marine salvage or towage;
     - a charter party of a ship or hovercraft;
     - a contract for the carriage of goods by ship or hovercraft; or,
     - a contract to which the next subsection relates, only to the extent that:
     - both parties deal or hold themselves out as dealing in the course of a business (and then only in so far as the contract purports to exclude or restrict liability for breach of duty in respect of death or personal injury).

(4) This subsection relates to a contract in pursuance of which goods are carried by ship or hovercraft and which either:

   - specifies ship or hovercraft as the means of carriage over part of the journey to be covered; or
   - makes no provision as to the means of carriage and does not exclude ship or hovercraft as that means,

   in so far as the contract operates for and in relation to the carriage of the goods by that means.

Section 16: Liability for Breach of Duty

- Subject to the next subsection, where a term of a contract, or a provision of a notice given to persons generally or to particular persons, purports to exclude or restrict liability for breach of duty arising in the course of any business or from the occupation of any premises used for business purposes of the occupier, that term or provision:
   - shall be void in any case where such exclusion or restriction is in respect of death or personal injury;
   - shall, in any other case, have no effect if it was not fair and reasonable to incorporate the term in the contract or, as the case may be, if it is not fair and reasonable to allow reliance on the provision.

- Nothing in the final paragraph of the above subsection shall be taken as implying that a provision of a notice has effect in circumstances where, apart from that paragraph, it would not have effect.

- The above subsection does not affect the validity of any discharge and indemnity given by a person, on or in connection with an award to him of compensation for pneumoconiosis attributable to employment in the coal industry, in respect of any further claim arising from his contracting that disease.

- Where under the first subsection above a term of a contract or a provision of a notice is void or has no effect, the fact that a person agreed to, or was aware of, the term or provision shall not of itself be sufficient evidence that he knowingly and voluntarily assumed any risk.
    - This section does not apply to:
        - a term in a consumer contract, or
        - a notice to the extent that it is a consumer notice,

(but see the provision made about such contracts and notices in sections 62 and 65 of the **Consumer Rights Act 2015**).

Section 17: Control of Unreasonable Exemptions in Standard Form Contracts

Any term of a contract which is a standard form contract shall have no effect for the purpose of enabling a party to the contract:

- who is in breach of a contractual obligation, to exclude or restrict any liability of his to the customer in respect of the breach;
- in respect of a contractual obligation, to render no performance, or to render a performance substantially different from that which the customer reasonably expected from the contract;

if it was not fair and reasonable to incorporate the term in the contract.

In this section "customer" means a party to a standard form contract who deals on the basis of written standard terms of business of the other party to the contract who himself deals in the course of a business.

This section does not apply to a term in a consumer contract (but see the provision made about such contracts in section 62 of the **Consumer Rights Act 2015**).

Section 18: Unreasonable Indemnity Clauses in Consumer Contracts

This section was repealed by the **Consumer Rights Act 2015**.

Section 19: "Guarantee" of Consumer Goods

This section was repealed by the **Consumer Rights Act 2015**.

Section 20: Obligations Implied by Law in Sale and Hire-Purchase Contracts

Any term of a contract which purports to exclude or restrict liability for breach of the obligations arising from:

- section 12 of the **Sale of Goods Act 1979** (seller's implied undertakings as to title, etc.);
- section 8 of the **Supply of Goods (Implied Terms) Act 1973** (implied terms as to title in hire-purchase agreements), shall be void.

Any term of a contract which purports to exclude or restrict liability for breach of the obligations arising from:

- section 13, 14 or 15 of the 1979 Act (seller's implied undertakings as to conformity of goods with description or sample, or as to their quality or fitness for a particular purpose);
- section 9, 10 or 11 of the 1973 Act (the corresponding things in relation to hire purchase), shall have effect only if it was fair and reasonable to incorporate the term in the contract.

This section does not apply to a consumer contract (but see the provision made about such contracts in section 31 of the **Consumer Rights Act 2015**).

Section 21: Obligations Implied by Law in Other Contracts for the Supply of Goods

Any term of a contract to which this section applies purporting to exclude or restrict liability for breach of an obligation such as is referred to below shall have no effect if it was not fair and reasonable to incorporate the term in the contract.

This section applies to any contract to the extent that it relates to any such matter as is referred to in section 15(2)(a) of this Act, but does not apply to:

- a contract of sale of goods or a hire-purchase agreement; or
- a charter party of a ship or hovercraft.

An obligation referred to in this subsection is an obligation incurred under a contract in the course of a business and arising by implication of law from the nature of the contract which relates:

- to the correspondence of goods with description or sample, or to the quality or fitness of goods for any particular purpose; or
- to any right to transfer ownership or possession of goods, or to the enjoyment of quiet possession of goods.

Notwithstanding anything in the foregoing provisions of this section, any term of a contract which purports to exclude or restrict liability for breach of the obligations arising under section 11B of the **Supply of Goods and Services Act 1982** (implied terms about title, freedom from encumbrances and quiet possession in certain contracts for the transfer of property in goods) shall be void.

This section does not apply to a consumer contract (but see the provision made about such contracts in section 31 of the **Consumer Rights Act 2015**).

Section 22: Consequence of Breach

This section was repealed by the **Consumer Rights Act 2015**.

Section 23: Evasion by Means of Secondary Contract

Any term of any contract shall be void which purports to exclude or restrict, or has the effect of excluding or restricting:

- the exercise, by a party to any other contract, of any right or remedy which arises in respect of that other contract in consequence of breach of duty, or of obligation, liability for which could not by virtue of the provisions of this Part of this Act be excluded or restricted by a term of that other contract;
- the application of the provisions of this Part of this Act in respect of that or any other contract.

Section 24: The "Reasonableness" Test

(1) In determining for the purposes of this Part of this Act whether it was fair and reasonable to incorporate a term in a contract, regard shall be had only to the circumstances which were, or ought reasonably to have been, known to or in the contemplation of the parties to the contract at the time the contract was made.

(2) In determining for the purposes of section 20 or 21 of this Act whether it was fair and reasonable to incorporate a term in a contract, regard shall be had in particular to the matters specified in Schedule 2 to this Act; but this subsection shall not prevent a court or arbiter from holding, in accordance with any rule of law, that a term which purports to exclude or restrict any relevant liability is not a term of the contract.

(2A) In determining for the purposes of this Part of this Act whether it is fair and reasonable to allow reliance on a provision of a notice (not being a notice having contractual effect), regard shall be had to all the circumstances obtaining when the liability arose or (but for the provision) would have arisen.

(3) Where a term in a contract or a provision of a notice purports to restrict liability to a specified sum of money, and the question arises for the purposes of this Part of this Act whether it was fair and reasonable to incorporate the term in the contract or whether it is fair and reasonable to allow reliance on the provision, then, without prejudice to subsection (2) above in the case of a term in a contract, regard shall be had in particular to:

- the resources which the party seeking to rely on that term or provision could expect to be available to him for the purpose of meeting the liability should it arise;
- how far it was open to that party to cover himself by insurance.

(4) The onus of proving that it was fair and reasonable to incorporate a term in a contract or that it is fair and reasonable to allow reliance on a provision of a notice shall lie on the party so contending.

Section 25: Interpretation of Part II

In this Part of this Act:

- "breach of duty" means the breach:
  - of any obligation, arising from the express or implied terms of a contract, to take reasonable care or exercise reasonable skill in the performance of the contract;
  - of any common law duty to take reasonable care or exercise reasonable skill;
  - of the duty of reasonable care imposed by section 2(1) of the **Occupiers' Liability (Scotland) Act 1960**;
- "business" includes a profession and the activities of any government department or local or public authority;

- "consumer contract" has the same meaning as in the **Consumer Rights Act 2015** (see section 61);
- "consumer notice" has the same meaning as in the **Consumer Rights Act 2015** (see section 61);
- "goods" has the same meaning as in the **Sale of Goods Act 1979**;
- "hire-purchase agreement" has the same meaning as in section 189(1) of the **Consumer Credit Act 1974**;
- "notice" includes an announcement, whether or not in writing, and any other communication or pretended communication;
- "personal injury" includes any disease and any impairment of physical or mental condition.

In relation to any breach of duty or obligation, it is immaterial for any purpose of this Part of this Act whether the act or omission giving rise to that breach was inadvertent or intentional, or whether liability for it arises directly or vicariously.

In this Part of this Act, any reference to excluding or restricting any liability includes:

- making the liability or its enforcement subject to any restrictive or onerous conditions;
- excluding or restricting any right or remedy in respect of the liability, or subjecting a person to any prejudice in consequence of his pursuing any such right or remedy;
- excluding or restricting any rule of evidence or procedure;

but does not include an agreement to submit any question to arbitration.

In sections 15, 16, 20 and 21 of this Act, any reference to excluding or restricting liability for breach of an obligation or duty shall include a reference to excluding or restricting the obligation or duty itself.

Schedule 2: Guidelines for Application of Reasonableness Test

Matters to which regard is to be taken for applying the reasonableness test are any of the following which appear relevant:

(a) The strength of the bargaining positions of the parties relevant to each other taking into account alternative means by which the customer's requirements could be met.

(b) Whether the customer received an inducement to agree to the term or to accepting it or had an opportunity of entering into a similar contract with other persons but without having to accept similar terms.

(c) Whether the customer knew or ought reasonably to have known of the existence and extent of the term (having regard to any custom of the trade and any previous course of dealing between the parties).

(d) Where the term excludes or restricts any relevant liability if some condition is not complied with, whether it was reasonable at the time of the contract to expect that compliance with that condition would be practicable.

(e) Whether the goods were manufactured, processed or adapted to the special order of the customer.

WASTE ELECTRICAL AND ELECTRONIC EQUIPMENT REGULATIONS 2013 (SI 2013 NO. 3113)

The Regulations were amended by the **Waste Electrical and Electronic Equipment (Amendment) Regulations 2018** and the **Waste Electrical and Electronic Equipment (Amendment) (No.2) Regulations 2018**. The changes have been inserted in the text below which gives an overview of the principal Regulations.

Part 1 deals with definitions of key terms.

Part 2 deals with the application of the Regulations. During the transitional period (defined in Regulation 2 as being from 1 January 2014 to 31 December 2018), the Regulations apply to EEE within Schedules 1 and 2. Regulation 6 makes provision for the application of these Regulations from 1 January 2019.

Part 3 deals with producer obligations and is concerned with financing the costs of collection, treatment, recovery and environmentally sound disposal of WEEE from private households and from other users. UK producers are obliged to join a Producer Compliance Scheme (PCS). Producers registered in the UK may also appoint an authorised representative in other Member States where the producer places EEE on the market, instead of registering as a producer in that Member State- this is particularly relevant to producers who use distance selling methods. Producers or their authorised representatives must pay PCSs according to their published fee structure and membership rules and must provide information to their PCS about the business and amounts of EEE placed on the UK market.

There is an exception from the requirement to join a PCS for 'small producers', i.e. those that place less than 5 tonnes of EEE on the market in any one compliance period. Instead, they are required to register directly with the relevant environment agency.

All producers must mark EEE placed on the UK market with the 'crossed-out wheeled bin' symbol and must provide information on reuse and environmentally sound treatment for products.

Part 4 deals with the obligations of the PCS. These obligations include the requirement for the operator of a scheme to register each scheme member and impose a responsibility on the scheme operator to finance the costs of collection, treatment, recovery and environmentally sound disposal of WEEE from private households and other locations.

Operators of schemes must also set up systems to prioritise the reuse of whole appliances. Where this is not possible, systems must be set up to provide for the separate collection and treatment of WEEE using best available collection, treatment, recovery and recycling techniques. All PCSs have to join a 'balancing scheme', under which the costs of collecting materials when requested by local authorities are shared among all PCSs. Procedures for approval of balancing schemes by the Secretary of State are provided in the Regulations.

If no contract is in place for the collection and treatment of WEEE between the scheme operator and the designated collection facility (operated by a local authority or a person acting on their behalf), where WEEE is in the same WEEE collection stream as deposited WEEE then the scheme operator of the WEEE is required to take action to collect and treat the WEEE. This Part also requires the operator of a scheme to make reports in a specified format to the appropriate authority concerning total tonnage of WEEE collected, delivered to a treatment facility, or returned or taken back to/by the operator. The amount of EEE placed on the market must also be reported. Where scheme operators have obligations in relation to WEEE from private households or other locations, they must provide a written declaration of compliance to the appropriate authority by 31 March following the end of the compliance period. A separate reporting requirement is present for the amount of WEEE that is exported for reuse or treatment outside of the UK.

Part 5 deals with the obligations and rights of distributors with respect to WEEE from private households. The distributor shall ensure that WEEE from private households can be returned to him free of charge and on a one-to-one basis by that person provided that any such WEEE:

- is of equivalent type to, and
- has fulfilled the same function as,

the supplied equipment.

Distributors:

- Have a right to return WEEE from private households free of charge to a system set up by a compliance scheme.
- Must make a range of information available in writing to users, such as information on the available collection and take-back systems, the meaning of the crossed-out wheeled bin symbol, etc.
- Are required to keep records of the number of units of WEEE returned and of the information made available to users.
    - Large distributors (those with a turnover for sales of electronic equipment in excess of £100,000) are required to take back waste electrical and electronic equipment in-store rather than through the National Take-Back Scheme.

Part 6 covers miscellaneous provisions such as financing obligations; the optimisation of reuse and recycling of WEEE; WEEE from private households that represents a health and safety risk; take-back from private households; prohibitions on showing costs of collection, treatment, etc. from private households; the final holder's right of return, free of charge, of WEEE from private households; notification of an intention to retain WEEE; and obligations on approved exporters of EEE to comply with the requirements of Schedule 9.

Part 7 deals with the approval of proposed schemes and withdrawal of approval of schemes.

Part 8 covers the approval of authorised treatment facilities and exporters.

Part 9 describes the powers and duties of the Secretary of State in relation to such things as take-back schemes, collection facility approval and preparing a code of practice on standards to be met by operators of collection facilities and schemes for collection of WEEE.

Part 10 deals with the duties of appropriate authorities, such as registration of producers and authorised representatives, monitoring, scheme approval, provision of information and approval of authorised treatment facilities and exporters.

Part 11 consists of a single regulation (Regulation 82), covering disclosure of information.

Part 12 is concerned with the right to bring appeals and the procedure for the same.

Part 13 covers enforcement. It is the duty of the Secretary of State to enforce these Regulations, although several of the regulations are enforced by the Environment Agency (England), Natural Resources Wales (Wales), SEPA (Scotland) or the Department of Agriculture, Environment and Rural Affairs (Northern Ireland).

Part 14 deals with offences and penalties, which are fines.

Schedules

Schedule 1 identifies the categories of EEE covered by these Regulations during the transitional period. These are:

1. Large household appliances.
2. Small household appliances.
3. IT and telecommunications equipment.
4. Consumer equipment and photovoltaic panels.
5. Lighting equipment.
6. Electrical and electronic tools (with the exception of large-scale stationary industrial tools).
7. Toys, leisure and sports equipment.
8. Medical devices (with the exception of all implanted and infected products).
9. Monitoring and control equipment.
10. Automatic dispensers.

Schedule 2 gives a list of products which fall under each category within Schedule 1, e.g. Item 1 (large household appliances) covers such items as:

- Refrigerators.
- Washing machines.
- Freezers.

Item 2 (small household appliances) covers such items as:

- Vacuum cleaners.
- Toasters.
- Fryers.

Schedule 3 identifies categories of EEE to be covered by these Regulations from 1 January 2019.

Schedule 4 gives a non-exhaustive list of examples of EEE that will fall within the categories set out in Schedule 3.

Schedule 5 is concerned with amendments to the 'first compliance period'.

Schedule 6 gives details of the 'crossed-out wheeled bin' symbol.

Schedule 7 covers Declaration of Compliance.

Schedule 8 covers the information to be included in applications for registration of producers or authorised representatives and the notification of new scheme members. It also deals with the reporting information to be supplied by a producer or authorised representative during the transitional period, as well as the requirements for registration of a small producer. Part A of the schedule covers approval of a producer compliance scheme balancing system.

Schedule 9 deals with the minimum requirements for shipments of used EEE suspected to be WEEE.

Schedule 10 covers the approval of proposed and existing compliance schemes.

Schedule 11 covers the approval of authorised treatment facilities and exporters.

Schedule 12 covers the criteria for approval as a designated collection facility.

Schedule 13 covers public register details (producers must provide certain information for the public register).

Schedule 14 covers the appeals procedure.

WORK AT HEIGHT REGULATIONS 2005 (SI 2005 NO. 735)

Citation and Commencement

These Regulations came into force on 6 April 2005.

Interpretation

"Access" and "egress" include ascent and descent.

"Construction work" has the meaning assigned to it by regulation 2(1) of the **Construction (Design and Management) Regulations 2015**.

"Fragile surface" means a surface which would be liable to fail if any reasonably foreseeable loading were to be applied to it.

"Ladder" includes a fixed ladder and a stepladder. "Line" includes rope, chain or webbing.

"Personal fall protection system" means:

- a fall prevention, work restraint, work positioning, fall arrest or rescue system, other than a system in which the only safeguards are collective safeguards; or
- rope access and positioning techniques.

"Suitable" means suitable in any respect which it is reasonably foreseeable will affect the safety of any person.

"Work at height" means:

- work in any place, including a place at or below ground level;
- obtaining access to or egress from such place while at work, except by a staircase in a permanent workplace;

where, if measures required by these Regulations were not taken, a person could fall a distance liable to cause personal injury.

"Working platform":

- means any platform used as a place of work or as a means of access to or egress from a place of work;
- includes any scaffold, suspended scaffold, cradle, mobile platform, trestle, gangway, gantry and stairway which is so used.

Regulation 3: Application

The requirements imposed on an employer shall apply in relation to work by employees, self employed, contractors but regulations 4 to 16 of these Regulations shall not apply to the master and crew of a ship, or to the employer of such persons, in respect of the normal ship-board activities of a ship's crew.

Regulation 4: Organisation and Planning

Every employer shall ensure that work at height is properly planned, appropriately supervised, and carried out in a manner which is so far as is reasonably practicable safe and that its planning includes the selection of work equipment (reg. 7) and planning for emergencies and rescue.

Every employer shall ensure that work at height is carried out only when the weather conditions do not jeopardise the health or safety of persons involved in the work. This does not apply where members of the police, fire, ambulance or other emergency services are acting in an emergency.

Regulation 5: Competence

Every employer shall ensure that any person in any activity involving work at height is competent to do so or, if being trained, is being supervised by a competent person.

Regulation 6: Avoidance of Risks from Work at Height

Every employer shall take account of a risk assessment under regulation 3 of **MHSWR 1999**.

Every employer shall ensure that work is not carried out at height where it is reasonably practicable to carry out the work safely otherwise than at height.

Where work is carried out at height, every employer shall take suitable and sufficient measures to prevent, so far as is reasonably practicable, any person falling a distance liable to cause personal injury.

- The measures required are ensuring that the work is carried out:
    - from an existing place of work, or
    - in the case of obtaining access or egress) using an existing means,
        safely and under appropriate ergonomic conditions; and
- where it is not reasonably practicable for the work to be carried out in accordance with these measures, sufficient work equipment must be provided for preventing a fall.

Where remaining risks are possible every employer shall:

- so far as is reasonably practicable, provide sufficient work equipment to minimise:
    - the distance and consequences; or
    - where it is not reasonably practicable to minimise the distance, the consequences, of a fall; and
- provide such additional training and instruction or take other additional suitable and sufficient measures to prevent, so far as is reasonably practicable, any person falling a distance liable to cause personal injury.

Regulation 7: Selection of Work Equipment for Work at Height

Every employer, in selecting work equipment for use in work at height, shall:

- Give collective protection measures priority over personal protection measures.
- Take account of:
    - The working conditions and where the work equipment is to be used.
    - In the case of work equipment for access and egress, the distance to be negotiated.
    - The distance and consequences of a potential fall.
    - The duration and frequency of use.
    - The need for easy and timely evacuation and rescue in an emergency.
    - Any additional risk posed by the use, installation or removal of that work equipment or by evacuation and rescue from it.

Every employer shall select work equipment for work at height which:

- has appropriate dimensions;
- is able to withstand foreseeable loadings;
- will allow passage without risk; and
- is the most suitable work equipment.

Regulation 8: Requirements for Particular Work Equipment

Every employer shall ensure that, in the case of:

- a guardrail, toe-board, barrier or similar collective means of protection;
- a working platform where scaffolding is provided;
- a net, airbag or other collective safeguard for arresting falls which is not part of a personal fall protection system;
- a personal fall protection system:
    - a work positioning system;
    - rope access and positioning techniques;
    - a fall arrest system;
    - a work restraint system;
- a ladder;

that the appropriate Schedules are complied with.

Regulation 8A: Dock Operations

In relation to work at height where people are engaged in dock operations, every employer shall ensure that Schedule 9 is complied with. (This provision was added by the **Health and Safety (Miscellaneous Revocations and Amendments) Regulations 2013** and came into force on 6 April 2014.)

Regulation 9: Fragile Surfaces

Every employer shall ensure that no person at work passes across or near, or works on, from or near, a fragile surface where it is reasonably practicable to carry out work safely and under appropriate ergonomic conditions without his doing so.

Where it is not reasonably practicable to carry out work safely and under appropriate ergonomic conditions without passing across or near, or working on, from or near, a fragile surface, every employer shall:

- ensure, that suitable and sufficient platforms, coverings, guardrails or similar means of support or protection are provided and used so that any foreseeable loading is supported by such supports or borne by such protection;
- where a risk of a person at work falling remains despite the measures taken under the preceding provisions of this regulation, take suitable and sufficient measures to minimise the distances and consequences of his fall.

Where any person at work may pass across or near, or work on, from or near, a fragile surface, every employer shall ensure that:

- prominent warning notices are so far as is reasonably practicable affixed at the approach to the place where the fragile surface is situated; or
- where that is not reasonably practicable, such persons are made aware of it by other means.

The provisions immediately above shall not apply where members of the police, fire, ambulance or other emergency services are acting in an emergency.

Regulation 10: Falling Objects

Every employer shall, where necessary to prevent injury to any person, take suitable and sufficient steps to prevent, so far as is reasonably practicable, the fall of any material or object.

Every employer shall take suitable and sufficient steps to:

- Prevent any person being struck by any falling material or object which is liable to cause personal injury.
- Ensure that no material or object is thrown or tipped from height in circumstances where it is liable to cause injury to any person.
- Ensure that materials and objects are stored in such a way as to prevent risk to any person arising from the collapse, overturning or unintended movement of such materials or objects.

Regulation 11: Danger Areas

Every employer shall ensure that:

- where a workplace contains an area in which, owing to the nature of the work, there is a risk of any person at work:
    - falling a distance; or
    - being struck by a falling object

    which is liable to cause personal injury, the workplace is so far as is reasonably practicable equipped with devices preventing unauthorised persons from entering such area; and
- such an area is clearly indicated.

Regulation 12: Inspection of Work Equipment

This regulation applies only to work equipment to which regulation 8 and Schedules 2 to 6 apply.

Every employer shall ensure that, where the safety of work equipment depends on how it is installed or assembled, it is not used after installation or assembly in any position unless it has been inspected in that position.

Every employer shall ensure that work equipment exposed to conditions causing deterioration which is liable to result in dangerous situations is inspected:

- at suitable intervals; and
- each time that exceptional circumstances which are liable to jeopardise the safety of the work equipment have occurred,

to ensure that health and safety conditions are maintained and that any deterioration can be detected and remedied in good time.

Every employer shall ensure that a working platform:

- used for construction work; and
- from which a person could fall 2 metres or more,

is not used in any position unless it has been inspected in that position or, in the case of a mobile working platform, inspected on the site, within the previous 7 days.

Every employer shall ensure that no work equipment, other than lifting equipment to which the requirement in regulation 9(4) of the **Lifting Operations and Lifting Equipment Regulations 1998 (LOLER)** applies:

- leaves his undertaking; or
- if obtained from the undertaking of another person, is used in his undertaking,

unless it is accompanied by physical evidence that the last inspection required to be carried out under this regulation has been carried out.

Every employer shall ensure that the result of an inspection under this regulation is recorded and kept until the next inspection under this regulation is recorded.

A person carrying out an inspection of work equipment shall:

- before the end of the working period within which the inspection is completed, prepare a report containing the particulars set out in Schedule 7; and
- within 24 hours of completing the inspection, provide the report or a copy thereof to the person on whose behalf the inspection was carried out.

An employer receiving a report or copy of an inspection report shall keep the report or a copy thereof:

- at the site where the inspection was carried out until the construction work is completed; and
- thereafter at an office of his for 3 months.

Where a thorough examination has been made of lifting equipment under regulation 9 of **LOLER**:

- it shall for the purposes of this regulation, be treated as an inspection of the lifting equipment; and
- the making under regulation 10 of **LOLER** of a report of such examination shall for the purposes of this regulation be treated as the recording of the inspection.

In this regulation "inspection":

- means such visual or more rigorous inspection by a competent person as is appropriate for safety purposes;
- includes any testing appropriate for those purposes;

and "inspected" shall be construed accordingly.

Regulation 13: Inspection of Places of Work at Height

Every employer shall so far as is reasonably practicable ensure that the surface and every parapet, permanent rail or other such fall protection measure of every place of work at height are checked on each occasion before the place is used.

Regulation 14: Duties of Persons at Work

Every person shall, where working under the control of another person, report to that person any activity or defect relating to work at height which he knows is likely to endanger the safety of himself or another person.

Every person shall use any work equipment or safety device provided to him for work at height by his employer, or by a person under whose control he works, in accordance with:

- any training in the use of the work equipment or device concerned which has been received by him; and
- the instructions respecting that use which have been provided to him by that employer or person in compliance with the requirements and prohibitions imposed upon that employer or person by or under the relevant statutory provisions.

Regulation 14A: Special Provision in Relation to Caving and Climbing

(1) Paragraph (2) applies in relation to the application of these Regulations to work concerning the provision of instruction or leadership to one or more persons in connection with their engagement in caving or climbing by way of sport, recreation, team building or similar activities.

(2) Where this paragraph applies, an employer, self-employed person or other person shall be taken to have complied with the caving and climbing requirements, if, by alternative means to any requirement of those requirements, he maintains in relation to a person at such work as is referred to in paragraph (1) a level of safety equivalent to that required by those requirements.

(3) For the purposes of paragraph (2), in determining whether an equivalent level of safety is maintained, regard shall be had to:

 (a) the nature of the activity;

 (b) any publicly available and generally accepted procedures for the activity; and

 (c) any other relevant circumstances.

(4) In this regulation:

 (a) "caving" includes the exploration of parts of mines which are no longer worked;

 (b) "climbing" means climbing, traversing, abseiling or scrambling over natural terrain or man-made structures; and

 (c) "the caving and climbing requirements" means regulation 8(d)(ii)[rope access and positioning techniques], so far as it relates to paragraph 1 in Part 3 of Schedule 5, and that paragraph.

Regulation 15: Exemption by the Health and Safety Executive

The HSE may, by a certificate in writing, exempt any person or class of persons, any premises or class of premises, any work equipment, or any work activity from the requirements imposed by paragraph 3(a) and (c) of Schedule 2 (height of top and intermediate guardrails).

Regulation 16: Exemption for the Armed Forces

The Secretary of State has the power to grant an exemption for the armed forces if in the interests of national security and then only if he is satisfied that the health and safety of employees is ensured as far as possible.

Regulation 17: Amendment of the Provision and Use of Work Equipment Regulations 1998

There shall be added to regulation 6(5) of the **Provision and Use of Work Equipment Regulations 1998** the following sub-paragraph:

*"(f) work equipment to which regulation 12 of the **Work at Height Regulations 2005** applies".*

Schedules

There are several detailed Schedules attached to these Regulations:

- Schedule 1 - requirements for existing places of work and means of access or egress at height.
- Schedule 2 - requirements for guardrails, toe-boards, barriers and similar collective means of protection.
- Schedule 3 - requirements for working platforms.
  - Part 1 - requirements for all working platforms.
  - Part 2 - additional requirements for scaffolding.

- Schedule 4 - requirements for collective safeguards for arresting falls.
- Schedule 5 - requirements for personal fall protection systems.
  - Part 1 - requirements for all personal fall protection systems.
  - Part 2 - additional requirements for work positioning systems.
  - Part 3 - additional requirements for rope access and positioning techniques.
  - Part 4 - additional requirements for fall arrest systems.
  - Part 5 - additional requirements for work restraint systems.
- Schedule 6 - requirements for ladders.
- Schedule 7 - particulars to be included in a report of inspection.
- Schedule 8 - revocation of instruments.
- Schedule 9 - requirements for work in docks (came into force on 6 April 2014).

WORKING TIME REGULATIONS 1998 (SI 1998 NO. 1833)

Introduction

The **Working Time Regulations** came into effect on 1 October 1998 as a result of **Council Directive 93/104/EC**, which dealt with the organisation of working time, and **Council Directive 94/33/EC**, concerning the protection of young people at work. In December 1999 further Working Time legislation was introduced amending the 1998 Regulations. The following takes the amendments into consideration.

The Regulations

These divide themselves conveniently into 5 Parts and 3 Schedules.

Amending Legislation

Working Time (Amendment) Regulations 2001 (SI 2001 No. 3256).

Working Time (Amendment) Regulations 2002 (SI 2002 No. 3128).

Working Time (Amendment) Regulations 2003 (SI 2003 No. 1684).

Working Time (Amendment) Regulations 2007 (SI 2007 No. 2079).

Part I

This contains the Definitions section of which the following are the most important in order to enable you to understand the text of the Regulations.

"Adult Worker" means a worker who has attained the age of 18.

"Calendar Year" means the period of 12 months beginning with 1 January in any year. "Day" means a period of 24 hours beginning at midnight.

"Employment", in relation to a worker, means employment under his contract, and "employed" shall be construed accordingly.

"Mobile Worker" means any worker employed as a member of travelling or flying personnel by an undertaking which operates transport services for passengers or goods by road or air.

"Night Time", in relation to a worker, means a period which is not less than seven hours, and which includes the period between midnight and 5am, which is determined for the purposes of these Regulations by a relevant agreement, or, in default of such a determination, the period between 11pm and 6am.

"Night Work" means a worker who works at least three hours of his daily working time during the night time, or who is likely, during night time, to work at least a proportion of his annual working time as may be specified in a collective agreement or a workforce agreement.

"Offshore Work" means work performed mainly on or from offshore installations (including drilling rigs), directly or indirectly in connection with the exploration, extraction or exploitation of mineral resources, including hydrocarbons, and diving in connection with such activities, whether performed from an offshore installation or a vessel.

"Relevant Agreement" means a workforce agreement which applies to a worker, any provision of a collective agreement which forms part of a contract between him and his employer, or any other agreement in writing which is legally enforceable as between the worker and his employer.

"Relevant Training" means work experience provided pursuant to a training course or programme, training for employment, or both, other than work experience or training the immediate provider of which is an education institution or a person whose main business is the provision of training, and which is provided on a course run by that institution or person.

"Rest Period" means a period which is not working time, other than a rest break or leave to which the worker is entitled under these Regulations.

"The Restricted Period", in relation to a worker, means the period between 10pm and 6am or, where the worker's contract provides for him to work after 10pm, the period between 11pm and 7am.

"Worker" means an individual who works under (or, worked under) a contract of employment; or any other contract, whether oral or in writing, whereby the individual undertakes to do or perform personally any work or services for another party to the contract whose status is not that of a client or customer of any profession or business undertaking carried on by the individual and any reference to a worker's contract shall be construed accordingly.

"Working Time" means any period during which a worker is working, at his employer's disposal and carrying out his activity or duties; any period during which he is receiving relevant training, and any additional period which is to be treated as working time under a relevant agreement and "work" shall be construed accordingly.

"Young Worker" means a worker who has attained the age of 15 but not the age of 18 and who, as respects England and Wales, is over compulsory school age.

The following are the main points of the Regulations.

Part II (Regulations 3 to 9)

Deals with the obligations imposed on employers, enforceable by the HSE and local authorities through the courts.

Regulation 4: Maximum Weekly Working Time

This states that subject to regulation 5, a worker's working time, including overtime, in any period of 17 weeks, shall not exceed an average of 48 hours for each seven days unless the employer has first obtained, in writing, the worker's agreement to perform such work. The employer must keep up-to-date records of all workers who have agreed in writing to carry out such work. An employer shall take all reasonable steps, in order to protect the health and safety of workers, to ensure that the above limit is complied with.

Where a worker has worked for less than 17 weeks, the time for which he has worked will be deemed to be the relevant reference period for the Regulations.

Where a worker is excluded from the scope of certain provisions of these Regulations by regulation 21 (Special Cases), each reference to 17 weeks will be substituted by a reference to 26 weeks.

A worker's average working time for each seven days during a reference period shall be calculated on the formula:

$$\frac{A + B}{C}$$

where:

A is the aggregate number of hours in the worker's working time during the reference period;

B is the aggregate number of hours in his working time during the period beginning immediately after the end of the reference period and ending when the number of days in that subsequent period on which he has worked equals the number of excluded days during the reference period; and

C is the number of weeks in the reference period. "Excluded Days" means days comprised in:

- any period of annual leave taken by the worker in exercise of his entitlement under regulation 13;
- any period of sick leave taken by the worker;
- any period of maternity, paternity, adoption or parental leave taken by the worker; and
- any period in respect of which the limits specified do not apply in relation to the worker by virtue of regulation 5.

Regulation 5: Agreement to Exclude the Maximum

This states that an agreement may either relate to a specified period or apply indefinitely and shall be terminable by the worker by giving not less than seven days' notice to his employer in writing or by agreement any different period of notice.

Where an agreement makes provision for the termination of the agreement after a period of notice, the notice period provided for shall not exceed three months.

Regulation 5A: Maximum Working Time for Young Workers

(1) A young worker's working time shall not exceed:

- eight hours a day, or
- 40 hours a week.

(2) If, on any day, or, as the case may be, during any week, a young worker is employed by more than one employer, his working time shall be determined for the purpose of paragraph (1) by aggregating the number of hours worked by him for each employer.

For the purposes of paragraph (1) and (2), a week starts at midnight between Sunday and Monday.

An employer shall take all reasonable steps, in keeping with the need to protect the health and safety of workers, to ensure that the limits specified in paragraph (1) are complied with in the case of each worker employed by him in relation to whom they apply.

Regulation 6: Length of Night Work

This states that a night worker's normal hours of work shall not exceed an average of eight hours for each 24 hours.

An employer shall take all reasonable steps, in keeping with the need to protect the health and safety of workers, to ensure that the above time limit is complied with in the case of each night worker employed by him.

The reference periods which apply in the case of a night worker are:

- in relation to successive periods of 17 weeks, each such period, or
- in any other case, any period of 17 weeks in the course of his employment.

Where a worker has worked for his employer for less than 17 weeks, the reference period applicable in his case is the period that has elapsed since he started work for his employer.

For the purposes of this regulation, a night worker's average normal hours of work for each 24 hours during a reference period shall be determined according to the formula:

$$\frac{A}{B-C}$$

where:

A is the number of hours during the reference period which are normal working hours for that worker; B is the number of days during the reference period; and

C is the total number of hours during the reference period comprised in rest periods spent by the worker in pursuance of his entitlement under regulation 11, divided by 24.

An employer shall ensure that no night worker whose work involves special hazards or heavy physical or mental strain works for more than eight hours in any 24-hour period during which the night worker performs night work.

The work of a night worker shall be regarded as involving special hazards or heavy physical or mental strain if it is identified as such in a collective agreement, or workforce agreement, which takes account of the specific effects and hazards of night work, or it is recognised in a risk assessment made by the employer under regulation 3 of the **Management of Health and Safety at Work Regulations 1999** as involving a significant risk to the health or safety of workers employed by him.

Regulation 6A: Night Work by Young Workers

An employer shall ensure that no young worker employed by him works during the restricted period.

Regulation 7: Health Assessment and Transfer of Night Workers to Day Work

This states that an employer shall not assign an adult worker to work which is to be undertaken during periods when the worker will become a night worker unless the employer has ensured that the worker will have the opportunity of a free health assessment before he takes up the assignment; or has already had a health assessment before being assigned to work to be undertaken and the employer has no reason to believe that that assessment is no longer valid. The employer shall also ensure that each night worker employed by him has the opportunity of a free health assessment at regular intervals of whatever duration may be appropriate in his case.

Any young worker assigned to work during the restricted period shall be treated accordingly.

For the purposes of health assessment, an assessment is free if it is at no cost to the worker to whom it relates.

Also under this regulation, no person shall disclose any such health assessment to any person other than the worker to whom it relates, unless:

- the worker has given his consent in writing to the disclosure, or
- the disclosure is confined to a statement that the assessment shows the worker to be fit either to take up an assignment or to continue to undertake an assignment.

Where a registered medical practitioner has advised an employer that one of his workers is suffering from health problems which the practitioner considers to be connected with the performance of night-work, and it is possible for the employer to transfer the worker to suitable work, the employer shall transfer the worker accordingly.

Regulation 8: Pattern of Work

This states that where the pattern of work is likely to put the health and safety of a worker employed by him at risk, because the work is monotonous or the work-rate is pre-determined, the employer shall ensure that the worker is given adequate rest breaks.

Regulation 9: Records

This states that an employer shall keep records which are adequate to show whether the limits specified in the Regulations for each worker are being complied with and retain such records for two years from the date on which they were made.

Part II (Regulations 10 to 17)

These confer certain rights on workers which are enforceable via employment tribunals.

Regulation 10: Daily Rest

This states that a worker is entitled to a rest period of not less than 11 consecutive hours in each 24-hour period. A young worker is entitled to a rest period of not less than 12 consecutive hours in each 24-hour period. The minimum rest period may be interrupted in the case of activities involving periods of work that are split up over the day or of short duration.

Regulation 11: Weekly Rest Period

This states that a worker is entitled to an uninterrupted rest period of not less than 24 hours in each seven-day period. If his employer so determines, a worker shall be entitled to either two uninterrupted rest periods each of not less than 24 hours in each 14-day period, or one uninterrupted rest period of not less than 48 hours in each such 14-day period.

A young worker is entitled to a rest period of not less than 48 hours in each seven-day period.

A seven-day period or (as the case may be) 14-day period shall be taken to begin at such times and on such days as may be specified in a relevant agreement or, where there is no relevant agreement, at the start of each week or (as the case may be) every other week.

In a case where 14-day periods are to be taken to begin at the start of every other week, the first such period shall be taken to begin:

- if the worker's employment began on or before the date on which these Regulations come into force, on 5 October 1998; or
- if the worker's employment begins after the date on which these Regulations come into force, at the start of the week in which that employment begins.

For the purposes of this regulation, a week starts at midnight between Sunday and Monday.

The minimum rest period to which an adult worker is entitled shall not include any part of a rest period to which the worker is entitled under regulation 10, except where this is justified by objective or technical reasons or reasons concerning the organisation of work.

The minimum rest period to which a young worker is entitled may be interrupted in the case of activities involving periods of work that are split up over the day or are of short duration and may be reduced where this is justified by technical or organisation reasons, but not to less than 36 consecutive hours.

Regulation 12: Rest Breaks

This states that where a worker's daily working time is more than six hours, he is entitled to a rest break. The details and duration of the break can be in accordance with any provisions which are contained in a collective agreement or a workforce agreement and, subject to those provisions, the rest break provided for shall be an uninterrupted period of not less than 20 minutes, and the worker is entitled to spend it away from his workstation if he has one.

Where a young worker's daily working time is more than four and a half hours, he is entitled to a rest break of at least 30 minutes, which shall be consecutive if possible, and he is entitled to spend it away from his workstation if he has one.

If, on any day, a young worker is employed by more than one employer, his daily working time shall be the aggregate number of hours worked by him for each employer.

Regulations 13 and 13A: Entitlement to Annual Leave and Additional Annual Leave

Read together, these two regulations state that a worker is entitled to a total of 5.6 weeks' annual leave in each leave year, as of 1 April 2009.

A worker's leave year, for the purposes of this regulation, begins on any date during the calendar year as may be provided for in a relevant agreement or, where there is no relevant agreement, on that date on which that employment begins and each subsequent anniversary of that date.

Where the date on which the employment begins is later than the date on which (by virtue of a relevant agreement) his first leave year begins, the leave to which a worker is entitled in that leave year is a proportion of the period equal to the proportion of that leave year remaining on the date on which his employment begins.

Leave to which a worker is entitled may be taken in instalments, but it may only be taken in the leave year in respect of which it is due and it may not be replaced by a payment in lieu except where the worker's employment is terminated.

Regulation 14: Compensation Related to Entitlement to Leave

This provides for compensation to be paid in lieu of annual leave where a worker's employment is terminated during the course of his leave year.

Where the proportion of leave taken by the worker is less than the proportion of the leave year which has expired, his employer shall make him a payment in lieu of leave in accordance with such sum provided for in a relevant agreement or, where there is no relevant agreement, a sum equal to the amount that would be due to the worker in respect of a period of leave determined according to the formula:

$$(A \times B) - C$$

where:

A is the period of leave to which the worker is entitled under regulation 13 and regulation 13A; B is the proportion of the worker's leave year which expired before the termination date; and

C is the period of leave taken by the worker between the start of the leave year and the termination date.

A relevant agreement may provide that, where the proportion of leave taken by the worker exceeds the proportion of the leave year which has expired, he shall compensate his employer, whether by a payment, by undertaking additional work or otherwise.

Regulation 15: Dates on which Leave is Taken

This states that a worker may take leave on such days as he may choose by giving notice to his employer subject to any requirement imposed on him by his employer.

A worker's employer may require the worker to take leave, or not to take leave on particular days, by giving the required notice to the worker.

Regulation 15A states that during the first year of employment, the amount of leave which has accrued is one twelfth on the first day of each month rounded up to the nearest half day.

Regulation 16: Payment in Respect of Periods of Leave

This states that a worker is entitled to be paid for any period of annual leave to which he is entitled at the rate of a week's pay for each week of leave.

A right to payment does not affect any right of a worker to remuneration under his contract ("contractual remuneration").

Regulation 17: Entitlements under Other Provisions

This states that when during any period a worker is entitled to a rest period, rest break or annual leave both under a provision of these Regulations and under a separate provision (including a provision of his contract), he may not exercise the two rights separately, but may, in taking a rest period, break or leave during that period, take advantage of whichever right is the more favourable.

Part III (Regulations 18 to 27)

These deal with exclusions and exceptions where certain workers are excluded, or where particular circumstances arise, or when employers and workers agree to modify or exclude certain aspects of the Regulations.

Regulation 18: Excluded Sectors

These Regulations do not apply:

- to workers to whom the **Merchant Shipping (Hours of Work) Regulations 2002** apply;
- to workers to whom the **Fishing Vessels (Working Time: Sea-fishermen) Regulations 2004** apply;
- to workers to whom the **Merchant Shipping (Working Time: Inland Waterways) Regulations 2003** apply.

Regulations 4(1) and (2), 6(1), (2) and (7), 7(1) and (6), 8, 10(1), 11(1) and (2), 12(1), 13, 13A and 16 do not apply:

- where characteristics peculiar to certain specific services such as the armed forces or the police, or civil protection services, inevitably conflict with these Regulations; or
- to workers to whom the European Agreement on the organisation of working time of mobile staff in civil aviation applies.

Regulations 4(1) and (2), 6(1), (2) and (7), 8, 10(1), 11(1) and (2) and 12(1) do not apply to workers performing mobile road transport services, as set out in **Directive 2002/15/EC**.

Regulation 24 does not apply to workers to whom the **Cross-border Railway Services (Working Time) Regulations 2008** apply.

Regulation 19: Domestic Service

This states that regulations 4(1) and (2), 5A(1) and (4), 6(1), (2) and (7), 6A, 7(1), (2) and (6) and 8 do not apply to a worker employed as a domestic servant in a private household.

Regulation 20: Unmeasured Working Time

This states that regulations 4(1) and (2), 6(1), (2) and (7), 10(1), 11(1) and (2) and 12(1) do not apply to a worker where the duration of his working time is not measured or predetermined or can be determined by the worker himself, as may be the case for:

- managing executives or other persons with autonomous decision-taking powers;
- family workers; or
- workers officiating at religious ceremonies in churches and religious communities.

Regulation 21: Other Special Cases

This states that regulations 6(1), (2) and (7), 10(1), 11(1) and (2) and 12(1) do not apply in relation to a worker where his place of work and place of residence are distant from one another including cases where the worker is employed in offshore work, or his different places of work are distant from one another. They do not apply where the worker is engaged in security and surveillance activities requiring a permanent presence in order to protect property and persons, such as security guards and caretakers or security firms.

Where the worker's activities involve the need for continuity of service or production, as may be the case in relation to services relating to the reception, treatment or care provided by hospitals or similar establishments (including the activities of doctors in training), residential institutions, prisons, work at docks or airports, press, radio, television, cinematographic productions, postal and telecommunications services and civil protection services, gas, water and electricity production, transmission and distribution, household refuse collection and incineration, or industries in which work cannot be interrupted on technical grounds, research and development activities, agriculture, the carriage of passengers on regular urban transport services, the above mentioned regulations do not apply.

Similarly, where there is a foreseeable surge in activities such as agriculture, tourism, and postal services, and where the worker's activities are affected by an occurrence due to unusual and unforeseeable circumstances, beyond the employer's control, or where the consequences of exceptional events could not have been avoided by the employer or, finally, where the worker's activities are affected by an accident or the imminent risk of an accident, where the worker works in railway transport and his activities are intermittent or he spends his working time on board trains or his activities are linked to transport timetables and to ensuring the continuity and regularity of traffic, the above mentioned regulations do not apply.

Regulation 22: Shift Workers

This states that:

- regulation 10(1) does not apply in relation to a shift worker when he changes shift and cannot take a daily rest period between the end of one shift and the start of the next one;
- regulation 11(1) and (2) do not apply in relation to a shift worker when he changes shift and cannot take a weekly rest period between the end of one shift and the start of the next one;

and neither regulation 10(1) nor regulation 11(1) or (2) apply to workers engaged in activities involving periods of work split up over the day, as may be the case for cleaning staff.

For the purposes of this regulation:

"Shift-work" means any method of organising work in shifts whereby workers succeed each other at the same workstations according to a certain pattern, including a rotating pattern, and which may be continuous or discontinuous, entailing the need for workers to work at different times over a period of days or weeks.

Regulation 23: Collective and Workforce Agreements

This states that certain of the regulations may be modified by a collective agreement or a workforce agreement.

Regulation 24: Compensatory Rest

This states that where a worker is required by his employer to work during a period which would otherwise be a rest period or rest break his employer shall wherever possible allow him to take an equivalent period of compensatory rest, and in exceptional cases in which it is not possible to grant such a period of rest his employer shall afford him such protection as may be appropriate in order to safeguard his health and safety.

Regulation 24A (added by the **Working Time (Amendment) Regulations 2003**) deals with adequate rest for mobile workers.

Regulation 25: Workers in the Armed Forces

This states that regulation 9 does not apply in relation to a worker serving as a member of the armed forces and that regulations 5A, 6A, 10(2) and 11(3) do not apply to a young worker serving in the armed forces.

Regulation 25A sets working times for doctors in training. This modifies regulation 4, to increase the time limit from an average of 48 hours to an average of 52 hours over a 26-week period.

Regulation 25B sets a reference period for offshore workers. For offshore workers, the reference period for working time is 52 weeks.

Regulation 26A: Entitlement to Additional Annual Leave Under a Relevant Agreement

Regulation 13A (Entitlement to additional annual leave) does not apply where workers are provided with an annual leave entitlement of 1.6 weeks or 8 days (whichever is the lesser) in addition to their entitlement under regulation 13, provided that such additional annual leave:

- may not be replaced by a payment in lieu except in relation to a worker whose employment is terminated;
- may not be carried forward into a leave year other than that which immediately follows the leave year in respect of which the leave is due; and
- is leave for which the worker is entitled to be paid at not less than the rate of a week's pay in respect of each week of leave.

Any additional annual leave in excess of 1.6 weeks or 8 days (whichever is the lesser) to which a worker is entitled, shall not be subject to the conditions outlined above.

Regulation 27: Young Workers - Force Majeure

This states that regulations 5A, 6A, 10(2) and 12(4) do not apply in relation to a young worker where he is required to undertake work which no adult worker is available to perform and which is occasioned by either unusual and unforeseeable circumstances beyond the employer's control, or the consequences of exceptional events which could not have been avoided by the employer, or is either of a temporary nature or must be performed immediately.

Under such circumstances, where a young worker is required to work during a rest period or rest break his employer shall allow him to take an equivalent period of compensatory rest within the following three weeks.

Regulation 27A: Other Exceptions Relating to Young Workers

(1) Regulation 5A does not apply in relation to a young worker where:

- the young worker's employer requires him to undertake work which is necessary either to maintain continuity of service or production or to respond to a surge in demand for a service or product;
- no adult worker is available to perform the work; and
- performing the work would not adversely affect the young worker's education or training.

(2) Regulation 6A does not apply in relation to a young worker employed:

- in a hospital or similar establishment, or
- in connection with cultural, artistic, sporting or advertising activities,

in the circumstances referred to in paragraph (1).

(3) Regulation 6A does not apply, except in so far as it prohibits work between midnight and 4am, in relation to a young worker employed in:

- agriculture;
- retail trading;
- postal or newspaper deliveries;
- a catering business;
- a hotel, public house, restaurant, bar or similar establishment, or
- a bakery,

in the circumstances referred to in paragraph (1).

(4) Where the application of regulation 6A is excluded by the above, and a young worker is accordingly required to work during a period which would otherwise be a rest period or rest break:

- he shall be supervised by an adult worker where such supervision is necessary for the young worker's protection, and
- he shall be allowed an equivalent period of compensatory rest.

Part IV (Regulations 28 to 35)

These deal with enforcement, offences, remedies, the right not to suffer detriment, unfair dismissal, conciliation, and contracting-out arrangements.

Regulation 28: Enforcement

This regulation gives a number of definitions of relevance to regulations 29 to 29E and to Schedule 3, and provides for enforcement of the Regulations by the Health and Safety Executive or the local authority, or by the Civil Aviation Authority, DVSA or the Office of Rail Regulation as appropriate.

Regulation 29: Offences

This states that an employer who fails to comply with any of the relevant requirements shall be guilty of an offence. An employer guilty of an offence under the Regulations shall be liable on summary conviction, to a fine not exceeding the statutory maximum or on conviction on indictment, to a fine.

Regulation 29A: Offences Due to the Fault of Other Person

Where the commission by any person of an offence is due to the act or default of some other person, that other person shall be guilty of the offence, and a person may be charged with and convicted of the offence by virtue of this paragraph whether or not proceedings are taken against the first-mentioned person.

Regulation 29B: Offences by Bodies Corporate

(1) Where an offence committed by a body corporate is proved to have been committed with the consent or connivance of, or to have been attributable to any neglect on the part of, any director, manager, secretary or other similar officer of the body corporate or a person who was purporting to act in any such capacity, he as well as the body corporate shall be guilty of that offence and shall be liable to be proceeded against and punished accordingly.

(2) Where the affairs of a body corporate are managed by its members, the preceding paragraph shall apply in relation to the acts and defaults of a member in connection with his functions of management as if he were a director of the body corporate.

Regulation 29C provides that proceedings for offences shall only be instituted by inspectors or by or with the consent of the Director of Public Prosecutions.

Regulation 29D gives inspectors the right to bring proceedings before the magistrates' court even though they themselves are not solicitors or barristers.

Regulation 29E gives the courts the power to order the cause of an offence to be remedied. This is in addition to their power to fine companies for non-compliance with the Regulations.

Regulation 30: Remedies

This states that a worker may complain to an employment tribunal that his employer has refused to permit him to exercise any right he has under the Regulations or has failed to pay him the whole or any part of any amount due to him under the Regulations.

An employment tribunal shall not consider a complaint under this regulation unless it is presented within three months (or in certain circumstances six months) beginning with the date on which it is alleged that the exercise of the right should have been permitted (or in the case of a rest period or leave extending over more than one day, the date on which it should have been permitted to begin) or, as the case may be, the payment should have been made.

The tribunal may consider a complaint within such further period as it considers reasonable in a case where it is satisfied that it was not reasonably practicable for the complaint to be presented before the end of that period of three or, as the case may be, six months.

Where an employment tribunal finds a complaint well-founded, the tribunal shall make a declaration to that effect, and may make an award of compensation to be paid by the employer to the worker.

Where on a complaint an employment tribunal finds that an employer has failed to pay a worker in accordance with the Regulations, it shall order the employer to pay to the worker the amount which it finds to be due to him.

Regulation 30A makes provision for the extension of time limits because of mediation in certain cross-border disputes, whilst **Regulation 30B** allows for an extension of time limits to facilitate conciliation before institution of proceedings.

Regulation 31: Right Not to Suffer Detriment

This inserts a new section 45A into the **Employment Rights Act 1996** giving a worker the right not to suffer detriment as a result of any act or deliberate failure to act on the part of his employer in connection with any requirement or right which is in contravention of these Regulations.

Regulation 32: Unfair Dismissal

This inserts a new section 101A into the **Employment Rights Act 1996** making any dismissal of an employee unfair if the grounds for dismissal are based on his refusal to comply with requirements imposed by an employer which are in contravention of these Regulations.

Regulation 33: Conciliation

This amends the **Employment Tribunals Act 1996** to permit complaints made under regulation 30 of these Regulations to be dealt with by the conciliation procedure.

Regulation 34: Appeals

This similarly amends the **Employment Tribunals Act 1996** to give the Employment Appeals Tribunal jurisdiction over appeals arising from decisions made on complaints under these Regulations.

Regulation 35: Restrictions on Contracting Out

This, as a general rule, makes void any provision in an agreement which is designed to preclude or limit the operation of these Regulations or to prevent any person from bringing proceedings under these Regulations before an employment tribunal.

Regulation 35A: Consultation

The Secretary of State must consult the two sides of industry and publish information and advice enabling those affected to understand their respective rights and obligations.

Part V (Regulations 36 to 43)

This deals with the application of the Regulations to special classes of persons, e.g. agency workers, Crown employees, armed forces, parliamentary staff, police service, non-employed trainees and agricultural workers in Wales or Scotland.

WORKPLACE (HEALTH, SAFETY AND WELFARE) REGULATIONS 1992 (SI 1992 NO. 3004)

Amending Legislation

The Regulations have undergone numerous minor amendments, usually in regard to specific industries, or where citation references have been updated in later legislation. Most recently, the **Health and Safety (Miscellaneous Repeals, Revocations and Amendments) Regulations 2013** have amended these Regulations to include the requirement for adequate lighting and safe access for workers on ships in a shipyard or harbour undergoing construction, repair or maintenance.

Workplace Definition

"Workplace" means any premises or part of premises which are not domestic premises and are made available to any person as a place of work, and includes:

- any place within the premises to which such person has access while at work;
- any room, lobby, corridor, staircase, road or other place used as a means of access to or egress from the workplace or where facilities are provided for use in connection with the workplace other than a public road.

A modification, an extension or a conversion shall not be a workplace or form part of a workplace, until the modification, extension or conversion is complete.

Note that "domestic premises" means a private dwelling. Factories, shops, offices, schools, hospitals, nursing homes, hotels, places of entertainment, etc., are all covered by the Regulations.

Locations Not Covered by the Regulations

The following are not covered by the Regulations:

- Workplaces in or on a ship, although there are exceptions where work is conducted in dockyards.
- Construction sites.
- Workplaces located below ground at a mine.
- Aircraft, locomotives or rolling stock, trailers or semi-trailers and vehicles for which a licence is in force under the **Vehicles (Excise) Act 1971**. In these cases, regulations 5 to 12 and 14 to 25 do not apply; regulation 13 applies where the aircraft, locomotive, etc is stationary inside a workplace.

Regulations 5 to 19 and 23 to 25 do not apply to outdoor workplaces forming part of an agricultural or forestry undertaking.

On temporary work sites, regulations 20 to 25 apply only so far as is reasonably practicable.

Employers' Duties

Employers have a general duty under section 2 of the **Health and Safety at Work, etc. Act 1974** to ensure, so far as is reasonably practicable, the health, safety and welfare of their employees at work. Persons in control of non-domestic premises also have a duty under section 4 of the Act towards people who are not their employees but use their premises. The Regulations expand on these duties. They are intended to protect the health and safety of everyone in the workplace, and to ensure that adequate welfare facilities are provided for people at work.

The following provisions are covered by the Regulations:

Regulation 4A: Stability and Solidity

Where a workplace is in a building, the building shall have a stability and solidity appropriate to the nature of the use of the workplace.

Regulation 5: Maintenance of Workplace and of Equipment, Devices and Systems

All workplaces and equipment must be maintained in an efficient state, in efficient working order and in a good state of repair.

Regulation 6: Ventilation

Effective and suitable provision must be made to ensure that every enclosed workplace is ventilated by a sufficient quantity of fresh or purified air. Ventilation plant must include an effective device for giving visible or audible warning of plant failure.

Regulation 7: Temperature in Indoor Workplaces

The temperature in all indoor workplaces must be reasonable at all times during working hours.

Workplaces must be adequately thermally insulated where necessary, having regard to the type of work being carried out. Excessive effects of sunlight on temperature must also be avoided.

A method of heating or cooling shall not be used which results in the escape into a workplace of fumes, gas or vapour of such character and to such extent that they are likely to be injurious or offensive to any person. A sufficient number of thermometers shall be provided to enable persons at work to determine the temperature in any workplace inside a building. The temperature in workrooms should normally be at least 16 degrees Celsius unless much of the work involves severe physical effort, in which case the temperature should be at least 13 degrees Celsius. These temperatures may not, however, ensure reasonable comfort, depending on other factors such as air movement and relative humidity. The temperatures refer to readings taken using an ordinary dry bulb thermometer, close to workstations, at working height and away from windows.

Regulation 8: Lighting

All workplaces shall have suitable and sufficient lighting and so far as is reasonably practicable, such lighting shall be natural light. In addition to the provision of suitable and sufficient artificial light, emergency lighting must be provided in the event of failure of artificial light and where persons at work are especially exposed to danger.

Regulation 9: Cleanliness and Waste Material

Every workplace, furniture, furnishings and fittings shall be kept sufficiently clean. This includes floor, walls and ceiling surfaces. So far as is reasonably practicable, waste material shall not be allowed to accumulate except in suitable receptacles.

Regulation 10: Room Dimensions and Space

Every room in which persons work shall have sufficient floor area, height and unoccupied space.

No room in the workplace shall be so overcrowded as to cause risk to the health or safety of persons at work in it. The number of persons employed at a time in any workroom shall not be such that the amount of cubic space allowed for each is less than 11 cubic metres. In calculating for this purpose the amount of cubic space in any room, no space more than 3.0 metres from the floor shall be taken into account and, where a room contains a gallery, the gallery shall be treated for the purposes of the Schedule as if it were partitioned off from the remainder of the room and formed a separate room.

Regulation 11: Workstations and Seating

Every workstation shall be so arranged that it is suitable for any person at work at the workstation and any work that is likely to be carried out there.

So far as is reasonably practicable, outdoor workstations shall be arranged:

- to provide protection from adverse weather;
- to enable anyone to leave them quickly in event of any emergency;
- to ensure that any person at the workstation cannot slip or fall.

Suitable seating must be provided for everyone whose work includes operations that can or must be done while sitting. The seat must be suitable for the person using it and the types of work he or she is carrying out. A suitable footrest must be provided where necessary.

Regulation 12: Condition of Floors and Traffic Routes

Floors and the surface of every traffic route in a workplace shall:

- be constructed so as to be suitable for use;
- not have holes or slopes;
- not be uneven or slippery;
- be kept free from obstructions, and articles or substances likely to cause persons to trip, slip or fall;
- have effective drainage.

Regulation 13: Falls or Falling Objects

Much of this regulation was revoked by the **Work at Height Regulations 2005**. The remaining requirements relate to ensuring that every tank, pit or structure where there is a risk of a person in the workplace falling into a dangerous substance (poisons, corrosives, etc.) shall be securely covered or fenced.

Regulation 14: Windows, and Transparent or Translucent Doors, Gates and Walls

Transparent or translucent surfaces in windows, doors, gates, walls and partitions shall be constructed of safety materials or be adequately protected against breakage where any part is at shoulder level or below in doors and gates or where any part is at waist level or below in windows, walls and partitions (with the exception of glasshouses). The material must be appropriately and conspicuously marked to make its presence apparent.

Regulation 15: Windows, Skylights and Ventilators

Windows, skylights and ventilators capable of being opened must be able to be opened, closed and adjusted safely without exposing the person performing the operation to any risk to health and safety. When open they must not present a risk to the operator's health and safety.

Regulation 16: Ability to Clean Windows, etc. Safely

All windows and skylights in a workplace shall be of such a design or construction that they may be cleaned safely. Account may be taken of equipment used in conjunction with the window or skylight or devices fitted to the building.

Regulation 17: Organisation, etc. of Traffic Routes

Workplace traffic routes must allow for the segregation of pedestrians and vehicles to allow both to circulate freely and safely. Routes must be constructed safely, clearly signed, and kept free of obstructions. Every workplace shall be organised in such a way that pedestrians and vehicles can circulate in a safe manner. So far as is reasonably practicable, traffic routes shall be suitable for the persons or vehicles using them, sufficient in number, in suitable positions and of sufficient size. Traffic routes shall not satisfy these requirements unless pedestrians or vehicles are able to use the traffic route without causing danger to the health and safety of persons at work near the traffic route and there is sufficient separation of any traffic route for vehicles from doors or gates or from traffic routes for pedestrians which lead on to it; where vehicles and pedestrians use the same traffic route there shall be sufficient separation between them and all traffic routes shall be suitably indicated.

Regulation 18: Doors and Gates

Doors and gates must be suitably constructed and fitted with safety devices where necessary, e.g. sliding doors and gates; powered doors and gates; and upward opening doors and gates. Doors and gates shall not comply unless any sliding door or gate has a device to prevent it coming off its track and any upward opening door or gate has a device to prevent it falling back. Any powered door or gate must have suitable effective features to prevent it causing injury by trapping any person.

Regulation 19: Escalators and Moving Walkways

These shall function safely, be equipped with any necessary safety devices and fitted with one or more emergency stop controls.

Regulation 20: Sanitary Conveniences

Suitable and sufficient sanitary conveniences and washing facilities must be provided at readily accessible places in workplaces. The rooms containing them must be adequately ventilated and lit; the rooms and conveniences must be kept clean and in an orderly condition; and separate rooms must be provided for men and women except where the convenience is in a separate room which can be locked from the inside.

Regulation 21: Washing Facilities

"Facilities" means sanitary and washing facilities; "sanitary accommodation" means a room containing one or more sanitary conveniences; and "washing station" means a wash-basin or a section of a trough or fountain sufficient for one person.

Where work activities result in heavy soiling of face, hands and forearms, the number of washing stations should be increased to one for every 10 people at work (or fraction of 10) up to 50 people; and one extra for every additional 20 people (or fraction of 20).

Where facilities provided for workers are also used by members of the public, the number of conveniences and washing stations specified above should be increased as necessary to ensure that workers can use the facilities without undue delay.

Regulation 22: Drinking Water

An adequate supply of wholesome drinking water shall be provided for all persons at work.

Regulation 23: Accommodation for Clothing

Suitable and sufficient accommodation shall be provided for any person at work's own clothing which is not worn during working hours and for special clothing worn at work but which is not taken home.

Regulation 24: Facilities for Changing Clothing

Sufficient and suitable facilities shall be provided for any person at work to change clothing in all cases where the person has to wear special clothing for the purpose of work and the person cannot, for reasons of health or propriety, be expected to change in another room. These facilities shall not be suitable unless they include separate facilities for use by men and women where necessary for reasons of propriety.

Regulation 25: Facilities for Rest and to Eat Meals

Suitable and sufficient rest facilities must be provided at readily accessible places which shall include suitable facilities to eat meals where food eaten in the workplace would otherwise be likely to become contaminated. Rest rooms and rest areas should include suitable arrangements to protect non-smokers from discomfort from tobacco smoke. Suitable facilities shall be provided for any person at work who is a pregnant woman or nursing mother to rest.

Regulation 25A: Disabled Persons

Where necessary, those parts of the workplace (including in particular doors, passageways, stairs, showers, washbasins, lavatories and workstations) used or occupied directly by disabled persons at work shall be organised to take account of such persons.

CASE LAW

Adsett v. K and L Steelfounders and Engineers Ltd (1953)

Significance: The meaning of the term 'Practicable'

Mr Adsett worked in a foundry, shovelling various casting sands and compounds through a grate onto a conveyor belt below. He freely breathed in the resulting atmospheric dust and contracted pneumoconiosis. Some time later, his employers installed an extractor system, as soon as its use in the circumstances had been thought of, but too late to prevent Adsett's condition. The question in this case was the meaning of 'practicable'. It was held that his employers were not in breach by failing to provide the extraction earlier as the system had not been invented. To be practicable meant that the measure or system had to be known for its application to workers in the industry concerned.

J Armour v. J Skeen (Procurator Fiscal, Glasgow) (1977)

Significance: Example of a prosecution under s.37 HSWA

A workman fell to his death while repairing a road bridge over the river Clyde. Mr Armour was the Director of Roads for the regional Council and as such the responsibility for supervising the safety of road workers was his. He had not produced a written safety policy for such work.

He was prosecuted under section 37(1) of the **Health and Safety at Work, etc. Act 1974** which imposes personal liability on senior executives.

Mr Armour's defence was that he was under no personal duty to carry out the Council's statutory duties, one of which was the formulation of a detailed safety policy for the roads department. This was rejected. Section 37(1) imposed upon Mr Armour the personal duty to carry out the Council's statutory duty to prepare a written policy. This he had failed to do and was therefore guilty of an offence.

Associated Dairies Ltd v. Hartley (1979)

Significance: HSWA - Reasonable practicability; cost of controls disproportionate to the risk

Following a fractured toe injury to an employee, the factory inspector issued an improvement notice (s.2(1)) to a supermarket company requiring the provision of safety footwear free of charge for employees who used roller trucks. At the time, the company made safety footwear available for purchase at cost, and offered a credit system for payment. The company appealed to the Industrial Tribunal on the grounds of cost outweighing the risk, and also that its current system was reasonable and in line with trade practice.

The tribunal held that the employer's duty under s.2(1) to ensure so far as is reasonably practicable the health, safety and welfare of employees is a general duty, and that it is right to consider the extent of the risk and the time, trouble and expense involved in any specific proposed solution. In this case, the company's existing policy was considered to be in proportion to the risk (considering the cost of provision for all employees at all stores). The law only prohibits a levy being placed on safety equipment provided under specific requirements, not under general duty clauses of **HSWA 1974**.

Baker v. T E Hopkins & Son Limited (1959)

Significance: The defence of *volenti non fit injuria*

The defendant had adopted a dangerous system of working, in allowing the cleaning of a well by lowering a petrol engine which emitted fumes. Two workers were overcome by fumes. The claimant's husband, a doctor, volunteered to go down the well, knowing of the existence of the fumes. He, too, was overcome by fumes but could not be lifted from the well because the rope that was attached to him became caught. All three men died. The defendant argued that the doctor consented.

It was decided that *"it is neither 'rational' nor 'seemly' to say that a rescuer freely and voluntarily takes on the risks inherent in the rescue attempt and created by the defendant's negligence"*. It was therefore held that the defendants were liable, not only in respect of the deaths of the employees, but also in respect of the death of the doctor- it was a natural and probable consequence of the defendant's negligence towards their employees that someone would attempt to rescue them.

Barber v. Somerset County Council (2004)

Significance: Employers' liability for work-related stress; trigger point for action to avert harm caused by excessive workloads

A local authority was in breach of its duty to its employee to take reasonable care to avoid injuring his health where it had become aware that his difficulties at work were having an adverse effect on his mental health, but had taken no steps to help him.

Mr Barber (B) appealed against a decision of the Court of Appeal that the local authority had not been in breach of its duty to take reasonable care to avoid injuring his health. B had been employed by the local authority as a teacher and, in September 1995, was given further responsibilities. He worked between 61 and 70 hours per week, and often had to work in the evenings and at weekends. In February 1996 B told his deputy head teacher that he was experiencing "work overload", and made enquiries about taking early retirement. In May B was absent from work for three weeks, his absence certified by his GP as being due to stress and depression. On his return to work B met with members of the school's senior management team and said that he was not coping with his workload and that the situation was becoming detrimental to his health. He was not met with an entirely sympathetic response and no assistance was provided. In November 1996 he left the school and did not return. Since that time B had been unable to work as a teacher, or to do any work other than undemanding part-time work. The issue was whether the Court of Appeal had been right to conclude that it was not foreseeable that, if B continued with his existing workload, he was liable to develop a psychiatric illness.

The House of Lords found in favour of Mr Barber, effectively agreeing with the trial judge that the local authority had been in breach and there was insufficient reason for the Court of Appeal to set aside that finding. The test was whether the local authority had fallen below the standard properly to be expected of a reasonable and prudent employer taking positive steps for the safety of his workers in the light of what he knew or ought to have known.

The duty to take action had arisen in June or July 1996 when B had seen members of the school's senior management team, and had continued so long as nothing had been done to help him. The senior management team should have made enquiries about B's problems and discovered what they could have done to ease them. The trial judge had been entitled to form the view that the school's senior management team were in a position of continuing breach of the employer's duty of care, and that had caused B's breakdown in November 1996. The Court of Appeal had accurately expressed the principles that ought to be applied where a complaint was made of psychiatric illness brought about by stress at work. (See **Sutherland and others v. Hatton and others**, below.)

Barkway v. South Wales Transport Co. Ltd (1950)

Significance: The absolute duty to maintain imposed by the Motor Vehicles (Construction and Use) Regulations; the application of the maxim *'Res ipsa loquitor'* (let the thing speak for itself) when establishing a causal link between a negligent act or omission and loss sustained

In this case, the appellant's husband was killed when a tyre burst, whilst travelling on a bus belonging to the respondent. The vehicles were regularly and thoroughly inspected and tested by South Wales Transport. However, the company was held liable as it did not have a system for reporting, or require drivers to report incidents which could have identified hidden defects that may have caused the tyre burst.

The provision and monitoring of safe plant and equipment includes therefore, both the monitoring of safety performance and the availability and use of a regular defects reporting system.

Bradford v. Robinson Rentals (1967)

Significance: Not necessary to foresee the precise harm that might arise - it is enough that some harm was foreseeable

The defendants in this case employed the complainant as a radio service engineer. The 57-year-old travelled between clients in a motor van, making frequent stops at clients' houses to perform maintenance service. In January 1963, he was sent out to change a colleague's old van, on a journey of between 450 and 500 miles. It was expected to involve some 20 hours of travelling, at a time when the weather was expected to be severe. Both the old van, and the new van were unheated and the radiator in the old van was defective, and had to be topped up frequently during the journey. In spite of expressing his view that the journey could be dangerous, and that he should not go, the claimant was instructed to undertake it. The lack of heater meant that his breath formed ice on the windscreen, so that he had to keep the window open. As a result of cold on the journey, and despite all reasonable precautions taken by the claimant, he suffered permanent injury to his hands and feet by frostbite, and sued his employers in negligence. Such an injury would be unusual in England.

It was held that the defendants had called on the claimant to carry out an unusual task that would likely expose him to extreme cold and fatigue, and that he had thereby been exposed to a reasonably foreseeable risk of injury from exposure to cold. As long as the damage is of a kind foreseeable, it does not matter that it is much greater in extent than the defendant could have contemplated, as liability did not depend on the precise nature of the injury suffered being itself reasonably foreseeable. The defendants were therefore held liable to the claimant in negligence.

British Railways Board v. Herrington (1972)

Significance: the common law duty owed to trespassers

A six-year-old boy was playing with his friends on land adjacent to an electrified railway line. He got through a fence in poor repair and fell onto a live line. The stationmaster had been warned of the condition of the fence and despite his knowledge that children frequented the area, the fence had not been repaired. The House of Lords held that, although the general rule remained that a person trespassed at his own risk, an occupier's duty was not limited to not harming the trespasser intentionally or recklessly. The occupier owed a duty of common humanity to a trespasser known to be present.

The House of Lords set out three criteria that should be established before a duty of common humanity exists:

1. The occupier must have knowledge that trespassers are getting onto his land.
2. That a hazard exists that would likely endanger the trespasser.
3. The risk is one that would compel a reasonable occupier to take action.

The Herrington decision was subjected to criticism and was referred to the Law Commission, whose report formed the basis of the **Occupiers' Liability Act 1984**. Thus, this case is no longer used as an authority for the proposition that a duty is owed to trespassers, since it has effectively been replaced by the 1984 Act.

Cambridge Water Co. Ltd. v. Eastern Counties Leather Plc (1994)

Significance: Strict liability; the addition of reasonable foreseeability to the rule in *Rylands v. Fletcher*

Cambridge Water Co. purchased a borehole in 1976 to extract water to supply to the public. In 1983, it tested the water to ensure that it met minimum standards for human consumption and discovered that it was contaminated with an organochlorine solvent. On investigation, it emerged that the solvent came from the Eastern Counties Leather Plc tannery, about 1.3 miles from the borehole. Since the tannery opened in 1879, until 1976 the solvent it used had been delivered in 40-gallon drums which were transported by forklift truck and then tipped into a sump. Since 1976, solvent had been delivered in bulk and stored in tanks. It was then piped to the tanning machinery. There was no evidence of any spills from the tanks or pipes, and it was concluded that the water had been contaminated by frequent spills under the earlier system. Cambridge Water Co. claimed damages against Eastern Counties Leather Plc alternatively for negligence, nuisance and under the rule in **Rylands v. Fletcher**.

At first instance, it was found that Eastern Counties Leather Plc could not have foreseen this type of damage and, therefore, the court disallowed the claims in nuisance and negligence. Further, it was found that the actions of Eastern Counties Leather Plc constituted a natural use of the land and consequently the court dismissed the claim based on the rule in **Rylands v. Fletcher**.

Cambridge Water Co. Ltd successfully appealed. Eastern Counties Leather Plc then appealed to the House of Lords.

The House of Lords unanimously found that Eastern Counties Leather Plc was not liable for the water contamination. The main issue was whether the foreseeability of the damage suffered by Cambridge Water Co. was relevant to a claim under the rule in **Rylands v. Fletcher**. The Lords accepted the original finding that a reasonable supervisor employed by Eastern Counties Leather Plc would not have foreseen that the solvent would leak from the tannery floors down into the water source. It was thought, at the time, that any spilt solvent would evaporate and that the only foreseeable risk was that if large quantities were spilt, someone might be overcome by the vapour.

Caparo Industries Plc. v. Dickman and Others (1990)

Significance: The nature of the duty of care; establishing when a duty is owed

The "neighbour principle" as set out in **Donoghue v. Stevenson (1932)** was inevitably too broad and has been refined several times. This case is the most significant recent decision in this area. The case involved the alleged negligent preparation of accounts.

The case established a three-stage test to establish if a duty of care exists between two parties:

- the harm suffered by the claimant must be reasonably foreseeable;
- there should be sufficient proximity between the claimant and defendant; and

- is it fair, just and reasonable to impose a duty?

This last step brings in the concept of policy, in which the courts have to balance the needs of a claimant against imposing excessive liability on a defendant, the problem being of "opening the floodgates" which means creating an indeterminate liability.

A good example within occupational health and safety relates to the issue of "nervous shock" nowadays better known as "Post Traumatic Stress Disorder" (PTSD). During the Hillsborough disaster of 1989 a number of football fans were killed or seriously injured due to the admitted negligence of the Chief Constable of South Yorkshire who was responsible for crowd control. There was no doubt that a duty of care was owed to those who sustained physical injury. However, there were many hundreds of others who suffered no physical harm but suffered PTSD as a result of witnessing the horrific sight of individuals being crushed and suffocated. These included fans at the ground, police officers who endeavoured to rescue those being crushed and the friends and relatives of those who died who were not at the ground but became aware of the disaster unfolding through the live TV broadcast.

In this case the number of possible claimants would have been very large and so the courts had to establish some rules to limit the liability of the defendant. The consequence of not limiting liability would cause the insurance system, which ultimately pays the compensation in such cases, to collapse as insurance companies would not be prepared to offer such cover to prospective defendants.

Corn v. Weirs Glass (Hanley) Ltd (1960)

Significance: Liability for personal injury - no link between breach and loss

A glazier was carrying a large sheet of glass with both hands. He overbalanced on the stairs and fell, causing himself injury. There was no handrail on the stairs contrary to the relevant regulations.

It was held that, since both the glazier's hands were involved in holding the glass, a handrail would not have been of use to him, and, therefore, its absence was not the cause of the injury.

Corr (Administratrix of the Estate of Thomas Corr, Deceased) v. IBC Vehicles Ltd (2008)

Significance: Damages for loss attributable to a spouse's death by suicide may be recoverable in an action against a former employer

Mr Corr had been employed by IBC Ltd as a maintenance engineer. Whilst at work, he had been struck on the head by a machine, resulting in a need for reconstructive surgery that left him disfigured. He suffered from post traumatic stress disorder and committed suicide nearly six years after the accident. Before his death, Mr Corr had begun a damages claim against IBC Ltd for his physical and psychological injuries. His claim survived his death (in accordance with s1 of the **Fatal Accidents Act 1976**) and Mrs Corr was awarded damages in respect of the financial loss attributable to the suicide. IBC Ltd appealed.

IBC Ltd accepted that they had breached their duty to Mr Corr, that his depressive illness was caused by the accident and that his depressive illness drove him to take his own life. The issue between the parties was whether the damages claimed by Mrs Corr were too remote. IBC Ltd argued that Mr Corr's suicide:

- fell outside the duty of care that they owed to him;
- was not reasonably foreseeable;
- broke the chain of causation;
- was an unreasonable act which broke the chain of causation;
- was the voluntary act of the deceased (and so allowed them to use the complete defence of *volenti non fit injuria*); and
- amounted to contributory negligence.

The House of Lords decided this case as follows:

(1) IBC Ltd owed Mr Corr a duty to avoid causing him psychological as well as physical injury. Its breach caused injury of both kinds. He would not have committed suicide had he not sustained his injuries. Therefore, his suicide fell within the scope of the duty of care that his employer owed him.

(2) Depression, possibly very severe, was a foreseeable consequence of the breach. Mrs Corr did not have to show that the suicide itself was foreseeable- a tortfeasor who reasonably foresaw the occurrence of some damage need not foresee the precise form which the damage might take. Suicide was not an unforeseeable consequence of severe depression.

(3) Mr Corr's suicide was the response of a man suffering from a severely depressive illness which impaired his capacity to make reasoned and informed judgments about his future, such illness being a consequence of IBC Ltd's tort. It was not unfair to hold IBC Ltd responsible for that consequence of its breach of duty.

(4) Since the suicide did not break the chain of causation (i.e. it was a foreseeable consequence of IBC's breach of duty), it was impossible to find that the damages attributable to the death were rendered too remote because the deceased's conduct was unreasonable.

(5) Mr Corr had not consented to the accident, nor had he consented to his injury. He did not consent to his suicide, which was the result of a psychological condition induced by IBC Ltd's breach of duty.

(6) It was not appropriate for the court to decide the contributory negligence issue on which the courts below had made no findings. A deduction for contributory negligence could be appropriate in circumstances of deliberate suicide committed in a state of depression induced by an accident.

IBC Ltd's appeal was dismissed.

Davie v. New Merton Board Mills Ltd (1959)

Significance: Employers' liability - the duty to provide reasonably safe tools and equipment; foreseeability of harm; the Employers' Liability (Defective Equipment) Act 1969

This case is worth closer examination to illustrate the position as it then was.

A firm of toolmakers (A) manufactured a steel bar, which was excessively hard. They sold the bar to a supplier (B), who in turn sold it to the employers (C) of Mr Davie. He was injured when a splinter flew off the bar when he was using it at work. He sued his employer and the manufacturer (A).

Initially judgment was in his favour against both (A) and (C), and (C) was to be compensated by (A). The employer (C) appealed and their appeal was upheld on the grounds that it was the duty of an employer to take reasonable care to provide reasonably safe tools and working appliances. If the employer was not himself the manufacturer of the tool, or the tool was not made to his specification, he did not fail in his duty of care to the employee by providing him with a ready-made tool which had been made by a reputable manufacturer. Under the circumstances the defendant, Davie, could only recover damages from the manufacturer.

This was an easy escape clause for the employer. Providing his employee with a tool which turned out to be faulty did not breach his duty of care to his employee and although the employee could, in theory, sue the manufacturer this would have depended upon his ability:

- to find the manufacturer (who might have gone out of business!), and
- to establish the manufacturer's negligence.

The situation changed ten years later with the introduction of the **Employer's Liability (Defective Equipment) Act 1969** which states:

"Where an employee suffers personal injury in the course of his employment in consequence of a defect in equipment provided by his employer for the purposes of the employer's business; and the defect is attributable wholly or in part to the fault of a third party (whether identified or not), the injury shall be deemed to be also attributable to negligence on the part of the employer (whether or not he is liable in respect of the injury apart from this sub-section), but without prejudice to the law relating to contributory negligence and to any remedy by way of contribution or in contract or otherwise which is available to the employer in respect of the injury."

The employer's breach of duty extends to failing to provide proper equipment for the job or failing to maintain it, and could possibly be coupled with failing to provide proper personal protective equipment. Under this interpretation of the law, Mr Davie would have been able to sue his employer successfully and his employer, in turn, would be able to take action against the manufacturer.

Donaldson v. Hays Distribution Services Ltd (2005)

Significance: the tort of breach of statutory duty - can a non-employee sue for breach of the Workplace (Health, Safety and Welfare) Regulations 1992?

The claimant was a customer who was sent to a loading bay to collect her purchases and was crushed by a reversing articulated lorry. She sued for breach of statutory duty under the **Workplace (Health, Safety and Welfare) Regulations 1992**, regulation 17, which states:

"Organisation, etc. of traffic routes

(1) Every workplace shall be organised in such a way that pedestrians and vehicles can circulate in a safe manner.

(2) Traffic routes in a workplace shall be suitable for the persons or vehicles using them, sufficient in number, in suitable positions and of sufficient size."

One issue at trial was whether the terms "pedestrians" and "persons" extended beyond workers to visitors?

The Court of Session held that non-workers could **not** rely on a breach of regulation 17 principally for the reason that the **Workplace Regulations** were enacted to give effect in the United Kingdom to the **Workplace Directive**, which applies exclusively for the protection of workers, and there was no indication that Parliament meant anything to the contrary.

This case was heard in the Scottish Court of Session and so the decision applies only in Scotland. However, there is a similar decision by the Court of Appeal that applies in England and Wales - *Ricketts v. Torbay Council (2003)*.

Donoghue v. Stevenson (1932)

Significance: The general duty of care at common law; the 'Neighbour Principle'

This case involved two ladies. A friend of the claimant purchased a bottle of ginger beer. The claimant drank some of the beer in which was found the remains of a decomposed snail. She was subsequently ill and sued the manufacturer. She was unable to sue the manufacturer for breach of contract because the only contract that existed was with the claimant's friend who had bought the ginger beer and the manufacturer.

The House of Lords held that the defendant being the manufacturer of the ginger beer owed a duty of care to the claimant as the consumer of the beer to take reasonable care to ensure that the bottle did not contain anything that might cause harm.

In this case the judge said that reasonable care must be taken to avoid acts or omissions which, with reasonable foresight, you would know would be likely to injure your neighbour. This is known as the **neighbour principle**. Therefore the test whether someone is a "neighbour", in the legal sense, can be established if it can be reasonably foreseen that the act or omission may cause harm to them.

Edwards v. National Coal Board (1949)

Significance: Definition of 'Reasonably practicable'

You need to be sure of the exact meaning of this phrase and to be able to distinguish it from other similar phrases which are quite different in interpretation. It appears early on in **HSWA** in section 2(1).

"It shall be the duty of every employer to ensure, so far as is reasonably practicable, the health, safety and welfare at work of all his employees."

Although a very important phrase in **HSWA**, the Act itself does not contain a definition of the expression. To find its precise meaning you have to refer to case law.

In *Edwards v. National Coal Board (1949)*, a miner was killed when a section of road on which he was working subsided. The section of the road concerned had no timber supports, although other sections were properly supported. Lord Asquith, the judge in the case, said that a balance had to be struck in deciding whether it would have been reasonably practicable to have taken the precaution of providing supports for the section of road which collapsed. The balance was struck by weighing the quantum of risk involved (the danger of collapse and loss of life) against the quantum of sacrifice involved (the cost, time and trouble). If there was a gross disproportion between the two and the risk was insignificant to the cost, there would be no requirement to take the additional precautions. The Coal Board did not present sufficient evidence to demonstrate that the cost was out of all proportion to the risk.

Therefore, to carry out a duty "so far as is reasonably practicable" means that the degree of risk has to be balanced against the time, trouble and cost involved in taking the measures necessary to avoid the risk.

If the measures are so disproportionate to the risk involved that it would be unreasonable to take the measures, then there can be no obligation to take them. The greater the risk the more likely it is that it would be reasonable to go to the expense of taking the measures. In a nutshell, if the consequences and the degree of risk are small and the cost of the measures to reduce the risk is very expensive, it would be unreasonable to incur that cost. The size of the company or its financial resources is not a consideration in arriving at a decision.

Fairchild v. Glenhaven Funeral Services Ltd and Others (2002)

Significance: Joint and several liability for damages in mesothelioma cases

Where a claimant suffers mesothelioma after being negligently exposed to asbestos dust during the course of employment with more than one employer, in circumstances where he could not prove which defendant's breach of duty was the cause of the disease, it was sufficient for the claimant to prove that a defendant materially increased the risk of injury. Such a claimant did not have to satisfy the "but for" causation test (i.e. the claimant does not need to show that, but for the particular employer's negligence, he would not have developed the disease).

The House of Lords were asked to hear appeals from three separate Court of Appeal decisions involving claimants who had developed mesothelioma after having been exposed to asbestos dust by more than one employer.

The House of Lords were asked to decide if, in cases where:

(1) a claimant (C) was employed at different times and for differing periods by both A and B; and

(2) both A and B were subject to a duty to take reasonable care or to take all practicable measures to prevent C inhaling asbestos dust; and

(3) both A and B breached that duty such that C developed mesothelioma, and

(4) where any other cause of mesothelioma could be discounted,

...could C recover damages against either A **or** B, or against A **and** B?

Given that current science cannot show which exposure caused the mesothelioma, the House of Lords decided that, where conditions (1) to (3) above were satisfied, C was entitled to recover against both A and B. The common sense view was that, in negligently exposing C to asbestos dust, **both** A **and** B materially contributed to the risk of C developing mesothelioma and so both should be liable. Each defendant would be liable in full for a claimant's damages, although a defendant could seek contribution against another employer liable for causing the disease.

Therefore, in a case where a mesothelioma sufferer had worked for several different employers, any of whom may have negligently exposed him or her to asbestos dust, and where only one of the employers can be traced (given that exposure may have occurred many years earlier), that one employer will be liable for the full amount of the damages claim. If, however, more than one employer can be traced, the amount of damages claimed will be apportioned between the defendants.

Ferguson v. John Dawson and Partners (Contractors) Ltd (1976)

Significance: Status as an 'employee' for the purposes of health and safety

Mr Ferguson was a subcontractor working for John Dawson and Partners (Contractors) Ltd. Whilst working on a flat roof with no guardrail, Mr Ferguson fell and was seriously injured. The respondent was found to be in breach of its statutory duty under the **Construction (Working Places) Regulations 1966**. The company based its appeal on two issues:

- Firstly, that Mr Ferguson was a subcontractor, working under a contract for services, and not an employee.

- Secondly, the company claimed that the roof was not going to be used for an 'appreciable time' and, therefore, did not have the necessary characteristic to be a 'workplace'.

The Court of Appeal applied the established tests and found that, although both the company and the contractor considered Mr Ferguson to be self-employed, he was employed under a contract of service. In compliance with the Regulations, the company was therefore held to owe him a statutory duty to provide a guardrail on the roof, and, as a result, was liable for damages to the claimant for breach of that duty. The 10 or 15 minutes required to do the work was held to be an 'appreciable time' and the roof was therefore considered to be a 'working place'.

This case shows that if, when the facts are considered and whatever name they may have given to their relationship, the relationship between two parties is seen to be that of employer and employee, the relevant obligations owed by an employer to an employee will apply.

General Cleaning Contractors Ltd v. Christmas (1953)

Significance: Employers' personal and non-delegable duty to establish a safe system of work

A window-cleaner was in the habit of standing on the outside window sill of a sash-type window and, having cleaned the top half, pushing it up almost to the top of the frame leaving just enough space for a handhold whilst he cleaned the lower half. On this occasion the sash dropped down and he lost his grip, which resulted in his falling and sustaining injury. He sued his employers for neglecting to provide a safe system of work.

The defendants had made safety belts available, but the claimant had not used one because there were no hooks to which it could be attached. The judgment in the case found in favour of the employee on the basis that it was the employer's duty to consider the situation, to devise a suitable system, to instruct his employees in what they must do, and to supply any implements that may be required such as, in this case, wedges to prevent the window from closing. Here the employers had done nothing, leaving any precautions to the discretion of the employee and were therefore in breach of their duty of care to take reasonable care to lay down a reasonably safe system of work.

Hudson v. Ridge Manufacturing Co. Ltd (1957)

Significance: The employer's duty to provide competent and safety-conscious co-workers; liability for foreseeable harm caused by practical jokers

The claimant, Hudson, was injured at work, as the result of a foolish prank played on him by a fellow employee, Chadwick. Such irresponsible horseplay at work had been the habitual conduct of Chadwick over a period of some four years. He had often been warned by his employers, who were aware of his behaviour, but he had not taken reprimands seriously. In spite of this, the employers kept him in their employ.

As a result, the claimant claimed damages for negligence from his employer at common law. At Manchester Assizes, the employers were in fact found liable for damages to the claimant for breach of their duty at common law to provide competent fellow employees. It was held that where an employee, in terms of his habitual behaviour, was likely to prove a danger to his fellow employees, the employer has a duty to remove that employee as a source of danger from the workplace. In this case, as the employer failed to stop Chadwick's behaviour or to remove him from the workplace, they were held responsible for the injury sustained by the claimant as a result of Chadwick's prank.

ICI v. Shatwell (1965)

Significance: The defence of *volenti non fit injuria*

George and James Shatwell were employed by the appellants to carry out work with explosives, for which they were both qualified. They ignored the appellants' instructions, and certain specific regulations which imposed a duty on them personally. They could not be bothered to wait for longer wires which would enable them to carry out tests from a shelter removed from the explosives, and both were injured in an explosion. George Shatwell sued the appellants stating that both employees were equally to blame and the employers were vicariously liable for the acts of the other employee, James. Whilst James' acts were considered to have contributed to injury, the appellants were held to be not liable because the principle of *volenti non fit injuria* gave them a complete defence. He had therefore gone willingly to his injury and was not entitled to damages.

Intel Corporation (UK) Ltd v. Daw (2007) (Court of Appeal)

Significance: Employers' liability for work-related stress; provision of counselling services

The claimant (Daw) had worked at Intel's UK head office in Swindon since 1988 and had been given a task which substantially increased her workload.

The following year, she claimed the workload was so high she was doing the job of nearly two people and suffered from a nervous breakdown in June 2001 which resulted in a claim for negligence in that she had received no help from the company.

Despite Intel offering free counselling to staff who felt stressed, Daw won her case. The harm to Daw's health was reasonably foreseeable. The indications of impending harm to health were clear enough for Intel to realise that immediate action was required.

At the original tribunal it was held that "the counselling service could be of little or no help to Miss Daw. It could not reduce her workload".

The Court of Appeal held: *"A very considerable amount of helpful guidance is given in Hatton. That does not preclude or excuse the trial judge either from conducting a vigorous fact-finding exercise, as the trial judge in this case did, or deciding which parts of the guidance are relevant to the particular circumstances. The reference to counselling services in Hatton does not make such services a panacea by which employers can discharge their duty of care in all cases."*

In other words, provision of counselling services alone will seldom if ever be enough to discharge the employer's liability in relation to work-related stress.

Jones v. Livox Quarries Ltd (1952)

Significance: Contributory negligence; lack of reasonable care by a claimant for his own safety

Mr Jones, the claimant, was employed by the defendants, Livox Quarries. Against instructions, he hitched a lift, unknown to the driver, on the tow bar of one of the defendants' 'traxcavators' (a kind of excavator). The vehicle stopped after turning a sharp bend and a dumper travelling close behind ran into it, injuring the claimant. Jones sued the defendants, alleging negligence on the part of both drivers.

The judge at first instance found negligence on the part of the dumper driver, in that he had failed to act as a reasonably careful driver and in particular in not keeping an adequate look-out. He found that Mr Jones was 20% contributorily negligent for his own injuries since he had placed himself in a position of danger on the traxcavator.

The Court of Appeal decided that:

(1) the driver of the dumper could not have been keeping any sort of look-out; it was his duty to keep a proper look-out, and that duty was owed to the claimant even though he was on the traxcavator;

(2) the judge had not been wrong in finding that the claimant, who deliberately put himself into a position which exposed him to this danger, was to some extent responsible for what had happened, and, therefore, the appeal should be dismissed.

A person will be contributorily negligent if he ought reasonably to have foreseen that, if he did not act as a reasonable, prudent man, he might hurt himself. He should also take account of the possibility that others might be careless. A person who is found to be contributorily negligent must bear his proper share of responsibility for the consequences. In deciding whether a claimant has contributed to his own injuries, the questions to ask are (1) what faults were there which caused the damage? and (2) was his fault one of them? As Lord Justice Denning stated: *"If a man carelessly rides on a vehicle in a dangerous position, and subsequently there is a collision in which his injuries are made worse by reason of his position than they would otherwise have been, then his damage is partly the result of his own fault, and the damages recoverable by him fall to be reduced accordingly."*

Knowles v. Liverpool City Council (1993)

Significance: the meaning of the term 'equipment' in relation to the Employer's Liability (Defective Equipment) Act 1969

Knowles was an employee of Liverpool City Council. He was injured when one of the flagstones he was laying broke. An action was brought against the employer under the **Employer's Liability (Defective Equipment) Act 1969** for providing equipment in a defective condition.

The employer appealed to the House of Lords. They held that the word "equipment" was to be construed widely to include every article provided to an employee for the purpose of the employer's business. The flagstone was therefore classed as 'equipment' for the purposes of the 1969 Act.

Latimer v. AEC Ltd (1953)

Significance: Provision of a reasonably safe place of work

You will appreciate that should an employer create a place of work, it follows that there should be some legal requirement on him to ensure that such a place of work shall be as safe as the standard of "reasonable care" demands. This liability is also extended to means of access and egress to and from the place of work. It would be unreasonable to expect an employee to be at risk on his employer's land while going to or leaving his place of work, whilst at the same time requiring that the same employee be made safe at such place of work.

A factory floor was flooded after heavy rainfall which left a slippery film when it subsided. The floor was treated with sawdust until it ran out but an employee slipped on the floor and was injured.

It was held that the supply of sawdust was sufficient for normal needs, therefore the employer had taken reasonable steps to keep the floor safe.

Lister v. Romford Ice and Cold Storage Co. Ltd (1957)

Significance: Vicarious liability; contract law - the implied requirement to use reasonable care and skill

An employee of Romford Ice and Cold Storage Co., not following rules, backed a truck over his father. The father could have sued his son but, instead, successfully sued his son's employer as being vicariously liable. The employer's insurers (acting in the employer's name) in turn sued the son for breach of contract, claiming there was an implied term in his employment that the son obey reasonable commands and use reasonable care. The House of Lords by a majority of three to two decided to accept the circular situation that the son had to pay the same as the employer.

Machray v. Stewart and Lloyds Ltd (1964)

Significance: Contributory negligence; safe systems of work

The claimant was an experienced rigger. In the course of his employment by the defendants, a loop section of pipe, weighing over 10 cwt., had to be fixed to a gangway 70 feet above the ground. The pipe needed to be moved some 14 feet along the gangway but the crane driver was not available to move it. The next choice for moving the pipe would then usually have been by chain block and tackle. The claimant tried to obtain two sets in order to move the pipe, but failed to get any, in spite of the site being supplied with two or three dozen sets. He managed to obtain a single set of rope blocks instead. Although moving the section of pipe by this means would be less safe, he had been told by the charge-hand that the job was urgent. In the course of moving the pipe with the rope block, the claimant was injured when the pipe swung out of control.

The court found the defendants negligent in failing to provide sufficient equipment for the job. They, however, claimed that the claimant had contributed to the accident through his own negligence. The court held that, although he was an experienced rigger and chose to adopt a method that was less safe, he had been prevented from following his usual preferences by the failure of the defendants to provide proper equipment. He had acted as he did with the purpose of getting on with his employers' business and, therefore, no contributory negligence was established on his part.

Marshall v. Gotham and Co. Ltd (1954)

Significance: Comparison of 'practicable' and 'reasonably practicable' duties

The first phrase leaves out the word **"reasonably"** and its omission implies a stricter standard.

The case concerned the collapse of a mine roof which had been subjected to earlier tests but which collapsed due to a rare geological fault.

The judges decided that the employers were not liable because they had taken some precautions but the trouble and expense involved in taking more precautions would have been prohibitive and even then would not have guaranteed safety. The judge ruled in this case that if a precaution is practicable it must be taken unless in the whole circumstances it would be unreasonable. The term is now generally interpreted to mean that whatever is technically possible in the light of current knowledge must be carried out. The cost, time and trouble involved are **not** to be taken into account in arriving at a decision.

McWilliams (or Cummings) v. Sir William Arrol and Co. Ltd (1962)

Significance: Breach of statutory duty - establishing the causal link between breach and loss

Mr McWilliams was an experienced steel erector working on a tower crane. He was working on a building about 70 ft high when he fell and died. His wife sued for breach of section 26 of the **Factories Act 1937**, which required that if a person could fall more than 10 feet, means such as fencing or safety belts should be provided unless adequate foot and hand holds existed. Safety belts had been available until two days before the accident but not used and had then been removed to another site. The House of Lords decided that although the defendants were in breach of their statutory duty in not providing a belt, they were not liable because the breach was not the cause of the accident, since on the evidence presented Mr McWilliams would not have worn the belt if it had been provided. (At that time there was no duty on employers to instruct or exhort employees to wear the belt.)

Mersey Docks and Harbour Board v. Coggins and Griffiths (Liverpool) Limited (1947)

Significance: Vicarious liability for a hired-out employee

A crane driver employed by a harbour board was hired, with his crane, by stevedores (Coggins and Griffiths) to load a ship. In working his crane the driver negligently injured an employee of the stevedores. The outcome of the case turned on the question of whether the employer/employee relationship had passed from the harbour board to the stevedores.

The House of Lords decided that the test was "*Who had the authority to direct or delegate to the workman the manner in which the vehicle was driven?*" Here, in operating the crane, the driver was using his own discretion which had been delegated to him by his regular employer (the harbour board). If he made a mistake in operating the crane, this was nothing to do with the stevedores company (Coggins and Griffiths).

The power to control the method of performing the work was not transferred from the harbour board to the stevedores, therefore the harbour board retained control over the driver and was vicariously liable for the driver's negligence.

Mitchell and Others v. United Co-operatives Ltd (2012)

Significance: Mental ill health and dealing with violence and aggression at work

Court of Appeal dismisses claim arising from shop robberies; the Claimants' employer had put appropriate precautions in place.

Implications

Unfortunately, some shops will be vulnerable to robberies. The issue for businesses, and for their insurers, is the extent to which precautions should be taken to protect employees against this risk. In this case, the Claimants submitted that a full-time security guard should have been employed, at an estimated annual cost of £30,000. This was in the context of a shop running at a loss of about £60,000 per annum.

This judgment will provide some reassurance. It will be necessary for businesses to carry out careful risk assessments, as the Defendant did in this case. However, provided reasonable measures are put in place, claims such as this can be successfully defended.

Background

The claim related to robberies at a convenience store. One or more of the Claimants were employed in the store when, on three occasions in 2004 and 2005, robbers entered and stole cigarettes and cash. The Claimants suffered post-traumatic stress and developed an anxiety state as a result.

Mrs Mitchell began work at the premises as a shop assistant in about 1988 when the shop was trading under the name "Dawn to Dusk". She was joined in 1999 by Mrs Benton. The shop was then sold to United Co-operatives Ltd (the Co-op) late in 1999. Mrs Goodwin was transferred to the shop as manager in February 2005. Whilst Dawn to Dusk was operating, the cash tills and the staff operating them were behind glass screens, which enclosed that area, access being obtained by the staff through a door which was locked behind them. The Co-op changed the layout and removed the glass screens. There were two robberies in the 11 years before the Co-op acquired the premises, but 10 robberies between 25 February 2000 and 7 December 2005. As a result of risk assessments in 2002 and 2003, the Co-op introduced a number of measures including CCTV monitoring and panic alarms.

At first instance, His Honour Judge Armitage QC dismissed the claim.

Decision

Ward LJ gave the leading judgment in the Court of Appeal, dismissing the appeal:

- The Co-op owed its employees a common law duty of reasonable care to keep them safe. The reasonable steps to be taken by the Co-op were to deter robberies: no employer could be expected to go so far as to prevent any robbery taking place at all.

- Security screens- it was not possible to say what part the presence or absence of screens played upon the criminal mind. The Judge was entitled to conclude that, although screens might have some deterrent effect, they carried risks for the staff (of being confined in an area with a determined robber) which outweighed that benefit.

- Security guard- it was necessary to strike a balance between the probable effectiveness of a precaution that can be taken and the expense that it involves. In addition, there was evidence that the Co-op's approach to risk management was standard practice for retail outlets of this kind. The Judge was entitled to find that the failure to provide full-time guarding did not amount to a failure to take reasonable care for the safety of the Claimants.

O'Toole v. First Quench (2005)

Significance: Manning levels - dealing with violence and aggression at work

It has always been recognised that people working alone are at a higher risk of workplace violence (a factor which must be taken on board during the risk assessment process). Consideration should be given to whether it is suitable for an employee to work on their own.

If it is, then ease of communication, raising an alarm and seeking assistance should be taken into account. In the Scottish case of **Collins v. First Quench** the Claimant won over £100,000 in damages when the trial Judge came to the dubious conclusion that the risk of the robbery would have been significantly reduced had a second member of staff been present.

Fortunately this decision was not followed in the case of *O'Toole v. First Quench* in August 2005 when an English Court found that it was unreasonable to 'double staff' purely as a deterrent against robberies.

Paine v. Colne Valley Electricity Supply Co. Ltd (1938)

Significance: Provision of a safe place of work

In this case, Colne Valley Electricity Supply Co. Ltd conveyed high voltage current to kiosks in which transformers were housed. British Insulated Cables Ltd manufactured and supplied the kiosks. The kiosks were arranged in three cubicles. In one of the kiosks, there was the transformer, in another switches and busbars, and in the third an oil switch. The cubicles were separated by insulating material, but in one kiosk the insulating material did not extend to the back of the cubicle and left a space of about six inches. One of the busbars in the adjoining kiosk came within two inches of this space. A workman, an employee of Colne Valley Electricity Supply Co. Ltd, came into contact with the busbar when it was live and was killed.

Colne Valley were found to be in breach of a statutory duty (**Factory and Workshop Act 1901**), as there was not efficient screening of the dangerous parts in accordance with the provisions of the Act. They were also found to be in breach of their common law duty of care to provide their employees with a safe place in which to work.

(British Insulated Cables Ltd, the manufacturers, were found not liable as there had been ample opportunity for examination of the kiosk by the employers, and, therefore, the proximate relationship of the manufacturers did not extend beyond their customer to the workman.)

Paris v. Stepney Borough Council (1950)

Significance: Special duty of care to vulnerable persons

A one-eyed garage worker became completely blinded after a chip of metal entered his good eye. Along with others working in the vehicle repair department, no protective equipment had been given to Mr Paris.

After the accident Mr Paris successfully claimed damages for his injury but this was overturned on appeal. Mr Paris then appealed to the House of Lords.

The House of Lords held that where an employer is aware that an employee has a disability which, although it does not increase the risk of an accident occurring, does increase the risk of serious injury, special precautions should be taken if the employer is to fulfil its duty to take reasonable care for the safety of that employee.

Stepney Borough Council owed a special duty of care to Mr Paris and had been negligent in failing to supply goggles to him, even though such equipment was not given to other employees.

Qualcast (Wolverhampton) Ltd v. Haynes (1959)

Significance: Employers' liability for injuries to very experienced, competent workers

A 38-year-old who had been a moulder all his working life was casting moulding boxes. The ladle of molten metal which he was holding slipped, and some of the metal splashed onto his left foot when he was wearing ordinary leather boots. The employers had a stock of protective spats and of reinforced boots at a price, but they never recommended the claimant wear them. At County Court, judgment was given to the claimant, subject to 75% contributory negligence, as the employer was bound to urge the use of the protective equipment. However, on appeal, Lord Denning stated that *"he knew all there was to know, without being told: and he voluntarily decided to wear his own boots, which he had bought for the purpose... this workman, after he recovered from the injury went back to work and did the same as before. He never wore spats. If the warning given by the accident made no difference, we may safely infer that no advice beforehand would have had any effect"*. He lost because he was experienced and should have guarded against the danger.

R. v. Associated Octel Co. Ltd (1996)

Significance: Application of section 3 HSWA; definition of 'undertaking' for the purposes of s.3

The defendant company engaged some contractors to carry out repairs of a tank during a shut-down period. A permit to work was issued by the defendant but it proved to be inadequate and was not monitored. A contractor took a flammable liquid into the tank to clean the inner surface. However, a flash fire developed and the contractor was seriously burned. The HSE successfully prosecuted Octel who were fined £25,000. The defendant appealed first to the Court of Appeal, who upheld the conviction, and then the House of Lords. The Lords held that if an employer engages a contractor who works on his or her premises then the employer, subject to reasonable practicability, must ensure the contractor's health and safety. The House of Lords appeal was concerned with the definition of the term 'undertaking', which effectively includes any work carried out on the employer's premises and may include work on other premises which is part of the employer's business.

R. v. British Steel Plc (1994)

Significance: HSWA s.3 - no defence of 'proper delegation'

In 1990, British Steel decided to move a steel platform by crane. Two workers were provided by sub-contractors to do the repositioning work. All equipment was provided by British Steel and a British Steel engineer, Mr Crabb, was made responsible for supervision.

The platform was cut free without being suspended from the crane. While one of the workers was underneath the platform, another worker walked on it causing it to collapse, fatally injuring the worker underneath.

Whilst British Steel accepted at Sheffield Crown Court that the incident constituted a breach of section 3(1) of **HSWA** they stated that the defence of reasonable practicability enabled them to submit a defence on the basis that the directing minds at senior management level had taken all reasonable care to delegate supervision to Mr Crabb.

The judge ruled that the defence of proper delegation did not arise and British Steel was convicted. British Steel appealed. The Court of Appeal held that section 3(1) imposes absolute liability subject to 'reasonably practicable' measures to avert the risk and the appeal was dismissed.

The case reinforces the concept that corporations cannot avoid liability simply because the act causing the breach was carried out by someone who was not the directing mind of the company. Nor can they avoid responsibility simply by taking reasonable care to delegate responsibility.

R. v. Chargot Ltd (T/a Contract Services) & Ors (2008)

Significance: The standard of proof in prosecutions for breaches of s2(1) or s3(1) HSWA

In prosecutions for breaches of s2(1) and/or s3(1) **HSWA**, the prosecution has only to prove that the result described in those sections had not been achieved or prevented. It is then up to the defendant to show that they had done what was reasonably practicable in the circumstances. Prosecutors need to do more than simply assert that a state of affairs existed, although they do not have to identify and prove specific breaches of duty.

One of Chargot Limited's employees had died when the dumper truck he was driving fell onto its side and buried him under a load of spoil that was being transported at the time. Chargot Ltd were tried and convicted for failing to comply with duties set out in **HSWA** s2(1), s3(1) and s37. They appealed their conviction and lost, so brought a further appeal before the House of Lords. The House of Lords decided that s2(1) and s3(1) described a result in which an employer had to ensure the health and safety at work of all his employees and had to ensure that non-employees were not exposed to risks to their health and safety. However, s2 and s3 do not say how that result should be achieved. To establish a breach, the prosecution merely has to prove that the result had not been achieved or prevented. The onus then passes to the defendant to demonstrate that they had done what was reasonably practicable in the circumstances.

Even where there has been an injury, it may not be enough for a prosecutor simply to claim that the injury was evidence of a health and safety risk; it may be necessary to identify and prove the respects in which there had been a breach of duty. It is not the case that prosecution allegations have to be specifically proved, nor is it necessary for a jury to agree unanimously on which allegations had been proved. As long as the jury agreed about the result that the employer had to achieve or prevent, they did not need to agree on all the details of the evidence.

The law did not aim to create an environment that was entirely risk-free. The word "risk" (as used in the 1974 Act) refers to material risks to health and safety that any person would appreciate and take steps to guard against (see **R. v. Porter (2008)** below).

In a prosecution under s.37 of the 1974 Act, there is no fixed rule as to what has to be proved to establish consent, connivance or neglect on the part of a senior manager. In cases where the senior manager works remotely, or where what is done is not under his or her immediate direction or control, more evidence in support of the allegation might be needed. Conversely, in cases where the circumstances under which the risk arose were under the senior manager's direction or control, the prosecution would need to show little more than what would be needed to establish a breach by the body corporate (see *R. v. P and Another* below). In either case, the prosecution would have to show that the manager knew the material facts that constituted the offence by the body corporate, and that he or she agreed to its conduct. Consent, connivance and/or neglect could be established by inference as well as by proof of an express agreement.

R. v. HTM (2006) (Court of Appeal)

Significance: HSWA s.2(1) - the relevance of foreseeability of an accident when deciding whether there has been a breach

Following a fatal accident, an employer was prosecuted for failing to discharge its duty under section 2(1) of the **Health and Safety at Work, etc. Act 1974** to ensure, so far as reasonably practicable, the health and safety at work of its employees.

To avoid conviction the defendant had to prove (on a balance of probabilities) that it would not be reasonably practicable to do more than they actually did (s.40 **HSWA**).

The defendant argued that the accident would not have occurred if the employees had followed the safety instructions that had been provided and that their conduct could not have been foreseen.

In contrast the prosecutor contended that foreseeability was not relevant to the question of whether there was a breach of duty under section 2(1) of the 1974 Act, and that regulation 21 of the **Management of Health and Safety at Work Regulations 1999** prevented the defendant from relying in its defence on any act or default of its employees.

The Court of Appeal held that in defending a prosecution under s.2(1) of **HSWA** it was not reasonably practicable to do more to eliminate the risk. It was necessary to take into account the likelihood of the event and therefore evidence of foreseeability could be presented against the cost of eliminating the risk.

R. v. Nelson Group Services (Maintenance) Ltd (1999)

Significance: Reasonable practicability

Although the circumstances where such a defence may be established are likely to be rare, the Court of Appeal in this case stated that an isolated act of negligence by an employee carrying out work on behalf of the company does not stop that employer from establishing a defence that it has done everything that is reasonably practicable.

The court said:

"It is not necessary for the adequate protection of the public that the employer should be held criminally liable even for an isolated act of negligence by the employee performing the work. Such persons are themselves liable to criminal sanctions under the Act and under the Regulations. Moreover it is a sufficient obligation to place on the employer in order to protect the public to require the employer to show that everything reasonably practicable has been done to see that a person doing the work has the appropriate skill and instruction, has had laid down for him safe systems of doing the work, has been subject to adequate supervision, and has been provided with safe plant and equipment for the proper performance of the work."

R. v. P and Another (2007) (Court of Appeal)

Significance: s.37 HSWA - 'Neglect' to be based not only on what one knew but also on what one ought reasonably to have known

A child was being carried as a passenger on a forklift truck. The truck collided with another vehicle and the child was thrown from the truck and killed. The employer was prosecuted for a breach of s.3 **HSWA** and the defendant 'P', who was the director of the company and was responsible for managing the area in which the accident occurred, was charged with a breach of s.37(1) in that the offence committed by the company was committed with the consent or connivance of or to have been attributable to any neglect on his part.

The Court of Appeal held that to establish neglect (in contrast to consent or connivance) it was necessary to establish *"if there had not been actual knowledge of the relevant state of facts, nevertheless the officer of the company should have, by reason of the surrounding circumstances, been put on enquiry as to whether or not the appropriate safety procedures were in place. That would depend on the evidence in every case"*.

Relevant matters to consider include:

- The functions of the post held by the defendant.
- Whether there was failure to take a step which could and should have been taken.

- The defendant's state of knowledge of a need for action.

R. v. Porter (2008)

Significance: 'Risk' within the meaning of HSWA 1974 needs to be real rather than fanciful or hypothetical

Where a person is charged with a breach of s3(1) **HSWA** (failing to ensure the health and safety of non-employees), the prosecution has to prove that the risk is a real risk as opposed to a fanciful or hypothetical one.

Mr Porter was the headmaster of a private school where a three-year-old child had suffered a head injury after jumping from a flight of steps. The judge felt that the jury could view the steps as a risk to the safety of the child, and that they could conclude that it would be reasonably practicable to put in place constant supervision to prevent the child from descending the steps. Mr Porter was convicted and brought an appeal against his conviction.

The Court of Appeal decided that the risk which the prosecution had to prove should be real as opposed to fanciful or hypothetical. There is no objective standard or test applicable to every case that shows what is 'real' and what is 'fanciful' when it comes to judging risks- juries have to consider the facts on a case-by-case basis. In this case, the fact that no previous accident had occurred despite the same allegedly inadequate level of supervision was highly relevant. Furthermore, there was nothing wrong with the construction of the steps. The fact that a young child might slip or trip or choose to jump from one height to a lower level was part of everyday life- that again was highly relevant. Overall, the evidence suggested that there was no real risk of the kind contemplated by the 1974 Act. Unless it could be said that the school's conduct had exposed the child to a real risk, no question of the reasonable practicability of measures designed to avoid that risk arose. In the circumstances, the jury's verdict was unsafe.

R. v. Swan Hunter Shipbuilders Ltd (1982)

Significance: The employers' duty to provide necessary information, instruction and training to non-employees under s.2(2)(c) HSWA

The employer's duty to provide information and instruction to ensure, so far as is reasonably practicable, the health and safety at work of his own employees also extends to providing such information and instruction to employees of a subcontractor, where necessary. The application of this is well illustrated by the following case.

A fire broke out on board a ship which was under construction by Swan Hunter Ltd. The fire was intense because the atmosphere inside the vessel had become oxygen enriched and eight men were killed. The oxygen had escaped from a hose left by an employee of a firm of subcontractors. Swan Hunter Ltd had distributed a book of rules to their own employees for the safe use of oxygen equipment, but this was not distributed to subcontractors' employees, except on request.

Swan Hunter Ltd were prosecuted under the **Health and Safety at Work, etc. Act 1974** for *"failure to provide a safe system of work"* (contrary to section 2(2)(a)), *"failure to provide information and instruction to ensure the safety of their employees"* (contrary to section 2(2)(c)), and *"failure to ensure that persons not in their employment were not exposed to risk"* (contrary to section 3(1)).

The trial judge ruled that all the above sections of the Act imposed a duty to inform or instruct employees other than Swan Hunter's own, with regard to all relevant safety matters. Swan Hunter Ltd appealed.

The Court of Appeal dismissed the appeal and upheld the trial judge's ruling. If, to ensure a safe system of work for an employer's own employees, it was necessary to provide persons other than his employees with information and instruction as to potential dangers, then he was under a duty to provide such information and instruction, so far as was reasonably practicable.

Rose v. Plenty (1976)

Significance: Vicarious liability

A milkman took a 13-year-old boy with him on his milk round to help with the work. This was contrary to a notice that the defendant, the milkman's employer, had displayed at the depot expressly prohibiting the employment of children to assist. Due to the milkman's negligent driving of the milk float the boy was injured.

It was held that as the milkman's employment of the boy was within the scope of his own employment and had been done for the purpose of his employer's business, the milkman's employers were vicariously liable. An employer's prohibition of the doing of an act is not necessarily such as to exempt the employer from liability, provided the act is done not for the employee's own purposes but in course of his service and for his employer's benefit.

Rylands v. Fletcher (1868)

Significance: Strict liability; private nuisance

The rule in this case is the most-often quoted example of strict liability. Basically it states that an occupier of land who brings onto it anything likely to do damage if it escapes, and keeps that thing on the land, will be liable for any damage caused by an escape.

The circumstances in the case were that Fletcher employed competent contractors to build a reservoir on his land. During the work, the contractors discovered an old mine whose shafts and passages connected with another mine on neighbouring land owned by Rylands. The contractors did not inform Fletcher and did not block up the shafts. When the reservoir was filled with water, the water escaped from Fletcher's mine shaft into Rylands' thereby causing damage.

Rylands sued on the grounds of Fletcher's negligence. Fletcher himself had not been negligent as he had no knowledge of the existence of the shafts. He was not vicariously liable for the actions of the contractors as they were not his employees.

The case eventually went to the House of Lords on appeal who upheld the original judgment that Fletcher was liable in tort. In the original judgment by Blackham J, it was stated that:

"We think the true rule of law is that the person who for his own purposes brings onto his lands and collects and keeps there anything likely to do mischief if it escapes, must keep it in at his peril and if he does not do so, is prima facie liable for all the damage which is the natural consequence of its escape".

During the appeal Lord Cairns, in agreeing with the above statement, added the qualification that the rule only applied to a "non-natural" use of the land, and not to circumstances where a substance accumulated naturally on the land. The word "natural" has since been extended to mean "ordinary".

Smith v. Baker and Sons (1891)

Significance: The defence of *volenti non fit injuria*

The claimant worked in a quarry, drilling in the rock face. While he did this a crane worked overhead and both he and his employers knew there was a risk of the rock falling from the crane. The claimant was not warned when the crane would operate. A rock fell and injured the claimant. The House of Lords held that although the claimant knew of the risk, the defence that he voluntarily assumed it was not proven because he was threatened with dismissal if he objected to the crane working overhead.

Smith v. Crossley Bros (1951)

Significance: Employer not liable where wilful misbehaviour on the part of employees cannot be foreseen

Smith, an apprentice, was seriously injured as a result of a practical joke played on him by two fellow-apprentices at the defendants' training school. He claimed negligence on the part of the defendants. However, the injury was as a result of an act of wilful misbehaviour that could not have reasonably been foreseen, and the defendants were held not to be vicariously liable.

Speed v. Swift (Thomas) and Co. Ltd (1943)

Significance: The employers' duty to provide a safe system of work and to ensure that it is updated to account for changing situations

The respondent received injuries while employed by the appellants to unload cargo from a ship. There were various weaknesses identified in the system of work provided by the employers:

- The starboard rail was broken, and was neither protected nor removed.
- The port winch was malfunctioning.
- Dunnage lying on the deck increased the risk of injury.

A hook caught on the rail, and either the rail itself or part of the cargo fell onto the respondent who was working in a barge alongside the ship.

The appellants contended that they should be exonerated from liability because the system of work was safe, and the accident and injury had been caused by the failure of a fellow worker to carry out this system correctly. However, it was held that the accident was due to the failure of the employer to supply a safe system of working, and not due to the behaviour of a fellow employee. The employers were therefore held liable in damages.

Stark v. The Post Office (2000)

Significance: The absolute duty to maintain work equipment in an efficient state, in efficient working order and in good repair

Mr Stark was a delivery postman and had been issued with a bicycle to help in deliveries. Whilst riding the bicycle in connection with work, the front brake broke and he was thrown over the handlebars, sustaining a serious injury. The cause of the failure was held to be either metal fatigue or a manufacturing defect, neither of which would have been revealed on even the most "perfectly rigorous" inspection.

Mr Stark argued that, notwithstanding the finding of fact concerning the cause of the failure, the Post Office was nevertheless under an absolute duty to maintain the bicycle in a state of good repair as set out in reg.6(1) **PUWER**, which states that *"Every employer shall ensure that work equipment is maintained in an efficient state, in efficient working order and in good repair"*. The Post Office, on the other hand, argued that the 'Work Equipment Directive' and the 'Framework Directive' to which **PUWER** was intended to give effect, contemplated something less than an absolute duty.

It was decided that **PUWER** clearly imposed an absolute duty on the employer, in this case the Post Office. Although the 'Work Equipment' and 'Framework Directives' set out minimum standards, there was nothing to stop a Member State from imposing more stringent requirements than the Directives required. Mr Stark's claim therefore succeeded.

Summers (John) and Sons v. Frost (1955)

Significance: Definition of 'Absolute' duty

The claimant's hand came into contact with a moving grinding wheel in breach of the **Factories Act 1961**, s. 14(1). The defendant argued that if a grinding wheel was securely fenced the machine would be unusable. The court rejected this proposition and refused to read the words 'so far as is reasonably practicable' into the statute.

This case created the bizarre situation that all grinding wheels were illegal unless all the wheel was contained within a guard. To overcome this the Government introduced the **Abrasive Wheels Regulations 1970** (since revoked) which permitted a lower standard of guarding than that required by the **Factories Act**.

Sutherland and others v. Hatton and others (2002)

Significance: Employers' liability for work-related stress

This series of appeals by four employers were heard together by the Court of Appeal concerning cases where damages had been awarded for stress-induced psychiatric illness, the others being **Bishop v. Baker Refractories**, **Barber v. Somerset County Council** and **Jones v. Sandwell Metropolitan Borough Council** (see also coverage of **Barber** elsewhere in this section). Two main questions were addressed:

- first, the scope of duty owed by the employer; and
- second, whether the employer had breached that duty.

After discussion, the court set out some general principles to apply in such cases.

They are (briefly):

- There are no special control mechanisms applying to claims for illness arising from stress. The ordinary principles of employer's liability should apply.
- The threshold question is whether this kind of harm was reasonably foreseeable.
- Foreseeability depends on what an employer knows or ought reasonably to know about the employee concerned.
- The test is the same whatever the employment.
- The employer is generally entitled to take what it is told by its employee at face value.
- To trigger a duty to take action, the indications of impending harm to health arising from stress at work must be plain enough for any reasonable employer to realise that it should do something about it.
- The size and scope of the employer's business, its resources and the demands it faces are relevant in deciding what is reasonable.
- An employer who offers a confidential counselling or treatment service is unlikely to be in breach of its duty.

- If the only reasonable step is to demote or dismiss the employee, the employer would not be in breach of its duty in allowing a willing employee to continue working.
- The claimant must show that the breach of duty caused or materially contributed to the harm suffered- occupational stress is not enough.

Following these principles, three of the employers' appeals were allowed. Sandwell MBC's appeal was dismissed. Mr Barber was given permission to appeal to the House of Lords (see above).

As a result of this case it became more difficult for an employee who had suffered work-related stress to succeed in a civil action, not least for the reason that offering a confidential counselling service could be deemed sufficient not to be in breach of the duty of care. More recent cases have to some extent redressed the balance- see **Intel Corporation (UK) Ltd v. Daw (2007)**.

Thompson and Others v. Smiths Ship Repairers (North Shields) Ltd (1984)

Significance: Liability for noise-induced hearing loss; date of knowledge

A number of men employed in the shipyards from about the 1940s to the 1970s suffered impaired hearing. The employers knew about the noise levels but no official guidance on the problem was available until 1963, and no protective equipment was provided until the 1970s. In 1980 and 1981, actions were brought against the employers for hearing damage due to negligence by the employers throughout this time.

The High Court held that an appropriate test should be used to establish the date from which the behaviour of the employer could be considered to be negligent. The test was determined to be what would have been done by a reasonable and prudent employer, in terms of what such an employer would or should have known about the issue of ear protection and noise levels at the time, and in line with common practice in the industry.

Using this test, the employer was held to be negligent only from 1963. Damages could only be recovered from this time, when the failure to provide protection against noise levels became a breach of the employers' duty of care. In this case, therefore, the claimants could only recover a portion of their loss, determined from 1963 onwards and taking into account the uncertainties involved in making such an apportionment.

Uddin v. Associated Portland Cement (1965)

Significance: Contributory negligence

A machinery attendant whilst attempting to remove a pigeon climbed up a steel ladder to a platform and then climbed on a cabinet which housed an unguarded revolving steel shaft. As he leant over the shaft his clothes became entangled and he was injured, losing an arm. The machinery attendant was in part of the factory in which he was not authorised to be. Although it was not foreseeable that an employee would get caught in the machine whilst chasing pigeons, it was foreseeable that a maintenance man would fail to turn off the machine when carrying out maintenance. The occupiers were in breach of s.14(1) of the **Factories Act 1961**. The Act protected *"every person employed or working on the premises"*. The claimant was entitled to protection even though not working or acting within the scope of his employment. However, it was held that the employee's damages would be reduced by 80% to account for his own contributory negligence.

Viasystems (Tyneside) Ltd v. (1) Thermal Transfer (Northern) Limited, (2) S&P Darwell Limited, (3) T Hall & C Day T/A CAT Metalwork Services (2005)

Significance: Vicarious liability - two separate employers could be vicariously liable for the negligence of a single employee

Viasystems Ltd had engaged Thermal Transfer Ltd to install air conditioning in their factory. Thermal Transfer had subcontracted ducting work to S&P Darwell Ltd who had contracted with a third company, CAT Metalwork Services, to provide fitters and fitters' mates on a labour only basis. A fitter's mate supplied by CAT Metalwork, but under the supervision of a fitter contracted to S&P Darwell, negligently caused a flood. Viasystems sued all three contract companies for damages arising from the flood.

At first instance the judge determined that CAT Metalwork Services (not S&P Darwell Ltd) was vicariously liable for the negligence of the fitter's mate. CAT Metalwork Services appealed against this decision.

The issue on appeal was whether both S&P Darwell Ltd and CAT Metalwork, rather than only one of them, could be vicariously liable for the negligence of the fitter's mate.

In allowing the appeal, the Court of Appeal held that the question to determine vicarious liability was who was entitled to exercise control over the relevant act or operation of the fitter's mate. The inquiry should concentrate on the relevant negligent act and then ask whose responsibility it was to prevent it: who was entitled and obliged to give orders as to how the work should or should not be done.

On the facts, both S&P Darwell's fitter and CAT Metalwork's fitter had been entitled, and, if they had had the opportunity, obliged to prevent the negligence.

There was no case law that bound the court to hold that dual vicarious liability was legally impossible. Dual vicarious liability was legally possible and both S&P Darwell Limited and CAT Metalwork Services were therefore found to be vicariously liable for the negligence. In this case, S&P Darwell and CAT Metalwork were found to have an equal measure of control over the fitter's mate and so were each ordered to contribute 50% of the damages awarded.

Walker v. Northumberland County Council (1994)

Significance: Foreseeability; liability for work-related stress

This was the first case where an employer was held liable for its employee's work-related stress.

In this case the claimant was employed as an area social services officer in an area with a high proportion of child-care problems. He suffered a nervous breakdown because of stress resulting from his high workload. On recovering, and before resuming work, it was agreed he would receive assistance in order to lessen his burden. He did not receive sufficient assistance and six months later, in part due to the backlog of work from his absence, suffered a second breakdown which forced him to cease work permanently. It was held that it was part of the employer's duty of care to provide a safe system of work. The employer chose to continue employing him, knowing he required additional effective help but did not provide effective help. It was reasonably foreseeable that in not providing the necessary assistance to alleviate the pressure from his workload further psychiatric damage could occur. The judgment was in favour of the claimant.

Westminster City Council v. Select Management Ltd (1984)

Significance: Application of s.4 HSWA - common parts of residential buildings to be considered "non-domestic"

Westminster City Council had served improvement notices on Select Management Ltd regarding the lifts and electrical installations in flats which they managed. They argued that section 4 of the **Health and Safety at Work, etc. Act 1974** applied to common parts of residential premises, such as lifts, and therefore placed a duty on Select Management Ltd, the controller of the premises, to ensure that the premises were safe and without risks to health.

Select Management Ltd appealed on the grounds that the flats were 'domestic premises' and therefore outside the jurisdiction of s.4 **HSWA** which only applied to non-domestic premises.

The Court of Appeal upheld that the common parts of residential premises could be considered non-domestic premises because they were available for use by others as a place of work or where they may use plant such as lifts. Consequently Select Management Ltd had a duty to persons who "use non-domestic premises made available to them as a place of work or as a place where they may use plant or substances provided for their use there" (s.4 **HSWA**) and the notices were upheld.

Wilsons and Clyde Coal Co. Ltd v. English (1938)

Significance: The employer's common law duty of care for his employees

The common law duties of an employer to his employees were identified in general terms in **Wilsons and Clyde Coal Co. Ltd v. English (1938)**. These duties comprise what is called employers' liability. In this case the employers were liable for injuries caused to a miner as a result of an unsafe system of working.

The claimant was working underground near the pit bottom at the end of his shift when the haulage equipment was switched on and the claimant was crushed between the equipment and the wall of the mine. The defendant claimed that the claimant could have got out of the pit by a different route or could have called to the operator of the haulage equipment telling him of his presence. The House of Lords held that the employer owes a duty of care to his employees, which encompasses the provision of a safe place of work, safe plant and equipment, a safe system of work and competent staff. This obligation is fulfilled by the exercise of due care and skill.

The case was also important because it stated that those duties were owed personally by the employer to each employee and were non-delegable, that is to say the performance of those duties could be delegated but the responsibility for their correct discharge could not.